THE WORLD WAR ONE SOURCE BOOK

THE WORLD WAR ONE SOURCE BOOK

PHILIP J. HAYTHORNTHWAITE

'. . . we feel we are utterly stuck and nobody seems to know what to do . . . the whole world is in a pretty good muddle, and we can only each try to do our best. How everybody longs for it to be over! . . .'

Revd. Oswin Creighton, Gallipoli
(killed in action, 15 April 1918)

'Kaiser Bill' – the Emperor
Wilhelm II.

ARMS AND
ARMOUR

Arms and Armour Press
A Cassell Imprint
Wellington House,
125 Strand,
London WC2R 0BB

Distributed in the USA by Sterling
Publishing Co. Inc., 387 Park Avenue
South, New York, NY 10016-8810.

Distributed in Australia by Capricorn Link
(Australia) Pty. Ltd, 2/13 Carrington Road,
Castle Hill, NSW 2154

First published 1992
Reprinted 1993, 1994
This paperback edition 1996

British Library Cataloguing-in-Publication
Data: a catalogue record for this book is
available from the British Library

ISBN 1-85409-351-7

All cartography by Richard Natkiel except
Jutland, by Sampleskill Ltd.

Designed and edited by DAG Publications
Ltd. Designed by David Gibbons; edited by
Michael Boxall; layout by Anthony A.
Evans; typeset by Ronset Typesetters,
Darwen, Lancashire; camerawork by M&E
Reproductions, North Fambridge, Essex;
printed and bound in Great Britain by
The Bath Press, Avon

Jacket illustration: *Canadians at Ypres*. The 'original' painting by
William Barnes Wollen is on display in the Princess Patricia's
Canadian Light Infantry Gallery located at the Museum of the
Regiments, 4520 Crowchild Trail S.W., Calgary, Alberta,
T3E 1T8.

CONTENTS

INTRODUCTION

As noted in the introduction of a previous Source Book, a brief explanation is necessary regarding the compilation of this work; as Gowing remarked, 'My object has been to compress the largest amount of information into the smallest possible space, and to insert . . . some of the most surprising and interesting events . . .'[1] With a subject so vast and so complicated as the First World War – truthfully styled 'The Great War' at least until that of 1939–45 – any such format must inevitably include generalizations which are not universally valid, and limitations of space preclude the most detailed coverage of any of the myriad aspects of the war which have provided the material for many thousands of volumes.

Within these limits, the *Source Book* is arranged in a number of sections. Section I comprises a brief chronological account of the war and a list of major engagements. Section II includes a survey of weaponry, its development and methods of use in what might be termed 'minor tactics', the basic operational practice which might be familiar to an ordinary line officer, rather than the concerns of higher strategy and generalship with which most campaign studies are concerned. Section III reviews the various combatant states, including where applicable their colonies, and a small number of states of some significance although not engaged officially in the war. These accounts concentrate on the nature of government and the principal administrations, with brief accounts of military, naval and aviation forces, to a degree inevitably superficial, especially in minutiae of unit-organization, uniform, equipment and technical data. Section IV comprises brief biographical notices of some of the most important military and naval personalities; Section V a review of source-material and associated subjects, Section VI miscellanea, and Section VII a glossary of some of the contemporary military terms and colloquialisms which might be difficult to interpret by reference only to a modern dictionary.

Many entries are accompanied by reference-lists to facilitate further reading; though it should be emphasized that for reasons of space these cannot be comprehensive, but simply a representative selection of some important or most accessible works. Almost all references have been selected for a basically English-speaking readership, so that for reasons of accessibility wherever possible English-language editions have been cited, although this inevitably necessitates the omission of many important works. For reasons of space, footnotes have been restricted largely to identification of quotations.

Some inconsistencies of spelling may be evident, especially in those cases where the original name was rendered in characters other than the Roman alphabet (hence Brusilov/Brusiloff, etc.); the selection has been somewhat arbitrary, and in some cases modern practice has been followed rather than complete anglicization as practised at the time; hence Emperor Franz Josef instead of Francis Joseph, etc.

Despite Gradgrind's philosophy that 'Facts alone are wanted in life', anecdotal material is interspersed throughout the text, partly to interrupt the recitation of fact and also to present contemporary attitudes and in some cases highlight the appalling nature of this most terrible of conflicts; although most are taken from English-language sources, the emotions they describe are probably universal. Almost exclusively this material is drawn from sources contemporary with the war, mostly obscure and some hitherto unpublished, instead of from the better-known, later accounts. In some cases these involve an element of humour, which might seem quite inappropriate for a subject so grave and even so immediate, yet is a feature of contemporary writings, as if it served as a temporary escape from the monstrous experience of war; although in many cases it is a somewhat 'gallows' style of humour:

> 'There was a young girl of the Somme,
> Who sat on a number five bomb,
> She thought 'twas a dud 'un,
> But it went off sudden –
> And her exit she made with aplomb!'[2]

(Significantly, most humour concerned the most desperate aspects of service: 'V Theatre, Twice Daily: ANNIE from ASIA, A screaming farce', a mock theatre notice referring to 'Asiatic Annie', a gun which regularly shelled 'V' Beach at Gallipoli).[3]

Unemotional facts and comments upon the comparable efficacy of weaponry and tactics should not disguise the essential nature of the war, which was unprecedented in scale and slaughter. A contemporary American comment on this is appropriate: that anyone who advocated war should first dig a trench in his garden, half fill it with water, stand in it for three days and nights without food or sleep, and hire a lunatic to shoot at him with a rifle; and only then, having experienced this simulation, contemplate war if still inclined! In contrast to the element of triumphalism which marks much contemporary (and some later) writing, with some notable exceptions those who had experienced the realities of war – the huge majority not soldiers by original profession – saw it for what it was. The editorial in *The Better Times* (a service journal produced on the Western Front), December 1918, remarked on the 'absolute apathy with which the end was received over here', in contrast to the armistice celebrations at home; 'though some may be sorry it's over, there is little doubt that the line men are *not*, as most of us have been cured of any little illusions we may have had about the pomp and glory of war, and know it for the vilest disaster that can befall mankind'.[4]

It is difficult to select one comment from a participant to encapsulate the enormity and destructiveness of the conflict, but a passage written one and a half centuries earlier seems not inappropriate. In March 1760 Frederick the Great, King of Prussia, one of the greatest of generals and who personally initiated some of the most sanguinary conflicts of his era, wrote to his confidant, Francesco Algarotti:

'. . . we run through the world to perform our bloody tragedies as often as our enemies permit us . . . We, poor fools, who have but a moment to live, render that brief space as mutually distressing as we can, and find pleasure in the destruction of every masterpiece which time and labour have produced, leaving behind us nothing but so many hateful memories of the havoc, desolation, and misery which we have wittingly occasioned!'[5]

Although written of the Seven Years War, it seems even more appropriate to 'the Great War for Civilization' of 1914-1918.

Footnotes

1. *A Soldier's Experience; or, a Voice from the Ranks.* (p. v, T. Gowing, Nottingham, 1907.
2. *Somme Times*, 31 July 1916.
3. *Dardanelles Driveller*, 17 May 1915.
4. Unsigned, but presumably by Lieutenant-Colonel F. J. Roberts.
5. English translation, given in *A Pictorial History of Germany during the Reign of Frederick the Great*. F. Kugler, London, 1845, pp. 432-3.

I
HISTORY OF THE WAR

HISTORY OF THE WAR

The modern equivalents of Emerson's 'shot heard round the world' were fired on St. Vitus's Day, 28 June 1914, in the Bosnian capital, Sarajevo; they struck and killed the Archduke Franz Ferdinand, heir to the Austro–Hungarian thrones, and his wife. The shots were fired by Gavrilo Princip, a Bosnian student revolutionary, in support of the ideal of the separation of Bosnia–Herzegovina from the Habsburg empire, and its union with Serbia, the inhabitants of which were ethnic fellows of the majority of Bosnia's population. The weapons with which Princip and his fellow-conspirators were armed were supplied by the Serbian secret society 'Black Hand', run by the arch-plotter Dragutin Dimitrijević, alias 'Apis'. It is debatable how deeply involved was the Black Hand; but whatever the case, the assassinations served to ignite a holocaust of unimaginable proportions.

It is impossible to ascribe a single principal cause for the beginning of the World War; theories range from a deliberate plan on the part of what became known as the Central Powers to precipitate a European conflict, to an almost accidental propulsion towards Armageddon, in which events went out of control of the statesmen of Europe.

The Balkans were a traditional focus for conflict, exacerbated by the decay of the Ottoman Empire during the 19th century; two Balkan wars had occurred in the two years prior to 1914, but their conclusion had not resulted in greatly increased stability. The Austro-Hungarian Empire, ruled by the same dynasty which had controlled the Holy Roman Empire it had succeeded, faced a challenge both from Serbia over the irredentist ideal of a 'greater Serbia', and from internal pressures from the many ethnic minorities within the empire, and thus it was inevitable that Austria–Hungary would take the strongest of lines towards Serbia in the wake of the Sarajevo murders. It was also inevitable that such action would involve other European states.

In the first decade of the 20th century the so-called 'Great Powers' of Europe each attempted to move forward by economic or technological prowess, so as to outdistance, or at worst keep pace with, its neighbours and rivals. Expansion in overseas colonies had led to confrontation, and this was not confined to the undeveloped world, but extended into Europe itself, with Russo–Turkish rivalry in the Caucasus and Italian designs on Albania. By 1914 the main European powers had divided into two opposing camps: the 'Triple Entente' of Britain, France and Russia, and the 'Central Powers' of Germany and Austria–Hungary.

Britain was at the height of her economic and colonial power, a world leadership which could only be challenged by the United States, Japan and Germany. Of these, confrontation was likely only with Germany, itself having an economic and technological base capable of rivalling Britain in time, and in course of constructing a fleet with which to question Britain's colonial superiority. Yet Germany itself feared Russian expansionism, and it has been speculated that a primary motivation for the beginning of the war in Europe was the German decision to launch a pre-emptive strike against Russia, before that nation's military reforms could be completed in 1917. The head of the German military establishment, General Helmuth von Moltke, saw Russia as the motivation behind Serbian and Slavonic aspirations, and at the end of 1912 advised the German Kaiser (emperor) that a war against Russia was the only solution, and moreover that the sooner it occurred, the better for Germany's prospects of success.

However, as France was an ally of Russia, the plan of campaign designed by the German chief-of-staff Alfred von Schlieffen in 1905–6 prepared for a war on two fronts: an initial, massive German strike to knock out France while containing the Russians in the east, before transferring the weight of Germany's formidable military machine to defeat

Assassination at Sarajevo:
Gavrilo Princip is arrested.

their greater enemy, Russia. Yet, although France still smarted from her defeat in the Franco–Prussian War, the election of April 1914 had returned a majority of Radicals and Socialists, with more pacific intentions, and the prospect existed of closer friendship between France and Germany. Many Germans, especially the industrialists, foresaw Germany becoming the leading European power from her growing economic strength, not requiring military action. Despite Anglo-German naval and colonial rivalry, Germany and Britain might be seen as becoming less antagonistic, and the prospect of the increase of Russian power did not preclude the possibility of a future alliance of Britain, France and Germany united in the face of the awakening Russian behemoth.

Nevertheless, many in the Central Powers followed von Moltke's idea that a war sooner was better than a war later,

and the nationalism present in most states denied the possibility of accepting unchallenged the actions of a perceived rival; though it is doubtful whether bellicose acts such as mobilization of forces, in response to heightened tension, were intended as more than a gigantic bluff, as had been made before, to check without hostilities the actions of a rival. If such mobilization orders were intended as merely raising the level of tension, to dissuade a rival from taking the ultimate step, then the statesmen of Europe made a gigantic miscalculation, in which the deterrence of armed might not only failed to deter but actually accelerated the pace towards conflict.

The murders at Sarajevo propelled Austria–Hungary to take its strongest stand yet against Serbia, which (rightly or not) was seen. as the culprit in the agitation which threatened the stability of the Empire. Because of known

Mobilization plans were completely dependent upon railways: German troops are even packed into the tender of this locomotive.

Russian support for the Serbs, Austria requested and received (5 July) a guarantee of German support if Russia moved to assist Serbia. The theory has been advanced that at this juncture both Germany and Austria–Hungary decided to turn the Balkan crisis into the war favoured by the 'better now than later' school; that only an Austrian strike against Serbia would end the internal unrest, and that only the military defeat of Russia before the completion of their re-armament would permit Germany to become dominant in Europe. Against this theory of deliberate provocation of a European war are the facts that threats alone had been effective before, and that both the Kaiser and von Moltke were on holiday at the time when the crisis was coming to a head. (The Austro–Hungarian chief-of-staff and war minister also departed on holiday at this date, but were advised to do so to conceal the fact that Austria–Hungary was planning military action; perhaps the same applied in Germany.) Henry Morgenthau, US Ambassador to Turkey, was convinced that Germany deliberately precipitated the war, based on information from Baron Wangenheim, Germany's Ambassador to Turkey, and denied all protestations of German innocence: 'I do not have reason to argue about the matter, I know.'[1]

Despite having no evidence that the Serbian government was implicated in the Sarajevo murders, on 23 July the Austro–Hungarian government issued an ultimatum to Serbia. Having ordered a mobilization of her forces as a precaution, Serbia accepted the Austrian conditions on 25 July, save for the most humiliating one, that Austro–Hungarian troops be allowed to enter Serbia in search of the Sarajevo conspirators. In response Austria–Hungary declared war on 28 July, probably under German persuasion, as the Austrian forces would not be ready for a further two weeks. (It is worth noting that the Kaiser regarded the Serbian reply as a great diplomatic success for Austria,

obviating the need for war; but the German 'war party' led by chancellor Bethmann-Hollweg did not relay the Kaiser's comments to Vienna until after the declaration of war.)

Once set in motion, the momentum of forces became unstoppable. Mobilization plans for all nations had been calculated precisely, involving the calling to the colours of the huge numbers of reservists maintained by most states, and were dependent entirely upon the use of railways. Timetables and schedules were such that partial mobilization precluded general mobilization; so that Austria–Hungary, for example, could either mobilize against Serbia, or against both Serbia and Russia; but to mobilize first against Serbia, and a short time later against Russia if necessary, was almost impossible because of the railway timetables. Thus general mobilization was in most cases the only possible course, which only increased the tension.

Afraid that Austro–German hegemony in the Balkans would threaten Constantinople and thus her trade route from the Black Sea, and to maintain her standing as protector of Serbia, Russia ordered general mobilization on 30 July. Russia was unprepared for war, and the mobilization was more bluff than bellicosity; but news of Russia's action propelled Germany towards her own mobilization on the following day. Austria–Hungary was already bombarding Belgrade, and it was probably at this point that extension of the war became inevitable. Aside from the theory of deliberate precipitation of the war, mobilization in Germany probably had a different implication than in other states. In most nations, plans for war demanded aggression, aiming for a rapid knock-out blow, and most armies were organized accordingly; and under the Schlieffen Plan, German mobilization demanded concentration of forces first against France; thus it might be said that in the German case, mobilization was not the turning of a diplomatic screw, but an inevitable step towards war.

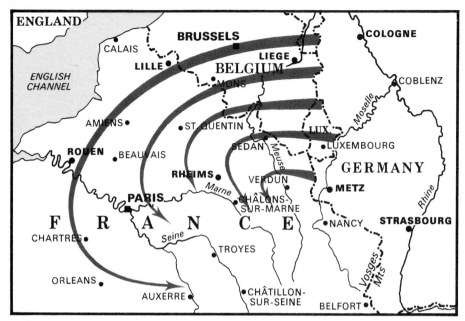

Germany's alternatives were now limited: to stop Russian mobilization by threat of war; to initiate a wider conflict, and neutralize France before concentrating upon Russia; or to lose the initiative and face a longer war on two fronts which Germany could not win. When Russia declined a demand to demobilize, Germany's hand was forced. War was declared upon Russia on 1 August 1914, and upon France, with barely any excuse, two days later. On 3 August Germany demanded free passage of its armies through Belgium, to facilitate their attack on France; Belgium refused, was invaded on 4 August, and this brought Britain into the war. Britain had been in some doubt how to react now that her allies were at war; the invasion of Belgium, a state whose neutrality had been guaranteed by Britain, removed the difficulty. On 4 August 1914 Britain declared war on Germany over the 'scrap of paper' which had guaranteed Belgium's neutrality. In a comment which recalled Pitt's 'roll up the map of Europe', British foreign secretary Grey remarked that, 'The lamps are going out all over Europe; we shall not see them lit again in our lifetime.'

Whether or not the cause was some deliberate plot, or a case of failed bluffs, inept statesmanship and the primacy of railway timetables and mobilization plans which once initiated could not be halted, Europe had crossed the threshold into a war of unprecedented magnitude. Few appreciated how such a war would progress, least of all the cheering crowds that greeted the declaration of war with elation. Although hostilities had been initiated by the Central Powers, there was no sense of it being a war of conquest: each state expressed the belief that it was acting defensively, to protect its own interests, even if the 'defence' necessitated invading other countries: thus, it was regarded throughout Europe as a matter of patriotic duty, to defend the Fatherland, Holy Russia, or whatever. Only Britain did

not feel under immediate threat, but acted from higher motives, in the protection of a smaller nation, and ultimately to wage a 'war to end war'. As the madness multiplied and the war dragged on, a level of disillusionment set in; yet the determination not to give ground was such that no matter how widespread the anguish, neither politicians nor the majority of the troops who carried out their directives lost the will to fight their corner. The early cries of 'On to Berlin!' or 'On to Paris!' were replaced by the resignation exemplified by the British verse (to the tune of *Auld Lang Syne*):

'We're here
Because
We're here
Because
We're here
Because
We're here',

and the slaughter continued.

None of this was apparent to the joyous crowds who waved off the departure of countless troop-trains in countless cities throughout Europe in August 1914; they could have had no inkling that the folly of Europe's statesmen was to result in the loss of getting on for fifteen million lives, and the ruination of countless millions more.

However, unlike the almost hysterical jingoism which marked much of this stage of the war, probably the reaction of those most closely affected by the mobilization orders was akin to that described by Ludwig Renn, who recorded a brief note from his mother on his departure, urging him to 'be true and play the man', and adding that she was enclosing with the message a pair of warm socks.[2]

An image which encapsulates the destructiveness of the war: a shell hits the medieval cathedral of Reims, 19 September 1914.

THE WAR

The following account covers military events only, and is not purely chronological as the main theatres of war cannot be regarded in isolation; and in some cases events are best covered in phases rather than by year. For example, the British Battles Nomenclature Committee, which issued a report in May 1921, identified seven phases of the war on the Western Front, ranging in length from Phase II (twenty months) to Phase VI (ten weeks).

The Western Front, 1914
Germany's strategy, decided long before the war, was to contain Russia on the Eastern Front and make a lightning attack on France; and having defeated that nation, transport the bulk of the German forces to mount an offensive against Russia, a plan made practical by the swift movement possible on the extensive railway system. As put into effect, however, the German offensive in the west was not the original Schlieffen Plan: chief-of-staff Moltke watered it down by keeping larger forces than planned originally on the Eastern Front and in Alsace–Lorraine (where it was predicted the main French offensive would be mounted), so as not to surrender the German territory which Schlieffen had been prepared to lose temporarily; by so doing, Moltke weakened the main offensive and made it impossible to carry out Schlieffen's reputed dying words, 'keep the right wing strong'. By avoiding a breach of Dutch neutrality, Moltke also limited the scope for manoeuvre of the German 'right hook' intended to swing around into the rear of the French army. The result was to concentrate only some 60 per cent of the German mobile force into the outflanking manoeuvre, whereas Schlieffen had intended that up to 90 per cent be used.

French strategy was for total offence, towards which French forces had been structured. Their 'Plan XVI' envisaged the German attack through Belgium, and prepared to counter it; but as the plan involved French violation of Belgian neutrality it was politically unacceptable, its designer (General Victor Michel) was replaced by Joseph Joffre as commander-in-chief, and a new 'Plan XVII' designed. By this, the main French effort was to be made in Alsace–Lorraine (as Schlieffen had predicted), with the Belgian corridor covered by a French force and the promised British Expeditionary Force to secure the left flank. Plan XVII was not bad, but greatly under-estimated the German capability to deploy its immense reserve forces, and catastrophe almost resulted.

Immediately following Belgian refusal to admit them, German troops began to pour over the Belgian border in the narrow gap between Holland and France, guarded by the Belgian fortress of Liège, on 3/4 August; the city was bombarded into submission by 16 August. On the extreme right of the German 'right hook' their First and Second Armies (Generals Alexander von Kluck and Karl von Bülow respectively) swept aside the small Belgian Army (which retired into the defences of Antwerp) and occupied Brussels (20 August).

In the interim, the main French assault had been mounted to the south, against Alsace–Lorraine, beginning the Battles of the Frontiers. The main strike was made roughly between Metz and Belfort, by (from north to south) the French Second Army (General Noël de Castelnau), First (General Auguste Dubail) and Army of Alsace (General Paul Pau), which drove into Alsace and Lorraine from 8 August. The Battle of Lorraine, however, had far from the predicted result: the German Sixth (Rupprecht of Bavaria) and Seventh (General Josias von Heeringen) Armies counter-attacked and repelled the French. The ferocity of this fighting helped to prevent Joffre realizing where the main German threat lay; or at least, where it should have lain had Moltke pursued the Schlieffen Plan to its ultimate. That he failed so to do prevented Germany from achieving the rapid knock-out whch they required so urgently.

Initially Moltke's 'right hook', intent on swinging round to envelope the French left and centre, met with success. North of the Alsace–Lorraine fighting, the 'pivot' of the German manoeuvre, their Fourth and Fifth Armies (Albrecht of Württemberg and Crown Prince Wilhelm respectively) defeated the French Third and Fourth Armies (Generals Pierre Ruffey and Fernand de Langle de Cary respectively) in the Battle of the Ardennes (20–25 August), the French retiring on the fortress of Verdun. As the German First, Second and Third (Baron Max von Hausen) Armies swept west and south-west, Joffre (in accordance with Plan XVII) ordered his Fifth Army (General Charles Lanrezac), with the newly arrived British Expeditionary Force (Sir John French) on its left, to meet the advance. Against some 750,000 Germans, Lanrezac and French mustered only about 350,000; Bülow and Hausen defeated Lanrezac in the Battle of the Sambre (22–23 August), and at Mons (23 August) the BEF held off Kluck despite being hugely outnumbered and suffering severe losses. Although French was prepared to stand, he had to fall back in line with Lanrezac, and the BEF fought a rear-guard action almost daily until Smith–Dorrien's British II Corps made a stand at Le Cateau and held off the whole of Kluck's First Army (27 August).

At this stage Moltke's amending of the Schlieffen Plan proved fatal. Observing the Allied line collapsing, he predicted the end of the war in six weeks; and instead of concentrating all his efforts on the right, to complete the envelopment, he diverted resources to Alsace–Lorraine, where German success had been somewhat unexpected, and even withdrew two corps for dispatch to the Eastern Front, a fatal diminution of the already weakened right of the Schlieffen Plan. Joffre's position was parlous, but with German strategy now becoming clear, he ordered his First and Second Armies to hold around Verdun and Nancy, ordered his left to continue to retreat before the German onslaught, and formed two new armies in their rear (Sixth, General Michel Maunoury, and Ninth, General Ferdinand Foch) in preparation for a counter-attack.

To relieve pressure on the BEF, still holding the Allied left, Joffre ordered his Fifth Army to attack the BEF's opponent, Kluck's First Army. Although not a success, elements of Lanrezac's army (Franchet d'Esperey's I Corps) inflicted a severe check uopn Bülow's Second Army at the Battle of Guise (29 August). Bülow requested assistance from Kluck who, unable to communicate with Moltke, and unaware of the new French Sixth Army gathering in the environs of Paris, acted upon his own initiative, deciding to assail Lanrezac in support of Bülow, and thus by-pass Paris to the east. (So convinced were the French of an imminent attack on the capital that the government had moved to Bordeaux on 28 August). As Kluck drove southwards, Joffre prepared his counter-attack, which brought about the Battle of the Marne (4–10 September). The French Sixth Army, temporarily under command of the Paris military governor, General Joseph Galliéni, moved towards Kluck's exposed right flank. Kluck halted his southward march and turned upon Sixth Army (their position was only held by Galliéni's rushing up reinforcements in a fleet of Parisian taxi-cabs), but in so doing opened a thirty-mile gap between himself and Bülow. As Joffre counter-attacked along the front to hold the other German armies, the French Fifth Army (Franchet d'Esperey: Lanrezac had been relieved) attacked Bülow's right, to prevent the closing of the gap between the German armies; into this gap moved the BEF.

At this stage, with Kluck about to be assailed in his left and rear, and fully occupied on his front, the whole of the German right could have crumbled; but Sir John French advanced the BEF only slowly, and his relations with the French were so strained that it required a personal visit from his superior, Lord Kitchener, to prevent him from withdrawing the BEF towards the Channel ports. Contrasting with Joffre's close communication with his commanders, which greatly facilitated his counter-attack, Moltke had so little communication from his forward commanders that German operations were disjointed, and he delegated authority to a staff colonel (Hentsch) who was sent to advise the army commanders. As Bülow was being forced back by Franchet d'Esperey, Hentsch approved Bülow's decision to retire, which necessitated Kluck retreating also, which at least saved him from a potentially devastating attack in his rear. With this German withdrawal to a defensible line, the Allies were saved; but despite the sterling service of their armies, Joffre's leadership and Galliéni's immortal taxi-cabs, it was as much the consequence of Moltke's mishandling of the Schlieffen Plan. As the Germans reorganized a new line Moltke was replaced in command, by war minister General Erich von Falkenhayn (14 September), who had noted somewhat acidly of his predecessor that once Schlieffen's notes had run out, Moltke was powerless. Casualties on both sides had been on a scale unimaginable before the war: the Allies about half a million men, the Germans something more.

But for the so-called 'miracle of the Marne' (tactically an inconclusive battle but a strategic success for the Allies), the war in the west might indeed have been 'over by Christmas' (a common slogan), with a defeat of the French as comprehensive as that achieved by Moltke's uncle at Sedan in 1870. As it was, the Western Front was to remain the principal theatre of operations for a further four years, involving a slaughter which dwarfed even that of the first six weeks of the war, and which ended the fluid 'war of manoeuvre' that had been predicted and which characterized the early battles. The change began with the 'race to the sea'.

Following the German withdrawal to their new positions along the Aisne, the Allies attempted to outflank the German right, but were stalled by hastily prepared fieldworks (First Battle of the Aisne, 15–18 September). Determining to seize the Channel ports and thus outflank the Allied left, Falkenhayn moved north-west; as he attempted to outflank Joffre, so Joffre attempted to outflank him, neither with success despite desperate fighting. In the south,

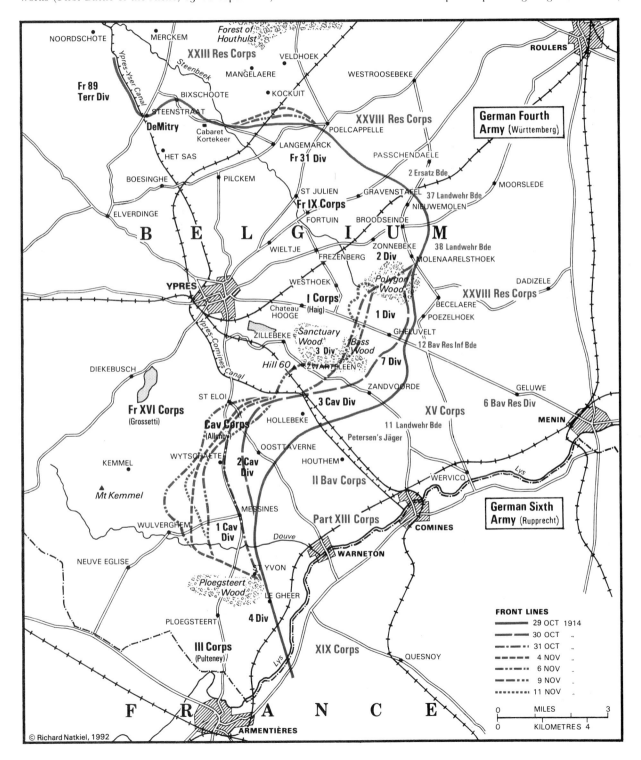

© Richard Natkiel, 1992

renewed attacks against Verdun were repelled, but the Germans did gain the St. Mihiel salient (24 September), and in the rear of the German front line, Antwerp fell (9 October), the Belgian garrison and its reinforcing British Naval Brigade escaping west along the Dutch border. In the final stages of the 'race to the sea' the Allies resisted German pushes in the Battle of the Yser (18 October–30 November), and the First Battle of Ypres (30 October–24 November), which almost destroyed the original BEF but which stopped the German progress. By early December the pattern of the next three and a half years had been set: opposing trench-lines stretching from the North Sea to Switzerland, seemingly impregnable, but which would be assailed time and again to little effect, with artillery constantly increasing in weight and machine-guns in number, so that the mobile actions of the first three months of the war became only a

An account of the 'Christmas truce' of 1914, from the anonymous diary of 2nd Battalion, Border Regiment noted on pp. ooo:

'On Xmas morning about 5.30 a.m. a German officer showed a white flag on the trench and about 10 mts after came on the top himself and walked half way across to our trench and asked to see one of our Officers . . . they talked for a time and then returned to there trenches, and no sooner had the German Officer returned where there voices shouted out a happy Xmas to all you English so we wished them the same . . . About 8 a.m. we saw them get out of there trench and asked us not to fire as they wanted to keep the Peace that day . . . At 9 a.m. they came half way and we went to meet them. And the first thing they asked us when are you going to give in you are beat. So we asked them who told you all this and they pointed to a paper they had . . . and they told us pointblank that they had troops reviewing in Hyde Park . . . Well me and my chum couldn't help laughing at them and they looked at us and couldn't make it out. So I said to them well I must admit that you have got troops in London but they are Prisoners of War. They would not take that so my chum gave them the News of the World and they thanked us and gave us a segar to smoke . . . At 11.15 . . . we all returned and found that we were to bury our Comrades that fell in the Charge on the 18th of Dec. so we all started diging and burying them side by side and made a Cross out of the wood of a Biscuit box . . . we all kneeled and offered up a Pray to God above for our Comrades who fell in Honour. We were having tea when the Germans started singing God save the King in as good English as they could. And then three cheers went up from our trenches. So we all had a good sing song that night in our trenches. But we did not forget to have our look out as I do not think we became friends . . .'

(Reproduced in *Made in the Trenches*, ed. Sir Frederick Treves Bt., pp. 86–7, London, 1916)

distant memory. By the end of the year the casualties on both sides were approaching an unbelievable one million.

The Eastern Front, 1914

German operations on the Eastern Front were regarded as a holding operation, secondary to those in the west; and Austro–Hungarian resources were similarly divided between Serbia and Russia. Russia's mobilized strength was formidable, but under pressure from their allies (principally France) they embarked on operations before they were ready, with disastrous consequences. There were two main theatres of operation, in East Prussia and Poland.

The Tsar's uncle, Grand Duke Nicholas (or Nikolai Nikolaevich), directed the advance of six Russian armies, two in East Prussia and four into Galicia. From 17 August the North-West Army Group of General Yakov Zhilinsky advanced against East Prussia; it comprised the First (Niemen) and Second (Narev) Armies of Generals Pavel Rennenkampf and Alexander Samsonov respectively. Immediately, Rennenkampf was checked by elements of the single German army which opposed him (General Max von Prittwitz's Eighth Army) at Stallupönen (17 August), while the widely spread German force conducted a gradual retirement. Prittwitz counter-attacked Rennenkampf at Gumbinnen (20 August) with some success, but fearful of the odds against him decided to retire to the Vistula. When Moltke was informed of this he dismissed Prittwitz and replaced him with General Paul von Beneckendorf und von Hindenburg, recalled from retirement, with General Erich Ludendorff as chief-of-staff (recently Bülow's deputy chief-of-staff in Flanders, and much celebrated for his seizure of Liège). This command partnership would become even more famous than that of Blücher and Gneisenau a century before.

Ludendorff determined to switch the concentration from Rennenkampf in the north to Samsonov in the south, and discovered that Colonel Max Hoffman, Prittwitz's senior staff officer, had made provision for identical dispositions (evidence, perhaps, of a unified tactical doctrine in the German high command). Utilizing railways to transfer troops, Ludendorff left only a screen in front of Rennen-kampf, concentrated against Samsonov, checked him at Orlau–Frankenau (24 August) and destroyed the Russian army totally at Tannenberg (26–31 August). Such was the level of unpreparedness and bad communication that Zhilinsky was unaware of the disaster facing him until the Battle of Tannenberg had begun. With his army routed at the cost of about 150,000 men (German losses only about one-tenth of that number), Samsonov killed himself; and the Germans again switched operations back to the north, smashing Rennenkampf at the First Battle of the Masurian Lakes, costing another 100,000 Russian casualties (about 10,000 German). By an almost Napoleonic strategy of defeat in detail of a larger force, the Hindenburg–Ludendorff partnership had inflicted such a blow upon the Russian army that it never fully recovered.

*German armoured train,
Galicia.*

In Galicia, operations went very differently. Directed by the Austrian chief-of-staff General Franz Conrad von Hötzendorf, the Austrian First, Third and Fourth Armies advanced on a 200-mile front, resources hopelessly spread and unable to provide mutual support, with Conrad commanding so far in the rear as to be almost a commander *in absentia*. The Austro–Hungarians were opposed by General Nikolai Ivanov's South-Western Army Group (Third, Fourth, Fifth and Eighth Armies), and despite initial Austrian success at Krasnik (23–24 August) and Zamosc–Komarów (26 August–1 September), were thrown back during the Battles of Lemberg (23 August–12 September). With the loss of about one-third of his effective forces (some 350,000), Conrad withdrew to the Carpathians, leaving only the fortress of Przemysl garrisoned amid the Russian advance.

This catastrophe exposed the German flank, so in haste Falkenhayn ordered Hindenburg to the assistance of the collapsing Austrians. Again exploiting the efficient German railways, Hindenburg rushed forces towards the Austrian left, forming a new German Ninth Army over which he took personal control. The Austro–German advance which followed in the latter part of September and October,

against greatly superior Russian forces, was ultimately unsuccessful, and their forces returned to the previous lines; but it had foiled Grand Duke Nicholas' plan to advance on Silesia (Germany's coal-mining centre) through Poland.

On 1 November 1914 Hindenburg was appointed overall commander in the east (including the Austro–Hungarian forces), as seven Russian armies renewed the assault. Using a 'scorched earth' policy to impede the Russian advance, the Germans withdrew and regrouped, until Ninth Army (now commanded by General August von Mackensen) struck at the Russian northern flank, driving between Rennenkampf's First and the Second Army at Lódz. The penetration was checked but inflicted severe losses upon the Russians, and Grand Duke Nicholas's projected offensive stalled. Although 1914 ended with neither side in the ascendant, it was overall a huge German success to hold a line against the immense weight of the Russian army.

The Balkan Front, 1914

The opening combat of the war began on 29 July 1914, with the Austro–Hungarian bombardment of Belgrade. From 12 August General Oskar Potiorek with the Austrian Second, Fourth and Sixth Armies pushed over the Rivers Save and Drina; he was opposed by about equal forces of Serbs (about 450,000) and some 40,000 wild and ill-trained Montenegrins, commanded by Marshal Radomir Putnik of Serbia. Again the imperfections of the Austro–Hungarian military system were exposed by a committed and experienced opponent, and Potiorek was thrown back at the Battle of the Jadar (12–21 August); a renewed advance (7–8 September) met the same result, but at least caused the withdrawal of the Serbian invasion of Bosnia. The third attack (Battle of the Drina, 8–17 September) was hardly more successful, although Putnik withdrew to new defensive positions south and west of Belgrade, which the Austro–Hungarians occupied on 2 December. Beginning the following day, Putnik and King Peter of Serbia mounted a huge counterattack at the Battle of the River Kolubara, which hustled the Austro–Hungarians back out of Serbian territory with considerable loss, and Belgrade was retaken on 15 December. Although Potiorek was not entirely culpable (Conrad had transferred part of Second Army to the Eastern Front in mid-campaign), he was relieved of command and replaced by the Archduke Eugene (22 December). The Austro–Hungarians had lost about half the forces committed; the Serbians about 170,000.

The Turkish Front, 1914

The entry of Turkey into the war on the side of the Central Powers (officially 31 October, although hostilities had begun on 29–30 October) had a serious effect upon Russia which, already severely mauled, was thus severed from British and French supplies by the closure of the Dardanelles. The first actions, however, were favourable to the Allies: the Turkish invasion of the Russian Caucasus, unwisely begun by Enver Pasha, suffered a severe defeat at

Sarikamish from the Russian army of General Count Vorontsov–Dashkov (29 December–3 January 1915). Britain responded to the Turkish action by annexing Cyprus and declaring a protectorate over Egypt; and began an invasion of Mesopotamia, Basra falling on 23 November.

The Western Front, 1915

The end of the 'war of manoeuvre' in the west allowed the combatants to review their strategy, greatly influenced by the entry of Turkey into the war. In the Allied camp, the necessity of re-establishing a supply route to Russia caused a division of opinion between those who wished to concentrate efforts on the Western Front (mainly the French and the British War Minister, Lord Kitchener), and those who saw the decisive blow as more effective in the east. Although it was impossible to concentrate fully in both areas, it was decided to continue offensives in the west while simultaneously mounting operations against Turkey. The Central Powers were also divided over their strategy:

Falkenhayn advocated concentration against the west, while Hindenburg and Ludendorff advised an attempt to break the already battered Russians. The latter won the argument, and Germany decided to hold on the Western Front and concentrate resources in the east.

From late December 1914 Joffre mounted a French offensive in Champagne, but despite a major effort little progress was made against the German Third Army, and some limited German counter-attacks were made along the La Bassée Canal and near Soissons in early 1915. A simultaneous British offensive north of La Bassée made initial progress at Neuve Chapelle (10 March), but the German Sixth Army (Rupprecht of Bavaria) recovered the line. French attacks against the St. Mihiel salient were unsuccessful (Battle of the Woëvre, 6–15 April), and before the Allies could co-ordinate another attack, Germany mounted its own, against Ypres, in April–May 1915. They made good progress following the first use in the west of poison gas (22 April), but the concentration of effort on the

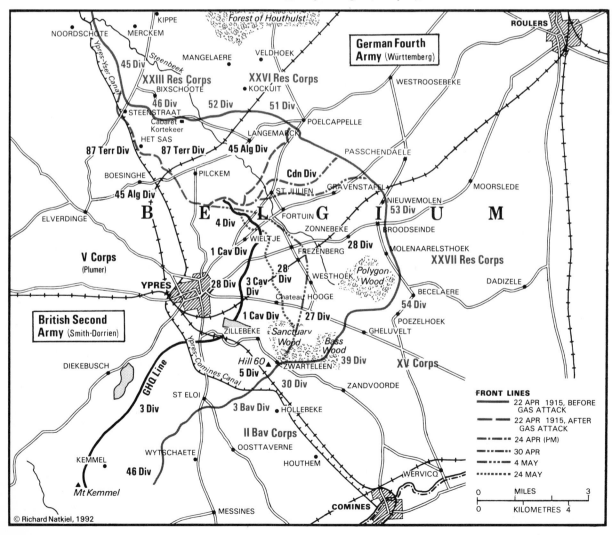

© Richard Natkiel, 1992

Eastern Front precluded the existence of sufficient reserves to capitalize on the initial success, and the British held on. The renewed Allied offensive around Festubert (British, 9–26 May) and in the Second Battle of Artois (French, around Souchez, 16 May–30 June) had very limited success and at severe cost in both lives and munitions: this was the period of the 'shell scandal' in which military commentators and the popular press castigated the responsible ministries for not ensuring an adequate supply of ammunition. In Britain, it resulted in David Lloyd George's appointment to head a Munitions Committee, from which position his importance in the political leadership of the Allies increased steadily.

After a period of recuperation, Joffre launched yet another co-ordinated assault, the British advancing against the German Sixth Army at Loos (25 September–14 October) and the French a short way south against Vimy Ridge (Third Battle of Artois), while the French made another attack in the Second Battle of Champagne. By the time fighting subsided in early November, the small Allied gains had cost about 60,000 British and approaching a quarter of a million French casualties, and about 140,000 German. Among the consequences of these immensely costly operations was the replacement of Sir John French as British commander-in-chief by Sir Douglas Haig (19 December). The reorganization of the British command structure also included the appointment of French's chief-of-staff, Sir William Robertson, as chief of Imperial General Staff, ensuring that the maximum effort would be concentrated in the western theatre at the expense of the subsidiary operations.

A remarkable photograph (if it is what it purports to be) published in June 1915, showing a German attack upon a position held by The King's (Liverpool) Regiment, near Ypres.

A type of 'casualty' photograph that was deemed acceptable for contemporary publication: German dead, Western Front.

An unprecedented munitions industry developed during the war: Cannon Workshop No. 5, Krupp Works, Essen.

The Serbian retreat: Putnik's caravan, with the ailing marshal being carried in a sedan chair, crossing the River Drin.

The Eastern Front, 1915

The first Austro–Hungarian objective was the relief of Przemysl with its garrison of about 125,000 men. In January Conrad von Hötzendorf initiated a major offensive, a diversionary attack by Baron Karl Pflanzer-Baltin's Army Group which captured Czernowitz (17 February), and the main thrust by the Austro–Hungarian Third Army (General Svetozar Boroević) and the Austro–German South Army (General Alexander von Lisingen). Despite Pflanzer-Baltin's limited success, the other thrust was a complete failure with appalling loss (about 100,000 men), and more than that number were captured when Przemysl finally had to surrender (22 March). As before, the near-destruction of the Austro–Hungarian Army demanded compensatory action from the Germans.

At the beginning of the year, German Ninth Army had made a feint towards Warsaw, resulting in the Battle of Bolimov (31 January) in which the first use of poison gas was made (to such little effect that the Russians never informed the Western allies that they had been attacked by it). Farther north, Hindenburg (in an operation planned by Hoffman) with Eighth and Tenth Armies won a considerable victory against the Russian Tenth Army in the Second Battle of the Masurian Lakes (or 'the Winter Battle'), beginning 7 February, elements of the defeated Russian army only escaping because of a counter-attack upon Hindenburg's right by a new Russian Twelfth Army on 22 February. A Russian push far to the south, into the Carpathians, was checked in March–April; and then the Central Powers launched their main offensive, Falkenhayn going in person to assume overall direction. The initial thrust was in the south, Mackensen's new German Eleventh Army driving into the Russian Third Army between Gorlice and Tarnow; Third Army cracked, the entire southern flank of the Russian line began to crumble, and Przemysl was

retaken in early June. The second phase of the German offensive extended farther north: Hindenburg had been occupying Russian attention north of Warsaw, and now German Twelfth Army (General Max von Gallwitz) drove onwards; Warsaw fell in early August, while Mackensen pushed on and took Brest–Litovsk (25 August). For the Russian army, this was 'the great retreat', the Germans driving back their lines even to Vilna (captured 19 September), before the autumn weather bogged-down the advance. Throughout this operation, however, despite immense losses, Grand Duke Nicholas had managed to salvage some order and prevent the total disintegration of the Russian Army; otherwise there was a real possibility that Russia could have been knocked out of the war by late 1915. Nicholas received scant recognition: on 5 September he was posted to the Caucasus, the Tsar taking personal command, with General Mikhail Alexeev as chief-of-staff.

To nations involved most heavily in the Western Front, the campaigns in the east have tended to be overlooked; but in these fluid operations, resembling somewhat the 'war of manoeuvre' which had been expected in the west, the combination of Hindenburg, Ludendorff, Mackensen and the often-overlooked Hoffman had performed supremely in stopping the Russian 'steamroller' despite the huge disparity in numbers. The Russian Army had been wounded fatally: they lost about two million men in 1915, half of these prisoners; the Central Powers, about one million.

The Balkan Front, 1915

The Balkans continued to be of significance in the wider strategy of the war, in that Turkey's supply-route from Germany ran through neutral Roumania (until it was closed in June), and Turkey's presence sealed the main Allied supply-route to Russia. Both camps courted Bulgaria, which joined the Central Powers in October following the

Allied reverses at the Dardanelles, and in the hope of securing Macedonia, which it had long coveted. Greece mobilized in response to the Bulgarian threat to Serbia, and requested Allied assistance; a Franco–British expeditionary force landed at Salonika from 9 October in response to this request, only for there to be a simultaneous Greek change of stance, the pro-German King Constantine dismissing his pro-Allied prime minister, Venizelos, and declaring Greek neutrality. In early October, in an operation planned by Falkenhayn and with Mackensen in command, four armies invaded Serbia (two Bulgarian under General Nikolai Zhekov, one Austro–Hungarian under Baron Hermann Kövess von Kövessháza, and one German under General Max von Gallwitz). Despite determined resistance, Putnik's Serbian army was driven south-west, ending in a terrible retreat in bitter winter weather into Montenegro and

Albania; their loss in casualties and prisoners was about half a million. In January 1916 the survivors were evacuated by Allied ships to Corfu, to be re-equipped and re-organized; but to all intents, both Serbia and Montenegro were knocked out of the war, and both countries were occupied by the Central Powers. The Allied contingents in Salonika (French under General Maurice Sarrail, British under Sir Bryan Mahon) did not operate under unified command, and being small and disunited were unable to offer material assistance to the Serbs. In the unusual predicament of being based in a state now neutral, they had no option but adopt a defensive posture against a possible Central Powers offensive.

The Dardanelles, 1915–16

The Allied expedition to the Dardanelles has been termed the one strategic idea of the war; yet it was also one of the most ill-managed in history. The 'easterners' within the Allied command – most notably British First Lord of the Admiralty Winston Churchill – conceived the Dardanelles expedition as a way of removing Turkey from the war and re-opening the supply-line to beleaguered Russia. The plan initially involved forcing the Dardanelles by an Allied fleet, thus gaining access to the Black Sea and opening Constantinople to bombardment, which would almost certainly have resulted in the fall of the Turkish government. From the outset, however, the operation was appallingly mishandled. The initial naval attacks by an Anglo–French fleet under Admiral Sackville Carden were mounted in February 1915; and by his successor, Admiral John de Robeck, a major attempt was made to force 'the Narrows' on 18 March, which was unsuccessful due to the strengthening of the Turkish shore-defences in the interim, the Turkish forces having profited greatly from German reorganization and

> 'We fixed bayonets and clambered out, and somehow got together some kind of formation and rushed towards the hedge . . . at last we arrived with a yell at the ditch where the German riflemen were concealed . . . being six feet below us, they had no chance. When we had each "done" our man we had to jump over the ditch and on towards the German guns. We were running like hell, when all of a sudden machine-guns poured into us from both sides, knocking dozens of us over in heaps. The officers gave the word to retire, and we came back at a run. When we came to the trench we had already jumped we found that we had not killed all the Germans in it, and as we passed over it again we were shot at, and my pal was nearly bayoneted. We got back, and did not do much good . . .'
>
> (Anonymous Cameron Highlander, in *The War Stories of Private Thomas Atkins*, p. 50, London, 1914)

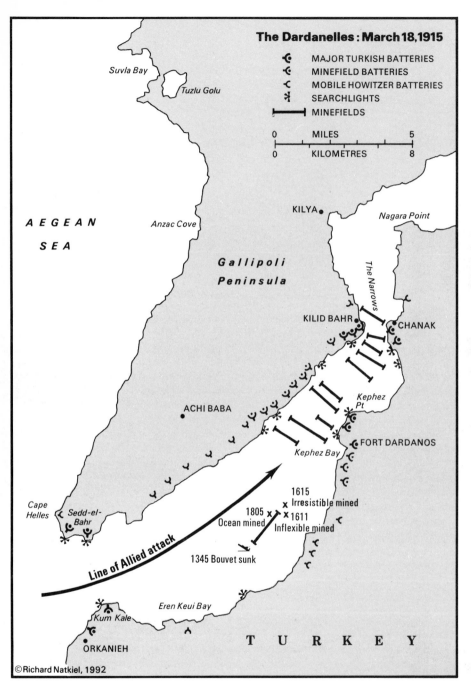

The Dardanelles : March 18, 1915

MAJOR TURKISH BATTERIES
MINEFIELD BATTERIES
MOBILE HOWITZER BATTERIES
SEARCHLIGHTS
MINEFIELDS

0   MILES   5
0   KILOMETRES   8

Suvla Bay

Tuzlu Golu

KILYA

Nagara Point

A E G E A N

S E A

Anzac Cove

*Gallipoli
Peninsula*

The Narrows

KILID BAHR

CHANAK

ACHI BABA

*Kephez
Pt*

Kephez Bay

FORT DARDANOS

*Cape
Helles*   *Sedd-el-
Bahr*

1615
x Irresistible mined
1805 x x 1611
Ocean mined Inflexible mined

1345 Bouvet sunk

Line of Allied attack

Eren Keui Bay

Kum Kale

T U R K E Y

ORKANIEH

©Richard Natkiel, 1992

HMS Irresistible sinking as a result of striking a mine, during the Allied attempt to force the Dardanelles on 18 March 1915.

An example of amphibious landing: French artillery being towed ashore at Gallipoli.

command. Ironically, when de Robeck called off the naval attack, the Turks were on the point of collapse.

The naval assault having failed, and much against the better judgement of those Allied commanders who wished to concentrate resources on the Western Front, it was decided to land an expedition on the Gallipoli peninsula, to drive up towards Constantinople. A force was assembled of British troops, a smaller French contingent, and the ANZAC (Australian and New Zealand Army Corps) from Egypt, all under the command of the experienced Sir Ian Hamilton, a man of considerable reputation, exceptional bravery, but lacking the decisive qualities needed for the leadership of such an expedition. Using bases on islands off the Turkish coast, the Allied force assembled with some difficulty, and sufficiently slowly for the Turkish defences to be overhauled by the German general Otto Liman von Sanders.

The Gallipoli landing was mismanaged from the outset: the first descent (25 April) was made by the British at Cape Helles, on the tip of the peninsula, and by the ANZACs at 'Anzac Cove' further north, upon the western shore; and

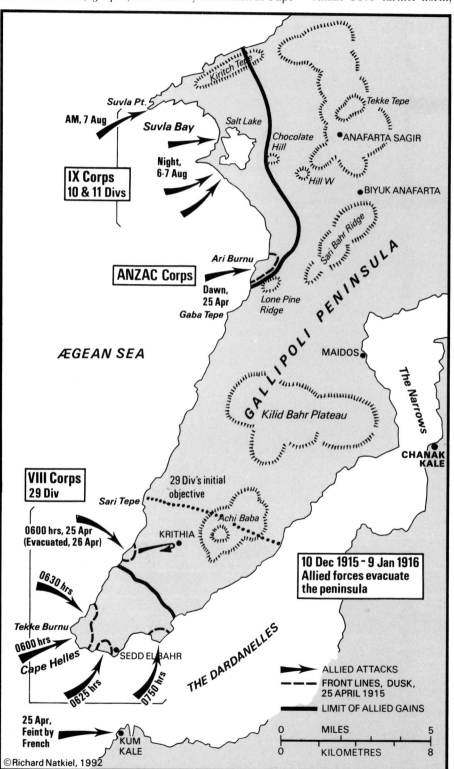

A rare photograph of the first landing at Gallipoli: HQ of 2nd Battalion, Royal Fusiliers on the cliffs above 'X' Beach, 25 April 1915. At the left is Lieutenant-Colonel Newenham, wounded later that day, and in the centre the battalion adjutant, Captain Thomas Duncombe Shafto, who was killed a week later, 2 May.

The converted merchant ship River Clyde *beached at Helles (Gallipoli) as a landing-vessel; troops attempted to storm ashore via ramps and doorways cut in the ship's sides.*

Map labels:

Kiritch Tepe

Suvla Pt.

AM, 7 Aug

Suvla Bay

Salt Lake

Tekke Tepe

Chocolate Hill

● ANAFARTA SAGIR

Night, 6-7 Aug

IX Corps 10 & 11 Divs

Hill W

● BIYUK ANAFARTA

Sari Bahr Ridge

ANZAC Corps

Ari Burnu

Dawn, 25 Apr

Lone Pine Ridge

Gaba Tepe

GALLIPOLI PENINSULA

ÆGEAN SEA

MAIDOS ●

The Narrows

Kilid Bahr Plateau

CHANAK KALE

VIII Corps 29 Div

29 Div's initial objective

Sari Tepe

● Achi Baba

0600 hrs, 25 Apr (Evacuated, 26 Apr)

KRITHIA ●

10 Dec 1915 - 9 Jan 1916 Allied forces evacuate the peninsula

0630 hrs

Tekke Burnu

0600 hrs

Cape Helles

SEDD EL BAHR

THE DARDANELLES

0625 hrs

0750 hrs

ALLIED ATTACKS

FRONT LINES, DUSK, 25 APRIL 1915

LIMIT OF ALLIED GAINS

25 Apr, Feint by French

KUM KALE ●

©Richard Natkiel, 1992

0   MILES   5

0   KILOMETRES   8

throughout the summer both forces, and the Turks, were involved in an attritional battle of quite dreadful proportions. After immense loss of life, a second landing was arranged farther north, at Suvla Bay, to coincide with further attacks upon Krithia in the south and by the ANZACs to break out of their bridgehead. Both the latter operations failed, and the Suvla landing established only another small bridgehead, which even though it later linked up with 'Anzac' had no chance of achieving the success desired. Hamilton was relieved of command on 15 October, and the new commander, Sir Charles Monro, recommended evacuation; and unlike the chaos of the earlier operations, the withdrawal was a masterpiece of planning, the Allies suffering not a single casualty in the operation, Suvla/Anzac being evacuated on 19–20 December and Helles on 8–9 January 1916. Both sides had suffered immense losses and had achieved miracles of heroism and fortitude in the most appalling of conditions; and in Mustafa Kemal, the Turks discovered a commander of real worth who was to make an indelible mark on the history of his nation. The predominant impression of Gallipoli, however, is one of useless, futile waste.

The Italian Front, 1915–16

1915 saw the opening of another front, following Italy's entry into the war. Originally favouring the Central Powers (in the old 'Triple Alliance' of Austria–Hungary, Germany and Italy), Italy entered the Allied camp in May 1915 in the

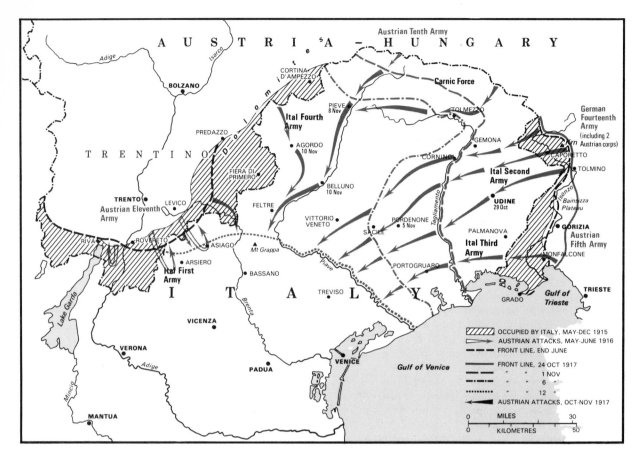

hope of achieving territorial gains at the expense of Austria and in the Balkans. Their army was numerous but not well-equipped, and suffered from poor leadership, which enabled the hard-pressed Austrians to contain them, initially with only limited German assistance.

Italy's plan was to operate in two main spheres: to hold the Trentino salient (butting into Italy) while making an offensive against the Isonzo salient (jutting into Austria). Conrad von Hötzendorf wished to attack Italy, but Falkenhayn forced him to adopt a basically defensive posture from lack of resources, which resulted in Italy being the offensive power of the war, striking against the heavily fortified Austrian frontier defences commanded by the Archduke Eugene. Italian operations were directed by their commander-in-chief, General Luigi Cadorna.

Operations in 1915 cost both sides heavily, but saw no substantial Italian progress, in the First to Fourth Battles of the Isonzo, lasting from June to December: Italy lost about 160,000 men, Austria–Hungary about 115,000. Despite the scale of these losses, there was really no option for Italy but to continue battering in the same area, although their operations were conducted with considerable ineptitude. The Fifth Battle of the Isonzo (11–29 March 1916) achieved no more, and was abandoned when the Austro–Hungarians launched their own attack, on the Trentino, from mid-May,

made possible by the Central Powers' success in Serbia. Considerable progress was made by Eugene's Third and Eleventh Armies against the Italian Fifth Army, but after a month the Austro–Hungarians withdrew somewhat and re-assumed the defensive, as resources were needed urgently on the Eastern Front. This gave Cadorna the opportunity to renew the offensive on the Isonzo, and although Gorizia was taken in the Sixth Battle (6–17 August), no major break-through was achieved, and the Seventh to Ninth Battles of the Isonzo (lasting until mid-November) were merely attritional actions which produced no concrete gains.

The Caucasus Front, 1915–17

With the destruction of much of his army at Sarikamish, due in considerable extent to his own ineptitude, Enver relin-quished command and returned to the capital to direct the war from there. Vorontsov–Dashkov failed to capitalize on the Turkish discomfiture, and was replaced by General Nikolai Yudenich. In April 1915 Armenia rose against the Turks (who had been massacring Armenians, suspecting them of aiding Russia), and seized Van. The new Turkish commander, General Abdul Kerim, counter-attacked and won a victory at Malazgirt (16 July), but was then checked and withdrew; but recaptured Van in early August. In September Grand Duke Nicholas arrived to take overall

The following diary extract was apparently written by an anonymous member of 2nd Battalion Border Regiment, and found in a German trench in 1915, which fact boded ill for the fate of the writer. The vivid account of a charge concerns that which occurred near Laventie on 18 December 1914:

'. . . the Officer came down the trench and told us there was going to be a charge . . . you could hear the men praying to God to look after there wife and children should anythink happen to them . . . our left was to soon with the charge and as soon as there voices went up so did the German lead and they let us have it . . . we were going down like raindrops as our trenches was only 70 yds apart so we retired and then made the second charge but received the same. We retired again and stopped in mid field and it was like being in a Blacksmith shop watching him swing a hammer on a red hot shoe and the sparks flying all round you but instead of them being sparks they were bullets . . . we lieyed there it was a pitiful sight to see and hear our comrades dyeing and could not get help to them as it ment serten death if we moved . . . We had to lay there from 6.20 [p.m] to 8.15 a.m. the next morning . . . it came over verry misty and this being our only chance we made good of it. So we crawl half way and then made a run for it. We could not see were we were going so fell over our comrades who were dead . . . And I must say I think it the first time I said my prayers in earnest which is nothing to my credit for when I looked round and saw my chums I thanked God he had spared me there fate.'

(Reproduced in *Made in the Trenches*, ed. Sir Frederick Treves Bt., pp. 84–5, London, 1916)

command, Yudenich retaining field command. Nicholas directed Yudenich's advance beginning in January 1916, which defeated Kerim's Third Army at Köprukoy on 18 January and stormed Erzerum (13–16 February). A Russian army and navy offensive along the Black Sea coast captured Trebizond (18 April), against which Enver planned a counter-attack by Third Army, with a new Second Army advancing against Yudenich's left. Yudenich, one of Russia's few truly capable generals, defeated Third Army completely at Erzinjan (25 July), and despite minor successes achieved by Mustafa Kemal (promoted from the Dardanelles to command a corps), Second Army made little progress and fighting on the Caucasus Front went into a lull in the autumn of 1916.

The Palestine Front, 1915–16

Operations in Palestine at this period hinged upon British possession of the Suez Canal, the reason for Britain's assumption of power in Egypt. The Turkish minister of marine, Djemal Pasha, and his German chief-of-staff Baron Kress von Kressenstein, made an attempt on the Canal by crossing the Sinai, but were repulsed easily (2–3 February

A major development during the war was the practice of women taking over many occupations previously the preserve of male workers: British munitions workers checking the hardness of shell steel.

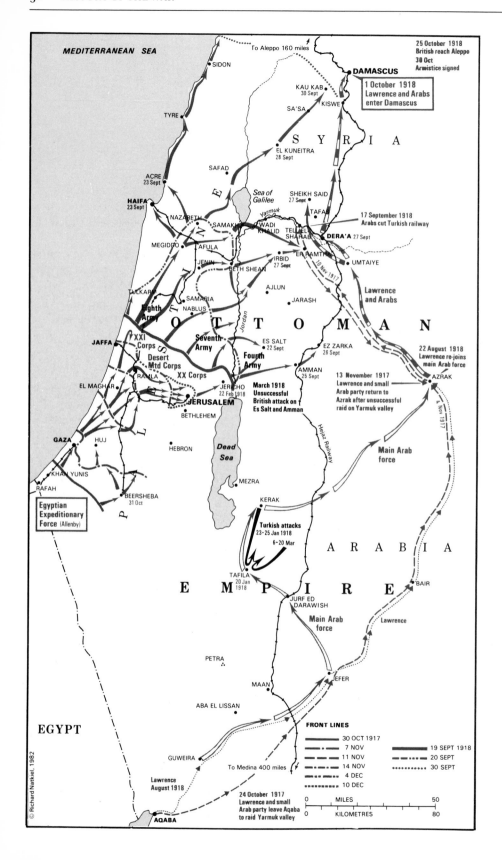

MEDITERRANEAN SEA

25 October 1918
British reach Aleppo
30 Oct
Armistice signed

To Aleppo 160 miles

SIDON

DAMASCUS

KAU KAB
30 Sept

KISWE

1 October 1918
Lawrence and Arabs
enter Damascus

SA'SA

TYRE

S Y R I A

EL KUNEITRA
28 Sept

SAFAD

ACRE
23 Sept

Sea of
Galilee

SHEIKH SAID
27 Sept

HAIFA
23 Sept

NAZARETH   SAMAKH   Yarmuk   WADI   TAFAS

17 September 1918
Arabs cut Turkish railway

KHALID   TELL EL
SHAHAB   DERA'A 27 Sept

MEGIDDO   AFULA

ER RAMTHA

UMTAIYE

JENIN   BETH SHEAN   IRBID
27 Sept

10 Nov 1917

TULKARM   AJLUN

SAMARIA   JARASH

Lawrence
and Arabs

**Eighth
Army**

NABLUS

O T T O M A N

Jordan

ES SALT
22 Sept

EZ ZARKA
26 Sept

22 August 1918
Lawrence re-joins
main Arab force

JAFFA   XXI
Corps

**Seventh
Army**

**Fourth
Army**

AZRAK

Desert
Mtd Corps

XX Corps

AMMAN
25 Sept

13 November 1917
Lawrence and small
Arab party return to
Azrak after unsuccessful
raid on Yarmuk valley

EL MAGHAR   RAMLA

JERICHO
22 Feb 1918

March 1918
Unsuccessful
British attack on
Es Salt and Amman

4 Nov 1917

JERUSALEM

BETHLEHEM

GAZA   HUJ

Hejaz Railway

Main Arab
force

KHAN YUNIS

Dead
Sea

RAFAH

HEBRON

BEERSHEBA
31 Oct

MEZRA

**Egyptian
Expeditionary
Force** (Allenby)

KERAK

A R A B I A

BAIR

Turkish attacks
23–25 Jan 1918
6–20 Mar

E M P I R E

TAFILA
20 Jan
1918

JURF ED
DARAWISH

Main Arab
force

Lawrence

PETRA

MAAN   JEFER

ABA EL LISSAN

FRONT LINES

EGYPT

FRONT LINES		
30 OCT 1917		19 SEPT 1918
7 NOV		20 SEPT
11 NOV		30 SEPT
14 NOV		
4 DEC		
10 DEC		

GUWEIRA

Lawrence
August 1918

To Medina 400 miles

24 October 1917
Lawrence and small
Arab party leave Aqaba
to raid Yarmuk valley

0   MILES   50

0   KILOMETRES   80

AQABA

© Richard Natkiel, 1982

1915). Although some eighteen months passed before the next major action between British and Turks, the threat to the Canal occupied resources needed more urgently in the Dardanelles; and throughout 1916 Britain pushed their defences into the Sinai, preparing for a possible drive against the Turks. Turkish operations were considerably hampered by the Arab Revolt in the Hejaz, encouraged by the Allies, from the last half of 1916 involving Arab guerrilla activity against Turkish supply-lines and garrisons throughout the area, into Syria. The head of the British positions in the Sinai was attacked by Kress von Kressenstein and a Turkish army (with German support) at Rumani on 3 August 1916, but the thrust was repelled with heavy Turkish loss.

Mesopotamian Front, 1915–16

Their forces directed from India, and including large numbers of Indian troops, Britain's Mesopotamian expedition under the command of Sir John Nixon was enlarged in its Basra bridgehead, and Turkish probes on the outposts at Qurna and Ahwaz were repelled easily. With the intention of advancing on Baghdad, Nixon sent Major-General Charles Townshend with a divisional force along the Tigris, from May 1915. His flank was protected by Major-General George Gorringe, advancing along the Euphrates, defeating a Turkish force at Nasiriya (24 July 1915). Reinforced, Townshend pressed on to take Kut-el-Amara on the Tigris, driving back the Turkish defenders on 27–8 September. Although this was a considerable victory, Townshend's communications were already stretched; but the successes achieved persuaded the British cabinet to back a full-scale advance on Baghdad, in an attempt to redress the decline in British prestige in the Muslim world as a result of the failures in the Dardanelles.

Despite the obvious weaknesses of the position, and the unavailability of reinforcements, Nixon was urged to push on to Baghdad. Townshend's attack on the reinforced Turkish forces entrenched at Ctesiphon (22–6 November) was unsuccessful, and he retired on Kut, holding off a somewhat half-hearted Turkish counter-attack at Umm-at-Tubai. Sending away his cavalry, Townshend waited in Kut for reinforcement, and was besieged there on 7 December 1915. A British attempt to break through to Kut, led by General Fenton Aylmer, failed in January 1916, and a second attempt by Gorringe (Aylmer's successor) in March was repulsed by the Turkish Sixth Army under the German veteran General Colmar von der Goltz, shortly before his death from tropical fever (or possibly poison at the hands of

the 'Young Turks'). With his supplies exhausted, Townshend surrendered Kut and his army on 29 April, a further very serious blow to British prestige; and not until the turn of the year were the British forces able to resume the offensive.

The Western Front, 1916

1916 witnessed two of the most costly and least-inspired military operations in history, at a time when both camps were already experiencing severe shortages of manpower (to the extent that in Britain it was necessary to institute compulsory military service for the first time). Both sides decided on offence: Joffre, anxious that the Allies should co-ordinate their strategies, called a conference at Chantilly

A popular slogan, especially during the earlier part of the war: 'Remember Belgium', as shown on a British recruiting poster. A verse in The Wipers Times, *26 February 1916, noted:*

'Oft we're told "Remember Belgium"
In the years that are to be;
Crosses set by all her ditches
Are our pledge of memory.'

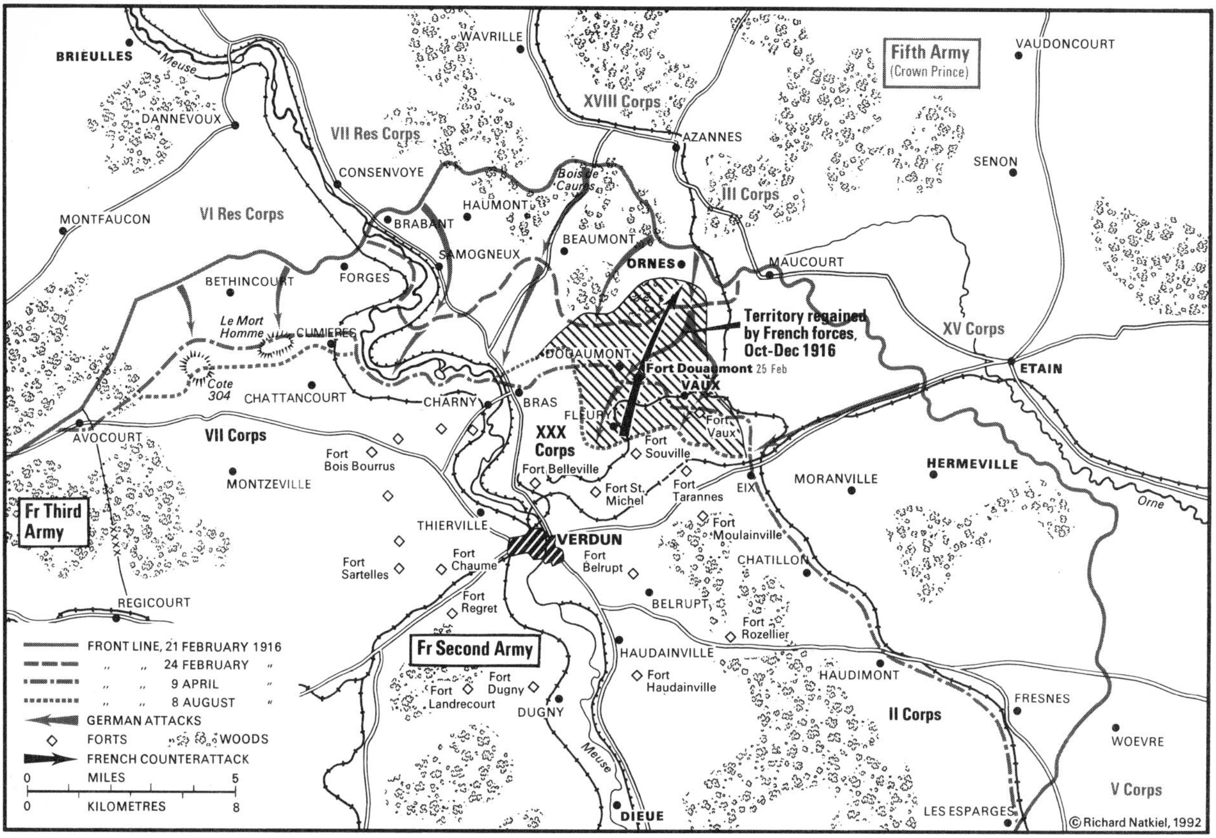
BRIEULLES
Meuse
DANNEVOUX
WAVRILLE
VII Res Corps
XVIII Corps
Fifth Army
(Crown Prince)
VAUDONCOURT
AZANNES
SENON
CONSENVOYE
Bois de Caures
III Corps
MONTFAUCON
VI Res Corps
BRABANT
HAUMONT
BEAUMONT
SAMOGNEUX
ORNES
MAUCOURT
BETHINCOURT
FORGES
Le Mort Homme
CUMIERES
Territory regained by French forces, Oct-Dec 1916
XV Corps
DOUAUMONT
Fort Douaumont 25 Feb
ETAIN
Cote 304
CHATTANCOURT
CHARNY
BRAS
VAUX
FLEURY
Fort Vaux
AVOCOURT
VII Corps
XXX Corps
Fort Souville
Fort Bois Bourrus
Fort Belleville
HERMEVILLE
MONTZEVILLE
Fort St. Michel
Fort Tarannes
EIX
MORANVILLE
Orne
Fr Third Army
THIERVILLE
Fort Moulainville
VERDUN
Fort Belrupt
CHATILLON
Fort Sartelles
Fort Chaume
Fort Regret
BELRUPT
REGICOURT
Fort Rozellier
FRONT LINE, 21 FEBRUARY 1916
" " 24 FEBRUARY "
" " 9 APRIL "
" " 8 AUGUST "
GERMAN ATTACKS
FORTS
WOODS
FRENCH COUNTERATTACK
0 MILES 5
0 KILOMETRES 8
Fr Second Army
HAUDAINVILLE
Fort Haudainville
HAUDIMONT
Fort Dugny
Fort Landrecourt
DUGNY
II Corps
FRESNES
WOEVRE
V Corps
DIEUE
LES ESPARGES
©Richard Natkiel, 1992

(December 1915) to arrange for a general offensive on Western, Eastern and Italian Fronts in about the middle of the year; Falkenhayn, believing that Germany could better survive a protracted war of attrition, planned a major effort on the Western Front which, even if it did not defeat the Allies, would cause France such casualties as to 'bleed them white'.

Falkenhayn took the offensive first, attacking the salient in the French line around Verdun. This, the most protracted battle of the war, began on 21 February with Crown Prince Wilhelm's Fifth Army offensive. Five days later he carried one of the most important positions in the defensive complex around Verdun, Fort Douaumont; and on the same day Joffre appointed General Henri Pétain to command the sector, with orders to hold at all costs. There developed in the Verdun area a slaughter in which attrition was the deliberate policy, pointless in terms of territory gained. Falkenhayn deployed up to forty divisions in the battle; the French, having to rotate units constantly because of casualties and exhaustion, used about two-thirds of their front-line infantry at some stage. Pétain's statement '*Ils ne passeront pas!*' was echoed by his subordinates, Generals Robert Nivelle and Charles 'Butcher' Mangin, as possession of the area, blasted almost out of existence (some 20 million shells were expended during the battle) became a symbol of French pride. With most communications severed, Verdun was supplied by a single minor road, the so-called *Voie Sacrée*, which became as famous as the strongpoints around Verdun over which so much blood was spilled. Attacks and counter-attacks on the west and east faces of the salient were relentless, with major German pushes being made in early March and throughout April and May. Pétain was promoted and command of Verdun was given to Nivelle; and the important Fort Vaux was finally captured by the Germans on 9 June. It was followed by renewed assaults, and the French almost cracked (Pétain recommended a withdrawal, refused by Joffre), but the tenacious defence at last brought its reward. Germany had to transfer resources to the Eastern Front, and on 29 August Falkenhayn was relieved of command, and replaced in the west by Hindenburg and Ludendorff; and after so much effort, the Germans decided to assume a defensive posture. This gave the French their first respite and opportunity to counter-attack: Forts Douaumont and Vaux were recaptured and by the end of the year their position was almost back to what it had been before the battle for Verdun began. For virtually no change in possession of this morass of mud and rubble both sides had lost immense numbers; statistics vary but the casualties were perhaps more than half a million French and more than 400,000 Germans.

The second period of almost pointless slaughter occurred farther north, along the Somme. Joffre had planned a joint

The utter devastation of many battlefields transformed the countryside into a nightmare landscape. This is the village of Guillemont, Somme, in 1916.

British casualty clearing-station, Western Front.

offensive, but with Verdun occupying so much of the French Army, the main attack had to be made by Britain, with assistance south of the Somme from Foch's French Northern Army Group. General Henry Rawlinson's British Fourth Army made the principal effort, with General Edmund Allenby's Third Army farther north also taking the offensive. On 1 July the attack was made against the German Second Army, and by nightfall the British had suffered 60,000 casualties (19,000 dead), the bloodiest day in the British Army's history and also the greatest loss by one side on any day of the World War. Attacking in waves towards the German wire – much undamaged despite a huge preparatory bombardment – the British troops were massacred to such an extent that it could be argued that 1 July 1916 was the day in which the old world was for ever

changed ('So ends the Golden Age' was the comment in the history of one battalion).[3] The loss was made more appalling in falling most heavily upon 'New Army' battalions recruited often from small communities like Accrington (11th East Lancashires), Barnsley (13th and 14th York and Lancaster) and Grimsby (10th Lincolns), battalions of 'Pals' and 'Chums' assembled on the promise of serving with their local 'pals', such communities being devastated by the losses sustained. The 10th (Service) Battalion, Prince of Wales's Own West Yorkshire Regiment, raised at York, with 710 casualties on 1 July, suffered probably the highest percentage unit-loss of any battalion during the war, but at least had one officer left at the end, albeit a wounded one; the 1st Battalion, Hampshire Regiment lost every one of theirs.

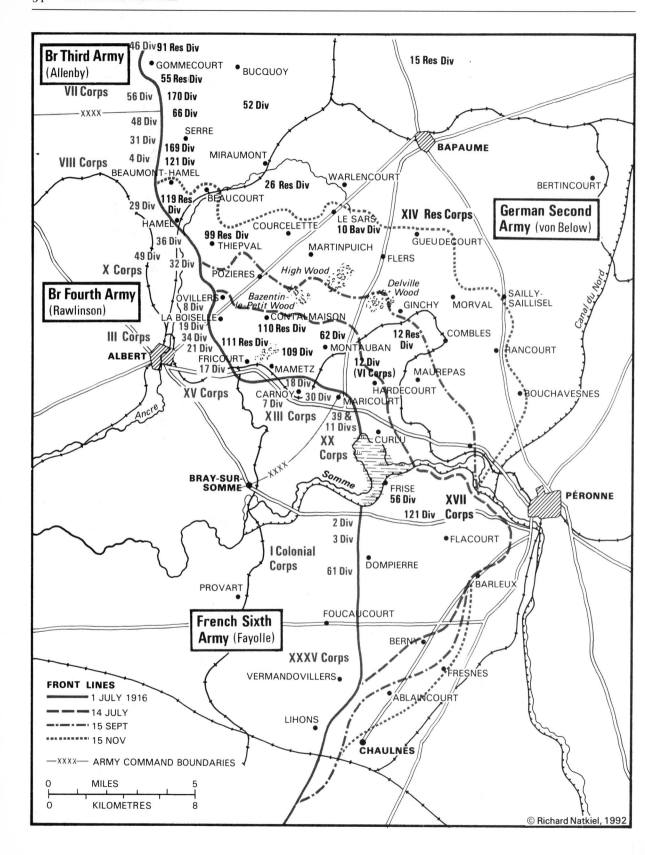

Br Third Army (Allenby)

VII Corps

46 Div 91 Res Div

GOMMECOURT   BUCQUOY

55 Res Div

56 Div   170 Div

66 Div

52 Div

15 Res Div

XXXX

48 Div

31 Div   SERRE

4 Div   169 Div

VIII Corps   121 Div   MIRAUMONT

BEAUMONT-HAMEL

26 Res Div   WARLENCOURT   BAPAUME   BERTINCOURT

119 Res Div   BEAUCOURT

29 Div   HAMEL   COURCELETTE   LE SARS   XIV Res Corps

99 Res Div   10 Bav Div   GUEUDECOURT   **German Second Army** (von Below)

36 Div   THIEPVAL   MARTINPUICH

49 Div   32 Div   FLERS   SAILLY-SAILLISEL

X Corps   POZIERES   High Wood

Br Fourth Army (Rawlinson)   OVILLERS   8 Div   Bazentin-le-Petit Wood   Delville Wood   GINCHY   MORVAL

LA BOISELLE   CONTALMAISON   GINCHY

III Corps   19 Div   110 Res Div   COMBLES   RANCOURT

34 Div   111 Res Div   62 Div   12 Res Div

ALBERT   21 Div   109 Div   MONTAUBAN   MAUREPAS   BOUCHAVESNES

FRICOURT   12 Div (VI Corps)

17 Div   MAMETZ   HARDECOURT

18 Div   MARICOURT

XV Corps   CARNOY   30 Div

7 Div   XIII Corps   39 & 11 Divs

Ancre   XX Corps   CURLU

XXXX   Somme

BRAY-SUR-SOMME   FRISE   56 Div   XVII Corps   **PÉRONNE**

121 Div

2 Div

3 Div   FLACOURT

I Colonial Corps   61 Div   DOMPIERRE   BARLEUX

PROVART

FOUCAUCOURT   BERNY

French Sixth Army (Fayolle)   XXXV Corps   FRESNES

VERMANDOVILLERS   ABLAINCOURT

LIHONS   CHAULNES

FRONT LINES

——— 1 JULY 1916
– – – 14 JULY
–·–·– 15 SEPT
········· 15 NOV

—XXXX— ARMY COMMAND BOUNDARIES

0   MILES   5
0   KILOMETRES   8

Canal du Nord

© Richard Natkiel, 1992

Despite these losses, Haig pushed on in a series of lesser attacks, almost breaking through the German second line on 13–14 July, and made considerable progress on 15 September at Flers–Courcelette (by the first use of armoured vehicles), but when the battle subsided in mid-November the total advance had been only some eight miles, at a cost of 615,000 Allied casualties (420,000 British), and German losses estimated at between 400 and 650,000. Comparatively early in the battle, Falkenhayn had to transfer units north to meet the Somme offensive, thus relieving pressure on Verdun, one of the objectives of the operation which was thus accomplished successfully; but such was the scale of the slaughter there and on the Somme that it could be argued that neither French, German nor British armies were ever the same again.

The Eastern Front, 1916–17

In response to French appeals for assistance to draw off German resources from Verdun, Russia made an offensive against the left of the German position on the Eastern Front,

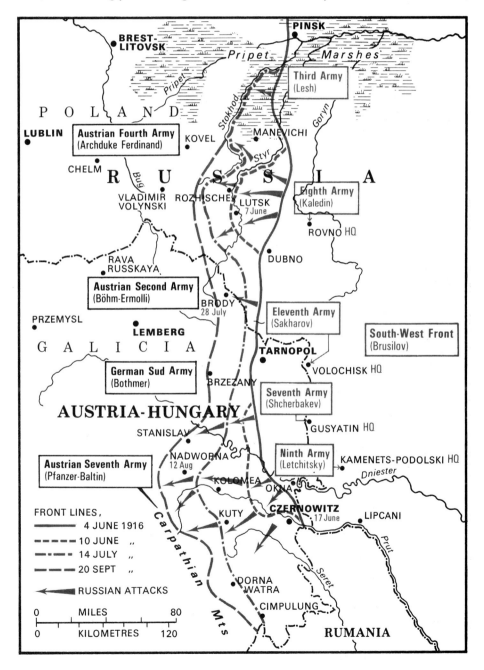

The German 125th Regiment (7th Württemberg) prepares to go into action near Metz, 22 August 1914:

'. . . that morning we received joyous tidings . . . Attack the enemy on sight!

'Although we had had an awful march that night, with just two hours' rest, we forgot hunger and exhaustion. Wood and vale were still shrouded with mist and the hills were wrapped in graceful veils.

'Silently we advanced in open formation. We were sternly confident of victory; and the predominant feeling was one of curiosity to see the enemy. Slowly the mist was dispelled, and behind us in the blue-grey morning sky, a fiery red cloud was to be seen.

'"That is the gate of Valhalla," said a man . . .'
(Unidentified German officer, ed. Dr. H. Cimino, *Navy & Army Illustrated*, p. 53, 1 May 1915)

by the First Army of General Alexei Kuropatkin; it failed, with huge loss, in the First Battle of Lake Naroch (18 March–14 April).

Again in response to Allied pleas (this time from Italy), Russia launched its major offensive in early June, led by the commander of the South-western Army Group, General Alexei Brusilov, one of the best Russian commanders. In a huge attack directed at the south of the Central Powers' front, Brusilov employed the Russian Seventh, Eighth, Ninth and Eleventh Armies in a double-headed attack, mounted upon the Austro–Hungarian First, Fourth and Seventh Armies, and the Austro–German 'South Army' (Südarmee), all under command of General Alexander von Linsingen. It was the best-planned and organized Russian operation of the war and, beginning on 4 June, the 'Brusilov offensive' had spectacular results: the Austro–Hungarian Fourth Army of the incompetent Archduke Joseph Ferdinand was virtually destroyed, and only the Südarmee (bolstered by its German units) resisted solidly, until forced to retreat by the collapse of the Austro–Hungarians around it. So catastrophic was the collapse that Falkenhayn had to hurry reinforcements from the west, and direct part of Hindenburg's command (farther north) to transfer south to bolster the defence of the Carpathians; and Austro–Hungarian reinforcements had to be moved from the Italian Front. Linsingen counter-attacked in mid-June and checked Brusilov's northern attack, but in late July and throughout August Brusilov pushed on, to the edge of the Carpathians, until the offensive finally halted as a result of lack of supplies, exhaustion and decimation of the Russian forces, and the lack of support Brusilov had received from other Russian Army Groups.

Apart from the territory gained, the Brusilov offensive had profound effects. Despite its success, it cost the Russian army about a million casualties, which was militarily unsustainable and encouraged unrest and demoralization. The near-collapse of the Austro–Hungarian Army resulted

in a change of concept of the Central Powers partnership which had already been largely the fact: that from being a dominant partner, Germany now assumed total control. In mid-September the Kaiser became nominal commander on the entire Eastern Front; Conrad von Hötzendorf was left to direct only the Italian Front, and in the following March was relieved of his duty as Austrian chief-of-staff.

The Brusilov offensive also brought another combatant into the war, and ironically gave the Central Powers a success to redress the balance of recent Eastern Front operations. Influenced by the early Russian progress, and after much negotiation with the Allies over the acquisition of Transylvania, Roumania entered the war on the Allied side on 27 August. Roumania's forces were not prepared for war, and required Russian assistance; yet by the time they declared war on the Central Powers, Brusilov's advance had already slowed. Predictably, the Roumanian campaign was brief. Falkenhayn (recently transferred after his replacement as overall commander) held the Roumanians with his Ninth Army, as Mackensen's Danube Army (Bulgarian, German, Austro–Hungarian and Turkish) left the operations against Salonika and drove north, through the Dobrudja, where the Roumanian General Alexandru Averescu had intended to make an offensive with his Third Army. Trapped between Mackensen and Falkenhayn, the Roumanians were unable to check either advance and were defeated overwhelmingly at the River Arges (1–4 December); both German commanders entered Bucharest in triumph on 6 December. Having lost about 350,000 of their initial 550,000 troops, the Roumanians were left in possession of only a tiny portion of their country, the remnant of the army retiring into Russia, leaving the valuable oil- and grain-producing resources of Roumania in German hands.

The war on the Eastern Front swung irrevocably in the direction of the Central Powers in 1917, although with the departure of Hindenburg and Ludendorff, German operations became less extensive (nominal control in the east was vested in Prince Leopold of Bavaria, though Hoffman retained his influential planning role). In March 1917 three years of war, and decades of ferment, resulted in the beginning of the Russian Revolution. The Tsar abdicated and was replaced by a Provisional Government, but its authority was undermined by the Soviets (revolutionary councils), and discipline within the armed forces collapsed. Disorder was fermented by Bolshevik agitators (most notably Lenin, who returned from exile with German assistance), and observing the collapse of order, Germany avoided offensive operations lest they caused the opposing factions to unite in the face of foreign aggression. The war minister and later leader of the Provisional Government, Alexander Kerensky, attempted to remain faithful to the Allied cause and instigated a new offensive in Galicia, led by Brusilov (now Russian chief-of-staff); from 1 July the Russian Seventh and Eleventh Armies roughly handled the Südarmee, but the offensive soon ground to a halt. From 19 July Hoffman staged a major counter-attack, and the

Russian forces collapsed. The German advance was not pressed; but in September the German Eighth Army of General Oskar von Hutier attacked the Russians in the north, using his infiltration tactics; the Russian Twelfth Army collapsed spectacularly, and to all intents Russian military power ceased to exist. A Bolshevik *coup* overturned the Kerensky government in November 1917, and their leaders began to negotiate peace with Germany, the preliminaries of which were concluded at Brest–Litovsk on 15 December, ending hostilities on the Eastern Front; Roumania signed an armistice on 12 December. Although this did not bring peace to Russia, but merely heralded the Russian Civil War in which a number of other nations became involved, in the wider context of the World War it relieved the Central Powers of one of their main concerns, so that attention now switched almost entirely to the Western Front.

The Balkan Front, 1916–17

The Allied forces around Salonika were increased by Franco–British reinforcements, and the arrival of the reformed Serbian Army in 1916, but relations between the Allied contingents were strained; despite Sarrail's nominal overall command, the British still took directions from home. In the second half of August 1916 Bulgarian–German forces mounted a limited offensive in the Battle of Florina, which drove back the Allied forward positions, but Sarrail counter-attacked from mid-September and, having gained ground, then halted. Towards the end of the year independent Italian operations against the Austro–Hungarians in Albania progressed so far to enable the Italians to join Sarrail's main army.

Similar conditions within the Allied camp prevailed in 1917, and although their strength increased to more than half a million, illnesses such as malaria were so rife that actual combat strength was only a fraction of that number; Macedonia (or 'Muckydonia' to the British) was an unpopular place. Limited Allied offensives in the spring (Battles of Lake Prespa, March, and the Vardar, May) were unsuccessful. Internal unrest in Greece between pro-Central Powers factions (supporting King Constantine) and pro-Allied factions (led by Venizelos) were concluded in June by the abdication of Constantine (under Allied pressure) and his replacement by King Alexander, who immediately installed Venizelos as prime minister; Greece entered the war on the Allied side on 27 June, though their forces were not fully prepared and no immediate Allied offensive resulted. The suspicions and rivalries which had beset Allied command in the Balkans were lifted by the replacement of Sarrail in December 1917; his successor, General Marie-Louis Guillaumat, instituted a reorganization and integrated the Greek forces into those of the other Allies.

The Western Front, 1917

Allied strategy on the Western Front had been considerably influenced by political changes. Asquith's British administration, which had been compelled to change from its original Liberal composition to a coalition as a result of the Dardanelles mishandling, had fallen at the end of 1916 and David Lloyd George had been installed as prime minister. In France, Joffre was promoted in December to serve as military adviser to the government, in effect retiring him from chief command, and Robert Nivelle was installed as chief of general staff, with responsibility for directing the war in the west. It was a most unfortunate choice, as despite his Verdun fame, urbane manners and fluent English, he was clearly unfit for the task. Relations between Lloyd George and Haig were cool, but despite the prime minister's dislike of his Western Front commander, he could not remove him; instead, much to the chagrin of the British military establishment, British forces were subordinated to Nivelle's command. The disagreements, and Nivelle's own pronouncements that the war could be won in 48 hours by a surprise attack(!) cost any chance of his planned operation remaining secret.

Ludendorff, with the approval of the Kaiser and Hindenburg, advocated a defensive posture on both Western and Eastern Fronts, concentrating on a push against Italy; and to this end abandoned the over-stretched German front line in the west, retiring some twenty miles to a newly constructed, layered defensive position, the 'Hindenburg Line', much stronger than the previous position and easier to maintain.

The most important development of 1917, however, was the entry into the war on the Allied side of the United States of America, partially as a result of US casualties from the Germans' unrestricted submarine warfare, and partly from the revelation of the 'Zimmermann note', named after the German foreign minister, in which a suggestion was made of German support should Mexico attempt a conquest of the southern USA. American entry into the war provided the Allies with an enormous boost to morale, and immense resources; but as the US forces were unprepared for war, it would obviously be a very considerable time before their troops could make any impact.

Nivelle's great offensive was planned for the spring of 1917, and as a preliminary British First and Third Armies (Generals H. S. Horne and Sir Edmund Allenby respectively) attacked German Sixth Army (General L. von Falkenhausen) at the Battle of Arras (beginning 9 April), in which the Canadian Corps captured Vimy Ridge (9–14 April); farther south, around Bullecourt, Fifth Army (General Hubert Gough) made less progress, and although Arras was a notable victory, it resulted in no breakthrough.

On 16 April the Nivelle offensive began, on a wide front in Champagne and along the Aisne, involving some 1.2 million men, French Fifth and Sixth Armies (Generals Olivier Mazel and Mangin respectively) leading the assault, supported by First and Tenth (Generals Marie-Emile Fayolle and Denis Duchêne respectively); against German First and Seventh Armies (Generals Fritz von Below and Max von Boehn respectively). Nivelle adopted his Verdun tactics, of

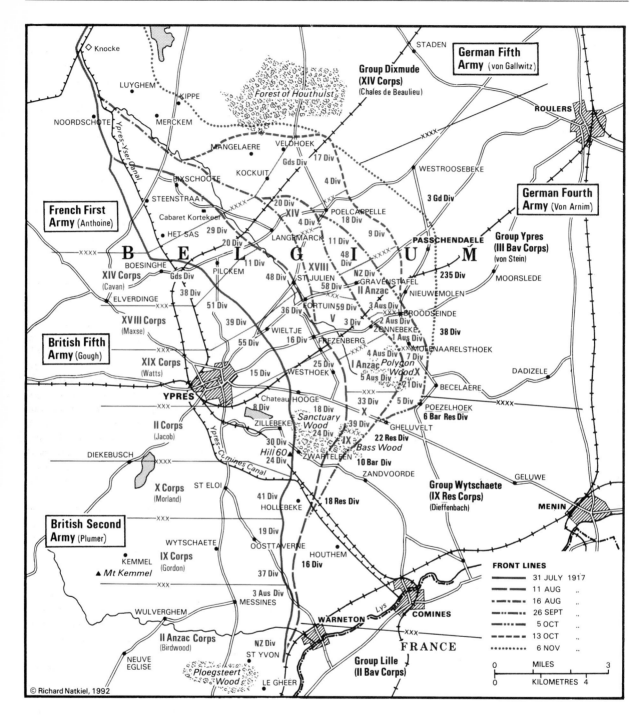

© Richard Natkiel, 1992

a heavy bombardment followed by massed infantry assaults behind a creeping barrage; but as the Germans were cognizant of his plans, thanks largely to his own pronouncements of imminent victory, they were ready. Despite the heroism with which the attack was pressed, the French managed only to reach the German first line, and suffered enormous casualties (118,000 by 20 April).

In comparison with other actions, even these casualties were not too excessive; but the futility of assailing near-impregnable positions, added to the appalling living conditions of the French Army, even when out of the line, caused the army's morale to crack, and mutiny flared along the front, with Sixth Army the worst affected. The situation was so critical that for some two weeks the French front was virtually powerless, but thanks to strict censorship by the time news reached German ears the mutiny had been quelled, and British diversionary attacks helped to occupy German attention during the crucial period. French courts-martial gave heavy sentences to leaders of the mutiny, though only some 49 death sentences were actually carried out. Nivelle was relieved of his command and replaced by Pétain, who did much to restore the army's morale by improving living conditions and pledging an end to attacks conducted without care for casualties.

Attention thus switched to the British sector, where Haig was determined to break through the German defences at the Ypres salient. The preliminary attack, capturing the Messines ridge, was accomplished successfully (beginning 7 June) by Second Army under the capable Sir Herbert Plumer. The main assault, generally styled the Third Battle of Ypres, began on 31 July, led by Sir Hubert Gough's Fifth Army, supported by Plumer and French First Army (General François Anthoine), against General Sixt von Arnim's German Fourth Army. Gough's attack was a considerable failure against German deep defensive positions and conducted over a sea of mud, the waterlogged terrain having been pulverized by artillery for three years. On 25 August Haig transferred overall command from Gough to Plumer who (after the fashion of his Messines operation) made careful plans and in a series of limited attacks succeeded in pushing on towards the village of Passchendaele, which was taken on 6 November, marking the end of the offensive and giving an alternative name to the battle: Passchendaele, synonymous in British annals for mud and useless waste. The operations had extended the Ypres salient by about five miles, for the cost of more than 320,000 casualties (about 200,000 or more for the Germans).

Despite these losses, Haig launched yet another attack, by General Julien Byng's Third Army against the German Second Army (General Georg von der Marwitz) at Cambrai on 20 November. This had no strategic objective, but was intended merely to score a victory before winter; but, by the first use of massed armour, it was a huge success, driving a wedge through the German line. Because it was not part of a major offensive, however, adequate support was not available to exploit the breakthrough, and German counter-attacks recovered almost all the lost ground by 3 December. It is easy to be critical with hindsight, but the unprecedented albeit temporary success of Cambrai highlights even further the utter futility of the Passchendaele operations.

The Italian Front, 1917

The death of the Emperor Franz Josef in November 1916 precipitated a major reform of the Austro–Hungarian military. The new Emperor, Karl, made changes in the administration of the empire and on 1 March 1917 replaced Conrad von Hötzendorf with General Arthur Arz von Straussenberg, while assuming personal command of the armies; he also ended the Austro–German agreement for unified command. This all tended to undermine his standing with his allies, and their disillusionment was completed in the following year with the publication of Karl's abortive attempts to persuade France to accept a negotiated peace. Because of Austria–Hungary's declining military power, Italy feared they would need German assistance, so themselves requested Allied help; Nivelle sent Foch to plan Franco–British reinforcement should Italy prove incapable of holding their front unaided.

Italy's contribution to the Allied offensive of 1917 only began in the middle of the year, Cadorna launching the Tenth Battle of the Isonzo (from 12 May); despite huge loss for little gain, he renewed the assault in the Eleventh Battle, in which the southern flank (the Duke of Aosta's Third Army) was halted by Boreović's Austro–Hungarian Fifth Army, but to the north the Italian Second Army (General Luigi Capello) made considerable progress until the offensive outran its supplies. With the Austro–Hungarians on the point of collapse, they appealed for German assistance, and a comparatively small force of German troops was assembled in an Austro–German Fourteenth Army (General Otto von Below), with the counter-attack prepared by Ludendorff's mountain warfare expert, General Konrad Krafft von Dellmensingen. The Austro–Hungarian Fifth and Tenth armies supported the attack on left and right respectively. From 24 October Krafft von Dellmensingen's twelve assault divisions attacked the Italians in the vicinity of Caporetto, in the battle bearing that name (or Twelfth Isonzo), using German surprise and infiltration tactics (also styled 'Hutier' tactics). Although outnumbered by the Italians over the whole front, the Austro–Germans achieved superiority in numbers in the sector attacked, and drove through the Italian line with ease, virtually destroying the Italian Second Army.

It is doubtful whether the Central Powers had imagined that such a collapse was possible, and consequently Conrad von Hötzendorf (now only commander in the Trentino since his demotion from chief-of-staff) had little support for his attack with Tenth and Eleventh Austro–Hungarian Armies, which seconded that on Caporetto, and lack of transport as well as mountainous terrain prevented rapid transfer of troops to the Trentino. Consequently, when the Austro–German attack staggered to a halt as it outran its supplies, Cadorna was able to patch together a defensive line north of Venice. It had been an immense defeat for Italy, however, with catastrophic losses (one estimate assesses casualties and prisoners at approximately 600,000), and much to Haig's despair six French and five British divisions under Plumer had to be sent to stiffen the crumbling Italian Army; had the Central Powers possessed the resources to exploit their victory, it is possible that Italy could have been removed from the war at a stroke.

Although Cadorna had handled the later stages of the Italian retreat with some skill (having initially refused to prepare for the attack which he was informed was coming), he was clearly demoralized and talking of further retreat and even a separate peace; under pressure from the Allies and his own prime minister, he gave up his command on 7 November and was replaced by General Armando Diaz.

The Middle East, 1917

In Palestine, the British hold on Sinai was secured by the Battle of Magruntein (8–9 January), and Sir Archibald Murray was ordered to advance upon the Turkish positions covering the main points of entry into Palestine, Gaza and Beersheba. The first attempt, at Gaza (26 March) was unsuccessful, but Murray presented it as a victory; accordingly he was ordered to try again, with similar lack of success (17–18 April). Murray was replaced by Edmund Allenby, transferred from the Western Front (June 1917). Given the responsibility of independent command Allenby prospered, and overhauled the Egyptian Expeditionary Force. In addition to his eight infantry divisions, one of his greatest resources was his Desert Mounted Corps, which Allenby (himself a cavalryman) employed to its best advantage. He was faced by the Turkish Eighth Army (Kress von Kressenstein) and the weak Seventh Army, bolstered by German technical and artillery units but weakened by the length of supply-lines and Arab guerrilla harassment.

Leaving a force to cover Gaza, Allenby attacked Beersheba with the greater part of his army on 31 October. The surprise attack, including a wide flank movement by the Desert Mounted Corps, was a total success, and was seconded by a rapid advance which struck between the two Turkish armies. They abandoned the Gaza positions to avoid entrapment, Seventh Army retiring on Jerusalem and Eighth up the coast. Initially, Allenby concentrated his pursuit on the latter, driving them back at Junction Station (13–14 November), but when he turned on Jerusalem was held up by Turkish reserves, and Falkenhayn, who had been sent to command the Turkish forces. It was but a temporary delay, for after an attack on Jerusalem (8 December) the city fell on the following day, and Allenby consolidated his position, holding off a counter-attack on 26 December.

These operations assisted the British in Mesopotamia, as Turkish troops intended to renew the assault had to be switched to the deteriorating situation in Palestine. The British commander in Mesopotamia, Sir Frederick Maude (appointed August 1916) advanced and defeated the Turks at the Second Battle of Kut (22–23 February); Halil Pasha's Turkish Sixth Army attempted to stand before Baghdad, but Maude pushed on and the city fell on 11 March. After a hiatus in major operations to avoid the worst of the climate (on 20 July a temperature of 123° F was recorded at Baghdad), Maude advanced up the Euphrates and defeated the Turks at Ramadi (27–28 September), but died of cholera (18 November) after drinking tainted milk. The loss of this energetic and talented commander was a severe blow, but his successor (Sir William Marshall) determined to continue the advance.

The Western Front, 1918

The near collapse of Italy emphasized the Allied need to co-ordinate their actions, to which end a 'Supreme War Council' was created at the Rapallo Conference (5 November 1917). The Council, established at Versailles, was to meet regularly and include the prime ministers of France, Britain and Italy, and the US president, or their representatives, and was the first step towards the Allied unity of command which evolved in 1918. The existence of the Council also provided Lloyd George with a military consultative body separate from his own commanders, with whom his relations were still poor. The installation of 'Tiger' Clemenceau as French prime minister on 16 November 1917 was also a crucial appointment, his motto being 'I wage war', and he was a vital reinforcement of French determination in the difficult days ahead. By this date, the Hindenburg–Ludendorff partnership had established a virtual dictatorship over not only Germany, but also her allies, as German resources were crucial in bolstering the tottering forces of Austria–Hungary, Turkey and Bulgaria.

The main combatant nations were all suffering severely from three years' war, and all their resources were stretched by the maintenance of more than one Front (Germany still maintained about a million men in the east, despite the cessation of major hostilities). The decisive factor would obviously be the resources of the USA, which when committed would turn the tide on the Western Front, but would be a considerable time arriving, and even then the Americans insisted on retaining a degree of autonomy and not integrating their troops into the Allied command structure. While the Allies were content to assume a defensive posture on the Western Front until the Americans arrived, Ludendorff realised that Germany's only chance was to defeat the British and French before they could be reinforced.

Accordingly, he planned a massive offensive, utilizing resources freed from the east, the operation to be named after Germany's patron saint, Michael, though it is perhaps better known as the *Kaiserschlacht* ('the Kaiser's battle'). Using surprise and infiltration tactics, he intended to strike the Allied line at the junction of British and French sectors, trusting that the different priorities of the Allied nations would assist the Germans in separating them, the British needing to protect their route towards the Channel ports, and the French to shield Paris. After the initial assault, Ludendorff planned to second it by attacks from Ypres to Champagne.

On 21 March 1918 Operation 'Michael' began with a huge assault by the Army Groups of Crown Prince Wilhelm and Rupprecht of Bavaria, some 65 divisions. The German Second, Seventeenth and Eighteenth Armies (Marwitz, Below and Hutier respectively) hit a 60-mile front of the British right flank between Arras and La Fère. Gough's British Fifth Army, its lines over-extended by recently taking over part of the French left, collapsed under the

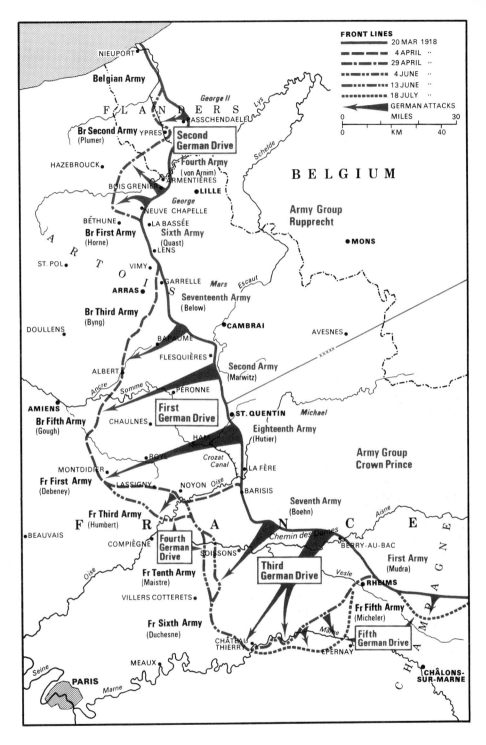

FRONT LINES

	20 MAR 1918
	4 APRIL "
	29 APRIL "
	4 JUNE "
	13 JUNE "
	18 JULY "
	GERMAN ATTACKS

MILES
0 ——————— 30
0 ——————— 40
KM

NIEUPORT

Belgian Army

George II

F L A N D E R S

PASSCHENDAELE

Lys

Br Second Army   YPRES

(Plumer)

Second German Drive

HAZEBROUCK

Fourth Army
(von Arnim)

Schelde

ARMENTIÈRES

BOIS GRENIER

LILLE

B E L G I U M

George

NEUVE CHAPELLE

BÉTHUNE

LA BASSÉE

Br First Army

(Horne)

Sixth Army

(Quast)

LENS

Army Group
Rupprecht

MONS

ST. POL

VIMY

A R T O I S

GARRELLE   *Mars*   *Escaut*

ARRAS

Seventeenth Army

(Below)

Br Third Army

(Byng)

CAMBRAI

AVESNES

DOULLENS

BAPAUME

FLESQUIÈRES

ALBERT

Second Army
(Marwitz)

Ancre   *Somme*   PERONNE

AMIENS

First German Drive   ST. QUENTIN   *Michael*

Br Fifth Army   CHAULNES

(Gough)

Eighteenth Army

(Hutier)

Army Group
Crown Prince

HAM

ROYE

Crozat Canal

LA FÈRE

MONTDIDIER

Fr First Army

(Debeney)   LASSIGNY   NOYON   *Oise*   BARISIS

F   R   A   N   Fr Third Army

BEAUVAIS   (Humbert)

Seventh Army

(Boehn)

Aisne

Fourth German Drive   SOISSONS   *Chemin des Dames*   C   E

COMPIÈGNE   BERRY-AU-BAC

First Army
(Mudra)

Oise   Fr Tenth Army

(Maistre)

Third German Drive

Vesle   RHEIMS

VILLERS COTTERETS

Fr Fifth Army

(Micheler)

Fr Sixth Army

(Duchesne)

Marne   **Fifth German Drive**

CHÂTEAU THIERRY   EPERNAY

C H A M P A G N E

Seine   MEAUX

CHÂLONS-SUR-MARNE

PARIS

Marne

pressure, and Byng's Third Army, its flank exposed, only just managed to contain the attack. With the British in full retreat and Pétain apparently more concerned with protecting Paris than helping them, Haig appealed to London for the appointment of a French commander who would do

more. With Paris itself under fire from German long-range artillery bombardment (which began on 23 March but which did comparatively little damage and did not break French morale), the situation was critical; at a meeting of the Supreme War Council, Ferdinand Foch was appointed

Allied 'co-ordinator' for the Western Front, and unity of command was established fully on 14 April when he was appointed Allied commander-in-chief, his control being extended to Italy, albeit in a more limited form, in June. The appointment of the offensively minded and indomitable Foch was a major benefit to the Allies cause; had the over-cautious Pétain remained in sole control of the French forces, the course of the next months could have been substantially different.

By 5 April Ludendorff's first offensive had ground to a halt, having cut a salient into the Allied line some 40 miles deep, but halting because of a combination of Foch's reserves stopping the drive at Montdidier, almost the westernmost point of the German advance, and because the assault had outrun its supplies. For all its success and the virtual destruction of the British Fifth Army, the 'Michael Offensive' had been undone by the terrain over which it had been forced to advance, the muddy morass created by three years of war prior to the German withdrawal to the Hindenburg Line, and not having recovered from its ravaging during that withdrawal as part of a deliberate 'scorched earth' policy. This terrain prevented the easy transport of reinforcements and supplies to the German fighting-line, and equally precluded a fast-moving exploitation of the breakthrough. Although Allied losses approached a quarter of a million, German casualties were not very much less, and the depletion of the specially trained assault troops was an irreparable loss. A major casualty of the operation was Hubert Gough, relieved of command of British Fifth Army against Haig's wishes, Fifth Army HQ coming under control of Sir Henry Rawlinson's Fourth Army, and the troops becoming the Reserve Army.

Ludendorff's second thrust, code-named 'Georgette', was mounted on 9 April, approximately between Ypres and La Bassée, German Fourth Army (Arnim) attacking British Second Army (now under Plumer, recalled from Italy) in the north, and German Sixth Army (General Ferdinand von Quast) against the left of Horne's British First Army. Again the Allied front buckled in the Armentières–La Bassée sector (the Portuguese Expeditionary Force virtually dis-solved before the attack); some British opinion advocated a defence of the Channel ports, and Haig issued his famous 'backs to the wall' exhortation, but the line held, and after a 10-mile advance Ludendorff suspended the assault. Again, despite a tactical victory, no strategic gain had been made.

Despite the casualties suffered in 'Georgette' (almost as many as the 100,000 lost by the British), Ludendorff renewed his attack on 27 May, in the assaults code-named 'Blücher' and 'Yorck', with German First and Seventh Armies (Generals Bruno von Mudra and Boehn respec-tively), against Duchêne's French Sixth Army on the Aisne, along the Chemin des Dames. Duchêne's position collapsed, and by 30 May the Germans had reached the Marne, a salient some 30 miles wide and 20 deep, until French counter-attacks held up the drive and Ludendorff sus-pended the attack on 4 June. The first US troops were

committed here, initially north-west of the 'Yorck' offensive at Cantigny (28 May) and, more significantly, on the Marne at Château-Thierry and Belleau Wood (30 May–17 June).

Before launching what was intended as the decisive blow against the British, Ludendorff determined to exploit his successes farther south by renewed attacks against the French. His fourth offensive, code-named 'Gneisenau', hit the Montdidier–Noyon sector of the new French line at the junction of the salients created by 'Michael' and 'Yorck–Blücher', on 9 June. The German Seventh and Eighteenth Armies made only limited progress as Foch had fore-knowledge of the attack, and Franco–American counter-attacks prevented the line being pushed as far back as Compiègne; 'Gneisenau' was called off on 13 June.

The final gasp of Ludendorff's great offensive was mounted in Champagne on 15 July; Operation 'Marne' against the southern front of the salient established by 'Blücher', and 'Rheims' to the east of that city. The latter made little progress, German First and Third Armies (Generals Mudra and Karl von Einem respectively) being halted by French Fourth Army (General Henri Gouraud); again, Foch had fore-warning of the operation from de-serters and aerial reconnaissance. Operation 'Marne' was initially more successful, German Seventh Army making progress against French Second; but again they were stopped by Franco–American counter-attacks. Having suf-fered some half a million casualties, Ludendorff had not achieved his breakthrough; his plan for a decisive attack in Flanders had little chance of proceeding, and although he had inflicted more casualties than the Germans had sustained, the Allies losses could be made up within about two months at the rate at which the Americans were

---

One of the most famous pieces of early-war propaganda was Ernst Lissauer's *Hymn of Hate*, a German patriotic poem which became equally well-known in Britain and was reproduced in a number of publications, including a translation by Barbara Henderson in the *New York Times*; the complete version appeared in German in *The Sphere*, 30 March 1915. This is an extract from the first verse:

French and Russian they matter not,
A blow for a blow and a shot for a shot;
We love them not, we hate them not . . .
We have but one and only hate,
We love as one, we hate as one,
We have one foe and one alone . . .
Come, let us stand at the Judgement place,
An oath to swear to, face to face,
An oath of bronze no wind can shake,
An oath for our sons and their sons to take . . .
We will never forego our hate,
We have all but a single hate,
We love as one, we hate as one,
We have one foe, and one alone –
ENGLAND.

arriving. As Ludendorff prepared to abandon the Soissons–Rheims salient created by 'Yorck–Blücher', Foch mounted his counter-attack, which with the German Marne–Rheims attack is sometimes styled the Second Battle of the Marne.

From 18 July Foch's counter-attack went in upon the German Marne salient, involving French Fifth, Sixth and Tenth Armies (Generals Henri Berthelot, Jean Degoutte and Mangin respectively), with Ninth Army in reserve; US forces led Tenth Army's attack. (Other US divisions operated with Sixth and Ninth Armies.) Despite stubborn defence, the German salient was eradicated; on 20 July Ludendorff finally abandoned any idea of a renewed assault in Flanders, and from this moment the Germans were on the defensive. The tide had at last turned in the west; and Foch was created Marshal of France as a reward for his victory.

Foch planned a remorseless drive against all sections of the German line. Haig attacked in the vicinity of Amiens, using Rawlinson's Fourth Army and French First Army

(General Eugène Debeney) against German Second and Eighteenth Armies, beginning on 8 August. Expecting an attack farther north, the Germans were taken by surprise and driven back by an attack led by tanks, and on 10 August the French attack was widened when their Third Army (General Georges Humbert) entered the combat on Debeney's right. A new experience occurred in the attack of 8 August: finally, worn down by attrition, German units showed evidence of demoralization, some surrendering with only token resistance. It was, Ludendorff wrote later, 'the black day of the German Army in the war', which 'put the decline of our fighting powers beyond all doubt'.[4]

Haig paused to reorganize, then advanced again, the front being widened by the participation of the British First and Third Armies on the left and the French on the right. Ludendorff ordered a general withdrawal from the Lys and Amiens sectors, but an Allied thrust which took Péronne (30–31 August) compelled the Germans to withdraw to

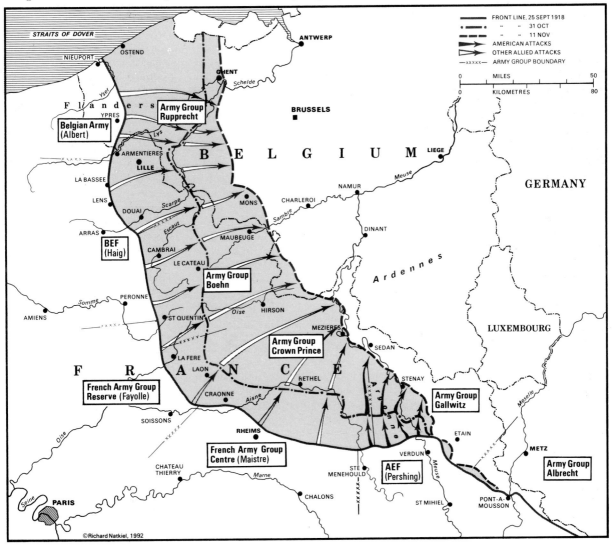

their 'Siegfried Line', a defensive position running approximately from the Scarpe to Rheims.

Prior to what Foch intended as the final attack along the front, he determined to reduce the St. Mihiel salient to the south of Verdun, which the Germans had held since 1914. As the US government remained unwilling to integrate their forces into the overall Allied command, they were assigned their own area of the front and allocated the task of taking the St. Mihiel salient. Although still unwilling to commit American forces to Allied command, Pershing agreed that after this operation the centre of American action would shift some 60 miles to the Argonne, to join the French in the coming battle. On 12–16 September the American First Army – almost twenty divisions – attacked both sides of the St. Mihiel salient, where eight weary German divisions were already withdrawing. The operation was accomplished with comparatively little loss (about 7,000 casualties) and provided the US Army with its first real victory, which had been the intention, boosting morale both at the front and at home. The elimination of the St. Mihiel salient also ended the jeopardy of the French rail communications between Paris and both Verdun and Nancy.

Foch's plan for the main attack involved a Franco–American assault in the Meuse–Argonne sector, aimed at capturing the German railway centre at Charleville–Mézières, and a British assault between Péronne and Lens; subsidiary attacks would be made by a Franco–British force in the Péronne–La Fère sector, and in Flanders by an Anglo–Belgian force. The first of these attacks began on 26 September in the Meuse–Argonne region; the American advance made some progress but stalled against determined defence. The assault was renewed in early October when more Americans from the St. Mihiel action were called up,

so that the forces in that area became too unwieldy to be administered by a single army, forcing Pershing to divide his troops into First and Second Armies. The First Army (General Hunter Liggett) continued to batter its way forward only slowly, much to Allied exasperation; Clemenceau tried to have Pershing replaced but was not supported by Foch.

Despite the slow progress, these operations sucked in German resources which could have been utilized elsewhere. On 27 September the second part of Foch's attack began, Haig beginning his offensive against Boehn's army group, which was pushed back inexorably as the Hindenburg Line was overrun; and from 28 September King Albert's Anglo–Belgian army group advanced in the Ypres–Armentières sector against Rupprecht's army group. By this time the outcome of the war had been decided; the new German chancellor, Prince Max of Baden, requested an armistice under the terms of the 'Fourteen Points' for peace announced by President Wilson on 8 January, but on behalf of the Allies, Wilson replied that there could be no negotiation with the virtual military dictatorship then running the German government.

As negotiations continued, so did the gradual collapse of the German positions along the Western Front. Ludendorff ordered a general withdrawal, hoping to establish a new line in front of the German border to permit negotiations from a position of some strength; but on 17–20 October British Third and Fourth Armies broke through Boehn's army group. On 27 October Ludendorff resigned to facilitate the peace negotiations, being replaced as chief-of-staff by General Wilhelm Groener, though Hindenburg retained his position as overall army commander. At the beginning of November, the American First and French Fourth Armies

Light railways were of great significance in transporting munitions to the front: a Canadian train on the Western Front.

finally burst through the last German positions on the left of the German line, bombarding the Mézières–Montmédy railway line which was of vital importance to the German supply system. The American Second Army began its push towards Montmédy on 10 November, but before it could become heavily engaged the war ended. With the German forces beset by mutiny, Max of Baden accepted Wilson's terms, a republic was proclaimed in Germany; the Kaiser abdicated and fled to Holland. The Armistice was concluded by a German delegation in Foch's railway carriage at Compiègne on 11 November 1918, and hostilities ceased at 11 a.m. on that day, with what amounted to a complete surrender by Germany.

The Italian Front, 1918

Austria–Hungary's domestic situation was deteriorating rapidly, including rebellions (an outbreak of naval mutiny at Cattaro on 1 February) and severe food shortages which encouraged violent unrest, exacerbated by marauding bands of ex-prisoners of war returned by Russia; yet despite this and the imminent material and moral exhaustion of the army, Conrad von Hötzendorf, commanding on the Trentino front, proposed another offensive, even though the German stiffening of the Austro–Hungarian forces had been withdrawn to bolster the Western Front. He urged that his sector be made the focus of the main offensive; as did Boroević on his Piave front. Archduke Joseph sanctioned an attack by both, so that neither had sufficient strength, and were prevented from assisting each other by the mountainous terrain between. Conversely, the Italians' 'interior lines' facilitated their transfer of forces from one area to another.

On 13–15 June both Austro–Hungarian attacks were mounted in the Battle of the Piave, Boroević towards Padua and Conrad von Hötzendorf towards Verona. The latter's Eleventh Army was rebuffed by the Italian Fourth and Sixth Armies, and although Boroević made some progress

'In the Quartier des Rivages ... the Germans had assembled a hundred civilians of all grades ... The officer in charge summoned Monsieur Edmond Bourdon, Clerk of the Court, and ordered him to proceed to the Left Bank and give out that if the French soldiers did not cease fire, the hostages would be shot ... During M. Bourdon's absence not one shot had been fired, yet [he] had barely time to rejoin his own family among the group when, from the machine-gun and the rifles of the soldiers, a wilful fire was directed at the crowd of innocent civilians. Not less than eighty-three persons were shot down like dogs; including twenty-six women and seventeen children under fifteen years of age. This wholesesale massacre was accomplished by the 101st Regiment of Grenadiers, of the Eleventh Saxon Army Corps ...'
(*The Atrocities at Dinant*, E. Gerard, Dinant n.d. (1919?))

against the Italian Third Army, Diaz brought up reinforcements, including Ninth Army, which had been held back for just such an emergency, and stabilized the position. Unable to get assistance from Conrad, Boroević withdrew on 22–3 June.

Despite the Austrian discomfiture and their increasing internal turmoil, Diaz made little exploitation of his success until the Central Powers' situation had declined even further. By the time it was obvious that the war was almost over, he had initiated a wide offensive against the Austro–Hungarian line, the Italian Fourth Army against its centre and Eighth, Tenth and Twelfth (bolstered by more reliable British and French divisions) to storm across the Piave. The first assault failed, Fourth Army being stopped at Monte Grappo (23 October), and from 24 October the Italian Eighth Army was stalled at Vittorio Veneto by the Austro–Hungarian Sixth. The Piave was finally crossed by French units of Twelfth Army and British units of Tenth (under the Earl of Cavan), who drove back the Austrian Fifth Army. As Italian reinforcements poured into the bridgehead Austro–Hungarian resistance collapsed, and an armistice was concluded on 3 November, coming into effect on the following day.

The Balkan Front, 1918

Operations in the Balkans were very limited after the confusions of 1917, Guillaumat's reorganization of the Allied forces having great effect, and the morale of the newly committed Greek forces being raised by their success (with French assistance) in the action at Srka di Legen (30 May). The crisis on the Western Front caused Guillaumat's recall to act as military governor of Paris; he was replaced by another Frenchman, Louis Franchet d'Esperey. One of the best of the Allied generals (who had suggested a Balkan 'Second front' as early as October 1914), his reputation had suffered from the rough handling of his army group along the Chemin des Dames in May 1918; but he was still a commander of resource. Persuading the Supreme War Council to sanction a major drive, he opened the Battle of the Vardar on 15 September, striking the Bulgarian line (by now denuded of almost all its German support) with First and Second Serbian Armies, with French and British formations operating on the flanks. The Bulgarians were routed and sued for an armistice (29 September), surrendering on the following day. Franchet d'Esperey determined to press on at full speed, advocating a drive not only into Hungary but through to Vienna and Dresden. With most Allied resources concentrated on the rapidly collapsing Western Front, however, the advance had to be limited, and his leading units were crossing the Danube as the war ended on 11 November. Roumania had re-joined the Allied camp on the previous day!

The Middle East, 1918

After the fall of Baghdad operations in Mesopotamia involved little serious combat. Operations in the Caucasus resumed after a hiatus following the Russian collapse, with Turks (assisted by Germany) and British vying for possession of the oilfields of western Persia. The British sent an expedition from Baghdad ('Dunsterforce', named after its commander, Major-General L. C. Dunsterville, Kipling's 'Stalky') which advanced from early 1917 and occupied Baku on 4 August. Unable to gain useful assistance, the British had to abandon the town in the face of increasing Turkish pressure on 14 September. (Baku was re-taken by a British force operating on the Caspian Sea in November.)

Similarly concerned with the possession of the Mosul oilfields, when the Turkish collapse appeared imminent a British force was rushed north from Baghdad in October 1918, Lieutenant-General A. S. Cobbe defeating the Turkish 'Tigris Group' (General Ismael Hakki) in a series of clashes at the end of the month, notably at Sharqat, the Turks surrendering on 30 October. Cobbe pushed forward to Mosul and, despite the fact that the armistice had officially ended hostilities, took the city (by negotiation) in early November.

The year's main operations in the Middle East were in Palestine, although initially Allenby's operations were limited severely by calls upon his resources from the Western Front. During this time of limited activity, the Arab guerrillas remained a constant drain upon the Turks, tying up huge numbers of troops, constantly severing communications and generally making themselves obnoxious to the Turks in every way. The Arab forces were assisted by small detachments of British specialists (armoured car, engineer and artillery personnel) and were inspired by Colonel T. E. Lawrence. By the time Allenby was able to resume the offensive, the Arabs had severed the Hejaz railway, isolating the Turkish garrison of Medina, and were ready to swarm north upon the right flank of Allenby's forces.

As before, Allenby's preparations were meticulous. He planned to blast through the Turkish defence-line along the coast, exploit the breakthrough with his cavalry, and swing north and east to destroy the remainder of the Turkish forces. These were now commanded by Liman von Sanders, who had replaced Falkenhayn, and comprised the Turkish Fourth, Seventh and Eighth Armies, though these were not strong and had to be bolstered by a small German contingent.

The operation was spectacularly successful. On 19 September the Turks were surprised at the Battle of Megiddo (Allenby's secrecy had been absolute), and by the following day Jerad Pasha's Eighth Army had virtually ceased to exist as the British left flank opened a gap on the Turkish right, the Desert Mounted Corps exploiting the breakthrough, and Turkish communications being wrecked by British aerial bombing. The Seventh Army (Mustafa Kemal) fell back upon the Jordan in chaos, and swept away Fourth Army with it; four days into the operation the Turks were in full retreat, with the Desert Mounted Corps leading the pursuit, and with the Arab irregulars of Lawrence and

Feisal bringing chaos and terror to the Turkish left and rear. Damascus fell on 1 October, Beirut shortly after, and as the pursuit continued relentlessly Turkey sued for an armistice, which was concluded (at Mudros) on 30 October, ending one of the most brilliant operations of the war.

The War in Africa
The operations in Africa are described in the 'national' section, under headings 'Africa' and 'North Africa'.

THE WAR AT SEA

The war at sea was of vital consequence, although it involved few major battles of the type that had been envisaged during the pre-war period. The most powerful fleets were those of Britain and Germany, and around these nations most of the main naval operations revolved; but the conservatism of most of the naval command of both sides made them unwilling to risk many large-scale actions, lest their nation's maritime capability be damaged irreparably by a single battle. Although naval commanders have been criticized for lack of offensive spirit, the charge may be countered by the truth of Churchill's remark that Admiral Jellicoe was the only man on either side who could lose the war in an afternoon.

Both Britain and Germany depended upon their fleets for the maintenance of overseas colonies, but Germany's were untenable given the weight of Allied sea-power ranged against them. Britain was also dependent upon naval power to keep open the sea-lanes along which a great proportion of the nation's food and raw materials was transported. Had Germany's pre-war strategy put greater emphasis upon submarines and less upon the belief that a surface fleet would have to engage an immediate British attack, their commerce-raiding might have had even greater effect than it did, when in the later stages of the war there was a real danger that the U-boat campaign could starve Britain into submission. Although the Germans were never able to threaten Britain's ability to transport troops and supplies to the continent and farther afield, the only real amphibious operation of the war was the landing in the Dardanelles; although the naval operations there were basically unsuccessful, the actual naval–military co-operation, in both landing and evacuation from Gallipoli, was conducted with conspicuous success (even though part of the Suvla landing was deposited in the wrong position).

Naval Operations: 1914
Operations in 1914 were largely a matter of the elimination of German colonial possessions and the naval forces which supported them; and exploratory moves by the main battle-fleets, both sides being unwilling to risk a major confrontation. The German maritime colonies fell quickly, there being insufficient forces to sustain them: in the Pacific, the Marshall, Mariana, Caroline and Palau Islands were

occupied by Japan, the German part of Samoa by New Zealand, and the German base of Tsingtao on the China coast (alias 'the Gibraltar of the East') was besieged by a Japanese force, with British assistance, and was captured on 7 November.

The German colonial naval support took considerably more effort to neutralize. Admiral Maximilian von Spee, commanding the German China Squadron, realized that Japan's entry into the war meant an end to the German presence in the Pacific, so sailed from Ponape in the Caroline Islands towards South America, intending to return to Germany via the Altantic. He dispatched the fast light cruiser *Emden* as a commerce-raider in the Indian Ocean; her exploits became almost legendary, and she wrought havoc with British shipping until caught and destroyed by HMAS *Sydney* at the Cocos Islands (9 November). Spee's squadron, the cruisers *Gneisenau* and *Scharnhorst* and light cruisers *Dresden*, *Leipzig* and *Nürnburg*,

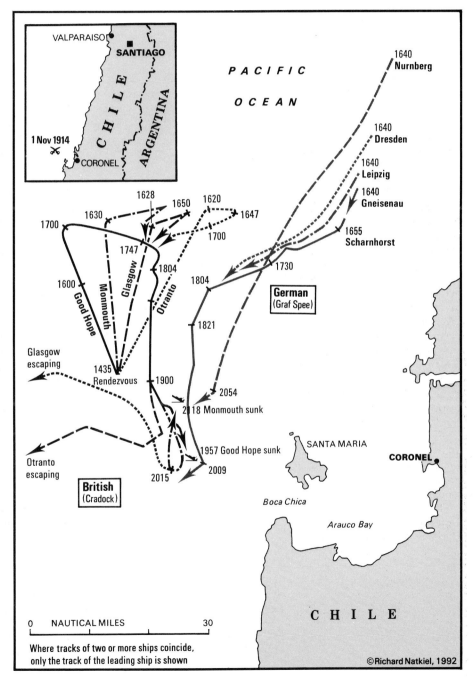

Where tracks of two or more ships coincide, only the track of the leading ship is shown

©Richard Natkiel, 1992

crossed the Pacific and on 1 November encountered a British force under Admiral Sir Christopher Cradock at Coronel on 1 November. Cradock led the cruisers *Good Hope* and *Monmouth*, the light cruiser *Glasgow* and the auxiliary merchant cruiser *Otranto*, and having discarded the old battleship *Canopus* as being too slow to keep up with the German squadron, Cradock was considerably outgunned. Spee's heavy cruisers sank both *Good Hope* and *Monmouth* before the lighter British guns could be brought within

effective range; *Glasgow* and *Otranto* ran and escaped.

British reaction was swift: Vice-Admiral Sir Frederick Doveton Sturdee was sent from Europe with the battle-cruisers *Invincible* and *Inflexible*, which with the cruisers *Kent*, *Cornwall* and *Glasgow* formed a squadron too powerful for Spee. The German commander, planning to raid the British station at Port Stanley in the Falklands, ran into Sturdee who was refuelling there; Spee attempted to escape but his squadron was destroyed almost entirely in the Battle of the

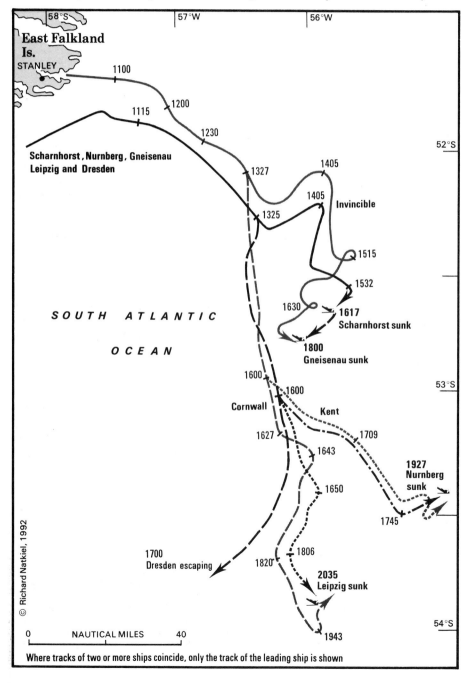

Where tracks of two or more ships coincide, only the track of the leading ship is shown

Falklands (8 December). Only *Dresden* escaped, and she was caught on 14 March 1915.

The last element of the German 'colonial' navy was the light cruiser *Königsberg*, stationed in East Africa; having sunk the British light cruiser *Pegasus* off Mombasa (6 August), she was blockaded in the River Rufiji, East Africa, and was destroyed in July 1915. Arguably the most important naval operation of the early war, however, was the transfer of the German battlecruiser *Goeben* and light cruiser *Breslau* to Turkish service, slipping through the Mediterranean and past the Dardanelles, helping to bring Turkey into the war on the side of the Central Powers.

The only serious action involving the main surface fleets was a British raid into German waters at Heligoland Bight (28 August); when the Germans responded to the thrust by the British 1st Light Cruiser Squadron, they were fallen upon by Vice-Admiral Sir David Beatty's supporting 1st Battlecruiser Squadron, the German light cruisers *Ariadne*, *Köln* and *Mainz* being sunk. Otherwise, operations in the North Sea were restricted to British blockade of German ports, and a raid launched by the commander of the German High Seas Fleet, Admiral Friedrich von Ingenohl, against the east coast of England, in which considerable civilian casualties were caused by German bombardments of Scarborough, Hartlepool and Whitby.

With some notable exceptions, by the end of 1914 the surface war had virtually ended; it was as if all the vast expense of constructing powerful navies had been wasted, as neither side was prepared to risk its main elements in an all-out action. The way ahead, however, was indicated by an action on 22 September in the English Channel, when the German submarine *U 9* commanded by Kapitänleutnant Otto Weddigen sank the British light cruisers *Aboukir*, *Hogue* and *Cressy*. Although an attempted submarine raid on the main British base of Scapa Flow (18 October) was unsuccessful (though forcing the British Grand Fleet to transfer temporarily to Rosyth), it indicated that submarine operations were potentially far more effective than those involving surface units, when it was considered that *U 9* and the submarine-laid mine which sank the battleship HMS *Audacious* on 27 October inflicted as much damage as the rest of the German fleet put together.

Naval Operations: 1915

The major action of the year was a further German raid into the North Sea, by Vice-Admiral Franz von Hipper's battle-cruiser squadron. Warned by radio intercepts, Beatty's squadron intercepted him at the Dogger Bank (24 January), where the German cruiser *Blücher* was sunk, but the remainder got away, Hipper's flagship *Seydlitz* suffering damage. The consequence of this action (apart from the replacement of Ingenohl by Admiral Hugo von Pohl as commander of the High Seas Fleet) was the installation of anti-flash doors in German ships, preventing the transmission of fire from turret to magazine, as a result of the experience with *Seydlitz*; thereafter, German ships became more resilient to damage, whereas the British remained vulnerable.

With Germany unwilling to risk any more of her surface units, in early February a submarine campaign was initiated, targeted at merchantmen (including neutrals) in the waters surrounding Britain. The campaign was considerably successful, most infamously in the sinking of the liner *Lusitania* on 7 May, but this and the loss of other American lives in British and neutral vessels provoked such protests from the USA that unrestricted submarine warfare was suspended on 1 September, having sunk about ¾ million tons of Allied shipping.

Lusitania, the Cunard liner *sunk off Kinsale by* U 20 *on 7 May 1915 with the loss of 1,198 lives, which provoked outrage among both Allies and neutrals.*

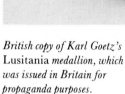

British copy of Karl Goetz's Lusitania *medallion, which was issued in Britain for propaganda purposes.*

The main Allied naval operation of the year was in support of the Dardanelles expedition, initially in the abortive naval attacks, and latterly in support of the land operations; but again, the powerful surface vessels were found to be vulnerable to submarine attack, and the larger Allied ships were withdrawn from the campaign. Allied submarines also had considerable success, slipping through the Dardanelles and wreaking havoc with Turkish shipping, up to the very anchorage of Constantinople.

Naval Operations: 1916

U-boat warfare was resumed in February 1916, but was curtailed in May in the face of further American protests. With this interruption in the submarine campaign, a number of hit-and-run raids were undertaken by German surface units against the east coast of England: Yarmouth and Lowestoft were bombarded on 24–25 April, and some minor forays took place in August and October. Apart from these and the continuing 'war of commerce' upon Allied merchant shipping, 1916 saw the one great naval battle of the war, at Jutland on 31 May–1 June.

Vice-Admiral Reinhard Scheer put to sea with the German High Seas Fleet, cruising northwards; the van of some 40 fast vessels, including five battlecruisers, was led by Hipper. The main body followed, including sixteen dread-noughts and six older battleships, with the usual accompanying force of cruisers and destroyers. Alerted by German radio traffic, Admiral Sir John Jellicoe's Grand Fleet immediately put to sea from Scapa Flow, and Beatty's faster battlecruiser fleet (and the 5th Battle Squadron of super-dreadnoughts) from the Firth of Forth. Hipper's and Beatty's scouting forces saw each other in mid-afternoon, Hipper turning away to draw Beatty on to the main High Seas Fleet. Beatty followed, a long-range gunnery duel ensued, which damaged Beatty's flagship *Lion* and sank the battlecruisers *Indefatigable* and *Queen Mary*, casualties to the lack of anti-flash doors. Despite the losses, Beatty continued his pursuit until the main German fleet was sighted; he then turned in the direction of Jellicoe's approach, attempting to lead the Germans into the Grand Fleet. A running fight continued until the leading elements of Jellicoe's fleet came up, whereupon Beatty turned east, to bring his ships into line with Jellicoe, and attempt to cut off Scheer from his route home. From about 6.30 p.m. a general action ensued, in which both sides took heavy punishment, the most notable casualty being the sinking of the British battle-cruiser *Invincible*. Facing annihilation, Scheer turned west-wards under cover of smoke and destroyer attacks, and passed out of British gunnery range. Jellico declined to pursue but continued south, knowing that he could thus interpose the Grand Fleet between Scheer and his route home. Suddenly, Scheer turned into range; again facing destruction, he turned away yet again, leaving his four battlecruisers still fit for action to cover his withdrawal. This they executed with heroism, and despite sustaining severe damage, none was sunk. Fearing torpedo attacks, Jellicoe

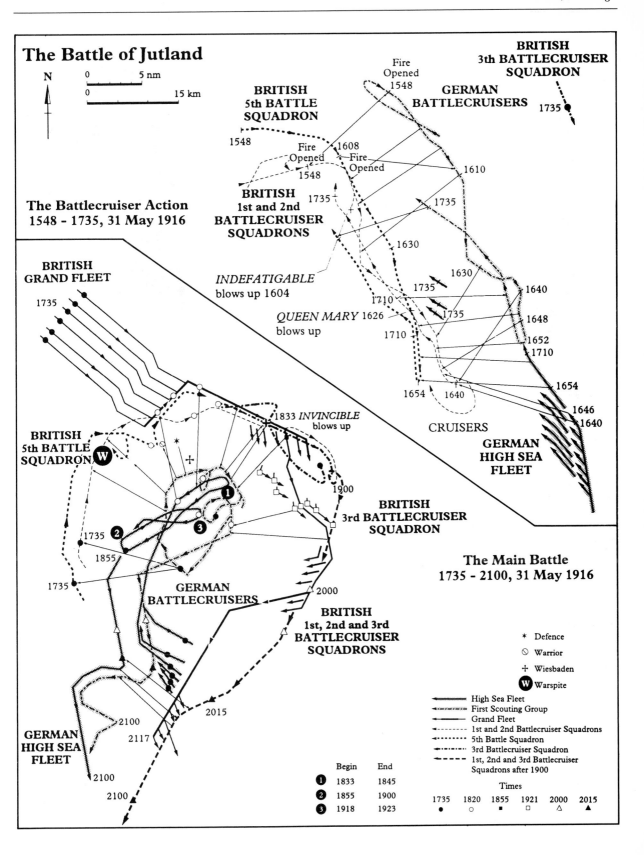

The Battle of Jutland

N

0   5 nm

0   15 km

The Battlecruiser Action
1548 – 1735, 31 May 1916

BRITISH
5th BATTLE
SQUADRON

1548

Fire
Opened
1548

Fire
Opened
1608
Fire
Opened
1548

BRITISH
1st and 2nd
BATTLECRUISER
SQUADRONS

1735

1735

BRITISH
3th BATTLECRUISER
SQUADRON

Fire
Opened
1548

GERMAN
BATTLECRUISERS

1735

1610

1735

1630

1630

1735

1735

1640

1648

1652
1710

1654

1646
1640

INDEFATIGABLE
blows up 1604

QUEEN MARY 1626
blows up

1710

1710

1654   1640

CRUISERS

GERMAN
HIGH SEA
FLEET

BRITISH
GRAND FLEET

1735

BRITISH
5th BATTLE
SQUADRON

W

1833 *INVINCIBLE*
blows up

1900

BRITISH
3rd BATTLECRUISER
SQUADRON

①

1735

②

1855

③

1735

GERMAN
BATTLECRUISERS

2000

BRITISH
1st, 2nd and 3rd
BATTLECRUISER
SQUADRONS

2015

GERMAN
HIGH SEA
FLEET

2100

2100

2117

2100

2100

The Main Battle
1735 – 2100, 31 May 1916

*   Defence
⊘   Warrior
✛   Wiesbaden
W Warspite

⟵ High Sea Fleet
⟵ First Scouting Group
⟵ Grand Fleet
⟵ 1st and 2nd Battlecruiser Squadrons
⟵ 5th Battle Squadron
⟵ 3rd Battlecruiser Squadron
⟵ 1st, 2nd and 3rd Battlecruiser
     Squadrons after 1900

	Begin	End
①	1833	1845
②	1855	1900
③	1918	1923

Times

1735	1820	1855	1921	2000	2015
●	○	■	□	△	▲

HMS Iron Duke, *a 'super-dreadnought' battleship which served as Jellicoe's flagship when he was commander-in-chief of the Grand Fleet. 25,000 tons, 10 × 13.5in, 12 × 6in, 2 × 3in. AA guns, 4 × 21in torpedo tubes.*

declined to follow, and during the night Scheer succeeded in fighting his way through the lighter elements of the Grand Fleet, in which action both sides again lost ships, most notably the old German battleship *Pommern*. By morning Scheer had regained his base; Jellicoe also returned home.

In material terms, Britain had suffered the most losses (three battlecruisers, three cruisers and eight destroyers, to Germany's one battleship, one battlecruiser, three cruisers and five destroyers), but the strategic victory was Jellicoe's. Although he has been criticized for not pressing the attack harder, his defence that the encroaching darkness prevented the action from being as decisive as Trafalgar has some validity; and as Churchill remarked, had the Grand Fleet been hit badly by torpedo attacks, Jellicoe had the capacity to lose the war in one action. Although the Kaiser acclaimed the battle as a German victory, it actually confirmed that the High Seas Fleet could not hope to operate in the North Sea without risking destruction, and effectively marked an end to German surface power; save for brief forays, the High Seas Fleet remained in port for the remainder of the war.

Naval Operations: 1917

Attention turned again to the U-boat campaign, unrestricted submarine warfare again being declared in February 1917, in the belief that if sufficient merchant ships were sunk, Britain could be starved into surrender, even though this policy was almost certain to bring the USA into the war. It was a gross miscalculation, by under-estimating the immense impact that US entry would make, and the ability of Britain to survive the huge losses of the submarine campaign. There were never enough U-boats to win the campaign, and resources were not used to the best effect: 'Wolf-pack' tactics were eschewed in an attempt to cover the maximum amount of ocean, instead of concentrating upon the most important shipping-lanes.

Nevertheless, the U-boat crews sustained the fight manfully, and Allied shipping losses mounted alarmingly. In 1914 64 British merchant ships were sunk, three by submarines, with a gross tonnage of 241,201 tons; in 1915, 277 ships, 227 by submarines, 855,721 tons; in 1916, 396 ships, 287 by submarines, 1,237,634 tons (the majority of other losses were to mines rather than to surface craft). In 1917, with the U-boat campaign in full swing, 1,197 ships were lost, 1,052 to submarines, gross tonnage 3,729,785. At the high point of the campaign, April 1917, more than half a million tons of British shipping were sunk, including 155 ships by submarine during the month, and losses of Allied and neutral ships were equally appalling. At the insistence of Lloyd George, the British Admiralty was compelled to adopt a convoy system, even though this meant denuding the Grand Fleet of its lighter elements for use as convoy-escorts; but, with US co-operation, it markedly improved the situation. More than 6½ millions tons of Allied and neutral merchant shipping were lost in 1917; of this, 3.8 million was in the first half of the year, and only 2.7 million in the second half. During 1918, British merchant losses declined to 544 vessels, 1,694,749 tons, testimony to the efficacy of the anti-submarine measures.

Surface actions during the year were restricted to minor German destroyer raids in the Channel (February–April), British bombardment of the U-boat bases at Ostend and Zeebrugge (May–June, with negligible effect), and German raids on Scandinavian convoys which forced the British to use battleships as a protecting force (December). Actions in the Mediterranean were greatly restricted by the Italian unwillingness to initiate offensive action, apparently in the belief that as Austria showed little offensive inclination, there was no need for Italy to do so. The one serious action occurred in the Straits of Otranto when the Austro–Hungarian Captain Miklós Horthy de Nagybánya mounted a daring raid and succeeded in reaching home safely; the fame he gained for it led to his promotion to admiral, ultimately to command the fleet, and he later became dictator of Hungary.

Naval Operations: 1918

After Jutland, the inactivity of the High Seas Fleet caused a serious decline in morale, which was not restored by amphibious support operations in the Baltic (October 1917 and from February 1918). Unrest appeared as early as July 1917, when a naval mutiny was suppressed, its cause being ascribed to bad conditions and socialist agitation.

Apart from the U-boat campaign, which became progressively less effective after the institution of the Allied convoy system, the main operation in northern waters was a British assault on the German submarine pens at Zeebrugge and Ostend, organized by Vice-Admiral Sir Roger Keyes, commander of the Dover Patrol and one of the most energetic and capable naval officers of his generation. On 23 April, in the 'St. George's Day raid', the light cruiser *Vindictive* with supporting vessels mounted an assault on the Zeebrugge mole, the ship and demolition parties being extricated after the infliction of some damage, in one of the most heroic naval episodes of the war. On 10 May *Vindictive* was scuttled inside the harbour mouth at Ostend, hoping to block the channel. The raids had only limited material effect, but were of immense morale significance, undermining further the shaky condition of the Germany navy. In the last stages of the war the U-boat campaign was abandoned (16 October), in accordance with US demands for the negotiation of an armistice. Hipper (chief of the High Seas Fleet from 11 August in succession to Scheer, promoted to supreme commander of the navy) conceived a scheme for a last *Götterdämmerung* of the German navy, of sailing out against the Grand Fleet in a defiant act of self-destruction; it came to nothing when the crews refused to sail. The naval mutiny of 29 October thus effectively ended the war at sea, although it was not until 21 June 1919 that the High Seas Fleet, captive at Scapa Flow, was scuttled to prevent the ships from being transferred to Allied navies.

In the Mediterranean, few major incidents occurred in 1918. In January *Goeben* and *Breslau* made a sortie into the Aegean, the former being mined (but salvaged) and the latter sunk; on 9 June an Austrian attempt from Pola against the Allied blockade ended with the sinking of the dreadnought *Szent Istvan* off Premuda Island, Dalmatia; and the Austrian *Viribus Unitis* was sunk at Pola on 1 November.

In summary, the naval war had been a disappointment on all sides; the immense expense of creating huge surface fleets had probably not been justified, as their main purpose had been to cancel out the enemy's fleet without a decisive victory; and damaging as the submarine campaign had

---

The 'Fourteen Points'
Probably the most famous political document of the war was the list of conditions proposed by Woodrow Wilson in an address to Congress on 8 January 1918, which specified his demands for peace and which formed the basis of the terms of the armistice:
(1) Open diplomacy, with agreements concluded openly.
(2) Freedom of navigation.
(3) Removal of economic barriers.
(4) Reduction of armaments.
(5) Colonial claims to be settled impartially and upon the interest of the populations concerned.
(6) Evacuation of Russian territory, and permittance of Russia to solve her economic and political problems independently.
(7) Evacuation and restoration of Belgium.
(8) Evacuation of occupied French territory, and restoration to France of Alsace–Lorraine.
(9) Italian frontier to conform to the nationality of inhabitants.
(10) Autonomous development for the nationalities in Austria–Hungary.
(11) Roumania, Serbia and Montenegro to be evacuated and restored, and Serbia guaranteed access to the sea.
(12) Turkish parts of the Ottoman Empire to be guaranteed sovereignty, but other nationalities granted autonomy, and the Dardanelles to be opened.
(13) Independence of Poland (including areas with predominantly Polish population), and access to the sea.
(14) Formation of an 'Association of Nations' with mutual guarantees of independence and territorial integrity.

---

been, it had neither starved Britain into submission nor had it interfered in the slightest with the transportation of American troops across the Atlantic.

CASUALTIES

Unlike previous European wars, when at least until the institution of mass compulsory service, casualties were concentrated upon those sections of the community for whom military service was a career, the protracted carnage of the Great War extended its reach throughout society. Taking Britain as an example: in commenting on casualties sustained to 1917, one periodical reported the deaths of the son of prime minister H. H. Asquith (Lieutenant Raymond Asquith, Grenadiers), the Labour leader Arthur Henderson (Captain David Henderson, Middlesex) and the Unionist leader Walter Long (Brigadier-General Walter Long), together with a number of Members of Parliament and countless members of the aristocracy. Emphasizing the backgrounds of the dead (in an interesting comment upon contemporary values), the article remarked that had the sufferers been old, or 'the thousands who crowd our lunatic asylums and fill our prisons', the loss would have been bearable; but, because 'the drunkard, the anaemic, or the feckless' were not the stuff of soldiers, the toll was borne instead by 'the flower of the race'.[5] It could be seen as unjust to concentrate in this way upon one section of the community, but the higher casualty-rate among officers makes such comparison inevitable (in 1916, for example, the chances of an officer being killed were about double those of an 'other rank'). The incidence of such casualties encouraged the popular belief of 'the lost generation', and where analysis has been possible, it appears that the upper social and educational groups did indeed bear the heaviest burden.[6] Inevitably, some cases attracted more attention than others. A case quoted at the time was that of the Woodroffe family of the Rifle Brigade, highlighted by the death at Hooge in July 1915 of 2nd Lieutenant Sydney Woodroffe (8th Battalion) in an action for which he was awarded the Victoria Cross. He had two brothers: Captain Leslie Woodroffe (8th Battalion), a Shrewsbury schoolmaster, died of wounds in France in May 1915; and 2nd Lieutenant Kenneth Woodroffe (6th Battalion), a noted fast bowler for Marlborough, Cambridge and Sussex, killed at Neuve Chapelle in May 1916. Although typical representatives, in contemporary eyes, of 'the flower of the race', their fate was no different from that of numberless thousands of more humble and unsung members of society throughout Europe.

It is impossible to give accurate casualty-figures for the war, as in many cases statistics were not collected, and civilian casualties are even harder to estimate. In some cases these greatly exceeded the military dead: more than 2 million civilians died as a result of the war in Turkey, for example, more than half Armenians as a result of persecution, as against about 325,000 military deaths in action. Russia, Serbia, Bulgaria and Greece all suffered more civilian dead than military, sometimes in huge proportions (Serbia, for example, lost probably about 45,000 troops in action and 80,000 from disease, but about 650,000 civilians).

The common perception of submarine warfare: a cartoon by Private A. H. Simmons, 7th City of London Regiment. The U-boat commander is saying to the whale: 'I beg your pardon, I thought you were a hospital ship.'

> 'We got to about 100 yards of their trenches, when the general passed the word that the brigade would fix bayonets and charge . . . we made a dash for it. The men were falling on each side of me. I was doubled up. There were only about half of us got there. When I got to their trenches I made a sort of dive at it with my bayonet leading, and it stuck in one of them, in the chest . . . We stopped in the trenches a while to get our wind, and we shook each other by the hand, and I said, "I will never be hit after that", and was confident of it. And I thanked God from my heart for being alive . . .'
>
> (Private Grace, Northumberland Fusiliers, in *The War Stories of Private Thomas Atkins*, p. 48, London, 1914)

Losses sustained in the war were unprecedented. In approximate figures of military battle-deaths, Germany lost more than 1.8 million, Russia 1.7 million, France 1.3 million, Austria–Hungary 922,000, Italy 460,000, the USA 50,500, Bulgaria 75,000. Statistics for the British Empire included Britain, 888,000; Canada 65,000; Australia 62,000; New Zealand 18,000; India 72,000; South Africa 9,300. Except for India and South Africa, these figures were approximately 50 per cent greater than for the Second World War, and in Britain's case 230 per cent greater.

Such statistics are bewildering until considered in terms of population: a contemporary British assessment remarked that every thousand casualties equated with the annihilation of every able-bodied man between the ages of 18 and 41 of a small market-town like Keswick or Calne. As 1759 was styled the *annus mirabilis*, it was suggested that 1916 might be termed the *annus cruentus* ('year of blood'), which would have been appropriate had not the previous and succeeding years been almost equally terrible.[7] Throughout this year, it was estimated that a serviceman of British birth or speech was killed or wounded every three-quarters of a minute; and that the average daily loss in August 1916 equated to the total casualties of Blenheim and Inkerman combined. Although some areas suffered especially heavily, there can scarcely have been a town of any combatant nation in which the male population was not ravaged. To take one unexceptional location in England: the town of Colne, Lancashire, lost some 517 men during the war, most fatalities falling upon the East Lancashire (131) and King's Regiments (32) and the Royal Artillery (38). At the 1911 census the population of the borough was 25,689, so that the military fatalities represent a loss of almost 2 per cent of the town. When the approximate number of wounded is included, perhaps as many as a third of the able-bodied men of military age became casualties during the war; and such a figure would be no way exceptional in any of the combatant countries.

Numbers of wounded almost always exceeded those of dead by between two and four to one. Approximate casualties included almost five million wounded in Russia, about 4.2 million in France and Germany, more than 3.6 million in Austria–Hungary, more than 2 million from the British Empire, 950,000 for Italy and 400,000 for Turkey; the fact that the latter figure is not much more than the total of fatalities is probably due to that nation's lack of adequate medical care. Apparently only Roumania lost more dead than wounded, their latter figure being about 120,000.

In addition to conventional battle injuries, there was a new variety in psychological damage or 'shell shock', varying from frayed nerves to complete mental collapse, and apparent physiological symptoms with psychiatric causes, such as paralysis. Although this was the first conflict in which psychiatric casualties were recognized (though it was not uncommon for such troubles to be ascribed to the sufferers being naturally 'windy'), it is interesting to reflect upon the reasons for 'shell shock' being so much more prevalent than in previous wars. The answer is probably in Lord Moran's analogy of courage being like a bank-balance, diminishing with each 'withdrawal' or period of combat pressure.[8] Previous wars were no more terrible to the individual, in that death and mutilation was just as horrific whether it came by high-explosive, bayonet, musket-ball or cloth-yard shaft; but, excluding siege operations, exposure to the danger of death was much less common in previous wars, and while actual combat was equally violent and terrifying, its duration was immensely less. To make a somewhat unscientific comparison:

During the Peninsular War two men, James Talbot and Daniel Loochstadt, qualified for the British Military General Service Medal with 15 clasps, the maximum awarded to

---

Allied propaganda made much of militaristic sentiments published in Germany, such as the following from *Jung Deutschland* (October 1913):

'War is the noblest and holiest expression of human activity. For us, too, the glad, great hour of battle will strike. Still and deep in the German heart must live the joy of battle and the longing for it . . . war is beautiful. Its august sublimity elevates the human heart beyond the earthly and the common. In the cloud palace above sit the heroes, Frederick the Great and Blücher and all the men of action . . . When here on earth a battle is won by German arms and the faithful dead ascend to heaven, a Potsdam lance-corporal will call the guard to the door and "Old Fritz",* springing from his golden throne, will give the command to present arms. That is the heaven of Young Germany.'
(Quoted in *Why We Went to War*, C. Gauss, p. 12, New York, 1918)
*'Old Fritz': Frederick the Great.

---

any one individual, each representing one battle in which they served. Although comparisons are wholly unsatisfactory, it is interesting to note that in the case of Talbot (of the 45th Foot), in the fifteen battles for which he was awarded a clasp, he was under enemy fire and in danger of losing his life for probably not more than a total of 24 hours, spread over eight years. In these actions his regiment suffered some 123 killed in action (plus the eventual deaths of many of those originally returned as 'wounded'). While not under-estimating Talbot's service or the heavy fighting in which he participated, the time he spent under fire and in physical danger from the enemy could easily have been exceeded by two days' service in a 'hot' portion of the line on the Western Front; and the casualties sustained by his battalion appear small when compared with those which might result from a single spell of trench-duty. In these terms, service in the front line during the World War was an unprecedented experience, and its consequence was to provide a steady drain on the 'bank balance' of courage, gradually wearing down the resilience of the men affected, and in many cases compounded by a degree of privation, lack of decent rations and sleep, which had not been encountered in even the meanest form of civilian life.

Footnotes

1. *World's Work*, June 1918, pp. 170–1; see also *Why We Went to War*, C. Gauss, New York, 1918, p. 86
2. *War*, London, 1929, p. 9
3. *History of the 9th (Service) Battalion The York and Lancaster Regiment 1914–19*, J. B. Montagu, 1934
4. *My War Memories 1914–18*, London 1919, p. 679
5. *The Great War*, ed. H. W. Wilson and J. A. Hammerton, London, 1917, VIII, pp. 550, 552
6. See 'Britain's "Lost Generation" of the First World War', J. M. Winter, in *Population Studies*, 1977
7. Wilson and Hammerton, op. cit., p. 536
8. *The Anatomy of Courage*, Lord Moran of Manton, London 1945 (2nd edn., London, 1966)

CHRONOLOGY

The following list of engagements identifies by date the most important actions, though it should be noted that in battles lasting weeks or months, different dates may be ascribed to their commencement or end. It is not possible to include all the smaller actions, but some of insignificant size are noted if they received much contemporary publicity: the action at Néry, for example (1 September 1914), was only a skirmish compared to the main battles and not even accorded the title of 'action' by the British Battles Nomenclature Committee (which styled it 'the Affair of Néry'); but which, from the heroic stand of 'L' Battery, Royal Horse Artillery, gained great fame at the time.

Western Front

1914:

16 August: German capture of Liège
18 August: action at Tirlemont
20 August: German capture of Brussels
14–25 August: Battles of the Frontiers, including:
   14–22 August: Battle of Lorraine
   20–25 August: Battle of the Ardennes
   22–3 August: Battle of the Sambre
   23–4 August: Battle of Mons
23 August: German capture of Namur
26–7 August: Battle of Le Cateau

Mass grave of fourteen German reservists in Belgium, killed in action 12 September 1914.

27 August: German capture of Lille
29 August: Battle of Guise
31 August–11 September: Battle of the Grande Couronne of Nancy
1 September: action of Néry
5–10 September: Battle of the Marne, including:
   5–9 September: Battle of the Ourcq
14–28 September: Battle of the Aisne
25–9 September: Battle of Albert
1–9 October: siege of Antwerp
2 October: Battle of Arras
10 October–2 November: Battle of La Bassée
11 October–30 November: Battles of Flanders, including:
   12 October–2 November: Battle of Messines
   13 October–2 November: Battle of Armentières
16 October–30 November: Battle of the Yser
19 October–17 November: First Battle of Ypres:
   21–4 October: Battle of Langemarck
   29–31 October: Battle of Gheluvelt
   11 November: Battle of Nonne Boschen
18–22 December: Battle of Givenchy
20 December: First Battle of Champagne (actions continuing to end of March 1915)

1915:

10–13 March: Battle of Neuve Chapelle, including:
   14–15 March: Battle of St. Eloi
6–15 April: Battle of the Woëvre
22 April–25 May: Second Battle of Ypres, including:
   22–3 April: Battle of Gravenstafel
   24 April–4 May: Battle of St. Julien
   8–13 May: Battle of Frezenberg
   24–5 May: Battle of Bellewaarde (or Bellewaerde)
9 May: Battle of Aubers
15–25 May: Battle of Festubert
16 May–30 June: Second Battle of Artois (or Souchez, or Vimy Ridge)
26 June–4 July: Battle of the Argonne
25 September–6 November: Second Battle of Champagne
25 September–8 October: Battle of Loos
29 September: French capture of crest of Vimy Ridge

1916:

21 February–18 December: Battle of Verdun, including:
   21 February: first German offensive
   26 February: German capture of Fort Douaumont
   6 March: second German offensive
   9 April: third German offensive

9 June: German capture of Fort
Vaux
24 October: recapture of Fort
Douaumont
2 November: recapture of Fort Vaux
2–13 June: Battle of Mount Sorrel
1 July–18 November: Battle of the
Somme, including:
  1–13 July: Battle of Albert
  14–17 July: Battle of Bazentin
  15 July–3 September: Battle of
  Delville Wood
  23 July–3 September: Battle of
  Pozières
  3–6 September: Battle of
  Guillemont
  9 September: Battle of Guinchy
  15–22 September: Battle of Flers–
  Courcelette
  25–8 September: Battle of Morval
  26–8 September: Battle of Thiepval
  1–18 October: Battle of Le Transloy
  1–11 October: Battle of the Ancre
  Heights
  13–18 November: Battle of the
  Ancre

1917:
9 April–15 May: Battle of Arras,
including:
  9–14 April: Battle of Vimy
  9–14 April: First Battle of the
  Scarpe
  23–4 April: Second Battle of the
  Scarpe
  28–9 April: Battle of Arleux
  3–4 May: Third Battle of the Scarpe
  3–17 May: Battle of Bullecourt
16–20 April: Nivelle Offensive,
including:
  16–20 April: Second Battle of the
  Aisne
  16–20 April: Third Battle of
  Champagne
7–14 June: Battle of Messines
31 July–10 November: Third Battle of
Ypres, including:
  31 July–2 August: Battle of Pilckem
  16–18 August: Battle of
  Langemarck
  20–5 September: Battle of the
  Menin Road
  26 September–3 October: Battle of
  Polygon Wood
  4 October: Battle of Broodseinde
  9 October: Battle of Poelcapelle
  12 October: First Battle of

Passchendaele
  26 October–10 November: Second
  Battle of Passchendaele
15–25 August: Battle of Hill 60
20 November–7 December: Battle of
Cambrai, including:
  23–8 November: Action of Bourlon
  Wood

1918:
21 March–5 April: the 'Michael'
offensive, or First Battle of the
Somme (1918) (or Second Battle of
the Somme, 1916 being the first),
including:
  21–3 March: Battle of St. Quentin
  24–5 March: First Battle of
  Bapaume
  26–7 March: Battle of Rosières
  28 March: First Battle of Arras (or
  Second, 1917 being the first)
  4 April: Battle of the Avre
  5 April: Battle of the Ancre
9–29 April: the Lys or 'Georgette'
offensive, including:
  2–29 April: Battles of the Lys
  9–11 April: Battle of Estaires
  10–11 April: Battle of Messines
  12–15 April: Battle of Hazebrouck
  13–15 April: Battle of Bailleul
  17–19 April: First Battle of Kemmel
  18 April: Battle of Béthune
  25–6 April: Second Battle of
  Kemmel
  29 April: Battle of the Scherpenberg
  24–5 April: action at Villers–
  Bretonneux
27 May–17 June: the Aisne or
'Blücher–Yorck' offensive,
including:
  27 May–2 June: Third Battle of the
  Aisne
  28 May: Battle of Cantigny
  2–4 June: Battle of Château–
  Thierry
  11–12 June: Battle of Belleau Wood
9–13 June: the Montdidier–Noyon or
'Gneisenau' offensive, including:
  9–13 June: First Battle of Lassigny
15 July–4 August: Second Battle of the
Marne, including:
  15–19 July: German 'Marne'
  offensive
  18 July–5 August: Allied Aisne–
  Marne offensive, including:
    20–31 July: Battle of Tardenois
    23 July–2 August: Battle of the

Soissonais and of the Ourcq
8 August–4 September: Allied Amiens
offensive, including:
  8–11 August: Battle of Amiens
  21 August–3 September: Second
  Battle of the Somme (1918) (or
  Third, 1916 being the first),
  including:
    21–3 August: Battle of Albert
    21 August–3 September: Second
    Battle of Bapaume
  9–15 August: Second Battle of
  Lassigny
  12–16 September: Battle of St. Mihiel
26 August–12 October: assault of the
Hindenburg Line, including:
  26 August–3 September: Second
  Battle of Arras, including:
    26–30 August: Battle of the
    Scarpe
    2–3 September: Battle of
    Drocourt–Quéant
  12 September–9 October: Battles of
  the Hindenburg Line, including:
    12 September: Battle of
    Havrincourt
    12–18 September: Battle of Epéhy
    27 September–1 October: Battle
    of the Canal du Nord
    29 September–2 October: Battle
    of the St. Quentin Canal
    3–5 October: Battle of Beaurevoir
    6–12 October: Second Battle of
    Le Cateau
    8–9 October: Battle of Cambrai
    (Second Battle of Cambrai
    sometimes stated as including
    actions from 27 September to 5
    August)
26 September–11 November: Meuse
Argonne offensive, including:
  26 September–12 October: Battle of
  Champagne
  1–11 November: Battle of the
  Sambre
28 September–11 November: Flanders
offensive, including:
  28 September–2 October: Battle of
  Ypres
  14–19 October: Battle of Courtrai
17 October–11 November: Picardy
offensive, including:
  17–25 October: Battle of the Selle
  1–2 November: Battle of
  Valenciennes
  4 November: Battle of the Sambre

Eastern Front

1914:

East Prussia: 7 August: Russian invasion of East Prussia

17 August: Battle of Stallupönen

20 August: Battle of Gumbinnen

23 August: Battle of Orlau–Frankenau

26–31 August: Battle of Tannenberg

9–14 September: First Battle of Masurian Lakes

26–8 September: Battle of the Niemen

1–9 October: Battle of Augustovo

1914:

Poland: 18 August: Russian invasion

An instruction card regarding the gathering of intelligence, noting the importance of German uniform distinctions.

of Galicia

23 August–1 September: Battles of Lemberg, including:

23–4 August: Battle of Krasnik

26–30 August: Battle of Gnila Lipa

3–11 September: Battle of Rava Ruska

6 September: Battle of Grodek

15–21 October: Battle of Warsaw

11–25 November: Battle of Lódź

7–13 December: Second Battle of Warsaw

1915:

31 January–2 February: Battle of Bolimov

7–22 February: Second Battle of the Masurian Lakes (or 'the Winter Battle')

17 February: Austrian capture of Czernowitz

22 March: Russian capture of Przemysl

2 May: Gorlice–Tarnow offensive (continued to late June)

3 June: recapture of Przemysl

22 June: Austrian capture of Lemberg

5 August: Austrian capture of Ivangorod; German entry into Warsaw

25 August: Austro–German capture of Brest–Litovsk

18–19 September: German capture of Vilna

1916:

18 March–14 April: Battle of Lake Naroch

4 June–20 September: Brusilov Offensive, including:

4 July: Ukraine offensive

28 July: second offensive

7 August: third offensive

1–4 December: Battle of the River Arges

6 December: Austro–German capture of Bucharest

1917:

1 July: Kerensky or Second Brusilov Offensive (begins)

19 July: beginning of German counter-attack in south

1 September: German northern offensive, including:

3 September: German capture of Riga

Balkan Front

1914:

29 July: Austrian bombardment of Belgrade

12 August: Austrian invasion of Serbia

12–21 August: Battle of the Jadar

7 September: second Austrian invasion of Serbia

8–17 September: Battle of the Drina

8 November: third Austrian invasion of Serbia

12 November: defeat of Montenegrins at Grahovo (Bosnian frontier)

2 December: Austrian occupation of Belgrade

3–9 December: Battle of the Kolubara (or Rudnik Malyen)

15 December: recapture of Belgrade

1915:

6 October: Austro–German invasion of Serbia

8–9 October: Austrian capture of
Belgrade

11 October: Bulgarian invasion of
Serbia

5 November: German capture of Nish

1916:

17–27 August: Battle of Florina

10 September–15 December: Allied
counter-offensive, including:

18 September: Allied capture of
Florina

13–18 November: actions around
Monastir

19 November: Allied capture of
Monastir

1917:

11–17 March: Battle of Lake Prespa
(or Doiran)

24–6 April: renewed action on Lake
Prespa

5–19 May: Battle of the Vardar

1918:

30 May: action at Srka di Lengen

15–25 September: Battle of the Vardar

29 September: French capture of
Uskub

12 October: Serbian capture of Nish

1 November: Serbian capture of
Belgrade

Caucasus Front

1914:

29 December–3 January 1915: Battle
of Sarikamish

1915:

20 April: Armenian capture of Van

16 July: Battle of Malazgirt

5 August: Turkish recapture of Van

1916:

18 January: Battle of Köprukoy

13–16 February: Battle of Erzerum

18 April: Russian capture of
Trebizond

25 July: Battle of Erzinjan

15 August: Turkish capture of Bitlis

24 August: Russian recapture of Bitlis

The Dardanelles

1915:

19 February: first Allied naval
bombardment

25 February: second Allied naval
bombardment

18 March: Allied naval attack

25 April: Allied landings at Helles and
Anzac

28 April: First Battle of Krithia

6–8 May: Second Battle of Krithia

12 May: second Allied naval attack

4 June: Third Battle of Krithia

12–13 July: British offensive at Helles

6 August: British landing at Suvla

6–9 August: ANZAC offensive at Lone
Pine

12 August: British offensive at Suvla

15 August: action at Kirich Tepe

21 August: British offensive at Suvla

19–20 December: evacuation of Suvla
and Anzac

1916:

8–9 January: evacuation of Helles

Italian Front

1915:

23 June–7 July: First Battle of the
Isonzo

18 July–3 August: Second Battle of the
Isonzo

18 October–4 November: Third Battle
of the Isonzo

10 November–2 December: Fourth
Battle of the Isonzo

1916:

11–29 March: Fifth Battle of the
Isonzo

15 May–17 June: Trentino offensive

9–28 June: Italian counter-offensive in
Trentino

6–17 August: Sixth Battle of the
Isonzo, including:

6–9 August: Battle of Gorizia

9 August: Italian capture of Gorizia

14–26 September: Seventh Battle of
the Isonzo

10–12 October: Eighth Battle of the
Isonzo

1–14 November: Ninth Battle of the
Isonzo

1917:

12 May–8 June: Tenth Battle of the
Isonzo

18 August–15 September: Eleventh
Battle of the Isonzo

24 October–12 November: Battle of
Caporetto (Twelfth Isonzo),
including

28 October: Austrian capture of
Gorizia

9–19 December: actions along the
Piave

1918:

13 June: actin at Cadi and Monticello
(Tonale Pass)

15–23 June: Battle of the Piave
(sometimes styled Second Battle)

2 July: beginning of Italian advance on
Piave

23 October: Battle of Monte Grappo

24 October–4 November: Battle of
Vittorio Veneto (or Third Battle of
the Piave)

Palestine Front

1915:

2–3 February: Turkish attack on Suez
Canal

1916:

10 June: capture of Mecca by Arab
Revolt

3 August: Battle of Rumani

1917:

8–9 January: Battle of Magruntein

26 March: First Battle of Gaza

17–19 April: Second Battle of Gaza

31 October: Battle of Beersheba (or
Third Gaza)

7 November: British capture of Gaza

13–14 November: Battle of Junction
Station

17 November: British capture of Jaffa

8 December: action before Jerusalem

9 December: British capture of
Jerusalem

1918:

21 February: British capture of Jericho

19 September: Battle of Megiddo or
Samaria (Battle of Samaria
sometimes taken as concluding 30
September)

20 September: British occupation of
Nazareth

23 September: British capture of Acre
and Haifa

30 September–1 October: Anglo–Arab
capture of Damascus

7 October: British capture of Sidon
and Beirut

26 October: British capture of Aleppo

Mesopotamian Front

1914:

7 November: British landing in
Mesopotamia

21–3 November: British entry into
Basra

1915:
12–14 April: action at Qurna
24 April: action at Ahwaz
24 July: Battle of Nasiriya
27–8 September: First Battle of Kut
22–6 November: Battle of Ctesiphon
1 December: action at Umm-at-Tubal
7 December: investment of Kut
1916:
29 April: surrender of Kut
1917:
22–3 February: Second Battle of Kut (sometimes taken as beginning 5 January, being commencement of operations)
24 February: Turkish abandonment of Kut
8–10 March: actions along River Diala in front of Baghdad
11 March: British capture of Baghdad
27–8 September: Battle of Ramadi (or Ramadiya)
1918:
5 April: Turkish occupation of Van (Armenia)
13 April: Turkish occupation of Batum
27 April: Turkish capture of Kars
7 May: British occupation of Kirkuk
14 June: Turkish capture of Tabriz
4 August: British occupation of Baku
1 September: Turkish attack on Baku
18 October: action at Fatha
24 October: action at Sharqat
3 November: British occupation of Mosul

Campaigns in Africa
1914:
22 August: action at Kamina, Togoland
26 August: surrender of German forces, Togoland
9 September: action at Karonga, Nyasaland
27 September: surrender of German forces, Duala (Cameroon)
2–5 November: action at Tanga, German East Africa
12 November: action against South African rebels, Mushroom Valley
1915:
18 January: action at Jasin, East Africa
3 February: surrender of South African rebels, Upington
3 February: death of Chelembe, leader of Nyasaland revolt
20 May: South African capture of Windhoek, German South-West Africa
9 July: surrender of last German forces in South-West Africa, at Tsumeb
1916:
1 January: Allied capture of Yaunde (Cameroon)
18 February: surrender of last German forces in Cameroon (Mora)
1917:
25 November: German evacuation of German East Africa
1918:
25 November: surrender of German forces, East Africa (Abercorn, Northern Rhodesia)

The War at Sea
1914:
5 August: first German loss of the war: minelayer *Königin Luise* destroyed
6 August: first Allied loss of the war; cruiser HMS *Amphion* sunk by mine, North Sea
28 August: Battle of Heligoland Bight
29 August: capture of German Samoa
13 September: Australian capture of Bougainville, Solomon Islands
22 September: HMSS *Aboukir*, *Hogue* and *Cressy* sunk by *U 9*
22 September: Madras bombarded by *Emden*
24 September: Australian capture of Friedrich Wilhelm, New Guinea
7 October: Japanese capture of Marshall Islands
1 November: Battle of Coronel
9 November: *Emden* sunk by HMAS *Sydney*
8 December: Battle of the Falkland Islands
16 December: German bombardment of Hartlepool, Whitby and Scarborough
25 December: French battleship *Jean Bart* destroyed by Austrian submarine, Straits of Otranto
1915:
24 January: Battle of Dogger Bank
19 February: first Allied bombardment, Dardanelles
25 February: second Allied bombardment, Dardanelles
14 March: *Dresden* sunk off Juan Fernandez (last of Spee's squadron)
18 March: Allied naval attack, Dardanelles
27 April: French battleship *Léon Gambetta* sunk by Austrian submarine, Adriatic
7 May: *Lusitania* sunk
12 May: second Allied naval attack, Dardanelles
11 July: destruction of *Königsberg* in River Rufiji, East Africa
18 August: action in Gulf of Riga (Russian navy inflicting some damage on German fleet)
19 August: liner *Arabic* sunk, prompting American protests resulting in suspension of German submarine campaign
1916:
25 April: German bombardment of Lowestoft and Great Yarmouth
31 May–1 June: Battle of Jutland
5 June: HMS *Hampshire* sunk, with death of Kitchener
18–19 August: abortive foray by High Seas Fleet
1917:
31 January: declaration of unrestricted U-boat warfare, effective from following day
25 February: German destroyer bombardment of Margate and Broadstairs
7–8 May: British raid on Zeebrugge
20 April: British victory in destroyer action in Channel
15 May: action in Straits of Otranto
17 November: minor action off Heligoland Bight
1918:
20 January: action at Dardanelles entrance (*Goeben* beached, *Breslau* sunk)
1 February: Austrian naval mutiny, Cattaro
22–3 April: Zeebrugge and Ostend raid
10 May: Ostend raid
9 June: Austrian *Szent-Istvan* sunk
29 October: German naval mutiny (at Kiel main outbreak was 3–4 November)
1 November: Austrian *Viribus Unitis* sunk at Pola

II
WEAPONS AND
TACTICS

WEAPONS AND TACTICS

As the development of weapons and tactics were linked inextricably, it is appropriate to consider the two together. There were only a limited number of major tactical variations applicable to any one nation, those that proved successful generally being adopted by others, facilitated by the organization of units being reasonably similar in all armies. While it is true that the war involved the maintenance of some outdated doctrines, the armies of the major combatant nations were eager to learn from observation and experience of recent campaigns, even if some of the examples quoted at the time dated back more than four decades: concern was paid to events in the Franco–Prussian and Russo–Turkish Wars, for example, as well as to more modern conflicts such as the Russo–Japanese War. As a distinction was made between the fighting of 'civilized' and 'savage' enemies, the guerrilla-style operations of most colonial campaigns provided only limited guidance to the development of 'regular' warfare, although the Boer War of 1899–1902 provided an immense shock to the British military system and had a number of salutary effects.

It is easy to consider the destructive powers of weaponry, and the intricacies of tactical development; but these should never conceal the realities of war. A newspaper editorial published more than a century before the Great War is more apposite than most comments made during the war:

'We frequently hear the subject of war treated with an unfeeling levity, and a battle or a siege, in which hundreds of our fellow creatures are killed or miserably wounded, described with the same apathy that the account of a route or a masquerade is detailed. But whatever cold calculators may urge, however lightly a commissary or contractor may talk of the effects of a state of warfare, still war has its *consummate horrors*.'[1]

Rifles

Despite the increasing emphasis upon other weapons, the rifle remained the universal infantry weapon; as Thomason of the US Marines observed, machine-guns could not always keep pace with infantry, their crews had a habit of being killed, trench-mortars and one-pounders were not always available, and men grew tired of carrying grenades; but the rifle and bayonet went wherever a man went.

Excluding the old, single-shot weapons pressed into service by second- and third-line troops in some armies, the rifles of all nations were basically similar in performance. All used the same basic system, bolt-action and a magazine to enable a number of shots to be fired without re-loading. Some had removable magazines but most were an integral part of the rifle, into which cartridges were inserted in a clip of 3 to 6 rounds, to speed the process of loading. Generally, rifles were loaded by withdrawing the bolt, inserting the clip into the breech, pushing the cartridges into the magazine, and ejecting the clip by the subsequent forward movement of the bolt; rounds were automatically pushed into the breech by a spring in the magazine, the spent cartridge cases being ejected by the action of the bolt after every shot.

There were two principal variations on this system: the widely used Mannlicher design involved the insertion of the entire clip into the magazine, the rounds being pushed upwards by a spring within the clip, which dropped out of the magazine when the last round had been fired; and the Lebel which used a tubular magazine holding 8 rounds, which had to be loaded individually, a slow process which caused the Lebel to be considerably out-dated and led to the French introduction of an improved rifle using the Mannlicher box magazine. The most important contributions to the development of these rifles were made by Mauser (the German 1898 pattern, *Gewehr 98*, was probably the best rifle of its type), and Lee, designer of the Lee box magazine. Apart from changes in the design of projectile, and the shortening of barrels on the most modern rifles (the US 1903 Springfield and British 1907 Short Lee-Enfield), the rifles used during the war were scarcely altered from those of fifteen or twenty years before.

Performance of the various patterns was similar under combat conditions. Maximum range approached 3,500 yards, but as the British musketry regulations stated, at ranges beyond 600 yards it was unprofitable to fire at a specific target with a single rifle. Similarly, although it was possible for a well-trained man to blaze off twenty or more rounds per minute, in normal circumstances aimed 'rapid fire' was between 8 and 12 rounds per minute; the 15 rounds of *aimed* fire sustained by the BEF of 1914 was a considerable achievement, and led the Germans to believe that they were facing many more machine-guns than were actually present.

To compensate the action of gravity, long-range fire involved the bullet using a high trajectory, depending upon the type of rifle, projectile and propellant. (Most effective was the pointed 'S' bullet introduced by Germany in 1905, termed *Spitz-geschoss* ('pointed bullet'), the initial letter being adopted by other countries to describe a pointed bullet (though it was termed 'D' in France). Being more streamlined, by reducing air resistance it had a flatter trajectory). For example, to hit a target at 700 yards (over even ground) an old Martini–Henry bullet had to travel in an arc in which the highest point was more than twenty feet from ground level; in the same circumstances a Lee-Enfield bullet reached a height of ten feet and a Mauser 'S' bullet approximately six feet.

Correct estimation of distance was paramount in maximizing effectiveness of rifle-fire, but at anything over close range other methods were used than that of marking an individual target. (Using British terminology, the general description of ranges were 'close' (0–600 yards), 'effective' (600–1,400), 'long' (1,400–2,000) and 'distant' (2,000–2,800). A rifle, even when fixed, would not project its bullet in exactly the same way every time, so that when the individual skills of a body of troops were taken into consideration, a volley of shots would be expected to straddle the target, and the bullets fly in an imagined, cone-shaped trajectory, the 'cone of fire' or 'cone of dispersion'. The ground upon which the hail of bullets fell was termed the 'beaten zone', which decreased in size as the target became more distant. Using statistics for a Lee-Enfield, at a target at 500 yards' range the 'beaten zone' formed an elongated oval around the target some 320 yards long; at a target at 1,500 yards it was 140 yards long. About 90 per cent of the bullets fired would fall within this area, and about three-quarters of the whole within a smaller area within the beaten zone, termed the 'effective zone' (with the above example, at 500 yards an oval 220 yards long, at 1,500 yards, 100 yards). At the centre of this zone was the 'nucleus' in which half the bullets landed (at 500 yards, about 120 yards long; at 1,500, 60 yards). Between the edge of the beaten zone and the marksman was the 'dangerous space', the area in which the lowest bullet of a volley would strike a man as it dropped, between head-height and the point where it hit the ground. This varied with the height of the man; at 1,000 yards' range, for example, the dangerous space for a mounted cavalryman would be 105 yards, but for a prone infantryman only 13 yards. As in war conditions very few standing targets were available, the dangerous space was only of consequence at close range. (Rising or falling terrain naturally affected the extent of the beaten zone or dangerous space.)

By using the 'cone of fire' it was possible for a body of troops to sweep an area with a continuous fusillade, inhibiting enemy movement even if it caused few casualties. A shower of bullets thus fired might not be as un-nerving as might be expected: in 1914, upon one Royal Irish Fusilier observing that it was raining bullets and they had better put on their greatcoats, one company continued to advance singing the comic song, *Put up your umbrella when it comes on wet!*

At longer range judgement of distance was crucial, and if uncertain of the actual range the fire-controller (officer or NCO in command) could order the use of 'combined sights', in which part of the detachment used one elevation on their rifle-sights and the remainder another, which enabled a greater extent of terrain to be swept, but with less effect since a proportion of shots would fall at the wrong range. Of the two basic methods of firing, a slow, continuous fusillade (perhaps 3 rounds per minute) was used as a continuous harassment and by troops skirmishing; bursts of rapid fire (8 to 15 or more shots per minute) were used for comparatively short periods, at the discretion of the fire-controller, often directed at specific targets rather than as a general 'sweep' of terrain. Rapid fire was most effective in short bursts, with a cessation of fire between to allow the fire-controller to assess the effectiveness of the previous bursts and switch to a new target.

Pre-war musketry theories were concerned primarily with mobile operations, not static trench-warfare, yet basic principles remained the same. In open terrain it was believed that prone was the best position for firing; kneeling was regarded as suitable only for shooting from behind cover, and firing from a standing position from behind cover upon which the rifle could be rested, or for firing on the move when it was not possible to lie down. Some held that troops in cover fired less accurately than those in the open, being unwilling to leave cover long enough to take proper aim, but pre-war statistics probably bore little relation to effectiveness in combat, when errors of judging distance might make some fire totally ineffective; it is possible that combat effectiveness might be as little as five per cent of that attainable under 'test' conditions.

Brief statistics involving some of the principal rifles in use during the war are tabulated here: Included by way of comparison are some of the outdated weapons in use by second-and third-line formations in some armies:

Nation and model	Calibre	Magazine capacity (rounds)	Length (overall) inches	Weight pounds	ounces	Muzzle velocity (fps)
Austria						
1895 Mannlicher	8mm	5	50	8	5½	2,034
Belgium						
1889 Mauser	7.65mm	5	50¼	8	¼	2,034
Bulgaria						
Berdan (Russian)	10.66mm	single	53	9	12½	1,444
1886 Mannlicher	11mm	5	52	9	15½	1,440
1895 Mannlicher	8mm	5	50	8	5½	2,034
Canada						
1907 Ross	.303in	5	52	8	1	2,060
1916 Ross Mk IIIB	.303in	5	50½	9	12	2,060
France						
1886 Lebel	8mm	8 (tube)	51.1	9	3½	2,380
1916 Mannlicher–Berthier	8mm	5	51.3	9	5½	2,380
Germany						
1898 Mauser	7.92mm	5	49¼	9		2,882 ('S' bullet)

Nation and model	Calibre	Magazine capacity (rounds)	Length (overall) inches	Weight pounds ounces		Muzzle velocity (fps)
Great Britain						
Lee–Enfield Mk I	.303in	10	49½	9	4	2,060
Short, Magazine, Lee–Enfield, Mk III	.303in	10	44½	8	10½	2,060
Greece						
1878 Gras	11mm	single	51¼	9	11	1,493
1903 Mannlicher–Schoenauer	6.5mm	5	48¾	8	5½	2,223
Italy						
1871 Vetterli	10.4mm (later converted to 6.5mm)	single	53½	9	9	1,430
1871–87 Vetterli	as above	4	54	9	13¾	1,525
1891 Mannlicher–Carcano	6.5mm	6	50¾	8	6½	2,395
Japan						
38th year Arisaka	6.5mm	5	50¾	8	10	2,396
Montenegro						
Berdan (Russian)	10.66mm	single	53	9	12½	1,444
1891 Moisin–Nagant	7.62mm	5	51¾	8	15¼	1,985
Portugal						
1904 Mauser–Verguiero	6.5mm	5	48	8	13	2,347
Roumania						
1893 Mannlicher	6.5mm	5	48½	8	12¾	2,400
Russia						
1891 Moisin–Nagant	7.62mm	5	51¾	8	15¼	1,985
Serbia						
1881 Mauser–Milanovic	10.15mm	single	50¾	10	4	1,580
1893 Mauser	7.65mm	5	48½	9	1	2,066
Turkey						
1874 Peabody–Martini	.45in	single (block breech)	49	9	10	1,380
1893 Mauser	7.65mm	5	48½	9	1	2,066
USA						
1903 Springfield	.30in	5	43¼	8	8	2,600
M1917 Enfield	.30in	5	46¼	9	3	2,600

The sights of the principal patterns were calibrated for the following maximum effective ranges:
US 1903 Springfield: 2,850 yards (2,187 metres); British 1907 Lee–Enfield: 2,800 yards (2,560 metres); Belgian 1889 Mauser, French 1886 Lebel, German 1898 Mauser, Greek 1903 Mannlicher–Schoenauer, Italian 1891 Mannlicher–Carcano, Japanese 38th year Arisaka, Portuguese 1904 Mauser–Verguiero, Roumanian 1893 Mannlicher, Turkish 1893 Mauser: 2,000 metres (2,187 yards); Austrian, Bulgarian and Greek 1895 Mannlicher: 2,600 paces (2,132 yards, 1,968 metres); Russian 1891 Moisin–Nagant: 2,700 paces (2,096 yards, 1,935 metres); Canadian 1907 Ross: 2,00 yards (1,846 metres).

The Bayonet
The bayonet existed in three basic styles: a knife-bladed version, the most common; the 'needle' bayonet, like that of the Lebel rifle (prone to breaking); and a pioneer version of a knife-bayonet with serrated rear edge for use as a saw (which was stated by Allied propaganda to be an example of Hun 'frightfulness'!). Despite the importance accorded to the bayonet (to the extent that when the beneficial shortening of the Lee–Enfield occurred, a longer bayonet was designed to compensate), and despite various nations claiming it as a weapon traditional to their forces, its use in combat was very limited. (One contemporary comment identified its uses as primarily for toasting, poking a brazier,

opening tins of peaches, scraping mud off boots, bread and puttees, candlestick and 100 other purposes, as well as for dealing with 'Fritz'!)[2]

Much emphasis was placed upon what a British manual termed 'the spirit of the bayonet', which 'must be inculcated into all ranks so that they go forward with that aggressive determination and confidence of superiority born of continual practice'.[3] This identified the essence of bayonet-work: '... essentially a weapon of offence which must be used with skill and vigour ... to await passively an opportunity of using the bayonet entails defeat, since an approaching enemy will merely stand out of bayonet range and shoot down the defenders. In an assault the enemy should be killed with the bayonet. Firing should be avoided, for in the mix-up a bullet, after passing through an opponent's body, may kill a friend who happens to be in the line of fire';[4] '... go straight at an opponent with the point threatening his throat and deliver the point whenever an opportunity presents itself'.[5]

Pre-war manuals stressed the importance of the bayonet against an 'uncivilized' enemy ('Apart from fanatics and from exceptionally brave savages like the Zulus, irregular warriors, be they Pathan hill-men or Somalis or Boxers or Boers, have no stomach for the infantryman's cold steel').[6] Thus, faith was still placed in the tactic of an advance employing musketry, followed by a charge with the bayonet: 'The rifle and bayonet is the weapon upon which every soldier must learn to rely both for attack and defence. Confidence in the bayonet carries men to the assault; confidence in the bullet beats off the counter-attack. These two are not separate, but one. The bullet supports the bayonet by its covering fire; the bayonet completes what the bullet begins.'[7] Contrary to those who believed that the primacy of the magazine-rifle would make bayonet-charges impossible, supporters of the bayonet cited actions in the Russo–Japanese War when Japanese troops carried positions at the point of the bayonet;[8] despite factors such as remarkably bad Russian marksmanship and artillery-direction which contributed to the success of such attacks, they were sufficient evidence to maintain the belief in the significance of the bayonet.

Although the theory of an orderly advance over open ground, ending in a bayonet-charge, was largely altered by the events of the war, the bayonet was of use in trench-fighting, which was often literally hand-to-hand; though even here it was subsidiary to other weapons (one veteran remarked that a sharpened entrenching-tool was immensely more effective!). It is difficult to assess the frequency of the use of the bayonet, but it is interesting to note that records of bayonet-injuries were not kept separately by British statisticians; they were consigned to the just over one per cent of casualties covered by miscellaneous injuries and accidents. Probably, as had been the case for the previous two centuries, the bayonet's value was more as a psychological than physical weapon, one side or the other giving way before steel could actually be crossed. A number of accounts

of bayonet-fights exist, though the number published in the early stages of the war probably greatly over-state the frequency and do not depict the full horror of such incidents: 'I saw one man single me out and come at me with his bayonet. He made a lunge at my chest, and, as I guarded, his bayonet glanced aside and wounded me in the hip; but I managed to jab him in the left arm and get him on the ground, and when he was there I hammered him on the head with the butt-end of my rifle.'[9]

The Machine-Gun

The heavy machine-gun was used by all the principal armies at the beginning of the war, but its tactical employment altered considerably during the conflict.

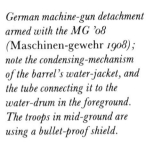

Italian sentry, wearing the Italian version of the Adrian helmet.

German machine-gun detachment armed with the MG '08 (Maschinen-gewehr 1908); note the condensing-mechanism of the barrel's water-jacket, and the tube connecting it to the water-drum in the foreground. The troops in mid-ground are using a bullet-proof shield.

Despite the large number of different patterns, principles of operation were the same, involving the weapon being positioned upon a low mount and delivering a large number of rounds (generally of rifle calibre) at a rapid speed. Ammunition was fed into the breech automatically, to keep up this rate of fire, by one of three means: by 'strip', in which the cartridges (30 was usual) were placed in a rigid metal tray or rack as for the French Hotchkiss; by a continuous belt of woven fabric into which rounds were inserted (250 per belt was usual); or by a belt composed of metal links, which belt separated into individual links as the spent cartridge-cases were ejected. The fabric belt was the most common; the link-belt was of especial use in aviation service, avoiding the danger of fabric belts trailing out of the gun and becoming entangled with the aircraft controls.

Performance and rate of fire were also reasonably standard, although performance depended to some extent upon the proficiency of the crew: a Russo–Japanese War estimate of one jamming of Maxim guns for every 300 rounds fired was attributed mainly to the inexperience of the crews. The firepower of a machine-gun was awesome, estimated by the French before the war to be the equivalent of 150–200 rifles at known range, or 60–80 rifles at estimated range; Germany calculated the fire of one gun to equal that of 80 riflemen. The difference between known and estimated ranges was due to the infantry 'cone of fire' being deeper than that of the machine-gun, the latter grouping its bullets more closely and thus at a known target was considerably more effective than at an estimated-range target when a greater percentage of rounds might be expected to miss. For a Maxim gun the 'effective zone' was estimated at 150 yards at 500 yards' range, 60 at 1,500 and 50 at 2,000. Accurate calculation of range was paramount, for if a two-gun section had to fire with 'combined sights' (i.e., different settings of range) at least half, perhaps three-quarters of the shots

would be totally without effect. However, a British instruction of 1909 cited the employment of 'combined sights' as an advantage of the assembly of machine-guns in batteries. Measuring-devices such as clinometers were affixed to guns, and range-taking instruments frequently accompanied machine-gun units.

The rapidity of fire – 600 rounds per minute was quite usual – resulted in severe heating of the barrel. Apart from the use of a very heavy barrel, two methods of cooling were employed, using air (with radiating fins attached to the barrel) or water. With the latter system, the barrel was surrounded by a 'water-jacket' into which water was poured as a cooling agent: with a Maxim, the 7½ pints of water it contained were raised to boiling-point after 600 rounds had been fired (i.e., one minute's continuous fire), and a further 1½ pints evaporated for every succeeding 1,000 rounds. (These statistics were not uniform for all guns: the Austrian Schwarzlose, for example, evaporated the contents of its water-jacket only every 3,000 rounds.) This entailed the regular re-filling of the water-jacket, which could have been difficult in combat, but provision of water was facilitated by the presence of a steam-vent on the water-jacket, which allowed condensed steam to be run off, via a tube, into a water-can, which could then be used to re-fill the jacket. Protracted service wore out gun-barrels, causing accuracy to decline; the Schwarzlose could fire 35,000 rounds without the efficiency becoming impaired.

Most guns were mounted on a detachable tripod or 'sledge', which greatly increased the weight (the German MG'08 'sledge', for example, was more than twice the weight of the gun). The Russian 1910 'Sokolov' Maxim had a trail and small wheels, allowing it to be trundled along the ground; others were carried by the crew, on mule-back or on horsed limbers. Shields were available for some guns, providing protection for the crew, but these were often

An anonymous German officer describes an advance under fire in the Vosges, late August 1914:

'"Twelfth Company, forward, march!"

'But we did not advance very far. We had hardly reached the border of the slope, when such a murderous volley burst upon us from their machine-guns, that we had to fling ourselves down flat immediately. It was out of the question to answer their fire. I don't know if those Maxims are ahead of us, or on our flanks, close at hand or far off; I only hear a terrific patter of bullets and suppressed groans among my men while I myself received three bullets . . . every one crawls behind tree and bush or rock. Again the bullets whistle and again I get a dose, this time in my chest to the left. I don't lose consciousness, and I feel my subaltern lifting me from behind to draw me behind a rock, where he applied First Aid.

'I do not feel the least pain, only I can hardly breathe, for now the right lung alone must do the work for both . . . For hours I lie behind that rock, while from time to time my brave subaltern appears to announce that our men are advancing . . . Then come the stretcher-bearers whom my subaltern has sent. I leave the field with an easy conscience, I had done my duty, knowing that for a little time I would be good for nothing . . .'

(ed. Dr. H. Cimino, *Navy & Army Illustrated*, p. 13, 24 April 1915)

removed as not only increasing the weight, but making the gun more visible to the enemy (mountings were low, so that the gunner either lay, crouched or sat on the mounting to fire). The need for more mobile guns not only produced the light machine-gun during the war, but also an important derivative of the German Maxim, the MG '08/15, the same basic gun but fitted with a butt and bipod mount, and portable by a single man.

Although one man could operate a heavy machine-gun, it normally involved a small team. Although two men could operate a gun for an unlimited period, a Maxim team (for example) might normally include four or six men. In British service the team was six strong, numbered 1 to 6. No. 1 was the principal gunner, who carried the tripod, mounted the gun, fired it and was responsible for direction, elevation and observation. No. 2 carried the gun and supervised the belt-feed of ammunition. Nos. 3 and 4 carried ammunition, No. 4 also being responsible for keeping the water-jacket filled; Nos. 5 and 6 acted as scouts and range-takers. Transportation of ammunition was a considerable problem, given the amount expended: a British ammunition-box, for example, contained a 250-round belt and weighed 22 pounds: for a two-gun section 32 belts were normally transported with the guns, with four extra belts and 15,000 loose rounds in the unit's ammunition-cart, plus a further 10,000 rounds per gun held by both the brigade and divisional ammunition column. The weight of ammunition (including boxes) immediately available for each gun was therefore 352 pounds, or more than 6 cwt for a two-gun section.

As the trajectory of machine-gun fire followed the same course as that of the rifle (although maximum range was considerably greater), it was possible to utilize this trajectory in indirect fire. Most hazardous was overhead 'supporting fire', in which the high trajectory was used to fire over the heads of friendly troops, to lay down a curtain of bullets upon the enemy in front of the friendly line. This was used most safely when the enemy was on higher ground: but provided that the greatest care was taken in ranging, overhead supporting fire could be used on level ground, though had to cease when the friendly troops approached the danger zone. A second type of indirect fire was that in which the gun-sights were aligned on some marker other than the target, most useful for night-firing. To sweep a section of terrain at night, to ensure that the correct area was hit during the dark, the gun would be aligned in daylight and the sights then turned upon some nearer object, the gun itself continuing to point towards the target. Thus, by keeping the sights set upon the nearer, visible aiming-mark, the flow of bullets would continue to hit the required area. A simple single-mark was the 'night-firing box', a battery-operated lamp visible only on the side pointing towards the gun.

Statistics for some of the principal heavy machine-guns are tabulated here; rate of fire is theoretical which does not take into account operational details such as reloading.

Type	Calibre	Ammunition	Weight (inc. mount) pounds	Cooling System	Rate of Fire (rpm)
German Maxim MG '08	7.9mm	belt	70–123½	water	600
German Maxim MG '08/15	7.92mm	belt	31–39	water	600
British Vickers Mk I	.303in	belt	73	water	500
French 1914 Hotchkiss	8mm	strip	88–115	air	600
Austrian Schwarzlose	8mm	belt	44	water	400
Russian 1910 Maxim ('Sokolov')	7.62mm	belt	90–152½	water	5–600
American Colt	.30in (or other for foreign armies)	belt	101	air	4–500
American 1917 Browning	.30in	belt	41	water	450–600

The British Army's principal machine-gun was the Vickers, which existed in a number of 'Marks'; this drawing of 1915 illustrates the belt-feed. (Drawing published anonymously in 1916)

(Differences in weight were according to mounting, presence of shield, etc.; for example, the MG '08 itself weighed 40½ pounds, the 1914 Hotchkiss 55 pounds, the Vickers 33 pounds, the 1910 Maxim 52½ pounds.)

The light machine-gun was largely a wartime development, more portable and able to keep pace with the infantry, into which the gunners were integrated. Although operating on the same principle as the heavy machine-gun, belts were not ideally suited for this service, and drums or magazines were preferred, so that the gunner and section of riflemen which generally supported him were laden with spare magazines; the Lewis gun, for example, had a 47-round magazine, the Chauchat 20, and the German *Muskete* (a Madsen derivative) 25. (The latter was a singular weapon in that it was not distributed throughout the army, but concentrated into special *Muskete–Bataillone*.) Not all such weapons were purely wartime developments: the Danish Madsen, for example, was already in use with the Russian Army in considerable numbers, and the Mondragon semi-automatic rifle had been invented as early as about 1891 by the Mexican general of that name, and had been fully developed by Germany by 1915. It resembled an ordinary rifle but had a capacity for automatic fire, using a 10-round magazine.

Statistics for important light machine-guns (all air-cooled) are tabulated here.

Type	Calibre	Weight pounds	Ammunition	Rate of fire (rpm)
Madsen	8mm	20	magazine	450
German 1915 *Muskete*	7.92mm	21¾	magazine	450
German Bergmann	7.92mm	30	belt	600
German MG '08/18	7.92mm	32	belt	600
(lighter, air-cooled version of the MG '08/15)				
Lewis	.303in	25	drum magazine	5–600
French Chauchat (CSRG)	8mm	20	magazine	250
American Chauchat	.30in	20	magazine	250
American Browning Automatic Rifle (BAR M1918)	.30in	19½	magazine	500

The only true submachine-gun to be used, in very limited numbers, was the German Bergmann MP 18, which appeared in 1918, classified as a 'machine-pistol' (hence the 'MP'), with a 32-round drum magazine and a rate-of-fire of 540 rpm. The Italian 9mm Villar Perosa, weighing only 14½ pounds, despite being double-barrelled, saw limited use as a military submachine-gun though it was designed for aviation service.

The role of the machine-gun evolved in a way which closely followed that of light artillery more than a century before, when the 'battalion guns' which had accompanied infantry were found to be more effective when assembled into massed batteries, following the old artillery maxim that the effect of a concentration of fire was greater than the sum of its parts.

Before the war, the more traditional view was to regard machine-guns as a mobile reserve of fire for infantry; as the British 1909 *Field Service Regulations* stated, 'machine guns are best used in pairs in support of the particular body of troops to which they belong', the 'particular body' being a battalion; but provision existed for the combination of the machine-gun sections of more than one battalion. The French system was similar, in that machine-guns were organized at section level, though employment was flexible. Germany also used the machine-gun as a fire reserve, but in addition to infantry guns also maintained separate machine-gun companies for support of those of the infantry. An additional bonus when compared to the British system was that although orders of 1909 confirmed the machine-guns as an integral part of the infantry, the guns of a German regiment of three battalions were not linked inextricably to each battalion, but under the command of the regimental commander, so that a regiment's six guns could be grouped in one battery. This is the principal reason why in the early stages of the war the Germans were believed to have far more guns they actually possessed, the employment of regimental batteries being much more effective than the British distribution in two-gun sections.

As the war progressed, other nations copied the superior German tactics, though in some cases the military establishments took some time to appreciate what should have been obvious. Initially, for example, no distinction was made in British service between the heavy machine-gun (the Vickers having replaced the Maxim as the principal weapon in the early months) and the newly-introduced Lewis, which being fired from the shoulder was not equal to the Vickers (overhead fire, for example, being too hazardous to be attempted); conversely, the Lewis was virtually as portable as a rifle. Eventually, such facts permeated among the military planners and dictated the disposition of guns later in the war.

To illustrate the development of tactics by reference to the British experience, the huge increase in number of guns and the development of the light gun led to the latter becoming the sole weapon of the infantry machine-gun sections. The heavy guns were formed into brigade companies, necessita-

ting the creation of a Machine Gun Corps and breaking the link between the infantry and the heavy machine-gun. To permit even greater concentration of fire, from March 1916 additional companies were formed at divisional level, to support the brigade companies. Because of the range of the heavy gun and its capacity for overhead fire, it was realized that as long as the bullets fell in the required position it did not matter where the guns were posted, enabling machine-gun units to be sited in positions different from those occupied by the infantry. Machine-gun fire had been regarded as primarily defensive, but in 1917 its offensive potential was demonstrated by the Canadians, who pioneered the tactic in British service of laying down offensive barrages during the Vimy Ridge and Messines operations, facilitated by having a divisional command for machine-gun units. Divisional machine-gun officers already existed in British formations, but their role was only advisory (and in commanding the single divisional company); not until January 1918 were divisional machine-gun commanders appointed, with control over the entire guns in the division.

The use of the barrage as an offensive tactic – in effect, turning the machine-gun into a form of artillery – led to a further refinement in disposition of guns, into forward and rear units. The proportions varied with circumstances, but in general the forward units were kept to a minimum, their role in offence to offer immediate support to the attacking infantry, and in defence to man the outpost line to disorganize and execute a temporary check upon the attacking enemy, who would ultimately be destroyed by the deeper defences of the system. The bulk of the guns, in rear deployment, using overhead barrage fire, were used in defence to protect specific strongpoints and used long-range fire to assist the defence of the forward positions. In attack, the rear guns would lay down barrages in front of the advancing friendly troops; as these tactics were designed for the conditions of the Western Front, objectives were generally sufficiently limited that the rear machine-guns would not have to be re-positioned more than once during an advance, given the long range at which their barrage could be laid. It was also important that guns be concentrated to direct their fire upon or from specific points (in defence, to protect the most important strongpoints and cover the most likely approach-routes of the enemy), rather than attempting to cover more lightly the entire front, resulting in a fatal dilution of fire. To guard against breakthroughs on an unprotected sector, a mobile reserve could be maintained; such was the role allocated originally to the German *Muskete* battalions.

Success of such machine-gun tactics depended upon co-ordination of movement and action, both between the different machine-gun units and between the guns and the infantry they supported; and it was found that the minimum size for a machine-gun unit was a section of four guns, anything less being unable to achieve its tactical objectives.

Infantry support was maintained by the light machine-guns able to keep pace with and crewed by the infantry, and generally disposed at the most basic level (i.e., accompanying each platoon rather than being concentrated into a battalion machine-gun company); in this role the Lewis, Chauchat, German Maxim MG '08/15 and '08/18, and automatic rifles like the American Browning, were ideally suited.

Whereas the rifle was the primary soldiers' weapon in 1914, by 1918 the machine-gun had become dominant. It is impossible to calculate exactly its respective influence, but the following is an extremely rough calculation. If, for example, a battalion's 'rifle' strength is estimated at 600, and each machine-gun the equivalent of 80 rifles, a British division in 1914 (twelve battalions) could field the equivalent of 9,120 rifles. In 1918, with nine infantry and one pioneer battalion, it could field the equivalent of 38,000 rifles, so greatly had the number of machine-guns multiplied. (If each gun were worth 150 rifles the comparison is even more startling: the equivalent of 10,800 rifles in 1914 to 66,000 in 1918).

The Grenade

The use of the grenade was revived by the Russo–Japanese War, as a result of which some nations (notably Germany) regarded the weapon with enthusiasm; others, like Britain, neglected it almost entirely until the World War had been in progress for some time. There were two basic types of grenade, those thrown by hand and those projected from a firearm; its most effective use was in the confined spaces of trench warfare, in which it could be lobbed over obstacles, enabling troops to kill their opponents without exposing themselves to the enemy's fire, and trench warfare provided the greatest impetus to the weapon's development.

Not at all the heroism of the war occurred in situations of armed conflict; 'passive resistance' also demanded courage. The following is a typical text circulated clandestinely in occupied Belgium: a handbill entitled 'Courage!':

'Belgians, your dignified attitude, your superb protests, have finally aroused the neutrals. If for several weeks the foreign press has not reached us, it is because it is unanimous in protesting against the cruel wrongs done to your liberty by the occupiers. Continue to exhibit to the world the example of a nation small in extent but great in the moral values and the untiring courage of its children.

'Crushed beneath the boot of a brutal aggressor, continue to oppose the Right to Might; this attitude will win you the sympathies of all true hearts and the admiration of history.

'Let no-one co-operate either directly or indirectly with the crime of the Teuton.

'Passive resistance in every way and always, this must be your watchword!

VIVE LA BELGIQUE'

Although a huge number of designs existed, all conformed to the same basic construction: a metal casing packed with explosives, a means of ignition, and usually some form of shrapnel to be distributed by the bursting of the charge, most effective when the casing was segmented to act as shrapnel itself. Some hand-grenades used blast alone, to avoid the thrower being injured by his own grenade, of which there was a considerable risk only in open warfare; in trench-fighting there was usually sufficient cover behind which the thrower could shelter to escape the danger of fragments. In open terrain, however, grenades were almost as dangerous to the thrower as to the target: the so-called 'Japanese' percussion grenade used by the Russian Army, for example, was so light that it could be thrown 45 yards, but its charge was such that its fragments were thrown 200 yards.

The two principal methods of ignition were percussion or impact fuzes, and timed fuzes. The impact fuze involved a plunger at the base of the grenade, which when striking the ground was forced against a detonator. This demanded that the grenade fall upon the plunger, which could be ensured by designing the casing so that the heaviest point was around the plunger, allowing gravity to ensure that it fell plunger-downwards; or by attaching fabric streamers to ensure that it hit the ground plunger-first. Another variety was the so-called 'all-ways' fuze, in which there was more than one plunger, as on the German 1914 'disc' grenade, resembling a discus with projecting lugs, any of which ignited the detonator when the grenade landed edge-on.

The time-fuze was a more reliable ignition, although one variety combined it with percussion-ignition, as in the French 'CF' model 1916 grenade, activated by rapping the base upon a hard object, which ignited a delayed-action explosion. Time-fuzed grenades were otherwise activated in a variety of ways, including a method similar to the principle of the safety-match, in which the detonator was dragged across a strip of matchbox-striker (usually tied around the grenadier's sleeve), as used in the British 'cricket-ball' grenade; or by a friction-fuze which performed the same function inside the grenade, activated either by pulling a cord hanging outside the grenade, or by having this cord attached to a wrist-loop, on the 'bracelet' grenade, which automatically pulled the igniter from the body of the grenade when it left the thrower's hand. Most effective was the spring-loaded igniter, activated when a pin was pulled from the grenade, releasing a spring to force a plunger upon a percussion cap, igniting a delayed explosion. This latter method was used in the British Mills grenade, probably the most effective munition of its type.

Excluding the discus and those resembling tubular rifle-grenades, there were two basic shapes: one with an ovoid or spherical casing, and one with a handle. Some of the most primitive were of the latter type, including the 'racket' or 'hair-brush' varieties made by Britain and France, in which the explosive was affixed to a wooden paddle shaped like a butter-pat. Although Germany made much use of the 'egg'-

grenade, their most famous type was the handled 'stick-grenade' (*Stielhandgranate*) or 'potato-masher', consisting of a metal cylinder containing explosive attached to a wooden handle, through which ran a cord to ignite the charge by friction when it was pulled.

A further variety was the home-made grenade. Whereas the German commission established to assess the lessons of the Russo–Japanese War recognized the potential of the grenade, the neglect of the weapon by Britain and France resulted in the production of improvised grenades, often by troops at the front, until official designs could be produced in quantity. Most commonly these involved packing explosives into empty tin cans (hence the common nickname 'jam-tin bombs'), or by strapping charges on to a wooden bat; these all employed friction-ignition and were often packed with nails, scrap metal or bits of barbed wire to act as shrapnel. Such improvised weapons were even used by the Germans, to supplement their ordinary grenades, for example by wiring a tobacco-tin filled with explosives on to a bat.

Rifle-grenades were available initially in greater quantities, but declined in importance because of lack of accuracy. Due to their longer range, all were of the fragmentation variety, employing a segmented casing. The earliest operated on the 'rod' principle, the grenade affixed to a steel rod which slid down the bore of a rifle and was projected by the firing of a blank cartridge; most famous was probably the British Marten Hale, though Germany and Russia also employed this style. An improved method of launching introduced later in the war was the *tromblon* or cup-discharger, in which a cylindrical metal cup was affixed to the muzzle of the rifle, into which a grenade was placed (the Mills or the French 'VB' – Viven–Bessières – were the most significant). The grenade was launched by firing an ordinary bullet, which passed through the grenade, activating its fuze, while the expanding gases in the rifle-barrel propelled the grenade from the cup. The cup-discharger reduced the range of rifle–grenades to about 180–200 yards (225 yards was maximum for a Mills), but to increase the range to almost 400 yards it was possible to employ a different cup and a finned grenade, like a mortar-bomb. Not until 1918 did the Germans replace the rodded grenade with a cup-discharger which gave a range of about 150 yards.

The hand-grenade was essentially a close-quarters weapon. British bombers were expected to land half their missiles in a 10 ft. by 4 ft. trench at 30 yards, using a 1½-pound grenade; some could greatly exceed this distance, and sometimes one bombing-party outranged another by using lighter grenades. In general, the bravest and most athletic men were selected as bombers, though technique was also important. Grenades were generally lobbed over-arm, though at shorter ranges stick-grenades could be thrown like a dart, and an action from the front of the shoulder like a shot-putt was recommended for use in confined spaces with percussion grenades, to avoid striking the detonator on the rear face of the trench as the arm was drawn back for a conventional throw. Training was also given in throwing the grenade from kneeling or prone positions. Except for time-fuzed grenades thrown after a couple of seconds' hesitation, to ensure that the four- or five-second fuze ignited the charge as the bomb dropped among the enemy, it was possible to throw back a live grenade, or even catch it in mid-flight: 'Trooper Bluegum' (Oliver Hogue) records a noted ANZAC cricketer named Renwick who was especially adept at this, and some Australians remarked that catching Turkish grenades at Gallipoli was the best slip practice they ever had! Rifle-grenades were fired with the rifle's-butt upon the ground and the stock braced against the firer's foot or leg; it was discovered that less damage occurred to the stock if the rifle were held with the magazine upwards.

In the attack, grenades for bombing-parties might be carried in boxes, pouched jerkins, pocketed belts (or looped belts into which rodded grenades could be slipped) or improvised satchels made from sandbags, the latter very common with German assault detachments. Although grenades might be carried by any infantry, there existed specialist bombing parties; in British service, for example, the official 9-man team comprised one NCO, two throwers, two carriers, two bayonet-men and two spares, which enabled a party to progress down a trench, lob grenades into the next bay, and after their detonation the bay would be entered by the bayonet-men who dispatched any enemy still capable of resistance, before signalling the throwers to move on to the next bay. Rifle-grenade parties were of similar size, but were used more as reserve artillery. A British manual described the essence of grenade tactics:

'The bomb is the auxiliary . . . for use in killing or dislodging the enemy from behind cover or underground, and driving him into the open where the rifle, Lewis gun and machine-gun can satisfactorily deal with him. The bomb is in no way a substitute for the rifle; its revival is the result of trench warfare, and the more open the warfare becomes, the fewer opportunities will occur for its useful employment . . . The rifle bomb may be regarded as the "howitzer" of the platoon and is used to support the attack by dislodging the enemy from behind cover or forcing him underground . . . Concentrations of rifle bombs can be used to put out of action machine-guns or other points of resistance . . .'[10]

Despite this classification of the grenade as a support weapon, by the later stages of the war it seemed to many observers that it had supplanted the rifle as the favoured weapon in both British and French Armies; Pershing remarked that whereas the Americans regarded the rifle as '. . . the American weapon, and it has other uses than as a stick for a bayonet',[11] the British and French seemed concerned only with the machine-gun, grenade and mortar, and another US observer remarked that the French appeared to regard the grenade as the main weapon, and the rifle as virtually an extended bayonet.

Grenade-throwing was potentially a most hazardous

Serbian infantry in a hilltop entrenchment.

occupation, and many accidents occurred of men being blown up by their own bombs. One of the most celebrated Victoria Cross awards, for example, the last for Gallipoli, was to Lieutenant A. V. Smith of the East Lancashire Regiment, who deliberately fell upon a grenade he had dropped rather than let its splinters mutilate his comrades.

In addition to blast and fragmentation grenades, others included smoke-bombs and even rifle-launched empty cylinders, used to transmit messages.

The Flame-thrower

The liquid fire projector was demonstrated by a German, Richard Fiedler, in 1906, having been under development for some years. Primarily intended as a siege weapon, although the static version might be regarded as 'trench artillery', in its more portable form the flame-thrower may be classed as an infantry-support weapon. Germany produced the first service version, which spurred the French and British to produce their own, though in the British case it was little-used (in some occasions on the Somme) and its presence was perhaps more to boost morale (so that the troops knew they also possessed the weapon) than for practical application.

The flame-thrower squirted a stream of inflammable oil and petrol mix, projected by gas under pressure (air, carbon dioxide, nitrogen; the latter was most suitable) and was ignited by a burning taper applied to the nozzle of the pipe, or later by automatic ignition. It was a very short-range weapon (in tests the maximum range ever achieved was 134 yards, but was generally restricted to very much less) and designed to make areas inaccessible to the enemy, both by the flame and surrounding heat.

The heavy flame-throwers were cylinders of gas and fuel mounted in emplacements; the German Grof (*Grossflammenwerfer*) had a range of about 40 yards, each canister burning for about one minute. The British version, tried experimentally but rejected and the equipment given to Russia (though not used), had a range of up to 90 yards. Another British pattern, named after its inventor, Captain Livens of the Royal Engineers, was designed to be shot from a dug-out and could deliver 240 gallons of fuel in four minutes, in three bursts. The main inhibiting factor was the huge quantity of fuel consumed, and the proximity to the enemy to which it had to be carried; for example, one mile of front line (requiring 30 Livens projectors) would consume about 1,000 gallons of petrol per minute, not including the oil also required, so that an hour of such operation using more fuel than the entire French army transport service's daily need in 1917–18.

Portable flame-throwers were far more useful, especially for trench-clearing, and were employed in about equal quantities by Germany and France; the British patterns (Norris–Menchen and Lawrence) were not used in combat save for a smaller version at Zeebrugge. Germany had two types of portable projector, the Kleif (*Kleinflammenwerfer*) and Wex. The Kleif was a portable version of the Grof, carried on the back of one member of the crew and with the nozzle generally directed by another, ranging to about 25 yards. The Wex was more portable, also carried on the back and shaped like a lifebelt with a spherical gas-container at the centre; its range was only about twenty yards, but unlike the others had automatic ignition. The French portable projector, carried on the back of the single crewman, was styled the Schilt (after its inventor, Captain Schilt of the Paris Fire Brigade, who also organized the flame-thrower companies); it carried more fuel (3 gallons) than the Wex (2¾ gallons) and could project eight or ten bursts up to 30 yards' range, or a single burst up to 100 yards. The portable projector was especially effective in hastening the surrender of troops sheltering in dug-outs, in attacking strongpoints or covering the advance and retreat of parties engaged in trench-fighting. In German service the *Flammenwerfer* was operated principally by the Guard Reserve Pioneer Regiment, whose personnel were lent to the assault units which normally operated flame-projectors.

Infantry Tactics

Although it is not possible for reasons of space to examine tactical development in great detail, it should be remembered that actions were invariably confused, and that no matter what the tactical theories employed, it was often impossible to carry them through with precision. Major F. W. Bewsher, writing of warfare on the Western Front, commented that combat never resembled that depicted in the illustrated papers or described by bayonet-instructors, but likened it to a situation in which 'two teams dressed in battle order play football in the dark on a ploughed field in a clay soil after three weeks of steady rain';[12] or, as in this German account of Loos: 'English on the right! Where? They are our men! No; by Heaven! they are Englishmen, quite near, not ten yards off, before their uniforms can be recognized . . . Often it was hard to say who was opposite, who was on the flanks or in the rear, friend or foe. And shrapnel burst wherever one turned one's steps'.[13]

When considering accounts of tactics, it is easy to overlook the fact that things rarely progressed as planned. Edmund Priestman of the 6th Battalion York and Lancaster Regiment described how his unit adopted 'artillery formation' for advance across country, in which platoons formed loose columns four abreast, to present the minimum target for artillery:

'Across the first field we kept this formation beautifully. Then we met a second hedge and then a wet ploughed field. On switching my attention from the ground to the platoon in front I found (by some unexplained means) they had disappeared and left not a sign of themselves! At this point a head poked over a hedge and saw me – and wanted to know what the —— I thought I was doing? To which I replied that I was under the impression that I was advancing in artillery formation. On closer examination I found my formation was more like a Mothers' Meeting out for a walk . . . the Colonel (for the head belonged to no less!) cursed me and my Mothers' Meeting most vilely for ten minutes and then went in search of the Major to repeat the best bits over again to him . . .'[14]

Despite the terrible ferocity of weaponry, they were not always as lethal as might be imagined. Erwin Rommel's *Infantry Attacks* describes how in 1914 his platoon advanced against French positions under a continuous fusillade, moving in rushes with each group being supported by the others, until they carried the position and found the defenders had fled; and so bad had been the French marksmanship that their shots had gone over the Germans' heads and caused no casualties. Similarly, many accounts described the ineffectiveness of artillery fire ('The noise was

Sturmangriff ('assault'): German 'war art' showing an assault detachment in action (print after Felix Schwormstadt).

simply deafening, but so little effect had the fire that the men shouted with laughter and held their caps up on the end of their rifles to give the German gunners a bit of encouragement'.[15] Continuing the account above, Rommel also described coming under an intense artillery bombardment for several minutes, but save for a few pieces of sharpnel in their knapsacks, and a shredded bayonet-tassel, again no hits were registered.

Nevertheless, the quantity of munitions expended did cause the most terrible damage, and it is interesting to note the increasing significance of artillery at the expense of infantry. German statistics (probably not accurate but useful even if only approximate) suggested that in 1914–15, 49 casualties were caused by artillery to every 22 by infantry, but in 1916–18 85 by artillery to every six by infantry (the latter figure being almost exactly the reverse of casualty assessments of the Franco–Prussian War).

The tactics employed during the war are sometimes styled those of 'the empty battlefield': i.e., with the advent of the magazine rifle, smokeless powder (so that positions were no longer revealed by musketry) and the machine-gun, manoeuvre of troops in tight formation was ended. Instead, by deploying troops in thin skirmish-screens, armies would advance (over much longer battle-fronts than before), utilizing all cover, and engage the enemy at long range (as Priestman described, 'away to the horizon are lines of men, each looking like a moving fence. Every now and then each line disappears, as the men drop into the heather to fire');[16] and hence, the battlefield appeared all but empty.

Nevertheless, much old tactical doctrine still prevailed, most theorists clinging to the idea that victory could best be won by an assault delivered at close range. French commanders were influenced by Clausewitz's assertion that offence and the achievement of 'local superiority' were keys to success, implying an old-style bayonet-assault at the end of an advance covered by fire. The French theorist Colonel C. J. J. Ardent du Picq convinced them that morale was the most significant factor, but it is not necessarily the bayonet-charge which demonstrates his point. Foch expressed the belief that it was impossible to lose a battle until the general believed himself defeated, and that a victory was a battle in which one refused to concede defeat; while this view has some merit, it could result in useless expenditure of life.

Trench warfare, virtually old-style siege operations, was scarcely envisaged at the outbreak of war. The French believed in a rapid war, employing all-out offence, with artillery a support for the national *élan* which was believed to be a peculiarly French attribute, in which a steady advance with covering fire approached to within about 400 yards of the enemy, followed by an irresistible final dash with the bayonet. The German concept envisaged a strong infantry firing-line advancing with artillery support to within about 600 yards of the enemy, and remaining there until the enemy was overwhelmed by volume of fire, when the advance would push on until the final dash over about

the last 100 yards. Although both French and German theories accepted the necessity for close artillery support, the British made co-operation between 'arms' paramount, involving a concentration of artillery, machine-gun and rifle fire upon the weakest part of the enemy line, with a constant advance by infantry until the enemy fire was seen to slacken, when the front line would be reinforced and drive forward with the bayonet. Thus, the three main protagonists on the Western Front had basically the same idea: that offence was necessary, and that if supporting fire were concentrated correctly, the impetus of the assault would succeed. By the end of 1914 the immense losses incurred on the Western Front proved these theories to be awry, and that with modern weapons properly used, defence predominated.

Although 'minor tactics' varied between armies, some general principles existed. Although it was usual for troops to lie down or shelter behind cover, once within 'effective' range of the enemy's fire it was held that a steady advance incurred less casualties than to halt under cover: a trace of the 'flight to the front' of Ardent du Picq's adherents: that if one will be mauled by staying still or retiring, one might as well push on and try to save oneself by overthrowing the enemy. The British *Infantry Training* (1914) stated that casualties decreased with a steady advance because of its morale effect upon the enemy (i.e., his fire would become erratic as he began to panic at the sight of an advancing foe) and because the range would be altering constantly. Although the advantage of attacking the enemy from the flank was one of the oldest tactical maxims, with the extended battle-lines envisaged it was clear that outflanking would have to be employed on a larger scale than battalion level, and in any case was hazardous by exposure to the enemy's enfilade fire; so the frontal attack continued to be advocated.

Infantry Training noted above described the 'artillery formation' already mentioned:

'Against frontal artillery fire, or direct long-range infantry fire, small shallow columns, each on a narrow front, such as platoons or sections in fours or file, offer a difficult target while admitting of efficient control, and may be employed during the earlier stages of an attack. These columns, making full use of the ground, should be on an irregular front, so that the range from the enemy's guns to each column is different';[17] and again stressed that fewer casualties would be incurred by pushing on than staying still. Such columns were to be maintained until approaching effective rifle-range, perhaps 1,400 yards from the enemy, when a thin line should be deployed. 'A formation in small columns should, however, be retained as long as it is applicable to the situation, for when once extended, a unit loses its power of manoeuvre. As a general principle deployment is necessary when fire is to be opened, the amount of extension depending upon the volume of fire which it is required to produce, and upon the effect of the enemy's fire. The greater the extension of a line, the fewer will be the casualties, but the less will be its fire effect.'[18]

The solution to this problem was to provide adequate covering-fire, but this was not always possible as it required a high level of experience for it to be effective. Initially, there was some belief instead in the 'mass attack' involving heavy bodies of troops rushing forward, rarely executed with success. One account describes German infantry being visible at 1,000 yards, lying down so that their helmets looked like mushrooms; then advancing, 'coming on in dense blocks – blocks which were probably companies – in echelon' until severely shot-up and driven back.[19] Another described the enemy appearing like a football crowd, swaying, half a mile away, but being unable to push nearer from the intensity of fire, the lack of a clear target resulting in the defenders having to blaze away at the given range, but unable to see if anything was being hit. Attacks in anything like 'mass' formation, however, were desperate: 'just like knocking dolls down at the fair ground'.[20] (An illustration was published in Britain in 1914 to prove that German tactics were so wasteful that if 100 Germans attacked 10 men over 800 yards, using the 'rush', every man would be shot within eight minutes, not one reaching the objective. It hardly needs to be added that such theoretical calculations were of little relevance in the field.)

When attacking, a theory accepted by all nations was for the force to be divided into three parts. At the front of the advance was the actual firing-line, virtually an extended line of skirmishers engaging the enemy with rifle-fire. Some distance behind was a line in support, to reinforce the firing-line; and the third part deployed farther back, generally in column, to act as general reserve and add weight to the attack when sufficient fire-superiority had been gained to permit the final bayonet-charge. In British service at least it was recommended that each of a unit's companies be represented in the firing-line, to facilitate command and reinforcement, 'by each company being distributed in depth rather than breadth'.[21] Sometimes it was suggested that formations should be divided into pre-determined strengths (in Russian service, for example, it was said that two platoons should provide the firing-line and its supports, to two platoons in reserve), but the British manual gave the best advice: 'A battalion . . . launched to the attack will be divided by its commander into (1) the firing line and supports; (2) local reserves. The relative strengths of these two parts will depend on the task allotted to the battalion and on the ground.'[22] The only exception was in the case of the surprise of the enemy, when the firing-line should be as strong as possible from the outset to exert maximum immediate pressure, while still retaining a sufficient reserve to meet counter-attacks.

The common method of attack was for small groups to advance in short rushes, covered by the rest, who would then themselves rush forward under similar cover. This whole method of action depended upon the proficiency of officers and NCOs in command of the small parties in question, placing a greater importance upon the initiative of sub-unit commanders than in previous modes of warfare.

The issuing of clear orders and the establishing of set objectives, at all levels of the chain of command, was thus paramount, as contemporary manuals stressed.

Trench Warfare

The conduct of 'minor tactics' altered rapidly with the emergence of trench warfare. The general conception of 'the trenches' is that each side manned a front-line trench, separated from the enemy by 'no man's land', fortified by barbed wire, and with support trenches running to the rear, permitting movement of troops and supplies under cover. To some extent this is accurate, at least until about late 1916, although the trench-systems were far more sophisticated constructions with not only communication-trenches leading to the rear but often entire additional defence-lines towards the rear, to act as a stop should the front-line system be over-run. The depth of such fortifications was a main reason why breakthroughs of the front line were rarely exploited in full.

Duty in the trenches was a mixture of boredom interspersed with terror. Although there were recognized 'quiet' sections of the front, the danger was ever-present. To prevent exhaustion and a decline in morale, trench-duty was generally conducted in spells: a number of days in the front line, a number in the reserve or support-trenches, and then a period at the rear for recuperation and training, before returning for the next period of front-line duty. In the less active sections of the front lines, almost an armed truce might exist, though this was dependent upon the type of troops occupying the opposing trenches. Trenches at Gallipoli were in some cases only a couple of yards apart, though there was no fraternization; whereas in the Carso, Italians and Austrians separated by a similar distance talked and threw each other presents (although Repington remarked that it was reckoned 'quite good form' among the Italians to throw over a pack of cigarettes, then a loaf, and thus having gained the Austrians' attention, follow these with a grenade!).[23]

Most movement to and from the front line, via communication-trenches and over-ground in the rear areas within enemy artillery range, was conducted at night, the continuous stream of nocturnal 'carrying-parties' replenishing front-line supplies often floundering in the dark over near-impossible terrain – a very unwelcome duty. Similarly, refurbishment of defences and installation of barbed wire was usually carried out at night. For those in the front line, unless a 'stunt' were planned, their day might comprise existence in the ill-lit, claustrophobic, stale atmosphere of dug-outs, the only refuge against artillery fire (although the Germans in particular created impressive underground chambers not so unpleasant to inhabit), interspersed by sentry-duty and the regular 'stand-tos' at dawn and dusk, to guard against an enemy attack under cover of half-light.

Even if no offensive were planned, there was often constant activity along the front, ranging from periodic artillery bombardments (to remind the enemy that the war was still on!), termed by the British as a 'hate', to nocturnal raids upon the enemy trenches, sometimes merely to keep a unit active or stir up the foe, but more often to take prisoners to gain intelligence. Raids could involve battalion-sized units, but smaller parties were more usual, generally lightly equipped but fully armed, including a selection of medieval-style weapons such as daggers and weighted clubs (the 9th Battalion, Royal Welsh Fusiliers even had swords with an 18-inch, leaf-shaped blade). A trench-raiding party would attempt to crawl through no man's land undetected, shielded by darkness and perhaps diversionary fire on another sector of the line, clip a path through the enemy wire, and fall upon the front-line trench, dispatching its occupants, bombing dug-outs, capturing prisoners and documents, and then withdrawing before the enemy could rally.

Techniques for a full assault varied with circumstance, but several standard practices existed. The popular idea of troops lining the front-line trenches and climbing out to go 'over the top' upon the blast of a whistle is not invariably accurate; for an attack mounted at dawn, it was a considerable advantage for troops to leave the trenches in darkness and lie down in no man's land until the moment of assault, thus being half-way to their objective before the attack began.

Co-ordination with artillery was essential. One theory held that the enemy line should be saturated with bombardment for days before the attack, destroying the wire and so

Undulating trench-lines, with fire-bays clearly visible, in a terrain pock-marked with shell-craters, near Flesquières, 24 September 1918. The 'crossroads' is in fact a railway-crossing, the intersection of the Havrincourt–Ribecourt line and the Havrincourt–Graincourt road.

Successive, crenellated trench-lines studded with rectangular bunkers: a defensive position, connected by zigzag or undulating communication-trenches, and thoroughly cratered with shell-holes: north-west of Flesquières, 24 September 1918.

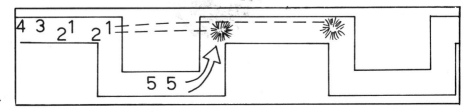

Tactics of trench-clearing by grenade. Protected by the zigzag traverse, bombers (1), each with a carrier (2) throw grenades into next bay of the trench; whereupon two bayonet-men (5) advance and clear any enemy still present. (3) is NCO in command of bombing-party, and (4) a spare man to replace any casualty. ▶

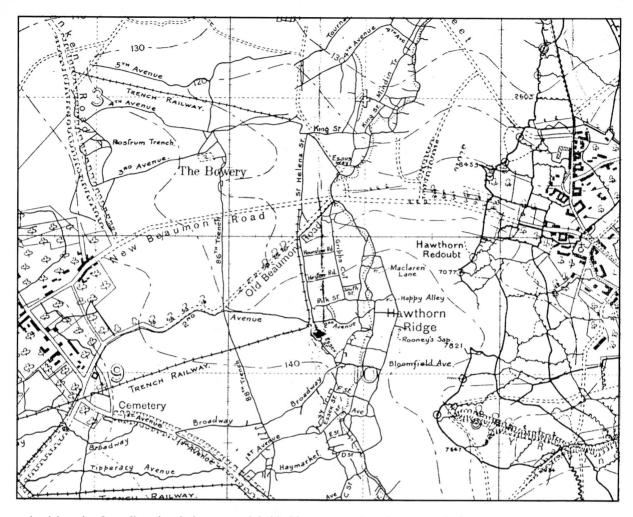

pulverizing the front line that it became uninhabitable, although some dug-outs were so deep as to survive anything but a direct hit. Days of bombardment sapped morale, but could be partially avoided if most of the front-line troops were withdrawn. To prevent their returning to meet the assault, the area behind the enemy front line could be saturated by fire; but often, as soon as the barrage ceased the defenders would emerge from their dug-outs, re-erect their machine-guns and be ready to meet the assault. There was a constant contest to out-wit the opponent: for example, after a heavy bombardment the guns might cease; the defenders would re-occupy their positions, anticipating an imminent assault; whereupon the artillery would fire another salvo at the front line, hoping to destroy the defenders before they had time to return to their shelters.

The closest co-operation between infantry and artillery was required if a 'creeping barrage' were planned, in which case artillery fire would precede the advancing troops (but casualties from 'friendly fire' were common). For an assault, a main artillery objective was to blow a path through the enemy wire (paths would be opened through the 'friendly'

A typical trench map: the web of opposing trenches on Hawthorn Ridge, Beaumont Hamel, 2 June 1916. Of especial note is the German Hawthorn Redoubt and the British lines (left) opposing it, and the location of narrow-gauge trench railways feeding the line. Although known German trenches are marked on this map (right), the British trenches were much more extensive than those shown: only those visible to the Germans were marked on trench-maps, so as not to reveal the location of others should the map fall into enemy hands. British trenches customarily were given homely names like those shown; note that 'Minden Trench' is mis-spelled, doubtless having been named by a regiment bearing that battle-honour (1759).

wire before an assault, and the route to be followed sometimes marked with tape), though in many cases the wire was insufficiently cut and (in the words of the song) whole battalions might end 'hanging on the old barbed wire'. Conversely, patches of enemy wire might have been constructed deliberately thinly, forming obvious paths of advance to create a 'killing ground' upon which machine-guns could concentrate fire.

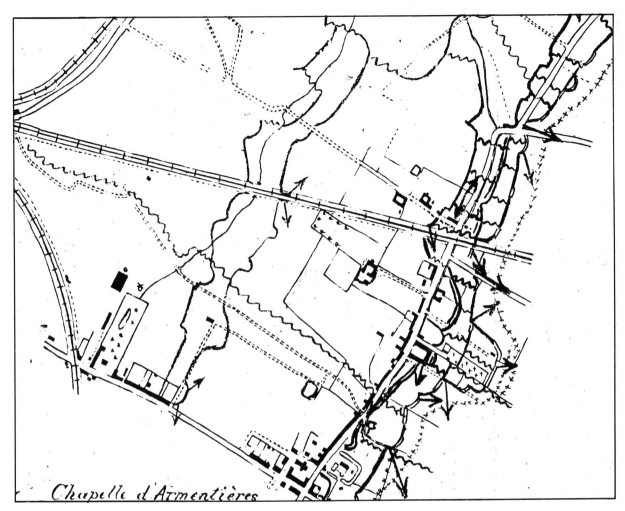

Chapelle d'Armentières

Hand-drawn trench-map of British positions around Armentières, October 1915; bold lines indicate main trenches, undulating lines communication-trenches, and lines of crosses represent belts of wire. Machine-gun positions are marked by arrows indicating the direction in which the guns would fire; note the intersecting fields of fire, and machine-gun positions in rear areas to cover any breakthroughs.

Once established in the enemy front line, an assaulting force could send out 'trench-stops', machine-gunners and bombers to seal off either side of their ingress, allowing the attacker to re-organize in the captured trenches without danger of immediate counter-attack; and would then spread along the trench-system rather than immediately rush forward. Successive waves would commonly 'leap-frog' over those in possession of the enemy front line, and press on towards the successive enemy defence-lines, as other supporting units 'mopped up' remnants of enemy resistance.

With the enemy able to call down his own bombardment, major exploitation of breakthroughs were rare, the superi-ority of defence resulting in the appalling carnage associated with major offensives. It might be said that the Allies chose to separate fire and movement, using infantry to exploit the effects of artillery rather than the German style of com-bining fire and movement simultaneously; thus failures to exploit breakthroughs were partly caused by limitations on movement caused by the effects of protracted artillery fire upon wet terrain, turning many battlefields into literal seas of mud. Confusion and the inability to transmit orders or inform higher command of progress was also a significant factor.

Despite the changes in tactics, the old principle of linear warfare remained: the necessity to hold a secure flank. Although it was true that units were most vulnerable from enfilade fire on the flank, the securing of flanks meant that large attacks could only progress at the speed of the slowest unit, so that the determined defence of one post might dislocate an entire offensive; but the importance of flank-security declined as tactics evolved further.

Probably the attacks on the Somme in 1916 marked a turning-point. Participants detected a change in the nature of warfare at about this period, the intensity of bombardment disrupting communications so that greater emphasis was placed upon the initiative of the sub-unit leader. Conversely, the *matériel* of war also increased in importance, and with it a greater impersonality of war: units could now fight for long periods without ever catching sight of their enemy; and both Ernst Junger and Edmund Blunden remarked that this increasing impersonality was epitomized by the adoption of the steel helmet, which seemed to reduce its wearers to mere working parts in the whole iron machinery of war.

Losses in such battles as the Somme caused a re-evaluation of tactics, leading to the Germans abandoning the theory of a continuous defensive front line for a system designed to minimize their casualties. This involved extending the width of the defensive zone, and no longer attempting to hold the forward positions. Instead of a continuous line, the front would be a lightly held series of outposts designed only to delay and disorganize an attack. Behind this outpost-line was a battle-zone, perhaps 1,000 to 2,000 yards deep, littered with fortified strongpoints (latterly reinforced concrete bunkers on the Western Front), sited to be mutually supportive. At the rear of this area was the final line of artillery and machine-gun nests, to take on any enemy who penetrated right through the battle-zone. The theory held that once the outpost line was overrun, the German artillery could drop a barrage upon it and no man's land, through which the attacker's supports would pass, and let the attacker exhaust himself assailing the strongpoints, before launching a counter-attack from behind the gun-line. The deliberate abandonment of the forward defences was taken a stage further from 1917, when the Germans would withdraw deliberately when a barrage opened, which would thus fall upon empty ground and serve only to make the terrain more impassable for the attacker, who would advance to find the forward line deserted and an unscathed defence-system awaiting him a short distance further on. Ludendorff commented on this 'web' system of defence: although, he noted, that the overall position would still be held at the end of a battle, the infantryman had no longer to think that his position had to be held at all costs, but could retire confidently as necessary, in the interests of the wider perspective.

Although this 'zonal' system of defence was adopted by all military theorists, it does not appear to have penetrated all the recesses of military thought. The failure of the British system of zonal defence in March 1918 was attributed in the Official History to the inherent trait of the British Army to fight it out where they stood, training and explanation of new tactics not having been sufficient for the troops to appreciate the principle of 'elastic' defence and the idea of withdrawing to deeper positions in the battle-zone. The majority would have preferred a clear sequence of lines of resistance; what were described scathingly as 'blob' tactics were both unpopular and misunderstood.

The Germans also turned the new theory into a system of offence. As early as mid-1915 a French infantry officer, Captain André Laffargue, postulated that as a result of his experiences attempting to assault German defences head-on at Vimy Ridge, a solution to deal with strongpoints would be to infiltrate squads of picked men between and behind them. His ideas were published, but ignored by the Allies; but a copy was captured by the Germans, translated, and seems to have laid the foundation for the evolution of infiltration tactics. These required the formation of companies (eventually battalions) of specialist 'storm-troops' or assault detachments, heavily armed with machine-guns, light artillery, mortars and flame-throwers. These troops would advance rapidly, under cover of terrain, and infiltrate throughout the enemy zones of defence, which had already been blanketed by a short but fierce bombardment. Pockets of resistance would simply be by-passed, the assault troops dashing to the enemy's rear areas to neutralize his artillery-line, which might already have been attacked with gas-shells. The storm-troops would be seconded by waves of supports which first overran the surrounded strongpoints and finally cleared the trench systems; after which the process could begin anew if a second tier of defences were to be assaulted. These tactics are often named after General Oskar von Hutier (1857–1934), who is credited with perfecting the methods of surprise infiltration and first employing them at Riga in September 1917. On the Western Front the tactic was first applied on a large scale in the counter-attack which recovered much of the ground lost to the Allied tank attack at Cambrai, demonstrating that determined infantry, handled imaginatively, was still an important force on the battlefield.

These tactics required a change not only in military thought but also armament: portable light machine-guns were essential to permit assault detachments to concentrate sufficient fire upon the flanks and rear of the positions they attacked. A British manual described the essentials of action against what it termed 'shell-hole defences' (i.e., fortified craters and strongpoints arranged checker-wise instead of linear trenches): first, each unit should be allocated an objective, and advance under artillery cover, as rapidly as possible. Next, covering-fire should assist one or more outflanking movements, using Lewis guns and rifle-grenades. When reinforcing a platoon that was held up, it was more useful to work on the flanks than by 'thickening' the unit being assisted: 'more may often be accomplished by reinforcing a platoon which is not held up than by directly supporting one which is; the surest means of helping a neighbour in battle is to push on'.[24]

With the acceptance of 'Hutier' or infiltration tactics, while the importance of flanking-fire was still crucial, the necessity of holding one's own flanks secure was no longer the shibboleth of the past, as deep penetration took precedence. Some older principles still applied, in that when a company advanced it would generally proceed in a sequence of platoons or sub-units, some held back as a reserve, and often preceded by a skirmish-line or scouts,

A survival guide to the trenches, issued by General Sir Edwin Alderson to his Canadian Division, 1915:

'Do not expose your heads, and do not look round corners, unless for a purpose . . . to lose your life without military necessity is to deprive the State of good soldiers . . . a soldier who takes unnecessary risks is not playing the game, and the man who does so is stupid . . . If you put your head over the parapet without orders, they will hit that head . . . When you are shelled, sit low and sit tight. This is easy advice, for there is nothing else to do. If you get out you will only get it worse . . . The Germans do not like the bayonet . . . If they get up to you, or if you get up to them, go right in with the bayonet . . .'

(The full text was published also in *The Great War*, ed. H. W. Wilson '& J. A. Hammerton, III, pp. 171–2, London, 1915)

and to restore the fight if any part of the position is overwhelmed'[25] was the advice to those commanding strongpoints.

Sniping

The practice of shooting opportune targets is ancient, but 'sniping' became more common in the Great War than ever before, and was especially prevalent in static warfare as in the trenches of the Western Front and Gallipoli. It was even pursued in 'quiet' sections of the line; as Ian Hay remarked, the sniper reminded everyone that they were at war, for without him the troops of both sides would have sat on their own parapets in their shirt-sleeves, without any malevolent intention towards the other camp, 'and that would never do'![26]

Snipers often worked in two-man teams, a marksman and an observer with telescope or binoculars; as a sniper could expect no mercy from the enemy, an escort of an infantry section might also be deployed. Sniping demanded exceptional qualities, including the patience to sit for hours, sometimes in a camouflaged hide, awaiting a target; and the will to shoot an enemy who was at that moment usually threatening neither the sniper nor his comrades (a Canadian sniper described to the author that, after shooting a German who was visiting a latrine, the realization came to him that he was simply an assassin). The concept of the sniper as a calculating specialist is not universally accurate, however; at Gallipoli the chief cook of the 7th Australian Light Horse, Sergeant Brennan, an ex-Dublin Fusilier, would stroll to the trenches and snipe until the time for his

who were also used to keep contact between the sub-units, maintaining the co-operation which was vital in this form of action. Infiltration tactics were also used in the semi-open warfare of the last months of the war, as the principles of rapid movement, the co-operation of small units and flanking-fire upon strongpoints were equally valid as in assaulting defensive systems. They did not, however, extend beyond infantry units with limited objectives: the application of the principle to strategic penetration required rapidly moving armoured columns and motorized infantry, which were not available until later in the century. The new tactics also emphasized the importance of training, morale and initiative; as the German storm-trooper Ernst Junger noted, a resolute platoon was more use than a mediocre company. Initiative of sub-unit commanders was vital: 'The soul of defence lies in offence . . . commanders must be ready to take the initiative, both to use the bayonet, when necessary,

Sniping was an ever-present hazard; this rare depiction shows a Canadian sniper on the Western Front, armed with a telescopically-sighted rifle.

next culinary duties. He would exhibit foul temper if he'd wasted a morning, but if he had killed one or more Turks 'he was as happy as Larry all day'.[27]

The prevalence of snipers often made it impossible to look over a trench in daylight, or to show a light at night; the superstitition regarding the bad luck of lighting three cigarettes with one match supposedly originates from this time, the flash of the match attracting the sniper, the lighting of the second cigarette allowing him to aim, and the third for his shot. The weapons used were sometimes more sophisticated than ordinary service rifles (the Canadian Ross, poor for ordinary use, was good for sniping), and the periscope device sometimes styled a 'sniperscope' allowed a marksman to fire over a trench without raising his head near the parapet. The effect of a proficient sniper could be devastating: accompanied only by a spotter but with his daily tally checked officially, Billy Sing of the 5th Australian Light Horse supposedly accounted for more than 150 Turks. The reaction of his comrades was shown by his nickname, 'the Murderer'.

Artillery

Artillery was classified according to the size of shell projected, and almost all guns were rifled breech-loaders operating with a recoil-system which caused the field guns to be styled 'quick-firers'. This was not concerned with speed of loading but by the absorption of recoil by a hydraulic mechanism which allowed the barrel, not the entire gun, to recoil, so that there was no need to re-lay after every shot. The old classification of guns and howitzers remained, guns firing high-velocity rounds using a flatter trajectory, and howitzers lobbing heavier shells with a higher trajectory. High-velocity rounds were especially

unpopular, as their rapid flight gave little notice of their arrival (hence the term 'whizz-bang'); whereas it was possible to hear the approach of a slower-moving shell and take cover accordingly.

The two principal types of projectile were high-explosive and shrapnel. High-explosive shells were packed with explosives and had an impact fuze which set off the charge when the shell landed; shrapnel shells were anti-personnel, packed with shrapnel (usually metal balls) and a bursting charge, with a time-fuze which caused the shell to explode in flight, spreading a lethal rain of metal in advance of the burst. (The velocity of the shell caused this forward-movement of shrapnel, so it was recommended when firing in support of infantry, that shells should be timed to burst directly over the heads of the friendly troops, to strike the area in front of them. Howitzer shrapnel, with shells dropping more vertically, fell closer to the spot over which it burst and scattered its contents less widely.) Although 'shrapnel' was a term used loosely to describe any metal fragments of artillery projectile, correctly it should be applied only to the anti-personnel shells; pieces of shell-casing (equally lethal) were correctly styled 'splinters'.

Artillery was divided into field and heavy guns, the former including light horse and mountain artillery; 'medium' guns (generally taken to mean those with a bore of 15cm or more) were intended to accompany the field guns, able to move at infantry pace and provide supporting fire with little or no special preparation. Allocation of the various types varied according to tactical doctrine (France, for example, envisaging an offensive war, was singularly ill-provided with heavy guns at the outset, necessitating the employment of old and originally fortress-based artillery). Field artillery provided the most immediate fire-support, and was capable of keeping pace with the main body of an

The famous French '75', showing the limber upended for action, allowing access to the ammunition.

army, horse artillery was lighter and intended to match the speed of march of cavalry. Field artillery was generally deployed at divisional level (though a reserve might be held at corps or army level); the heavier guns, intended for less mobile warfare, were more effectively concentrated at corps level. To facilitate ammunition-supply, howitzers were usually organized in their own batteries, rather than (as in the past) forming part of batteries otherwise equipped with guns.

Artillery was classified either by bore-diameter (e.g., 75mm) or weight of shell (e.g., 18pdr), and ammunition by the terms 'fixed' or 'semi-fixed': smaller shells had the propellant 'fixed' (i.e., in an attached shell-case) while larger projectiles often had separate propellant. Artillery carriages originally had a single or 'pole' trail, which restricted the possible elevation of the barrel; heavier pieces requiring greater elevation might have a 'box' trail with an open space below the breech to allow depression of the breech-end of the barrel, or (latterly) a split trail, which became standard after the war. There was a constant process of improvement during the war, involving basically the ability to deliver a greater weight of shell at longer range.

Statistics for representative field and medium artillery are noted below, with classification in the terms preferred by the individual nation (e.g., poundage, millimetres or centimetres); ranges are approximate and could vary with the projectile or model of gun:

Type	Weight of shell (pounds)	Range (yards)	Notes
Austria			
10.4cm M14	38½	13,670	rate-of-fire 4rpm
15cm howitzer M14	28	8,850	
France			
Model 1897 75mm	16 (shrapnel) 11¾ (HE)	9,000	most celebrated field gun of the war, with fastest rate-of-fire: 15 to 30rpm in extremis
Schneider 105mm howitzer	35	6,000	
Model 1897 105mm	35	13,400	6rpm
155mm howitzer 1898	88	7,650	
Schneider 155mm howitzer	95	10,500–13,300 depending on shell	30 rounds per hour; main medium howitzer
Germany			
7.7cm (various patterns)	15	5,800–11,700 depending on pattern	principal German field gun
10.5cm light field howitzer 98/09	34	7,600	
10.5cm howitzer model 1916	34	9,200–10,900 depending on shell	4rpm
10cm 04/14	39½	12,085	2rpm
15cm howitzer (various patterns)	95	7,000–9,400	principal medium howitzer
Great Britain			
Mk I 18-pdr	18	7,000	standard field-gun of the war; cal. 3.3in; 8rpm; late improved version ranged 9–11,000 yds.
4.5in howitzer	35	7,000	4rpm
13pdr	12½	5,900	horse artillery gun
60pdr	60	10,300	standard medium gun; cal 5in; 2rpm; late improved version ranged to 15,000 yds.
12½pdr mountain	12½	5,800	cal 2¾in
20-pdr mountain howitzer	20	5,800	cal 3.7in
6in howitzer	100	10–11,600 depending on shell	main medium howitzer
Russia			
Model 1909 light field howitzer	52	8,100	cal 122mm

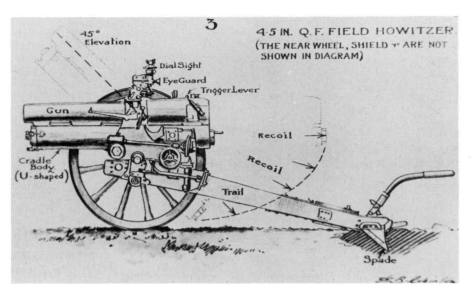

Diagram of a British field howitzer, showing the extent of barrel recoil; print by B. Robinson, published 1915.

The heavier artillery, used for bombardment, ranged from guns with ordinary wheeled carriages to immense pieces best transported by rail and then set up on reinforced beds. Guns heavier than the 8in and 9.2in howitzer were styled 'super heavy' in British terminology, an apt description: the French 370mm mortar, for example, weighed more than 30 tons, of which the gun weighed 9.27 tons, the carrige 9.4, the bed 9.9 and the transporter 2.5. Examples of some of those used in the war were:

Type	Weight of shell (pounds)	Range (yards)	Notes
Austria			
30.5cm howitzer	846	13,100	10 rounds per hour
38cm howitzer (1916)	1,320	16,700	
France			
155mm GPF (Filloux)	97	19,650	2rpm
270mm mortar model 1885	204–384	8,800	
370mm mortar	1,076	8,800	
220mm Schneider (model 1917)	200	24,500	
370mm howitzer	900–1,120	8,900–11,500 depending on shell	
Germany			
21cm Mörser	184	10,280–11,150 depending on shell	2rpm
42cm heavy howitzer	2,052	15,500	10 rounds per hour; known as *Dicke Berta* ('Big Bertha')
42cm light howitzer	900–1,750	10,300–13,600 depending on shell	
15cm L/40	about 100 (varied)	14–19,000 depending on shell	originally designed for naval use
15cm model 1916	28	23,500	
17cm	140	30,000	
21cm long Mörser	261	11,200	
28cm howitzer	750	11,200	
Great Britain			
6in (various patterns)	100	17,700	
9.2in howitzer	290	10–12,700 depending on shell	

British howitzer dug into a typical gun-pit, with camouflage to shield it from aerial observation.

Schneider light field howitzer.

A rare photograph of a shrapnel-burst in mid-air, photographed over Belgian trenches on the Western Front.

The heaviest guns fired from mobile railway mountings. Some had an 'all-round' mount which allowed the gun to traverse on its truck; others had a fixed direction of fire and were aimed by moving the truck along a curved section of track. Although these guns and attendant vehicles could be camouflaged, it was almost impossible to conceal the construction of sidings and rail-spurs from enemy aerial observation. (In addition to these immense, often ex-naval guns, considerable use was made on the Western Front of field guns mounted on railway cars, operating at night as mobile batteries, firing a salvo and then moving before the enemy could reply, but these were mostly only of 'nuisance' value.)

Among the rail-mounted heavy guns used on the Western Front were as tabulated here.

Type	Weight of Shell (pounds)	Range (yards)	Notes
France			
274mm	561	29,000	
520mm Schneider howitzer	3,130	20,000	heaviest shell used in the war
Germany			
280mm	630	30,800	
380mm	785	about 28 miles	
'Paris gun' (210–240mm)	264	about 80 miles (though these were known generically as '100-mile guns')	longest-ranging gun of the war
Great Britain			
9.2in	380	26,000	
12in howitzer	750	16,000	
14in	1,400	35,000	
USA			
14in	1,560	22–30 miles depending on shell)	

The 'Paris guns' (so named because they were used to bombard Paris) had varying calibres as the barrels could be rebored as they became worn; accuracy was not great, declining after about 20 shots, and the projectile was comparatively light. From March to August 1918 320 to 367 shells were fired at Paris (French and German statistics conflict); material damage was not great, and after the initial shock, the morale effect declined. (Contrary to popular belief, these guns were not styled 'Big Bertha' or 'Long Max' – the latter was a 15in naval gun which shelled Dunkirk – but were officially the 21cm *Lange Kanone*, unofficially 'William's gun'.)

Transportation of most artillery still depended upon horse teams, despite the great increase in motorization. Motorized artillery was either dragged by tractors (both wheeled lorries and caterpillar-tracked vehicles), or carried on the back of lorries, known as 'portee' mounting.

Although the positioning of artillery for action depended upon circumstances, some traditional principles remained: the importance of concealment by features of terrain (there being no longer any necessity for guns to be within sight of their target), and deployment of a battery in staggered formation to lessen the effect of enemy enfilade fire, and sufficiently spread to prevent two guns being hit by one shell-burst, although a compromise was sometimes necessary to ensure the requisite number of guns on a given frontage. The attendant ammunition-wagons had to remain within range of easy supply to the guns, but far enough away to lessen their chance of destruction by counter-battery fire. The guns' armoured shields gave protection, and to take advantage of this limbers were usually positioned as near to the gun as possible; limbers might also be armoured, the additional weight being more than offset by the protection afforded.

Crewing of guns depended upon the size, but for an ordinary field gun six men was a typical team: an NCO in command, who received and transmitted orders; a layer, responsible for the gun's alignment and elevation; a gunner who opened and closed the breech (shell-cases were ejected automatically upon the opening of the breech after firing), and three men to set fuzes and handle shells.

Excluding very long-range guns, artillery targeting was directed by observation of fall of shot. Only at very short range or in open terrain was it possible for a battery-commander to view the fall of his shot in person; usually, this was performed by a forward observation officer (FOO) who occupied a post nearer the enemy or at a higher level, whose directions could be relayed to the battery by telephone or even signal flags. As the war progressed, aerial artillery-observation increased, using light-signalling, dropped messages or radio. The procedure for 'ranging' varied, though in general one or two shells would be fired at the approximate distance of the target, the fall of shot observed, and corrected until the target was struck, whereupon the whole battery would fire. This could be a protracted process, so when immediate fire was required a battery might open at approximate range with each gun having a different setting, in order to blanket a larger area;

Vast pieces of ordnance were mounted upon rails during the war; this French Schneider howitzer is a small and early (1914) example of the principle.

in French service this 'bracketing' of a target with rapid fire was termed a *rafale* (squall). A variation was 'sweeping fire' (*tir fauchant*) in which each gun fired series of three rounds, the second and third to the right and left of the original round. A salvo of sixteen such series (48 rounds) could be fired in as little as 75 seconds from a 75mm gun, but this rate could not be maintained (a battery at maximum rate would expend its entire ammunition-supply in thirteen minutes); it was calculated that such 'sweeping fire' would bracket an area 600 × 200 metres, in which the casualty-rate on men not under cover was estimated at 19 per cent.

Ordinary battery fire was usually either 'section fire' (in which pairs of guns fired alternately), or 'rapid fire', in which all guns fired a specified number of rounds as quickly as possible. Generally, a gun would fire at the sector of target directly in its front, so that the whole battery-frontage would be bombarded evenly. The preferred ranges may be deduced from the terminology of British service:

Range (yards)	Field artillery	Heavy artillery
close	0–2,500	0–2,500
effective	2,500–4,000	2,500–5,000
long	4,000–5,000	5,000–6,500
distant	5,000–6,500	6,500–10,000

Initially, high-explosive was used for the destruction of buildings or fieldworks, and shrapnel against personnel; so prevalent had the latter come before the war that it was styled the projectile *par excellence* by the German field artillery regulations, and it was carried exclusively by British field batteries, although HE was also used by the field artillery of a number of armies. As the war progressed, high-explosive was found to be much more effective and the use of shrapnel declined markedly, so that it represented only 5 per cent of French field-gun ammunition, for example. With ordinary field-gun ammunition the radius of explosion of HE was about 25 yards, and the 'cone' of effective shrapnel from 100 yards at short range to 50 yards at long range. Casualty-rates are almost impossible to determine with accuracy, given that many shells on a particular occasion may not have been aimed against personnel (if fired to cut wire, for example), and estimates range from about 30 to 1,400 shells required, on average, to kill one enemy.

In trench warfare it was usual for one field artillery brigade to be allocated per infantry brigade (often representing a 1,000-yard frontage, of which three battteries of the brigade covered their own units, and the fourth acted as a 'swinger', i.e., a battery capable of assisting any of the others or the units on the immediate flanks of the brigade; most howitzer batteries were used as 'swingers'. Field artillery was generally deployed in three positions, forward (in the battle-zone, supporting the outposts), in the main position (about 3,000–4,000 yards behind the front line, to bombard the 'front'), and in reserve, 2,000–3,000 yards further back, to bombard the friendly second-line trenches in the event of an enemy breakthrough. Reserve positions

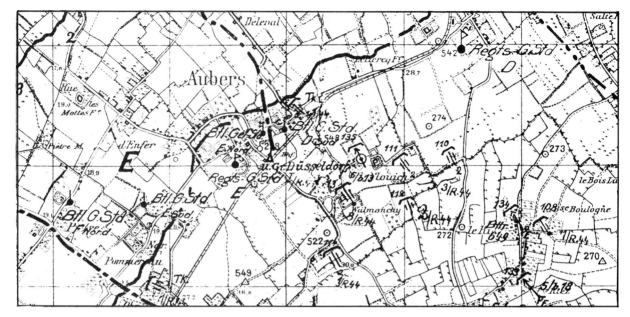

Trench-map showing the artillery dispositions of the German 44th Reserve Field Artillery Regiment, 44th Reserve Division, in the area around Aubers in November 1917. The staggered disposition of emplacements is shown, with the armament of each position indicated by the symbols shown in the key:
(1) 7.7cm field gun
(2) 10.5cm light field howitzer
(3) 13cm gun
(4) 15cm heavy field howitzer

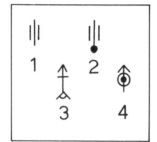

were stocked with ammunition but not normally occupied; about one-third of the field artillery was deployed in the forward position, and the remainder in the main position. It was not usual to sub-divide four-gun batteries, but with six-gun batteries (as in British service) each battery might cover its own frontage by deploying two guns in the forward position and four in the main position. Medium and heavy guns and the wagon-lines were generally much farther back, perhaps five miles from the enemy field artillery. Latterly all guns at the front were sited in earthern emplacements or 'gun-pits', with camouflage to conceal them from aerial observation, the whole network connected by telephone lines. Wherever possible additional emplacements were constructed to accommodate reinforcements.

During the war there was a general trend towards the employment of heavier artillery, as it was found that HE from a field gun was insufficient to do much damage against earthern fortifications. The most useful trench-bombardment weapon was found to the the 6in or 15cm howitzer,

and the proportion of howitzers increased markedly (the howitzer's steep trajectory required less propellant and thus reduced barrel-wear). There was also a considerable extension of range, largely by the designing of streamlined shells, increasing in extreme cases by up to 95 per cent (the German 7.7cm field-gun range, for example, was extended from about 6,000 to 11,700 yards); this was especially necessary when linear trenches were succeeded by defences in depth. A further consequence of trench warfare was the employment of barrages of increasing size and duration, bombardments often being measured not in hours but days. Some believed that overwhelming bombardment was the only key to victory, Robertson noting in late 1915 that given sufficient guns and munitions any front could be broken, and that what really counted was the ability to move enough forces sufficiently quickly to penetrate the rear lines, having by force of bombardment exhausted the enemy and used up his reserves.

On average, on the Western Front a scale of one gun per 30 yards was regarded as normal, increased about threefold for an offensive. In October 1917 French instructions for supporting an offensive recommended one field gun per 15 yards, one medium or heavy gun for demolition per 30 yards and another for counter-battery fire per 35 yards, one super-heavy gun per 170 yards and one piece of 'trench artillery' per 30 yards. The increased range of artillery made major offensives on limited fronts impossible (to prevent the attackers being enfiladed), consequently requiring a huge artillery concentration to saturate a wide front. The great German attack of March 1918, on a 50-mile front, required approximately the following per mile: 92 field-guns, 31 field howitzers, 14 medium howitzers, 14 heavy guns, 7 heavy howitzers and 3½ super-heavy howitzers, not including an increment of two extra field guns per battery, where

> *It's a Long Way to Tipperary* is perhaps the most famous song of the Great War, but its popularity with the troops had declined markedly by late 1914:
>
> '. . . there are certain soldiers lying in a hospital which I visited in Paris who would never like to hear "Tipperary" again. The sound of it, they say, plunges them into the deepest gloom, for to them and many of their comrades it has become nothing but a death dirge.'
>
> ('VVV' in *The Sphere*, p. 294, 19 December 1914)

possible, which were without transport or crews but pushed into the line for the opening bombardment only. This immense concentration was doubled by the practice of bombarding alternate stretches of Allied line, the untouched sections being by-passed by infiltration, so that those sectors under attack were pounded by the equivalent of one gun per five yards. Expenditure of ammunition was huge: for a six-hour bombardment it was calculated that the following was a reasonable quantity for every mile of front attacked:

50,000 field-gun shells, 10,000 field howitzer, 2,000 heavy gun and 5,700 heavy howitzer, with a minimum of the same quantity in reserve. Weight of bombardment was sometimes unimaginable in its intensity: prior to the Messines assault, from 26 May to 6 June 1917 British artillery fired more than 3½ *million* shells in support of the attack, something in the order of the explosion of 3½ shells per second for a twelve-day period. Apart from material damage, such bombardments had a considerable effect from damage of morale and deprivation of sleep on those underneath the bombardment:

> 'I hate all Huns, yet most hate I, that surly-livered blighter,
> Who with persistence breaks my sleep, with his ten-times-a-nighter;
> When fast asleep, and in the arms of Morpheus or some other,
> The rotter looses off and then – oh damn it, there's another.'[28]

In addition to general bombardment there existed counter-battery fire aimed at the enemy artillery. This

A German experiment of 'portee' mounting of artillery, upon the bed of a specially designed lorry.

A German shell-burst some distance from a French 155mm Rimailho howitzer; the black smoke gave rise to the nicknames 'coal-box' and 'Jack Johnson'.

required the location of enemy guns by aircraft, sound-ranging or spotting of muzzle-flashes, greatly complicated by the camouflaging of gun-pits and the construction of dummy emplacements, sometimes complete with flashes, to suggest that they were in use, the intention being to encourage the enemy to dissipate his fire against empty positions. Germany had considerable success against Allied artillery by gas-shelling, guns being almost unworkable in heavily gassed atmosphere. Another artillery duty was wire-cutting, effective only up to about 1,800 yards with shrapnel, and only with HE after reinforced wire came into use during the war (much HE merely blew a crater in the ground into which the wire fell, largely undamaged).

The theory that an attack could only be attempted after a prolonged bombardment was disproved by the short bombardment and 'surprise' attack of infiltration tactics, and heavy bombardment could be counter-productive, rendering the terrain almost impassable in wet weather, alerting the enemy, and with the constant danger that a 'creeping barrage' to cover an infantry attack might fall upon friendly forces. The key to success was co-ordination of fire and movement (either by telephone, signal-rockets or 'runners') and a plentiful supply of ammunition, with field artillery laying down the barrage which supposedly protected the advancing infantry and the heavier guns bombarding the enemy's artillery and rear areas.

Gas

A weapon almost restricted to the Great War, toxic gas could be released towards the enemy from cylinders positioned in or in advance of the front line, but being dependent upon wind direction was hazardous to the releasers in that it could blow back. Much more effective was the use of the gas-shell, which could be dropped upon the enemy at will. Cylinder gas was released in vapour form; shell-gas was liquid, being scattered and evaporating after the explosion of the bursting-charge. Dependent upon climatic conditions, some gases dispersed quite rapidly; others of 'high persistence' might remain active much longer, such as mustard gas oozing from the surface of the ground for days after its deposition. The best weather conditions included little wind, moist atmosphere and no sun, inhibiting dissipation of the gas; the first gas attack, at Bolimov in January 1915, was of little effect because of the coldness of the weather which prevented the xylyl bromide from evaporating.

Gas was classified into lethal and irritant, the former including those compounds which caused instant death but which were unstable (for example, the cyanides used primarily by France, less by Britain and not by Germany). The other lethal types were delayed-action, largely respiratory irritants, such as phosgene. The irritants were less immediately lethal, but to describe them as such conceals the fact that if inhaled in quantity, while not causing death, could result in years of suffering. They included lachrymators (causing the eyes to water) sternutators (causing

The power of an exploding shell is demonstrated by this limber, flung up on a shattered tree.

sneezing) and vesicants (causing blistering). The first two were temporarily incapacitating, but were additionally hazardous if they prevented a man from donning his gas mask, leaving him vulnerable to other gases employed at the same time.

Most gas was produced and used by Germany (more than 68,000 tons), France (almost 37,000) and Britain (more than 25,000); production by other combatants was much less. The most prolific were the acute respiratory irritants, more than nine times the quantity of the next most common, the vesicants. Among the gases used were:

Benzyl bromide: powerful German lachrymator, first used March 1915.

Bromacetone: powerful lachrymator, used by Allies and

Austria, asphyixiating in concentration; moderately persistent; introduced 1916.

Chlorine: introduced 1915, used only from cylinders, by Allies and Germany. Acute respiratory irritant, forming hydrochloric acid on contact with moisture; caused vomiting and in concentration could be fatal from spasm of the larynx.

Chloromethyl chloroformate: respiratory irritant (shells), used by Allies and Germany, introduced 1915.

Chloropicrin: introduced 1916, used by Allies and Germany, a more acute form of chlorine; shell or cylinder, most often in shell in conjuction with other gases. German term 'green cross I'.

Cyanogen compounds: immediately fatal in concentration, but only mildly incapacitating when weaker, causing dizziness, headache and pulmonary pains, but leaving no permanent damage. Introduced 1916; used by Allies in shells, as mixtures of hydrogen cyanide, arsenic trichloride, chloroform, stannic chloride; cyanogen bromide used by Austria.

Dichlormethylether: respiratory irritant used by Germany, introduced 1918.

> If the Hun lets off some gas –
>   Never mind
> If the Hun attacks in mass –
>   Never mind
> If your dug-out's blown to bits,
> Or the C.O.'s throwing fits,
> Or a crump your rum jar hits –
>   Never mind.
> ('Minor Worries', in *Wipers Times*, 1 May 1916)

No man's land; a view of the front line around Hill 60, 1915.

Dibrommethylethylketone: powerful German/Austrian lachrymator, fatal in concentration; introduction 1916.

Dichlorethylsulphide ('mustard gas'): used by Allies, Germany and Austria; also known as 'yellow cross' or 'Yperite'; introduced 1917. One of the most effective, though not officially lethal: blistered and burned the skin, even through clothing, causing blindness (usually temporary) and if inhaled could cause death from bronchial pneumonia, burning the respiratory system. Shell-carried; remained potent for several days in favourable climate.

Diphenylchloroarsine: German shell-carried solid chemical, dispersed in clouds of fine particles which could not be kept out of ordinary gas masks; powerful sternutator, causing retching and vomiting, and severe headache in concentration; introduced 1917, known as 'blue cross'.

Diphenylcyonoarsine: similar to diphenylchoroarsine, but more powerful, replacing the latter as filling for 'blue cross' shells in 1918.

Ethyldichloroarsine: German sternutator, introduced March 1918, less powerful than diphenylchloroarsine; used in 'yellow cross I' shells, later styled 'green cross III'.

Ethyl iodoacetate: powerful British lachrymator, introduced 1916; high persistence, but effect ceasing immediately the area affected by gas was left.

Monobrommethylethylketone: German/Austrian lachrymator, introduced 1916; more powerful incapacitator than bromacetone.

Phosgene (carbonyl chloride): used in cylinder with chlorine, and in shells; acute respiratory irritant used by Allies and Germany, introduced 1915. Especially dangerous due to delayed action, causing sudden death as long as 48 hours after exposure, the victim often not realizing that he had been gassed.

Trichloromethylchloroformate (diphosgene): effect similar to phosgene; used in shells, sometimes in combination with other gases, by Allies and Germany; introduced 1916.

Xylyl bromide: powerful German lachrymator, introduced 1915.

The use of progressively more effective gas masks and respirators became universal from the middle part of the war. Early protection was often nothing more than goggles and a mouth-pad impregnated with chemicals (the earliest recommendation was to hold a urine-soaked handkerchief over the nose and mouth!); the next development was a hood which tucked inside the tunic-collar, and the ultimate protective helmet was a face mask with air-tube or valve which drew in air through a chemical filter which neutralized the gas. Even such comparatively sophisticated protection left the wearer vulnerable to mustard gas, which could even penetrate clothing, and the wearing of masks was a considerable inhibitor of movement, with eye-pieces prone to steaming-up; the difficulty of operating artillery under such conditions led to the widespread German shelling with gas of known battery positions immediately before an attack.

Chemical warfare also had a morale effect: when first encountered on the Western Front, gas-attacks caused widespread panic, as no dug-out or shelter was impervious to heavier-than-air gas. It was found to be so effective that, for example, for the German attack on the Aisne in late May 1918, eighty per cent of the long-range bombardment shells contained gas (mostly 'blue cross'), seventy per cent of the barrage on the rear of the front line, and even forty per cent

---

An account of the routine of a trench-mortar battery recalls the meaning of the title of Remarque's *All Quiet on the Western Front*:

'. . . when you watch the bomb sailing over gloriously . . . to the German lines, watch it fall gracefully, and then it goes off, and you look out with Machiavellian glee for bits of Germans and sausages in the huge funnel of stuff that erupts, it is simply great . . . it is the strain that is so wearing. The pretty continuous job and tear at the nerves will pull the best man to pieces. In the trenches a man is continually stretched on an intangible rack . . .

'. . . the daily strafe . . . consists of an hour or so when the exchange of civilities between the lines is more violent than during the rest of the day. A few men are blown to pieces, some more crippled, a woman's heart is broken, a father's hopes are withered, and the report is issued that there is "nothing doing" on that particular sector . . .'

('Bombardier Drew', in *Made in the Trenches*, ed. Sir Frederick Treves Bt., pp. 65–6, London, 1916)

---

of the creeping barrage which preceded the attack. The fact that only an estimated three per cent of gas casualties proved fatal should not conceal its nature: Wilfred Owen's *Dulce et Decorum Est* portrays a gas casualty in all its obscene horror.

A further type of chemical warfare was the limited use of incendiary shells. German shell-filling of white phosphorus (spread by air-burst) was less effective than the British compound thermit (iron oxide/aluminium mixture), ignited by a bursting-charge of the explosive ophorite. This was most effective when fired from a low-velocity mortar, as ignition was more difficult to achieve from an artillery shell.

Trench artillery

Not until the beginning of trench warfare was the necessity realized for portable weapons providing more immediate fire-support than artillery. As a result of observation of the Russo–Japanese War, Germany had a small number of such weapons available at the outset; but France had to press into service a range of ancient, smoothbore mortars dating to the beginning of the 19th century, and when trench artillery was required at Gallipoli, all that were available to the British were half a dozen Japanese mortars with limited ammunition.

The earliest devices for projecting explosive charges short distances were termed 'bomb-throwers', miniature medieval-style siege-engines using coiled springs, rubber or tensioned wire as catapults to hurl grenades. Some of these resembled large crossbows, such as the rubber-powered British Leach catapult which threw a 1½lb grenade up to 200 yards, and the less powerful, spring-driven French Sauterelle. Others, like the British West spring-gun, acted like a medieval mangonel, capable of throwing a 2lb bomb about 240 yards, about the maximum distance attainable with this type of propulsion. Most were used only in 1915, until the provision of more modern ordnance; but a later version, the Minucciani bomb-thrower, used the unique motive power of centrifugal force, grenades being ejected from a revolving interior when a handle was turned.

Proper trench-mortars, for which the main criteria were ease of use and portability, were in service from 1915. All projected an explosive bomb, usually fitted with fins for stability in flight, from a short barrel or tube, using a very high trajectory and with limited range: the early models were effective from 200–500 yards, and even the latest had an effective range of less than 2,000 yards. In the early types the bomb had a rod which fitted down the bore of the mortar-tube in the manner of a rifle-grenade, and which was projected by ignition of a propellant charge at the base of the barrel, by means of friction-tube, percussion cap or even by the lighting of a length of combustible match. High-pressure trench-mortars, firing missiles of this type, resembled small, smoothbored howitzers on flatbed carriages; the most prolific was the French Dumézil mortar, used also by Italian, Russian and US armies.

Low-pressure mortars achieved the same effect with

Statistics for examples of trench artillery were:

Type	Weight of projectile (pounds)	Maximum range (yards)	Notes
Batignolles 240mm	192	1,125	weighed 2,080lb
Batignolles 240mm (longer)	179	2,265	
Batignolles 340mm	430	2,250	required concrete bed and light railway to transport bombs
Brandt pneumatic	1½	250 (with accuracy)	
Dumézil no. 2	35–99	715	weighed 818lb
Granatenwerfer	4	330	weighed 88lb
Granatenwerfer	5½ bouncing bomb	275	
7.6cm Light Minenwerfer	9	1,150	weighed 312lb
7.6cm Light Minenwerfer (longer)	9	1,422	
17cm Medium Minenwerfer	109	980	weighed 1,064lb
17cm Medium Minenwerfer (longer)	109	1,250	weighed 1,232lb
24.5cm Heavy Minenwerfer	210	612	weighed 1,362lb
24.5cm Heavy Minenwerfer (longer)	210	990	weighed 1,693lb
3in Stokes	10	1,250	
4in Stokes	25	1,250	

(Elevation was commonly 45°, but different elevations gave different ranges with the same propellant; the 240mm Batignolles, for example, at 45° could reach 1,125 yards, but only 1,045 yards at 55⅓°.)

much thinner walled tubes, thus decreasing weight and increasing mobility. The most common were the French Batignolles (used also by Britain, Italy and the USA) and the British Stokes, probably the most famous trench-mortar of the war, designed in 1915 by Sir Wilfred Stokes. It existed in several varieties, characterized by portability (the tube having a metal base-plate to absorb recoil but otherwise only a light, bipod mount) and automatic ignition, in which the bomb was dropped into the tube and ejected immediately by the action of a percussion cartridge at the base of the bomb upon a fixed striker at the base of the tube. In British service the 3in Stokes was used primarily for firing HE and latterly smoke; the 4in was used only for gas, smoke and incendiary; supplemented by the 6in Stokes-Newton, they provided the bulk of the army's trench artillery in the latter part of the war. The Batignolles 240mm mortar, one of the leading heavy weapons of its type, fired a bomb sufficient to create a crater 30 feet in diameter and 10 feet

Early 19th-century mortars pressed into service by the French Army in 1914, because of shortages of modern equipment.

deep, consequently requiring a more substantial and thus less-portable framework.

All the Allied weapons were smooth-bored, but the majority of German mortars (*Minenwerfer*) were rifled. As with Allied weapons, improvements were made during the war, notably in lengthening barrels and the late (1917–18) conversion of light weapons to direct fire, for use as light field guns. *Minenwerfer* were designed as miniature howitzers and had wheeled, horse-drawn carriages, though the lighter ones could be manhandled. Calibres ranged from 7.6cm to 24.5cm, the larger ones being almost field artillery (the 24.5cm heavy *Minenwerfer*, for example, weighed almost 1,700 pounds). Much more mobile were the grenade-projectors (*Granatenwerfer*) which propelled a finned grenade about 300 yards; a late (1918) projectile had a small charge at the head which burst on impact, causing the grenade to bounce and burst in the air like shrapnel. Germany also used rudimentary smoothbored mortars, such as the 9.2cm Lanz, the Ehrhardt, and the curious Albrecht *Mörser* (25, 35 and 45cm calibres), which had a wooden tube, bound with wire. The 24cm *Flügelminenwerfer* was the largest, weighing almost 3,000 pounds and firing a vaned bomb; it was sufficiently hazardous to use that it was fired by a 50ft lanyard. There were also 17cm *Flügelminenwerfer* and 18cm *Minenwerfer* which were also smoothbored.

The oddest trench artillery were the pneumatic guns which used compressed air as a propellant. Dependence upon supplies of bottled carbon dioxide and limited range (the Brandt was effective only up to 250 yards) led to only the French Brandt being used in any quantity. German weapons (*Pressluft Minenwerfer*) existed in 10cm and 15cm calibres, with ranges of about 540 and 490 yards respectively.

Cavalry

Once one of the most important arms on the battlefield, during the war, in all but a few theatres, cavalry was relegated to the least significant. Initially much importance was placed upon the mounted troops, despite tactical theories that had eroded the traditional importance of shock action, in favour of dismounted 'fire' tactics: virtually all cavalry were equipped with firearms and trained to fight on foot.

At the beginning of the war the usual deployment was in two groups: 'divisional cavalry', usually individual squadrons attached to infantry divisions to provide a communication and reconnaissance facility; and in independent cavalry divisions, complete with their own mobile supporting services, to act as a mobile supporting, reconnaissance, protecting or striking-force alongside or in front of the infantry divisions. Although cavalry forces were kept in reserve by most armies in the hope of exploiting a breakthrough, the nature of the warfare that was evolving made the opportunities for use very rare, and in several armies many of the mounted personnel were converted to infantry.

Russian Steppe Cossack, whose uniform was akin to that of the ordinary Russian army, not the exotic costume of the Caucasian Cossacks. The rough, hardy pony is typical.

Initially, however, there were opportunities for old-style cavalry action. At Moncel on 6 September 1914, the British 9th Lancers (advance-guard of the 2 Cavalry Brigade) charged through some squadrons of the German 1st Guard Dragoons, piercing the German line and rallying in their rear. By strange irony, the 9th's machine-gun officer, Lieutenant Frederick de V. B. Allfrey (whose duty represented the modern face of war) left his position and was killed while extracting a German lance from the shoulder of the 9th's adjutant, Captain G. F. Reynolds. A short time later, in the neighbouring village of Faujus, the British 18th Hussars demonstrated the futility of old-fashioned tactics: 'B' Squadron, formed a firing-line amid a field of corn-stooks and was charged by a German squadron 'in perfect order, in line at close order',[29] which was 'almost annihilated' by the 18th's fire: 32 German casualties were counted on the immediate front of 'B' Squadron, yet so resolute were the German troopers that some charged right through the firing-line and were shot by the 18th's horse-holders at the rear. Of about 60 or 70 who charged, not more than a dozen survived.

Despite cavalry being outdated by trench-warfare, mounted action still occurred on the Western Front, most notably at Moreuil Wood on 30 March 1918, when the ability of cavalry to move rapidly to plug a gap in the line (long recognized as one of their key abilities even in 'modern' warfare) prevented a German breakthrough. In this action the Canadian Cavalry Brigade under General J. E. B. 'Galloper Jack' Seely combined mounted and dismounted action. Most notably, three troops of Lord Strathcona's Horse, commanded by Lieutenant Gordon Flowerdew, charged two lines of German infantry and machine-guns about 200 yards apart, rode through both lines, turned and charged back until the Germans fled; having suffered about 70 per cent casualties, the survivors dismounted and, joined by a troop dismounted previously as a reserve, occupied the position themselves. About 70 Germans were killed by sword-thrusts; Flowerdew died of wounds the following day and was awarded a posthumous Victoria Cross. Haig described the action as 'a brilliant counter-attack'; which could not have been made by other than mounted troops, proving that under exceptional circumstances, cavalry was still of value.

In more open warfare, mounted forces were of much greater use, notably in Palestine, where Allenby's army contained a high proportion of superb horsemen, albeit many classified as 'mounted rifles' (mounted troops equipped as infantry). The Australian Light Horse and New Zealand Mounted Rifles represented the best type of such troops, whose mobility was of crucial importance. Beersheba demonstrated the combination of foot and mounted action: the 2nd and 3rd Australian Light Horse traversed a long stretch of open country in troop columns at wide intervals, an advance so rapid that the Turkish gunners could not correct their ranging sufficiently to cause heavy casualties. Some 1,500 yards from the Turkish position the Australians rode into a depression, where they dismounted and completed the advance on foot, a classic example of 'modern' cavalry tactics.

A more traditional attack was made later in the day by the 4th and 12th Australian Light Horse, which charged a Turkish position in squadron columns, about 300 yards between squadrons and five paces between each man. They covered the 3,000 yards to the Turkish trenches under cover of the fire of two artillery batteries, and having no swords charged with bayonet in hand; this so unnerved the Turks that few casualties were inflicted at long range, and almost none as the Australians bore down upon the trenches. The leading squadrons rode over the two lines of trenches, dismounted and began to clear them, as the succeeding squadrons galloped right into Beersheba, causing havoc among the Turkish transport-lines. The effect on defenders' morale in facing so uncommon a sight as a mounted charge would seem to be confirmed by the action of the Dorsetshire Yeomanry at El Mughar in November 1917, when a Turkish position was carried by one dismounted and two mounted squadrons; by far the heaviest casualties were

suffered by the dismounted men.

Strategically, only in open country was it possible to use the mobility of cavalry to the full; in Allenby's 1918 offensive its potential was demonstrated in the advance of the Desert Mounted Corps, whch was composed of some of the best mounted troops of the war: Australians, New Zealanders, British Yeomanry, Indian and Imperial Service cavalry, and a regiment of French Chasseurs d'Afrique. As Allenby wrote of Beersheba, what would not cavalry on the Western Front have given for such an opportunity; but wire, mud and machine-guns proved to be the obituary of the cavalry soldier.

Armoured warfare

Armoured warfare began in 1914, with the employment by the Allies of armoured cars, initially ordinary vehicles with armour-plating added, and later specially designed cars. Their original function was as mobile machine-gun and artillery positions, for reconnaissance, raiding and the provision of fire-support. Britain, France and Belgium employed these to some effect, but the beginning of trench warfare removed most of their opportunities for action. Thereafter, they were employed principally in the more open terrain of Egypt, Palestine, Mesopotamia, East and South-West Africa, and in smaller numbers in Roumania and southern Russia (the armoured-car crews were almost the only British representatives in the two latter theatres); and some use was made again of them on the Western Front after the German breakthrough of March 1918. Considerable importance was placed upon the 'all-round' armouring of such vehicles, hence the effectiveness of traversible turrets in which the machine-guns were situated: open-topped vehicles were extremely vulnerable, as was proven in 1918 by the casualties sustained by 1 Canadian Armoured Machine-Gun Brigade, equipped with light trucks produced by the Autocar Company of Pennsylvania, which had folding armoured side panels but no overhead protection.

True armoured warfare began only with the development of the tank, perhaps the only real innovation of the war. It originated with the British Landships Committee established by Winston Churchill at the Admiralty in February 1915, to develop the theory of Lieutenant-Colonel Ernest Swinton for the creation of an armoured assault vehicle. Swinton, who had already gained some reputation as a military theorist for his minor classic *The Defence of Duffer's Drift*, was not the first to postulate such a machine (as early as 1912 an Australian, L. E. Mole, had submitted such a plan to the War Office but had been ignored), but it was under Swinton and other innovators that the tank was developed. The major development was the acceptance that tracks were of more use than wheels for rough terrain, Swinton demonstrating the abilities of the Holt caterpillar tractor which was already in use as artillery transport.

The first design – known as 'Little Willie' – was a metal box with tracks mounted at the sides, upon which it was intended to mount a rotating gun-turret. As this would have

created too high a silhouette, a second design was tried (largely the invention of Lieutenant W. G. Wilson and William Tritton, managing director of Foster's, the company contracted for the development of military tracked vehicles), of a rhomboid armoured box with caterpillar tracks encircling the body and armament mounted on sponsons on each side. From this ('Mother') was developed the first practicable tank, the Mark I, which existed in 'male' versions (with 6pdr naval guns mounted in the sponsons), and 'female' (armed with machine-guns). The term 'tank' was adopted during the secret construction and trials, to give the impression that mobile water-tanks were under development, not fighting vehicles.

The basic pattern remained in use for the British heavy tank throughout the war, though improvements were made, most notably in the early removal of the two artillery wheels at the rear, which were found to be an unnecessary aid to steering. At Swinton's behest the armour plating was designed to stop a reversed bullet at 10 yards (bullets fired back-to-front had greater armour-piercing capability, the armour stopping the hard outer casing but being more vulnerable to the lead core), and the minimum capability required was a speed of 4mph and the ability to cross an 8-foot trench and climb a 5-foot parapet of 1 in 1 gradient. All machinery was inside the armoured box, and steering was by gears which varied the speed of tracks independently of each other.

To operate the tanks, a new unit was formed, originally the Heavy Branch of the Machine-Gun Corps, later the Tank Corps. Their situation was unenviable: badly-ventilated, the machines became so hot and fume-ridden (even soldered joints warped, releasing noxious gases) that crews suffered delirium, vomiting, unconsciousness and burns from hot machinery, and in the light tanks, where the heat was even more concentrated, ammunition might explode. Fighting in such unpleasant conditions was described aptly by a Canadian quoted by the tank officer Frank Mitchell: 'A regular pocket-hell'.[30]

The tank was essentially an offensive weapon, and in retreat a liability: in the German March 1918 offensive, for example, of about 370 tanks which attempted to cover the British withdrawal, 180 broke down and had to be burned and abandoned, so that the Tank Corps briefly became merely a screen of machine-gunners. Mechanical breakdown was very common, and far more costly than enemy fire: in the first armoured attack, for example (15 September 1916), of 49 tanks deployed, only 32 reached the start-line, of which nine broke down, five were 'ditched', nine preceded the infantry into the German positions and nine were unable to keep pace with the infantry but helped in the mopping-up. 'Ditching' occurred when a tank became bogged in soft ground or a collapsed trench; each tank carried a large wooden boom or 'unditching beam' to be pulled under the tracks to provide something upon which to grip. If stuck on a firm object which raised the tracks off the ground, a tank was said to be 'bellied'. Even a ditched tank, however, was a formidable obstacle: at Third Ypres the British tank bearing the ironic name 'Fray Bentos' became bogged down 500 yards ahead of the British line; for two nights and almost three days its crew held off repeated German attacks, resorting to firing revolvers through loopholes, until the machine was finally abandoned when the crew (one dead, six wounded) escaped under cover of darkness.

The military establishment initially showed little enthusiasm for tanks: Kitchener, for example, described them as mere 'pretty mechanical toys'. Consequently, the first employment was in small numbers, but despite the breakdowns and ditchings the success of the weapon had been demonstrated.

Swinton regarded tanks as a way simply of breaching the enemy line, as an auxiliary support for infantry. An opposite view was taken by Lieutenant-Colonel John F. C. Fuller, chief of tank staff, who believed that mechanism was the key to future wars, and that the mobility of the tank made it virtually an armoured, mechanical horse which could be used like cavalry, not only to penetrate front lines but to

British-built tanks outnumbered 'native' machines in German service, large numbers of Mark IVs and others being captured due to the difficulty of recovering damaged or bogged-down machines, especially during the 1918 spring offensive. These were mostly refurbished at the German workshops at Charleroi. These views show British tanks in German hands; note the entry-doors at the rear of the sponsons, the extended track-plates, and the wooden rollers placed on the road to assist traction. (Peter Kilduff)

drive right through defence-systems which, because of their increasing depth, could not be opened by artillery alone. Even so, in Fuller's 'Plan 1919' for armoured warfare, emphasis continued to be placed upon the shock effect of armoured assault rather than upon what was probably the ultimate advantage of armoured vehicles, the rapid transportation of men and equipment over ground impassable at such speed by other means, striking not only through the enemy rear areas but into the supporting communication system. The limited speed and frequent breakdown of the early tanks, however, confirmed the general perception of the vehicle as suitable mainly for the attainment of limited objectives and the support of infantry.

For the attack at Cambrai (the largest armoured assault to that date), Fuller devised a supremely successful method of attack which was adopted almost universally. To increase the gap-crossing ability (ten feet for a Mark IV), each tank was equipped with a 10-ton brushwood fascine which could be dropped from the nose of the tank into a trench to form a bridge. The tank force was divided into units of three vehicles, one 'advanced' and two 'main body'. The advanced tank approached the German front line or 'fire-trench', flattening the wire in front of it, then turned to the left and raked the trench to keep its occupants under cover. The first main body tank then went through the path in the wire, dropped its fascine in the fire-trench, crossed it, then turned left to rake the rear of the fire-trench and front of the support-trench. The second main body tank then advanced over the fire-trench, dropped its fascine in the support-trench, crossed it, then turned left and raked the rear of this trench. Meanwhile, the advanced tank had swung round, passed over the fire- and support-trench fascines, and dropped its own fascine in the third-line trench. Infantry in small parties followed under cover of the main body tanks, first the trench-clearers who marked with red flags the gaps in the wire, and then entered the trenches to neutralize their defenders; secondly the 'trench-stops' who blocked-off the occupied area to prevent counter-attack; and finally the

trench garrisons which consolidated the captured positions. The success of such tactics is shown by the progress on the first day of the Cambrai attack (20 November 1917); 378 combat tanks and 98 supply-carriers and supports led a 9,500-yard advance on a 13,000-yard front, at the cost of about 1,500 casualties; at Third Ypres a similar advance by conventional means had taken three months and cost almost 400,000 casualties.

Panic often ensued among troops attacked by tanks. Undoubtedly the tank had a major effect on the war (a German general remarked that it was not Marshal Foch who had defeated them, but General Tank), yet by no means all regarded the tank with awe. The stormtrooper Ernst Jünger, for example, believed that artillery and machine-guns represented the real technological key, and regarded the situation of tank crews with pity. In as far as a combination of artillery and infiltration could prove as effective in its way as armoured attacks, there is some justification for Jünger's beliefs; yet for some time after the end of the war tanks were known in Germany as 'Germany's Death'.

The German defence against tanks included obstacles such as pits which could not be crossed, and attempts to destroy them with artillery. The only weapon designed specifically as an anti-tank gun was the single-shot, bolt-action Mauser 13mm rifle, fired prone from a bipod mount; latterly a few were equipped with magazines. Modifications were made to the ordinary 7.7cm and captured Russian 7.62cm field guns (reducing the wheel-diameter to give a lower silhouette) for anti-tank use; 2cm, 3.7cm 'revolver cannon' and 5.7cm guns were also produced. These were not especially successful, but a 3.7cm light anti-tank gun ('Pak': *Panzerabwehrkanone*) was better, yet not produced in large numbers. Ordinary ammunition was of little use against tanks, though a shortish range impact on the outside of the armour could dislodge 'splashes' of metal from the internal face to fly around the interior of the tank; hence the chain-mail face-veils used by tank crews as eye-protection.

A stranded tank: the damaged right-hand track is visible clearly, as is the metal-shod, chained unditching beam, which appears to have slipped down the rear of the vehicle from its original position. Note the open door at the rear of the 'male' sponson. (Peter Kilduff)

A damaged tank thoroughly bogged-down in typical Western Front battlefield conditions. Damaged track was forced into this looped shape by the motion of the wheels before the vehicle stopped; no machine-guns are visible in the sponsons of this 'female' tank as crews were expected to remove them when abandoning a wrecked vehicle. (Peter Kilduff)

The drainpipe-like object protruding from the forward turret of this 'female' tank is the unmistakable shape of the barrel of a Lewis gun, not an ideal weapon for tank use as its large barrel was damaged easily by enemy fire, and its fumes were drawn into the gunner's face by the engine fan, hence its eventual replacement by the Hotchkiss gun. As 'female' sponsons occupied less room than the 'male' version mounting an artillery piece, escape-doors could be accommodated below the 'female' mounting, clearly shown here. (Peter Kilduff)

Brief statistics of some of the tanks in use are:

Model	Armament	Armour (max.)	Weight (tons)	Speed (mph)	Crew
Mks I–IV male	2×6-pdrs, 4 MG	12mm	28	3.7	8
Mks I–III female	5 MG	12mm	27	3.7	8
Mk IV female	6 MG	12mm	27	3.7	8
Mk V male	2×6-pdrs, 4 MG	14mm	29	4.6	8
Mk V female	6 MG	14mm	28	4.6	8
Medium Mk A (Whippet)	4 MG	14mm	14	8.3	3
Medium Mk B	4 MG	14mm	18	7.9	4
Schneider	1×75mm, 2 MG	11.4–17mm	14½	5	6
St. Chamond	1×75mm, 4 MG	11mm	24	5	9
Renault FT17	1 MG; later 37mm gun	16mm	6½	5–6	2
A7V	1×5.7cm, 6 MG	30mm	32	8	16

German infantrymen were supplied with clips of 'K' bullets (armour-piercing), and machine-guns with belts of the same; but the development of a high-velocity machine-gun capable of firing 13mm armour-piercing rounds (*Tuf* ammunition: *Tank und Flieger*, for use against tanks and aircraft) was not sufficiently rapid for these to be used before the armistice. Minefields were also used as anti-tank defences: for example, the US 301st Battalion lost almost one-third of its strength in an attack on the Hindenburg Line, when running into rows of buried trench-mortar bombs. Against anti-tank artillery, snipers might be deployed to protect tanks by shooting the gun-crews.

With the USA using tanks of British design, only two other nations produced their own designs. French tanks were conceived and developed independently, both the main heavy patterns (St. Chamond and Schneider) being basically armoured boxes upon Holt caterpillar tractors, similar to the 'Little Willie' design rejected by Britain. These *chars d'assaut* ('assault vehicles') were not a success, and production was switched to the Renault *char léger*, a two-man light tank intended to act as a quicker moving cavalry-style tank. It was produced in large quantities, but the British equivalent was superior, the three-man Medium A or 'Whippet', which though not as heavily armed was capable of sufficiently rapid motion to exploit a breakthrough made by the heavy tanks. It could even be handled by a single crewman: a Private Bussey of the Tank Corps, the sole unwounded member of his crew, fought for four hours in August 1918, leaving the tank to steer itself and manning its guns alternately. Germany was late in emulating the Allied success, and produced only a small number of their A7V tank, though they used a quantity of captured and refurbished British vehicles.

Transport

Transportation of men, munitions and supplies was of paramount importance, and was structured on several levels, from the vehicles of individual battalions, to brigade, divisional and army 'trains' or transport columns. The number of vehicles was huge: for a British division in 1914,

for example, it included 877 vehicles, nine motor cars and 5,594 horses. Despite the increasing use of motor vehicles, by 1918 the equivalent establishment still included 822 horsed vehicles and 8,838 horses, three motor lorries, eleven motor cars and 21 motor ambulances.

Of equal significance was the network of light railways laid to supply the front lines. These had existed as early as the Crimean War, but the extent of use during the World War was unprecedented. Some advocated the use of the standard gauge (4ft 8½in), but the majority of railway track was of the 'soixante' gauge (60cm wide), employing light locomotives and rolling-stock. This required considerably less effort than for the construction of the standard gauge: British construction varied between 1,760 and 2,400 man-days per mile, whereas an American figure for construction of standard gauge was 4,300. Germany speeded the process by converting existing civilian standard-gauge lines, which required no new road-bed and involved only the moving of one length of track. Motive power was provided by both steam locomotives and gasoline-powered tractors.

Speeds of movement varied with the terrain, most calculations being based on movement over level ground, a rough contemporary guide being that infantry could march about 100 yards per minute. The following were official British statistics for movement in the field (1914):

Troops	Yds. per min.	Mins. to cover 1 mile	mph including halts
Infantry	98	18	3
Cavalry, walk	117	15	3½
Cavalry, trot	235	8	7
Cavalry, gallop	440	–	–

Speed of march of vehicles was given as: wheeled transport (horses) 2½mph; bullock-carts 1½mph; pack-mule or horse 3mph; pack-bullock 2mph; coolie 2mph; motor lorry 6mph; tractor 3½mph. Field artillery speeds were approximately 4mph at a walk, 9mph at a trot and 15mph at a gallop, not including halts; heavy artillery was slower than infantry pace. Marching pace (a mixture of trot

The war produced a large number of ingenious inventions, and a number of bizarre pieces of equipment, such as this Italian 'hydro-ski' undergoing French military trials: by moving the feet forwards a paddle-wheel at the stern was activated, driving the soldier over water.

and walk, including halts) for field artillery was about 4mph, 5mph for horse artillery; German calculations indicated that a 14-mile march could be made by a field battery in 5 hours, and by a horse battery in 4 hours. German statistics (1912), expressed in metric measures, indicated a speed of march of infantry (small units) at 5–6 kilometres per hour, cavalry (trot and walk alternating) 8–9 kph, and that an average day's march (22.5km) was covered by infantry in 5–6 hours and by cavalry in 3–5 hours, though noted that in exceptional circumstances a cavalry division could cover 40–50 kilometres per day.

For distances taken up by troops on the march, the British calculations were: infantry, ½ yard per man (normally marching in fours); cavalry, 1 yard per riding horse; 4 yards per pack animal; 15 yards per 4-horse vehicle, 20 yards per 6-horse vehicle, including spaces between. Six yards was the space calculated for a motor lorry, with a minimum of 15 yards between vehicles (40 yards on gradients, 100 yards at full speed). The total distances tabulated here were those occupied by units in normal marching formation (vehicles in single file):

Unit	'Fighting portion'	1st line Transport	Ammunition Column
Divisional HQ	20 yards	80 yards	–
Cavalry Div HQ	30	100	–
Infantry Brigade HQ	15	50	–
Cavalry Brigade HQ	40	55	–
Cavalry Regiment	570	480	–
Horse Artillery Brigade (2 batteries)	910	1,120	830
Field Artillery Brigade (18pdrs)	1,230	860	615
Horse Artillery battery	440	90	–
Field Artillery battery (18pdrs)	390	65	–
Heavy Artillery battery (60pdrs)	360	55	90
Divisional Ammunition Column	–	–	2,400
Engineer Field Company	400	90	–
Bridging Train	–	1,200	–
Infantry battalion	590	200	–
Infantry company	125	15	–
Cavalry Field Ambulance	–	290	–
Field Ambulance	–	380	–
Divisional Train	–	1,755	–

The space allocated for higher units was:

Unit	'Fighting portion'	Transport
Cavalry Division	6 miles	5½ miles
Cavalry Brigade	1 mile	7/8th mile
Infantry Division	8 miles	6⅔ miles
Infantry Brigade	1½ miles	¾ mile

German calculations (1912) indicated that an infantry battalion (marching four abreast) would occupy 330 metres, a cavalry regiment 450 metres, a foot battery 300 metres and a horse battery 400 metres. Their rule-of-thumb for calculating space occupied was, for troops marching four abreast: infantry, strength divided by three = length in metres; cavalry, number multiplied by ¾ = length in metres.

When marching along roads, it was usual to keep close to walls, trees or buildings on one side of the road, using cover shadows to conceal the nature of the column from aerial observation.

Communications

Most armies had signal services organized in independent companies, deployed at all levels from brigade upwards. The older methods of signalling, by flag and heliograph, were generally not appropriate for European war, and with radio in its infancy, the usual method of communication was by telephone. Great importance was placed on the maintenance of cable-lines, often buried many feet deep, transmitting either by voice communication or by 'buzzer' (using Morse Code). Bombardment frequently broke the cables, however, so that the signal units had a constant and most hazardous task in attempting to keep the lines open. Portable handsets and cables carried by moving troops were even more vulnerable, necessitating the use of runners, carrier-pigeons and signal-rockets, the latter especially useful in calling down bombardments upon pre-set co-ordinates. This was at best a haphazard method of communicaton, resulting in one of the anomalies of 'modern' war, in that generals were often deprived of the ability to alter plans according to circumstance simply because of lack of communication with their troops. Unlike earlier wars, when the scale of operations were such that it was possible for a general to traverse the entire battlefield and personally conduct the action, the commanders of the World War had at their disposal the full range of modern technology, yet hardly any means of directing it once the initial plans had been laid and the first orders issued. On innumerable occasions operations went awry because of lack of support or the ability to change plans centrally due to lack of adequate communication between front and rear areas, a typical consequence of a system in which command and control had not kept pace with the developments in weapons-technology and the immense increase in the size of battles. The British *Infantry Training* (1914) commented on this from the perspective of the battalion commander, whose control was so limited once an action began, that 'success will depend, in a great measure, on the clearness of the order which commits his leading companies to the attack, and the definite objectives he gives';[31] which was equally true for all levels of command.

Engineers

Before the war considerable importance was placed upon fortification, influenced by the work of such engineers as the noted Belgian officer Henri Alexis Brialmont (1821–1903). His perception of defending a country included fortifying the capital and important harbours, the points where lines of communication crossed a strategic barrier (mountain-chain, etc.), and any points through which an enemy might pass, and constructing fortified camps from which a defending army could operate. Because of increased ranges of artillery, it was no longer possible to base fortifications upon a continuous enceinte; the strategic place had to be protected by mutually-supportive detached forts some distance away, such forts having guns mounted in armoured cupolas (thus protected from overhead fire), with support from batteries between the main fortifications. Much use was made of concrete (more resistant than stone or brick) and soft earth, the latter best at absorbing fire.

Defences of this nature were used in Belgium for the strategic centres of Antwerp, Liège and Namur, which were protected by chains of pentagonal forts and smaller, triangular fortlets or *fortins*. The defences of Antwerp were based upon the 1859 enceinte and detached forts some 3,500 yards away, a series of Brialmont forts built from 1879, and a further series (filling the gaps) in 1913, at which time the old forts received increased concrete defences and new cupolas. Antwerp had 31 forts and further defence in an area which could be flooded. Liège and Namur were intended as 'barrier' fortresses, to delay rather than block an invasion, but under Brialmont were turned into positions of more significance, Liège having a ring of six forts and six *fortins*, and Namur four and five respectively; forts were armed with two 6in, four 4.7in and four light quick-firing guns, and two 8in mortars; *fortins* with two 6in, two 4.7in, three light quick-firers and one or two 8in mortars. Together with supporting artillery, Liège mustered about 400 guns and Namur 350. Considerable faith was placed in these defences, but ordnance had progressed markedly since the last great siege (Port Arthur), and the increased weight of shell demonstrated in 1914 that such defences were vulnerable. The ease with which the Belgian forts were overcome undermined confidence in permanent fortifications to the extent that Verdun was considerably denuded of its artillery in late 1915, yet it was the rings of fortifications around Verdun which stopped the Germans from capturing the position: these were mutually supportive and equipped with heavy artillery in retractable steel turrets, supported by a web of fieldworks and bunkers.

In most armies engineers were deployed at divisional level and upwards, with field companies providing divi-

Victorious German troops pose on the wreckage of a typical fort-cupola: Maubeuge, 1914.

sional support and the specialist units (bridging-train, tunnellers, etc.) concentrated at higher levels. From the end of 1914 fieldworks became the dominant feature of the war, notably on the Western Front. Construction of trenches was normally supervised by engineers, but any troops could be used to provide muscle-power, and the maintenance of fieldworks was often the responsibility of the unit in occupation. Of materials used, statistics quoted in the British *Field Service Pocket Book* (1914) noted distances of maximum penetration with a pointed 'S' bullet: hard steel plate 7/16in; mild steel plate ¾in; brickwork with cement mortar 9in; chalk 18in; compressed sand (i.e., sandbags) 18in; hard wood 38in; loose earth 40in; soft wood 58in; clay 60in. Approximate time required for the construction of fieldworks was given as:

Digging one cubic foot: three minutes, for one man averaged over four hours (amount declining with fatigue).

Digging two paces of narrow fire-trench (45 cu. feet): 100 minutes for one man, 70 minutes for two.

Digging two paces of medium fire-trench (90 cu. feet): 300 minutes for one man (150 minutes for two pairs, the first relieved after two hours).

Digging two paces of wide fire-trench (110 cu. feet): 420 minutes for one man (180 minutes for two pairs, as above).

Digging two paces of communication-trench (80 cu. feet): 240 minutes for one man, 135 minutes for two pairs, as above.

Shovelling loose earth (as in spreading spoil at the rear of a trench): 1 cu. foot per man per minute (averaged over eight hours).

Filling one sandbag: three minutes for one man (averaged over two hours, when a 3-man party could fill 120 sandbags).

Filling one gabion (2 feet high, 2ft 9in wide) with earth (to be dug): five minutes for one man per cu. foot.

Cutting sods (18×9×4in): 30 sods per hour per man, averaged over four hours.

Making one gabion (weight 50lb, using 75lb brushwood, the remainder being offcuts and waste): 360 minutes for one man (3-man team).

Making a fascine, 18ft × 9in diameter, weight 140lb (from 200lb brushwood, 60ft wire or 40ft iron hoops): 240 minutes for one man (4-man team).

Loopholing brick wall (up to 18in thick): 30 minutes per loophole for one man, using pick and crowbar.

Making wire entanglement: 30 minutes per square yard for one man (3-man team).

A simple fire-trench was specified as three feet wide, although the sides could be sloped to be wider at the top than the bottom, and might incorporate a shelf for the elbow (to facilitate firing), one at the rear for equipment and a recess for ammunition; excavated spoil made a parapet on the enemy's side of the trench. Communication-trenches were specified as three feet wide at the base and four feet at the top, with a 2½-foot parapet on both sides in addition to the 4½-foot depth. As the war progressed, trenches became much more elaborate, with duck-board footings, reinforcements of sandbags, chicken-wire and beams, dug-outs (sometimes of considerable sophistication), and with the straight trench-lines interrupted by zigzag traverses and fire-bays. Trenches required constant upkeep, very soon falling into disrepair (especially in wet weather), and were often so bombarded as to consist of shell-holes connected by remnants of trench.

Initially a typical trench-system might include three lines of trenches about half-a-mile apart, connected by a network of communication-trenches, the front line being a fire-trench, the second the support-trench and the third the reserve, with artillery emplacements at the rear. In the later part of the war the system was altered totally. The positions

Cross-section of a Western Front dug-out; unsigned illustration published 1915.

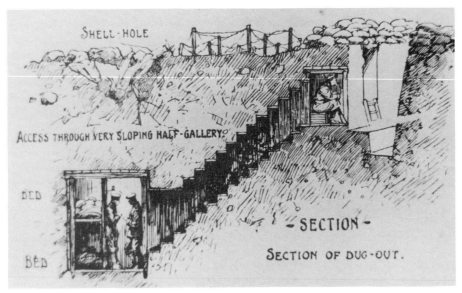

A simple trench dug-out with German inhabitants, 1914.

An anonymous Canadian wonders about the enemy:

'Our friends opposite are almost rude – they cut us dead; ignore us . . . They have a sense of humour, though; one day they stuck up on the parapet a wooden horse such as a child might play with. Our chaps shot it down; they put it up again with a bandage round its neck, and one round a hind leg. They call out at times such things as "We no shoot, you no shoot. We are Saxons and you are Anglo-Saxons. If you come half-way we'll give you cigarettes."'

(In *With the First Canadian Contingent*, p. 68, Toronto & London, 1915)

nearest the enemy were only outposts, varying from shell-holes to concrete or armoured pillboxes, intended to delay and disrupt an enemy. The actual 'front line' could be a mile behind these outposts, dug on a reverse slope where possible (concealment from the enemy was important, for although a position was visible by aerial observation, its garrison could only be estimated from the immediate vicinity): a line 100 yards from the crest of a ridge provided a sufficient 'killing zone' for machine-guns to cut down the attackers as they appeared over the crest. This 'front line' was likely not to be continuous but instead a series of short trenches or strongpoints which could be enfiladed from the rear (in the event of capture); and behind this line, one or two miles deep, was the 'battle zone' littered with short fire-trenches, communication-trenches and reinforced strong-points capable of all-round defence. At the rear of the battle-zone, the second-line trench formed the front of the 'reserve-zone', behind which there might be one or two further complete trench-systems as well as the heavy artillery emplacements. The deepening of the zone of action made attacking immeasurably more difficult, while the defender's munitions and supplies could be conveyed to the battle-line by light railways, a modern version of the old principle of 'interior lines' being easier to maintain than those of the attacker. The strongpoints within the battle-zone were like miniature forts, sited to be mutually supportive and with clear fields of fire, studded by machine-guns at strategic points; those 'pillboxes' built of reinforced concrete and roofed could be extremely difficult to overcome.

Although many engineering tasks could be performed by working-parties from other arms, mining was the responsi-bility of specialist tunnelling companies. One of the most hazardous tasks, this involved driving subterranean pas-sages under the enemy line, to be packed with explosives and detonated before an attack, to destroy an entire section of the enemy's fieldworks. In some areas of the Western Front mining continued for months, with counter-mining aimed at cutting into and destroying the enemy mines before they could be completed, even resulting in subter-ranean combat between opposing gangs of miners. The most proficient tunnellers were probably those recruited from the British mining industry, or the 'clay-kickers' employed in excavating the London underground railway and sewerage systems ('clay-kicking' was a method of excavation in which the tunneller lay upon his back on an angled board, and kicked the blade of his spade into the clay, which was then removed by a colleague).

The most famous result of mining was the detonation of 19 mines at Messines on 7 June 1917, involving some 500 tons of explosives, blown up simultaneously, the shock-waves felt in England. The mine at Spanbroekmolen, the third corner of a triangle formed with Wytschaete and Messines, was begun some 18 months earlier, was 88 feet below ground and contained 91,000 pounds of explosives; it formed 'Lone Tree Crater', 40 feet deep and 250 feet across, and devastated a diameter of 430 feet. At the instigation of 'Tubby' Clayton, this example of mankind's destructiveness was purchased in 1930 by Lord Wakefield, presented to Toc H, and transformed into the 'Pool of Peace'.

Reinforced concrete pillboxes became a common feature of deep defensive zones; this is a very much smaller and earlier (1915) French version of the same principle, an armoured sentry-box or machine-gun post set into a trench system.

A camouflage screen shielding the tracks of a light trench railway; with Belgian troops observing on the ladder, 1917.

A British camouflaged field-gun emplacement near Martinsart, 1915, a style of fieldworks basically unchanged for several centuries.

Naval Warfare

The philosophy of naval warfare at the beginning of the war was dominated by the importance of the 'Capital Ship', the huge battleships which had evolved over the previous half-century. The most recent examples of combat involving numbers of such ships had occurred in the Russo–Japanese War and had culminated in the annihilation of the Russian Baltic Fleet at Tsushima (27 May 1905), yet despite the influence of smaller Japanese craft, in this action most energies were still directed towards the improvement of the capital ship.

From the later 19th century warships had developed rapidly. Defensively, the use of armour-plating produced vessels protected by steel more than a foot thick, which in turn required an improvement in offensive capacity in order to penetrate it, so that guns increased in calibre up to 15 inches' diameter. The invention of the rotating, armoured gun-turret mounting two or three guns permitted fire to be directed ahead and astern of the ship, although in some vessels turrets located between or on one side of the superstructure were limited to the earlier broadside direction of fire. Rate of fire was increased by the improvements in breech-mechanism, and fire-control improved by central direction and ranging aids and tables which supplanted the earlier system of fire dependent upon the eye and experience of the gunnery officer. In addition to main armament, larger ships carried 'secondary' (and in some cases 'intermediate') armament, guns of smaller calibre.

The most significant development in the capital ship was the building of the British HMS *Dreadnought*, completed in 1906. Based on the ideas of Admiral Sir John Fisher (appointed First Sea Lord in 1904), this was a break with the previous system of 'mixed armament': *Dreadnought* was the first of the 'all-big-gun' ships, with ten 12in guns in five turrets, capable of delivering a salvo immensely greater than that of any other ship. Her foot-thick armour (eight inches on turrets) was as effective as any in use, yet her speed (the first large warship powered by steam turbines and four

screws) at 21 knots was two knots faster than any other capital ship, and her endurance (4,000 nautical miles at 16 knots) was one-third again as great as the best previous ship. *Dreadnought* was thus the most impressive fighting machine yet devised, and rendered all other naval vessels obsolete.

The effect of *Dreadnought* was profound, to such an extent that 'dreadnought' became a generic term for all similar ships, earlier battleships being described as 'predreadnoughts'; yet ironically it virtually wiped out British naval supremacy. With all previous capital ships being now outdated, all major naval powers turned to the construction of dreadnoughts, beginning almost from a level of parity, resulting in an arms-race between Britain and Germany. Thanks to the earlier start, at the beginning of the war Britain had 24 dreadnoughts to Germany's fourteen (with three more completed by November 1914), a smaller advantage than if the main ships had been predreadnoughts, of which Britain had 2½ times as many as Germany.

The next category of vessel down from the battleship was the cruiser, a term describing a ship which cruised some distance from the battle-fleet in patrol, scouting and commerce-protection duties. Of these, the 'armoured cruiser' was of considerable size (up to about 15,000 tons displacement) and was intended to form part of the battle-fleet; the second variety was the 'protected cruiser' with only vital parts (engines, magazines, etc.) shielded by armour-plated decks and by coal-bunkers running along the sides of the vessel. These (generally older) vessels had improved performance resulting from the limited use of heavy armour-plating, and were used as commerce-escorts and as the naval presence in colonial outposts.

If *Dreadnought* reduced older battleships to the category of vessels which (as was said) could neither run away nor fight effectively, the older cruisers were rendered obsolete by another British development under the aegis of Fisher, the battlecruiser. Closely related to the dreadnought, this was intended to be more powerful than an armoured cruiser but with reduced armour to permit enhanced speed: in effect a fast capital ship able to destroy the enemy while keeping out of range. Although originally designated 'fast armoured cruisers', they generally resembled battleships (with one less turret) but were considerably longer and more powerfully engined; instead of supplanting the armoured cruiser, during the war they were pressed into the main line of battle. Their speed and long-range gunnery proved ideal in situations such as the Battle of the Falkland Islands, but as the spearhead of the British Grand Fleet and German High Seas Fleet they were less successful. Having better armour but suffering little in terms of performance, the German battlecruisers were probably the more effective: learning from the Dogger Bank action, German warships had anti-flash doors fitted during the war, obstructing the transmission of explosion from turret to magazine, a lesson not learned by the British. British ships remained vulnerable to internal explosion, which claimed *Indefatigable*, *Invincible* and *Queen Mary* at Jutland, for example (and, perhaps most famously, *Hood* in 1941). Battlecruisers were not constructed by many other nations before the war: the US *Lexington* class, though designed in 1916, was not built before the armistice; the Japanese had some ships classed as battle-cruisers, but lacking the speed which was an essential part of their ability, only the *Kongo* class actually qualified for the term; and the four Russian examples launched in 1915 were not completed. A further British development, 'light battle-cruisers', were designed originally with reduced draught for Baltic service; but the three constructed ultimately became aircraft carriers, not being used for the original purpose.

As destroyers developed in the early 1900s from large torpedo-boats into effective and fast warships, a new type of cruiser was required, able to match the speed of destroyers in forming the scouting-screen for the battle-fleet (the task of frigates in the earlier age), yet sufficiently powerful to be able to engage the enemy. The resulting light cruiser was armed with nothing larger than 6in guns (4.1in for German vessels, which outranged the British); although Britain assembled 35 and Germany 37 before 1918, they were not much in evidence in other navies: Austria had four, Japan three and Italy two.

A wartime development was the monitor, virtually a floating battery, largely for coastal bombardment, mounting a small number of large-calibre guns; older 'coast defence battleships' existed in a number of navies, but the construction of ships for this specific role was new. Three 'river monitors' constructed for Brazil by Vickers (each with 3 × 6in guns) were taken over by Britain in August 1914, and from these a range of vessels grew, using guns from various sources. The four *Abercrombie*-class vessels of the Royal Navy, for example, used American 14in guns intended for the Greek battlecruiser *Salamis*, being built in Germany; others received guns from pre-dreadnought battleships, and 18in guns were mounted in three monitors, two from the light battlecruiser *Furious* which was found incapable of

sustaining such immense weapons. Some of these vessels were given 'bulged' protection: bulges added to the sides to absorb the impact of torpedoes. These proved exceptionally effective; no 'bulged' British ship struck by a torpedo was sunk. The monitors *Erebus* and *Terror* received only limited damage from attacks which otherwise would have destroyed them, and similarly old cruisers of the *Edgar* class were torpedoed in the Mediterranean, again with the bulges absorbing the impact and permitting the vessels to survive to be repaired.

The smaller vessels were to an extent dependent upon, or derived as protection against, the torpedo. This self-propelled missile with a range of up to 10,000 yards was powered by a compressed air engine and equipped with mechanism to control its direction and depth, and was probably the most destructive maritime weapon of the war. Most navies maintained flotillas of small, fast torpedo-boats, and the destroyer (originally 'torpedo-boat-destroyer' or 'TBD') evolved as a larger version of the torpedo-boat, armed with guns as well. Torpedoes were also carried by most capital ships, and during the war acquired the ability of launch from an aircraft.

The torpedo, however, was launched most effectively from a submarine. At the beginning of the war, Britain and France together possessed about half the submarines then existing, Germany having constructed only 24 before 1914. The development was comparatively recent: the first British boats were completed in 1902 and the first German in 1906 (although three Russian boats had been built in Germany from 1904). British submarine design was based originally upon the American Holland pattern, initially small craft with surface displacement under 200 tons, intended primarily as coast-defence vessels. The *D* class vessels (built 1910–12) were the first to exceed 500 tons, whereas all but the first four German boats were well in excess of this size. Despite the disparity in numbers, Germany had the lead in submarine development, and preferred large submarine 'cruisers' which could operate independently in an offensive role; British perspective throughout the war was for reconnaissance vessels primarily intended to work in conjunction with the fleet. In 1914 an intensive construction programme was begun by Germany: the number of boats was almost doubled by the end of the year (fifteen completed) and many were built in succeeding years.

British submarines scored a number of successes during the war (for example, the havoc caused by those which penetrated the Dardanelles was out of all proportion to the number of boats used), but the main effect of submarines was that of the German U-boats. Especially in the post-Jutland period, when the surface fleet was virtually unused, almost all German naval effort was sustained by sub-marines, a remarkable achievement when it is considered that the most in service at any one time was 140 (October 1917). Despite some remarkable successes against warships (the destruction of HMSS *Aboukir*, *Cressy* and *Hogue* by *U 9* on 22 September 1914, the sinking of the battleship

Blücher, *the German heavy armoured cruiser conceived to match British battle cruisers (15,500 tons, 12 × 8.2in, 8 ×* 5.9in, 16 × 24pdr guns, 4 × 18 in torpedo tubes). *Considerably outgunned, she was sunk at Dogger Bank.*

Formidable, 1 January 1915, and the threat to Allied warships in the Dardanelles, leading to the withdrawal of all capital ships save *Triumph* and *Majestic*, which were duly sunk), the main U-boat threat was against Allied merchant shipping.

The German submarine campaign attracted much opprobrium, especially in the destruction of nine hospital ships, most infamously perhaps the sinking of *Llandovery Castle* on 27 June 1918 (which was clearly lit and unmistakable for what she was), and in the sinking of *Lusitania* which had wider implications, but did immense damage to Allied commerce. Despite a decline after the institution of the convoy system and enhanced anti-submarine capability, the importance of the U-boats is clear:

Number of Allied and neutral ships lost during the war:

	1914	1915	1916	1917	1918
To submarines	3	396	964	2,439	1,035
To surface craft	55	23	32	64	3
To mines	42	97	161	170	27
To aircraft	–	–	–	3	1

Of the above (gross tonnage 12,739,000), some of the mine losses might also be attributed to submarines, as a number of minelaying submarines were employed.

The primary defence of commercial shipping was the convoy system, though it is surprising that the Allies took so long to institute it, given that it had been standard practice during the Napoleonic Wars and was already used successfully for troop-transportation and cross-Channel commerce. The first counter to the U-boat campaign was an increase of patrolling by warships, armed merchant cruisers and Q-ships; with only limited effect.

The armed merchant cruiser was a large commercial vessel given reasonable armament and employed as a warship: until December 1917, for example, such ships formed the British 10th Cruiser Squadron. Seventeen such British vessels were lost during the war, all to submarines save two mined, one foundered, one sunk by a surface-raider and two wrecked off the Scottish coast. These should not be confused with other armed merchantmen: Commissioned Escort Ships and Armed Boarding Vessels (under naval command) and the much larger number of Defensively Armed Merchant Ships, commercial vessels with anti-submarine armament. Germany had a smaller number of merchant cruisers, and actions between vessels of this type were rare, although a notable exception was the sinking of the Hamburg South America Line *Cap Trafalgar* by the Cunarder HMS *Carmania* in the South Atlantic in September 1914.

Q-ships were designed as decoys, and originated as early as November 1914 with the British *Victoria* and French *Marguerite*. As submarines preferred not to waste torpedoes but sink smaller merchant vessels by gunfire, they usually surfaced before attacking. The earliest attempts to frustrate this were to send out a trawler with a submerged submarine following; when the U-boat surfaced to destroy the trawler, the hidden submarine would attack: the destruction of *U 40* off Aberdeen by the hired trawler *Taranaki* (armed with a 1pdr gun) and the British submarine *C 24* was the first success for this tactic. A Q-ship, however, was a small merchantman, tramp-steamer or coaster (even a small sailing-ship) with concealed guns and torpedoes, sometimes sailing under false colours; a few were purpose-built. The first successful action was the sinking of *U 36* off the Hebrides by the Q-ship *Prince Charles* in July 1915. Q-ships accounted for some eleven U-boats between that date and late 1917 (when they were withdrawn), but were only a limited success, and frustrated in part by a change of German tactics from gunnery to torpedo attack when Q-ship operations became known.

Germany also maintained a small number of disguised merchantmen, used to raid Allied shipping. Among the best-known were two which survived, *Moewe* (ex-SS *Pungo*, 4 × 5.9in guns and mines) and *Wolf* (ex-SS *Wachtfels*, 2 × 5.9in, 4 × 4.1in guns), and three which did not: *Greif* (ex-SS *Guben*, sunk two days after leaving Hamburg on a raid in 1916 by HMS *Comus* and two Armed Merchant Cruisers); *Leopard* (ex-SS *Yarrowdale*, originally captured by *Moewe*, sunk off the Shetlands in 1917 by HMS *Achilles*); and *Seeadler* (ex-*Pass of Balmaha*, a sailing-ship with concealed auxiliary engines, wrecked in the Fiji islands in August 1917).

A convoy system was finally introduced in May 1917, but because of lack of escorts did not operate fully until the end of the year, and could not have been carried out without the participation of the US Navy. The decline in loss of merchant vessels was most marked, more so when it is remembered that many of the losses incurred after mid-1917 were of vessels not participating in convoys. From January to July 1917 inclusive, 1,700 Allied and neutral merchant ships were sunk by submarines; from August to December only 739, an average monthly loss declining from 242.8 for the first seven months to 147.8 for the next five; the monthly average for 1918 was only 103.5.

The convoy system involved the escorting of numbers of merchant ships in as cohesive formation as could be achieved. The vessels used as escorts were primarily destroyers, with trawlers and a small number of larger ships, generally cruisers. A typical assembly would be for the merchantmen to form two columns, in echelon, with armed trawlers on the outside and beyond them destroyers on a zigzag course; between the two lines might be more trawlers (including one or two towing reconnaissance kite-balloons), with a destroyer and light cruiser in the lead. Larger convoys, usually consisting of 25 to 32 ships, were arranged in five or six columns, with 500 yards separating each ship from the one ahead, and 800 yards between the columns, with destroyers at the sides and head of the formation. The proportion of destroyers eventually common was eight to a convoy of 22 ships and six to a convoy of less than sixteen. Usually a convoy would cross the Atlantic on its own and rendezvous with its naval escort some 300 miles out; if submarines were suspected to be in the area, the whole convoy would adopt a zigzag course. By the end of October 1917, 99 convoys had come to Britain for a loss of only ten vessels out of 1,502, plus a further fourteen sunk when the convoys had dispersed for individual destinations upon entering coastal waters. This had forced the U-boats to restrict operations to nearer the British mainland, increasing the hazard to them: numbers of U-boats lost rose from five in 1914 to nineteen in 1915, 25 in 1916, 66 in 1917 and 74 in 1918 (plus fourteen destroyed to prevent capture). Some areas became terribly hazardous: in the last year of the war anti-submarine activity from Dover had become so effective that the German Flanders Flotilla (which lost 24 boats during the year) became known as 'the Drowning Flotilla', with the life-expectancy of its submarines only

> A by no means unique occurrence: the ultimate 'SIW':
> 'Thursday April 15/15.
> 'My first experience of a ship's Funeral. A Quarter-Master with the Troops, a Scotchman named McClay, a fine tall chap, shot himself at 5.30 a.m. with a revolver. Bullet went right through his head, through the bulk-head & into the adjoining cabin. Fortunately no-one was in the latter.
> 'The body was sewn up in canvas, covered with a Union Jack & weighted & at 11 a.m. was committed to the deep. Captain Prentice read the service, a firing party fired a volley & the Last Post was sounded on the bugle. Very sad case. Engines were stopped while service was on.'
> (Purser's log, SS *Wiltshire*, 15 April 1915)

three to four trips. Despite one criticism of the convoy system (that it slowed the Atlantic crossing by up to a week until ships were arranged into fast- and slow-sailing groups), the effect was startling: from its institution, more than 88,000 ships were conveyed, and only 436 of these were lost.

The frustration of the U-boat campaign prompted Germany to attack with surface craft, only possible on the UK–Scandinavia route. The effectiveness of such an attack was demonstrated on 17 October 1917 when a convoy of twelve merchantmen escorted by the destroyers *Mary Rose* and *Strongbow* was attacked by the German light cruisers *Brummer* and *Bremse*; both destroyers and nine merchant ships were sunk. An attack on a Lerwick–Norway convoy by German torpedo-craft was similarly successful (13 December 1917), which compelled Britain to institute closer co-operation between covering cruiser forces and merchant shipping. The final foray of the German fleet in strength, in April 1918, was conceived similarly as a raid against North Sea convoys, but in this case the British covering force was in position and the Germans turned back, the battlecruiser *Moltke* being torpedoed by *E 42* on her way home.

Generally laid by surface craft, the mine accounted for the loss of many more ships than gunfire, minelaying and sweeping being among the most important duties of naval forces. Minefields or barrages were most effective when laid for a specific purpose, both to sink enemy shipping or inhibiting movement. An example of the effect is provided by the string of twenty laid by the Turkish mine-expert Geehl parallel to the Asiatic shore of the Dardanelles on 8 March 1915. When the Allies mounted their great naval attack on 18 March, these unsuspected mines accounted for the French battleship *Bouvet* and the British *Irresistible*, damaged the British *Inflexible* and probably sank the British *Ocean* as well, causing the abandonment of the entire attack which, if successful, would have rendered unnecessary the entire Gallipoli débâcle.

Most common was the contact mine, moored to the sea bed, which exploded when a ship's keel struck one of the detonator 'horns' protruding from it. Less common was the controlled mine, detonated by an observer, and used for the protection of shore installations. Magnetic mines, detonated by the magnetic field of a ship which passed over it, were devised by Britain but introduced only in the last year of the war. Although Britain had taken second place to Germany in mine technology, her minesweeping became extremely proficient, using either purpose-built vessels or, more commonly, hired trawlers or drifters (at the armistice 120 fast sweepers and 606 trawlers and others were employed in home waters). Minesweeping generally utilized a serrated wire stretched between two vessels; this severed the mooring wires of the mines which then floated to the surface, to be destroyed by gunfire. The minesweeping force became so expert that at the armistice a flotilla of British minesweepers cleared some 600 British and Turkish mines. in the Dardanelles and cleared a passage for the fleet to Constantinople within 24 hours. British vessels destroyed almost 24,000 mines during the war; 595 British ships were sunk or damaged by mines, 214 of them minesweepers, and although these losses were considerable an equal consequence of minelaying was the absorbing of resources in mine counter-measure activity.

In calculating the comparisons between ships, many variable factors had to be considered (thickness of armour, calibre of armament, proficiency of crew, etc.), but as a rule-of-thumb a French naval officer, Lieutenant Baudry, propounded the theory that when ships of equal strength were opposed, their fighting force should be calculated as a square of their numerical strength. Thus, for example, if four ships were opposed to two of equal strength, the odds would not be two-to-one but four-to-one (square of $4 = 16$, versus square of $2 = 4$; 16:4 or 4:1). This difference was even more marked if three ships opposed one: square of $3 = 9$, versus square of $1 = 1$: or nine-to-one against the single ship.

Although ships might act independently, for concerted action the traditional squadron organization was employed, these comprising vessels of similar class or capability. This is exemplified in the orders of battle for Jutland, tabulated here, showing a typical organization and illustrating the attachment of supporting and reconnaissance vessels to the squadrons of capital ships: '*' indicates a squadron or divisional flagship.

British Grand Fleet
Battle Fleet

1ST BATTLE SQUADRON (Battleships): *Agincourt, Collingwood, Colossus,* Hercules, Marlborough,* Neptune, Revenge, St. Vincent.*

2ND BATTLE SQUADRON: *Ajax, Centurion, Conqueror, Erin, King George V,* Monarch, Orion,* Thunderer.*

4TH BATTLE SQUADRON: *Iron Duke* (fleet flagship, Admiral Sir John Jellicoe), *Bellerophon, Benbow,* Canada, Royal Oak, Superb,* Téméraire, Vanguard.*

3RD BATTLECRUISER SQUADRON: *Indomitable, Inflexible, Invincible.**

1ST CRUISER SQUADRON: *Black Prince, Defence,* Duke of Edinburgh, Warrior.*

2ND CRUISER SQUADRON: *Cochrane, Hampshire, Minotaur,* Shannon.*

4TH LIGHT CRUISER SQUADRON: *Calliope, Caroline, Comus, Constance, Royalist.*

ATTACHED LIGHT CRUISERS: *Active, Bellona, Blanche, Boadicea, Canterbury, Chester.*

4TH DESTROYER FLOTILLA: *Acasta, Achates, Ambuscade, Ardent, Broke, Christopher, Contest, Fortune, Garland, Hardy, Midge, Ophelia, Owl, Porpoise, Shark, Sparrowhawk, Spitfire, Tipperary,* Unity.*

11TH DESTROYER FLOTILLA: *Castor** (light cruiser), *Kempenfelt, Magic, Mandate, Manners, Marne, Martial, Michael, Milbrook, Minion, Mons, Moon, Morning Star, Maunsey, Mystic, Ossory.*

12TH DESTROYER FLOTILLA: *Faulknor,* Maenad, Marksman, Marvel, Mary Rose, Menace, Mindful, Mischief, Munster, Narwhal, Nesses, Noble, Nonsuch, Obedient, Onslaught, Opal.*

OTHERS: *Abdiel* (minesweeper), *Oak* (destroyer tender to *Iron Duke*).

Battlecruiser Fleet

FLAGSHIP: *Lion* (battlecruiser) (Vice-Admiral Sir David Beatty).

5TH BATTLE SQUADRON: *Barham,* Malaya, Valiant, Warspite.*

1ST BATTLECRUISER SQUADRON: *Princess Royal,* Queen Mary, Tiger.*

2ND BATTLECRUISER SQUADRON: *Indefatigable, New Zealand.**

1ST LIGHT CRUISER SQUADRON: *Cordelia, Galatea,* Inconstant, Phaeton.*

2ND LIGHT CRUISER SQUADRON: *Birmingham, Dublin, Nottingham, Southampton.*

3RD LIGHT CRUISER SQUADRON: *Birkenhead, Falmouth,* Gloucester, Yarmouth.*

1ST DESTROYER FLOTILLA: *Fearless** (light cruiser), *Acheron, Ariel, Attack, Badger, Defender, Goshawk, Hydra, Lapwing, Lizard.*

9TH & 10TH DESTROYER FLOTILLAS (COMBINED): *Landrail, Laurel, Liberty, Lydiard,* Moorsom, Morris, Termagent, Turbulent.*

13TH DESTROYER FLOTILLA: *Champion** (light cruiser), *Moresby, Narborough, Nerissa, Nestor, Nicator, Nomad, Obdurate, Onslow, Pelican, Petard.*

OTHER: *Engadine* (seaplane carrier).

German High Seas Fleet
Battle Fleet

1ST BATTLE SQUADRON: *Friedrich der Grosse* (fleet flagship, Vice-Admiral Reinhard Scheer), *Heligoland, Nassau, Oldenburg, Ostfriesland,* Posen,* Rheinland, Thüringen, Westfalen.*

2ND BATTLE SQUADRON: *Deutschland,* Hannover,* Hessen, Pommern, Schlesien, Schleswig-Holstein.*

3RD BATTLE SQUADRON: *Grosser Kurfürst, Kaiserin, König,* Kronprinz Wilhelm, Markgraf, Prinz Regent Luitpold.*

4TH SCOUT GROUP (Light Cruisers): *Frauenlob, Hamburg, München, Stettin,* *Stuttgart.*

TORPEDO FORCE: *Rostock** (light cruiser), 1st Torpedo-Boat Flotilla (four vessels), 3rd (seven), 5th (eleven), 7th (nine).

Battlecruiser Fleet

1ST SCOUT GROUP (Battlecruisers): *Derfflinger, Lützow** (flagship, Vice-Admiral Franz Hipper), *Moltke, Seydlitz, Von der Tann.*

2ND SCOUT GROUP (Light Cruisers): *Elbing, Frankfurt,** *Pillau, Wiesbaden.*

TORPEDO FORCE: *Regensburg** (light cruiser), 2nd Torpedo-Boat Flotilla (ten vessels), 6th (nine), 9th (eleven).

Wherever possible, allocation of ships was made according to their capability: the British 5th Battle Squadron, for example, attached temporarily to the Battlecruiser Fleet, comprised faster battleships or 'super-dreadnoughts' which could keep pace with the swifter battlecruisers; in the German fleet, the 2nd Battle Squadron was composed of predreadnoughts, the 1st and 3rd of dreadnoughts, and so on.

The tactical deployment of a fleet continued to include the traditional 'line of battle', in which ships were arrayed in line and pounded the enemy with broadsides. This originated in the first days of naval gunnery, and although the efficacy of other tactics had been demonstrated (for example the 'pell-mell battle' advocated by Nelson), manoeuvre in line was still used. A variation, practised with great effect at Tsushima, was the so-called 'crossing the "T"', in which one fleet (the horizontal bar of the 'T') manoeuvred to concentrate its gunnery upon the head of the enemy fleet (the vertical part of the 'T'), thus achieving local superiority against one part of the enemy's force. Although communications had improved markedly, the distances over which naval battles were fought had increased so greatly that a fleet commander might be no more sure of the overall situation than his 18th-century counterpart whose view of a battle, although at much closer range, was obscured by smoke. The most profound modern development was the range at which fire could be opened, so that naval combat was no longer the close-quarter affair as in the past: the battlecruiser action at Jutland, for example, opened at 18,500 yards and the British 5th Battle Squadron joined in at almost 20,000 yards' range. Not all action was at such long range, however: when HMS *Kent* sank *Nürnberg* at the Falklands, the last salvoes were fired into the burning German ship when *Kent*'s captain was within sufficiently close range to see that *Nürnberg*'s ensign was still flying.

The criticism most often levelled at Jellicoe for the failure to win a decisive victory at Jutland is that he was over-cautious and relied too much on pre-determined courses of action, which is in part justified (Beatty's comment that there was 'something wrong with our ships' was followed by a remark that there was also something wrong with the system). Nevertheless, Jellicoe had reasons for his caution, fearing that he might be led into a trap of submarines or

mines, and more importantly that to risk more than a few of his nation's major naval assets could jeopardize the entire outcome of the war: in effect, the possibility of destroying the High Seas Fleet was not worth risking the whole of the overall strategy against Germany.

This leads on to the wider aspect of naval strategy. In July 1915 Arthur Balfour, then First Lord of the Admiralty, identified the seven major tasks of a fleet: (1) to attack the enemy's commerce; (2) to defend its own commerce; (3) to render impotent the enemy fleet; (4) to inhibit the enemy's capacity for transporting troops by sea; (5) to transport its own troops at will; (6) to supply its own troops; (7) to support land operations. To these ends, both Britain and Germany concentrated upon the construction of capital ships, but after mid-1916 the High Seas Fleet could not risk venturing out of port, and the Grand Fleet had to remain ready in case it did; it was to a large extent stalemate. Following Jutland, German naval strategy developed upon the use of the submarine as a way of performing the first of the tasks listed by Balfour, causing a switch of emphasis from capital ships to smaller vessels capable of waging underwater commerce-raiding and submarine counter-measures. Although not obvious at the beginning of the war, most of Balfour's list could have been achieved by the use of submarines and smaller surface vessels, whereas only the support of land operations (in the form of naval bombardment) was best performed by large ships capable of delivering a substantial broadside. Ironically, the most obvious use of capital ships in this way, at the Dardanelles, was frustrated by the threat of submarines and mines. Although battle-fleets had to be maintained as long as similar forces were possessed by the enemy, and although submarine tactics were condemned by the British Admiral Sir Arthur Wilson as unfair and 'damned un-English', the course of the war demonstrated that the future of naval warfare lay with the submarine and its counter-measures.

Aerial Warfare

War in the air was not entirely new in 1914: aerial observation by balloon had been practised for more than a century, and the first anti-aircraft fire in history was as early as 1794, when an Austrian roundshot glanced off the bottom of the balloon-basket manned by J. M. J. Coutelle of the French *Compagnie d'Aérostiers* at Maubeuge. In effect, however, military aviation began less than eight years after the Wright Brothers' first powered flight: on 22 October 1911 an Italian Nieuport made the first military reconnaissance flight in the Italo–Turkish war, and on 1 November an Italian Etrich Taube dropped the first bombs in action.

Early aviation development was almost entirely civilian. Exemplified by Louis Blériot's first air crossing of the English Channel, France was the early leader in aircraft design, but the triumph in the seaplane race for the Schneider Cup of Thomas Sopwith's Tabloid in 1914 (albeit powered by a French Gnôme engine) demonstrated the importance of the British aviation industry. Despite the

Henri Farman 'pusher', aircraft suitable only for reconnaissance and by 1915 relegated to training duty, although the F20, F21 and F22 saw considerable early service with several Allied nations: they were operated by 3, 5, 6 and 7 Squadrons RFC, and 1–3 Squadrons RNAS in British service. The RFC sergeant in the foreground wears the corps' 'maternity jacket' but an ordinary cap instead of the distinctive unit side-cap.

advances in civilian recreational aviation, the military applications were not accepted in all quarters: Sir William Nicholson, British Chief of General Staff 1908–12, declared: 'Aviation is a useless and expensive fad advocated by a few individuals whose ideas are unworthy of attention.'[32]

Consequently, at the outbreak of war the combatants had at their disposal fleets of aircraft that reflected the importance placed on military aviation: Russia (which had virtually no independent national aircraft-industry) had about 300 machines, Germany about 240, France some 150; Britain managed to assemble about 60 aircraft, some having been purchased before the war for the infant Royal Flying Corps, and others recently in civilian hands (one bore the legend 'Daily Mail' on its wings!).

'. . . when I had descended to a height of 500 feet, the machine suddenly turned its toes up, promptly fell to pieces, and dived nose first to earth . . . On reaching the ground, I ceased to take any active interest in the state of health of my machine. When I regained consciousness, I found myself in a recumbent position with something biting my back. This proved, on investigation, to be the engine. At this moment the Village Idiot appeared, and having removed the engine from my spine, politely inquired "Has anything happened?" As I brushed the blood from my eyes, I casually replied "Oh, no! the d——d engine fell out," to which he hotly retorted, "Ah! you should not use such language – you have been nearly dead!" Then, and not till then, did I explain my intense dislike of himself and his ancestors to forty places of decimals and in thirty different positions. At this juncture the ambulance arrived and claimed me – "And that was the end of a Perfect Day".'

('A.V.H.' – presumably Lieutenant A.V. Heywood, RFC, in *The Return*, 18 May 1917)

The function of these aircraft was almost entirely reconnaissance, and thus the only capabilities required were stability and a capacity to fly slowly; the concept of using aircraft offensively was alien to all but a few far-sighted or wild individuals who wished to pursue a more active form of warfare, like the British Lieutenant Louis Strange, an early exponent of the fitting of a machine-gun to an aircraft, and who in August 1914 manufactured and dropped some rudimentary petrol-bombs upon some German vehicles. The ingenuity of pilots remained an important factor in the development of the aircraft as a fighting machine: an example of the miscellaneous evils dropped from the air were large iron ragbolts which a Lancashire pilot obtained from his father's loom-manufacturing company, which he flung out in handfuls upon the heads of German troops. Slightly more sophisticated aerial darts or 'flechettes' were provided officially, although *The War Illustrated* noted that the weapon was used only experimentally by the RFC, partly because of the remote chance of hitting the target, but was shunned mainly out of 'sportsmanlike feeling': 'some of the officers say that it is a dirty way of fighting, because the enemy cannot hear them coming, and because they make such nasty wounds'.[33]

When the war became static and cavalry patrolling was thus impossible, aerial reconnaissance became the only feasible method and increased the importance of aviation even in the eyes of those who had thought it an expensive fad. Initially reconnaissance involved a laborious process of sketching and annotating maps, until aerial photography was developed. This field was led initially by France; Britain trailed behind and their first photo-reconnaissance pictures were produced by the initiative of aircrew, until the value was realized officially. By mid-1915 aerial cameras had been produced which, braced into position on the aircraft, not only ensured a vertically photographed image but overcame the problem of vibration which had resulted in blurred images. Photographs of amazing clarity were produced which, aided by an increasingly sophisticated ability of interpretation, presented a view of enemy dispositions never before available to a general: by the armistice more than two-thirds of all intelligence was gathered by this means.

In the early stages of the war various methods of airborne artillery spotting had been attempted (the indication of a target and corrections to aim being made by reporting the fall of shot), including the use of signal-flags (difficult for gunners to see when waved from an aircraft), Klaxon horns signalling in code (difficult to hear and dependent upon wind-direction to carry the sound to the gunners), light-signalling and, more successfully, the use of coloured, coded flares. The process was really only made effective by the development of wireless telegraphy, using wireless sets carried in the aircraft and devices like the British 'clock code', a transparent celluloid disc bearing concentric circles identified by letter and radial lines identified by number. This was laid over a map and the exact point of the fall of a shell in relation to a specified target was relayed to the gunner, who had a similar 'clock', simply by sending the message 'Z2', 'D4', etc.

For general reconnaissance and artillery-ranging, aircraft became invaluable; and from this developed the concept of air combat. Anti-aircraft fire, by artillery or small arms, was persistent but not effective:

'F stands for "Fritz" who flies in the sky,
To bring down the brute we've had many a try,
But the shells we shoot with, all pass him by
And fall in Mesopotamia'.[34]

The interdiction of aerial reconnaissance was thus best achieved by other aircraft. The first aircraft armament was no more than small arms carried by the observer or pilot, with which to take pot shots at the enemy, a most ineffective system, and hence the mounting of machine-guns on aircraft. The first victim of air combat fell as early as 5 October 1914 when a German Aviatik scout was shot down near Rheims by the Hotchkiss gun mounted at the front of Sergeant Joseph Frantz's French Voisin, and operated by his observer, Corporal Quénault. However, aerial combat only developed fully after the development of forward-firing machine-guns which could be operated by the pilot of a single-seater 'scout' aircraft, producing the first 'fighters'. Previously, guns were fired by the observer (in the front cockpit of a 'pusher' aircraft, i.e., with the propeller at the rear, or the rear cockpit of a 'tractor', with the airscrew at the front); guns mounted on the upper wing of a single-seater to fire over the propeller, or sideways from the cockpit, were not very successful. In order to fire the gun through the propeller, an interruptor-gear had to be devised, so that the gun would fire only when the propeller was out of line; the French manufacturer Raymond Saulnier made a rudimentary version, but it persisted in shooting propellers to pieces. A cruder solution, designed in con-

The detail attainable by aerial photography was minute: in this photograph of an unidentified canal-crossing on the Western Front, individual soldiers are visible by the barricade at one end of the bridge, and behind them, on the road beside a destroyed building, a lorry.

junction with the pre-war racing pilot Roland Garros, was to affix deflector plates to the blades of the propeller to turn away rounds which hit it. On 1 April 1915 Garros, flying a Morane–Saulnier near Ostend, shot down a German with his forward-firing gun. It remained a secret weapon for less than three weeks: Garros was forced down behind German lines on 18 April and the deflector-plates were copied immediately. Within months, however, the Dutch designer Anthony Fokker had perfected the interruptor-gear and by August 1915 the Fokker EI monoplane had achieved dominance by means of their synchronized machine-guns, enabling the pilot to aim his entire aircraft at the enemy.

This initiated a struggle for dominance of the air: at times over the Western Front (the only part of the war in which major aerial combat occurred) air superiority was achieved by one side of the other, but generally this was localized or very brief, as each side continually improved their aircraft, the balance of superiority swinging continually from one side to the other. The original 'Fokker Scourge' was cancelled by the next generation of Allied fighters such as the Nieuport Scout; then Germany responded with the 'D-type' fighters so that by late 1916 the Allies were again losing aircraft in numbers like those which fell to the early Fokkers. Following 'Bloody April' 1917, in which the Royal Flying Corps was decimated, new Allied machines (notably the Sopwith Camel and SE5) caused the pendulum to swing again, though the re-emergence of Allied superiority was due not only to quality but quantity of their aircraft, the Allies having the manufacturing capacity to produce larger numbers of machines than Germany during the closing stages of the war.

Air warfare produced a phenomenon almost unique, in the 'ace', a high-scoring pilot. Although for propaganda reasons those who performed brave deeds on land or at sea might be accorded the status of popular hero, the position of

the 'ace' was more enhanced, such men being regarded as the cavaliers of modern war. Although, appropriate to this perception, an element of chivalry probably did exist between opposing fliers in the early stages of the war, it is at odds with the awful reality of air combat: that if the instability of the aircraft were survived, there was always the prospect of burning to death in the air (no parachutes were carried), or of inexperienced pilots being literally massacred by aces with the ruthlessness of an executioner. Although those in the trenches found it difficult to believe, the pressures upon pilots were probably just as intense as those upon the infantry subaltern.

The entire structure of aviation services was altered by the emergence of the forward-firing machine-gun. Originally aircraft were all general-purpose machines; now, with the development of 'scouts' or fighters, aircraft were designed for specific tasks. As the 'pusher' became outdated, it was usual (though not universal) to seat the pilot in the

Fokker EII, one of the **Eindecker** *(monoplane) aircraft which temporarily achieved complete dominance over Allied machines. The black cross on wings, tail and fuselage was the universal German recognition-symbol.*

Maurice Farman MF11, known as the 'Shorthorn' in British service; seen here in Mesopotamia.

front cockpit, with the observer at the rear with a traversible machine-gun on a pillar or, later, a ring mounting, to act as defence for a reconnaissance machine or for additional offence for a two-seater fighter. (Classifications were not rigid: it was always possible for one machine to perform a number of functions). Increasing importance was given to technical characteristics, speed, rate of climb or manoeuvrability, as aircraft were no longer basically stable observation-platforms; such factors attained relevance equal to the armament and skill of the pilot.

Organization and tactics changed with the advances in aircraft design. Although individual expeditions always continued, formation flying developed, the common tactical unit being a flight of six aircraft, employed offensively in seeking out enemy aircraft, or defensively in protecting less-manoeuvrable reconnaissance or light bomber aircraft. Such tactics could be conducted with considerable sophistication, the various elements flying in formation and 'layers', each component part of a force with an allotted task

'I would especially warn you against going out with a cheap watch. An unreliable article is worse than useless and may be the means of getting the owner of the watch into very serious trouble. This is a point well worth the attention of the lady friends of officers. If the allowance from pater will not allow of the purchase of a really good article, find some other present for your young hero – say a waterproof writing-case and a good fountain pen. Of course, the wrist-watch is the fashion of the moment. The only drawback I have heard urged against it is that if you are wounded some low-bred Pomeranian (soldier, I mean, not dog) may be tempted to cut off the hand as the quickest way of getting at the booty. The risk, however, is small, if existent, and, after all, war is a game in which one takes one's chances . . .'

('The Oracle', in *Navy & Army Illustrated*, 24 April 1915)

One of the most important developments in aviation warfare was the interrupter-gear which permitted a machine-gun to fire forward through the propeller arc; this is the propeller, gun and interrupter-mechanism on a German Rumpler.

A German Parabellum machine-gun with drum-magazine, as operated by the observer of a two-seater aircraft.

British FE2b, a two-seater 'pusher' which although outclassed by later generations of German fighters, remained in use with the RFC and later Independent Air Force as a night bomber, and for anti-Zeppelin, home-defence work.

The fragility of aircraft is evident from pictures of the remains of crashes; this is the Henri Farman F27 which crashed on 17 June 1915 after its pilot and passenger (neither strapped in) fell out at 700 feet. The pilot was Rex Warneford, VC, who had been the first to shoot down a Zeppelin; he died before his injuries could be treated. The manufacturer's 'HF' monogram is visible on the remains of the rudder.

Aerial photograph of a French trench-line, shell-craters producing an almost lunar landscape.

1909 'Portable Hotchkiss' machine-gun as fitted in the front cockpit of a 'pusher' aircraft; in US Army service this weapon was known as the Benèt-Mercié machine-rifle.

The giant aircraft was largely a Russian development; Professor Igor Sikorskii (or Sikorsky), on the right of the cockpit in this illustration, designed a number of varieties of huge bomber, noted both for their enclosed cabins and their four engines, the Ilya Mourometz series developing from Sikorskii's twin-engined 'Great Baltic'.

'Sergeant, addressing his squad with a very serious air during a few moments' "stand easy" – "I don't know whether all you men read orders carefully last night, but in case you didn't, it may be well to remind you that in the event of General Joffre passing a message down the line that peace has been concluded, there is to be no demonstration of any kind – no shouting, no cheering or anything like that. The sanitary squad will immediately fall in and fill up the trenches, and the rest will go back to their respective homes as quietly as possible!" And one or two open-mouthed heroes took it all in!'

(*The Return*, p. 17, 16 June 1916)

determined by the attributes of the aircraft. In the last year of the war, for example, a British fighter force (operating in squadrons twelve strong) could be 'layered' so that SE5s at 12,000–14,000 feet had higher-flying Bristol fighters above them (at about 18,000 feet) and Sopwith Camels below, engaging lower-flying enemy aircraft and performing ground attacks. Massed operations involving 'circuses' of 30 or more fighters were not uncommon in the later stages of the war.

Bombing assumed increased importance (especially on the part of Germany and France) as the war progressed. Light bombing was aimed principally at the enemy front-line troops and immediate supports; strategic bombing was made feasible by the development of longer-range aircraft

The skeleton framework of a burned Zeppelin: the consecutively numbered LZ32 and LZ33 were both lost over Essex on 24 September 1916, LZ32 shot down with the loss of all her crew near Billericay, and LZ33 being destroyed by her crew after a forced landing near Little Wigborough.

No. 1 Sqdn., RAF at Clairmarais, 1918; the aircraft are SE5as, probably Britain's best all-purpose fighter; 200hp Wolseley Viper or 200–240hp Hispano–Suiza engine, maximum speed 132mph at 6,500 feet, ceiling 20,000 feet, rate of climb 765ft/min; forward-firing synchronized Vickers and Lewis gun fixed on top of upper wing.

capable of carrying a worthwhile bomb-load. The German 'Gotha' raids on Britain took over this role from the airships when these became vulnerable to improved Allied aircraft, though improved British air defences forced the Germans to suspend daylight raids after a few months. Neither side profited greatly from strategic bombing, the fear it induced among a helpless civilian population and the defensive resources it occupied (urgently required elsewhere) probably far outweighing any temporary damage caused to industrial targets.

The airship was probably one of the greatest disappointments of the war, and was used primarily by Germany. (The term 'Zeppelin' applied officially only to those based on Count Zeppelin's design: the naval Schütte-Lanz airship,

for example, was not a Zeppelin although often classed under the incorrectly-used generic term 'Zepp'). Although also used for reconnaissance, it was as a strategic bomber that the Zeppelin attained its infamous and sinister reputation: in popular opinion there was something almost unearthly about these gigantic, slow-moving craft which could steal up under cover of darkness initially at an altitude which made them almost impervious to air-attack, and drop bombs indiscriminately upon sleeping civilians. They became much less effective when aircraft were developed that were capable of reaching their altitude and of shooting them down with incendiary rockets; and they were also much more dependent upon meterological conditions than were aircraft. Despite the number of raids mounted (some in strength: the largest, September 1916, involved sixteen airships), damage caused was low in relation to effort. The combined number of heavy bomber and airship raids on Britain was only just in excess of 100; conversely, Anglo-French raids on Germany from 1915 numbered 675.

Smaller, 'captive' balloons were used for observation and aerial defence. The former, generally moored a short distance behind the front line, were protected by anti-aircraft artillery and were targets sufficiently hazardous to engage that the destruction of one was usually counted as a 'kill' in an ace's score; some pilots became especially expert in this duty, such as Belgium's top-scorer, Willy Coppens. (The crews of observation-balloons were the only personnel customarily issued with parachutes, as tethered balloons could not be winched down sufficiently quickly to save their lives in the event of air attack.) Smaller balloons, and occasionally kites, were used as aerial obstacles, with wires hanging from them, forcing enemy aircraft to fly around or above. Although the Italians claimed great success for this device, its significance was probably limited, although German defences of this nature did claim a Handley-Page bomber near Bruges.

An aircraft role which increased in prominence was ground-attack and army co-operation. Although from the beginning reconnaissance or 'contact patrols' had been flown, as the war progressed aircraft were developed specifically for operation against the enemy ground forces, involving the armour-plating of aircraft fuselages (as a protection against small-arms fire from the ground upon the low-flying ground-attack aircraft), and even downward-angled machine-guns to fire upon troops.

Naval aviation also developed during the war, with the facility for flying aircraft off purposely converted carriers; and seaplanes could also be accommodated on ordinary warships. The principal use of maritime aviation was for reconnaissance, though heavily armed flying-boats carried out anti-submarine patrols, and naval units also flew raids or patrols from coastal or other stations.

In the techniques of air warfare, although tactics changed with technical developments, certain features remained standard. The manoeuvrability of 'scouts' was paramount, both to attack and to evade destruction, and by 1916 even spinning nose-dives were used deliberately to throw off an attacker, whereas previously this had indicated a loss of control and speed and was the prelude to a crash. By 1917, originated by French pilots, the 'rolling' of aircraft (rolling along the logitudinal axis) was commonly practised, and 'looping' enabled rapid turns to be made while gaining height, most famously the 'Immelmann turn', named after its legendary progenitor.

The D1 was the first of the Albatros scouts, which regained the aerial domination once enjoyed by the Fokker monoplanes. Powered by a 160hp Mercedes engine, it had a maximum speed of 110mph at sea level, and carried twin, forward-firing synchronized Spandaus.

The enormous size and almost eerie appearance of the Zeppelin airship is evident from this study; the crew was accommodated in the gondolas on the underside.

The British Handley Page 0/100, and the improved and more prolific 0/400, was one of the principal heavy bombers of the war, the 0/400 having a bomb-load of 1,792lb. Twin-engined with the 266hp Rolls-Royce Eagles, later more powerful engines including the Eagle VIII or 275hp Sunbeam; maximum speed rose to 98mph. Three crew; armament included 2 or 4 Lewis guns in the nose and rear cockpit, and one firing below and behind from a trapdoor in the fuselage.

Such aerobatics were not possible for the slower, less manoeuvrable two-seaters, whose prime defence was not eluding the enemy but the observer's machine-gun(s); two-seater pilots were also often less experienced. When attacking two-seaters, tactics depended upon whether the assailant was alone. The ideal point of attack was from below and to the rear, thus shielded from the observer's view. When flying in pairs, one fighter would approach broadside-on and open fire at long range, to distract the observer, while the second came up from behind and opened fire at 30 to 50 yards' range. When attacked from this direction, a two-seater would almost always turn in an attempt to bring the gun to bear on the fighter; to frustrate this, the fighter would then turn in the opposite direction before turning back, using its extra speed and manoeuvrability, and again come up from below and behind to make a second attack.

When attacking alone, the best tactic was to dive upon the target out of the sun, which demanded considerable skill. Although the pilot of a fighter would bank and dive as soon as he became aware of the attack, many air combats were decided in the first seconds: 'Beware the Hun in the sun!' was a salutory warning. Later in the war some observers fixed mirrors in line with their gun, which if focused accurately could reflect back the rays of the sun and blind an attacking pilot. Given the speed, rate of climb and manoeuvrability of the later fighters, it should have been easy to dispose of less-experienced crews flying inferior two-seaters; yet a resolute crew could make a two-seater a formidable opponent, and a number of aces fell to such 'inferior' combinations.

In combat between aircraft of approximately equal ability, the pilot's skill and experience were even more crucial. The most skilled made use of cloud, ideally flying on the very edge to render themselves invisible but able to see below. Cloud-cover enabled a pilot to swoop upon an enemy and then return to invisibility, but increased the risks of being ambushed by others taking advantage of the clouds. Maximum altitude was also important, as combats would descend as they progressed, often reaching almost ground level.

On the Western Front, it was the Allies who were almost always on the offensive, so most combat occurred over German-held territory, which increased Allied casualties as damaged machines that were able to land generally came down in German territory. The losses of 'Bloody April' 1917, when the RFC sustained casualties approaching 30 per cent per week, were not caused exclusively by the obsolescence of aircraft and inexperience of crews; the insistance by the military command of continuous reconnaissance, contact and offensive patrols was a main contributory factor. With a more defensive strategy, as used by the Germans, the losses would not have been so catastrophic. (The inexperience of aviators was a problem difficult to overcome, given the necessity for a constant supply of reinforcements: the French estimate of the time needed to train a proficient pilot was about four months' flying training, and four months' patrol-work at the front; many were lucky to survive a quarter of the latter period.)

The development of air warfare was perhaps the most important military result arising from the war. In a progression of remarkable speed, air warfare had evolved from a little-regarded adjunct to ground forces to a major factor in its own right, to the extent that aerial superiority

became an essential part of a successful military campaign; and the aviation services began to develop into independent entities, no longer administered wholly by the ground forces. The British Royal Air Force, by 1918 the first independent force as well as the largest, at the armistice numbered some 22,500 aircraft and almost 300,000 personnel, almost three times the magnitude of the entire BEF of 1914.

Footnotes

1. *The News*, 23 November 1906.
2. *The Listening Post*, quoted in *Made in the Trenches*, ed. Sir Frederick Treves Bt., London, 1916, p. 126.
3. *Bayonet Training* (1916), pp. 5–6.
4. Ibid., p. 19.
5. Ibid., p. 5.
6. *Small Wars: Their Principles and Practice* C. E. Callwell, London, 1896; 1906 edn., p. 399.
7. *The Training and Employment of Platoons* (1918), p. 22.
8. For example, see eye-witness reports by Ian Hamilton in *A Staff Officer's Scrap Book during the Russo–Japanese War*. London, 1905.
9. Unidentified KOYLI private, in *The War Stories of Private Thomas Atkins*, London, 1914, p. 76.
10. *The Training and Employment of Platoons* (1918), pp. 22–3.
11. *Our Army at the Front*. H. Broun, New York, 1918, p. 120.
12. *History of the 51st (Highland) Division 1914–18*. Edinburgh, 1921, p. 114.
13. *Berliner Tageblatt*, quoted in *The Times History of the War*, London, 1916, VI, p. 382.
14. *With a B-P Scout in Gallipoli*. E. Y. Priestman, London, 1916, pp. 34–5; published in the year following Priestman's death at Suvla.
15. *Atkins at War*, ed. J. A. Kilpatrick, London, 1914, p. 31.
16. Priestman, op. cit., p. 53.
17. *Infantry Training* (1914), p. 127.
18. Ibid., p. 128.
19. Unidentified KOYLI private, in *The War Stories of Private Thomas Atkins*, London 1914, p. 76.
20. Kilpatrick, op. cit., p. 31.
21. *Infantry Training* (1914), p. 139.
22. Ibid., p. 138.
23. *The First World War*, Lieutenant-Colonel C. à C Repington, London, 1920, I, p. 229.
24. *The Training and Employment of Platoons* (1918), p. 28.
25. Ibid., p. 30.
26. *The First Hundred Thousand*. Ian Hay, London and Edinburgh 1915; Paris edn., p. 237.
27. *Trooper Bluegum at the Dardanelles*. O. Hogue, London, 1916, p. 91.
28. Anonymous poem, *BEF Times*, 20 January 1917.
29. *1914*. Field Marshal Viscount French, London, 1919, p. 120.
30. *Tank Warfare*. F. Mitchell, 1933 (rep. Stevenage, 1987), p. 264.
31. *Infantry Training* (1914), p. 139.
32. Quoted in *The Royal Flying Corps: a History*, G. Norris, London, 1965, p. 14.
33. *The War Illustrated*, 23 January 1915, p. 558.
34. *BEF Times*, 20 January 1917.

References

The sources listed below are concerned with weapons, equipment, tactics and associated subjects. Contemporary manuals (which are of great value) are not listed; naval and aviation subjects are listed in Section V.

Ashworth, T. *Trench Warfare 1914–1918: the Live and Let Live System*. London, 1980.

Barrie, A. *War Underground*. London, 1962

Baynes, J. *Morale: A Study of Men and Courage*. London, 1967

Bidwell, S., and Graham, D. *Fire Power: British Army Weapons and Theories of War 1904–1945*. London, 1982.

Brooks, S. *Armoured Warfare: the Development and Role of Armoured Fighting Vehicles*. London, 1980

Brown, D. G. *The Tank in Action*. London and Edinburgh, 1920

Chamberlain, P., and Ellis, C. *British and German Tanks of World War I*. London, 1969

Ellis, C., and Bishop, D. *Military Transport of World War I*. London, 1970

Ellis, J. *The Social History of the Machine-Gun*. London, 1975

Fitzsimons, B. (ed.). *Tanks and Weapons of World War I*. London. 1973 (extracted from Purnell *History of the First World War*)

Fletcher, D. *Landships: British Tanks in the First World War*. London, 1984

— *War Cars: British Armoured Cars in the First World War*. London, 1987

Foulkes, Major-General C. H. *'Gas!': The Story of the Special Brigade*. London, 1934

Fries, A. A. and West, C. J. *Chemical Warfare*. New York, 1921

Fuller, Colonel (later General) J. F. C. *Tanks in the Great War*. London, 1920

Grieve, W. G., and Newman, B. *Tunnellers: the Story of the Tunnelling Companies, Royal Engineers*. London, 1936

Griffith, P. *Forward into Battle: Fighting Tactics from Waterloo to Vietnam*. Chichester, 1981 (excellent general survey)

Haber, L. *The Poisonous Cloud: Chemical Warfare in the First World War*. Oxford, 1986

Haldane, J. B. S. *Callinicus: A Defence of Chemical Warfare*. London, 1925 (a defence of the humane nature of poison gas!)

Hesketh-Pritchard, Major H. *Sniping in France*. London, 1920 (personal memoir much concerned with marksmanship)

Hogg, I. V. *The Guns 1914–18*. New York, 1971

Hogg, I. V., and Weeks, J. *Military Small Arms of the Twentieth Century*. London, 1973, rep. 1991.

Holmes, R. *Firing Line*. London, 1985 (the experience of war over a wider period)

Knötel, R., Knötel, H., and Sieg, H. *Handbuch der Uniformkunde*. Hamburg, 1937, rep. 1964; English edn. *Uniforms of the World*. London, 1980 (general history of military uniforms)

Liddell Hart, Sir Basil. *The Tanks: The History of the Royal Tank Regiment and its Predecessors, Heavy Branch Machine Gun Corps, Tank Corps and Royal Tank Corps 1914–1945*. London, 1959

Liepmann, H. *Death from the Skies: A Study of Gas and Microbial Warfare*. London, 1937

Lloyd, A. *The War in the Trenches*. London, 1976

Mirouze, L. *World War I Infantry in Colour Photographs*. London 1990

Mitchell, F. *Tank Warfare: the Story of the Tanks in the Great War*. London, 1933; rep. Stevenage, 1987

Mollo, A. *Army Uniforms of World War I*. Poole, 1977 (the best work on the subject)

Newman, B. *The Cavalry Went Through*. London, 1930. (Novel based on the discovery of a military genius who won the war in 1917 by a massive Allied victory; basically the emergence of a figure like the Napoleon of the era of the Italian campaign. Interesting tactical scenario)

Prentiss, A. M. *Chemicals in War*. New York, 1937

Purves, A. A. *The Medals, Decorations & Orders of the Great War 1914–1918*. 1975; rev. edn. Polstead, Suffolk, 1989

Rogers, Colonel H. C. B. *Tanks in Battle*. London, 1965

Rommel, E. *Infantry Attacks*. London, 1990

Terraine, J. *White Heat: The New Warfare 1914–18*. London, 1982

Walter, J. (ed.). *Guns of the First World War*. London, 1988 (reprint of *The Text Book of Small Arms*. London, 1909)

Wintringham, T., and Blashford-Snell, J. *Weapons and Tactics*. London, 1973 (enlargement of Wintringham's original study, published 1943; general survey which puts the tactics of 1914–18 excellently into perspective)

Wynne, C. W. *If Germany Attacks: Lessons from the Western Front 1915–17*. London, 1940

III
THE WARRING
NATIONS

THE WARRING NATIONS

This section, which comprises a review of the states involved in the war, cannot be comprehensive; military organization, equipment and uniform is not covered exhaustively, and many exceptions to generalizations are not examined in depth. For a much more exhaustive survey of uniforms, reference is recommended to *Army Uniforms of World War I*, A. Mollo, Poole, 1977, but even this does not cover all combatant states. Similarly, it has not been possible to list all naval vessels, so for the larger navies only some 'capital ships' are mentioned; for those detailed individually, only main armament has been listed (for example, for *Friedrich der Grosse*, listed here with armament consisting of 12 × 12in and 14 × 5.9in guns, also included in its complete armament 12 × 24pdrs, 4 × 14pdrs (anti-aircraft), and 5 × 20in torpedo tubes). In conventional British terminology of the period, naval armament is classified with calibre in inches (i.e., '12in') irrespective of the system of measurement in use with the state in question, as being the most convenient way of comparing vessels' armament, even though this occasionally involves the use of conflicting statistics (in the above case, for example, secondary armament may be found described as either 6in or 5.9in). Aircraft are noted only briefly, identifying only type and function, as technical details (engine, armament, performance, etc.) are available in specialized publications. The references listed after many entries include some of the recognized 'standard works', biographical or autobiographical material not covered in the references to Section IV, and some titles primarily of use in providing a contemporary perspective (usually obvious from date of publication). As noted in the introduction, most references quoted are in English; exceptions include important official histories or the uniform-references of Moritz Ruhl, etc.

ADEN

From its annexation in 1839 Aden had been part of British India, under the authority of the governor of Bombay; its position was of considerable significance, as a station serving the Suez Canal and as a trading depot for the interior of Arabia and the Somali coast. Its garrison comprised the Aden Brigade of the Indian Army (23rd Sikh Pioneers, 109th Infantry, the Aden Troop of cavalry and one British battalion, which from December 1914 was the 1/1st Brecknockshire Battalion).

The first offensive against Aden by Turkish forces in the Yemen (commanded by a most active Circassian, 'Ali Sa'id Pasha) was driven off in November 1914 by 29 Indian Brigade, then at Aden en route to India. A more serious operation was made in July 1915, when the Turks and Arab allies moved into the sultanate of Lahej, friendly to Britain, some 25 miles from Aden. The Aden Brigade marched out to meet them, but stricken by the climate and after accidentally killing the Sultan of Lahej, they were forced to retire on another outpost, Sheikh Othman, which also had

to be abandoned. In response, 28 (Frontier Force) Brigade was dispatched from India, under the command of Major-General Sir George Younghusband, ex-commander of the Corps of Guides and an officer of immense experience. He drove the Turks from Sheikh Othman on 20 July, and skirmishing continued throughout the year. In January 1916 troops from Aden supported local Arabs against the Turks and fought a successful small action at Subar, near Lahej. The defensive perimeter around Aden was extended to a radius of eleven miles, and although skirmishes occurred until the end of the war, there was no further major action. To support the garrison, small units of Arabs were taken into British service, including an Arab Legion (1st Yemen Infantry), but their service was limited to patrolling.

AFGHANISTAN

The presence of Afghanistan on its frontier had been the cause of much trouble for British India, and the outbreak of the World War caused consternation lest the Afghans took the opportunity of Britain's preoccupation to interfere with the frontier province. As soon as hostilities commenced, the Government of India requested the Amir Habibulla Khan of Afghanistan to maintain his state's neutrality, which he pledged to do in return for a guarantee of Afghan independence.

The entry of Turkey into the war placed the Amir in a difficult situation, as religious fanatics and others within his country began to agitate for support of their co-religionists and to take advantage of British preoccupation elsewhere. Recognizing the potential, Germany and Turkey sent a joint mission to Kabul in 1915, led by the geologist, explorer and artillery captain, Oscar Niedermayer, who eluded the Russian troops detailed to intercept him and reached Kabul in late September. Despite internal pressures, Habibulla kept the Anglo-Indian authorities informed of developments, and after weeks of prevarication spent even longer in negotiations with Niedermayer. In January 1916 he agreed a draft treaty with Germany, but demanded such huge subsidies and material assistance that it was clearly pointless, and Niedermayer left empty-handed in May 1916. For the remainder of the war, Habibulla kept his dissidents in order, maintained Afghan neutrality, and used his influence to discourage insurrection in the British frontier territories (disturbance was restricted to comparatively minor risings by the Mohmands and Mahsuds, 1915–17). In return for this remarkable achievement, Habibulla requested a seat at the Versailles peace conference (which was rejected, as Afghanistan had not been engaged actively in the war), and for favours from Britain. The Viceroy of India, Lord Chelmsford, grateful for Habibulla's wartime diplomacy, was sympathetic; but the Amir was shot to death in his bed on 20 February 1919. His brother was blamed, but the circumstances are unclear; but whatever the case, the removal of Habibulla led directly to the Third Afghan War (1919).

Reference
McMunn, Lieutenant-General
  Sir George F. *Afghanistan, from
  Darius to Amanullah.* 1928

AFRICA

Military operations in central and southern Africa centered around the four German colonies, the largest in area and population being German East Africa (acquired 1885), the others Cameroon, Togoland and South-West Africa (all 1884). That conflict should spread here was inevitable, as they were surrounded by colonies belonging to Britain, France, Belgium and Portugal. With the exception of South Africa, where the armed forces were predominantly of European origin, most of the colonies employed large numbers of native troops or Askaris; and although some European units were employed in Africa, most forces were raised in the continent or (like the German colonial troops) formed specifically for service there.

Togoland

Togoland, on the Gulf of Guinea, was bounded by the French colonies of Senegal, Niger and Dahomey, and by the British Gold Coast; its harbours and coastal radio stations were of considerable strategic value, and thus their possession was of great importance to the Allies. Lome, the capital, was founded by Germany on the site of a small fishing village. For some time before the war there had been an exodus of natives to the Gold Coast and Dahomey, a reaction to the harsh treatment by the German administration; at the outbreak of war the governor, Adolf Friedrich, Duke of Mecklenburg, was on leave, and Major von Döring was in command; he had at his disposal some 300 European troops and 1,200 askaris.

Although Britain had a strong garrison at Freetown, Sierra Leone, to protect the maritime coaling-station (including 1st West India and West African Regiments), only the West African Frontier Force was available for service in the German colonies: the Nigeria Regiment (33 companies), the Gold Coast Regiment (eight companies), the Sierra Leone battalion and Gambia company, some of which could not be spared from internal security duties; the French troops in French Equatorial Africa (about 7,600) and Dahomey/Ivory Coast (about 3,500) were restricted similarly.

At the outbreak of war Döring proposed that his and the adjoining Allied colonies should be declared neutral, thus securing the important German radio station at Kamina. When this was rejected, he abandoned the coastal region and fell back upon Kamina, before which post he was engaged by converging Allied forces, about 590 of the Gold Coast Regiment and some 160 Senegalese Tirailleurs. The

Germans beat off an attack on 22 August 1914, but on the approach of stronger Allied columns, Döring blew up the Kamina radio station and surrendered on 26 August. Little opposition was encountered in the remainder of Togoland, which during the war was divided into British and French zones of control.

Cameroon

The German colony of *Kamerun* was bordered by Nigeria, French Equatorial Africa, and (neutral) Spanish Guinea; the principal target for Allied attention was the harbour and radio station of Duala. The garrison, commanded by Colonel Zimmermann, consisted of some 200 German and 1,550 native troops, about 40 German and 1,250 native police, and newly formed units of German settlers and sailors and askaris. After the first Allied probes were repulsed, a stronger force was organized under the command of the Inspector-General of the West African Frontier Force, Major-General Charles Dobell, initially with about 4,300 British and French native troops (about equal in proportion), with Allied naval support. Allied forces landed on the coast near Duala on 25 September, shelled the town next day, and on 27 September the German authorities capitulated, having destroyed the radio station; but Zimmermann (with materials to open a new radio station in the interior) withdrew, leaving the Allies in control only of the coastal regions. Little progress was made by Allied columns in the north, and further reinforcements were required before an attempt could be made upon the next main town, Yaunde, as Zimmermann's command had increased to some 2,800 Germans and up to 20,000 natives. Allied strategy involved an advance by Dobell from Duala with some 750 Europeans and 7,500 native troops (about half of them French and Belgian); by General Aymerich (commander-in-chief in French Equatorial Africa) with about 7,000, from the east; and Brigadier-General Cunliffe with 4,000 troops from the north. Belgian forces from the Congo were added to Aymerich's command, and the reinforcements included troops from Freetown (West India Regiment) and the Indian 5th Light Infantry. Against determined German resistance progress in both northern and southern regions was slow; but faced with an impossible situation, Zimmermann and the German governor, Ebermaier, abandoned Yaunde (occupied by the Allies on 1 January 1916) and, evading Allied attempts to intercept them, took their surviving 800 German and 6,000 native troops into Spanish Guinea, where they were interned. Having been besieged for some eighteen months, the final German outpost, Mora in the extreme north, surrendered on 18 February 1916.

South-West Africa

The colony of South-West Africa (now Namibia) had two main ports, Lüderitz Bay or Angra Pequena, and Swakopmund. Upon the outbreak of war, the Germans abandoned the coast and retired on the capital, Windhoek, some 200

German Camel troops, South-West Africa. In combat the distinctive slouch hat was sometimes worn with both sides of the brim upturned, making it a very difficult target.

miles from Swakopmund, German strength being about 2,000 troops and 7,000 reservists. Following the South African rebellion (see 'South Africa'), Louis Botha, commanding the South African forces, launched a double-pronged offensive against South-West Africa, one under his own command from Swakopmund, and one (originally of three columns from Lüderitz Bay and South Africa) under Smuts. The German commander, General von Heydebreck, withdrew into the interior, and following the capture of Windhoek by Botha (20 May 1915) the German governor, Dr. Seitz, proposed a partition of the colony, on the strength of the German forces still at large in the north. Botha refused, continued his advance, and the last German forces surrendered at Tsumeb on 9 July 1915.

German East Africa

In contrast to the rapid collapse of Togoland and South-West Africa, and the delayed collapse of Cameroon, the German colony of East Africa was by far the most difficult to overcome, partly because of the strength of the German forces (probably around 10,000 initially) and partly because of the German commander, Colonel Paul von Lettow-Vorbeck, who proved himself a master at guerrilla warfare.

The colony, about nine-tenths of which later formed British Tanganyika, was bordered by British East Africa in the north, Portuguese East Africa in the south, and Uganda, Belgian Congo, Northern Rhodesia and Nyasaland in the west. The chief towns were Dar-es-Salaam and the port of Tanga, both on the eastern littoral. From early 1914 Lettow-Vorbeck was military commander, and from July 1912 the civil governor was Dr. Albert Schnee. The most important strategic feature, however, was the Uganda railway, just over the northern border, connecting Uganda with the British port of Mombasa. Initially the British forces available to confront the Germans were only about 1,500

Europeans and 2,300 natives (in Uganda and British East Africa combined), and the Germans were able to attack the railway without threat of a serious counter-offensive.

To reinforce the British presence, two Indian Army expeditionary forces were sent to East Africa: Brigadier-General J. M. Stewart's 'Force C', to support the troops holding the border between British and German East Africa (29th Punjabis, two composite Imperial Service battalions comprising half-battalions from Bhurtpore, Jind, Kapur-thala and Rampur), and artillery; and Major-General A. E. Aitken's 'Force B' comprising 27 Bangalore Brigade and an Imperial Service Brigade, including Indian troops of very poor quality. This force landed at Tanga on 2 November 1914; the Germans, reinforced by rail from the interior, beat off the assault with some ease, some of the Indians behaving badly, and 'Force B' was withdrawn on 5 November, covered by the most reliable units, 2/Loyal North Lancashire and Kashmir Rifles. The vast quantity of munitions they abandoned was an invaluable asset to Lettow-Vorbeck's isolated command.

Britain adopted a defensive posture, awaiting reinforcement; but Lettow-Vorbeck waged an effective guerrilla war against the Uganda railway, including a successful action at Jasin (18 January 1915), which forced Britain to divert more resources to East Africa, which was the Germans' main aim. Sir Horace Smith-Dorrien was nominated to take command of the British forces, but was prevented by illness, and command was given to Lieutenant-General Jan Smuts, whose forces included not only Indian and East African units, but reinforcements from Britain, West Africa and South Africa.

Despite a considerable numerical superiority, and an excellent leader in Smuts, British operations were rendered extremely difficult by the nature of the terrain and the unwillingness of Lettow-Vorbeck to engage in a major

His Majesty's armoured train Simba, *used to protect the Uganda railway.*

action, seeking only to evade capture and thus tie down the maximum Allied resources. So resourceful were the Germans that they were able to manufacture what they could not capture (even producing their own whisky and cigars!), and utilized the guns of the cruiser *Königsberg*, destroyed in East African waters, to augment their artillery, which included a plentiful quantity of machine-guns.

Smuts planned an advance on multiple fronts, his own force and that of the South African Major-General Jacob van Deventer advancing from British East Africa, amphibious forces occupying the coast and advancing south from Lake Victoria, the Nyasaland and Rhodesia Field Force advancing north over the southern border of German East Africa, and a Belgian force moving from the Congo to seize

Ruanda and Urundi on the north-west border. Gradually Lettow-Vorbeck was forced out of the highlands, but this supremely skilful leader could not be cornered; but, forced into the south-east corner of the colony, he lost about one-third of his force which was isolated and forced to surrender on 28 November 1917. Before that, to escape destruction, Lettow-Vorbeck withdrew his surviving troops into Portuguese East Africa (25 November 1917), from where he continued to wage a guerrilla war until after the armistice; when informed of the end of hostilities, he surrendered his surviving 175 Europeans and about 3,000 natives at Abercorn in Northern Rhodesia on 25 November 1918. Lettow-Vorbeck's effort had been quite astonishing: in a hopeless position, he had occupied the attention of some

Operations in East Africa: a machine-gun position of the Northern Rhodesia Police.

130,000 Allied troops, inflicted great losses on them, and was still at large when the war ended; in many ways, it was the most outstanding performance by any commander during the entire war. After the war, almost all of German East Africa was transferred to Britain, as Tanganyika; Ruanda and Urundi were added to the Belgian Congo.

Armies

The German colonial forces were formed in 1889, with personnel from the army or marines, or volunteers from colonial settlers; styled *Schütztruppen*, units were composed of German officers with 'other ranks' partly German (including NCOs) and mostly natives, organized in independent companies of three platoons each, with their own transport. Companies were styled either as *Feldkompagnie* (FK) or *Schützkompagnie* (SchK); at the outbreak of hostilities in East Africa, for example, there were fourteen such companies comprising some 260 Germans and 2,500 natives, numbers enlarged greatly by recruitment at the beginning of the war. Their uniform was of a similar cut to that of the German army in Europe, but in 'sand grey', a khaki-yellow drill (which remained in use for some time even though field-grey was ordered in 1913), with Swedish cuffs, ordinary German arm-of-service piping, and facing-colours of cornflower-blue for South-West Africa, poppy-red for Togoland and Cameroon, and white for East Africa. Head-dress was a low, grey felt hat edged with the colony colour, with a national cockade on the upturned right brim; natives wore a fez of the uniform-colour; equipment was generally as used in Europe. Weaponry was rather outdated; in East Africa, for example, some eight companies were armed with 1871-pattern rifles using black powder propellant, far more conspicuous than the usual smokeless cartridges; but these defects were remedied in part by British equipment captured at Tanga. Each company had from two to four machine-guns, which thus considerably outgunned the British in the early stages. In addition to the combatants, as with all forces operating in Africa, each company required about 250 native porters to carry equipment.

The British forces in Africa were a mixture of a limited number of European units, some volunteer corps formed from the white settlers (e.g., the East Africa Mounted Rifles and East Africa Regiment), and native corps such as the West African Frontier Force. The most important of the 'native' units was the King's African Rifles, formed in 1902 by the amalgamation of the Uganda, Central Africa and East Africa Rifles; commanded by British officers (usually on secondment from British regiments) and some British NCOs, the rank-and-file were recruited from the so-called 'martial races' of central Africa and the Sudan. These troops were dispersed widely at the beginning of the war, throughout British East Africa and Uganda, and despite their great qualities in bush fighting, by early 1917 there were still only five regiments, in thirteen battalions; but in February 1917 the number was ordered to be increased to 20 battalions, ultimately 22, some being recruited from captured German

askaris. Having borne the brunt of the early operations in East Africa, the KAR continued to serve with great distinction. Their uniform was either a khaki drill long shirt and shorts, or a khaki long pullover, with a khaki pillbox cap (often with neck-cover) and blue puttees and sandals (although many preferred to go barefoot on campaign, being unused to wearing boots), with leather equipment. Officers wore khaki drill uniform of the ordinary British style, with either a tropical helmet or, somewhat unusually, a khaki peaked kepi with neck-curtain.

In addition to the military forces, both British and Germans employed their quasi-military police in a purely military role.

Other African colonies

Brief details of some of the other European colonies are included below, although apart from the campaigns already described, their contribution to the war was limited.

Basutoland: British crown colony, of which the High Commissioner for South Africa was governor; administered by a British resident commissioner; capital Maseru.

Bechuanaland: British protectorate, the northern part of Bechuanaland (the southern part, British Bechuanaland, was part of Cape Colony, chief town, Mafeking). Administered by a resident commissioner, with a small force of quasi-military police recruited in Basutoland and commanded by Europeans.

Belgian Congo: The Congo Free State was annexed by Belgium in November 1908, and thereafter was controlled by a minister responsible to the Belgium parliament, and administered by a governor-general and four provincial vice-governors-general. At the beginning of the war Belgium attempted to secure neutrality for the Congo, but after German incursions an army of about 10,000 was raised to participate in the East African campaign. The north-western part of German East Africa was administered by Belgium from September 1916, and in September 1919 an Anglo–Belgian agreement transferred most of Ruanda and Urundi to the Congo.

East Africa: British East Africa (renamed Kenya in July 1920) was administered like a British crown colony, with a governor, lieutenant-governor and provincial commissioners; the chief town and port was Mombasa. Also included in British East Africa was the protectorate of Uganda and Zanzibar, over which the sultan of the latter state remained sovereign.

French Equatorial Africa: 'AEF' (*Afrique Equatoriale Française*), formerly French Congo, was an immense colony stretching from the Atlantic to Egypt and from the mouth of the Congo to Tripoli, some 870,000 square miles. It was administered by a governor-general who supervised the administration of the separate colonies, Gabun (capital Libreville), Middle Congo (capital Brazzaville), and Ubangi-Schari (capital Bangi); a fourth province, Chad, was added officially in March 1920.

French West Africa: 'AOF' (*Afrique Occidentale Française*) was a common name for the colonies of Senegal, Upper Senegal and Niger, Guinea, Dahomey, Mauretania and the Ivory Coast; it was administered by a governor-general from Dakar. By 1921 the territory had been resolved into four groupings: Senegal, Upper Senegal/Niger (capital Woulouba), Upper Volta (capital Ouaga Dougou); Guinea (capital Konakry), Ivory Coast (capital Bingerville); Dahomey (capital Porto Novo), Mauretania; and Niger (capital Zinder). Details of some of the individual colonies: *Dahomey:* administered by a resident at Abomey; French rule completed following their deposition of a client-chief in 1911. Small columns of French troops operated from Dahomey against German Togoland in 1914, and for the remainder of the war the population remained quiet, contingents being sent from Dahomey for the campaigns in Cameroon and Europe. *Ivory Coast:* part of French Equatorial Africa in 1889, and an independent colony from March 1893; administered by the government of French West Africa, though with a separate budget and ruled by a lieutenant-governor. Principal town and port was Grand Bassam, although the capital was Bingerville (ex-Adjame). *Senegal:* comprised two sections, Senegal, and Upper Senegal and Niger; the territory north of the River Senegal was a separate region, Mauretania. The chief towns in Senegal were St. Louis and Dakar; seat of government for Upper Senegal and Niger was Bamako. The colonies were administered by their own lieutenant-governors, and Senegal returned one deputy to the French parliament. Senegal provided France with recruits for the Senegalese Tirailleurs, who established a formidable reputation during the war.

Gold Coast: British crown colony, administered by a governor; capital Accra. Defence was entrusted to the Gold Coast Regiment of the West African Frontier Force, which participated in the operations against Togoland and the Cameroons, and from July 1916 to September 1918 it served in East Africa. More than half of Togoland was placed under British control during the German surrender, but in July 1919 almost all was ceded to France, the Gold Coast gaining only a few frontier districts.

Nigeria: British crown colony, the largest British possession in West Africa, formed in January 1914 by the amalgamation of the previous protectorates of Northern and Southern Nigeria. The colony was divided into two provinces, each administered by a lieutenant-governor, with a governor-general over them; administrative centres were Lagos (the principal port) for Southern Nigeria and Zungeru for Northern Nigeria. Defence was conducted by the Nigeria Regiment, comprising four battalions, two mounted infantry companies and an artillery battery, which participated in the Cameroon and East Africa campaigns and was preparing to go to Palestine when the armistice was signed. One outbreak of unrest occurred during the war, a rising in Egbaland (capital Abeokuta, north of Lagos) in which some railway-track was destroyed, but the revolt was suppressed without difficulty by the Nigeria Regiment.

Nyasaland: British protectorate, known as British Central Africa until 1907; administered by a governor under orders from the colonial office. Capital, Blantyre. The protectorate was virtually defenceless in 1914, until almost every Briton of military age enrolled in the Nyasaland Volunteers; after a minor German incursion was repelled at Karonga in September 1914, no further hostilities occurred. Defence was bolstered in September 1915 by 1,000 Imperial Service troops, and Nyasaland acted as a base for operations against German East Africa, in which the Nyasaland battalions of the KAR were involved. Early in 1915, while the colony was still in danger, a rising occurred in the Shiré highlands, led by John Chelembe, a Nyasaland native who had been educated by the American Baptist Mission and who had studied at university in America. His followers killed three Europeans at Magomera on 23 January 1915; a force of 40

The British armed motor-boat Mimi *is pushed off a sandbank; with its companion* Tou-Tou *it was hauled overland by traction-engine to Lake Tanganyika, where the force under Commander G. B. Spicer-Simpson, RN sank two German gunboats.*

European volunteers and 100 KAR recruits dispersed the rebels, and Chelembe was tracked and killed on 3 February by native police. The rising, seen as a symptom of a general movement for African independence rather than specifically anti-British, was an isolated event.

Portuguese East Africa: Previously and subsequently named Mozambique, the Portuguese colony on the eastern coast of Africa had been styled 'the State of East Africa' from 1891. It was administered by a governor-general from the principal port, Lourenço Marques. It maintained a force of about 4,000 men, about 1,200–1,400 of whom were Europeans. The first German raiding parties entered the colony early in 1917, followed in November by Lettow-Vorbeck, who for the next year carried on his guerrilla war from there.

Rhodesia: In August 1911 the three Rhodesian colonies were reduced to two, Southern and Northern (the latter an amalgamation of North-Eastern and North-Western Rhodesia); the largest town was Salisbury, capital of Southern Rhodesia, and administration was still in the hands of the British South Africa Company. Military forces before the war consisted of the British South Africa Police (the commandant-general of which was paid by the British government), a mixed European and native force about 1,000 strong; and two divisions of Southern Rhodesia Volunteers, about 1,800 strong. During the war, early raids from German East Africa were contained by Rhodesian volunteers, the BSAP and troops from the Belgian Congo; and Rhodesians participated in the operations under General Northey launched against the Germans from Northern Rhodesia. The 1st Rhodesian Regiment was formed for service in the South African rebellion and the campaign in South-West Africa, and the 2nd Regiment served in East Africa; in all more than 6,850 European Rhodesians saw active service during the war, over half the total male population. A native combatant battalion was raised in Northern Rhodesia (more than 2,700 served in East Africa), and many thousands served as 'carriers' in the various African campaigns. The final act of the war occurred in Northern Rhodesia, which Lettow–Vorbeck had entered from Portuguese East Africa prior to learning of the armistice.

Sierra Leone: British crown colony, capital Freetown; headquarters of the British Army in West Africa. The colony itself provided a battalion of the West African Frontier Force; it was used as a base during the war, and the Sierra Leone forces were involved in the Cameroon campaign.

(For other states, see separate entries on Eritrea, North Africa, Somaliland and South Africa.)

References

Clifford, Sir Hugh. *The Gold Coast Regiment in the East African Campaign.* London, 1920 (contains much general information on the nature of 'bush' warfare)

Collyer, J. J. *The South Africans with General Smuts in German East Africa 1916.* Pretoria, 1939

Crowe, Brigadier-General J. H. V. *General Smuts' Campaign in East Africa.* London, 1918

Dane, E. *British Campaigns in Africa and the Pacific 1914–18.* London, 1919

Dolbey, Captain R. V. *Sketches of the East African Campaign.* London, 1918

Downes, Capt. W. D. *With the Nigerians in East Africa.* London, 1929

Farwell, B. *The Great War in Africa 1914–1918.* London, 1987

Gardner, B. *German East: The Story of the First World War in East Africa.* London, 1963

Haywood, Colonel A., and Clarke, Brigadier F. *History of the Royal West African Frontier Force.* Aldershot, 1964

Hordern, Lieutenant-Colonel C. *Military Operations, East Africa.* London, 1941 (official history)

Hoyt, E. P. *Guerilla: Colonel von Lettow-Vorbeck and Germany's East African Empire.* London, 1981

Lettow-Vorbeck, Colonel P. E. *My Reminiscences of East Africa.* London, 1920

Moberley, Brigadier-General F. J. *Military Operations, Togoland and the Cameroons.* London, 1931 (official history)

Mosley, L. *Duel for Kilimanjaro: the East African Campaign 1914–18.* London, 1963

Moyse-Bartlett, Lieutenant-Colonel H. *The King's African Rifles: A Study in the Military History of East and Central Africa.* Aldershot, 1956

Page, M. E. (ed.). *Africa and the First World War.* London, 1987

Young, F. B. *Marching on Tanga.* London, 1917

ALBANIA

Albanian independence from the Ottoman Empire was finally achieved as a result of the Balkan Wars, and Albania was recognized as a sovereign and neutral state on 29 July 1913. Several of the great powers, however, remained concerned about their influence over Albania, and so disrupted was the country that at the beginning of 1914 there existed three governments in various parts of the country. An attempt at unification by the appointment of an independent prince, agreed by the great powers, was not a success: Prince William of Weid, who arrived in Albania in March 1914, was an ineffective leader and at loggerheads with his minister of war, Essed Pasha, an adventurer who had governed in central Albania by force. Prince William was supported by Austria–Hungary, Essad by Italy and Serbia; the rivalry, complicated by bands of marauding Greeks in the south, resulted in a conflict which at first caused Essad's flight to Italy, then a rebellion by his supporters, who besieged Prince William in the port of Durazzo, until he abandoned his briefly adopted country in September 1914.

Essad re-established his rule in central Albania, Serbia occupied the north and Greece the south; but despite his precarious position, Essad was regarded as the legitimate Albanian ruler in the eyes of the Allied nations. In later 1915, however, Austria–Hungary moved into north and central Albania, Essad being chased to Salonika, where he remained until his true status became apparent and he ceased to be regarded as Albania's leader. Areas of the country remained under control of local chieftains, but support for the Central Powers was evinced by such guerrilla leaders as Bairam Tsuri, who harassed Allied lines of communication. In June 1917 Italy declared Albanian independence under their protection; this caused disquiet in France, which responded by proclaiming the establishment of a very ephemeral Republic of Koritsa. With the retreat of the Austro–Hungarian forces in late 1918, most of Albania fell under Italian control, upon whom Bairam Tsuri turned his attention. When Italy declined to expend any more effort in maintaining a military presence in Albania, she recognized the country's complete independence in August 1920; Serbia moved down from the north upon Tirana, but withdrew after considerable fighting. Despite the instability of the government, Albania remained independent; an attempt to find another neutral head of state having failed (it was said that the English cricketer C. B. Fry had been offered the position of king!), in 1924 the former prime minister Ahmed-i-Zog seized power, and proclaimed himself King Zog in 1928.

Army

During its brief initial period of independence, the Albanian army wore a light-blue uniform with black facings and braid, and a fur cap, though on active service ordinary national dress was worn. The Italian intervention in Albania included the creation of an Albanian Legion, formed 1916, comprising two regular battalions and some units of irregulars; uniform and equipment was of Italian style, plus the Albanian national head-dress of a white fleece cap.

ARABIA

Arabia comprised a number of states on the Arabian peninsula, and extended north into Syria and Iraq. The most important areas on the peninsula were Oman and Hadhramaut, bordering the Arabian Sea; Yemen and Asir, bordering the Red Sea north of Aden; Hejaz, extending north along the Red Sea to Aqaba; and Nejd, the hinterland between Yemen and Hejaz and the Persian Gulf states of (north to south) Kuwait, Bahrein, El Qatar, and Trucial Oman.

Although officially part of the Ottoman Empire, many of the states were virtually autonomous, with spheres of influence divided between Turkey and Britain (Trucial Oman, for example, had been under British protection since 1892, which extended to British control of foreign policy). At the beginning of the war Turkish control extended effectively only to the two holy cities of the Hejaz (Mecca and Medina), some garrisoned ports and towns, and the Hejaz railway, ostensibly intended to transport pilgrims to Mecca but actually used to increase Turkish control of the region. The independent attitude of the local rulers was traditional, but the Arab Revolt had its genesis farther north, in Arab secret societies persecuted by the Turks. The execution of Arab nationalists in Syria, and Turkish pressure to declare a *jihad* (holy war) upon the Allies, forced the hand of the Sherif of Mecca, Husein Ibn 'Ali. Husein (or Hussayn), head of the Hashemite clan which ruled the holy cities, had been building up the power of his sherifiate with

a view to independence; and with British encouragement and with the Red Sea controlled by the Royal Navy, he not only refused to proclaim the *jihad* but in mid-1915 expressed to the Allies his desire for revolt, and in return received pledges of support. After a long delay, the revolt began in June 1916, and after the capture from the Turks of Mecca and Jedda, he was proclaimed as 'Sultan of the Arabs' (October 1916); he exchanged this title for that of King of the Hejaz in 1917.

The Allies provided financial and material help to what became known as the Arab Army, and military missions which grew into supporting units of British and French artillery, armoured cars, machine-guns and even a flight of British aircraft which served with the Northern Arab Army in the Jordan/Palestine area. The most famous of these Allied aides was T. E. Lawrence, whose significance is still in question, some regarding him as an almost irrelevant self-publicist and others as the inspiration of the Arab Revolt; the truth lies somewhere between these two extremes. The Arab Army, the main military force of the revolt, was composed primarily of volunteers aged between 12 and 60 from the various tribes, both domiciled peasants and Bedouin nomads. These were quite without military training, often poorly armed (until weapons were captured or received from Britain), and capable only of guerrilla-style operations; and although some tribal distinctions in costume existed, their dress was entirely civilian. The disciplined nucleus of the Arab Army were two weak regular brigades, the great majority of whom were ex-prisoners of war, Syrians or Iraqis who had been conscripted into the Turkish Army but whose sympathies lay with the Arabs. Ex-Ottoman officers provided much of the leadership: commander of the regulars in the Arab Army was Ja'afar al Askari, who had been captured by the Dorset Yeomanry at Aqqaqia in February 1916 when commanding the regulars in the Senussi attack on Egypt. These troops wore a mix of British khaki uniform and native styles, including the khaki *kafiya* (head-cloth) which was an especial distinction of the regular Arab Army. Finally, the army included units of *Agayl*, professional mercenaries recruited from Hejaz and Nejd, as fierce as but more disciplined than the Arab irregulars, though motivated more by profit than idealism; Lawrence formed his own bodyguard of such men.

In late 1916 the 'Sherifian' or Arab Army was reorganized into three commands: a Northern Army, commanded by the Sherif's third son, Feisal, including a regular brigade and four artillery batteries; a Southern Army, under 'Ali, the eldest son, including one camel and two infantry battalions and four batteries; and the Eastern Army, under the second son, Abdullah, including a camel battalion and a mountain battery. To each of these were added large bodies of irregulars. The Northern Army operated primarily against the Hejaz railway and marched on Damascus; the Southern besieged the Turkish garrison of Medina (which surrendered only in January 1919) and operated against those posts farther south, into Yemen; and the Eastern

Typical Arab irregular troops: followers of the Sheikh of Mohommerah. The rifles displayed are single-shot Martini-Henrys.

watched the Turks' most loyal ally, Ibn Rashid of the Shammar tribe of central Nejd, who saw a Turkish alliance as the best way of maintaining his position against both the Sherifians and Ibn Sa'ud.

Ibn Sa'ud of Riyadh, whose Sa'udi kingdom was in effect established just before the World War, was a leader of the Wahhabi sect which originated in Nejd, a puritanical Islamic movement founded by Ibn 'Abd ul-Wahhab, who is said to have died in 1791, which was opposed to all luxury and the worship of saints (and even Mohammed). Ibn Sa'ud was antagonistic towards the Ottomans, the Shammar, the Sherifians and the pro-British Gulf states; but, anxious to support the winning side, he forsook his original pledge to support the Turks, received British assistance, but remained largely uninvolved in the war, save for minor actions against the Turks and, in the last year of the war, a drive against the Shammar. Ibn Sa'ud came to dominate the Arabian peninsula, being strong enough to challenge the forces of the Sherif; he was proclaimed king of the Hejaz and Nejd in 1926, the territory being re-named Saudi Arabia in 1932. But for the possession of firearms, the Sa'udi forces were almost medieval in composition and tactics, though possessed of a formidable nucleus of Wahhabi fanatics, the *ikhwan*, communities of recently-settled Bedouin, almost the Janissaries of the Sa'udi regime. Their ferocity was such that Ibn Sa'ud disbanded these settlements of Wahhabite fundamentalism after the war.

One of the Arab Army's greatest assets was its capacity for rapid movement, of great value in the guerrilla war which wrought such havoc to Turkish outposts along the Hejaz railway and elsewhere. Apart from the regular nucleus, the majority of the army had a somewhat amorphous character, with members likely to drift away before returning for the next fight; but as the Northern Army progressed northwards, other tribes began to support the revolt, such as the Druze of the mountains south of Damascus; and Syrian and Armenian members of the Ottoman Army deserted in large numbers to join the revolt, continuing to wear their Turkish uniform even after joining the Arab Army. Having occupied vast numbers of Turkish troops needed elsewhere, in the final advance on Damascus the Arab Army formed the right flank of the British drive through Palestine. The forward element of the Northern Army (Lawrence's bodyguard, an Arab mobile column and British, French and Egyptian elements) reached Damascus a day before the main British forces, and Feisal himself arrived one day later. He had hoped to become king of Syria, but British and French intentions for the region ran counter to those of the Arabs, and the friction which developed originated with what in Arab eyes was regarded as a betrayal. Nevertheless, although their aspirations were unfulfilled, the contribution of the Arab Revolt to Allied victory in the theatre was very considerable. (*See also* the separate entry on Aden.)

References

See Section V for sources on the campaigns. *Lawrence and the Arab Revolts.* D. Nicolle, London, 1989 is an excellent guide to the forces and composition of the various Arabian tribes; Lawrence's *Revolt in the Desert*, 1927, expanded to *The Seven Pillars of Wisdom*, 1935, contains much on the nature of the Arab forces.

AUSTRALIA

Australia entered the war behind Britain on an equal upsurge of patriotism. Although Australian troops had participated in earlier colonial wars – notably the Boer War

– the World War was the first real opportunity to prove their loyalty: 'To be allowed to share in the perils and glories of the battlefield as part of a British army, was regarded at once as a distinction of which Australia might be proud, and as a guarantee of their future position as British subjects.'[1] This attitude is hardly surprising, given that the population of Australia of European descent was something over 96 per cent British; but despite Andrew Fisher's declaration that Australia would support Britain 'to the last man and the last shilling', a small minority of the population of Irish descent (about a third of those of British origin) followed the Irish Nationalist opposition to support of British interests in the war.

The Federal Commonwealth of Australia was formed on 1 January 1901 by the association of the hitherto autonomous states of New South Wales, Queensland, South Australia, Tasmania, Victoria and Western Australia, with a parliament of a lower House of Representatives and an upper house of an elected Senate, with a governor-general acting as the King's representative. The 1913 election resulted in the defeat of the Labour administration of Andrew Fisher, a Scottish-born ex-coal miner who had emigrated to Queensland at the age of 23. The new Liberal ministry was led by Joseph Cook, born in Staffordshire and also an ex-miner; but his government was beset with difficulties and on 30 July 1914 the governor-general dissolved both Houses. The Labour Party won the ensuing election convincingly, and Fisher resumed office as prime minister. He pursued the war with enthusiasm, but resigned in late 1915 in the wake of the Dardanelles disaster, and became Australian High Commissioner in London, which post he held until 1921. He was succeeded as prime minister by his colleague and ex-attorney-general William Morris Hughes (1864–1952), a small, deaf and irascible Welshman who, in the course of his life had been a knife-grinder, teacher and barrister.

'Bill' Hughes was unashamedly supportive of Britain's interests. He visited Britain in 1916 on a recruiting drive, and was welcomed with the acclamation he never received in Australia; and undertook to introduce conscription. Two referenda on the subject, however, failed to achieved the majority he required, and after losing the support of his own party (which opposed conscription), Hughes was forced to form a new administration in coalition with Cook, and including only a few of his former Labour colleagues. One reason for the rejection of conscription was said to be a belief that Hughes would resign if it were not passed, and so many Australians were hostile to his combative style of leadership that they took it as a way of being rid of him! Also exerting an influence were radical socialist politicians (one of whom, from Queensland, stated that every Irish–Australian who enlisted was simply helping an oppressor), and certain members of the Roman Catholic Church, but the second (1917) referendum was decided by less than 167,000 votes. The troops abroad could have swayed the issue, but only a small majority of them voted in favour of conscription,

> The 5th Australian Light Horse at Gallipoli:
> 'Anyone who has used a periscope knows that unless the periscope is held well up before the eyes, instead of the landscape one sees only one's own visage reflected in the lower glass. Bill did not hold the periscope up far enough, and what he saw in it was a dark, dirty face with a wild growth of black stubble glaring straight back at him. He dropped the periscope, grabbed his rifle, and scrambled up the parapet, fully intending to finish the Turk who had dared to look down the other end of the periscope. He had mistaken his own reflection for a Turk's.'
> (Anonymous artilleryman – address 'Sea View', Shell Green, Anzac, in *The Anzac Book*, p. 24, London, 1916)

presumably having such pride in the fact that all were volunteers that they did not welcome the prospect of drafts of pressed men.

Hughes formed another new cabinet in January 1918, and remained prime minister until 1923. He was a most robust defender of Australia's position at Versailles, where he clashed with Woodrow Wilson over the policy to be adopted towards Japanese expansionism in the Pacific. Making his point in a typically forthright manner, Hughes caused Wilson to ask him what right he had to speak in such a manner? Hughes replied that he spoke on behalf of 60,000 dead Australians . . .

In addition to military resources, Australia contributed to the British war effort by shipping vast quantities of meat and metals to Britain: during the war some 97 per cent of Australia's meat production was consumed by Britain, and 35 per cent of Britain's requirement of copper was supplied by Australia.

Army

The qualities of the Australasian soldier in the war were unique, and in contemporary opinions resulted from the independent spirit of those who colonized the frontiers of civilization, the 'men from the bush', even though many recruits were either recently arrived immigrants from Britain or from the urban centres. C. E. W. Bean, the Australian official historian who observed them at first hand, believed that the word 'ANZAC' (an acronym from 'Australian and New Zealand Army Corps') represented reckless heroism, enterprise, resourcefulness, fidelity and 'mateship', the latter perhaps the most significant: the belief that come what may, one's mates should never be let down. Some British comments tended to patronise their rough and independent cousins (Sir Frank Fox, writing as 'GSO' in *GHQ.*, London 1920, observed that the greatest successes in Australia were the breeding of new sheep from the Spanish merino, and the conversion of Britain's black sheep into 'good white stock',[2] and to criticize them for lack of conventional discipline and respect for authority, but none

The Australian uniform is illustrated excellently in this study of an ANZAC and two South African recruiters at Durban; the comfortable but not smart appearance (especially the slouch hat) led one British officer to remark that no discipline could be kept among troops who looked like dustmen!

perception of the Anzac attitude is the remark attributed to Major-General Granville Ryrie at Gallipoli, when wounded by a shot through the throat: 'Holy Moses, they've got me where the chicken got the axe!'[5] The contraventions of conventional disciple caused problems, such as enthusiastic 'scrounging' and near riotous behaviour like that on Good Friday 1915 which devastated the Cairo red-light district Haret el Wasser, alias 'the Wozza'; but the most accurate reflection on the qualities of the Anzac is that expressed by Sir William Birdwood: 'I, personally, shall always regard the time I have been privileged to be a comrade of the brave and strong men from Australia and New Zealand, who have served alongside of me, as one of the greatest privileges that could be conferred upon any man, and of which I shall be prouder to the end of my days than any honour which can be given me.'[6]

The Australian military establishment was directed entirely towards home defence. From 1 March 1901 all existing state forces came under control of a unified Department of Defence. The 1903–4 Defence Act provided for the enrolment of all men between the ages of 18 and 60 in time of war, for service only within the Commonwealth; the 1909 Defence Act decreed universal training, confirmed by a report presented to parliament in 1910 following a survey by Kitchener. His recommendations included the establishment of a part-time 'citizen army' of 80,000, a military college (created at Duntroon in 1911) and a small-arms factory (established in 1912 at Lithgow). Apart from a tiny 'permanent force' or regular army, Australia's military resource was the militia, the older force existing before the 'citizen army' which was under construction in the immediate pre-war period. From 1911 provision was made for compulsory training of junior cadets, all those of twelve years of age being liable for 90 hours' drill per year for two years, and from the age of fourteen, 96 hours' drill per year for four years. The militia was some 45,000 strong in 1914, 90 per cent of whom were aged between 19 and 21. Because of this low age, it was decided that when war began, the troops to be sent overseas should not be based upon the existing units, but (as in Canada) be part of a newly created, independent force. Its title was devised by Australia's senior military commander, Major-General Sir William Bridges (who was killed by a sniper at Gallipoli); the Australian Imperial Force or AIF. Recruiting remained entirely voluntary throughout, and the response from the Australian population was magnificent. Some 332,000 troops served overseas, of whom more than 212,000 were wounded and almost 60,000 killed, a casualty-rate of more than 82 per cent (only some 42 per cent were discharged as fit at the end of the war); this was the highest proportion of casualties sustained by any army during the war, and is in itself sufficient testimony to the contribution of Australia, contradicting the detractors who saw the non-implementation of conscription as evidence of a lukewarm attitude.

questioned their indomitable spirit. Oliver Hogue quoted Colonel McCay of 2 Brigade at Gallipoli: 'The way, the cheerful, splendid way, they face death and pain is simply glorious . . . I said in effect to them (my own brigade), "Come and die", and they came with a cheer and a laugh. They are simply magnificent.'[3] 'GSO' repeated the belief that this was the product of 'living close up to Nature', where the 'back-country Anzac' learned 'to be wary and enduring and sternly true to the duties of mateship',[4] and these qualities were demonstrated throughout the war.

Conversely, the independent and self-reliant attitude infuriated the more traditional members of the British military establishment: British officers could never become used to the Australian habit of addressing their officers by a first name, or for showing scant concern for the usual military ranks and conventions. The story of the Anglo–Turkish truce-negotiations at Gallipoli being interrupted by an Anzac who marched in to inquire whether any of the bastards present had seen his kettle is well-known, and similar anecdotes are legion. Perhaps typical of the common

The AIF included 60 numbered infantry battalions, four to each of fifteen consecutively-numbered brigades, in five autonomous divisions on the British model: 1st Division (1–3 Brigades); 2nd Division (5–7 Brigades); 3rd Division (9–11 Brigades); 4th Division (4, 12, 13 Brigades); 5th Division (8, 14, 15 Brigades). Battalions retained a state identity, for example:

2nd Division:
5 Brigade: 17th–20th Battalions, all NSW;
6 Brigade: 21st–24th Battalions, all Victoria;
7 Brigade: 25th Queensland, 26th Queensland/Tasmania, 27th S. Australia, 28th W. Australia Battalions.

Supporting services were deployed at divisional level, heavy artillery and transport at corps level. There were two Anzac Corps: I comprised the 1st, 2nd, 4th and 5th AIF divisions, and II the 3rd AIF, the New Zealand Division, and one British division. At the Gallipoli landings, however, I Anzac Corps comprised 1st and 2nd Australian Divisions, and a combined New Zealand and Australian Division (of the 4th AIF, New Zealand Infantry and New Zealand Mounted Rifles Brigades); and after November 1917 there was just one Australian Corps.

The cavalry was the Light Horse, whose organization was confirmed by the first GOC Australian forces upon federation, Sir Edward Hutton. These splendid troops were among the best of the Australian forces, essentially mounted infantry adept at fighting on foot yet utilizing the skills of the boundary-riders and bushmen; their mounts were the sturdy 'stock-horse' or 'waler' (from New South Wales), whose endurance matched that of the legendary cossack pony. The Light Horse were organized in regiments of three squadrons of four troops each, with a total strength of about 500, usually with three regiments to a brigade, and with units retaining a 'state' identity. They served in the Dardanelles (as infantry) and on the Western Front, but found their true role in the Desert Column in Sinai, and in the reorganized Desert Mounted Corps in later 1917:

Desert Mounted Corps
Anzac Mounted Division: 1 Light Horse Brigade (1st NSW, 2nd Queensland, 3rd S. Australia/Tasmania Regiments); 2 Light Horse Brigade (5th Queensland, 6th and 7th NSW Regiments); New Zealand Mounted Rifles Brigade.
Australian Mounted Division: 3 Light Horse Brigade (8th Victoria, 9th Victoria/S. Australia, 10th W. Australia Regiments); 4 Light Horse Brigade (4th Victoria, 11th Queensland/W. Australia, 12th NSW Regiments); later with 5 Light Horse Brigade (14th and 15th Regiments)
Yeomanry Mounted Division; Imperial Camel Corps.

The Australian effort at Gallipoli provides the most telling popular perception of the Anzac of the Great War (Australia's national day, Anzac Day, is the anniversary of the first landing at the Dardanelles), and indeed few troops could have sustained what they did with equal cheerfulness; but their efforts on the Western Front and in Palestine were equally valuable. Australia produced its national heroes, some of whom became equally famous outside their own country (such as Albert Jacka, who won the Victoria Cross for clearing a trench at Gallipoli), and great leaders (such as 'Light Horse Harry' Chauvel, who led the largest body of cavalry deployed in modern times with the skill of his hero, J. E. B. Stuart). Most significant, however, was Sir John Monash, who rose to command the Australian Corps, an example of a man rising to a high level without any experience of regular soldiering before the war. From an unlikely background (a civil engineer of Jewish parentage, born in 1865 and with his only military background being militia service from 1887), at the time he was knighted on the battlefield by the King he had been a full-time soldier for

Australian Light Horse on the march from Bethlehem to Jerusalem.

Reverend Oswin Creighton writes of his fears before going into action:

'I simply dread the first few days. Slaughter seems to be inevitable. We had a printed message from Hunter-Weston, our Divisional General yesterday. He said the eyes of the world are on us, and we must be prepared to face heavy losses by bullets, shells, mines and drowning. Cheery, isn't it? People's eyes seem perfectly open . . . at least three-quarters, it seems to me, will probably be casualties the first day. They are quite prepared for it. I feel very gloomy about it all at the present moment. One thing I feel certain of, and that is that the men will do their duty and cover themselves with glory, even if they are to be exterminated; and even if they had gone to France it would have been the same. Extermination is going on everywhere, and nothing can stop it now.'

(Padre Creighton's fears were realized, though the men did do their duty. Creighton survived Gallipoli but was killed in action on 15 April 1918).

(With the Twenty-Ninth Division at Gallipoli, pp. 42–3, London, 1916)

ANZAC intelligence 'office', a sandbag shelter at Gallipoli.

only four years. He left the army immediately after the end of the war and returned to engineering; the naming of Monash University, Victoria, is a fitting tribute.

Organization, uniform and equipment was like that of Britain, but the uniform included some jealously guarded features which, together with a personal appearance which European observers took as representing an outdoor life, gave the Anzacs the distinctive, easy yet purposeful demeanour remarked upon by contemporary writers. Most notable was the slouch hat, often worn upturned on the left side, which became the most characteristic mark of Australian troops during (and after) the war, although it was not universal: caps, often with neck-covers, were common in the Dardanelles, and presumably in an attempt to confer individuality, when commanding the 3rd Division, Monash ordered his men to wear the brims of their slouch hats down, not upturned. The Australian tunic was likewise quite distinctive, having voluminous exterior pockets and, being manufactured from drab serge, flannel or cord dyed khaki, faded with use to attain a blue-grey shade. Australian

Queensland recruits to the ANZAC Corps: the uniforms are distinctive but the equipment is the British 1908 pattern.

regiments used a universal badge, the so-called 'rising sun' (a derivation of that used during the Boer War) which became the proud distinction of the AIF. Typical, perhaps, of the Australian sense of humour, the 'rising sun' name appears to have been taken not from the design of the badge itself, but from the trademark of Hoadley's 'Rising Sun' jam, quantities of which had been sent to Australians serving in the Boer War!

Reverend Oswin Creighton tries to work out the war:
'. . . we feel we are utterly stuck and nobody seems to know what to do . . . It looks like a question of stalemate and nothing happening. We must advance, but how? The only thing to do seems to be to try and cheer people up as much as possible, and remind them that it is not our fault, and that the whole world is in a pretty good muddle, and we can only try to do our best. How everybody longs for it to be over! You seem to hear nothing else. But it is a great thing to have fine weather, plenty to eat, no lice, and to feel well. I feel so sure that, though it is impossible to see how, somehow or other some day good will come of the whole war . . .'
('W' Beach, Gallipoli, 18 May 1915; *With the Twenty-Ninth Division in Gallipoli*, p. 100, London, 1916)

Navy

The Australian Navy originated with small vessels purchased by Victoria and New South Wales in the mid-1850s. Other states followed suit (South Australia's 'navy', *Protector*, served in the Boxer Rebellion), and in 1887 the colonies formed a Royal Navy Auxiliary Squadron, for which they contributed a subsidy to Britain (by an agreement of 1903, Australia contributed £200,000 annually and New Zealand £40,000; the vessels were to remain in Australian waters and some served to train personnel recruited in Australia). In July 1911 the title 'Royal Australian Navy' was granted to the independent squadron decided upon in 1909, and in 1913 the navy truly came into being with the arrival in Australian waters of *Australia*, *Melbourne* and *Sydney*. Nevertheless, it was not entirely independent: Cook's Liberal ministry put it at British disposal in the event of hostilities, and accordingly *Australia* served as flagship of the British 2nd Battlecruiser Squadron (but was undergoing a refit at the time of Jutland).

The surface vessels included the 1913 battlecruiser *Australia* (built at the John Brown yard, Clyde; 18,000 tons, 8 × 12in, 14 × 4in guns); the Chatham-class light cruisers *Melbourne* (1913, Cammel Laird, Birkenhead), *Sydney* (1913, London & Glasgow yard, Glasgow) and *Brisbane* (1915, built at Cockatoo Dockyard, Sydney), all of 5,400 tons, 8 × 6in guns; and the I-class destroyers *Paramatta* and *Yarra* (1910, built by Fairfield Yard, Clyde, and by Denny of Dumbarton), *Warrego* (1911, Fairfield but erected from sections in Sydney), and *Huon* (1914), *Swan* and *Torrens*

(1915) (all Cockatoo); all these were 700 tons displacement, 1 × 4in, 3 × 12pdr guns. Older vessels were the Pelorus-class cruisers *Pioneer* and *Psyche* (1900, 2,200 tons, 8 × 4in, 8 × 3pdr guns, the latter transferred to *Australia* in 1917), and the Challenger-class cruiser *Encounter* (1905, 5,880 tons, 11 × 6in, 9 × 12pdr guns) was stationed in Australia but not presented to the Australian Navy until 1919. The service of these ships included duty in the Mediterranean, Atlantic, Pacific, North Sea and Indian Ocean. *Pioneer* participated in the destruction of *Königsberg* off East Africa, and *Australia*, *Melbourne* and *Sydney* were present at the surrender of the High Seas Fleet in 1918; but the most famous service probably occurred as early as November 1914, when HMAS *Sydney* destroyed the German surface-raider *Emden*.

Equally important was the cruise of the Australian submarine *AE2*, which penetrated the Dardanelles into the Sea of Marmara on 25 April 1915, at the very moment when the commanders of the Gallipoli landing were urging withdrawal. The feat of *AE2* under Lieutenant-Commander H. S. Stoker was heralded as a major achievement, and was used by Hamilton to put heart into his subordinates. It may have turned the course of the campaign, for few could contemplate withdrawal after Stoker's achievement, but the cruise of *AE2* was brief: on 30 April a fault in the main ballast tank caused her to be scuttled to prevent her from falling into Turkish hands. (The other Australian boat, *AE1*, sank for an unexplained reason in September 1914.)

Aviation Service

The Australian Flying Corps was established in 1912, but not so titled until 1914, in which year the first flying school was instituted. Typical of the independent attitude pervading most Australian policy, the AFC was the only aviation service of the British Empire to remain independent of the Royal Flying Corps. The first use of Australian military aircraft was a half-flight sent to Bombay to operate in Mesopotamia in early 1915; the two aircraft of the Australian Naval and Military Expeditionary Force

---

'One mornin' early while we was standin' to arms 'e lights up a bumper, so I tells 'im not to let the officer cop 'im or there'd be trouble. Just then along comes the bloomin' officer, so 'Enessy sticks 'is lighted bumper down south into 'is overcoat pocket, and 'olds it there out of sight. The officer sniffs about a bit, then 'e asks 'Enessy: "Are you smoking?"
'"No sir!" says 'Enessy.
'"Well, I can smell smoke!" says the officer. Then 'e looks pretty 'ard at 'Enessy and says: "What's your name?"
'"'Enessy, sir."
'"Well, Henessy, your pocket's on fire!"'
('E.A.M.W.' in *The Anzac Book*, pp. 47–8, London, 1916)

(ANMEF) to New Guinea and New Britain in 1914 were not required due to lack of German resistance. No. 1 Squadron AFC went to Egypt in 1916 and served in Palestine, flying BE12s and later RE8s and SE5s. Three squadrons were formed for the Western Front: 3 (Reconnaissance) and 2 and 4 (Fighters) arrived at the front in September 1917. Four more (5–8) were formed as the Australian Training Wing in England, to support those operating on the continent, and another squadron was established in Australia at the Central Flying School at Point Cook. The AFC lost some 60 aircraft on the Western Front, and the RE8s of 3 Squadron broke new ground in the parachuting of machine-gun ammunition to Australian troops in the advance on Hamel. The AFC was disbanded in 1919, but resurrected as the Royal Australian Air Force in 1921. Their uniform was similar to that of the AIF, although some pilots wore the 'maternity jacket' of the RFC; the pilots' brevet ('wings') was like that of the RFC, except for the letters 'AFC' in the centre.

Footnotes

1. *Her Majesty's Indian and Colonial Forces: A Descriptive Account*, W. Richards, London, n.d., p. 349.
2. *G.H.Q.*, 'GSO', London, 1920, p. 188.
3. *Trooper Bluegum at the Dardanelles*. O. Hogue, London, 1916, p. 159.
4. 'GSO', op. cit., pp. 193–4.
5. Hogue, op. cit., p. 256.
6. *The Anzac Book*. London 1916, p. x.

References

Anon. *Australia in Palestine*. Oxford, 1920 (produced by soldiers in the field)
Anon. *The Anzac Book*. London, 1916 (produced by Anzacs at Gallipoli)
Adam-Smith, P. *The Anzacs*. Melbourne, 1978
Bean, C. E. W. *Anzac to Amiens: A Shorter History of the Australian Fighting Services in the First World War*. Canberra, 1946
— *The Official History of Australia in the War of 1914–18*. Sydney, 1921–43
Brugger, S. *Australians in Egypt 1914–19*. Carleton, Victoria, 1980
Charlton, P. *Pozières 1916: the Australians on the Somme*. London, 1986
Cutlack, F. M. *The Australian Flying Corps in the Western and Eastern Theatres of War*. Sydney, 1923 (Vol. VIII of the official history)
Denton, K. *Gallipoli: One Long Grave*. Sydney, 1986
Evans, A. *Royal Australian Navy*. Sydney, 1988
Gullett, H. S. *The Australian Imperial Force in Sinai and Palestine*. Sydney, 1944 (Vol. VII of the official history)
Hill, A. J. *Chauvel of the Light Horse*. Carleton, Victoria, 1978
Hogue, O. *Trooper Bluegum at the Dardanelles*. London, 1916
Jones, I. *The Australian Light Horse*. Sydney, 1987
Jose, A. W. *The Royal Australian Navy 1914–18*. Sydney, 1928 (Vol. IX of the official history)
Laffin, J. *Digger: Legend of the Australian Soldier*. Melbourne, 1986
— *The Australian Army at War 1899–1975*. London, 1982
— *Western Front 1916–1917: the Price of Honour*. Sydney, 1987
— *Western Front 1917–1918: the Cost of Victory*. Sydney, 1988
McKernan, M. *The Australian People and the Great War*. Melbourne, 1980
Monash, General Sir John. *The Australian Victories in France in 1918*. London, 1920
— *War Letters*. Sydney, 1935
Pedersen, P. A. *Monash as Military Commander*. Melbourne, 1985
Preston, R. M. P. *The Desert Mounted Corps*. London, 1921
Robson, L. L. *The First A.I.F.: a Study of its Recruitment 1914–1918*. Melbourne, 1970
Smithers, A. J. *Sir John Monash*. London, 1973
Wedd, M. *Australian Military Uniforms*. Kenthurst, 1982

AUSTRIA–HUNGARY

The most venerable of European monarchies, descendant of the Holy Roman Empire, was presided over by the most venerable of sovereigns, the Emperor Franz Josef I (1830–1916), who had been on the throne since the 'year of revolutions', 1848. The Austro–Hungarian Empire embraced about one-eighth of the population of Europe, ranging from the Poles of Galicia, the Germans of the Austro–German border, Czechs, Slovaks, to Dalmatians, Italians, Croats and Bosnians, a wide mix of religions, cultures and languages which inevitably caused severe internal pressures. The Empire comprised two separate states sharing a sovereign, army and foreign policy: Austria or Cisleithania, administered from Vienna; and 'the lands of St. Stephen's Crown', Hungary or Transleithania, administered from Budapest. The sovereign held the titles of Emperor of Austria and Apostolic King of Hungary, and unofficially the two states were often styled 'the Dual Monarchy'. Relations between the two were governed by the 'Compromise' (*Ausgleich*) or agreement dating from 1867.

Three ministries existed for the administration of common policies: foreign affairs, war (controlling only those forces common to the Dual Monarchy) and finance (which presided over joint expenditure, not the internal finances of either state).

In Austria, the Emperor was head of the executive, a council of eight ministers with portfolio (including defence, which administered the Austrian forces) and two without, for Galicia and Bohemia, headed by a president of the council or prime minister. Legislative power resided in the *Reichsrat* or 'council of the empire', comprising an upper chamber (*Herrenhaus*) of hereditary princes and peers, and life-peers nominated by the emperor; and a lower chamber (*Abgeordnetenhaus*) of members elected by male Austrians aged 24 and over. Civil administration was performed by provincial governors, and there also existed seventeen provincial parliaments. The seventeen 'crown lands' included three kingdoms (Bohemia, Dalmatia, Galicia), two archduchies (Lower and Upper Austria), six duchies (Bukovina, Carinthia, Carniola, Salzburg, Silesia, Styria), two countships (Görz–Gradisca and Tirol), two margraviates (Istria, Moravia) and the territory of Vorarlberg; plus Trieste as an independent city. For administration, Tirol and Vorarlberg were united; and Istria, Görz–Gradisca and Trieste formed the district of Küstenland.

Hungary, just over half the area of the empire, consisted of Hungary itself (Magyarország), including the largely autonomous town and district of Fiume, the principality of Transylvania and the province of Croatia–Slavonia. The nationalities were Magyars (just over half the total), Roumanians (about 17 per cent), Germans and Slovaks (about 12 per cent each), Croatians and Serbs (together less than 5 per cent) and Ruthenians (less than 3 per cent). The Emperor, as King of Hungary, headed the executive and

The symbol of empire: the illusion of Austrian imperial power as portrayed in a gold coin of 1915, considerably different from the reality of the empire's power.

The Emperor Franz Josef (1830–1916).

shared legislative power with the parliament. The executive consisted of a cabinet of ten ministers, headed by a president or prime minister, and including a defence minister who controlled the Hungarian forces. The parliament (*Országgyülés*) consisted of an upper 'House of Magnates' (*Förendiház*) of hereditary princes and peers, clerics and life members appointed by the king or elected by the house, plus three representatives from the semi-autonomous Croatia–Slavonia; and a lower House of Representatives (*Képviselöház*), elected by a franchise limited to about 5 per cent.

Franz Josef's life had been beset by personal tragedy: his brother Maximilian had been executed in Mexico in 1867; his wife Elizabeth, duchess of Bararia, was stabbed to death by the Italian anarchist Luccheni at Geneva in 1898; his only son Rudolf committed suicide in 1889; and his heir (though never recognized officially), Franz Ferdinand and his wife, were assassinated by Princip at Sarajevo.

The Austrian prime minister at the outbreak of war was Count Karl von Stürgkh (1859–1916), in power from November 1911 and responsible for the suspension of the *Reichsrat* from March 1914, following obstruction from Czech and Social Democrat members. Despite this and the agitation of anti-war, nationalist and Italian irredentist factions, there was widespread popular support for the state at the outbreak of war. In the last stages of Stürgkh's ministry the military increased in power, to the extent of almost ruling the country; and on 21 October 1916 Stürgkh was shot to death by Friedrich Adler, son of the Social Democrat leader, to cries of 'Down with absolutism! We want peace!' In Stürgkh's place, Ernst von Körber (1850–1919) was appointed prime minister (having held the post 1900–4). During his brief tenure, Franz Josef died (21 November 1916), depressed and pessimistic about the war. He was succeeded by his grand-nephew Karl Franz Josef (1887–1922), who became Emperor Karl I. A humanitarian young man, who wanted peace at almost any price, and whose wife Zita of Bourbon-Parma (who had two brothers in the Belgian Army) was to exert influence regarded as dangerous by the military establishment, Karl lacked the judgement and experience needed at such a critical juncture. Körber resigned on 14 December 1916 after Karl insisted on a moderate Compromise with the Hungarian government. He was replaced by Count Heinrich von Clam–Martinic (1863–1932), who had been Körber's agriculture minister. As a Czech, he endeavoured to form a coalition ministry to embrace all nationalities, and reconvened the *Reichsrat* (31 May 1917); but the Czechs and southern Slavs who attended made this impossible by constitutional demands which the German faction could never support; and with no hope of achieving his coalition, Clam–Martinic resigned (19 June 1917) to become military governor of Montenegro. Negotiations for a separate peace in spring 1917, conducted via the Empress' brothers, were unsuccessful, Allied governments fearing that a peace with Austria–Hungary might increase the demands for a total cessation of hostilities, at a time when the USA's entry into the war seemed to ensure victory, and that an Austrian peace might cause Italy to withdraw from the Allied camp.

Karl continued to exert a wide influence upon the government: having replaced foreign minister Count Istvan Burian von Rajecz (1851–1922) with Count Ottokar Czernin (1872–1932) (Burian resumed office in April 1918), and chief of staff Count Franz Conrad von Hötzendorf (1852–1925) with the more pliable Arthur Arz von Straussenburg (1857–1935), he now appointed his former tutor, Ernst von Seidler, as prime minister. Seidler was unable to suppress the growing agitation for regional autonomy, temporarily adjourned the *Reichsrat*, and faced with the establishment of an independent Czechoslovak state, resigned on 22 July 1918. He was succeeded by Baron Max Hussarek von Heinlein (1865–1935), who proposed a federal system of semi-autonomous states; this met with no success and he resigned on 27 October 1918. He was succeeded by the pacifist Heinrich Lammasch (1853–1920), but by this time the opportunity for a negotiated peace was long gone, and only total collapse faced Austria–Hungary. The last foreign minister of the empire, Count Julius Andrássy von Csik-Szent (1860–1929), who held office only from 24 October to 1 November, dissolved the German alliance which had been created by his father, also foreign minister, in 1879; and Lammasch resigned on 11 November.

From June 1913 the Hungarian prime minister was Istvan Tisza de Boros–Jëno (1861–1918), who maintained the Hungarian parliament and worked constantly for the rights of Hungarians within the empire, securing the legalization of the Hungarian language for official purposes and the adoption of a new flag and coat of arms. He was prepared to grant concessions to Italy and Roumania to keep them neutral, and became increasingly unpopular not only with the opposition in Hungary (declining the offer to co-operate in a coalition ministry in 1915) but with Austria, at a time of wrangling over the joint economic agreement; his haughty manner and Calvinist religion (in a Catholic state) served also to alienate support. Karl dismissed Tisza

on 23 May 1917; he took the field as a colonel in the Hungarian Army, and was murdered by Red Guards in Budapest on 31 October 1918. Karl – who reigned in Hungary as King Karl IV – appointed the inexperienced Count Maurice Esterhazy as prime minister; he attempted to introduce electoral reform but his health collapsed under the strain, and was succeeded on 20 August 1917 by Alexander Werkele (1848–1921). He supported Czernin over his proposal that Germany surrender Alsace–Lorraine to France to bring about peace, and succeeded in widening the electoral franchise in Hungary, but was unable to maintain the Dual Monarchy. Although Werkele proclaimed Hungarian independence on 19 October 1918, he was forced to resign on 23 October, to be replaced on 31

The Emperor Karl and his wife, Zita of Bourbon–Parma.

October by Count Mihály Károlyi von Nagkároly (1875–1955). On 11 November he proclaimed the Hungarian republic, but was deposed as head of state by a Communist revolution in March 1919.

The final collapse of the empire was precipitated not only by the internal, nationalistic pressures from within, but also by the reverses and financial exhaustion of the war; with an inefficient system of agriculture, there had been worsening food shortages from 1915. Franz Josef had been about the only force for cohesion and stability; with him gone, the empire fragmented, and the measures proposed by Karl and his ministers were too little, too late. Karl handed over command of what remained of the imperial army to Baron Hermann Kövess von Kövessháza (1854–1924), and relinquished his position as head of state on 11 November; on the following day the Republic of Austria was proclaimed. The empire was dismantled officially by the Treaty of St. Germain (10 September 1919, part of the Versailles settlement), with Austria reduced to a fragment of its former size. Karl fled to Switzerland in March 1919 and renounced his decree of 11 November; in 1921 he twice attempted to return to Hungary, was arrested on the latter occasion and deported to Madeira, where he died in 1922.

In March 1919 a Communist dictatorship under Béla Kun was established in Hungary, which was followed by a Hungarian invasion of Czechoslovakia (March 1919), a Roumania invasion of Hungary (to forestall a Hungarian attempt to re-take the Roumanian-occupied Transylvania), and an anti-Communist revolution. The Communists were driven from power and a government instituted under Archduke Josef (1872–1962) as Regent of Hungary; as a representative of the old regime he was unacceptable to the Entente powers, and from March 1920 was replaced by Admiral Miklós Horthy de Nagybánya (1868–1957), who remained in power until 1944.

Army

The armed forces of the empire had been starved of resources in the pre-war period, so that despite the size of Austria–Hungary the military establishment was comparatively weak. The army was divided into three main bodies. The 'Common Army' ('Imperial and Royal', *kaiserlich und königlich* or 'KuK') was the regular force recruited from both parts of the Dual Monarchy, and under central command. This was supported by two national armies, controlled by their respective state governments: the Austrian *Landwehr*, styled 'Imperial Royal' or 'KK', and the Royal Hungarian Landwehr, known as *königlich ungarische* or 'KU', more commonly styled the Honved. Although all three were regular formations, it was intended that the Common Army would be deployed abroad in event of war, and the others used for home defence; but from 1890 it was realized that in order to wage war effectively, the *Landwehr* would have to be upgraded into first-line troops, and a new force organized for home-defence, the Austrian ('KK') and Royal Hungarian ('KU') *Landsturm*.

Recruits were raised by limited conscription from age 21, though by no means all of those eligible actually served (important occupations and sole supporters of families received only basic training and then passed to the Ersatz Reserve, to be used only in wartime). Service was three years with the colours and ten in the reserve (cavalry and horse artillery four and seven respectively), then five years in the *Landsturm* first reserve before passing into the second reserve. Volunteer service was also possible, mostly in the Common Army, which permitted the recruit to choose his unit; and the educated classes could serve as 'one-year volunteers' only, maintained at their own expense in exchange for the shorter enlistment. Bosnia–Herzegovina had no *Landwehr* or *Landsturm*: after service with the colours their men passed into the first to third reserves of the regulars. Less than one-third of the army was German; almost half, and approaching three-quarters of the infantry, were Slavs. Officers were trained at a military academy, and the one-year volunteers formed a reserve of candidate officers for wartime. Shortage of leaders was a serious problem: with the army suffering almost 42 per cent losses in the first year of the war, there were insufficient NCOs to be promoted, resulting in untrained conscripts with inexperienced junior officers, which in turn resulted in a greater rate of surrenders and desertions than in other armies (almost half a million were taken prisoner in the first year of the war). Lack of enthusiasm was also a factor: in April 1915 almost all the members of the 28th Infantry (Viktor Emmanuel III, König von Italien) surrendered to the Russians, which created quite a stir, as its headquarters was in Prague and its personnel Czechs with no great loyalty to the empire, typical of the attitude of some of the nationalists within the empire.

The army was divided into sixteen corps, each with a military district from which its recruits were drawn (except XV Corps, based in Bosnia–Herzegovina, which drew its personnel from other districts; Bosnian and Herzegovinian units served elsewhere). Headquarters were: I Corps Cracow, II Vienna, III Graz, IV Budapest, V Pressburg, VI Kaschau, VII Temesvár, VIII Prague, IX Josefstadt, X Przemysl, XI Lemberg, XII Hermannstadt, XIII Agram, XIV Innsbruck, XV Sarajevo, XVI Ragusa. Others were formed during the war, XVII and XVIII in 1914, XIX 1915 (though originally assembled as *Corps Krauss* in the Balkans in September 1914), XX and XXI in 1916 (against Italy), XXII and XXIII also 1916, and XXIV–XXVI in 1917. The initial plan was for six Armies, with a seventh formed in the Carpathians in 1914; in the same year the Fifth and Sixth Armies in the Balkans were amalgamated. Three armies were formed in 1915 (a new Fifth, 'Group Rohr' and Tirol), and Third Army dissolved on the Eastern Front, to be re-created in Serbia. First Army (Eastern Front) was dissolved in 1916 and re-formed against Roumania; Eleventh and Twelfth Armies were formed and 'Group Rohr' numbered Tenth. Fifth Army became the First and Second Isonzo Armies, and a new Sixth Army was

Austrian encampment in the Carpathians.

formed on the Italian Front in late 1917. In 1918 the Eastern Front armies were reformed into 'General Kommandos', and Second Army (Ukraine) re-styled 'KuK Eastern Army'.

Corps organization was generally of two infantry divisions, each of two brigades of two or more infantry regiments and a *Jäger* battalion, with an artillery brigade and usually a cavalry brigade of two regiments, though in 1914 I, II and X Corps each had a cavalry division of two brigades, and XI Corps two cavalry divisions. Basic divisional organization remained largely unchanged, but during the war cavalry divisions were reduced to single-brigade formations.

Divisions were numbered consecutively, 49 (infantry) existing in 1914 and nine more being formed before the end of the year: these included 1st–12th, 14th–19th, 24th, 25th, 27th–36th, 47th–50th, 52nd–56th, 1st–4th Cavalry and 6th–10th Cavalry, all Common Army; 13th, 21st, 22nd, 26th, 43rd–46th, all 'KK' *Landwehr*; 20th, 23rd, 37th–42nd, 51st, 5th and 11th Cavalry, all Honved; and 95th and 106th *Landsturm*. Upon mobilization, extra brigades were added, including 32 of 'KK' and seventeen of 'KU' *Landsturm*, some nominated as line-of-communication forces only, though despite the original intention the *Landsturm* was pushed into the front line almost from the outset. By the turn of 1917–18 there were 44 Common Army divisions, 10 'KK' *Landwehr* (re-titled *Schützen*), twelve Honved, nine Common Army cavalry, one 'KK' *Schützen* cavalry, and two Honved cavalry.

Infantry

In 1914 there were 102 consecutively numbered line regiments in the Common Army, four Tirolean *Kaiserjäger*

and four Bosnian–Herzegovinian regiments; they were also known by the name of the *Inhaber* (colonel-in-chief), or a few retained the title of a famous personage (e.g., Regiment General Paul Kray, Nr. 67, named after the Napoleonic general). Each comprised four battalions of four companies each, plus a machine-gun company. Regiments nos. 2, 5, 6, 12, 16, 19, 23, 25, 26, 29, 31–34, 37–39, 43, 44, 46, 48, 50–53, 60–72, 76, 78, 79, 82, 83, 85, 86, 96 and 101 were Hungarian. There were 30 *Jäger* battalions (styled *Feldjäger*), one of which was Bosnian–Herzegovinian, and six independent frontier companies from that region. The 'KK' *Landwehr* had 40 regiments (including three of Tirolean *Jägers* or *Landesschützen*) and the Honved 32, all of three battalions each. The Tirolean *Jägers* and 'KK' *Landwehr* Regiments 4 and 27 were specialist mountain troops. The Tiroleans were not supposed to be moved from the Italian frontier, but in 1914 were sent to the Eastern Front, being replaced by reserves drawn from local rifle clubs (*Standschützen*).

Peacetime establishment was about 1,600 per regiment; in wartime, each company was augmented to 240 men, giving a battalion strength of about 1,000 (*Landsturm* about 800). Regimental machine-gun companies had three sections, with a fourth mobilized for war, each battalion having two guns; machine-gun detachments were only added to some *Landsturm* formations in 1915. In 1916 the numbers of guns was doubled, and trebled in 1917, when light machine-guns were also added, each battalion having a platoon of eight guns. Reinforcement was provided by '*marsch*' regiments, of which the Common Army originally had 28 and the Honved sixteen; *Jäger* battalions had a *marsch* company. During the war, every regiment received a monthly reinforcement of a *marsch* battalion (about 800–1,000 strong), which was distributed among the ordinary battalions when it joined the regiment. Mobilized at the outbreak of war, 38 Austrian and 32 Honved *Landsturm* regiments were formed, as well as independent units, increasing in number when the age of service of *Landsturm* men was later extended to 18–55.

New units were created during the war: 103rd Infantry in 1915, 104th 1916 and 105th–109th 1917; three *Feldjäger* and two Bosnian–Herzegovinian *Jäger* battalions in 1915, the 4th–8th 1916 and 5th Bosnian–Herzegovinian Infantry 1916. In 1915 some ephemeral Bosnian–Herzegovinian garrison battalions were formed, and in 1916 the frontier *Jäger* companies were extended to battalion strength. In October 1917 all line regiments were reduced to three battalions, new units being formed from the 4th battalions and the four most junior Bosnian–Herzegovinian *Jägers*, so that by early 1918 there were 138 infantry regiments (139th formed in May), four Tirolean *Jäger* and eight Bosnian–Herzegovinian regiments, each of three battalions. The 'KK' *Landwehr* was retitled *Schützen* in early 1917, the Tirolean *Landesschützen* re-styled *Kaiserschützen*, and the 4th and 27th 'KK' *Landwehr* Regiments re-titled 1st and 2nd Mountain Regiments (*Gebirgsschützen*). The Honved (an official designation after early 1917) formed seventeen new regiments (300th–316th); by 1918 the *Landsturm* included 23 regiments (eight Hungarian) and 217 independent battalions, of which four were Tirolean, sixteen Hungarian, and 156 for line-of-communication duties (65 Hungarian).

Each battalion's pioneer section was expanded from 1916 into a 'technical company', each of a searchlight, trench-mortar and grenade section; telephone sections were added to each battalion. Storm-troops were formed from early 1916, with organization formalized in later 1917 so that by early 1918 each division possessed a storm-battalion assembled from the storm-detachments of the component units.

From 1909 a new field uniform was introduced, in pike-grey (*Hechtgrau*), consisting of a soft kepi with black or grey peak and a flap to cover the ears, bearing a cockade with the Emperor's cipher ('FJI', later 'K', in brass or black, bullion for officers, and a horn badge for *Jägers*); a single-breasted tunic, with fly-front, standing (later stand-and-fall) collar, patch breast- and side-pockets and facing-coloured *Paroli* (collar-patch, also worn on the double-breasted greatcoat), trousers with combined ankle-gaiters and ankle-boots (knee-breeches, grey wool stockings and climbing-boots for mountain troops). For Hungarian regiments the cap-cipher was 'IFJ', later 'IK', and trousers bore a yellow welt and thigh-knot (grey for Honved). Bosnian–Herzegovinian units wore a red or pike-grey fez with black or pike-grey tassel respectively, and loose pantaloons (white trousers in summer). *Paroli* were coloured as follows: crimson: Regiments 1, 18, 52, 53; imperial yellow 2, 22, 27, 31; sky-blue 3, 4, 19; rose-pink 5, 6, 13, 97; dark-brown 7, 12, 83, 93; grass-green 8, 28, 61, 62, 'KK' *Landwehr*, all *Jägers*; apple-green 9, 54, 79, 85; parrot-green 10, 46, 50, 91; ash-grey 11, 24, 33, 51; black 14, 26, 38, 58; madder red 15, 34, 44, 74; sulphur-yellow 16, 41, 99, 101; red-brown 17, 55, 68, 78; lobster-red 20, 35, 67, 71; sea-green 21, 25, 70, 87; cherry-red 23, 43, 73, 77; light-blue 29, 32, 40, 72, 75, 104 and all after; pike-grey 30, 49, 69, 76; light-red 36, 57, 65, 66; scarlet 37, 39, 45, 80; orange-yellow 42, 59, 63, 64; steel-green 47, 48, 56, 60; carmine 81, 82, 84, 96; amaranth 86, 90, 95; wine-red 88, 89; white 92, 94; fawn 98, 100; sea/grass-green 102; alzarin red, all Bosnians; grey Honved and Hungarian *Landsturm* (pink after 1917). Buttons were yellow for Regiments 1, 2, 4, 5, 8, 9, 11–16, 21, 26, 27, 30, 32, 35, 40, 43–6, 48, 51, 52, 55–57, 59, 61, 64, 65, 68, 70–73, 76, 84–86, 89–91, 93, 94, 96, 99, 100, 102, *Jägers*, Bosnian infantry, Honved and Hungarian *Landsturm*; and white for the remainder.

Austrian troops manning a trench-system.

Rank-insignia was borne on the collar or *Paroli* in button-coloured lace and stars (bone or composition stars in white for NCOs): 1st class private one star, corporal two, sergeant three, sergeant-major (*Feldwebel*) three and yellow collar-edge, cadet-sergeant same with inner gold lace, ensign (*Fähnrich*) one silver star and gold collar-edge, company officers one to three button-coloured stars, field officers button-coloured metallic lace edging and one to three contrastingly-coloured stars, general officers the same but gold zigzag lace edging. Staff officers retained the stiff-sided pike-grey kepi. A feature of Austrian uniform throughout the war was the continued use of the *Feldzeichen* ('field-sign', green foliage worn in the head-dress, a recognition-symbol pre-dating the invention of national uniforms).

From 1915 the pike-grey uniform began to be replaced by a similar one in field-grey (with stand-and-fall collar and puttees); from the same year German steel helmets were issued to storm troops, later to all infantry, manufactured in Austria and named 'Berndorfer' after the designer. The *Paroli* became simply a strip of cloth sewn to the collar, and from 1917 grey patches bearing unit-number and identity were sewn to the shoulder-straps of tunic and greatcoat, and on the side of the cap. In addition to unit-numbers the letters used on these badges included 'BH' (Bosnian–Herzegovinian infantry), 'BHJ' (ditto *Jägers*), 'FJ' (*Feld-jäger*), 'GrJ' (frontier or *Grenzjäger*), 'J' (*Jägers*), 'KJ' (*Kaiserjäger*), 'KS' (*Kaiserschützen*), 'LSB' (independent *Land-sturm-Bataillone*) and 'TJ' (*Tirolerjäger*). These identifications were dark-blue, green for 'KK' *Landwehr* and *Jägers*, grey for Honved (red from late 1917) and pink for 'KK' *Landsturm*. Other changes included a tunic with cloth-covered buttons on the breast, styled a *Karlsbluse* after the emperor.

Equipment was medium-brown leather, the waist-belt with a buckle, eagle-plate or plate bearing the Hungarian arms; the 1888 pattern had one cartridge-pouch on each side of the buckle, each holding 20 rounds, the 1909 pattern two 10-round pouches on each side. A rolled greatcoat was strapped over the top of the tanned hide knapsack, below which was a smaller hide knapsack containing 50 rounds and canned food. Bread, canteen and personal equipment was carried in a canvas haversack at the left; mountain troops used a rucksack instead of the ordinary equipment, and carried climbing gear. The standard rifle was the 8mm 1895 Mannlicher, but older 1888–90 and 1890 patterns were used by third-line formations, and the 1890 or 1895 *Stützen* (carbine) by mountain troops. Officers carried the pistol of their choice, generally the 8mm Steyr or 9mm Steyer-Hahn automatic; their stirrup-hilted, slightly curved swords with 30in blade (24in for mountain troops) were soon discarded or replaced by a bayonet. The standard machine-gun was the Schwarzlose, manufactured at Steyr, a notably simple machine easy to maintain, adopted in 1907.

Cavalry

Of the eleven cavalry divisions, all were Common Army save 9th and 11th (Honved), and 5th was formed only during mobilization. The eight standing divisions comprised 19 brigades, generally each of two brigades, totalling four regiments; the remainder were distributed as divisional cavalry. Regiments were organized into half-regiments, each of three field squadrons about 160 strong; each regiment possessed a telegraph and pioneer section, and each division had one or two machine-gun sections (generally four guns) and a horse artillery division (three batteries, total twelve guns).

The regiments comprised: 1st–15th Dragoons, 1st–16th Hussars and eleven *Uhlan* (lancer) regiments numbered 1–8, 11–13; the 'KK' *Landwehr* included six *Uhlan* regiments (renamed mounted *Schützen* 1917) and two half-regiments of Mounted Rifles, one Tirolean and one Dalmatian; the Honved included ten hussar regiments, and upon mobilization ten half-regiments of Honved *Landsturm* hussars were formed. Other regiments received two reserve squadrons at the same time. Austrian cavalry tactics were outdated and unsuccessful against the more modern Russian system, which favoured dismounted fire-fighting instead of mounted 'shock', and by early 1915 some Austrian regiments were already fielding dismounted sections. By late 1917 only one mounted squadron was maintained in each infantry and cavalry division. The remaining regiments were formed into two half-regiments styled cavalry *Schützen-divisionen* of four dismounted squadrons each, two machine-gun squadrons (eight guns each), two light machine-gun sections, a technical (pioneer) section; an infantry support section of one searchlight, two trench-mortar and two grenade squads; and a mounted telephone squad. Cavalry divisions henceforth comprised four dismounted regiments, a storm battalion, an engineer detachment, a telegraph company and one mounted squadron. A 12th Division was created in March 1918.

Although a service uniform had been planned from 1909, it had only been issued to machine-gun detachments, others wearing full-dress helmets and coloured uniforms at the beginning of the war. Dragoons wore a single-breasted, light-blue tunic with facing-coloured cuffs and standing collar, madder-red trousers, black knee-boots and black leather combed helmet with brass eagle-plate and chinscales (gilt fittings and comb for officers), worn with a grey cover, or painted grey, for active service. In winter, a double-breasted, light-blue pelisse (*Pelz*) was worn over the tunic, with facing-coloured cuffs and black fleece collar and lining (white for officers). Facing-colours were: dark-red, Regiments 1, 3; black 2, 6; grass-green 4, 9; imperial-yellow 5, 12; sulphur-yellow 7, 10; scarlet 8, 11; madder-red 13, 14; white 15. Buttons were white for Regiments 1, 2, 5, 7, 11, 13 and 15, and yellow for the remainder. Greatcoats were brown.

Hussars wore a single-breasted hussar tunic (*Attila*) in dark-blue (light-blue for Regiments 2, 4, 6, 7, 10, 12, 14, 16) with yellow and black cord decoration (officers, gold and black) and yellow olive-shaped toggle-buttons (white for Regiments 4, 5, 7, 9. 11–13), madder-red trousers with piping and thigh-knots as on the *Attila*, a winter pelisse like the *Attila* but with fleece as for dragoons, black hussar boots, and a low felt shako of regimental colour with brass eagle-plate and a regimentally-coloured American-cloth service cover: dark-blue Regiments 1, 13; white 2, 3, 9, 12; madder-red 4, 5, 8, 14; ash-grey 6, 11, 15, 16. The Honved hussars wore the same with dark-blue *Attila* with red cords (officers, gold and red), yellow toggles, shakos grey (Regiment 1), light-blue 2, white 3, madder-red 4, 5, 8–10, grass-green 7, bearing the Hungarian arms badge. The Honved *Landsturm* hussars had the same with white toggles and madder-red shako for all regiments.

The *Uhlans* wore a single-breasted light blue tunic (*Ulanka*) with regimental facings, and a double-breasted winter version with coloured cuffs and fleece collar and lining; legwear as before, and a small square-topped *czapka* in black leather with facing-coloured cloth top, brass chinscales and eagle plate, and a grey service cover. Facing-colours were: imperial-yellow, Regiments 1, 6; dark-green 2, 7; madder-red 3, 8; white 4; light-blue 5; cherry-red 11; dark-blue 12, 13. Buttons were yellow (6–8, 11, 13 white). The 'KK' *Landwehr Uhlans* all had madder-red facings and white buttons. The Tirolean and Dalmatian Mounted Rifles wore a pike-grey tunic with grass-green collar and cuffs, white buttons, a matching fleece-lined pelisse for the Tirolean Regiment, blue-grey trousers piped grass-green, pike-grey greatcoat with grass-green *Paroli*, and a field cap or shako on service. All branches wore a red, peak-less side-cap on active service, and from 1915 the coloured uniforms were replaced by a field-grey service uniform like that of the infantry, including riding-breeches worn with ankle boots and leather gaiters; facing-colours were retained as a *Paroli*. In the 1917 identity-patches, lettering was blue for Common Army (letters 'D', 'H' and 'U' according to branch), green for Mounted Rifles ('RDS' and 'RTS' for Dalmatian and Tirolean regiments), red for 'KK' *Landwehr* and Honved (the latter with 'HH'), and grey ('HO') for *Landsturm* hussars.

Equipment was brown leather, with ammunition-pouches on the waist-belt. All carried sabres (of various patterns), and from 1908 the 'M7'-pattern Roth-Steyr automatic pistol. Carbines were of the 1890 or 1895 pattern, with no provision for a bayonet, or latterly the 1895 short rifle (*Stützen*).

Artillery

Despite attempts to remedy the defects in the two years before the war, artillery equipment was under-strength and outdated. Initially, each Common Army division included a field artillery brigade of a field regiment and field howitzer half-regiment; each 'KK' *Landwehr* division had a Common Army field regiment and half-regiments of *Landwehr* field guns and field howitzers; and each Honved division one or two Common Army field half-regiments and a Honved field regiment (the Honved had no howitzers). Each cavalry division had a horse artillery division (three batteries of four

guns each); heavy and mountain artillery was deployed at corps level.

Initially there were 42 consecutively numbered Common Army field regiments (nos. 10–21, 34–39 Hungarian). Each consisted of five batteries, each of four guns, rising to eight on mobilization; there were eight 'KK' *Landwehr* and eight Honved field regiments, each of four batteries. The fourteen Common Army field howitzer regiments (4th–7th, 12th and 13th Hungarian) each had four batteries of six howitzers each; upon mobilization each formed two half-regiments of two batteries each (the 14th into a half-regiment of field howitzers and another of mountain guns); there were eight 'KK' *Landwehr* field howitzer half-regiments. The nine Common Army half-regiments of horse artillery (numbered 1–11, no 3rd or 8th, the 4th–7th Hungarian) each had three batteries, four upon mobilization, each of four guns; there was one Honved horse half-battery. The Common Army had fourteen heavy half-regiments (two batteries each) and 10½ mountain regiments, each of six batteries including two of mountain howitzers, each forming an additional battery of guns on mobilization; these were numbered 3–14 (no 1st, 2nd, 5th or 9th), of which 6, 7, 12 and 13 were Hungarian, as was the Dalmatian half-regiment, which had no howitzers. The fortress artillery included six regiments (three battalions each, the 6th Hungarian) and ten battalions (2nd, 3rd and 7th Hungarian), all Common Army.

The field gun at the outbreak of war was a 9cm quick-firer, introduced in 1905, but except for the twelve 2-gun batteries of 305mm mortars (some of which went to Western Front) the heavier guns were obsolete, principally the 1899 105mm field howitzer and 1899 mountain gun. By early 1915 new 100mm light and 150mm heavy field howitzers, and 100mm and motor-drawn 150mm field guns had been introduced; some of the re-equipment was achieved by the appropriation of ordnance being manufactured for the Chinese and Turkish governments: units so equipped were styled 'Chinese' or 'Turkish' batteries. New mountain artillery was introduced (1915-pattern 75mm gun and 100mm howitzer), and by late 1916 some fortress artillery was being upgraded. Some of this was astonishingly archaic: 1861 pieces were still in use, and most modern fortification pieces (240mm guns) were dismantled for use on the Eastern Front, leaving only the turret-mounted 100mm howitzers on the Italian border as modern artillery. The outdated pieces were replaced by 240mm and 350mm guns and 210mm, 380mm and 420mm mortars.

The artillery establishment expanded greatly, with an increase in weight and of howitzers in relation to field guns: the 28 heavy batteries increased to 328 at the armistice (the lighter batteries were not much more than doubled), and as howitzers increased to outnumber guns by three to one, some field-gun batteries were converted to howitzers. Mountain batteries increased from 74 in 1914 to 324. By February 1918 all regiments were styled 'Field Artillery'; each division henceforth had two field regiments (each of two gun, three howitzers and one AA or TM battery), one

Austrian 42cm howitzer on bed for firing.

heavy regiment (4–5 batteries, 150mm howitzers with one 104mm gun battery), and a mountain group (two gun and one howitzer battery). There were fourteen independent mountain regiments (each of six gun and three howitzer batteries), the fortress artillery was re-named 'heavy' and organized into regiments of four groups, each of four batteries; and the horse artillery was re-titled 'mounted field artillery', each unit of four howitzer, two gun and one TM battery.

The artillery wore the ordinary field uniform (horse artillery with cavalry legwear), with scarlet *Paroli* and yellow buttons. The 1917 identification-patches had blue numbers and letters (*Landwehr* red), 'FAR' or 'SFAR' for field and heavy field regiments, 'FSR' fortress, and crossed cannons badge for horse and mountain artillery.

Supporting services

Initially the engineer service consisted of eight pioneer battalions (four companies each), fourteen sapper battalions (three companies each), and a pontoon battalion. Additional units were created at the outbreak of war (new battalions plus an increase of companies per battalion), and combat units were formed (trench-mortars, grenades, searchlights and in 1917 a gas battalion). The 1917–18 reorganization disbanded the pioneers, so that henceforth there were 60 sapper battalions (three companies each) including one per division, plus pontoon units and a flame-thrower battalion. Service uniform had cherry-red *Paroli* and yellow buttons; the 1917 patches had blue lettering (*Landwehr* red) with letters 'S', 'P' or 'Br' for sappers, pioneers and pontoon (bridging) units respectively, and crossed pick and shovel for labour companies.

Each division maintained its own train; an increasing number of motorized units were created during the war.

The Railway Regiment was increased from 34 to 71 companies during the war; it also manned the armoured trains used in Galicia. The Telegraph Regiment's four battalions increased to 249 companies. The Train service wore service uniform with light-blue *Paroli*, white buttons, and patch with blue 'T' and numeral; medical services had a madder-red *Paroli*, yellow buttons, and patch bearing the unit-number and cross in blue.

Navy

The navy existed largely for coastal defence, and was limited in size due to the comparatively short coastline, along the Adriatic; the main base was at Pola, but there was a significant installation at Trieste, and a fleet of monitors on the Danube. Operations were limited, largely to patrol and raiding in the Adriatic, but the presence of the capital ships expended Allied resources to keep them in port. The following ships of 2,000 tons displacement or more existed in the first year of war:

Date	Name & displacement (tons)	Main armament only
Battleships		
1896–7	Budapest, Monarch, Wien (5,600)	4 × 9.4in, 6 × 6in
1903–4	Arpad, Babenberg, Habsburg (8,340)	3 × 9.4in, 12 × 6in
1905–7	Erzherzog Ferdinand Maximilian,	4 × 9.4in, 12 × 7.6in
	Erzherzog Friedrich, Erzherzog Karl (10,600)	
1910–11	Erzherzog Franz Ferdinand, Radetzky,	4 × 12in, 8 × 9.4in,
	Zrinyi (14,500)	20 × 4.1in
1912–15	Prinz Eugen, Szent Istvan, Tegetthof, Viribus Unitis (20,000)	12 × 12in, 12 × 6in
Cruisers		
1899	Kaiser Karl VI (6,325)	2 × 9.4in, 8 × 6in

Viribus Unitis, fleet flagship, 20,000-ton dreadnought battleship (12 × 12in, 12 × 6in, 18 × 12pdr and 2 × 12pdr AA guns, 4 × 21in torpedo tubes); sunk 1 November 1918.

An Austrian poster, 'Subscribe to the 5½ per cent Third War Loan', a powerful evocation of the Empire breaking lances bearing the flags of Italy (top) and Russia, upon a shield bearing the Imperial arms. Drawn by Erwin Puchinger.

1900–1	*Aspern, Szigetvar, Zenta* (sunk Adriatic 1914) (2,350–2,400)	8 × 4 .7in
1905–6	(reconstructed) *Kaiser Franz Josef, Kaiserin Elizabeth* (sunk 1914) (4,060)	8 × 6in
1906	*Sankt George* (7,400)	2 × 9.4in, 5 × 7.6in, 4 × 6in.
1907	(reconstructed) *Kaiserin und Königin Maria Theresia* (5,200)	2 × 7.6in, 8 × 6in
1910	*Admiral Spaun* (3,500)	7 × 4.1in
1914	*Helgoland, Novara, Saida* (3,500)	9 × 4.1in

There were also five torpedo-gunboats, eleven submarines, eighteen destroyers and 91 torpedo-boats.

Aviation service

Like most branches of Austro–Hungarian service, the flying corps (*Luftfahrtruppen*) was neglected and under-funded. Not until 1913 was a flying company (six aircraft) established to supplement the existing balloon companies, and despite the growth of aircraft-manufacturing (home-designed as well as German machines produced under licence), the aviation service always remained behind requirements. A total of 37 companies existed by late 1916, and in the following year specialized units were formed, priority being given to reconnaissance (deployed at divisional level), with a limited number of fighter and bomber companies.

The following provides very brief details of aircraft built by Austria–Hungary:

Albatros: the 21–24 series were two-seater reconnaissance biplanes, based on the German Albatros B-type by the OAW company (*Oesterreichische Albatros Werke*), used in the earlier years of the war. The 22/23 series of Knoller–Albatros alone was armed (with a Schwarzlose gun for the observer).

Aviatik: built by the Austrian subsidiary of the German Aviatik company (O-UFA, *Oesterreichische-Ungarische Flugzeugfabrik Aviatik*). BII and BIII: two-seater reconnaissance biplanes used until early 1916, as trainers thereafter; both could carry a small bomb-load, but only the BIII had a machine-gun. CI: two-seater reconnaissance biplane used from early 1917 and ultimately manufactured by other companies; known as the 'Berg' from its designer, Julius von Berg. The 1918 photo-reconnaissance version was a single-seater. DI: the first single-seater biplane fighter designed and built in Austria; known as the 'Berg Scout', in service in later 1917.

Hansa-Brandenburg: the CI was a German two-seater reconnaissance biplane produced in considerable numbers by the Austrian manufacturers Phönix and Ufag; known as 'Big Brandenburg' to differentiate it from 'Little Brandenburg', the BI trainer; used from early 1916. CC: German-designed single-seater flying-boat built by Phönix for the Austrian Navy; the three-seater Brandenburg FB flying-boat was also used. DI: German-designed single-seater biplane fighter used exclusively by Austria–Hungary, 1916–17; built by Phönix and Ufag.

Knoller CI/II: two-seater reconnaissance biplane which never saw active service because of structural defects.

Lloyd CI–V: two-seater reconnaissance biplanes produced by *Ungarische Lloyd Flugzeug und Motorenfabrik* and WKF (*Wiener Karosserie und Flugzeugfabrik*), of which the CII and CIII (1915–16) were the most prolific; the CV was used as a trainer. Initially unarmed, later fitted with rear Schwarzlose.

Lohner: the BI–VII and CI were two-seater reconnaissance and trainer biplanes, produced by Jakob Lohner of Vienna; BII used principally as a trainer, BIV the first to be armed (Schwarzlose for observer). E and L: two-seater biplane pusher flying-boat/reconnaissance/bomber, the E

ZEICHNET

5½% dritte
KRIEGS-
ANLEIHE

casualties, including probably more than 920,000 dead, though exact figures are impossible to determine.

References

Anon. *Handbook of the Austro–Hungarian Army in the War.* General Staff, London 1918

Andrássy, Count J. *The Collapse of the Austro–Hungarian Empire.* London, 1930

Crankshaw, E. *The Fall of the House of Habsburg.* London, 1966

Czernin, Count O. von. *In the World War.* London, 1919

Gooch, G. P. *The Races of Austria·Hungary.* London, 1917

Hanak, H. *Great Britain and Austria–Hungary during the First World War.* London, 1962

Lucas, J. *Austro–Hungarian Infantry Uniforms 1914–18.* London, 1973

— *Fighting Troops of the Austro–Hungarian Army 1868–1914.* Tunbridge Wells, 1987 (Concentrates on pre-war period but is an excellent study of the army as it stood at the outbreak of war)

Manteyer, G. de (ed). *Austria's Peace Offer 1916–17.* London, 1921 (Prince Sixte de Bourbon's attempt to broker peace)

Pribram, A. F. *Austrian Foreign Policy 1908–1918.* London, 1923

Ruhl, M. *Die Osterreichische-Ungarische Armee.* Leipzig, n.d. (leading source on uniforms)

Strauss Feuerlicht, R. *The Desperate Act: the Assassination of Francis Ferdinard at Sarajevo.* New York, 1968

Taylor, A. J. P. *The Habsburg Monarchy 1815–1918.* London, 1949

Zeman, Z. A. B. *The Break-up of the Habsburg Empire 1914–1918.* London, 1961

operational in the early war and the L 1915–18. A successful design: crew sat side-by-side, the observer with a Schwarzlose. The Lohner R was a purely reconnaissance version.

Oeffag CI/II: two-seater reconnaissance biplane produced by Oeffag (*Oesterreichische Flugzeugfabrik*); CI produced 1915, but not successful, and used only as a trainer; improved CII used 1917–18.

Phönix: the CI was a two-seater reconnaissance biplane apparently based on the Hansa–Brandenburg CII, produced 1918. DI–III: single-seater biplane fighters developed from Hansa–Brandenburg DI; limited ability to climb and manoeuvre, so employed mainly on escort and reconnaissance duties, and by the navy.

Ufag CI: two-seater reconnaissance biplane similar to the Phönix CI and probably similarly derived from the Hansa–Brandenburg CII; tested against the Phönix CI and although both were accepted, the Ufag was probably the better machine. In service from spring 1918.

In addition to home-produced aircraft, some of German construction were also employed, for example the Etrich Taube.

By the armistice there were 82 aviation companies, 32 balloon companies, and a smaller naval air service operating flying-boats.

The total mobilization of the empire during the war was in the region of 7.8 million men, of whom 4.5 million became

A view of Austro–Hungarian discipline is provided by a British military internee working in a Hungarian military hospital:

'I kicked up a row about the Colonel's pleasing habit of doing minor operations, such as lopping off fingers and toes without using any anaesthetic. The officers in the Austrian army are not quite so arrogant as their Prussian brethren, but they seemed to me to be utterly callous and often brutal in their treatment of the men under their care . . .

'One of the two men of the Labour Corps got "mad drunk" one day and chased the cook with a huge carving-knife. I heard the screams of the latter whilst I was talking to the Colonel one evening, and he sent me to investigate. I found the cook flying round the building with "Josef" hard on her heels with the knife and evidently meaning business, so I yelled to "cookie" to make for the room where the Colonel was, and tried unsuccessfully to lay hands on "Josef". The game finally came to an abrupt conclusion when "cookie" burst into the room, closely followed by "Josef" and the carving-knife. I was just in time to see the old Colonel deal with the situation in a masterly manner . . . he ignored the cook, took one step forward and caught "Josef" between the eyes as hard as he could hit, then, before he could recover, turned him round and propelled him into my arms by means of a series of whole-hearted kicks . . . Next day "Josef" lost his "cushy" job and left the Hospital for his depot . . .'

('J.G.' (J. Gardiner), in *The Return*, 25 October 1918, pp. 12–13)

BELGIUM

A small country refusing to be crushed by a great power, 'plucky little Belgium' occupied a special place in Allied popular sentiment. Baden Powell, quoting the David and Goliath analogy and comparing Belgium to a peaceful little tailor set upon by 'a big, beery loafer', remarked that the reason for Britain's admiration was because 'There are two things above all others which Britons, down to the very lowest among them, inherently appreciate, and those are Pluck and Fair Play.'[1] Asquith stated that the Belgian people had 'won the immortal glory which belongs to a people who prefer freedom to ease, to security, even to life itself',[2] and it is this image of Belgian resistance, overlaid with gory accounts of atrocities perpetrated on the civilian population, that has coloured many accounts of Belgium's participation in the war.

Belgium's neutrality had been guaranteed by the great powers, and it was this declaration, the 'scrap of paper', over which Britain went to war. Belgium was a constitutional monarchy, whose king, Albert I (1875–1934) had succeeded his uncle, Leopold II, in December 1909; the son of Prince Philip of Saxe–Coburg, Albert was a cultured and capable monarch whose life had been spent in the army. His country was prosperous, and despite its small size and population (less than 7½ million in 1910) as a commercial nation ranked sixth in the world. Government was by a parliament of two houses, senate and national assembly, elected by proportional representation, electors (males of 25 years and over) having one to three votes according to their circumstances. The king was nominally head of the government, delegating executive powers to a cabinet, but had the right to initiate laws. The Catholic Party had been in power since 1884, and its head was Baron Charles de Broqueville (1860–1940). Internal administration was based upon nine provinces, each with a governor nominated by the king and each sub-divided into cantons, of which 342 existed in all.

A route through Belgium being necessary for their attack upon France, on 2 August 1914 Germany issued an ultimatum demanding access through Belgian territory and the use of the fortresses of Liège and Namur; Belgium's refusal resulted in immediate invasion. Belgium's neutral status prevented her joining the Entente powers immediately, and in fact upon mobilization (31 July) her forces were deployed to resist not only the declared threat from Germany but also against possible French incursions. The German Army crossed the Belgian frontier during the night of 3–4 August, and despite resistance advanced to capture Brussels (20 August), until only the very north-west of the country remained outside German control. The invasion was accompanied by great destruction and, whilst the 'atrocity' stories were exaggerated, by much barbaric treatment inflicted upon the civilian population, only in part as reprisals against armed civilians (*francs-tireurs*) who had resisted the invaders. The wider aim was presumably to overawe the civilian population and forestall organized resistance behind German lines, but while achieving this objective it aroused widespread condemnation, not only in those countries already engaged against Germany.

The Belgian government retired from Brussels to Antwerp, thence to Ostend and finally to Le Havre; the diplomatic community followed save for the representatives of the USA, the Netherlands and Spain, who remained in Brussels. More than a million civilians fled, the bulk to Holland (from where all but about 50,000 returned upon German promises of good treatment), some 200,000 to France and 100,000 to Britain. The surviving part of the army was withdrawn to the small enclave not under occupation, and to France, and remained in the Allied line throughout the war. To maintain it, the king's appeals brought thousands of recruits who had escaped from occupied Belgium, and on 1 March 1915 universal conscription was enacted on Belgians aged 18–25 and living in free Belgium, France and Britain, and on 21 July 1916 this was extended to those aged 18–40 and resident in Allied or neutral countries. The plight of the refugees was recognized by the Allied nations and numerous funds were established for their relief.

The German administration was harsh, and Belgium's resources were plundered. An attempt was made to exploit ancient Flemish/Walloon rivalry, Germany intending to establish an independent Flanders under German protection, governed by a German-inspired political movement, *Raed van Vlaenderen*, with its own Flemish army to serve alongside that of Germany; Brussels was intended to be the capital of Flanders and Namur for the remainder. The plan failed when it became obvious that but for a small minority, even the most ardent Flemish-speakers regarded their loyalty as being primarily to the greater Belgium. There was no armed resistance in the occupied areas, but passive resistance was widespread, encouraged by clandestine news-sheets such as *La Libre Belgique*. More than 115,000 Belgians were deported to labour in Germany, beginning October 1916, but they were so unenthusiastic that their efforts were not worth their maintenance. Repatriation began in June 1917, but the workers involved were either compelled to labour in Belgium in the German interest, or were deported anew, many to occupied France.

With the ruination of the Belgian economy, food shortages among the civilians increased to the level of starvation. Throughout the war, hundreds of thousands of Belgians were dependent upon humanitarian aid received (with permission of the occupying Germans) from Allied and neutral nations, via organizations such as the Commission for the Relief of Belgium (CRB) and the *Comité national de secours et d'alimentation* (CN), administered initially by the US and Spanish governments. (When the USA entered the war, Holland took over their participation, and the CRB was retitled the *Comité Hispano–Neerlandais*). Nevertheless, by 1917 it was estimated that up to one-third of the ¾-million inhabitants of Brussels were destitute and kept alive only by

in the 1917 offensive on the grounds that it would only bring more devastation upon occupied Belgium. This brought him into conflict with his cabinet, especially de Broqueville, who favoured closer co-operation with the Allies. Albert was prepared to consider a separate, negotiated peace with Germany as early as the winter of 1915–16, and by late 1917 had even persuaded de Broqueville to contemplate it. The remainder of the cabinet, however, were so firmly against any compromise that amid mutterings of treason de Broqueville was forced to yield his portfolio as foreign minister (January 1918) and premier (May 1918), to be succeeded as foreign minister by Paul Hyams (1865–1941), previously Belgian Ambassador to Britain. Hyams became the most influential member of the cabinet, and (while a public split was avoided) exerted pressure on Albert, who finally relented. Belgian forces co-operated in the final offensive of 1918, and Albert's conversion to the Allied cause was confirmed by his appointment by Foch in late 1918 as commander of the Flanders Army Group, with some British and French forces under his command. Returning to his capital eleven days after the armistice, Albert actually began to advocate the abandonment of Belgium's traditional neutrality. Throughout the war he had been regarded by the public of the Allied nations as an unsullied hero, his obstruction of Allied plans of campaign remaining generally unknown. He was mourned universally upon his death in a mountaineering accident in February 1934.

Army

Belgium's military forces had not kept pace with her economic development, the 'guaranteed' neutrality providing little incentive for the improvement urged by King Albert.

In accord with legislation of 1902, recruitment was by a mixture of voluntary enlistment and limited conscription by ballot, although service was not compulsory as the provision of substitutes was permitted. Under pressure from the king and against the beliefs of their party, in 1912 the government accepted the principle of compulsory service, enacted in 1913, which demanded only one member from each household. The term of service decreed in 1912 was fifteen months with the colours (21 months for field artillery, 24 for horse artillery); but married men or those who supported families served only four months. In 1913 an army reorganization reformed training, equipment and command, and created a supervisory body, the *Conseil Supérieur de la Défense Nationale*, but as these reforms were scheduled to be completed only in 1918, they had little effect on the war. The active army was intended to number almost 43,000, with 100,000 reservists; by 1918, with the wider annual training, the mobilized army was intended to number about a quarter of a million, plus an additional 100,000 garrison troops. At the outbreak of war, only about 117,000 reservists were available, and many units were greatly under-strength.

The Belgian forces comprised the regular army, the Gendarmerie, and the *Garde Civique*. The Gendarmerie,

King Albert I (1875–1934).

soup-kitchens, and such privations had a severe effect: before the war there was a weekly average of 150 births and 140 deaths in Brussels; in 1917 these figures were 120 and 279 respectively. The monthly requirement of foodstuffs (excluding potatoes which were obtained locally) estimated by the CRB in April 1915 amounted to 79,000 tons.

King Albert remained a somewhat uneasy ally of the other Western Front powers, maintaining a stance which saw Belgium as a neutral nation compelled by invasion to fight. Collaboration by the Belgian forces was therefore limited: Albert declined to co-operate with Joffre in 1914, maintained a separate command and refused to participate

organized in three divisions and recruited from selected personnel, formed an élite cavalry more than 3,000 strong, but the *Garde Civique* was of little military value. Administered by the Home Department, not the War Department, it included all able-bodied men aged 21–32 not already in the army or reserve, with a reserve of those aged 33–50. From about 90,000 who had attended the statutory ten drills per year, probably only 37,000–40,000 were actually available for service. Some of the older volunteer corps and artillery could be regarded as decent Territorial troops; the remainder existed only as a deterrence to social unrest, and were not even accepted as part of the army by the Germans; thus, before the occupation of Brussels, the local *Gardes* laid down their weapons at the town hall to avoid being treated as *francs-tireurs*.

Prior to reorganization, the army comprised eight light cavalry regiments (two guides, two *chasseurs à cheval*, eight lancers); nineteen infantry regiments (including one of grenadiers, one carabiniers, three *chasseurs à pied*), each of three or four active and three or four reserve battalions; and 104 artillery batteries, including 30 field, four horse and the remainder garrison.

The new organization encompassed six infantry and one cavalry division (1st Ghent, 2nd Antwerp, 3rd Liège, 4th Namur, 5th Mons, 6th and cavalry Brussels), plus separate 13 (Namur) and 14 (Liège) mobile brigades. Each division was to comprise three brigades, each of two three-battalion regiments and three field batteries integrated at brigade level; divisional troops included a cavalry detachment,

engineers, commissariat and an artillery 'group' of three field and two 9.5in howitzer batteries. However, only one howitzer group had been formed, and none with the proposed 15cm howitzers, so that all the remainder were equipped with 75mm Krupp field guns. Wartime mobilization included the expansion of each regiment into two (six battalions); strength of a division was about 22,000 (cavalry 5,000). Each cavalry brigade comprised two 6-squadron regiments, a gendarmerie regiment, a cyclist battalion, a bicycle-mounted engineer detachment, three horse batteries and a motorized field-ambulance; but because not all the planned new cavalry regiments had been· formed, the cavalry division fielded only three brigades instead of the planned four. There were insufficient Maxim guns to make it the universal weapon as planned, and some units were armed with Hotchkiss guns removed from fortress service, and also used was the light Berthier gun, often carried on carts pulled by dogs, a form of transport common to Belgian milkmen.

Great importance was placed upon the fortresses of Antwerp, Liège and Namur; it was intended that the field army should number 150,000 men, with as many as 128,000 in the fortresses (90,000 in Antwerp) and 60,000 in reserve; the expected shortfall in numbers was to be remedied by mobilizing local *Gardes Civiques* for the fortress garrisons.

Following the withdrawal to the Yser, reorganization was necessary, with only about 32,000 front-line troops being under arms (the stand on the Yser, the Belgian Army's most notable exploit, cost about 18,000 casualties). Infantry

Belgian armoured car with traversible, cupola-style turret, of use only in the 'open' warfare which preceded the establishment of trench-lines. Note the odd tyres!

divisions comprised three mixed regiments (each of an infantry regiment and a field artillery group); the excess artillery for the infantry available led to the loan of two regiments to the British. In early 1917 another reorganization was possible, due largely to the adoption of the French Chauchat light machine-gun (six, later nine per company) which permitted a reduction in company-strength without a decrease of firepower. Divisions henceforth comprised three brigades of two infantry regiments, each of three battalions, each comprising three rifle companies (about 180 strong) and one machine-gun company with six guns; an artillery brigade of two regiments, two engineer battalions, two light cavalry squadrons and a cyclist company.

Stricter conscription permitted the army to maintain a front-line strength of about 170,000 for the remainder of the war. Training and medical facilities were largely in France, although three general hospitals were opened in Britain, in addition to the four in France. (The Cabour Hospitale, opened near Adinkerke in April 1915, had none other than Marie Curie as its head of radiography.) The total number of men mobilized during the war was about 267,000, of whom almost 14,000 were killed and about 45,000 wounded.

The original Belgian uniform was among the most outdated in Europe. In 1913 a single-breasted tunic (*vareuse*) with standing collar and brass buttons had been introduced, but many retained the previous double-breasted tunic. For infantry it was dark-blue with red piping (grey-blue on the 1913 uniform), with blue-grey trousers (dark-blue for

grenadiers) and a shako (on campaign covered in oilskin, with the regimental number painted on the front); light infantry wore the same in dark-green with yellow piping and blue-grey trousers piped green (*chasseurs à pied*) or yellow (carabiniers), and black leather gaiters; grenadiers wore bearskin caps and red tunic-piping, and carabiniers Tyrolean-style hats (kepis for their cyclists). The shako was soon discarded in favour of a peakless, round, dark-blue forage-cap with red piping and band, often worn with the double-breasted dark-blue greatcoat with brass buttons, instead of the tunic.

Cavalry uniforms included a short-skirted, double-breasted tunic introduced in 1913, worn in green with crimson piping and trousers and fur busbies by the two Guides regiments. The others had blue tunics and blue-grey trousers, with piping crimson (1st and 2nd Lancers), white (3rd and 4th Lancers), red (2nd and 4th Chasseurs), blue (4th Lancers) or yellow (1st Chasseurs) (the 3rd Chasseurs had still not been formed by the outbreak of war), with white trouser-stripes (Guides, 3rd–5th Lancers yellow). The lancers wore *czapkas*, the remainder shakos. Artillery and engineers wore the new tunic in dark-blue, piped scarlet, train and administration with light-blue piping; blue-grey trousers (red stripe for artillery and engineers); and shakos, save for administration (kepi) and field and horse artillery, which wore a small fur busby (*talpack*) with red bag at the left. Medical personnel wore a kepi, blue tunic piped crimson, and black trousers; gendarmerie blue tunic piped red, blue-grey trousers, and bearskin cap. Equipment was in

Belgian Chasseurs à Cheval *in their outdated 1914 service uniform, with the 'Portable Hotchkiss' light machine-gun.*

Belgian Chasseurs à Cheval
*in the 1914 uniform, with
undress caps, around a field-
kitchen.*

the collar and one to three stripes on the kepi; field officers the same with a gold bar on the collar and additional braid on the kepi.

In late 1914 the so-called 'Yser' uniform was adopted, a more functional, single-breasted dark-blue or grey tunic with grey metal buttons, dark-red corduroy trousers, blue puttees, and a soft dark-green or blue kepi with arm-of-service piping around the crown. From early 1915 a new uniform was introduced, of khaki cloth supplied by Britain, including single-breasted tunic and double-breasted great-coat with bronzed buttons, and British-style cap. Collar-badges were: infantry red piped blue, light infantry green piped yellow, artillery blue piped red, engineers black piped red, Guides crimson piped green, lancers white piped blue, *chasseurs à cheval* yellow piped blue, and train light-blue piped dark-blue. Rank-badges were two red cuff-bars (corporal), one or two silver cuff-chevrons (sergeant) and a varying number of collar-stars for officers, with an additional bar for field ranks. The equipment was brown leather, with smaller multiple cartridge-holders on the waist-belt for cavalry and cyclists, and latterly the 1915-pattern webbing equipment, like the British 1908-pattern but with four cartridge-pouches at each side of the waist-belt clasp. French gas masks were used, and from late 1915 the Adrian helmet was introduced, painted khaki and bearing a lion-mask on the front. The armoured car personnel sent to

black leather with a brass rectangular waist-belt plate, a single cartridge-box at the front, a tanned hide knapsack, Linnemann entrenching-tool and oval, fabric-covered canteen. The 1889 7.65mm Mauser rifle was retained throughout the war; gendarmerie, cavalry and garrison artillery carried one of several variants of 1889-pattern carbine; and the *Garde Civique* had a further variety with downturned bolt-handle. Cavalry sabres were carried on the saddle, and from 1913 all cavalry had lances with pennons in the national red/yellow/black colours. Rank-markings were chevrons on the sleeves (white or yellow lace, silver or gold for sergeants), and for company officers one to three stars on

> 'When you've sung yourself hoarse with a war that is won,
> When you've reckoned what valour and courage have done,
> When the best of the foe has been laid in the dust,
> And you feel God has prospered the cause of the just;
> And your weather-stained barques o'er the perilous sea,
> Carry their freights 'neath the flag of the free
> And afar in the silence, real, loyal and true
> Our heroes lie sleeping: What, then, will you do?
> We gave you our dear ones – the best we could –
> Sons, brothers, husbands – all brave Britain's blood
> In disdain of all hardships, contented to go
> In defence of our country to fight a stern foe;
> When they come back and the fighting is done
> (IF they come back and the battle IS won!)
> Maimed, crippled, disabled but honest and true
> All victims of Honour! Britain! What will YOU do?
> Will England forget what her children have done?
> Will she forget when victory is won?
> Tommy has fought in the cold and the rain,
> He has cheerfully suffered again and again;
> He has willingly given his best in the fight
> For England, for Honour, for Empire, for Right.
> To those that are broken, now what of the debt?
> Will she Remember – or simply Forget?'
> (Anon. – signed 'W' – in *The Mesopoluvian*, 24 November 1917)

Russia in late 1915 wore Belgian uniform but with Russian rank-insignia.

Navy
Belgium possessed no naval forces, but did have a small contingent of marines, artillery and infantry, whose duties were largely as garrison troops.

Aviation service
At the outbreak of war the *Compagnie des Aviateurs* comprised only a single squadron of about a dozen aircraft, instead of the intended four squadrons. In 1915 the reorganized service was re-titled *Aviation Militaire*, of five squadrons; specific fighter units were created in 1917, organized into a 'fighter group' of three squadrons in 1918. Ultimately there were eleven squadrons, about 140 aircraft; those in use were largely French, including the Breguet 14, Farman F40 (retained by Belgium after it had been deemed outdated by the French) and HF20, Franco–British Type H, Hanriot HD1, Morane-Saulnier Al, Nieuport Baby, and Spad XI. British aircraft in use included the BE2c, DH9, RE8 and Sopwith Camel and 1½-Strutter. Belgium's leading aviator was 2nd Lieutenant Willy Coppens de Houthulst, who registered 37 victories before he lost a leg while attacking a balloon on 18 October 1918.

Footnotes
1. *King Albert's Book*, ed. H. Caine, London, 1914, p. 176.
2. Ibid., p. 13.

References
Anon. *Military Operations of Belgium*. London, 1915
Caine, H. (ed). *King Albert's Book*. London, 1914 (collection of essays, etc. in support of Belgium)
Cammaerts, E. *Albert King of Belgium: Defender of Right*. London, 1935
Essen, L. van der. *The Invasion and the War in Belgium from Liège to the Yser*. London, 1917
Galet, E. J. *Albert, King of the Belgians, in the Great War*. Boston, 1931
Millard, O. E. *Uncensored: the True Story of the Clandestine Newspaper 'La Libre Belgique'*. London, 1937
Pirenne, H. *La Belgique et la Guerre Mondiale*. Paris, 1928
Powell, E. A. *Fighting in Flanders*. New York, 1915 (American war correspondent with the Belgian Army)
Toynbee, A. J. *The German Terror in Belgium*. London, 1917
Whitlock, B. *Belgium under the German Occupation*. London, 1919 (author was US Ambassador to Belgium)

BRAZIL

Brazil was the only South American republic to participate in the war: Bolivia, Ecuador, Peru and Uruguay severed diplomatic relations with Germany, while Argentina, Chile, Paraguay and Venezuela delcared their neutrality.

Following the deposition of the monarchy by a military *coup* in 1889, the United States of Brazil (*Estados Unidos do Brazil*) was a federal republic, governed by a president and executive cabinet, supported by a senate and national congress. There had been recent unrest (in 1910 elements of the fleet had bombarded Rio de Janeiro, there had been election disturbances in 1912, and a revolt of unemployed rubber-workers in Ceara province in 1914), but the 1914 election was peaceful and installed Dr. Wenceslóo Braz as president. He remained president until November 1918; his intended successor died before taking office and an election had to be held in April 1919, when the chief Brazilian delegate at the Paris peace conference, Dr. Epitacio Pessôa, was appointed.

Popular sympathy was almost entirely on the side of the Allies, despite the volume of trade with Germany (in 1913, for example, Germany was Brazil's second best customer with exports (in sterling) of more than £9 million, against more than £21 million to the USA and £8½ million to Britain; imports from Germany totalled £11¾ million, against £16½ million from Britain and £10½ million from the USA). German U-boat warfare tipped the scales from neutrality to belligerence. On 4 April 1917 the steamer *Paraná* was sunk near Cherbourg; anti-German demonstrations occurred in Rio de Janeiro, and when the German minister attempted to present an explanation, the Brazilian foreign minister, Dr. Lauro Müller, refused to receive him. The following day diplomatic relations were broken and Müller resigned, lest his German ancestry embarrass the government. After the sinking of the Brazilian ship *Tijuca*, in late May some 150,000 tons of German shipping was seized, having previously been interned in Brazilian waters. The sinking of the *Macao* led to a declaration of war on 26 October 1917.

Brazil's main contribution to the Allies was in trade, especially meat (export of frozen and preserved meat rose from some 8,600 tonnes in 1915 to 78,000 in 1918), and Allied markets helped compensate the complete cessation of exports to Germany (in 1915 they were worth £23, and did not recommence until 1919). In as far as the armed forces were in a position to make an active contribution, warships served in the Atlantic and some medical and aviation personnel were attached to other Allied armies.

Army
The peacetime establishment of the army was about 25,500 but as some units were kept as a cadre the actual strength was about 15,000. Recruitment was by compulsion, a law of January 1908 decreeing that able-bodied males aged 21 to 44 served two years, followed by seven in the reserve, seven in the 'second line' and eight in the national guard; but this was difficult to implement and sometimes convicts were impressed to make up the numbers. In December 1917 a selective conscription was introduced for those aged 21–30, and the national guard was incorporated into the 'second line'. Pre-war organization included 40 infantry battalions, fourteen cavalry regiments (four squadrons each), six artillery regiments (four batteries each) and two engineer battalions. At the end of the war total strength was about 54,000, but a complete mobilization would have produced about 120,000. There was in addition a 26,000-strong gendarmerie. In 1908 a universal, light khaki field uniform was adopted, a tunic with standing collar and fly front (with

black buttons for officers), the regimental number on the collar; a French-style kepi with khaki top, dark-blue band and red piping; and natural leather equipment. Cavalry and other arms wore the same; legwear was breeches and leather knee-gaiters. In 1917 the kepi was replaced by an American-style khaki peaked cap with crossed rifles badge and khaki peak and chinstrap, and khaki webbing belts replaced the leather. Rank-markings were in the form of 1–6 black laces on the shoulder-strap; NCOs had black insignia above the cuffs. The principal weapon was the Mauser rifle. Although the president was nominally commander-in-chief, actual command was exercised by the general staff (resident in the capital) and the commanding general of each of the country's seven military districts.

Navy

Following the destruction of the armoured ship *Aquidaban* in 1905 (when its magazine blew up accidentally, off Rio de Janeiro), which deprived Brazil of half its effective navy, a building programme was instituted (Rio de Janeiro arsenal boasted a shipbuilding yard), so that by the outbreak of war Brazil possessed a navy considerably more modern than some of her neighbours (Argentina had only three vessels of cruiser size or above constructed during the 20th century, Peru two, Chile one, for example). Brazil had two dreadnoughts, completed 1910 (*Minas Geraes* and *São Paulo*, both of which had mutinied in 1910 when Rio de Janeiro was shelled; principal armament 12 × 12in, 22 × 4.7in guns), two 1902 coastal battleships (2 × 9.2in, 4 × 4.7in guns), two 1910 cruisers (10 × 4.7in), two old cruisers (6 × 6in, 4 × 4.7in; and 10 × 6in, 2 × 4.7in guns respectively), ten destroyers, four torpedo-boats and three modern (1912) submarines. Five destroyers and three more submarines were under construction by the end of the war. The lighter vessels (principally destroyers) were those used during the war, because re-fits of the capital ships had not been completed by the armistice.

BULGARIA

As one of the most powerful Balkan powers, Bulgaria was courted by both Allies and Central Powers, yet had been independent for only six years before the outbreak of the war. A province of the Ottoman Empire, its revolt in 1876 helped precipitate the 1877–8 Russo–Turkish War; by the treaty of San Stefano, which ended hostilities, Bulgaria was accorded the status of an autonomous province of the Ottoman Empire, and appointed Prince Alexander of Battenburg as its first sovereign. The assistance received from Russia helped create a very pro-Russian atmosphere within Bulgaria.

In 1866 Alexander abdicated under Russian pressure, and the Bulgarian National Assembly (*Sobranie*) elected in his place Prince Ferdinand of Saxe–Coburg–Gotha (1861–1948), maternal grandson of King Louis–Philippe of France

King Ferdinand of Bulgaria (1861–1948), wearing German uniform.

and currently a lieutenant in the Austrian Army. Initially he was dominated by the great Bulgarian statesman Alexander Stambulov, but his assassination in Sofia on 15 July 1895 (perhaps with Ferdinand's complicity) left the prince in the leading position in Bulgarian affairs. His policy was expansionist, directed towards the acquisition of the Turkish province of Macedonia, to which Bulgaria had historic and ethnic claims. On 5 October 1908, taking advantage of the confused internal situation in Turkey, Ferdinand declared the independence of Bulgaria, which was recognized by Russia and Turkey in April 1909; Ferdinand styled himself Tsar of Bulgaria, although in Western Europe he was usually referred to as 'King Ferdinand'.

Ferdinand took Bulgaria into the Balkan League, which in 1912 declared war on Turkey on the pretext of protecting the inhabitants of the remaining Turkish provinces, principally Macedonia, from the barbarities of Turkish rule. The war resulted in Turkey's loss of almost all her Balkan provinces, but dissent arose among the Allies over the division of Macedonia; dissatisfied with the outcome, on 29 June 1913 the Bulgarian Army attacked the Serbs virtually without warning. This Second Balkan War was of short duration: Roumania, Greece and Turkey became involved and the Bulgarians had to sue for peace. The Treaty of Bucharest (10 August 1913) deprived Bulgaria of almost all the gains of the first Balkan War.

In July 1913 Ferdinand appointed as prime minister Vasil Radoslavov, who had led the government 1899–1901, had acquired a reputation for corruption and brutal suppression of dissent, and was markedly pro-Austrian. Although Bulgaria had an elected parliament, it was dominated by Ferdinand, and Radoslavov survived despite failing to win a majority in the December 1913 election, and another election in March 1914 gave him the mandate to rule. The Bulgarian drift away from Russia and towards the Central Powers was confirmed in June 1914 by the declaration of a loan from Germany and Austro–Hungary, vital for the Bulgarian economy and accepted instead of loans from the Entente powers. By accepting the loan, Bulgaria handed over control of her coal industry and a vital railway to the consortium advancing the loan, which caused such uproar in the *Sobranie* that it was impossible for the necessary bill to be read.

With the outbreak of war both camps bid for Bulgaria's support or neutrality, as part of an auction in which both bargained away territory that was not theirs in an effort to gain the allegiance of the uncommitted Balkan states, including also Greece and Roumania. Despite Serbia's objections at the suggestion of ceding territory to a recently defeated enemy, the Allies were able to advance a proposal to enlist Bulgarian support; but the sentiments of Ferdinand and Radoslavov lay with the Central Powers, and from Bulgaria's geographical position it was clear that her neutrality could not be preserved once Turkey had entered the war. Accordingly, on 6 September 1915 Bulgaria signed a military convention with the Central Powers, pledging co-operation in an attack on Serbia in return for Serbian Macedonia, and also territory from Greece and Roumania should either nation show hostile intentions towards Bulgaria. On 17 September Ferdinand met the leaders of the opposition in the *Sobranie*; the pro-Russian Democrat Alexander Malinov, who had been premier 1908–11, urged Bulgarian neutrality, while Alexander Stamboliski, head of the Agrarian Party (BANU) spoke against the Central Powers alliance with such vehemence that he was imprisoned and sentenced to death, later commuted to life imprisonment. On 5 October Bulgaria attacked Serbia, declaring war officially on 12 October; Britain responded by declaring war on 15 October, and France and Italy on the succeeding two days.

Although initially successful and acquiring Macedonia, from late 1916, with the war widened by declaration of war on Roumania (1 September), Bulgaria began to falter. Though bolstered by German assistance, food stocks were depleted to supply Germany and Austria, and were compounded by a bad harvest, so that severe rationing had to be imposed. By early 1917 the opposition in the *Sobranie* urged that, as Macedonia and the Dobruja had been gained,

Bulgaria should withdraw from the war; but despite worsening relations with Germany, the alliance was maintained. In January 1918 Germany withdrew the annual subsidy paid since Bulgaria entered the war, and after March sent no further supplies or munitions upon which the Bulgarian military had depended. In an attempt to stifle growing unrest, in June 1918 Ferdinand dismissed Radoslavov and appointed the pro-Allied Malinov in his stead, but Malinov was unable to form a broad-based government as Ferdinand refused to release Stamboliski and other BANU leaders, so had to maintain the existing foreign policy. The complete collapse of the Bulgarian forces on the Macedonian Front compelled Malinov to request an armistice, which was signed on 30 September 1918.

Released on 25 September, Stamboliski, at Ferdinand's behest, went to the front where there was growing unrest among the army; he found them mutinous and was himself declared (probably unwillingly) as president of a Bulgarian revolutionary government. The revolution was crushed almost immediately: rebel troops were defeated (with German assistance) outside Sofia, but Ferdinand's position was hopeless. Advised by his ministers (at the instigation of the Allies) that he should abdicate, he acceded to the demand on 4 October and left the country, followed by Radoslavov. Malinov remained as premier until 28 November, when he resigned in protest against the installation of a Roumanian administration in the Dobruja, in contravention of the terms of the armistice. The Bulgarian crown passed to Ferdinand's son, Boris; Stamboliski formed a minority government in late 1919, and on 27 November signed the Treaty of Neuilly-sur-Seine, which reduced Bulgarian territory, restricted its military forces, and imposed a reparation of £90 million sterling. Stamboliski's attempt to negotiate amicably with Bulgaria's neighbours infuriated nationalist and military groups, and he was murdered following a *coup d'état* in 1923. Malinov, imprisoned briefly before the *coup*, again took the highest office in 1931; both Radoslavov and Ferdinand died in exile in Berlin, in 1929 and 1948 respectively.

Army

The strength of the army led to Bulgaria's nickname 'the Prussia of the Balkans'. A militia was organized by Russian officers immediately upon the creation of the Principality of Bulgaria, transformed by successive laws (1880, 1891 and 1904) into a modern standing army. By the Army Law of 1 January 1904 it comprised the permanent, active army (*deistvuyushta armia*); the active army reserve; the reserve army; and the territorial militia (*narodno opolchenie*). All able-bodied males were liable for conscription (Muslims could purchase exemption), although less than half of those called were actually trained. Beginning at age 21, two years were spent in the active army and eight in the active reserve (three and six respectively for technical services and cavalry), then seven years in the reserve army, and finally *opolchenie* service until age 46. In peacetime the standing army was about 85,000 strong, yet from a population of under six million, more than 400,000 men could be fielded upon mobilization, over half a million if *opolchenie* were included. Morale was not always high (there was some disquiet about an alliance with the traditional Turkish enemy and opposition to the traditional ally, Russia), but organization was good, and as officers in general came from a lower social strata than in many armies, they had a greater rapport with their men. Almost a quarter of the national budget was spent on maintaining this force.

There were nine divisions grouped in three Inspectorates, which in wartime formed the basis of three field armies. Divisional headquarters were at Sofia, Dupnitza, Philippopolis, Plevna, Rustchuk, Shumla, Sliven, Stara-Zagora and Vratza. Each divisional area was divided into four districts, each supporting an infantry regiment and its reservists. Peacetime establishment included 36 infantry regiments (each of two battalions, a non-combatant company and machine-gun section), eleven cavalry regiments (three squadrons each), nine field artillery regiments (six batteries each), three mountain artillery regiments (four batteries each), three howitzer batteries, three siege batteries and three pioneer battalions; there was no independent train, transport being integrated into each unit. On mobilization each of a battalion's four companies expanded into a battalion, and the cavalry (reinforced by mounted gendarmerie) formed a cavalry division as well as supplying divisional cavalry for the infantry; the pioneers increased to nine battalions. The siege and howitzer batteries were under independent command; the field batteries were permanently deployed at divisional level.

The mobilized strength of a division was equivalent to a corps in some armies; in Bulgarian service there was no intermediate formation between division and army. In general, war strength of a division was: two infantry brigades (sixteen battalions, each about 1,000 strong), one reserve infantry brigade (eight battalions), two cavalry squadrons, a field regiment of nine batteries (36 guns) of 75mm Creusot guns, a field regiment of six batteries (24 guns) of 75 and 87mm Krupp guns, two or three mountain batteries (eight or twelve guns), 2–4 machine-gun companies, two engineer companies and sometimes a howitzer battery, with a total of about 24,000 infantry. The cavalry division comprised two brigades of two regiments each, each of four squadrons of 130 men and a machine-gun. Upon mobilization, 72 battalions (each about 500 strong) of older reservists were formed for garrison and line-of-communication duties, but these were not assigned to individual divisions. New formations were also created: the 10th (Aegean) Division had been formed after the Balkan Wars; the 11th (Macedonian) was raised in 1916, largely from Bulgars resident in Macedonia, and by the armistice there were fourteen divisions, with a total strength (according to the Bulgarian Army) of 877,000 men, considerably more than some Allied estimates.

A grey-green, Russian-style field uniform was introduced in 1908, but it was not universal, and the expansion of the army necessitated the use of German supplies, the previous brown field uniform, and the peacetime coloured uniforms: dark-green double-breasted tunic and trousers for infantry; the same with black facings for artillery and engineers, and blue with red facings for cavalry (4th Regiment green with raspberry facings). The 1908 uniforms included a fly-fronted, single-breasted tunic with pockets and standing collar, breeches and knee-boots, or ankle-boots with puttees and gaiters (blue breeches were often worn by cavalry and technical troops); shortages of footwear resulted in widespread use of the traditional civilian sandal (*opanka* or *palanka*) with rudimentary cloth leggings, often cross-gartered. The Russian-style cap (of the uniform-colour) had a black or grey-green leather peak and chinstrap and bore an oval national cockade on the front (red/green/white from the centre out). Arm-of-service colours were present as crown-piping and band on the cap, piping on the collar, and on the shoulder-straps of the older uniform: infantry and gendarmerie dark-red, cavalry red, artillery, technical troops and staff black. Regimental numbers were carried on the shoulder-straps of infantry (Regiments 1, 4–6, 8, 9, 17 and 22 a royal cipher instead, with German-style lace loops (*Litzen*) on the collar) and artillery (Regiments 3 and 4 a cipher), and a battalion-number by engineers. Equipment was brown leather, generally the German 1895 pattern; the double-breasted grey-brown greatcoat had a single row of buttons and rectangular collar-patches in the arm-of-service colour (officers, light-grey with two rows of buttons, dark-green collar (blue for cavalry) and red piping for general officers). Rank-distinctions were metallic lace edging to collar and cuffs for NCOs, one to three red bars on the shoulder-strap for 1st class private and junior NCOs, and a metallic bar for sergeants. Officers' shoulder-straps were metallic lace with a stripe of arm-of-service colour (two stripes for field ranks) and one to three stars of contrasting colour; cadets had other ranks' straps with metallic lace edge. General officers had gold straps with one to four silver stars.

The principal weapon was the 8mm Mannlicher rifle, of 1888 and 1895 models in about equal quantities, and the 1891 Mannlicher carbine for cavalry and machine-gunners; a few old Russian Berdan rifles were also in use, issued originally to engineers and *opolchenie*. Automatic pistols were carried by all officers, and senior cavalry NCOs; all officers and cavalry carried sabres, but only the guard cavalry had lances. The machine-gun in general use was the 8mm Maxim on a wheeled carriage (a minority on tripods). Artillery was largely French, with a minority of German, patterns: 75mm Schneider–Creusot field guns, 105mm Schneider–Creusot field howitzers and 75mm Schneider mountain guns; also in use were older 75mm and 87mm Krupp field guns, 120 and 150mm Krupp howitzers and 75mm Krupp mountain guns. In addition to the subsidies which were vital in financing the Bulgarian war effort, and large quantities of German munitions (losses in the recent

The main vessel of the Bulgarian Navy: the 715-ton, unarmoured torpedo-gunboat Nadiedja, *built in Bordeaux in 1898 (2 × 4in, 2 × 9pdr, 2 × 3pdr guns, 2 torpedo tubes).*

Balkan Wars had been considerable), Germany also contributed some units for integration in the Bulgarian Army: as the bulk of the Bulgarian rank-and-file was poorly educated or completely illiterate, and as the very limited nature of Bulgarian industry provided insufficient technicians, the German support was in the form of artillery, machine-gun, communications, railway-construction and medical personnel. Aviation units also had German personnel and German machines, such as the AEG CIV.

German influence extended so far that at Bulgaria's entry into the war less than half her forces were under control of the commander-in-chief, General Nikola Zhekov (1864–1949). The remainder were under German command in the person of August von Mackensen, according to the military convention agreed before Bulgaria entered the war. At the beginning the three field armies were composed as follows:

Mackensen:
First Army (General Boyadzhiyev): 1st, 6th, 8th, 9th Divisions: Serbian frontier; Second Army (General Todorov): 3rd, 7th and Cavalry Divisions: south of First Army, to operate in Macedonia;
Independent:
Third Army (General Toshev): 4th and 10th Divisions: for operations in Thrace.

Other divisions were held within Bulgaria; but of the troops deployed on the frontier, seven out of nine divisions were ultimately under German control.

The total personnel mobilized during the war was about 1.2 million, of whom almost 76,000 were killed (and perhaps 25,000 more dying of disease) and more than 150,000 wounded; with perhaps 275,000 civilian deaths in addition. The peace terms imposed a drastic disarmament on Bulgaria, forces reduced to 33,000 armed personnel in only three infantry divisions and four cavalry regiments, with no heavy artillery, no imported munitions and only one authorized armaments factory. The duties of the army were limited to maintenance of public order and border-guard duty.

Navy

The weak Bulgarian navy played no active role in the war. It comprised two flotillas, those of the Danube (patrol- and gunboats) and the Black Sea (one large gunboat and a few torpedo-boats). The largest vessel was the torpedo-gunboat

On the bitterness against staff officers:
    'I love this war. Perhaps you think that
    Is strange. Well I am different from the rest
    Of you poor blighters. I live at the Base,
    And use the Brain inside my nice, red hat.'
    (*Arma Virumque Cano*, 'C.L.P.', *B.E.F. Times*, 10 April 1917)

Nadiedja (715 tons, 2 × 4in, 2 × 9pdr, 2 × 3pdr guns); the six 1907 Creusot torpedo-boats (one of which had the singular name of *Smeli!*) were 98 tons displacement and armed with 2 × 3pdrs and 3 × 8in torpedo tubes. There were also a few launches. By the terms of surrender Bulgaria was permitted to retain only four torpedo-boats, manned by civilians and with torpedoes prohibited.

References

Anon. *Die Bulgarische Armee.*
    Vienna, 1912
Logio, G. C. *Bulgaria Past and
    Present.* Manchester, 1936

Protić, S. *The Aspirations of
    Bulgaria.* London, 1915
Ruhl, M. *Die Armeen der Balkan-
    Staaten.* Leipzig, n.d. (includes
    Bulgaria)

CANADA

The Dominion of Canada was formed in 1867, and enjoyed virtual autonomy despite having a governor-general appointed by the British crown, who retained the right to veto legislation considered harmful to British Empire interests. It consisted of the provinces of Alberta, British Columbia, Manitoba, New Brunswick, Nova Scotia, Ontario, Prince Edward Island, Saskatchewan and Quebec, and some districts. Executive authority was vested in a cabinet which nominally served the governor-general; the parliament consisted of an elected House of Commons and a Senate nominated by the governor-general and his council. The Duke of Connaught was succeeded as governor-general in June 1916 by the Duke of Devonshire. The Liberal government of Sir Wilfred Laurier (prime minister since 1896) was defeated in the 1911 election, and was succeeded by the Conservative Robert (later Sir Robert) Borden, who formed a Conservative–Liberal coalition 'Union' government in October 1917 (Laurier having called 'a truce to party strife'), which was confirmed by the election of December 1917. Borden was a member of the Imperial War Cabinet and remained in office until his resignation due to ill-health in 1919.

Canada made no individual declaration of war, but automatically followed Britain. Laurier declared at the outbreak of war that there was in Canada but one mind and one heart, supportive of Britain; but despite the existence of French–Canadian battalions, British commentators expressed reservations about the commitment of the French-speakers. (Before the introduction of conscription there were an estimated 13,000 French-speakers in the army; the first contingent contained only about 1,200 French-speakers, and whereas the 1.6 million 'French' inhabitants of Quebec provided less than 7,000 recruits, the 400,000 'English' provided 22,000. It was regarded as significant, though, that one of the early Canadian heroes of the war was Lieutenant Papineau of the Princess Patricia's Light Infantry, a descendant of Louis Papineau, leader of the 1837 rebellion.) In addition to the military contribution, Canada produced huge quantities of foodstuffs for the Allied war effort, and by 1917 more than half Britain's shrapnel, 42 per cent of the

Canadian troops in a trench revetted with sandbags and corrugated iron; note the periscope, and the leather jerkin worn by the man third from left.

4.5in shells, more than a quarter of the 6in shells, and one-fifth of the 60pdr shells were made in Canada.

Army

The Canadian military establishment was almost entirely part-time militia, in which all able-bodied men aged 18–60 were nominally enrolled; service was voluntary and for three years, although the government had the power to apply compulsion. Under the 1904 Militia Act the military forces comprised active and reserve militia, the former divided into permanent and non-permanent forces. The permanent force or 'regular army', only 3,110 strong at the outbreak of war, consisted of training cadres and garrisons (the fortified harbours of Halifax, Nova Scotia, and Esquimalt, British Columbia, had passed from British to Canadian control in 1905). The active militia trained for 12 to 16 days per year; the reserve militia was not organized.

When it was decided to send a Canadian Expeditionary Force (CEF) to Europe, instead of mobilizing existing units, volunteers were organmized into new, consecutively

numbered battalions of eight companies each, in four brigades of four battalions each. Mobilization was carried out under the aegis of Samuel (from 1915 Sir Samuel) Hughes (1853–1921), Minister of Militia and Defence from 1911, who had served in the Boer War and was promoted to major-general in 1915. A man of strong personality and opinions, despite his experience he was a difficult colleague and resigned from Borden's administration in 1916. Under his direction, the volunteers assembled in a huge camp at Valcartier, outside Quebec, an unnecessary expenditure of effort in its construction as assembly could have been equally well achieved piecemeal, instead of gathering more than 32,000 men (including 750 US volunteers) in one vast camp.

In all, some 260 numbered CEF battalions were formed during the war. Most represented specific areas, but in some cases they were formed almost exclusively from militia units; thus the 15th Battalion, raised from the 48th Highlanders (Toronto), was titled as the 15th Battalion (48th Highlanders of Canada). Battalions were numbered

as follows, with titles or place of origin:

Battalions 1, 34 Western Ontario; 2, 39 Eastern Ontario; 3, 19; 35, 37, 58, 74, 81, 95, 166, 169 Toronto; 4 Central Ontario; 5 Western Cavalry; 6 Fort Garry House; 7 1st British Columbia; 8, 27, 61, 90, 107, 144, 190, 200, 203, 221, 250, 251 Winnipeg; 9, 49, 51, 63, 66, 138, 218 Edmonton; 10, 31, 50, 56, 82, 137 Calgary; 11, 65, 152, 188, 209, 214, 217, 232 Saskatchewan; 12 Maritime Provinces; 13, 42 Montreal (Royal Highlanders of Canada); 14 Royal Montreal Regiment; 15, 134 Toronto (48th Highlanders); 16 British Columbia Scottish; 17 Nova Scotia (Seaforth Highlanders); 18, 33, 70, 142 London; 20 1st Central Ontario; 21, 80, 253 Kingston; 22, 57, 167, 171, 178, 189, 258 Quebec; 23, 41, 60, 69, 87, 148, 163, 206 Montreal; 24 Montreal (Victoria Rifles); 25, 64 Halifax; 26, 104, 115, 140, 145, 165 New Brunswick; 28 North-West; 29, 47, 62, 72 Vancouver; 30 2nd British Columbia; 32 Manitoba & Saskatchewan; 36, 120, 205 Hamilton; 38, 77 Ottawa; 40, 112 Nova Scotia; 43, 174, 179 Winnipeg (Cameron Highlanders of Canada); 44 Brandon; 45 Manitoba Rangers; 46 South Saskatchewan;

48, 103 Victoria; 52, 94 Port Arthur (New Ontario); 53, 243 Prince Albert; 54, 225 Kootenay & British Columbia; 55 New Brunswick & Prince Edward Island; 59 Brockville; 67 Victoria (British Columbia Highlanders or Western Scots); 68, 249 Regina; 71 Woodstock; 73 Montreal Highlanders; 76 Barrie; 78, 100 Winnipeg Grenadiers: 79, 108, 184, 222 Manitoba; 83, 255 Toronto (Queen's Own Rifles of Canada); 84 Oshawa; 85, 193, 219, 246 Nova Scotia Highlanders; 86 Hamilton MG Battalion; 88 Victoria Fusiliers; 89, 192 Alberta; 91 Elgin; 92 Toronto Highlanders, 93 Peterboro; 96 Saskatchewan Highlanders; 97, 213 Toronto Americans; 98 Lincoln & Welland; 99 Essex; 101 Winnipeg Light Infantry; 102 North British Columbia; 105 Prince Edward Island Highlanders; 106 Nova Scotia Rifles; 109, 247 Victoria & Haliburton; 110 Perth; 111 South Waterloo; 113 Lethbridge Highlanders; 114 Haldimand County (Brock's Rangers); 116, 182 Ontario County; 117 Eastern Township; 118 Kitchener; 119 Saulte St. Marie; 121 British Columbia (Western Irish); 122 Muskoka; 123 Toronto Royal Grenadiers; 124 Toronto (Governor-General's Bodyguard); 125 Brantford; 126, 234 Peel County; 127, 220 York Rangers; 128, 229 Moose Jaw; 129 Wentworth County; 130, 240 Lanark & Renfrew; 131 Westminster; 132 North Shore, New Brunswick; 133 Norfolk County; 135 Middlesex County; 136, 235 Durham County; 139 Northumberland; 141 Rainy River; 143 British Columbia Bantams; 146 Frontenac County; 147, 248 Grey County; 149 Lambton County; 150 Montreal (Carabiniers Mont-Royal); 151, 187 Central Alberta; 153 Wellington County; 154 Cornwall (Stormont, Dundas & Glengarry Highlanders); 155 Prince Edward County; 156 Brockville (Leeds & Grenville); 157, 177 Simcoe County; 158 Duke of Connaught's Own British Columbia; 159 Sudbury; 160 Bruce County; 161 Huron County; 162 Parry Sound; 164 Halton & Dufferin; 170 Toronto (Mississauga Horse); 172 Kamloops (Rocky Mountain Rangers); 173 Hamilton Highlanders; 175 Medicine Hat; 176 Welland County; 180 Toronto Sportsmen; 181 Brandon; 183 Winnipeg (Manitoba Beavers); 185 Cape Breton Highlanders; 186 Kent County; 191 South Alberta; 194 Edmonton Highlanders; 195 City of Regina; 196 British Columbia (Western Universities); 197 Manitoba (Vikings of Canada); 198 Toronto (Canadian Buffs); 199 Toronto/Montreal (Duchess of Connaught's Own Irish Rangers); 201 Toronto Light Infantry; 202 Edmonton Sportsmen; 204 Toronto Beavers; 207 Carleton; 208 Toronto (Canadian Irish); 210 Moose Jaw (Frontiersmen); 211 Alberta American Legion: 212 Winnipeg American Legion; 215 Brant County; 216 Toronto Bantams; 223 Manitoba Scandinavians; 224 Ottawa Forestry; 226 Manitoba Men of the North; 227 Algoma & Sudbury Men of the North; 228 Nippising (Northern Fusiliers); 230 Ottawa (Voltigeurs Canadiens Français); 233 North West; 236 New Brunswick Highlanders (Maclean Kilties of America); 237 Nova Scotia Americans; 238 Forestry Battn.; 239 Railway Battn.; 241 Windsor (Canadian Scottish Borderers); 242 Montreal Forestry; 244 Montreal (Kitchener's Own); 245 Montreal Grenadiers; 252 Lindsay; 254 Hastings & Prince Edward Island; 256 Toronto Railway Construction Battalion; 257 Montreal Railway Construction Battn.; 259, 260 Siberian Expeditionary Force.

Two regiments were outside the CEF: the Royal Canadian Regiment, the regular battalion which served in Bermuda until it joined the 3rd Canadian Division in late 1915, and the Princess Patricia's Canadian Light Infantry. The latter, 'Pat's Pets', was raised from ex-British soldiers resident in Canada at the expense of a private individual, Hamilton Gault of Montreal, and named after the daughter of the governor-general. It served with the British 27th Division until December 1915, when it joined the 3rd Canadian; Gault, a major in the regiment, was an early casualty, being wounded twice within a short time.

The 1st Division assembled for service overseas comprised the 1–4 Brigades (1st–4th, 5th–8th, 13th–16th and 9th–12th Battalions respectively), three field brigades (each of three 6-gun 18pdr batteries), a cavalry squadron drawn from the 19th Alberta Dragoons, the 1 Automobile Machine-Gun Brigade (armoured cars with Colt guns), and a Canadian Mounted Brigade of the Royal Canadian Dragoons, Lord Strathcona's Horse and the British 2nd King Edward's Horse (formed from colonials in Britain), the latter replaced by Fort Garry Horse in February 1916. There was a further cavalry regiment, the Canadian Light Horse, whose four squadrons each wore the badge of a militia unit: 1st Hussars, 16th Light Horse, 19th Alberta Dragoons and Royal North-West Mounted Police (a quasi-military unit with HQ at Regina); and thirteen Mounted Rifle regiments: 1st Brandon, 2nd Victoria, 3rd Medicine Hat, 4th Toronto, 5th Sherbrooke, 6th Amherst, 7th London, 8th Ottawa, 9th Lloydminster, 10th Portage, 11th Vancouver, 12th Calgary and 13th Pincer Creek.

'As you know, we are rather an Irish regiment, and as we have an Irishman in command, the men were convinced that we should make an attack during the day. This did not come off, but the men had to celebrate St. Patrick's Day somehow. They started off by sticking the Irish flag, the Union Jack, and the tricolour on the parapet . . . They then sang the National Anthem, the Marseillaise, the Maple Leaf, and Wearing o'the Green. The Germans riddled the tricolour with bullets, but left the other two alone. Our men have found a sure way of annoying the Germans. They shout across to them, and the following remarks are sure to draw a reply in the form of some perfectly ineffective rifle fire. "Hi, Fritz, bring the menu!" or "Herr Lieutenant, why don't you pay your washing bill?"'

(Anonymous officer of 90th Winnipeg Rifles, in *With the First Canadian Contingent*, p. 55, Toronto & London, 1915)

After training in England, 1st Division landed in continental Europe in February 1915; the Canadian Army Corps was formed when 2nd Division arrived in September 1915, with 3rd early the following year and 4th in August 1916. These four divisions were maintained at full strength instead of forming additional, weaker divisions (5th Division, formed early 1917, was broken up a year later to reinforce the others). More than 595,000 men were enlisted in Canada, of whom 418,000 CEF men served overseas; in addition, 14,500 reservists resident in Canada returned home to join up, and more than 21,000 Canadians served outside the CEF, including almost 13,000 in the British aviation service. Voluntary enlistment was maintained until winter 1917/18, when the Military Service Act introduced conscription, but this brought in fewer than 86,000 men in all, some of whom volunteered anyway (although there was some opposition to conscription, especially among the French-speakers). More than 210,000 casualties were sustained, including more than 56,500 dead, a casualty-rate of about 48 per cent of those Canadians who served overseas.

The Canadian Corps performed a number of remarkable feats on the Western Front. The commander from May 1916 to June 1917, the Hon. Sir Julian Byng, led them with distinction and when ennobled after the war took as his title Baron Byng of Vimy, one of the Canadians' most notable victories; from 1921 to 1926 he was governor-general. His successor in command was Lieutenant-General Sir Arthur Currie, an Ontario-born pre-war militiaman, the first Canadian to rise to such command. Other units included the medical services (including sixteen establishments in Britain), the Forestry Corps (created 1916, serving in France and Britain), and railway battalions, which constructed all the light railways, and more than half the standard-gauge railways, used by the British Army on the Western Front. Canadian troops also provided the garrisons of Canada (12,000) and St. Lucia. Relations between the Canadians and British were cordial, despite the difference in pay: Canadian other ranks received almost 5s. per diem, against the British 1s. 2d!

Uniform and equipment was generally of British pattern, although the Canadian 1903 service uniform had nine buttons on the breast instead of five, a standing collar, pointed cuffs and detachable shoulder-straps (worn by the original CEF 'First Contingent' for about a year: infantry dark-blue, rifles green, artillery red, cavalry yellow). The CEF badge was a bronze maple-leaf bearing a crown and 'Canada', but battalion-badges soon appeared and by 1917 their expense was underwritten by government, having previously been provided from regimental funds. Many of the Scottish battalions wore badges of Scottish design, and Scottish bonnets and kilt. Three patterns of equipment were worn initially: the old British leather 'valise equipment', a Canadian version of the British 1908 webbing equipment, modified to accommodate Ross ammunition; and an improved 1913 version issued to the 'permanent force' and the Princess Patricia's. The old leather equipment was largely replaced by British sets before the 'First Contingent' left Britain, though it remained in use in Canada and briefly with 4th Division. A further variety was the 'tump-line'

'Fix bayonets!': Canadian troops prepare to go 'over the top', a scene almost undoubtedly staged for the benefit of the photographer.

Canadian troops resting in a ditch; the armoured vehicle is a French Renault light tank.

design, which included a strap which supported part of the weight on the forehead, as used by miners, trappers and Indians in the Canadian backwoods.

Initially the Canadian forces were armed with the Ross rifle, a home-produced weapon derived from the 1890 Mannlicher, which though an excellent target-rifle was mechanically inferior to the Lee-Enfield, prone to jam during cartridge-extraction and with problems of ammunition-supply on active service. Despite the production of some 30,000 Ross Mk III rifles for the CEF, by 1916 they had been re-equipped with the Lee-Enfield, contracts for further Ross arms were cancelled and the company closed. (A few Ross rifles were retained for specialist tasks such as sniping, for which their accuracy made them ideal). Other equipment was of British pattern, though shortage of Vickers guns led to the use of Colt machine-guns in 1914–15; ordnance was of British pattern, but the original CEF used only 18pdrs as there were insufficient 4.5in howitzers.

The spirit of Newbolt's *Vitaï Lampada* is recalled in an article by Field Marshal Sir Evelyn Wood, VC, on fox-hunting and sport as a means of traning for military leadership; to which the editors of the publication in which it appeared added that it:

'. . . invites reflection on the whole question of the effect of British sports on the resource and morale of the greatest army this country has ever called into existence. A man no doubt makes the better soldier for being a good cricketer or football player, and the casualty lists have borne eloquent witness to the heroes in happier times of the bat and the ball. Who but a British officer would have thought of taking his men into action by literally kicking off a football as was done by Captain Nevill of the East Surreys?'

(E. Salmon & J. Worsfold, eds., *The British Dominions Year Book*, p. 286, London, 1917)

Navy

The Royal Canadian Navy was founded by the Laurier administration in 1910, with the purchase of two British cruisers, but plans for extension were shelved by Borden. Instead, in 1912 Borden proposed that Canada finance the construction of three battleships for Britain, to revert to Canadian control in the event of the creation of an entirely independent Canadian navy; but this expenditure was defeated by the Senate. When hostilities commenced the

RCN had only two submarines (built in San Francisco, originally for the Chilean Navy), and the two cruisers bought in 1910: *Niobe* (11,000 tons, 1898, 16 × 6in, 14 × 12pdr guns), stationed at Halifax; and *Rainbow* (3,600 tons, 1892, 2 × 6in, 6 × 4.7in, 8 × 6pdr guns), stationed at Esquimalt. Further vessels were added during the war, for minesweeping and patrol duty only. At the armistice the RCN comprised, in the Atlantic, *Niobe* (a depot ship after the first year's service), two submarines and the depot ship

Shearwater (1900, 980-ton sloop, 6 × 4in guns, transferred from Royal Navy 1915), the torpedo-boat *Grilse* and 125 smaller vessels, trawlers, drifters and minesweepers; and in the Pacific *Rainbow* (serving as a depot ship), the British sloop *Algerine* (only attached to the RCN: 1895, 1,050 tons, 6 × 4in, 4 × 3pdr guns) and the auxiliary patrol-vessel *Malespina*. There were in addition a considerable number of motor-launches, principally on the Atlantic station. Crews were drawn principally from the Royal Canadian Volunteer Reserve; of more than 5,100 Canadian personnel serving at the armistice, less than 750 were members of the regular RCN. In addition, almost 3,000 Canadians served in the Royal Navy, including some 580 in the Royal Naval Air Service, before recruiting for the Royal Air Force began in Canada. The Canadian Naval Air Service was founded in mid-1918, and co-operated with the US Navy in coastal patrol duties.

Canada's shipyards contributed significantly to the re-pairing and refitting capacity of the Allies, and almost 1,000 vessels were manufactured in Canada, mostly of the smaller type; the two modern steel shipbuilding yards existing before the war had increased to seventeen by the armistice.

The Canadian national symbol, the beaver, which was used on a number of Canadian regimental badges, is seen here representing industry in a poster advertising 1918 Victory Bonds.

References

Anon. *With the First Canadian Contingent.* Toronto & London, 1915

Aitken, M. (Lord Beaverbrook). *Canada in Flanders.* London, 1916–17 (Vol. III, 1918, by Major C. G. D. Roberts)

Nicholson, G. W. L. *Canadian Expeditionary Force 1914–1919.* Ottawa, 1962

Sheldon-Williams, I., and Sheldon-Williams, R. F. L. *The Canadian Front in France and Flanders.* London, 1920

Steele, Captain H. *The Canadians in France.* London, 1920

Swettenham, J. *Canada and the First World War.* Toronto, 1969

Upper Canada Historical Arms Society (various authors): *The Military Arms of Canada.* Ontario, 1963

Babin, L. L. *Canadian Expeditionary Forces Cap Badges 1914–18.* London, n.d.

Duguid, A. F. *Official History of the Canadian Forces in the Great War 1914–18.* Ottawa, 1938

Goodspeed, D. J. *The Road Past Vimy: The Canadian Corps 1914–1918.* Toronto, 1969

Haycock, R. G. *Sam Hughes: the Public Career of a Controversial Canadian.* Ottawa, 1986

Nasmith, Colonel G. G. *Canada's Sons and Great Britain in the World War.* Toronto, 1919

CEYLON

Ceylon was a British crown colony, administered by a governor assisted by executive and legislative councils. Although a British military establishment was maintained in Ceylon, attempts to provide an indigenous military force were not successful, largely due to the lack of martial enthusiasm among the Sinhalese people: the Ceylon Rifle Regiment, despite sending recruiting-parties as far afield as Madagascar, found such difficulties in providing recruits that it was disbanded in 1874. Such military force as existed were volunteers (the Ceylon Planters Rifle Corps served at the HQ of I Anzac Corps at Gallipoli, for example), and the lack of martial feeling among the Sinhalese would seem to be confirmed by the recruiting statistics for the World War: almost 1,600 of the 2,182 who served in the war were Europeans, although 1,200 more were recruited as clerks and mechanics. The Ceylon Sanitary Company (formed 1917) served in Mesopotamia.

CHINA

Although ultimately part of the Allied camp, China's internal problems made it quite impossible for her to participate militarily in the war. China's political history during the period was extremely complicated, and only the briefest summary is possible here.

Revolutionary sentiments grew in China following the Boxer Rebellion, caused largely by pressures placed upon China by the victorious European powers. In January 1912, amid great civil strife, the child emperor Hsuan Tung abdicated, and on 10 March Yuan Shih-kai, head of the military forces, became president of China in the place of Dr. Sun Yat-sen of the republican Kuo Min-tang movement. Yuan Shih-kai's reign as president was troubled, beset by local rebellions, and his rule never extended to the

Chinese labourers ('coolies') formed that nation's greatest contribution to the Allied war effort: here a gang of them are loading British military lorries, bearing the 'WD' signifying 'War Department'.

provinces controlled by semi-autonomous military governors. The interference of foreign powers only exacerbated the situation, Germany attempting to encourage China into hostilities with Japan, which after the fall of Kiaochow claimed the privileges previously enjoyed by Germany. War was averted only by China's concessions to Japan's '21 Demands', greatly injurious to China, such as the granting of a 99-year lease on the South Manchurian railway.

Lacking the financial and military strength to impose his rule on the rebellious provinces, Yuan Shih-kai transferred civil authority to Tuan Chi-jui as prime minister; in response to which the Kuo Min-tang set up their own government in Canton under the vice-president Li Yuan-hung. Civil war was averted only by the death of Yuan Shih-kai (6 June 1916); Li Yuan-hung succeeded to the presidency, and Tuan Chi-jui remained as premier. Yuan's death, however, also removed all possibility of there existing a strong central government; the provinces were increasingly under the complete domination of the military governors (*tuchuns*). Yuan had already been making overtures to the Allies regarding China's entry into the war, in the hope of relieving China of the indemnities still being paid for the Boxer Rebellion, and of gaining assistance against Japanese expansionism; this policy was pursued by Tuan (against president Li's inclinations), and on 14 March 1917 diplomatic relations with Germany were severed, German ships in Chinese ports were seized, and the action justified by a protest against unrestricted U-boat warfare.

Declaration of war, however, was delayed by another outbreak of factionalism and chaos. Tuan's cabinet and the *tuchuns* voted for war in April 1917; opposed to this and backed by the Kuo Min-tang, Li dismissed Tuan who fled to his military support in Tientsin, where a provisional government was established in June 1917. Under pressure from one of the most powerful *tuchuns*, General Chang Hsun from Hsuchowfu, Li dissolved parliament on 13 June; on 1 July, in defiance of his *tuchun* colleagues, Chang replaced the boy emperor on the throne and named himself as regent. Tuan and the other military leaders marched on Peking and after some fighting Chang capitulated, the emperor again going into retirement (12 July). Having acted thus in defence of the republic, and having had the support of vice-president General Feng Kuo-chang, Tuan was able to resume his premiership with increased powers; Li's position was no longer tenable, and he was succeeded as president by Feng on 18 July.

With prime minister and president in accord, China declared war on 14 August 1917, in return for a suspension of the Boxer indemnity and financial assistance from the Allies. Because of the intransigence of Tuan and the northern *tuchuns*, no accommodation was reached with the Kuo Min-tang, so the south remained in a state of insurrection, and it was obvious that despite the size of her military forces, China could not participate actively in the war. The presidential election of September 1918 replaced Feng with the sometime viceroy of Manchuria, Hsu Shih-chang, but with Japan gaining more influence over the northern military forces and the south still in open opposition, by the time Tuan was driven from power in 1920 China had degenerated into an almost medieval society of independent factions and warlords, presaging decades of sanguinary conflict.

Army

Prior to 1905 the Chinese military establishment comprised the 'Manchu Army' based at Peking and the chief provincial centres, and the 'army of the Green Standard', provincial forces. After the Boxer Rebellion a total reorganization was intended to produce a force trained and equipped in a western manner, responsible to the central government, but in practice the provincial forces remained largely dependent upon the local governors. Apart from the Manchus who performed a sort of hereditary military service, recruiting was by voluntary enlistment for three years, followed by three years in the reserve and four in the third-line territorials, the reserve training for 30 days per year and the territorials 30 days every other year. Two armies were created, North and South, of 36 divisions; Yuan Shi-kai's Northern Army was markedly superior in training and equipment. The 'army of the Green Standard' was reformed from 1907, with control officially vested in the minister of war, but the provincial allegiances remained and after the death of Yuan Shi-kai all cohesion broke down and the forces commanded by the *tuchuns* took on the characteristics of private war-bands. At the end of the World War there were probably about 1¼ million men under arms, of whom more than half a million were supposedly commanded by the central government; but as the government was unable to collect its revenues from the provinces, the troops relied for maintenance upon the local *tuchun* or impressments levied from their province. As there was thus no effective national army, no effective participation in the war was possible, and apart from periodic internal conflict, the only operations of the Chinese army during the period was the ejection of Russian Bolsheviks who had moved into northern Manchuria.

From about 1910 the Chinese Army adopted a European-style uniform of single-breasted tunic with standing collar, trousers and peaked cloth cap, in dark-blue for winter and light khaki for summer, with knee-length white gaiters and brown boots and leather equipment. Shoulder-straps and cap-band were in arm-of-service colours (infantry red, cavalry white, artillery yellow, engineers blue, transport dark-brown); NCO rank-insignia comprised one to four red laces around the cuff and black stripes on the cap-band. Officers for field service wore a dark-blue tunic, breeches and cap, with rank-insignia of 1 to 3 black stripes around the cuff and 1 to 3 gold discs above, the latter identifying company, field and general grades respectively. The Guards Division had a similar uniform in light-grey with red arm-of-service distinctions. Ordnance and small arms were produced at the arsenals of Tientsin and Shanghai.

Navy

The Chinese Navy had never fully recovered from the destruction of Admiral Ting Ju-ch'ang's 'Northern Fleet' by the Japanese at Weihaiwei in February 1895, in the closing stages of the Sino–Japanese War. At the outbreak of the World War, excluding four cruisers under construction, the navy's principal vessels were two 1912, 2,750-ton cruisers (*Ying Swei* and *Chao-Ho*, main armament 2 × 6in, 4 × 4in guns); the cruiser *Hai-Chi* (1899, 4,300 tons, 2 × 8in, 10 × 4.7in guns); three 1898 cruisers (*Hai-Yung, Hai-Chu, Hai-Chen*, 3,000 tons, 3 × 6in, 8 × 4.1in guns); three gunboats (the heaviest-armed having 2 × 4.1in guns); four torpedo-boat destroyers (2 × 12pdr, 4 × 3pdr guns); and eight torpedo-boats. Naval administration was reformed in 1909–10, and coastal defences were made the responsibility of the naval department; the main defences were the Kiangyin forts at the mouth of the Yangtsze, the Bogue forts on the River Canton, and the Min forts on the River Fuchow; ordnance was supplied by Krupp and Armstrong.

Other services

Although the Chinese troops that served in the World War were limited to the Military Mission sent to Europe (which for tours to the front wore Chinese uniform with French Adrian helmets), immense numbers of Chinese served with Allied armies as labourers or 'coolies' (the latter term is deceptive: among the Chinese labour corps were engineers and artisans with experience of work in Chinese arsenals). Chinese labour corps had been formed for Allied service before China entered the war, and the number increased when China joined the Allies; by early 1918 almost 100,000 were serving with the British on the Western Front, about the same number with the French, and some 5,000 with the Americans. Others served in East Africa and Mesopotamia, the number serving with British and Empire forces totalling about 175,000. They performed a valuable service and were generally liked by the Allied troops for their pleasant nature (if regarded as notably unhygenic!), but many were not noted as being the most enthusiastic of workers. Some Chinese medical personnel also served with the British forces.

References

Ch'en, J. *Yuan Shi-k'ai*. Stanford, 1961
La Fargue, T. E. *China and the*
World War. Stanford, 1937
Wheeler, W. R. *China and the World War*. London 1919

COSTA RICA

Despite the presence of a considerable German colony and German influence, the republic of Costa Rica was one of the first Latin American states to support the Allies. It had been fully independent since 1848, though from 1895–8 had been part of the Greater Republic of Central America (with Honduras, Nicaragua and El Salvador). Despite boundary disputes (that with Panama escalated into conflict in 1921), Costa Rica had remained out of international conflict since 1860, but some internal unrest had occurred. Under the 1870 constitution, government was nominally by a House of Representatives, but with a president and cabinet constituting the executive, which did not necessarily have to pay any heed to the House. Elections were by popular vote, but after an inconclusive election Alfredo Gonzáles was nominated president in 1914 by the legislature. His policies led to his deposition by Federico Tinoco in 1917, whose prestige suffered a severe blow when he was not recognized by the USA. Although Tinoco suppressed risings in 1918, he was himself deposed in 1919 by Julio Acosta, who became president in his stead in 1920. Despite these internal troubles, Costa Rica declared for the Allies in 1917, breaking diplomatic relations with Germany on 21 September and declaring war on 23 May 1918.

Even had the will to participate actively in the war been present, Costa Rica's size (population less than ⅓-million in 1904) would have prevented any effective military effort. The standing army was only 600 strong, backed by an active militia (to which all able-bodied males aged 18–40 belonged), a militia reserve (ages 40–50) and a national guard (those under 18 and over 50 years); service was compulsory for all in wartime. The total forces that could theoretically have been mobilized would only have been some 36,000. The navy, although requiring an admiral to command it, was scarcely worth the name, consisting of only a gunboat and a torpedo-boat.

Hints on Cooking in the Field:
  'C.O.'s Pudding
  'Take two ration biscuits and grind them to a powder. Add one tea-spoonful of Baking Powder and two of Sugar. Add water and stir to stiff paste, thoroughly flavouring with Rum. Boil for one hour and serve hot with plenty of Rum Sauce. Take two helpings of the Sauce and none of the pudding.'
  (*The Mesopoluvian*, 5 January 1918)

CUBA

Cuba declared war on Germany immediately after the United States, on 7 April 1917, following a very close connection between the two countries. After the Spanish–American War, an American military administration had controlled Cuba until the establishment of a Cuban constitution and government in 1902, and in 1906 the USA had to intervene again and re-establish a provisional government, following an insurrection. American forces were withdrawn in April 1909 following the resumption of power by a Cuban administration in January, but the succeeding years were beset by continuing unrest, a Negro revolt in May 1912 leading to a concentration of US warships in case intervention again became necessary. The election of November 1916 occasioned further unrest (US forces were landed at Santiago in 1917 to help restore order), but General Mario Menocal was re-elected and took Cuba into the war. Cuba's situation prevented any active participation, but German vessels in Havana harbour were impounded (just in time to forestall a plot, it was reported,

to block the harbour entrance by scuttling the merchantman *Bavaria*), a war loan announced and military conscription authorized in 1918. Cuban naval and military forces were not extensive; most impressive was their single light cruiser, *Cuba* (2 × 4in, 4 × 3pdr guns). Otherwise, there existed seven gunboats, the most powerful of which (*Patria*) carried but two 12pdrs.

CZECHOSLOVAKIA

In 1914 the territory which became Czechoslovakia was part of the Austro–Hungarian empire, the provinces of Bohemia, Moravia, Slovakia and Ruthenia. The Czechs and Slovaks were generally unwilling members of the empire, but were compelled to perform their military service, and with the Austrian parliament suspended most agitation on behalf of the long-repressed desire for nationhood came from outside. Most influential of the Czech *émigré* leaders was Thomas Masaryk (1850–1937), son of a Slovakian, born in Moravia, who had represented the liberal Young Czech Party in the Austrian *Reichsrat*, and later the moderate-left Realist Party. At the outbreak of war he decided to remain in exile, working for the ideal of Czech independence; his principal ally was Eduard Beneš (1884–1948), a leader of the Czech independence movement before the war. In 1915 he went to Paris, initially to work as a journalist in the pro-Czech, pro-Entente cause, and in the same year was appointed general secretary of the Czecho-slovakian National Council, which provided the political leadership of the independence movement.

Masaryk's hopes for a liberation of Czech and Slovak territory by Russian arms did not come to fruition. Although the Russians were prepared to incorporate Czech units in their army – and some Austro–Hungarian units of Czech composition deserted en masse – in 1915 the Slovak–Russian Society in Moscow proposed the incorporation of Slovakia as a province of the Russian empire, which to the Czech nationalists was simply the exchanging of one master for another. Masaryk moved from Geneva to London in March 1915 and began to place more reliance upon the western Allies, and in February 1916 the French prime minister Briand declared his support for an independent Czechoslovakia after the war. Masaryk also gathered much support from Czechs and Slovaks in the USA.

From the outset, Czech military units had served against the Austro–Hungarians. A small Czech unit, attaining regimental strength in December 1915 and brigade strength in mid-1917, had been formed in the Russian Army. The 1917 revolution gave Masaryk the opportunity of negotiating with the Bolshevik regime, which resulting in the formation of the 'Czech Corps', later styled the Czech Legion, largely from the ex-POWs of the Austro–Hungarian Army, which formed an army on the Eastern Front approaching 100,000 strong by late 1918. Recognized as part of the Allied forces and nominally under French control, in March 1918 the Legion was ordered by Foch to march to Vladivostok, to be shipped from there to France. With friction increasing between the Czechs and the Bolsheviks, and suspicion of German–Bolshevik collusion, the Legion revolted against the 'Red' regime in Russia in May 1918 and decided to shoot its way through. The Czechs secured the Trans–Siberian railway, and were compelled to collaborate with Kolchak's 'Whites' to protect their own lines; after fighting against the 'Reds' in the civil war which followed, after the collapse of the Kolchak regime they were evacuated from Vladivostok, where Japanese and smaller British and American contingents had been landed to protect the Czechs' line of withdrawal.

Other Czech formations, of less strategic importance, served with the French and Italians. It was the presence of these three forces which ultimately caused the Allies to declare publicly their support for an independent Czechoslovakia; the National Council, located in Paris, became a provisional government in exile, and a supporting National Council was formed in Prague in July 1918. Masaryk's lobbying in the USA resulted in a declaration of support named after the US Secretary of State, Robert Lansing, in May 1918, reinforced the following month by the Pittsburgh Declaration which pledged the support of Slovak–American leaders; but the first declaration of Czech nationhood, and recognition of all three Czech Legions as part of the same independent army, was made by Britain on 9 August 1918. In September the USA and Japan made similar declarations, and on 14 October the National Council was constituted officially as the provisional government of a sovereign state. On 18 October the provisional government issued a declaration of independence, recognized on 27 October by Austria–Hungary, and the National Council at Prague took over the administration of the country. A National Assembly met at Prague on 14 November, decided that the new state should be a republic, and that Masaryk should be president; Beneš became foreign minister. The existence of the Czechoslovakian state was confirmed when the Slovak National Council decreed that Slovakia should be included, and in May 1919 the Central Council of the Ruthenians accepted the same for Ruthenia.

A recruiting poster issued by the Czechoslovak Recruiting Office, New York, in 1918; note the unmistakable silhouette of the Adrian helmet. Drawn by V. Preissig.

Army

The uniform and equipment of the three Czech Legions resembled those of the armies with which they operated. The Russian Czech Legion wore a khaki uniform, including a single-breasted tunic with falling collar bearing a patch scalloped at top and rear, coloured cherry-red (infantry), white piped red (cavalry) or scarlet (artillery); the cavalry wore red trousers piped white in full dress. The head-dress was a Russian-style peaked cap displaying the red and white Czech national colours either as a stripe around the base of the cap-band, or a frontal badge, either a diagonal red and white stripe or the Russian cockade covered with cloth divided diagonally into red and white; fur caps were also used. The double-breasted khaki greatcoat also bore patches on the folding collar. Rank-insignia was originally Russian but changed on 30 December 1917 to inverted chevrons piped red on the upper arm, one to four narrow or one broad and one to three narrow, yellow for NCOs, silver for company officers and gold for field ranks; Russian arms and equipment.

The French Legion wore French horizon-blue uniform and Adrian helmet, with dark-blue collar patch with red piping and numeral (silver or gold for officers and NCOs), with badges on the shoulder-straps of both tunic and greatcoat of a dark-blue oval edged red, bearing 'CS' in red or silver. Officers wore a red kepi with black velvet band and silver braid; other ranks wore a dark-blue French beret, although red berets are shown in recruiting-posters for the Legion. Rank-insignia was French, in dark-blue (silver for officers).

The Czech Corps (or 6th Czech Division) of the Italian Army was constituted in April 1918, labour battalions having been enlisted earlier from Czech POWs; these wore the ordinary Italian field uniform with a vertical red and white stripe on the cap and a red and white brassard on the left arm. The Czech Corps also used Italian uniform and equipment, the tunic with a horizontally striped red and white collar-patch, with a white metal crossed rifles badge; the double-breasted greatcoat bore the same collar-patch. Head-dress was an Alpini-style hat, and the Adrian helmet with a red and white Czech badge painted on the front; rank-insignia consisted of short horizontal bars on the lower sleeve, in number as for the 'Russian' Legion, in violet (silver for officers). From mid-1918 a badge was added to the left upper arm, a grey-green or light-blue shield edged violet, bearing 'C.S.' in violet (silver for company officers, gold for field officers), some with the regimental number in black. The uniforms of the three Legions was later commemorated by use with the presidential bodyguard of the Czechoslovakian republic.

References

Baerlein, H. *The March of the Seventy Thousand*. London, 1926 (the Czech Legion)

Beneš, E. *Bohemia's Case for Independence*. London, 1917

— *My War Memoirs*. London, 1928

Bradley, J. F. N. *Czechoslovakia: a History*. Edinburgh, 1971

Lowrie, D. A. *Masaryk of Czechoslovakia*. Oxford, 1930

Masaryk, T. G. *Austrian Terrorism in Bohemia*. London, 1916

— *The Making of a State*. London, 1927

Seton-Watson, R. W. *History of the Czechs and Slovaks*. London, 1943

EGYPT

Although nominally part of the Ottoman Empire, Egypt had to all intents been under British control since 1882, the security of the Suez Canal being vital to British interests. Egypt had traditionally enjoyed almost complete autonomy from the Ottoman Empire, and was ruled by a hereditary prince or Khedive, assisted by a council of ministers, to which was added a British adviser with power to veto all financial decisions of the cabinet; since 1882 no measures had been instigated without the consent of the British plenipotentiary. Internal administration resided with the governors and heads of the provinces into which the country was divided. From 1913 there was a unified legislature, the Legislative Assembly, comprising the cabinet ministers, 66 elected representatives and seventeen nominated members representing the minorities.

From September 1911 Britain's representative in Egypt had been Lord Kitchener, whose career had been built on his military operations there; he was on leave when the World War began, and never returned to Egypt. The Legislative Assembly, supported by the Khedive, Abbas Hilmi, was nationalistic and hostile to the prime minister, Husein Rushdi Pasha, and to the British presence, and was suspended upon the outbreak of war. Martial law was imposed on 2 November. The entry of Turkey into the war

Abbas Hilmi, the pro-Ottoman Khedive, deposed on 19 December 1914.

made Egypt's previous status insupportable, and on 18 December 1914 Britain announced that henceforth Egypt was a British protectorate. On the following day, Khedive Abbas Hilmi was deposed in his absence (ardently pro-Turkish, he was convalescing in Constantinople after an assassination attempt by an Egyptian fanatic), and his uncle, Prince Hussein Kamel, was installed as Sultan of Egypt.

Although Egypt remained tranquil during the war (save for the Senussi hostilities: see 'North Africa'), and was held secure from Turkish attacks on the Suez Canal by the British and Empire garrison, nationalist sentiments prospered and an independence movement grew. With its new status, Egypt acquired a British administrator or High Commissioner; early in 1915 the acting commissioner, Sir

of the war was originally hostile to the Declaration of Independence arranged by Lord Allenby in 1922, by which the Protectorate was dissolved. The Wafd's objections lay with the continuing British control of the Suez Canal and all military and security affairs; but it was pushed through, the sultan became King Fuad I (reigning until 1936), and Zaghlul became first prime minister of the 'independent' state after the 1924 election. Full independence was achieved only in 1936, and even then Britain obtained a military occupation of the Suez Canal zone for a further 20 years.

Army

The Egyptian Army had been reorganized under British command, with its best elements being Sudanese, but was never very numerous (18,000 strong in 1908). When Turkey entered the war, Britain declared that it would protect Egypt and not call upon the Egyptian people for assistance, although a number of Egyptian gunners volunteered to defend the Suez Canal and participated in the repulse of the Turkish attack. Otherwise, the Egyptian Army was used to maintain internal tranquillity in the Sudan, which was ruled by an Anglo–Egyptian administration. In 1914 it comprised seven Sudanese, one southern Sudanese, one Bedouin Sudanese and eight Egyptian infantry battalions; three mounted infantry companies, the élite Camel Corps (largely Sudanese), supporting services and a number of para-military gendarmerie units; there were many British officers throughout the army. Uniform and equipment was similar to British tropical styles, although the red fez (worn with a khaki cover, including neck-cloth), coloured cummerbund and winter-wear khaki pullover were distinctive. The Camel Corps wore the Arab *kafiya* (head-cloth). Weapons were generally of British pattern, though not until later in the war did the Lee-Enfield finally replace earlier rifles such as the Martini-Henry.

Despite the declaration not to involve the Egyptian people, agricultural resources were requisitioned. A volunteer Egyptian Labour Corps, ultimately some 117,000 strong, was formed to support British forces in Palestine and on the Western Front, and from 1917 the Frontier Districts Administration formed an Egyptian security force (under British officers) to patrol the Arabian and Libyan desert frontiers. Some units, notably the Camel Corps, supported the Arab Revolt.

References
Elgood, Lieutenant-Colonel P. G. *Egypt and the Army*. Oxford, 1924

Nicolle, D. *Lawrence and the Arab Revolts*. London, 1989

Hussein Kamel, Sultan of Egypt from the deposition of his uncle, the Khedive, in December 1914, until his death in October 1917.

Milne Cheetham, handed over to the commissioner, Sir Henry McMahon; in December 1916 he was succeeded by General Sir Reginald Wingate, previously *Sirdar* (commander) of the Egyptian Army and governor-general of the Sudan. Sultan Hussein Kamel was never universally popular (attempts were made on his life), and upon his death in October 1917 he was succeeded by his brother Ahmad Fuad, who had been educated in the Italian military academy at Turin. (Hussein Kamel's son, Kamel ed Din. who had married the ex-Khedive's sister, had declined the sultanate.) Husein Rushdi Pasha remained as prime minister throughout the war.

Sa'ad Zaghlul Pasha's nationalist party, the Wafd ('delegation') was in the forefront of nationalist agitation, which broke into some violence in 1918; yet in the aftermath

ERITREA

The Italian colony of Eritrea was so named in 1890, although the Italian settlement had originated twenty years earlier; it was administered by a civil governor responsible to the Italian foreign ministry. It played little part in the war, although Italian possession of that part of the Red Sea coast helped ensure that Turkish vessels were unable to operate there, the other Allied force being the Royal Navy operating from Egypt. However, Eritrean troops were the best of Italy's colonial forces, and were of considerable use in the operations against the Senussi in North Africa, whereas the Italian colonial troops recruited there were much more unreliable and prone to desertion. The Eritrean askaris had traditionally worn a red fez and a white uniform including a long 'skirt' worn over trousers; but for service in the war they may have worn Italian tropical uniform instead. Eritrean troops also served in Italian Somaliland.

Reference
Nicolle, D. *Lawrence and the Arab Revolts*. London, 1989

ESTONIA

Estonia had been a Russian province since 1721, but only from the 1880s was there a deliberate attempt at 'Russification', to diminish the importance of the existing German–Est culture. Following the fall of the Tsar, Estonia was granted local self-government in the *Maapen* or Diet (12 April 1917) and was permitted to form an Estonian army by recalling Estonians from the Russian Army; but in the face of Bolshevik agitation the National Council (established July 1917) declared independence (28 November 1917). Having failed to win much support in the January 1918 election, the Bolsheviks tried to regain control by force, whereupon the Estonian nobility called on German assistance (28 January); the Germans occupied Revel on 25 February and the Bolsheviks were expelled. An Estonian provisional government was established on 24 February, but this was not recognized by Germany, which set up a military occupation. Germany evacuated Estonia at the armistice, leaving the country virtually defenceless (Germany having disbanded its army in April 1918), and the Russians (nominally Estonian Communists) invaded. An Estonian Soviet Republic was established in the occupied areas; but with the aid of 3,000 Finnish volunteers, the Royal Navy (which prevented the Russians from taking Revel) and their own re-organized forces, the Estonians halted the Red advance and by January 1919, co-operating with White Russian forces, had driven the Reds back into Russia. Fighting continued until late 1919, when an armistice was declared, and Russia recognized Estonian independence by the Treaty of Dorpat, 2 February 1920.

Army
The First Estonian Army was that formed under the permission of the Russian Provisional Government in 1917; its uniform and equipment was basically Russian, plus the Estonian cap-cockade (blue/black/white); brassards in these colours (or white) were common. When the Germans withdrew from Estonia the only defence force extant was a

A typical report, which could have been written by any nationality, concerning a not unusual night's activity:

'After almost 2 days' incessant bombardment on the part of the enemy of our trenches S. of TOUVENT FARM, a large party of the enemy were seen at 5·30 p.m. on the 19th Feb. 1916 working on their wire along their front line trench . . . The O.C. Lancashire Fusiliers at once ordered the machine-guns, Lewis guns and Artillery, to open fire on this party . . .

'This was followed almost immediately by a heavy bombardment by the enemy of our front and support line trenches S. of TOUVENT FARM. Later a barrage was formed with gas and other shells, in the vicinity of the reserve Company, who were forced to put on their smoke helmets . . .

'During this bombardment a party of the enemy estimated at about 110 strong entered a small part of our trench (trench 82) which had been previously rendered easy of access by a heavy bombardment early in the morning, by heavy trench mortars directed on this one spot. Large craters had been formed and the wire very badly damaged. This place having been thus damaged was only held by a listening post of two men supported close in rear by a post of 7 men.

'The enemy on entering, after disposing of this listening post, as well as the group in rear, who were all

volunteer force about 600 strong, the Baltic Regiment under a Colonel Weiss, formed to oppose Bolshevism. To these were added the 3,000 Finnish volunteers under General Wetzer, enlisted by a loan of 20 million marks guaranteed by the Revel banks. Under their influence the khaki uniform of the re-formed Estonian Army took on a Finnish style, the tunic having four patch pockets and a folding collar (blue piped white for officers), with badges on the point of the collar; one to three officers' rank-stars were carried on the shoulder-strap, with additional smaller stars on the collar for field ranks. The Russian-style peaked cap was retained, but German steel helmets and khaki fore-and-aft caps bearing the national cockade were also worn.

FINLAND

By the Treaty of Fredrickshavn (17 September 1809) Finland was transferred from Sweden to Russia, the territory becoming a semi-independent grand duchy with its own senate, a Russian-appointed governor-general, and the Tsar as Grand Duke. Russian influence did not intrude to a degree to cause Finnish disquiet until the end of the 19th century. Upon the outbreak of war, only some 2,000 Finns volunteered for Russian service; about the same number joined the German Army, and were concentrated into *Jäger* Battalion Nr. 27.

killed, turned with the evident intention of bombing northwards along the front line trench . . .

'Capt. Gamon, Lancashire Fusiliers, the Officer in command of the Company taking the situation well in hand, at once ordered Lt. MacMullan to move up the platoon to the counter-attack. This was promptly carried out and after a hard hand to hand fight drove the enemy out of the trench at the point of the bayonet.

'The whole operation was well carried out, & as the Company supports moved forward to the counter-attack, the men of the Reserve Company still wearing their smoke helmets moved slowly forward to replace them.

'Our casualties were 7 killed, 1 Officer and 17 men wounded, 1 Officer and 4 men missing.

'The enemy's casualties are unknown, but are believed to be heavy as throughout this period the Artillery kept up a very effective barrage in front of and along their trenches. So far 7 dead Germans have been counted lying out in front of our trenches, whilst more dead may yet be found in the numerous shell holes and in the trenches themselves, which are in a bad state.

'Nothing was taken away by the enemy.

(Sgd) D. Burt-Marshall, Captain
General Staff, 48th Division.'

(Captain Maurice Partridge Gamon was killed in action, 1 July 1917)

As the new Russian government could not decide who should assume the power previously accorded the Tsar, on 18 July 1917 the Finnish parliament (Diet) declared itself supreme in all but military and foreign affairs. This being unacceptable to the Russian Provisional Government, Kerensky ordered the Diet dissolved and a new election called, which resulted in the rise of right-wing or middle-class parties at the expense of the Social Democrat Party, which advocated Finnish autonomy within Russia. On 6 December 1917 the new Diet declared Finnish independence, which was recognized by the Soviet government on 1 January 1918, believing that the Socialist faction would institute the same system as evolving in Russia. In mid-1917 a defence force had been organized in Finland, the White Guard, largely to control the large numbers of Russian troops in the country; to balance this the Social Democrats organized their own Red Guard, and on 28 January 1918 staged a *coup d'état*, seized the government installations in Helsingfors, and proclaimed Finland a Socialist Workers' Republic.

The government of Pehr Svinhufvud fled to Vassa, which was taken from the Russian garrison by the ex-Russian general Carl Gustav Mannerheim (1867–1951), who on 18 January had been appointed to command the White forces (which included the Finnish-recruited 27th *Jägers*). In a response to a request from the government, the German 'Baltic Division' of Count Rüdiger von der Goltz (1865–

1946) arrived in Finland on 3 April, assisting the 'Whites' in expelling the 'Reds', Mannerheim winning a decisive victory at Viborg (28–29 April). Germany sought to make capital from their position, but the armistice caused their troops to be withdrawn in December 1918; Mannerheim replaced the pro-German Svinhufvud on 12 December, at the head of a provisional government. Mannerheim organized a 100,000-strong security force (the *Skyddskorps* or 'Protective Guard'); although skirmishes occurred until 1920, Mannerheim's suggestion that Finnish troops should participate on the 'White' side in the Russian Civil War did not find favour with the other Allied nations already involved. In July 1919 a presidential election installed Professor Kaarlo Ståhlberg, a moderate coalition government took power, and a republic was proclaimed; independence was confirmed by the Treaty of Dorpat (14 October 1920).

Army

The 27th *Jägers* continued to wear German uniform when transferred to Finnish service, with the new Finnish cockade (white with light-blue ring), and soon Finnish rank-badges (one to three rosettes on the point of the collar). The White troops wore improvised uniform, including some Russian and some manufactured from grey Swedish cloth, with fur caps and greatcoats; white brassards were borne on both arms, bearing a variety of coloured devices and lettering, for example a Finnish lion upon a shield. A common White Guard style comprised a single-breasted tunic with four pockets and turn-down collar, breeches with puttees (riding-boots for officers) and a peaked kepi. The diversity of uniform is exemplified by the two cavalry regiments: the Nyland Dragoons wore light-grey tunics with dark-blue facings and breeches, and grey Swedish tricorns with blue lining; the Kexholm Cavalry had Russian peaked caps with yellow band and piping, a similar tunic with red-brown facings piped yellow, dark-red loops on the breast and dark-red breeches with double yellow stripe.

Reference
Smith, C. J. *Finland and the Russian Revolution 1917–22*. Athens, Georgia, 1958

FRANCE

A republic since the fall of Napoleon III, the French legislature was the National Assembly of two houses: a 584-member Chamber of Deputies elected by almost universal male suffrage for a four-year term, and an upper house of 300 Senators, elected for a nine-year term. The head of state was the president, elected for seven years by a majority in the National Assembly, who had the power to dismiss the Chamber of Deputies (with the consent of the Senate) and who nominated the prime minister, president of the council of ministers chosen by the prime minister. There were twelve ministries (one headed by the prime minister), with an advisory council of state of which the justice minister was president. Local administration was based upon 87 *départements*, each sub-divided into *arrondissements*, each headed by a prefect and sub-prefect respectively.

President of France throughout the war was Raymond Poincaré (1860–1934), who was elected in January 1913. Determined to increase the significance of the presidential office, Poincaré played an important role during the war, guiding the somewhat ineffectual prime ministers in the first part of the war, although his influence declined latterly and never extended to the military command. The 1914 election resulted in the eventual appointment as prime minister of the Algerian-born René Viviani (1862–1925), a somewhat indecisive and pliant character subordinated to Poincaré in the immediate pre-war negotiations, and not an obvious leader. (An alliance between the Radical Joseph Caillaux and the Socialist Jean Jaurès had seemed more likely, but Caillaux was involved in a scandal after his second wife had shot to death the editor of *Figaro* for revealing correspondence between her and Caillaux from the time when she was his mistress, and Jaurès was murdered by the appropriately named assassin Villain.) Under pressure from Poincaré Viviani presided over the reconstruction of the government in late August 1914, into the *Union Sacrée*, a broad coalition of 'national defence'.

Viviani found himself almost powerless in the face of Joffre's insistence on running the war without interference, and resigned on 29 October. He was succeeded by Aristide Briand (1862–1932), ex-prime minister and an ally of Poincaré, whose tenure of office was beset by public criticism of both government and military, and by worsening relations with Poincaré. Briand succeeded in loosening Joffre's hold on the military control, and supported the appointment of Nivelle; but war minister General Louis Lyautey, finding himself unable to prevent or influence Nivelle's disastrous plans, resigned on 14 March 1917, precipitating the collapse of the Briand regime two days later. The new premier was Alexandre Ribot (1842–1923), previously finance minister. He oversaw the installation of Pétain and Foch as commander-in-chief and chief of general staff respectively, but suffered bad publicity over his interior minister, Louis Malvy (1875–1949), who was widely believed to be a defeatist and was even accused of selling plans of the Nivelle offensive to Germany (he was acquitted of treason in 1918 but convicted of criminal negligence). Ribot resigned on 7 September 1917 but retained the foreign affairs portfolio for some time, and was succeeded by Paul Painlevé (1863–1933), war minister from March 1917. The *Union Sacrée* broke up when Socialists refused to join his cabinet as a protest to Ribot's continuing as foreign minister, and although Painlevé presided over the establishment of the first inter-Allied war council, his government collapsed on 13 November.

Poincaré chose instead Georges Clemenceau (1841–1929), ex-premier (1906–09), ex-champion of Dreyfus and

Raymond Poincaré (1860–1934), President of France from January 1913 to January 1920.

ardent supporter of the war in his journal *L'Homme Libre*, leading Radical and untiring critic of previous ministries. Clemenceau formed his cabinet on 16 November 1917, and in him Poincaré found a prime minister to carry France through the final year of the war with a resolution previously absent. Clemenceau's declaration upon taking office that 'I wage war' was a blunt statement of the truth: he arrested Caillaux for defeatism, and took such a leading role in the cabinet that his robust policy of pursuing the war to its end, despite vociferous but ineffective political opposition, carried the nation behind him in a manner

Georges Clemenceau (1841–1929), the indomitable French prime minister in the last year of the war, whose motto was 'I wage war'.

Army

The French Army was one of the cornerstones of the Allied war effort; mobilizing almost half a million men less during the war than the British Empire, French fatalities were almost half as much again, and the wounded more than twice as numerous. The offensive spirit regarded as characteristic of the French resulted in enormous early casualties (almost three times as many in 1914 in comparison with combatant strength as in any of the succeeding years), and necessarily gave way to a more defensive mode of operation.

The concept of universal military service had been established in France after the Franco–Prussian War. As finalized in 1905 when exemptions were removed, the 'two years' law' decreed that all fit men aged 20 to 45 would serve in the army: two years' service with the colours, eleven with the army reserve, and the remainder with the territorial army. In 1913, to redress the imbalance between the French and German Armies (to oppose which all French planning was directed), the 'three years' law' was passed to extend the term of service with the colours to three years. Voluntary service was also permitted, from age 18, and those whose compulsory service had expired could re-engage for up to 15 years, such *rengagés* receiving a bounty, improved pay and pension, a system which provided a cadre of experienced men: almost all NCOs were *rengagés*.

The army comprised some 823,000 men (three-year conscripts, and including 46,000 colonial troops); 2,887,000 reservists were mobilized in the first two weeks of August 1914 (which, inclusive of officers, brought a total of 3,780,000), and from then until the end of June 1915 a further 2,700,000 were called up. In order to mobilize so many, classes from 1889 had to be called, which at worst included men aged 45 who had received a total of 69 days' training over the previous 23 years. Such men were obviously unfit for immediate service, and competent officers and NCOs were in short supply (it was possible to provide cadres of officers from the active army for the reserve, but not for the territorials). The reserve divisions, and even more the territorials, were in no state to undertake active campaigning immediately; but the best men were assigned to the 'Covering Army' on the frontiers, to resist the early attacks. Call-ups became less frequent: against those mobilized by mid-1915 noted above, the total figure for the entire war was only 8,317,000, of whom 475,000 were colonials. Officers were commissioned from the various military colleges (infantry and cavalry at St. Cyr, artillery and engineers at the *Ecole Polytechnique*), plus about one-third from NCOs, trained for commissions at their own establishments. There was also a staff college (*Ecole supérieure de Guerre*) and other specialist establishments.

Command was vested nominally in the president, but the war minister and his council of senior generals (*Conseil supérieure de la guerre*) provided actual direction; the vice-president of this body was the commander-in-chief of the field army, and the chief-of-staff was also on the council.

impossible for his predecessors. At last a politician was able to subordinate the military to the government, and Clemenceau's belligerence caused the military to fall into line without protest. He supported Pétain, and under his aegis the Allied nations accepted Foch as head of a unified Allied command. Under the fierce resolve and determined leadership of 'Tiger' Clemenceau (the nickname was appropriate), France pursued the war to the end, eschewing any negotiated peace that left the Allies short of total victory. His popularity declined after the war and he was defeated in his attempt to succeed Poincaré; but without him the Allied cause would have been much the poorer.

Despite the official political control, until the advent of Clemenceau the general staff virtually ran the war, and at times deliberately failed to co-operate with their supposed political superiors.

Pre-war organization was based upon numbered Army Corps, with headquarters as follows: I Corps Lille, II Amiens, III Rouen, IV Le Mans, V Orléans, VI Châlons-sur-Marne, VII Besançon, VIII Bourges, IX Tours, X Rennes, XI Nantes, XII Limoges, XIII Clermont-Ferrand, XIV Lyons, XV Marseilles, XVI Montpellier, XVII Toulouse, XVIII Bordeaux, XIX Algiers and XX Nancy. From 1910 some reorganization was instituted to counter the increase of German forces in Alsace–Lorraine, including the formation of XXI Corps to act as a 'covering force' for the Vosges, and the assembly of five armies in which the 'covering force' corps acted as advance-guards (I, II, VI, VII, XX and XXI). Organization at the outbreak of war was:

First Army (Dubail): VII, VIII, XIII, XIV, XXI Corps
Second Army (Castelnau): IX, XV, XVI, XVIII, XX
    Corps; 2nd *Groupe de Divisions de Réserve* (GDR).
Third Army (Ruffey): IV-V, 3rd GDR
Fourth Army (Langle de Cary): XII, XVII
Fifth Army (Lanrezac): I–III, X, XI.

Upon mobilization, active units were brought to full strength by reservists, and on average one reserve division was created per corps, assembled into the GDR formations. XIX Corps, as the garrison of Algiers, was not available for deployment *en masse*, but during the war two African divisions were sent to Europe for service with Fifth Army. Armies were created and dispersed according to need, including forces overseas, for example the Army of the East formed at Salonika. A larger formation was the Army Group, by which armies were brought under central authority: in 1915, for example, there were three (Centre, East, North), and in 1917–18 'reserve army groups' (GARs) were created, such grouping extending to Allied forces such as that commanded by King Albert in 1918.

Each Army Corps generally comprised two infantry divisions, a cavalry regiment, four groups of field artillery (each of three 4-gun batteries), a reserve infantry brigade (two regiments, styled *éléments non endivisionnés* or 'ENE'), and supports including eight field hospitals. Exceptions in 1914 included VI and VII Corps with three divisions each, and XIX with three plus one in Tunis, allowing it to maintain the North African garrison while still sending troops to Europe. There were eight cavalry divisions (HQs Paris, Lunéville, Meaux, Sedan, Melun, Lyons, Rheims and Dôle), later ten; and the military governments of Paris and Lyons, separate from the corps system; the former included 3½ divisions from II–V Corps, a colonial division, and the 1st and 3rd Cavalry Divisions, and the latter much of XIV Corps and 6th Cavalry Division. During the war the number of divisions in a corps varied, as units were transferred according to circumstances.

French infantry in their outdated blue uniform, worn 1914–15; the man in the foreground is preparing to throw a bracelet-grenade.

Infantry

An infantry division initially consisted of two brigades, each of two regiments of three battalions, a field artillery regiment of three groups (each of three 4-gun batteries), a cavalry squadron, engineer company and supports, totalling about 15,000 men, 36 field and 24 machine-guns. In order to increase the ratio of guns to infantry, divisions were later reduced to three regiments. Active divisions (*divisions d'infanterie* or DI) were numbered 1–43; reserve divisions were numbered 51–75 and styled *divisions de réserve* (DR) until 1915; territorial divisions bore numbers above 80. When existing divisions were reorganized from 1915, the new formations were given numbers over 100. Allocation of divisions in Europe in 1914 was: I Corps: Divisions 1, 2; II: 3, 4; III: 5, 6; IV: 7, 8; V: 9, 10; VI: 12, 40, 42; VII: 14, 41; VIII: 15, 16; IX: 17,18; X: 19, 20; XI: 21, 22, 52, 60; XII: 23, 24; XIII: 25, 26; XIV: 27, 28; XV: 29, 30; XVI: 31, 32; XVII: 33, 34; XVIII: 35, 36; XX: 11, 39; XXI: 13, 43; 1st GDR: 58, 63, 66; 2nd GDR: 59, 68, 70; 3rd GDR: 54–56; 4th GDR: 51, 53, 69; North-East Mobile Force: 57, 71–73; others: 44, 61–65, 67, 74, 75.

A 1907 St. Etienne machine-gun mounted for the anti-aircraft role, illustrating the use of ammunition fed into the breech in strips or racks, the alternative mechanism to belt-feed.

The infantry of the 'active army' comprised 173 numbered line regiments, of which 164 had three battalions of four companies each, eight garrison regiments had four battalions each, and a regiment garrisoning Corsica a fluctuating number. Upon mobilization each regiment formed a two-battalion reserve regiment, numbered by adding 200 to that of the parent regiment. There were 31 *chasseur à pied* battalions (thirteen of which were élite *Chasseurs Alpins*, mountain troops) all with six companies per battalion; four Zouave regiments with a varying number of 4-company battalions (recruited in France despite their North Africa origin and dress); nine native *tirailleur* regiments of a varying number of battalions of one depot and four active companies each; five African disciplinary light battalions; and two Foreign Legion regiments. The territorial infantry comprised 145 regiments (numbered 1–145), organization varying with size of recruiting-district, including twelve Zouave and seven *chasseur* battalions. Each battalion had a machine-gun section, but these had not extended to the territorials before the outbreak of war.

Brigades were numbered consecutively through the numbered divisions, which at two brigades per division in

French Chasseurs Alpins *in a trench in the Vosges: the legendary 'blue devils', distinguished by their large berets. The man in the foreground is wearing a leather jerkin.*

1914 meant that, for example, 15th Division would automatically contained the 29 and 30 Brigades. Typical divisional composition for 1914 for an active corps was:

VIII Corps:
15th DI: 29 Brigade: 56th, 134th Regiments
30 Brigade: 10th, 27th Regiments
16th DI: 31 Brigade: 85th, 95th Regiments
32 Brigade: 13th, 29th Regiments
Corps troops (ENE): 210th, 227th Regiments

Reserve corps included three divisions, and reserve brigades three regiments instead of the two of the 'active army', because of the lower number of battalions in reserve regiments: thus both 'active army' and reserve brigades each fielded six battalions.

The 1st–3rd Zouaves had six battalions each and the 4th Regiment seven; on mobilization these were augmented by reserve battalions and formed into *régiments de marche* (RM) or provisional regiments, those in France forming 37th and 38th Divisions (outside the corps organization) and 45th Division (not immediately deployed):

37th Division:
73 Brigade: RM of 2nd Zouaves (1st, 5th, 11th Battalions)
74 Brigade: RM of 3rd Zouaves (1st, 5th, 11th Battalions)
38th Division:
75 Brigade: RM of 1st Zouaves (4th, 5th, 11th Battalions)
76 Brigade: RM of 4th Zouaves (4th, 5th, 11th Battalions)

Others served in the Moroccan *Division de Marche* in North Africa.

The native *tirailleur* regiments were numbered consecutively, the 4th and 8th Tunisian (RTT: *Régiment de Tirailleurs Tunisiens*) and the remainder Algerian (RTA: *Régiment de Tirailleurs Algériens*). These had three battalions, except: 6th and 7th four each; 3rd five; 2nd, 4th and 8th six. For war they were organized into *régiments de marche* (RMT: *régiment de marche de tirailleurs*, or RMZT: *régiment de marche de Zouaves et tirailleurs*). Additional battalions were formed until by early 1918 there existed regiments numbered 1–15, 17 and 21, mostly of three battalions (15th RMT comprised one *tirailleur* battalion and three of the 228th Line). In all, some 155,000 Algerians and Tunisians were mobilized during the war, of whom 35,900 were killed. The North African *tirailleurs* were generally though unofficially styled 'Turcos'.

The two Foreign Legion regiments were based at Sidi-bel-Abbès and Saïda, with a *régiment de marche* in Morocco. The influx of recruits at the beginning of the war permitted the formation of four RM, each of four battalions. (The 4th RM of the 1st Foreign Legion Regiment (RE: *régiment étranger*) was known as the Garibaldi Brigade, almost entirely Italian and commanded by members of the Garibaldi family; it was mauled so severely that it was disbanded in 1915, most survivors transferring to Italian service.) In late 1915 losses had been so severe that the Legion battalions were amalgamated into a single RMLE (*régiment de marche de la Legion étrangère*). In addition to these units, the Legion continued to act as the garrison of Morocco, involved in continual hostilities with the local tribes; the majority were Germans and Austrians, who were thus permitted to avoid fighting against their countrymen.

The number of infantry as a proportion of the army declined during the war, though still remained most numerous despite the increase in artillery to almost three-quarters of the infantry strength. From more than 1.5 million combat infantrymen in spring 1915, the number reduced to only 850,000 by the armistice.

Despite earlier experiments with semi-camouflage uniform, at the beginning of the war the infantry was clothed in a very outdated style. The tunic was single-breasted with a standing collar, black for officers and dark-blue for other ranks, but almost universally was discarded by the latter in favour of the double-breasted, dark-grey–blue greatcoat; the regimental number in blue or black was carried on a red collar-patch on both garments. The red kepi had a dark-blue band bearing the regimental number in red, usually

worn with a grey-blue cover on service. The conspicuous red trousers which had distinguished French infantry from 1829 were retained, but within a few weeks of the beginning of the war there is evidence that blue-grey or blue linen overalls were being worn over the red; short black gaiters were worn with ankle-boots (longer gaiters by officers, who had wide black stripes on their trousers); drab puttees sometimes replaced the gaiters. Buttons were brass. *Chasseurs* had blue kepi and collar-patch, white buttons and blue-grey trousers with yellow stripe, the *Chasseurs Alpins* with a voluminous dark-blue beret, sometimes with white cover, and optional white trousers. Zouaves wore their traditional Arab costume: soft red fez (*chéchia*), dark-blue collarless shirt and short-tailed jacket bound with red braid, red baggy trousers with blue knots and piping on the seam, short gaiters and blue girdle; in North Africa they wore white trousers, of which some use seems to have been made in Europe, but by September 1914 these were replaced by khaki or blue, and the caps received blue covers. The North African *tirailleurs* wore light-blue Zouave uniform with yellow lace, white *chécia* and red girdle. The Foreign Legion wore infantry uniform with collar-numerals, '1' or '2', of the parent unit.

Rank-markings were diagonal bars on the cuff, usually red or metallic lace of the button-colour: private 1st class one bar, corporal two, sergeant one or two metallic, warrant officer (*adjutant*) metallic lace ring (opposite of button-colour) with red stripe. Officers: subalterns one or two metallic lace cuff-rings, kepi with one to three horizontal lace rings; captain, three cuff-rings, kepi same plus two vertical laces; field officers four or five cuff-rings (alternately in opposing colour for lieutenant-colonel), four or five kepi-rings, three vertical laces and knot on crown; generals had bright scarlet trousers, black facings, two or three silver stars on tunic-cuff and greatcoat-collar, one or two gold oak-leaf rings and three vertical laces on kepi; marshals the same, with seven silver stars and three kepi-rings.

A new colour was devised to replace the unsuitable infantry uniform, originally a mixture of red, white and blue threads, known originally as 'tricolour grey' or more commonly 'horizon-blue', used from late 1914 for the kepi, peakless fore-and-aft side cap, tunic, trousers, puttees and greatcoat (originally double-breasted, but soon a single-breasted version with breast-pockets was introduced). The collar-patch was ordered to be yellow with dark-blue numeral and double chevron for infantry, iron-grey with these in yellow for light infantry, but very quickly this was amended to ground-coloured patches, with the *chasseur* device changing to green numeral, hunting-horn badge and double chevron from 1915. On the new greatcoat the patch was shaped to fit the point of the folding collar, with the double chevron above. Light infantry kept their blue uniform until at least mid-1916. Rank-badges were reduced in size and amended: warrant officers, a lace bar with interwoven red squares; officers one to five metallic lace bars on the cuff and chevrons on the side-cap; general officers two to seven gilt stars; all these also worn on the front of the

kepi. 'Trade' badges were worn on the tunic- and greatcoat-sleeves, embroidered or cut from cloth, e.g., pioneers had a grenade over crossed spade and axe, in the unit colour. From mid-1915 the steel helmet was adopted (*casque Adrian*, named after its designer), painted horizon-blue and with a comb and embossed metal badge on the front, indicating the arm-of-service; this replaced bowl-shaped iron skull-caps worn with the kepi. For African troops (including Foreign Legion) this uniform was ordered to be of mustard-coloured khaki from December 1914, but was initially worn alongside horizon-blue items and was not universal until mid-1916; the Foreign Legion continued to wear green rank-chevrons, and their traditional blue girdle over the coat for parade.

Equipment was black leather, including a waist-belt with cartridge-pouch at each side of the rectangular plate, with shoulder-braces and 1893-pattern knapsack to which was strapped a mess-tin, rolled blanket and tent-section; a drab cloth haversack was carried over the right shoulder and a double-spouted canteen over the left. The equipment became brown by 1916, and a double-size canteen (originally designed for tropical service) became general from mid-1915. A metal-framed knapsack was introduced for light machine-gunners in 1917, to support the weight of magazines.

French infantry in a trench near Maurepas, wearing the horizon-blue uniform and Adrian helmet; note the grenades and the overhead wire. The narrow tin box worn by the man at extreme left was the container for the 'Tissot' gas mask.

The rifle used originally was one of the most famous of the era, but it might not be unjust to comment that although the French Army might have had twenty ways of cooking potatoes, they were provided with a rifle as outdated as the 1914 uniform. The Lebel rifle originated in 1886, the product of the 1883 Commission for Repeating Weapons, and bore the name of the commandant of the Châlons-sur-Marne Weapons School. It was the first small-bore (8mm) military rifle to be adopted by any nation and was superbly produced, and was probably too good in that it was retained even though the superior Lee magazine was coming into service in other armies. The Lebel was an 8-shot weapon with cartridges carried under the barrel (a ninth could be placed in the breech), but rounds had to be loaded individually and thus had an inferior rate-of-fire when compared to the superior clip-loading method, and when taking into account the time needed to load eight rounds individually it had only a small advantage over a single-shot weapon. Minor adjustments were introduced in 1893, giving the official designation '1886 M.93'. It had a needle-like épée bayonet with hooked quillon, removed to produce the 1916-pattern; the thin bayonet had a propensity for breaking off in action, hence the preference by the Senegalese of a broad-bladed knife for close-quarter combat.

Colonial troops (Indo–Chinese) were issued with the 1902-pattern rifle, known as the Mannlicher-Berthier, which was the basis for the Lebel successor, the Berthier 1907/15 with three-round clip, and the 1916 with five-round clip.

Several patterns of machine-gun were used, the most famous being the Hotchkiss; the Model 1900 used a rigid brass ammunition clip holding 24 or 30 8mm cartridges; the Model 1905 Puteaux and Model 1907 St. Etienne (both named from the factories which designed them) used metal bands of 25 cartridges. Being air-cooled the St. Etienne was especially useful in hot climates; the Hotchkiss was modified to produce the Model 1914. Unlike many Allied armies, the French used the Lewis gun only in an aviation role; the first French light machine-gun was the 1907 Chauchat (named after its designer), which was modified to produce the Model 1915 CSRG (Chauchat-Sutter-Ribeyrolles-Gladiator: the last was a bicycle-manufacturer!), which, with its distinctive semi-circular magazine, was produced in huge quantities from that date (some quarter of a million, many supplied to Allied forces). Although prone to jamming, its 240 rounds per minute made it a most effective close-support weapon, and by early 1918 each company had up to twelve Chauchat teams (originally two men per team, later four to share the ammunition-load). Other light

machine-guns included the Model 1908 Berthier–Pacha and the 1909 lighter Hotchkiss, the latter restricted to fortification, tank and aviation use. Automatic rifles, all of limited use, included the 7mm Model 1910 A-6 gun (first issued 1917), the Model 1917 RSC gun, and a lighter Model 1918. The increase in numbers of machine-guns was remarkable: from 2,158 in September 1914, by 1918 there were more than 19,000 heavy and 47,000 light machine-guns in front-line service.

Grenades varied from simple 'jam-tin' and 'racket' types, to spherical grenades ignited by friction-fuze when the bomb was thrown, egg-grenades like the Model 1916 CF and can-shaped Model 1916 incendiary, ignited by striking the base (to depress an internal plunger) before throwing, and more conventional varieties such as the Model 1915 egg-grenade and Model 1916 'automatic' incendiary, with ignition via a spring-loaded plunger held in place by a pin. Rifle-grenades were also used.

Cavalry

The 91 cavalry regiments comprised twelve of cuirassiers, 32 of dragoons, 21 of *chasseurs à cheval*, fourteen of hussars, six of *Chasseurs d'Afrique* and six of *Spahis* (Algerian light horse), each regiment of four squadrons (*Spahis* five). Generally, each infantry division included one cavalry squadron (often the mobilized 5th and 6th reserve squadrons of a regiment), plus a full regiment with each Army Corps; the remainder formed cavalry divisions (ultimately ten), each of three brigades of two regiments each. Heavy divisions had four dragoon and two cuirassier regiments; 'mixed divisions' two regiments each of cuirassiers, dragoons and light cavalry; and light divisions four regiments of dragoons and two of light cavalry. Attached to each division was a horse artillery brigade (two 4-gun batteries), supporting services and a *chasseur à pied* cyclist company. There were six machine-guns per division; total strength was about 4,500 men. Additional machine-guns were added in 1915, and the force declined in numbers as regiments were dismounted for service as infantry; there were more than 106,000 mounted cavalrymen at the beginning of the war, but only 33,500 by early 1918.

Uniforms were initially even more outdated than those of the infantry. Cuirassiers wore a maned helmet (usually covered with fabric on service), dark-blue tunic (black for officers) with red collar, cuff-flaps and epaulettes, blue collar-patch bearing regimental number, yellow buttons, iron cuirass, and red trousers with black stripe; dragoons the same minus the cuirass, with white collar, cuff-flaps, trefoil shoulder-knots and buttons, and red trousers with light-blue stripe. The *chasseurs* wore a light-blue shako with horn badge, light-blue tunic with crimson collar and cuff-flaps, white buttons and trefoils, and red trousers with light-blue stripe; hussars wore the same, but for light-blue facings and Austrian-knot decoration on the front of the shako. Alternative head-dress for light regiments was a red kepi with light-blue band, or the 1910 helmet, similar to that

Among a number of ancient catapults and the like used in the early stages of the war, this steel and wire crossbow with a stock shaped like that of a rifle was used to hurl grenades from 20 to 80 yards; l'arbalète lance-grenade *was known colloquially in the French Army as a 'grasshopper'.*

French cavalry with British troops at a barricade, 1918; note the ammunition-bandoliers carried around the horses' necks.

worn by dragoons, though the issue of the latter was only very partial. Cuirassier units dismounted in November 1914 to form *cuirassiers à pied* wore the ordinary helmet with comb removed. Rank-insignia was as for infantry, except that NCO badges were in the form of chevrons. The *Spahis* wore a turban and voluminous red, hooded cloak, red Zouave jacket and waistcoat with dark-blue lace, red sash and blue baggy trousers, and officers European-style uniform in the same colours, with light-blue kepi and trousers; the *Chasseurs d'Afrique* wore chasseur uniform with yellow collar and cuff-patch, and red kepi with light-blue band. The Model 1890 carbine existed in cavalry, cuirassier and gendarmerie varieties (only the latter with provision for a bayonet), with 3-round Mannlicher clip. Swords were soon discarded: some, like those of the light cavalry, were still based on the 1822 pattern, while the 1880 modification of the 1854-pattern was also common. The lances used were the patterns of 1823 (triangular blade, ash shaft), 1890 (quad-

rangular blade, bamboo shaft, largely used for training), and 1913 (triangular blade, browned steel shaft, the most common).

The cavalry adopted horizon-blue service uniform like the infantry, with dark-blue collar patch and trouser-piping, the collar numeral and double chevron in crimson, white, green and sky-blue for cuirassiers, dragoons, *chasseurs* and hussars respectively; the greatcoat was single-breasted and much longer than the infantry version. Gendarmerie wore black collar-patches bearing a white grenade, and white trouser-piping. *Spahis* and *Chasseurs d'Afrique* adopted mustard-khaki instead, the former retaining their cloaks and wearing voluminous khaki trousers; collar-patches were dark-blue with yellow numeral and double chevron, with yellow buttons for *Spahis* and white for *Chasseurs d'Afrique*.

Artillery

At the outset, artillery composition reflected the French offensive philosophy, in that there was a greater prepon-derance of mobile field artillery (4,098 field, 192 mountain and 389 heavy guns in September 1914). There were 62 field regiments, of three or four groups of three 4-gun batteries, with five groups in North Africa; plus 30 horse batteries, 24 medium howitzer, 35 heavy and 75 foot batteries. Three

French 120mm model 1878 Système de Bange heavy gun, 1915; the plates around the wheels (ceintures de roue, lit. 'wheel-belts') were to give additional traction and prevent the wheels sinking.

field groups were part of each division, with four groups deployed at corps level, and a horse brigade (two 4-gun batteries) to each cavalry division.

The principal field gun was the 75mm 1897-pattern, probably the most famous piece of ordnance of the war: with a rate of fire of 15 rounds per minute (rising to 30 *in extremis*) and a range of 9,000 yards, it was a superb weapon and known universally as the *Soixante-Quinze* or '75'. Initially there was no mobile field howitzer, so the 1898 155mm howitzer was used mainly in that role; the horse artillery Schneider gun fired the same projectile as the '75' with only two-thirds of the charge; the 1906 mountain gun was of 65mm calibre. Medium artillery included the Rimailho 155mm howitzer, the only modern heavy gun in use at the start of the war, available only in small numbers and supplemented by the Schneider and St. Chamond weapons of the same class. For heavy artillery, the 1878 *Système de Bange* guns had to be used initially, followed by the 155mm GPF gun (*greande puissance Filloux*). The 220mm 1917 Schneider gun was used on a road mounting, and the 220mm Schneider siege howitzer was introduced to replace the earlier expedient of 190mm guns re-bored to take British 8in shells. A 240mm howitzer was designed by St. Chamond, and a 370mm howitzer by Filloux. Largest of all were the rail-mounted Batignolles 320mm (projectile up to 1,100 pounds) and the 400mm St. Chamond, the largest land-based gun of the war, with a 10-mile range and a projectile up to 1,980 pounds in weight.

For infantry support, the 37mm Puteaux 'trench gun' was manufactured from 1915, which was transported in three sections and equipped either with wheels or tripod; the 1916 pattern was hand-loaded, the 1917 semi-automatic and the 1918 fully automatic. Initially no modern trench artillery was available, so that ancient mortars dating back to the 1830s were pressed into service. A wide variety of mortars was developed from 1915, most famously the series designed by Edgar Brandt, of which the 90mm 'Type 90' was probably the best. Stokes and Belgian Van Deuren mortars were also used, and by the end of the war the most common were the light 150mm (Pattern '150T', Models 1916 and 1917, known as the Fabry), the heavy 240mm (Types '240CT' and '240LT'), and a 75mm mortar for mountain use. A range of more unusual weapons included projectors using compressed air as a propellant.

Artillery was principally horse-drawn, though a variety of motorized tractors were adopted, beginning with the equipping of the 13th Regiment with American Jeffery tractors in June 1915 (a French design, the Latil tractor, was widely used to replace the Jeffery). Earlier attempts to tow artillery had not been successful (the tractors traversed muddy ground but the guns stuck), a problem overcome by loading the guns on to the rear of flatbed tractors; units so equipped were styled *portée* artillery, and in August 1917, it was decided to convert all 75mm batteries to this method of transportation. Twenty regiments had been converted by

March 1918, and 33 by the armistice, involving 8,600 motor vehicles. The majority were lorries: tracked vehicles were present in much smaller numbers (Renault and Schneider *Porteur* tractors), their manufacture restricted by the armoured vehicles' first call upon the track-making factories.

Artillery strength increased greatly during the war (from some 395,000 men in early 1915 to more than 600,000 by late 1918), and there was also an increase in weight of ordnance: heavy guns represented 8.3 per cent of the artillery in 1914, but almost half in 1918 (more than 7,100 heavy and 6,600 field, 260 mountain and more than 970 37mm; plus 4,100 pieces of trench artillery including more than 1,800 Stokes mortars).

The original artillery uniform was like that of the infantry, a blue tunic with scarlet collar, cuff-flaps, great-coat collar-patch and trefoil epaulettes, yellow buttons, blue trousers piped scarlet, and either a blue kepi piped scarlet or a beret for mountain artillery. The horizon-blue artillery uniform had scarlet collar-patch and trouser-piping, the former with numeral and double chevron in bright-blue, green, dark-blue and white for field, foot, horse and mountain artillery respectively.

Supporting services

The engineers originally comprised six ordinary, one railway and one telegraph regiment, totalling 26 battalions of between three and seven companies each. Initially each division had an engineer company (cyclists in cavalry divisions), with four companies, telegraph and searchlight

sections assigned to each Army Corps. Total combatant strength grew from some 104,000 in early 1915 to about 117,000 by late 1918. Originally they wore infantry-style uniform with black facings and collar-patch bearing red number, yellow buttons and blue trousers with scarlet piping; the horizon-blue uniform had black collar-patches with scarlet double chevron and number, and black trouser-piping.

There were originally 20 squadrons of train, initially deployed as divisional columns, corps columns and additional artillery and infantry ammunition-columns. Vehicles increased in number from some 19,000 in 1914 to more than 88,000 in 1918, and motorization expanded greatly during the war: in 1914, for example, more than 6,000 trucks, 2,500 cars and 1,000 omnibuses were acquired from civilian sources, and the commandeering of the Parisian taxis to rush troops to the Marne was one of the great epics of the war. The train originally wore a light-blue tunic with crimson facings and collar-patch bearing grey-blue numeral, crimson trousers with grey-blue stripe, kepi and white buttons; the horizon-blue uniform had green trouser-piping and green collar-patch with crimson number and red double chevron.

Medical services were deployed at divisional level (divisional bearer unit or field ambulance), with each corps originally including eight field hospitals, six hospital units, a corps bearer unit and a motorized medical unit. The original uniform was of infantry style with crimson facings and kepi-band and yellow buttons; the horizon-blue uniform had crimson collar-patch with grey-blue numeral.

Many armies commandeered civilian vehicles for transport, some of which remained in use throughout the war, such as this French bus.

Armoured troops

Although armoured cars were used from 1914, French heavy armoured vehicles first saw action on 16 April 1917. Originally, Colonel J. E. Estienne conceived a scheme for building an armoured body on a Holt tractor, and from February 1916 orders were placed with the Schneider–Creusot and St. Chamond works, each of which designed a heavy tank. The Schneider CA1 had a crew of seven and was armed with a 75mm Schneider gun and 8mm Hotchkiss; the St. Chamond had a 75mm gun at the front and a Hotchkiss on each of the four faces. The latter was the better vehicle, but the tracks of both were too narrow, resulting in poor cross-country performance. Production was halted in October 1917 to concentrate upon the new Renault light tank, conceived by Estienne as an armoured version of the cavalry skirmisher, with a two-man crew and either a 37mm gun or Hotchkiss in a revolving turret; it weighed only 7 tons and was good across country, but had a road-speed of only 5–6mph and compared unfavourably with the British Whippet. French tanks were styled *chars d'assaut* ('assault vehicles') and the corps termed *artillerie d'assaut*; the tactical unit was a *groupe* of four 4-tank batteries of heavy tanks, with a Renault command tank. Four Schneider or three St. Chamond *groupes* normally formed a *groupement*. The Renault was regarded as an infantry weapon and was organized in companies of 25, three of which formed a battalion.

Colonial forces

The forces covered above were styled 'metropolitan', the army of metropolitan France. There were in addition

Algerian Tirailleurs, colloquially 'Turcos', photographed near Reims in 1914; their original sky-blue Zouave coat and white trousers were ultimately replaced by the mustard-khaki worn by all French 'African' troops.

colonial forces, which also formed an expeditionary corps in France, about one-third being based there normally. Corps headquarters was Paris, and divisional HQs Paris, Brest and Toulon. They included sixteen colonial infantry regiments (formerly marines) of voluntarily recruited Europeans, of which twelve were stationed in France; five independent battalions in the colonies; twelve native *tirailleur* regiments (four Senegalese, four Tonkinese, three Madagascan and one Annamite); four cavalry squadrons (two Senegalese *Spahis*, one Congolese, one Indo–Chinese); in France, three artillery regiments (36 batteries, including six mountain), and four regiments and two independent artillery groups in the colonies. There were also six 'mixed regiments' in Morocco, each of two Senegalese *tirailleur* and one colonial infantry battalion. Uniforms were like those of the metropolitan army, colonial infantry with blue kepi piped red, blue-grey trousers piped red, yellow buttons and epaulettes for full dress; the Senegalese had yellow lace edging to collar and cuffs, red collar-patches bearing 'TS' (*Tirailleurs Sénégalais*), and Zouave *chéchia*; the most unusual distinction was the umbrella-shaped Indo–Chinese hat worn by the Annamites. Colonial artillery was distinguished from metropolitan only by the collar insignia of a fouled anchor (a relic of marine origin). The colonials adopted mustard-khaki instead of horizon-blue, initially with regimental distinctions (the Senegalese originally retained their yellow lace), infantry having khaki collar-patch with red numeral, anchor and double chevron, and the artillery red with blue anchor; the anchor was also worn on the Adrian helmet.

A sandbagged French trench-mortar post near Verdun; the shape of the finned projectile resulted in the name 'aerial torpedo'.

British infantry retire past a French machine-gun position, 1918; the gun is a Hotchkiss with the 1916-pattern tripod mount, which dispensed with the elevating-wheel present on some earlier mounts.

A French signal-rocket post in a trench: a common method of signalling. The soldier is wearing a fabric cover over his Adrian helmet.

Navy

The French coast was divided into five *arrondissements*, each with its own headquarters (Brest, Cherbourg, Toulon, Lorient and Rochefort), each commanded by a naval prefect who was a vice-admiral. There were also bases in Algeria (Oran), Indo–China (Saigon and Hongaj), Madagascar (Suarez), Martinique (Fort de France), New Caledonia (Nouméa), and Tunisia (Bizerta). Control was vested in the minister of marine, assisted by a civilian cabinet responsible for policy and a naval general staff (for organization and operations); the minister was also president of the Naval Council, a professional advisory body including the chief of naval staff. Although there was some voluntary enlistment and transfer of conscripts from the army, recruiting was mainly by the *inscription maritime*, introduced in 1681, by which all mariners (including those working on rivers and canals navigable by sea-going vessels) between the ages of 18 and 50 had to be enrolled, being liable for a period of seven years' active service from age 20 (in practice it was normally five years).

The fleet comprised regional squadrons (Mediterranean, Northern, Atlantic, Pacific, Indian Ocean, Far Eastern and Cochin–China), but the main concentration (and scene of operations during the war) was in the Mediterreanean, initially to ensure communications with the North African colonies. After a period of stagnation, a building programme was instituted before the war, pursued enthusiastically by Admiral Auguste Boué de Lapeyrère (1852–1924) during his term as minister of marine (1909–11). Concentrating upon capital ships and cruisers, under his guidance France neglected the important smaller vessels, and after an unimpressive showing as commander in the Mediterranean he asked to be relieved of duty in late 1915, retiring the following year. French Mediterranean operations included not only maintaining communications with North Africa but a significant participation in the Dardanelles operation (when *Bouvet* was sunk), the containment of the Austrian Navy, and the evacuation of the Serbian Army to Corfu.

Ships of over 4,000 tons displacement existing in the first year of the war included those tabulated here.

Date	Name and displacement (tons)	Main armament only
Predreadnought battleships		
1893	*Jauréguiberry* (11,900)	2 × 12in, 8 × 5.5in
1893	*Charles Martel* (11,882)	2 × 12in, 2 × 10.8in, 8 × 5.5in
1894	*Carnot* (12,150)	2 × 12in, 2 × 10.8in, 8 × 5.5in
1896	*Bouvet* (12,007)	2 × 12in, 2 × 10.8in, 8 × 5.5in
1897	*Henri IV* (8,948)	2 × 10.8in, 7 × 5.5in
1898	*Massena* (11,924)	2 × 12in, 2 × 10.8in, 8 × 5.5in, 8 × 4in
1899–1900	*Charlemagne, Gaulois, St. Louis* (11,260)	4 × 12in, 10 × 5.5in, 8 × 4in
1903	*Suffren* (12,750)	4 × 12in, 10 × 6.4in, 8 × 4in
1906	*République, Patrie* (14,865)	4 × 12in, 18 × 6.4in
1907–8	*Vérité, Démocratie, Justice* (14,900)	4 × 12in, 10 × 7.6in
1911	*Danton, Concordet, Diderot, Mirabeau, Vergniaud, Voltaire* (18,400)	4 × 12in, 12 × 9.4in

Date	Name and displacement (tons)	Main armament only
Dreadnoughts		
1912	*Bretagne, Lorraine, Provence* (23,550)	10 × 13.4in, 22 × 5.5in
1913–14	*Courbet, France, Jean Bart, Paris* (23,467)	12 × 12in, 22 × 5.5in
Armoured cruisers		
1896	*Pothua* (5,360)	2 × 7.6in, 10 × 5.5in
1902–03	*Montcalm, Dupetit Thomas, Gueydon* (9,517)	2 × 7.6in, 6 × 6.4in, 4 × 4in
1903	*Jeanne d'Arc* (11,270) (training ship)	2 × 7.6in, 14 × 5.5in
1903–4	*Dupleix, Desaix, Kléber* (7,700)	8 × 6.4in, 4 × 4in
1903–4	*Amiral Aube, Condé, Gloire, Marseilles* (10,000)	2 × 7.6in, 8 × 6.4in, 6 × 4in
1906	*Leon Gambetta* (sunk April 1915), *Jules Ferry, Victor Hugo* (12,416)	4 × 7.6in, 16 × 6.4in
1908	*Ernest Renan* (13,644)	4 × 7.6in, 12 × 6in
1908	*Jules Michelet* (12,000)	4 × 7.6in, 12 × 6.4in
1910	*Edgar Quinet, Waldeck-Rousseau* (14,000)	14 × 7.6in
Protected cruisers		
1893–6	*Latouche-Treville, Briux* (4,750)	2 × 7.6in, 6 × 5.5in
1896	*Descartes* (4,000)	4 × 6.4in, 10 × 4in
1898	*Du Chayla* (4,000)	6 × 6.4in, 4 × 4in
1898	*D'Entrecasteaux* (8,114)	2 × 9.4in, 12 × 5.5in
1901	*Jurien de la Gravière* (5,685)	8 × 6.4in
1902	*Guichen* (8,277)	2 × 6.4in, 6 × 5.5in

Other vessels over 4,000 tons displacement included the protected cruiser *Chateaurenault* (8,018, 2 × 6.4in, 6 × 5.5in) acting as a minelayer, and the aircraft carrier *Foudre* (6,086, 8 × 4in). Vessels of lesser tonnage included three cruisers, three torpedo-gunboats, four gunboats (one sunk at Tahiti, October 1914), 80 destroyers (four 1915, one sunk October 1914), about 280 torpedo-boats, eight minelayers (one sunk 1915) and 65 submarines (twelve 1915, six sunk 1915). Naval construction was almost halted by the war, even the Toulon naval ammunition works being turned over to army munitions, reflecting the comparative importance of the services. During the war some 166 vessels were lost (49 accidentally), including four battleships (*Bouvet, Danton, Gaulois, Suffren*), four armoured or battlecruisers and *Chateaurenault*. At the end of the war almost 1,300 vessels

The French battleship Suffren; *12,750 tons, 4 × 12in, 10 × 6.4in, 8 × 4in, 22 × 3-pdr guns, 4 × 18in torpedo tubes. In November 1916* Suffren *was lost with all hands when torpedoed off Lisbon by* U 52.

were in service, the majority small craft employed on convoy, minesweeping and anti-submarine duty.

Aviation service

The aviation service was originally an engineer battalion, but in 1910 received independent identity as the *Corps d'Aérostation*, operating balloons. At the outbreak of war the aviation service (*Aviation Militaire*) comprised about 200 aircraft in 23 squadrons (*escadrilles*), each of six machines, normally of the same type throughout the squadron, mostly general-purpose two-seaters, but two 'cavalry squadrons' flew single-seat Blériot monoplanes. Personnel increased from 8,000 in May 1915 to 52,000 at the armistice, and specialization was introduced comparatively early. General, reconnaissance and artillery-spotting duty was assigned to 'corps squadrons' (*escadrilles de corps*), and others formed fighter (*escadrilles de chasse*) and bombing (*de bombardement*) squadrons; the strength of each squadron was up to ten aircraft, and the total deployed in 1918 was almost 3,400. Three or more *escadrilles* formed a *groupe*, two or more of which formed a wing (*escadre*), a number of which might be formed into a *groupement* of 20 or more squadrons. Losses during the war amounted to some 3,700 aircraft, of which almost 2,000 were sustained in 1918. Squadrons were normally identified by a number, and initials representing the aircraft they flew ('C' for Caudrons, 'B' Breguets, 'MS' Morane-Saulniers, 'MF' Maurice-Farmans, 'N' Nieuports, 'SPA' Spads, etc.), but more famous were nicknames like *Les Cigognes* (the Storks), the élite fighter group, each *escadrille* of which painted a different version of the stork symbol upon its aircraft.

The aviation service originally wore engineer uniform, with dark-blue collar-patch bearing scarlet numerals for balloon personnel and vice-versa for aircraft personnel. The *Aviation Militaire* had a variety of specialist branch-badges, and many officers who transferred from other corps retained their previous uniform with the addition of such badges. The horizon-blue uniform had black collar-patch with red number and double chevron coloured green for fighter squadrons, bombers red, reconnaissance light-blue, balloons orange, meterological service white and ground personnel violet. Flying clothing included black leather jackets and trousers like those of the Paris fire brigade; the pilots' gold, winged propeller badge (red, white and gold for NCOs) was worn on a blue brassard with this jacket.

The service included a number of the most famous early pilots: René Fonck, a superb marksman and tactician who claimed his score to be more than half as many again as the 75 'kills' with which he was credited; Georges Guynemer, who disappeared over Poelcapelle in 1917; and Charles Nungesser, an audacious pilot who painted a skull, crossed bones and coffin on his aircraft and who, despite severe injuries, survived the war only to die attempting to fly the Atlantic in 1927.

The naval air service in 1914 comprised only eight machines and 200 men; at the end of the war it had more

One of the most famous posters of the war: Jules Faivre's 'On les aura!' ('We'll get them!'), for the Second French National Defence Loan.

than 1,250 aircraft (370 in active service), more than 250 dirigibles and captive balloons, and more than 11,000 personnel.

As France was in the forefront of aircraft development, many of the machines used were of indigenous manufacture, but even the French aircraft industry could not supply all requirements, necessitating the use of some foreign aircraft and engines such as the Hispano–Suiza. Among the home-produced aircraft were:

Blériot XI: single-seater unarmed reconnaissance monoplane resembling Louis Blériot's Channel-crossing machine, used until mid-1915; two- and three-seater *Artillerie* and *Génie* models also existed.

Breguet: the Breguet 2, 4 and 5 were two-seater pusher biplane bombers in service from 1915; the 14 was a two-seater reconnaissance (Type A2) and light bomber (Type B2) biplane used from mid-1917, one of the best and most widely used bombers; the Breguet 1914 was a metal-fuselaged two-seater reconnaissance biplane used briefly in 1914, known as the 'tin whistle' in British service!

Caudron: the G2 was a single-seater reconnaissance

biplane, from which was developed the G3, an unarmed two-seater reconnaissance/light bomber biplane in service until 1917; the G4 was an enlarged version used 1915–16 (to 1917 with British RNAS), with guns; the G6 was a version with more powerful engines, in service from spring 1917. The Caudron R4 was a three-seater, twin-engined biplane designed as a bomber but relegated to reconnaissance use 1916–17, being insufficiently powered as a bomber; the improved R11 was designed as a night bomber but its heavy armament (five Lewis) made it an ideal escort for other bombers.

Deperdussin TT: two-seater reconnaissance monoplane, used in small numbers at the beginning of the war.

Dorand: two-seater reconnaissance biplances, the DO1 used 1914–15, and the improved AR1 and AR2 1917–18.

Farman F series: co-operation between the brothers Henri and Maurice Farman produced a series of two-seater pusher reconnaissance/light bomber biplanes from 1915, variants styled F30, F40, F56, F60, F61; not successful in having no defence against attack from behind, but remained in service until 1917 (with the Belgians until the armistice). The Farman F50 was a two-seater, twin-engined tractor heavy bomber in limited use in late 1918.

Franco–British: the Franco–British H was a reliable three-seater pusher biplane flying-boat used in considerable numbers by France and several Allied nations; improved S Type (1918) had increased bomb-load.

Hanriot HD1: single-seater biplane fighter used by French Navy (and more widely by Italy and Belgium) from 1918.

Henri Farman: F20–22 were underpowered two-seater pusher reconnaissance biplanes in use at the outbreak of war, relegated to training in 1915 despite extensive use with Allied forces (RNAS had a floatplane version); the F27 was a four-wheeled steel bomber useful in tropical climates (with no wood to warp), used by RFC and RNAS in the Middle East and Africa to 1918.

Letord: the Letord 1 was a three-seater twin-engined biplane designed as a bomber but incapable of carrying sufficient load, and used for reconnaissance in limited numbers from spring 1917; versions 4 and 5 were improved.

Maurice Farman: the MF7 was a two-seater pusher reconnaissance/light bomber biplane used 1914–15, unarmed; the MF11 (with Lewis or Hotchkiss for observer) was used operationally 1915 and thereafter as a trainer. The MF7 and 11 were known respectively as 'Longhorn' and 'Shorthorn' by the British, from the length of landing-skids.

Morane–Saulnier: the A1 was a single-seater monoplane fighter used only in early 1918. The L or 'Parasol' was an outstanding two-seater reconnaissance monoplane, 1914–15, initially unarmed but from early 1915 with forward-firing Hotchkiss; the LA was an improved version (1915–17) and the P a larger variety. The N was a single-seater monoplane fighter used in small quantities 1916, known as the 'Bullet' by the British. The T was a three-seater, twin-engined reconnaissance biplane, from 1916.

Nieuport: the 6M was a single-seater reconnaissance monoplane used in small numbers early in the war (longer in Russian service). The Nieuport 10 was a two-seater reconnaissance biplane (1915), often flown as a single-seater to permit the weight of a Lewis gun on top wing; the 12 was a larger version (1915–17), also used as a light bomber. The Nieuport 11 was a single-seater biplane fighter 1915–17, known as *Bébé* (from small size); the 16 was a larger and more powerful version, 1916–17. The 14 was a two-seater biplane bomber, 1916. The Nieuport 17 was one of the best single-seater biplane fighters of the war, used spring 1916–autumn 1917, known as *Superbébé*; the type 23 was an improved version, and the 21 a two-seater trainer version; the type 24 was a 1917 development of the 17, but the further improved 27 was basically obsolete before its introduction in late 1917 and was used only as a trainer. The Nieuport 28 was a single-seater biplane fighter different from the others in not having their characteristic V-shaped struts; used 1917–18, and became one of the principal fighters of the AEF.

R.E.P.: the type N was a two-seater reconnaissance monoplane, unarmed, used in small numbers until early 1915; the designation came from the designer, Robert Esnault-Pelterie. The R.E.P. Parasol, a 1915 two-seater reconnaissance monoplane, was probably not used by France but saw limited service with the RNAS.

Salmson: the *Société des Moteurs Salmson*, the company of the industrialist Emile Salmson, was the producer of the Canton-Unné aircraft-engine. In 1916 the company produced its first aircraft, the SM1 (Salmson–Moineau, the latter the designer), a three-seater long-range reconnaissance biplane with two propellers mounted between the wings and powered from a central engine; only four saw service, December 1917–April 1918. The SAL2 was a two-seater reconnaissance biplane used from early 1918, so successful that it was adopted as the standard US reconnaissance machine; also used in ground-attack light-bomber role.

Schmitt: the type 7 was a large two-seater biplane heavy bomber based on Paul Schmitt's pre-war *Aérobus*, already obsolete when introduced in spring 1917, and soon replaced; the 7/4 was a four-wheeled version. The large size resulted in the ability to carry only a small bomb-load.

Spad: produced by the *Société Anonyme pour l'Aviation et ses Dérivés*. The Spad VII was an extremely successful single-seater biplane fighter, autumn 1917–mid-1918, also serving with Allied forces; the XI was a two-seater reconnaissance version, 1917–18, but less successful with poor rate of climb and danger of stalling; the 'improved' XVI (limited use 1918) was no better. The Spad XIII was a larger development of the VII, principal French fighter from spring 1918 and used in large numbers by the USA; a very few of the uprated version, type XVII, were used in later 1918.

Voisin: one of the most successful and versatile aircraft of the war, two-seater pusher reconnaissance/light bomber biplane used throughout the war in successive marks: Types

1 and 2 unarmed, Type 3 (1914–15) with Hotchkiss for observer, Type 4 (late 1914) for ground attack, Type 8 (late 1916) night bomber, Type 10 (1918) heavy bomber.

In addition to home-produced aircraft, foreign aircraft included the Caproni Ca3 and Ca5 and Sopwith 1½-Strutter, the latter used in far greater numbers by France than by Britain.

> '. . . the average French soldier, when off parade, looks rather slovenly. The baggy trousers go a long way towards the creation of this impression . . . The 'pas-de-flexion' [a] bent-knee, slouching method carries men along with a swing . . . at such a pace that they cover about thirty miles a day . . . the rank and file . . . carry their rifles . . . in any fantastic position that makes for ease . . . a man drops back to the rank in his rear to talk to a comrade, or goes forward . . . to light his cigarette. They smoke and sing and joke; they eat bread and drink wine . . . the fetish of smartness is non-existent here; comfort and use are the main points . . .'
>
> (Anon. ('Ex-Trooper'), *The French Army From Within*, pp. 21–3, London, 1914)

References

Anon. *Les Armées Françaises dans la Grande Guerre*. Paris (French official history, basically a collection of historical documents)

Anon. ('Ex-Trooper'). *The French Army from Within*. London, 1914.

Bruun, G. *Clemenceau*, Hamden, Connecticut, 1968

Cassar, G. H. *The French and the Dardanelles: A Study of Failure in the Conduct of War*. London, 1971

Clemenceau, G. *Grandeur and Misery of Victory*. London, 1930

Foch, Marshal F. *The Memoirs of Marshal Foch*. London, 1931

Gide, C. (ed.). *Effects of the War upon French Economic Life*. Oxford, 1923

Gorce, P.M. de la. *The French Army*. London, 1963

Hall, B., and Niles, J. J. *One Man's War: the Story of the Lafayette Escadrille*. London, 1929

Joffre, Marshal J. J. C. *The Two Battles of the Marne*. London, 1927

King, J. C. *General and Politicians: Conflict between France's High Command, Parliament and Government 1914–1918*. University of California, 1951

Lintier, P. *My Seventy-Five: Journal of a French Gunner August–September 1914*. London, 1929

Marshal-Cornwall, General Sir

James. *Foch as Military Commander*. London, 1972

Neuville, Colonel M. *Collections Historiques du Musée d l'Armée: La Grande Guerre 1914–18*. Paris, 1982

Pétain, Marshal H. P. *Verdun*. London, 1930

Pierrefeu, J. de. *French Headquarters 1915–18*. London, 1924

Poincaré, R. *The Memoirs of Raymond Poincaré*. London, 1926–9

Powell, E. A. *Vive la France*. London, 1916 (war correspondent with the French Army)

Recouly, R. *Joffre*. New York, 1931

Ruhl, M. *Die Französischen Armee*. Leipzig, 1915

— *Die Französischen Armee in ihrer Uniformerung vor dem Weltkrieg*. Leipzig, 1914.

Sheahan, H. *A Volunteer Poilu*. Boston, 1916

Spiers, Sir Edward. *Liaison 1914: a Narrative of the Great Retreat*. London, 1930 (British liaison officer with the French Army)

Ward, H. *Mr. Poilu: Notes and Sketches with the Fighting French*. London, 1916

Watt, R. M. *Dare Call it Treason*. London, 1964 (the 1917 mutinies)

Williams, J. *Mutiny 1917*. London, 1962

GERMANY

Formed in 1871, the German Empire was a confederation of 26 states, including the kingdoms of Prussia, Bavaria, Saxony and Württemberg; the grand-duchies of Baden, Hesse, Mecklenburg–Schwerin, Mecklenburg–Strelitz, Saxe–Weimar and Oldenburg; the duchies of Anhalt, Brunswick, Saxe–Altenburg, Saxe–Coburg–Gotha and Saxe–Meiningen; the principalities of Lippe, Reuss–Greiz, Reuss–Schleiz, Schaumburg–Lippe, Schwarzburg–Rudolstadt, Schwarzburg–Sonderhausen and Waldeck; the free cities of Bremen, Hamburg and Lübeck; and the 'imperial territory' of Alsace–Lorraine gained by the Peace of Frankfort (10 May 1871). The most important of these was Prussia, with 40 million out of the 65 million population (1910), whose Hohenzollern king was German Emperor or Kaiser, and under whose aegis the empire had been formed.

Although the title 'German Emperor' was used rather than 'Emperor of Germany', to show that the Kaiser was only one of a number of German sovereigns, he was very much the ruler of the empire. He was assisted by a federal council (*Bundesrat*), to which all states appointed members, in which Prussia had seventeen seats, Bavaria six, Saxony and Württemberg four each, Baden and Hesse three each, Brunswick and Mecklenburg–Schwerin two and all the others one seat); and a lower house, the elected *Reichstag* or Diet, in which Prussia again dominated (236 out of 397 seats; the next largest representation was Bavaria with 48 and Saxony 23). Excepting the two Mecklenburgs and Alsace–Lorraine, all other states had their own assemblies, though all foreign policy, military and naval forces and commerce was controlled by the imperial government. The Kaiser controlled foreign policy and had the right to declare defensive war, needing the consent of the *Bundesrat* to declare offensive war. All laws had to be passed by both houses, but the emperor retained the right of veto. Chief minister was the chancellor (*Reichskanzler*), the head of the Prussian delegation to the *Bundesrat*, the link between parliament and Kaiser, and in control of all but military affairs: although advisory committees existed on major topics (foreign affairs, military, finance, etc.), each having members from at least four states, these did not form a cabinet.

Kaiser Wilhelm II ('Kaiser Bill' to the British) (1859–1941) succeeded his father Friedrich III in 1888 (who had ruled but 99 days from the death of Wilhelm I). His advisers were not particularly well-chosen, and his leadership before and during the war was unsuccessful, and had the result of virtually delivering the German government into the hands of the army's high command. Chancellor from July 1909 was Theobald von Bethmann Hollweg (1856–1921), who was similarly unsuccessful in both internal and external politics, his foreign policy being founded upon the necessity of preventing 'encirclement' of Germany by unfriendly powers and marked by such undiplomatic statements as that describing Belgian neutrality as a 'scrap of paper'. At the beginning of the war he propounded a list of aims which would have given Germany little less than total domination of Europe, and his assurance of unqualified support for Austria–Hungary severely limited Germany's options in the immediate pre-war period.

Perhaps in emulation of his ancestor Frederick the Great, the Kaiser spent most of the war at army headquarters, albeit largely as a figurehead. The original chief of the general staff was Helmuth von Moltke (1848–1916), less able than his more famous uncle, the victor of Sedan. Appearing to suffer from mental depression, he was replaced in mid-September 1914 by Erich von Falkenhayn (1861–1922), who also served as Prussian war minister until February 1915. His task was difficult, in attempting to sustain war on three fronts while attempting to deflect criticism from both military and politicians at home, and following the losses of Verdun and the Brusilov offensive he was dismissed by the Kaiser on 29 August 1916. He was replaced by Field Marshal Paul von Hindenburg (1847–1934) as chief-of-staff, and Erich Ludendorff (1865–1937) as

'Kaiser Bill': Emperor Wilhelm II (1859–1941).

quartermaster–general, who together formed one of the most famous command partnerships in history, and henceforward the military to a large extent took control of the war.

A crucial decision was reached at the crown council at Pless on 9 January 1917, when both the Kaiser and Hindenburg concurred with the naval chief-of-staff Admiral Henning von Holtzendorff (1853–1919) that an unrestricted U-boat campaign would reduce Britain to its knees, even though it was predicted (correctly) that it would result in the entry into the war of the USA. Bethmann Hollweg was apprehensive but acceded to the demands of the military; and with the majority of the Reichstag urging peace and with his position undermined, he resigned on 13 July 1917. The appointment of a career civil servant as chancellor, Georg Michaelis (1857–1936), did little to relieve growing internal tensions; he was forced to accept the *Reichstag*'s peace declaration of 19 July 1917 (which called for an end to the war without indemnitites) and, unable to control the *Reichstag*, resigned on 31 October 1917. He was replaced next day by Count Georg von Hertling (1843–1919), previously Bavarian chancellor, who was unable to check Ludendorff's expansionist plans which followed the Russian revolution. The Kaiser's influence declined even further: when Hindenburg and Ludendorff threatened to resign unless the head of the Kaiser's civil cabinet was dismissed (Rudolf von Valenti, 1855–1925), Wilhelm II had to accede to their wishes; and so powerful had the military become (supported by the Kaiser's heir, Crown Prince Wilhelm, alias 'Little Willie', 1882–1951) that the treaties of Brest–Litovsk and Bucharest were concluded almost without reference to the Kaiser. The military also undermined and forced the resignation of the foreign minister, Richard von Kühlmann (1873–1948) on the grounds of defeatism.

With the failure of Germany's 1918 offensive, even the most militant realized that the war was lost. Hertling resigned on 3 October and was replaced by Prince Max of Baden (1867–1929). On 26 October Ludendorff, regarded by many as the covert dictator of Germany since 1916, was forced to resign by the government and the Kaiser, and went into exile in Sweden; he was succeeded as deputy chief-of-staff by General Wilhelm Groener (1867–1939). With military revolt and civil unrest appearing, Hindenburg and Groener advised the Kaiser that he could no longer count upon the support of the army, and on 9 November Prince Max pre-empted the Kaiser and announced that both emperor and crown prince had abdicated. Wilhelm raged against this 'treason', but went into exile in Holland on the following day. Max's hope for a constitutional monarchy under Wilhelm's eldest grandson and a regent were frustrated immediately when the Social Democrat Philipp Scheidemann (1865–1939), a member of Max's cabinet, announced the creation of the German Republic. After a period of great instability the Social Democrat leader Friedrich Ebert (1867–1939) was elected as first president of the republic (11 February 1919).

The end of the Hohenzollern empire ushered in a period of social unrest, including the revolutionary–socialist Spartacist rebellion led by Karl Liebknecht and Rosa Luxemburg, resulting in the economic ruination of Germany and eventually its renaissance as a National Socialist state, in which the old *eminences grises* of the empire collaborated: Hindenburg became president of the republic in 1925 and had the misfortune to be remembered as the one who appointed Adolf Hitler as chancellor (1933); Ludendorff was politically more active, participating in the abortive beer-hall *Putsch* in 1923 and becoming leader of the Nazi Party in the *Reichstag*.

Prussia was not the only state to lose its hereditary monarchy as a result of the war. King Otto I of Bavaria, who had succeeded his insane brother in 1886, was himself mad and the state was administered by Prince Ludwig as regent, who declared himself king on 5 November 1913, even though Otto lived until November 1916. On 7 November 1918 a republic was proclaimed in Bavaria, and Ludwig abdicated on 13 November. King Friedrich August III of Saxony, who had reigned since 1904, also abdicated on 13 November 1918 following the fall of his cabinet on 26 October, the installation of a liberal government, and the outbreak of revolution on 9 November. King Wilhelm II of Württemberg, who had succeeded his cousin in 1891, abdicated on 30 November 1918 and took the title Duke of Württemberg instead; he had reamined popular with all shades of political opinion throughout the war and his abdication was the result of the fall of the Hohenzollerns rather than from any internal unrest.

Army

The military forces of the empire were under unified command, with only Bavaria maintaining a separate establishment. At the beginning of the war the German Army was one of the most professional in Europe, and despite terrible attrition remained formidable almost to the end; and in spite of the outbreaks of mutiny and revolution which occurred at the very end of hostilities, it was remarkable that the army should have remained stalwart for so long.

Prussia refined the system of universal service after the débâcle of Jena (1806). The regulation of 1895, in force at the beginning of the World War, imposed a liability for military service: from the age of 17 to 20 men were liable for service in the *Landsturm* (home guard); from 20 they spent two years in the regular army and five in the reserve (three and four respectively for cavalry and horse artillery). From age 27 a man transferred to the 1st class (*Ban*) of the *Landwehr*, and at 32 to the 2nd class; from age 39 to 45 *Landsturm* service was again a liability. In practice barely half of those eligible were actually trained or served in the regulars, as the population was too numerous for the army's establishment; untrained men were posted to the *Landsturm* or the *Ersatz Reserve*, the latter consisting of men excused ordinary service for domestic reasons or because of minor disabilities; they trained thrice-yearly and after twelve years passed to the *Landsturm*. Despite increasing industrialization, most recruits continued to be drawn from rural communities or small towns (before the war only some 6 per cent were from industrial areas), as it was believed that countrymen were physically more suited to military service, more loyal and conservative than city-dwellers and less susceptible to exposure to socialist or revolutionary propaganda. When the demands of war forced the enlistment of urban personnel, the traditional and very conservative attitude of the army was diluted, and some believed the unrest and mutinies of 1918 were attributable to these politically suspect city-dwellers.

Upon mobilization, regular regiments were raised to war

The greatest command partnership of the war: Hindenburg (left), Ludendorff (centre) and Max Hoffman (right).

directed towards the formation of a reserve of trained officers of good family and education. Strictures on the recruiting of regular officers were not relaxed, so that while the number of reserve officers multiplied more than eight-fold during the war, the regulars only doubled, despite the casualty–rate of more than three-quarters of the total. A solution to the dearth of officers was the appointment of NCOs as *Offizierstellvertreter*, who were accorded the responsibility of subalterns but not the status. By the end of the war units might have only one regular officer in command, assisted by reserve officers and NCOs holding this appointment. Senior NCOs were career soldiers, consequently enjoying considerable social standing, and increased in importance during the war as the number of officers declined. During the war it was possible for even conscripts to rise to the highest non-commissioned rank, and at least in the front-line units the excellent calibre of NCO was maintained despite the heavy losses, these in many cases being largely unaffected by the unrest which afflicted the lower-grade units at the rear in 1918–19. Such was the shortage of officers that it was not uncommon for companies to be commanded by sergeants.

Despite the proficiency of the recruiting system, losses were such that even by late 1915 the reservoir of reservists was running low. To remedy the shortages, classes which would have been called in future years were conscripted, so that by 1917 those due to serve in 1919 were being sent to the east and the Balkans, to release more experienced men for the Western Front.

Higher formations

At the outbreak of war the largest autonomous formation was the Army (AOK: *Armee Oberkommando*), of which eight existed, based on the eight 'inspectorates' of the pre-war army; these embraced 25 army corps (numbered I–XXI, Guard and I–III Bavarian). A further ten AOKs were formed during the war, numbered 9–12, 14–19, plus the *Bugarmee* and *Sudarmee* ('army of the Bug', Eastern Front, and 'army of the south', Carpathians); AOKs 1, 8, 9 and 11 were disbanded and re-formed during the war. In addition there were five *Armee–Abteilungen*, named after their commander or identified by a letter (for example, A–A Stranz became A–A 'D' in February 1917). Two to four AOKs might be formed into army groups (*Gruppen*), generally named after their commander; above these were theatre headquarters (Western Front, Eastern Front, Italy, Balkans, Middle East), and above them the Kaiser's general headquarters responsible for directing all operations. The total number of army corps increased during the war, with some being formed entirely of reserve divisions; each comprised two or more infantry divisions with all necessary supporting units (heavy artillery and engineers deployed at corps level, etc).

At the beginning of the war there were two Guard, 42 infantry and six Bavarian divisions; usual divisional strength included two infantry brigades (three in the 2nd

German infantry in a trench, c. 1914, wearing their unmistakable Pickelhauben *with fabric covers, the cross* *visible on the front of one identifying these troops as* Landwehr.

establishment by the recall of recently discharged reservists; the other reservists were formed into duplicated regiments for front-line service. The *Landwehr* acted as a support for the regular army, the *Ersatz Reserve* served as a source of replacements (though in the event some units were pushed into the front line at an early stage), and the *Landsturm* served within the boundaries of the empire, freeing other forces for wider service. Within the first week of mobilization in 1914 the standing army of 700,000 had been augmented to more than 3.8 million, more than two million of whom were deployed upon the western and eastern fronts, demonstrating the excellence of organization which was evident throughout the war.

Despite the introduction of middle-class members, the officer corps remained largely an aristocratic and land-owning élite in the regular forces. The reserve officers were mostly of a lower social group, but included a large number of 'One-Year Volunteers', conscripts who had reduced their period of service to one year in return for maintaining themselves and purchasing their equipment, a policy

Guard, 10th, 11th, 14th, 17th and 29th), a field artillery brigade, and a cavalry brigade (two cavalry brigades for 2nd, 12th and 34th). Upon mobilization the cavalry were concentrated into their own divisions, so that for active service a division comprised two or three infantry brigades, each of two regiments, and a field artillery brigade. The number of divisions increased during the war, beginning with a 3rd Guard and 45 reserve divisions by October 1914; reserve divisions had the same organization but with nine batteries per field brigade instead of the usual twelve. Early in 1915 the divisional structure was altered, so that each comprised one infantry brigade of three regiments and one field artillery regiment of three battalions, hence the term 'triangular' division, but the reduction from four to three infantry regiments per division was not completed until 1917; the regiments thus transferred helped to create the many new divisions. There were 240 divisions at the armistice, not all consecutively numbered: numbers used during the war included:

Infantry: 1–5 Guard, *Jäger*, 1–42, 50, 52, 54, 56, 58, 83, 84, 86–89, 91–96, 101, 103, 105, 107–09, 111, 113, 115, 117, 119, 121, 123, 183, 185, 187, 192, 195, 197, 199–208, 211–28, 231–43, 255, 301, 302; Bavarian, 1–6, 10–12, 14–16.

Reserve: Guard, 1, 3, 5–7, 9–19, 21–26, 28, 33, 35, 36, 43–54, 75–82; Bavarian 1–5, 6, 8, 9, 30, 39.

Ersatz: Guard, 4, 5, 10, 19, Bavarian.

Landwehr: 1–5, 7–26, 29, 38, 44–48, 85; Bavarian 1, 2, 6.

To exemplify changes of organization and different types of division, the following orders-of-battle show three typical divisions, and also illustrate the attachment of further supporting services in the later part of the war:

5TH DIVISION (Western Front 1914–18 save for brief period on Eastern Front and Italy 1917):

1914:
9 Brigade: 8th Grenadiers, 48th Infantry
10 Brigade: 12th Grenadiers, 52nd Infantry
Cavalry: 3rd Hussars (three squadrons)
Artillery: 5 Brigade (18th and 54th Field Regiments)

1918:
10 Brigade: 8th and 12th Grenadiers, 52nd Infantry
Cavalry: 3rd Hussars (three squadrons)
Artillery: 142 Group (18th Field Regiment, three batteries 67th Foot Battalion, 848th, 879th, 792nd Light Ammunition Columns)
Support: 116th Pioneer Battalion (two companies 3rd Pioneers, 14th Bavarian Pioneer Company, 5th Trench Mortar Company, 35th Searchlight Section); 5th Signal Group (5th Telegraph and 29th Wireless detachments); 9th Field Ambulance Company, 26th and 27th Field Hospitals, 5th Veterinary Hospital; 538th Motor Transport Column.

45TH RESERVE DIVISION (Western Front):

1914:
89 Reserve Brigade: 209th, 212th Reserve Regiments
90 Reserve Brigade: 210th, 211th Reserve Regiments
Cavalry: 45th Reserve Cavalry Detachment
Artillery: 45th Reserve Field Regiment
Support: 45th Reserve Pioneer Company

1918:
90 Reserve Brigade: 210–212th Reserve Regiments
Cavalry: 45th Reserve Cavalry Detachment
Artillery: 45th Reserve Field Regiment, three batteries 20th

The campaign appearance of the German Army in the earlier part of the war, including the Pickelhaube *with spike removed, and the 1910-pattern field-grey tunic with the cuffs of Saxon units, with 1909-pattern leather equipment. The original of this photograph was captioned by a British soldier, 'Not a bad looking lad for a Boche' and states that he had a number of photographs 'on him', and was thus taken from the subject as a prisoner or from his body.*

Foot Regiment, 772nd, 839th, 1210th Light ammunition columns

Support: 345th Pioneer Battalion (One Company 21st Pioneers, 45th Reserve Pioneer Company, 245th Trench Mortar Company, searchlight section); 445th Signal Group (445th Telegraph and 141st Wireless Detachments); 527th Ambulance Company, 76th and 77th Reserve Field Hospitals, 445th Veterinary Hospital, 732nd Motor Transport Column.

11TH LANDWEHR DIVISION (Eastern Front 1914–18)

1914:

33 *Landwehr* Brigade: 75th and 76th *Landwehr* Regiments

70 *Landwehr* Brigade: 5th and 18th *Landwehr* Regiments

Cavalry: 92nd *Landwehr* Cavalry

Artillery: 98th Field Regiment

1918:

70 *Landwehr* Brigade: 18th, 75th and 424th *Landwehr* Regiments

Cavalry: 11th Dragoons (one squadron)

Artillery: 98th Field Regiment, 1018th Light Ammunition Column.

Support: 4th *Landsturm* Pioneer Company, 79th and 359th Searchlight Sections, 511th Telegraph Detachment, 217 Ambulance Company, 105th and 150th Field Hospitals, 211th Veterinary Hospital.

Infantry

An infantry regiment consisted of three battalions (numbered I–III), each of four companies, plus a battalion machine-gun company. Each company comprised five officers and 259 men, organized in three platoons (*Zugen*) numbered 1–3, each of four sections (*Korporalschaften*) numbered 1–12; the MG company comprised 99 men (four officers) and six guns. Usually (though not invariably) all three battalions served together; thus a German regiment was roughly equivalent to a British brigade, and a 'triangular' division to a British division. Excluding the eleven Guard regiments existing at the outbreak of war (plus the Guard instructional unit or *Lehr Batallion* which was expanded to regimental strength), the other regiments were of similar character despite the various appellations of Grenadiers, Fusiliers, *Leib* regiments (those which had been Guards in the old state armies) and the 108th *Schützen* Regiment.

New regiments were formed following the mobilization of the reserve, *Ersatz* and *Landwehr*, these bearing numbers separate from those of the regular line and bearing their title, the reserve normally identified by the number and letter 'R', i.e., *Nr. 212 R*. Each regimental district formed two *Ersatz* companies from personnel surplus to reinforcement needs, and thus each brigade district formed a *Brigade–Ersatz–Bataillon* or 'BEB'. Other *Ersatz* units were mobilized complete.

During the war, personnel was reduced but firepower maintained by the increase of machine-guns and trench artillery. In mid-1916 the establishment of the regimental MG company was increased to fifteen guns (it is interesting to observe that initially the scale of issue was like that in other armies, the German concentration of fire giving the impression of superior numbers); shortly afterwards a 6-gun company was attached to each battalion. There were also independent MG *Abteilungen* deployed in the manner of supporting artillery (including the two *Muskete* battalions, 1915–18, armed with a derivative of the Madsen gun, intended to block breakthroughs in the line, and the companies of 'machine-gun marksmen' (*Maschinengewehr-Scharfschützen-Abteilungen*), the best-trained men deployed at divisional level). During 1916 the total number of machine-guns in service rose from 8,000 to 16,000, and instead of the 24 guns per division in 1914, the number was 358 by early 1918. In February 1917 eight *Granatenwerfer* and four light *Minenwerfer* were authorized for each battalion; in March the effective strength of a battalion was officially reduced to 750, a reduction offset by the issue of two light machine-guns per company, increased to six by February 1918. Regimental pioneer companies were formed from 1915–16 (duties latterly taken over by specialist units), and in September 1918 the battalion trench-mortar platoons were assembled into one company. The reorganization into battalions of three rifle and one MG company, specified in October 1918, probably had no time to take effect.

Landsturm battalions either operated independently or were formed into regiments; they bore the designation of their Army Corps district and their own number, e.g., I/2; some were ultimately converted to line or *Landwehr* regiments. Also independent battalions were those (701st–703rd) formed for service in Palestine, each of three rifle, one MG and one support company, the latter including platoons of *Minenwerfer*, light artillery and cavalry.

Assault detachments of 'storm-troops' were a major development. Squads of trained trench-fighters were formed by individual regiments from 1915, the *Sturm–Bataillone* being a development of later 1915–16, each comprising two to four companies and MG, flame-thrower and *Minenwerfer* companies; but the concentration of the best men into élite units served to diminish the calibre of the ordinary infantry, so that eventually most storm-battalions were dispersed. These should not be confused with the 'shock divisions', those in 1917–18 recognized as better than others and styled *Grosskampfdivisionen* or *Eingreifsdivisionen* (counter-attack divisions); the more ordinary ones were styled 'sector' divisions, i.e., capable of holding a sector but not initiating an offensive.

The eighteen *Jäger* battalions were intended to form mobile units for use with cavalry, a number doubled by reserve battalions upon mobilization. Each comprised four rifle, one MG and one cyclist company, expanded by an extra MG and *Minenwerfer* company in 1916; the cyclists were concentrated into cycle battalions in 1917–18, and some units were grouped into 3-battalion regiments, concentrated into three *Jäger* divisions. The five ski battalions

German infantry in the 1916 steel helmet, which became the characteristic symbol of the German Army much as the Pickelhaube had done earlier.

The officer (left) wears the 1910 tunic (Waffenrock) with 'Brandenburg' flapped cuffs; the others have the 1915 amendment with deep, turned-back cuffs.

(1st Pomeranian), 6–7 (1st–2nd West Prussian), 8 (1st Brandenburg *Leib*-Grenadiers), 9 (2nd Pomeranian, Colberg Grenadiers), 10–11 (1st–2nd Silesian), 12 (2nd Brandenburg), 89 (Mecklenburg), 100 (1st Saxon *Leib*-Grenadiers), 101 (2nd Saxon), 109 (1st Baden *Leib*-Grenadiers), 110 (2nd Baden), 119 (1st Württemberg).

Infantry: 13, 15–17, 53, 55–57 (1st–8th Westphalian); 14, 21, 42, 49, 54, 61 (1st–8th Pomeranian); 18, 19, 58, 59 (1st–4th Posen); 20, 24, 48, 52, 60, 64 (3rd–8th Brandenburg); 22, 23, 62, 63 (1st–4th Upper Silesian); 25, 28–30, 65, 68–70, 160, 161 (1st–10th Rhenish); 26, 27, 66, 67 (1st–4th Magdeburg); 31, 32, 71, 72, 94–96, 153 (1st–8th Thuringian); 41, 43–45 (5th–8th East Prussian); 46, 47, 50, 51, 154, (1st–5th Lower Silesian); 74, 77, 78, 164, 165 (1st–5th Hanoverian); 75, 76 (1st–2nd Hanseatic); 78 (East Frisian); 81–83 (1st–3rd Hessian); 84 (Schleswig); 85 (Holstein); 87, 88 (1st–2nd Nassau); 91 (Oldenburg); 92 (Brunswick); 93 (Anhalt); 97, 99 (1st–2nd Oberheim); 98 (Metz); 102–07, 133, 134, 139, 177–79, 181 (3rd–15th Saxon); 111–14, 142, 169, 170 (3rd–9th Baden); 115–18, 168 (1st–5th Hessian Grand-Ducal); 120, 123–27, 180 (2nd, 5th–8th Württemberg); 121 (Old Württemberg); 128 (Danzig); 129, 140, 148, 149, 155, 175, 176 (3rd–9th West Prussian); 130, 131, 135, 136, 144, 145, 156, 157, 173, 174 (1st–10th Lorraine); 132, 137, 138, 143 (1st–4th Lower Alsace); 141 (Kulmer); 146, 147 (1st–2nd Masuria); 150, 151 (1st–2nd Ermland); 152 (Deutsch–Ordens); 156, 157 (3rd–4th Silesian); 162 (Lübeck, 3rd Hanseatic); 163 (Schleswig–Holstein); 166 (Hesse–Homburg); 167, 171, 172 (1st–3rd Upper Alsace).

Fusiliers: 33 (East Prussian), 34 (Pomeranian), 35 (Brandenburg), 36 (Magdeburg), 37 (Westphalian), 38 (Silesian), 39 (Lower Rhenish), 40 (Hohenzollern), 73 (Hanoverian), 80 (Hessian), 86 (Schleswig–Holstein), 90 (Mecklenburg), 108 (Saxon), 122 (4th Württemberg).

Jägers: 1 (East Prussian), 2 (Pomeranian), 3 (Brandenburg), 4 (Magdeburg), 5, 6 (1st–2nd Silesian), 7 (Westphalian), 8 (Rhenish), 9 (Laurenberg), 10 (Hanoverian), 11 (Hessian), 12, 13 (1st–2nd Saxon), 14 (Mecklenburg).

A field-grey service uniform was introduced in 1910 (grey-green for *Jägers*, MG battalions and *Schützen*, save Bavarians who wore field-grey), including a single-breasted tunic with eight breast-buttons, turn-down collar, and piped cuffs in four styles: Brandenburg (with rectangular, three-button flap); Swedish (two buttons set horizontally, no flap: worn by Guard Regiments 1–4, *Jägers*, MG battalions, Regiments 100, 101, 109, 119, 123); Saxon (two vertical buttons, no flap: Saxon units); and French (with three-pointed flap: *Guard* Jägers and 2nd MG Battalion). The lace loops (*Litzen*) which traditionally indicated Guard status were worn by those units. Shoulder-straps bore a red regimental numeral or cipher (for example, in the case of Regiment 47 quoted above, the badge was a crowned 'L', the cipher of Ludwig of Bavaria). Piping was generally determined by the Army Corps to which a regiment belonged: I, II, IX, X, XII and I Bavarian white; III, IV, XI, XIII, XV, XIX and II Bavarian red; V, VI, XVI and

were part of the *Jäger* organization, the 1st–4th (formed 1915) being part of the 3rd *Jägers*, and the 9-company Württemberg Ski Battalion independent.

The infantry regiments bore a number, a state number and often a title; for example, '*Infanterie–Regiment König Ludwig III von Bayern (2 Niederschlesisches) Nr. 47*': named after the King of Bavaria, it was the 47th in the line and also the 2nd Lower Silesian. State numbers and units at the outbreak of war were:

Prussian Guard: 1st–5th Foot Guards; 1st–5th Guard Grenadiers; Fusiliers; *Jägers*; *Schützen*.

Grenadiers: Regiments 1, 3–5 (1st–4th East Prussian), 2

Stormtroop tactics. Phase 1: assault detachments (A) rush forward under cover of rapid, heavy bombardment of 1st–3rd lines of enemy trenches (1–3); assault troops bypass defended posts (B) and move rapidly to rear areas, the artillery and strongpoints of which (C) were simultaneously gas-shelled (D). In phase 2, successive waves neutralise the bypassed strongpoints (E) and support assault troops in penetrating farther (G) to prevent withdrawal of enemy defenders.

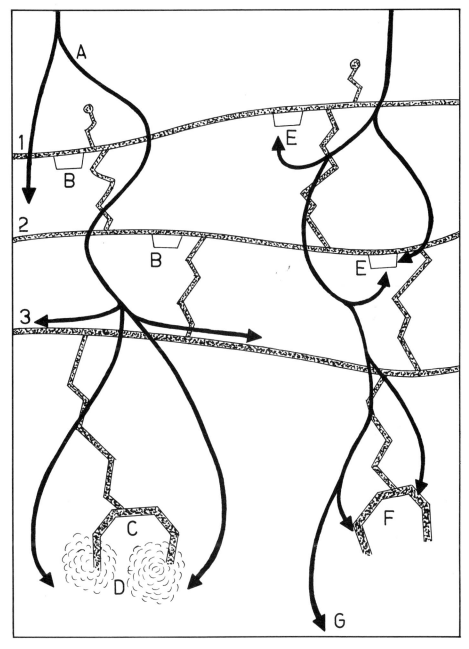

III Bavarian yellow; VII, VIII, XVIII and XX blue; XXI, *Jägers* and *Schützen* light-green. In 1915 a modified tunic was introduced, with plain deep cuffs, rear piping removed, and the remaining piping generally white for infantry and light green for *Jägers*, with a few exceptions. In September 1915 a completely new tunic was ordered, the *Bluse*, with fly-front to conceal the buttons. Shortages of equipment resulted in all three patterns remaining in use throughout, and for training units even the old blue dress tunics were pressed into service. The trousers were worn with knee boots, with puttees coming into use for active service from about 1915.

Personal equipment was generally of the brown leather 1909 pattern (blackened officially from September 1915 though this had already occurred widely), with three ammunition-pouches at each side of the waist-belt plate; the 1895-pattern pouches (one large box at each side of the plate) were issued to second-line troops, and were even retained by some front-line formations. The grey, single-breasted greatcoat (with coloured collar-patches discontinued 1915) was carried rolled atop the hide knapsack; the bottle-shaped canteen had a fabric cover, and the entrenching-tool was carried next to the bayonet, which had a

'Dear Wilhelm,

'I send you greetings from my grave in the earth. We shall soon become mad in this awful artillery fire. Day and night it goes on without ceasing. Never has it been so bad as this before. We sit all day deep down in the earth with neither light nor sunshine, but just waiting for death, which may reach us any moment. I ought not to write like this to you dear Wilhelm, but I must. Again a big attack is coming on! Shall we ever meet again? God alone knows! This is awful! . . .'

(Anonymous soldier, Regiment No. 66 (3rd Magdeburg), 104 Brigade, 52nd Division, around Beaumont-Hamel, autumn 1916; quoted in *The Great War*, ed. H. W. Wilson & J. A. Hammerton, VIII, p. 174, London, 1917)

fabric knot (*Troddel*) in a combination of colours which identified the owner's company.

The head-dress was originally the dress *Pickelhaube* with field-grey cover, usually bearing the regimental number ('R' and number for reserve, 'L' and number for *Landwehr*, Iron Cross for *Landsturm*; not used by Guards), initially red but in green from August 1914. The leather *Pickelhaube* had a brass or white-metal plate (of which many state or regimental varieties existed) and cockades behind the chinscale-bosses of the imperial and state colours; during the war economy patterns were produced, made of pressed metal or blocked felt, with spike removed and with cheaper, grey-metal fittings. *Jägers* and machine-gun battalions wore a shako with service dress cover, and some *Landwehr* units wore the 1860-pattern shako with their distinctive cross badge. The undress cap (*Mütze*) was commonly worn on active service, field-grey with coloured piping and band (the latter often covered by a field-grey strip), generally red (*Jägers* and Bavarian MG battalions light-green, *Schützen* black), with both imperial and state cockades; officers' and NCOs' caps had a peak. In 1916 the 'coal-scuttle' steel helmet came into use.

Rank-markings were: senior private (*Gefreiter*), small button on collar; corporal (*Unteroffizier*, *Oberjäger* in *Jägers* and *Schützen*), gold or silver lace edge to collar and cuffs; sergeant same plus large collar-button; lance-sergeant-major (*Vizefeldwebel*) same plus officers' sword, knot and cap-cockades; sergeant-major (*Feldwebel*) same with double cuff-lace; *Offizierstellvertreter* same but lace edge to shoulder-straps; ensign (*Fähnrich*: officer-cadet) as *Unteroffizier* plus officers' bayonet-knot and cap-cockades; company officers, grey metallic lace on shoulder-straps with none to two gilt stars; field officers same but plaited cord lace; general officers same but gold with central silver cord on scarlet ground, none to four silver stars; field marshal same but silver crossed batons.

The principal arm was the 1898 7.9mm Mauser rifle (*Gewehr 1898* or '*Gew 98*'), with five-round magazine (a

clumsy 20-round magazine could be used); second-line formations often used the 1888 Mauser ('*Gew 88*'). The main machine-gun was the 1908 *Maschinengewehr*, which when lightened and fitted with a shoulder-stock produced the 08/15 model, the main light machine-gun; an even lighter version, 08/18, was prone to overheating. The 1915 *Muskete* (based on the Danish Madsen gun) was used only in small quantities, as was the 1915 Bergmann automatic rifle and the Bergmann MP18 submachine-gun. The standard pistol

Body-armour was worn by a number of armies, but not widely so: this is the German pattern introduced in 1916 (a reinforcing-plate could also be added to the front of the helmet), but it was never popular because of its great weight, about 35 pounds.

(carried by officers, senior NCOs, machine-gunners and some storm troops) was the 9mm 1908 Parabellum (or Luger), although the 7.63 or 9mm 1898 'broomhandle' Mauser also continued in use. The most famous grenade was the 'potato-masher' stick-grenade (*Stielhandgranate*), but also used in considerable quantities were the egg-grenade (*Eierhandgranate*) or the type known to the British as a 'cricket-ball', the spherical *Kugelhandgranate*.

Cavalry

Cavalry regiments consisted of four active and one depot squadron, the active totalling 724 of all ranks per regiment. Apart from the Guard cavalry division, the cavalry was deployed in brigades attached to infantry divisions, but upon mobilization most were grouped into eleven cavalry divisions (numbered 1–9, Guard and Bavarian), organized in corps (*Höheren–Kavallerie–Kommandeure*) of two or three divisions plus *Jäger* battalions, with the remainder allocated to the infantry as divisional cavalry. Each division comprised three brigades of two regiments each, a *Jäger* battalion, a machine-gun detachment, three horse batteries, and pioneer, signal and train units. Although the divisional cavalry attached to the infantry remained mounted, more than 80 per cent of the remainder was dismounted progressively and formed into *Kavallerie Schützen* regiments, each of three battalions of four rifle and one MG squadron, each battalion formed from one of the old mounted regiments. Some 33 reserve, one *Ersatz* and two *Landwehr* regiments were formed on mobilization (all only three squadrons strong), and some nineteen *Ersatz* and 33 *Landwehr* independent squadrons. All the remaining regiments had been in existence pre-war, and although the role of all was the same, they were divided into different categories:

Cuirassiers: ten regiments. Tunic similar to infantry pattern, but Swedish cuffs and standing collar, piping: Garde du Corps, 4th Westphalian Regiment red; Guard Cuirassiers, 6th Brandenburg blue; 1st Silesian black; 3rd East Prussian crimson; 5th West Prussian pink; 7th Magdeburg yellow; 8th Rhenish green. Collar and cuffs edged with field-grey lace with two facing-coloured lines, piped white; shoulder-straps with facing-coloured piping outside white piping; *Mütze* with facing-coloured band piped white. White-metal spiked helmet (yellow tombak, zinc/copper alloy for Garde du Corps, Guard and 6th Regiments). In the 1915 uniform the shoulder-straps were white with facing-coloured piping, with yellow cipher or numeral (2nd crimson).

Dragoons: 28 regiments. Tunic as for cuirassiers, with regimental colours: 1st and 2nd Guard, 1st (Lithuanian), 5th (Rhenish), 13th (Schleswig–Holstein), 17th (1st Mecklenburg), 20th (1st Baden), 23rd (Hessian Guard) red; 2nd (1st Brandenburg), 6th (Magdeburg), 14th (Kurmark), 18th (2nd Mecklenburg), 19th (Oldenburg), 22nd (3rd Baden) black; 3rd (Neumark), 7th (Westphalian), 15th (3rd Silesian) pink; 4th, 8th (1st and 2nd Silesian), 16th (2nd Hanoverian), 21st (2nd Baden), 26th (2nd Württemberg) yellow; 9th (1st Hanoverian), 10th (East Prussian), 24th (2nd Hessian), 25th (1st Württemberg) white; 11th (Pomeranian), 12th (2nd Brandenburg) crimson. Shoulder-straps piped in regimental colour, with black inner for 22nd; collars piped white 13th–16th, black 22nd. *Pickelhaube* with square-cut peak. In 1915 uniform, light-blue shoulder-straps piped in regimental colour, bearing red numeral or cypher (3rd, 7th and 15th pink).

Saxon Heavy Cavalry: two regiments, dressed as cuirassiers with tombak helmet; regimental colours white (*Garde-Reiter*) and black (*Karbiniers*); 1915 shoulder-straps blue with facing-coloured piping.

Lightly-wounded German casualties passing through Conflans, autumn 1914, on their way home to Germany, conveyed in horse-drawn open wagons.

Hussars: 21 regiments. Single-breasted field-grey hussar tunic (*Attila*) with grey braid on collar, cuffs with Austrian knots and five breast-loops; red and yellow collar- and cuff-lace for Guard Regiment. Shoulder-straps of plaited braid of facing- and button-colour, the former being that of the full-dress *Attila*: Guard, 3rd (Brandenburg) red; 1st, 2nd (1st–2nd *Leib*-Hussars), 17th (Brunswick) black; 4th (1st Silesian) brown; 5th (Pomeranian) crimson; 6th (2nd Silesian), 10th (Magdeburg) green; 7th, 9th (1st–2nd Rhenish), 8th (1st Wesphalian), 12th (Thuringian), 13th, 14th (1st–2nd Hessian), 15th (Hanoverian), 16th (Schleswig–Holstein), 18th, 19th (1st–2nd Saxon), 20th blue; 11th (2nd Westphalian) dark-blue. Buttons yellow for Guard, 3rd–7th, 9th–11th, 17th, 18th, white for remainder. The low fur busby was worn with a grey service cover, obscuring the dress badges. The *Mütze* band was of the regimental colour (11th green), piped in the button-colour (3rd, 5th and 11th white).

Uhlans: 24 regiments. Double-breasted field-grey lancer tunic (*Ulanka*) with piping in regimental colour: 1st Guard, 1st (West Prussian), 5th (Westphalian), 9th (2nd Pomeranian), 13th (1st Hanoverian), 17th (1st Saxon) white; 2nd Guard, 2nd (Silesian), 6th (Thuringian), 18th (2nd Saxon), 19th (1st Württemberg) red; 3rd Guard, 3rd (1st Brandenburg), 7th (Rhenish), 11th (2nd Brandenburg), 15th (Schleswig–Holstein), 20th (2nd Württemberg), 21st yellow; 4th (1st Pomeranian), 8th (East Prussian) blue; 10th (Posen), 14th (2nd Hanoverian) crimson. The 12th (Lithuanian) and 16th (Altmark) had white regimental colour but blue tunic-piping. Shoulder-straps were piped in the regimental colour, from 1915 red with similar piping and yellow number. The square-topped *czapka* (lancer-cap) was worn with a grey cover; the *Mütze* had regimentally-coloured band and piping (12th and 16th, blue piped white).

Jäger zu Pferde (Mounted *Jägers*): thirteen regiments. Grey-green cuirassier tunic with light-green collar and cuffs, with similar lace edged in regimental colour, centre regimental colour edged yellow; shoulder-straps of regimental colour: 1st, 8th white; 2nd, 9th red; 3rd, 10th yellow; 4th, 11th light-blue; 5th, 12th black; 6th, 13th dark-blue; 7th pink. From 1915 shoulder-straps were light-green piped in regimental colour; *Mütze* had light-green band and piping. Regiments 8–13 wore the dragoon *Pickelhaube*, the others the metal helmet enamelled black.

Bavarian cavalry: *Uhlan* tunic with pointed cuffs for *Uhlans* and Swedish for *Chevaulegers*. Piping in regimental colour: 1st, 2nd *Uhlans* crimson; 1st, 2nd *Chevaulegers* orange; 3rd, 6th *Chevaulegers* peach; 4th, 5th *Chevaulegers* red; 7th, 8th *Chevaulegers* white. Shoulder-straps piped in regimental colour, from 1915 of regimental colour, piped steel-green. The two heavy cavalry regiments wore cuirassier tunics with yellow shoulder-straps piped dark-green from 1915; *Uhlans* wore the *czapka*, the rest the *Pickelhaube*. *Mütze* with regimentally-coloured band and piping (heavy regiments red).

Equipment was brown leather, like that of the infantry but with 1911-pattern pouches (carrying six clips, not the twelve of the infantry) and no knapsack; the steel helmet was adopted from 1916. The *Kavallerie Schützen* wore infantry uniform and equipment, with green shoulder-straps bearing red regimental number. The firearm was a short version of the *Gew 98*, although the cavalry version (*98 Karabine* or *98 Kar*) with 18in barrel was not a success, and from 1909 rearmament was undertaken with the artillery *Karabine 98* (*Kar 98*). Despite the introduction of the Parabellum, 1883-pattern and Saxon Cavalry revolvers were still used; all mounted units carried lances of the tubular steel 1890 pattern, with pennon either rolled or (after 1914) discarded.

Artillery

Until February 1917 the artillery was divided into field, deployed at divisional level, and foot, the heavier guns at corps and army level. From February 1917 the two branches were amalgamated into the *Arko* (*Artillerie-Kommandeure*) which controlled all guns within a divisional sector.

Initially field regiments consisted of two 'battalions' (*Abteilungen*) each of three 6-gun batteries; horse batteries had four guns. As part of the mobilization in 1914, many 4-gun batteries were formed, and in 1915 the 4-gun battery was made standard, the excess guns creating new batteries; by the following year the number of howitzers had increased so that each regiment had one *Abteilung* equipped exclusively with it. The formation of 'triangular' divisions was complemented by the creation of some regiments of three *Abteilungen*, so that divisional artillery consisted of one regiment of nine batteries, instead of two of six each; 9-battery divisions had originated in the reserve divisions formed on mobilization, and by early 1917 the 9-battery division became standard. The expansion of field artillery reached its maximum by 1916, after which most new guns were used to replace battle-casualties rather than create new batteries; the number of field-gun batteries rose from 782 in 1914 to 1,691 at the armistice, and field howitzer batteries increased from 159 to 1,103. The 1896 7.7cm field gun remained in use throughout, despite the widespread introduction of the new FK16 (*Feldkanone* 1916); the 1909 version of the 1898 10.5cm field howitzer similarly remained in use alongside the 1916 light field howitzer (lFH16: *leichte Feldhaubitze*) and the Krupp howitzer (lFHKp).

The number of Foot Artillery batteries (of four guns each) increased from less than 150 on mobilization to about 1,100 by late 1915, and 1,550 by the Armistice. There were initially 24 regiments, each of two *Abteilungen* of four batteries (two batteries for those equipped with the 21cm *Mörser*). *Abteilungen* and batteries were deployed individually, and a number of independent batteries were formed. The foot artillery employed four types of 15cm howitzer, the heavy field howitzer (*Schwere Feldhaubitze*) models 1900, 1902 and 1913 (sFH, sFH02 and sFH13 respectively), and the 1913 'long heavy field howitzer' (*Lange Schwere Feldhaubitze*, lgsFH13), and a variety of 10cm and 15cm guns and some

German 21cm. Mörser manhandled by Foot Artillerymen; they wear the artillery Pickelhaube *with ball top instead of the spike of the infantry and cavalry.*

Austrian 30.5cm howitzer and mount, sent to the Western Front in 1918 to supplement the German siege artillery in reducing the Belgian forts; these immense pieces were nicknamed Schlanke Emma *('slim Emma')!*

German 15cm heavy field howitzer.

captured ordnance. The other principal weapon was the 21cm *Mörser*, a large-calibre howitzer, which existed in a number of varieties, and was supplemented by even more massive pieces, from the 30.5cm *Mörser* and 42cm 'Big Bertha' to rail-mounted 21cm guns intended for bombardment at the longest range.

Close-support weapons included the ephemeral 'infantry batteries' (1916–17, manned by field artillery and equipped with 7.7cm guns) and the seven *Abteilungen* of mountain artillery (*Gebirgs-Artillerie*), most armed with the 7.5cm mountain gun, about half of which were of Austro–Hungarian (Skoda) manufacture, and a few with the 10.5cm mountain howitzer. Specific anti-tank weapons were not a success and were not produced in large numbers, but after experiments with Russian 57mm and 76.2mm guns and a 2cm gun, a 3.7cm *Panzerabwehrkanone* (Pak) was developed. Trench artillery included the 7.6cm, 17cm, 24cm and 24.5cm *Minenwerfer*, the grenade-projector (*Granatenwerfer*) and some other varieties, including compressed-air mortars and the somewhat bizarre 25cm, 35cm and 45cm *Albrecht Mörser*, which had a wooden barrel bound with wire. Anti-aircraft artillery was generally ordinary ordnance adapted to fire skywards, but included the heavier Flak 8cm and 8.8cm guns.

Artillery wore a uniform like that of the infantry, the *Pickelhaube* with a ball top instead of a spike (Bavarian artillery was ordered to use the ball only from 1915), and with Swedish cuffs for field artillery, Brandenburg for foot, and Saxon for Saxon regiments. Shoulder-straps were field-grey with corps piping as for the infantry (white for foot, and white, red and yellow for I–III Bavarian Corps), with grenade-badge in addition to the numeral or cipher. The 1915 shoulder-straps were red for field and yellow for foot, with piping white, yellow and blue for Guard Regiments 1, 2 and 4 respectively. The field cap for all branches had a black band and red piping.

Armoured corps

Armoured units were not formed until September 1917, the nine *Sturm-Panzerkampfwagen-Abteilungen*, each of five tanks (two with guns, three with machine-guns); three *Abteilungen* were equipped with the huge German A7V tank and the remainder with captured British tanks (*Beute-Panzerkampfwagen*).

Engineers

Two engineer units consisted of officers only, and were concerned with fortress construction (*Ingenieur Korps* and *Festungsbauoffiziere*). Field engineering was performed by the Pioneers (*Pioniere*), of which 35 battalions existed before the war (officers were interchangeable between the three corps). Upon mobilization each battalion split into two new battalions, which had the somewhat unusual designations of *I* or *II Bataillon, Pionier-Bataillon I*, and so on. Each battalion comprised three companies, which were deployed individually, so that with wartime expansion it was possible to attach at least two companies to each division, instead of three companies per army corps as at the outset. By mobilization of *Ersatz*, *Landwehr* and *Landsturm* companies, the number rose to almost 700 by late 1917, with III and IV battalions being added to most of the original units. Ten pontoon or bridging trains were formed (1915–17), and from 1916 tunnelling companies. Pioneers crewed the *Minenwerfer* companies (one company attached to each division from 1915, each company with two heavy, four medium and six light pieces), which were transferred to the infantry only in August 1918; 23 independent *Minenwerfer Abteilungen* were also formed for deployment at corps level. Pioneers also crewed the flame-throwers (ten projectors and a machine-gun section per company), usually deployed as individual *Flammentruppe* (a section of two projectors), often attached to storm battalions; and the chemical companies with gas-projectors, ultimately eight battalions (numbers

The first tank versus tank action was fought on 24 April 1918 at Villers–Bretonneux, when a German armoured force was repelled by the British 1st Tank Battalion. This German A7V tank, Elfriede, *was abandoned when it became bogged in no man's land, and was recovered at night by two British tanks. 'A' Company, 1st Tanks, have inscribed their name upon it!*

German mobile field-kitchen; the position of the chimney, here stowed for transport, resulted in the nickname Gulasch-kanone *('stew-guns') for such vehicles.*

35–39, 94–96), deployed as individual companies. From 1915 each infantry regiment also maintained a pioneer element, and from 1916 *Landsturm* battalions were mobilized primarily as labour units. Pioneers wore infantry-style uniform with Swedish cuffs and *Pickelhaube*, black shoulder-straps with red piping and battalion-number (and pick, shovel and axe badge for Saxons), and field cap with black band and red piping.

Supporting services

The original 25 train battalions were expanded and deployed at divisional and corps level, until in 1916 they were removed from corps control and assigned permanently to specific sectors of the front, so that when a corps moved its position the train remained in place for the relieving corps; this greatly facilitated supply and reduced the amount of movement necessary. Motor transport remained

separate, a smaller service deployed at divisional and corps level. The railway troops were also separate, both construction and traffic companies; they ran the military railways in occupied territories, the German rail network remaining under civilian control. The telegraph service, which became independent only in July 1917, ran all signals and communications. The medical service was composed exclusively of officers and NCOs, one NCO being attached to each company and two officers to each battalion; stretcher-bearers were found by the individual units, and transportation-personnel by the train. Bearer companies and a dressing station were attached to each division, plus additional 'sanitary companies' deployed where required; there were generally two field-hospitals per division and two additional per corps.

The supporting services wore infantry-style uniform, the railway battalions with the *Pickelhaube* and the remainder with peaked caps and Swedish cuffs (Saxon cuffs for Saxon train), the cap with black band and red piping, veterinary black band and crimson piping). Shoulder-straps had light-grey piping, 'E' and numeral for railway troops; telegraph troops, black with red piping, 'T' and numeral; train light-blue straps and piping, red numeral; motor transport light-grey piping and 'K' (*Kraftfahrtruppen*); red piping for medical officers, crimson for veterinary, dark-blue piped light-blue for medical orderlies, crimson straps for stretcher-bearers. The 1915 shoulder-straps were blue with yellow number for train, stretcher-bearers crimson with yellow number, and light-grey with red numeral and 'T' or 'K' for telegraph and motor transport.

Post-war

During the immediate post-war period the existing divisions either demobilized themselves or served on. Forces formed shortly after the armistice were the eastern frontier guard (*Grenzschutz Ost*), and the *Sicherheitstruppen*, formed from the 1918 class and soldiers with no civil employment. The latter were so unreliable that volunteer units (*Freikorps*) had to be formed by officers of the old army to counter the Spartacist rising and other civil unrest. In April–May 1919 a provisional army (*Reichswehr*) began to be assembled, with allied volunteers (*Volkswehr*); the *Sicherheitstruppen* were either disbanded or, like the *Grenzschutz Ost*, ultimately merged with the *Reichswehr*.

Navy

The German Navy became the second most powerful in the world, and its challenge to British supremacy was a contributory cause of the war. The architect of the navy was Grand Admiral Alfred von Tirpitz (1849–1930), who enlarged upon his First Navy Law of 1898 (which provided for a fleet capable of opposing France and Russia) with the Second Navy Law of 1900, which planned a greatly increased fleet designed to challenge Britain. The building programme was dislocated by the development of the *Dreadnought*, and was behind schedule in 1914.

From 1889 the navy was controlled by the admiralty, headed by the naval secretary of state who controlled dockyards and supply; the fleet and its personnel were controlled by the naval officer in chief command. The principal stations were at Kiel (Baltic) and Wilhelmshaven

(North Sea), connected by the Kaiser Wilhelm Canal across the Schleswig–Holstein peninsula; Cuxhaven, Heligoland and Sonderburg were other depots, and others were established during the war in occupied territory, like that at Zeebrugge. Recruiting was by a combination of volunteering (by those preferring naval to army service) and conscription from the inhabitants of the maritime areas.

The principal naval force was the High Seas Fleet, of three battle and one battlecruiser squadrons, which was confined largely to the North Sea after 1914, although some operations were undertaken in the Baltic. After Jutland the main naval effort was transferred to the submarine campaign.

The following ships of 4,500 tons displacement served during the war:

Date	Name and displacement (tons)	Main armament only
Pre-dreadnought battleships		
1891–2	*Brandenburg, Worth* (10,060)	6 × 11in, 8 × 4.1in
1898–1901	*Kaiser Friedrich III, Kaiser Barbarossa, Kaiser Karl der Grosse, Kaiser Wilhelm II, Kaiser Wilhelm der Grosse* (10,790)	4 × 9.4in, 14 × 5.9in (*Karl* 18 × 6in)
1902–3	*Wittlesbach, Mecklenburg, Schwaben, Wettin, Zahringen* (11,830)	4 × 9.4in, 18 × 5.9in
1904–6	*Braunschweig, Elsass, Hessen, Lothringen, Preussen* (13,200)	4 × 11in, 14 × 6.7in
1906–8	*Deutschland, Hannover, Pommern, Schleswig–Holstein, Schlesien* (13,200)	4 × 11in, 14 × 6.7in

Date	Name and displacement (tons)	Main armament only
Dreadnought battleships		
1909–10	*Westfalen, Nassau, Posen, Rheinland* (18,900)	12 × 11in, 12 × 5.9in
1911–12	*Heligoland, Oldenburg, Ostfriesland, Thüringen* (21,000)	12 × 12in, 14 × 5.9in
1912–13	*Kaiser, Friedrich der Grosse, Kaiserin, König Albert, Prinz Regent Luitpold* (24,700)	12 × 12in, 14 × 5.9in
1914	*König, Grosser Kurfürst, Kronprinz Wilhelm, Markgraf* (25,500)	10 × 12in, 14 × 5.9in
1916	*Baden, Bayern* (28,075)	8 × 15in, 16 × 5.9in
Battlecruisers		
1909	*Blücher* (sunk Dogger Bank 1915) (15,500)	12 × 8.2in, 8 × 5.9in
1910	*Von der Tann* (19,400)	8 × 11in, 10 × 5.9in
1911–12	*Moltke, Goeben* (transferred to Turkey 1914) (22,460)	10 × 11in, 12 × 5.9in
1913	*Seydlitz* (25,000)	10 × 11in, 12 × 5.9in
1914–17	*Derfflinger, Hindenburg, Lützow* (sunk Jutland) (28,000)	8 × 12in, 12–14 × 5.9in
Cruisers		
1892	*Kaiserin Augusta* (6,060)	12 × 5.9in
1897	*Fürst Bismarck* (10,700) (training ship)	4 × 9.4in, 12 × 5.9in
1898	*Freya, Hansa, Victoria, Luise, Vineta* (5,660–5,885) (used largely as training ships)	2 × 8.2in, 6 × 5.9in

German armoured cruiser Scharnhorst (11,600 tons, 8 × 8.2in, 6 × 5.9in, 20 × 3.4in guns, 4 × 17.7in torpedo tubes); sunk at the Battle of the Falkland Islands.

Date	Name and displacement (tons)	Main armament only
1900	*Prinz Heinrich* (8,930) training ship)	2 × 9.4in, 10 × 5.9in
1903	*Prinz Adalbert* (sunk Libau 1915), *Friedrich Karl* (mined Baltic 1914) (9,050)	4 × 8.2in, 10 × 5.9in
1905–6	*Roon, Yorck* (mined Jade Bay 1914) (9,350)	4 × 8.2in, 10 × 5.9in
1907	*Scharnhorst, Gneisenau* (both sunk Falklands) (11,600)	8 × 8.2in, 6 × 5.9in
1912	*Breslau* (to Turkey 1914, mined Imbros 1918), *Magdeburg* (sunk 1914), *Stralsund, Strassburg* (4,550)	12 × 4.1in
1913	*Karlsruhe* (blown up 1914), *Rostock* (sunk Jutland) (4,900)	12 × 4.1in
1914	*Regensburg, Graudenz* (4,900)	12 × 4.1in, later 7 × 5.9in
1915	*Frankfurt, Wiesbaden* (sunk Jutland)	8 × 5.9in
1915–16	*Königsberg* (2), *Emden* (2), *Karlsruhe* (2) *Nürnberg* (2) (5,300)	8 × 5.9in

A remarkable close-range action, which recalled the sea battles of a century before, occurred when the raider *Emden*, disguised by a dummy funnel as HMS *Yarmouth*, surprised the Russian light cruiser *Jemtchug* (known to the Allies as 'Cream-Jug') at Penang, 28 October 1914. This account was written by an anonymous eye-witness on shore:

'It was a quarter past five and the first streaks of a crimson sunrise were lighting the east. Silhouetted indistinctly against the sky was the black outline of the Russian cruiser, and the outline of a second cruiser, moving slowly round the first-named and spitting forth lightning flashes of flame. With the rapidly gaining light the staggering truth dawned upon us, and for twenty minutes or so we were amazed and spellbound witnesses of two ships doing battle almost at point-blank range. One or two shells that missed their objective fell hissing into the sea not far from where we stood, while two or three others passed shrieking over the town. The ships were obscured in smoke, which was pierced only by the stabbing flashes of fire from the guns. Suddenly there was an extremely brilliant gleam, followed immediately by a report more bursting and awesome than any we had yet heard, a lurid blaze of yellow, a belch of *débris* and blackest smoke with human forms hurled high above all! Then *silence* – a silence which could be felt . . .'

(Having destroyed *Jemtchug*, *Emden* sank the French torpedo-boat *Mousquet* and also shelled the Penang customs patrol boat, but upon realizing that the latter was unarmed, *Emden* not only ceased fire but sent an apology for having attacked a defenceless vessel!)

(*The 'Emden' Raid upon Penang*, in *Navy & Army Illustrated*, p. 330, 2 January 1915)

Von der Tann, the first German battle cruiser (19,400 tons, 8 × 11in, 10 × 6in, 16 × 24pdr guns, 4 × 18in torpedo tubes); present at Jutland, she was scuttled in 1919.

There were some twelve earlier protected cruisers (1894–1903) and 21 light cruisers (all named after towns); although some were adapted as minelayers, two were built specifically for the task, *Bremse* and *Brummer* (1916, 4,000 tons). Only one cruiser (*Stuttgart*) carried aircraft, as naval air reconnaissance was largely by airship. The destroyer force comprised more than 230 vessels, bearing numbers, and there was a considerable fleet of smaller vessels, torpedo-boats, minesweepers, etc.

The submarine branch was organized in four flotillas: North Sea or High Seas Fleet; Flanders, based at Zeebrugge, operating from Flamborough Head, through the English Channel to Waterford; Mediterranean, based at Pola, Cattaro and Constantinople; and Baltic or Kurland, based at Libau. There were three basic types of boat, U, UB (coastal) and UC (small minelayers), with many varieties: those bearing U numbers, for example, varied from *U 1* (1906), displacement 238 tons, to *U 142* (1918), displacement 2,158 tons. Size grew progressively towards the large 'U-cruiser' boats of 1,000–2,000 tons, with a range of up to 13,000 nautical miles, although most of these were constructed too late to see much service. The UB and UC classes were considerably smaller than the later U series, though at 400–500 tons and above the late UB and UC boats also exhibited the same growth in size. The number of boats at sea simultaneously peaked at 61 (June 1917); normally about half that number were at sea, including, say, two or three ocean-going boats around the Azores and west coast of Africa, eight or nine in the Atlantic approaches, four or five in the Channel and approaches, about seven UB and UC boats in the North Sea, and about six in the Mediterranean.

At the beginning of the war with the field army contained one Naval Division, comprising the 1st–6th Naval (or Marine) Fusilier Regiments with naval artillery and support; these were recruited from seamen or the inhabitants of ports and had only a mediocre combat value until 1917 when drafts from the army were received. In November 1914 a 2nd Naval Division was formed, and a third from drafts of these divisions in September 1916, a provisional force until regularized as the 3rd Naval Division in April 1917. The 1st and 2nd were posted on the Flanders coast during the war; the 3rd served on the Somme.

Aviation service

Despite the German concentration upon the airship which somewhat retarded the development of aircraft units, Germany had more machines available for front-line service in 1914 than either Britain or France. Until 1916 the aviation service was regarded as part of the communications troops; a separate command was established as early as March 1915, though it was never unified: military and naval aviation remained separate, and even in the former there was division of command (the Württemberg government, for example, ordered its aviation depot to post personnel only to Württemberg units!). Initially detachments were controlled by the individual armies to which they were attached, but on 8 October 1916 General Ernst von Hoeppner was appointed *Kommandierender–General* of the air force, and reorganizations were undertaken to unify command.

Originally there were just 'general' units, based on the standard flight of six aircraft. In mid-1915 specialized units came into existence, at first units of two-seater fighters for defensive patrolling, and later of single-seaters (sometimes styled *Fokker Abteilungen*) for offensive action. Reconnaissance units (*Flieger Abteilungen*) were also divided, with artillery-liaison units being crewed largely by artillery personnel. The single-seater fighters evolved into 'pursuit' or 'hunting' flights (*Jagdstaffeln* or *Jastas*), formed into

Arguably the most famous German ship of the war, the light cruiser Emden *(3,650 tons, 10 × 4.1in guns, 2 × 18in torpedo tubes) wrought havoc in the Indian Ocean before encountering* HMAS Sydney *at the Cocos Islands on 9 November 1914, when she was sunk.*

temporary groups of about four flights in 1917 (*Jagdstaffel-gruppen*), replaced in 1918 by squadrons of four flights (*Jagdgeschwader*). Escort flights (*Schutzstaffeln* or *Schusta*) were transformed into 'battle flights' (*Schlachtstaffeln*) for ground-attack duty. Bombers were separate, forming *Kampfstaffeln* from early 1916, assembled into *Kampfgeschwader OHL* (*Kagohl*); from late 1916 these were transformed either into *Schutzstaffeln* or long-range bombing flights, titled *Bombenstaffeln* in December 1917 and grouped in *Bombengeschwader* (*Bogohl*). The aviation service was finally classified into pursuit or fighter units (eighteen machines); ground attack (six–twelve aircraft); long-range bombers (about 24 machines); reconnaissance flights; artillery-spotting units (*Flieger Abteilungen-A*); and single-seater *Kampfeinsitzerstaffeln* for home defence. The number of aircraft available for use (not including reserves) rose from about 220 in 1914 to 1,100 by 1916 and 3,500 by 1918; more than 47,000 aircraft were used during the war, of which more than 3,000 were lost. The highest number of flying personnel in service was 5,500 (1918), with the same number training. A total of 6,840 were killed and 7,350 injured.

The independent naval aviation service operated flying-boats from ultimately 32 stations on the German and occupied coasts; and a number of flights for land service participated in the defence of the Yser and Belgian coastal areas.

The efforts expended on airship development were not justified by results obtained during the war. Although known by the generic name 'Zeppelin', not all were constructed by that company: a smaller number of Schütte–Lanz craft, and smaller Parseval craft were used by military and naval air services in both reconnaissance and strategic bombing roles. The early craft were comparatively small: the first to raid Britain, the naval L-3, had a volume of less than 800,000 cubic feet; in the last raid, the X-type lost (August 1918) had a volume of almost 2.2 million cubic feet. Until aircraft were developed capable of attaining the altitude of a Zeppelin, the airships were able to operate almost unhindered; but results were largely disappointing, and the military airship service was discontinued in 1917, their surviving craft being transferred to the navy, which continued to operate them until the end of the war (virtually all naval air reconnaissance was by airship). A principal difference in construction was that the Zeppelin type was metal-framed and the Schütte–Lanz plywood which tended to absorb moisture; the total numbers from the four manufacturers used during the war were: Zeppelins, navy 67, army 43; Schütte–Lanz, army ten, navy eight; Parseval, army six, navy three; Gross–Basenach, army one, navy one. Not all these were actually used on service.

As part of the army, the military aviation service wore army uniform. Initially there were five Airship Battalions of 3–4 companies, wearing shako, Swedish cuffs and Guard lace, field-grey shoulder-straps with light-grey piping and red battalion-number and 'L' (*Luftschiff*), and forage-cap with black band and red piping. The four Flying Battalions (*Flieger-Bataillone*) of aircraft personnel wore the same but with a winged propeller and battalion-number in red on the shoulder-straps, which were piped white, red, yellow and blue for the 1st–4th Battalions respectively. From 1915 Airship and Flying personnel had light-grey shoulder-straps with devices as before.

The following were among the aircraft used by Germany, all home-produced:

AEG: produced by the Allgemeine Elektrizitäts Gesellschaft. The B and C series were two-seater reconnaissance and occasional escort biplanes, the BI and BII in 1914, CI and CII from 1915, and the most effective CIV 1916, which remained in use to the end. The G series (*Grossflugzeug*) were 3- or 4-man twin-engined bombers, GI and GII 1915, GIII and GIV 1916; the larger GV was a fine heavy bomber with enhanced load-capacity introduced at the very end of the war. The JI and JII were two-seater biplanes based on the CIV, used 1917–18 for infantry co-operation, armour-plated against ground fire and some with twin Spandaus to fire through the floor for ground-attack.

A most effective German poster drawn by Otto Lehmann: 'Support our Field-Greys: Rend England's Might: Subscribe to the War Loan'. Climbing upon the shoulders of industrial and agricultural workers, a German soldier tears the British flag.

STÜTZT UNSRE FELDGRAUEN

ZEREISST ENGLANDS ~MACHT~ ZEICHNET

KRIEGSANLEIHE

AGO: Aerowerke Gustav Otto produced a series of two-seater pusher reconnaissance biplanes with unusual twin-fuselage design: CI 1915, heavier CII 1915–17, and smaller CIII 1916–17 (also existing in maritime floatplane version). The CIV was a conventional two-seater tractor reconnaissance biplane which saw limited service.

Albatros: Types BI, BII and BIII were two-seater, unarmed reconnaissance biplanes used 1914–15, and being excellent fliers were used thereafter as trainers. The C series were reconnaissance and general-purpose armed two-seater biplanes: CI (1915–17) a larger version of the BII; CIII derived from BIII (1916–17), also used as a light bomber; CV was a new design (1916–17) but less successful; CVII (1916–17) was much better and more popular; CVIII was a larger version intended as a night bomber. CX was used for reconnaissance and artillery co-operation, and CXII an improved version. Others in the C series never went into full production, and the CII was of a different configuration, being an outdated pusher. The D series were single-seater biplane fighters: DI from autumn 1916, DII slightly later, DIII from early 1917; these reasserted German dominance originally held by the Fokker monoplanes. The DV and DVa (from mid-1917) and DVII (1918) were less successful and never regained the ground lost to the later generations of Allied fighters. The JI (1917) and improved JII (1918) were armoured two-seater ground-attack biplanes; the W4 a single-seater biplane seaplane fighter based on the DI and used for coastal patrol in limited numbers 1917–18.

Aviatik: two-seater reconnaissance biplanes, the BI and BII (1914–15) unarmed, BIII (1915–17), CI (1915–17) and CIII (1916–17) with guns for the observer; unusually both B and C series originally had the observer at the front. CIII saw some service as a light bomber.

Brandenburg: biplane flying-boats: CC (1916) a single-seater pusher; FB (from 1916) two-seater pusher; W12 (from 1917) two-seater tractor. W29 (from spring 1918) was a monoplane version of the W12.

DFW: produced by the Deutsche Flugzeugwerke, B and C series of two-seater reconnaissance biplanes: BI and BII unarmed (1914–15); CI and briefly-used CII (1915) were improved, armed versions; CV (1916–18) was most successful, used in large numbers, and for ground attack. The RI and RII were four-engined heavy bombers (1916–18) which were unsuccessful and very few were produced.

Fokker: named from the Dutch designer Anthony Fokker. Small numbers of the AI and AII single-seater reconnaissance monoplanes (designed before the war) were used in 1914. The E (*Eindecker*) series were single-seater monoplane fighters which gained complete domination over the Allied aircraft from mid-1915 to early 1916: EI and EII (1915), most effective being the later EIII; the first single-seaters to carry a synchronized machine-gun. The heavier EIV was an unsuccessful attempt to re-establish the earlier dominance. The D series were single-seater biplane fighters designed to replace the monoplanes: DI and DII (1916) were out-matched by their Allied opponents, DIII and DV were

slight improvements, and DIV a DI with improved engine. DVI (1918) was produced only in limited numbers, but DVII was perhaps the best of all German fighters, used from spring 1918 and a most formidable, manoeuvrable and stable aircraft. The DVIII was basically an alternative designation for the EV monoplane. The DrI (*Dreidecker*) was a single-seater triplane fighter, 1917–18.

Friedrichshafen: the FF (Flugzeugbau Friedrichshafen) series were two-seater biplane seaplanes for reconnaissance, fighter and light bomber duties, FF33 from 1915, FF49 from mid-1917; an unarmed bomber version of the latter also existed. The G series were three-seater, twin-engined heavy bombers in service from late 1916: GII had a limited load capacity, the much larger GIII being more effective and remaining in service from early 1917; the GIV and GV saw only limited service (1918).

Gotha: the twin-engined, three-seater Gotha biplane bombers became somewhat infamous for the raids on Britain. The GI was a curious machine with the fuselage level with the upper wing, and saw only limited service (autumn 1915); GII and GIII (1916) were less prolific than the main variant, GIV (from mid-1917); GV was an improved version with biplane tail to give the rear gunner an improved field of fire. Although not easy to fly, these took over long-range bombing from the Zeppelins. A number of three-seater, twin-engined biplane seaplanes were designed by Gotha, but only the WD14, a torpedo-attack aircraft (1917–18) made any impact, but mainly in a long-range reconnaissance role as the torpedo role was ineffective.

Halberstadt: two-seater reconnaissance biplanes, the CLII and CLIV were used for escort and ground-attack 1917–18, the CV for long-distance reconnaissance from mid-1918. The DI–DV series were successive variants of single-seater fighter and escort biplanes, in service from early 1916 to late 1917.

Hannover: two-seater escort and ground-attack biplanes, marks CLI–III in service from 1917.

Junkers: the DI single-seater monoplane fighter was the first all-metal military aircraft, in limited use from spring 1918, a most effective machine. The CLI was a two-seater escort and ground-attack derivative, from mid-1918; the JI (in service from late 1917) was an all-metal, infantry-support and reconnaissance biplane, with armour-plating which increased the weight and led to the nickname *Möbelwagen* ('furniture van'); some had two Parabellum guns firing down through the armour for ground-attack duty.

LFG Roland: Luftfahrzeug Gesellschaft adopted the name Roland to prevent confusion with LVG. The CII was a two-seater reconnaissance and escort biplane, late 1915–late 1917; known as *Walfisch* ('whale') in Germany and 'the Slug' to the British, from its shape. The D series (DI–II and DVI) were single-seater biplane fighters, in service from 1916; compared unfavourably with other machines so use was limited.

LVG: two-seater reconnaissance biplanes produced by the

A most graphic illustration of the collapse of the Central Powers was the outbreak of civil war in Germany; this is a defended barricade in the Potsdamer Platz, Berlin, during the Spartacist revolt.

Luft-Verkehrs Gesellschaft, originally designed by the Swiss Franz Schneider who patented the first movable gun-ring, which became standard on all German two-seaters. BI and BII were unarmed reconnaissance machines in service 1914–15, and BIII (1917) a trainer; CI–III used 1915–17, the CII also serving as a light bomber (executing the first daylight raid on London, 28 November 1916); the improved CV (from mid-1917) and CVI (from early 1918) were the most successful.

Otto B: unarmed two-seater pusher reconnaissance and light bomber used in limited numbers 1914–15; notably slow.

Pfalz: A and E series were Bavarian-built single-seater monoplanes based on Morane–Saulnier designs, initially unarmed; used for reconnaissance, fighter-escort and light bombing. The EI and EII were similar in appearance to the Fokker *Eindecker*, but the A series were of parasol design. The D series were single-seater biplane fighters used 1917–18, the DIII (from August 1917) and DXII (from August 1918) being the most prolific.

Rumpler: two-seater reconnaissance biplanes used throughout the war: BI (unarmed) 1914–15; CI/Ia 1915–18; CIII 1916–17 (not a success); CIV (from late 1916) and CVII (from late 1917) were more successful, the latter existing in a high-altitude photo-reconnaissance version (*Rubild*) with oxygen generator and heated suits for crew. The CVIII was a purpose-built trainer, used from late 1917; the 6B1 and 6B2 were single-seater seaplane versions of the CI and CIV, used from mid-1916. The GI–III were three-seater biplane heavy bombers used in small numbers from mid-1915.

Siemens–Schuckert: the D series were single-seater biplane fighters used in relatively small numbers, the DI (from late 1916) a copy of the Nieuport 17; DIII from late spring 1918, improved DIV from August 1918. The R was an immense biplane heavy bomber, 'R' indicating *Riesenflugzeug* ('giant aircraft'); only seven produced, 1915–17.

Taube: the Taube ('Dove', named from shape of wings) was produced by a number of companies: two-seater reconnaissance monoplane, designed 1910, unarmed but the first 'combat' aircraft by virtue of bomb-dropping in Libya in 1911–12. Sometimes styled the 'Etrich Taube' (after its designer, Igo Etrich), among the companies to manufacture it were Albatros, Rumpler and Gotha.

Zeppelin: R series were giant heavy bombers with up to five engines, seven crew, in service from August 1916; used in small numbers, and conducted raids on London 'escorted' by Gothas.

References

Anon. *Der Weltkrieg, 1914 bis 1918.* Berlin (German official history)

Anon. *Histories of the 251 Divisions of the German Army which participated in the War 1914–18* (Intelligence section, AEF), US War Office 1920, rep. London, 1989

Bethmann Hollweg, T. von. *Reflections on the World War.* London, 1920

Dupuy, T. N. *The Military Lives of Hindenburg and Ludendorff of Imperial Germany.* New York, 1970

Falkenhayn, General E. von *General Headquarters 1914–1916 and its Critical Decisions.* London, 1919

Feldman, G. D. *Army, Industry and Labor in Germany 1914–1918.* Princeton, 1966

Fischer, F. *Germany's Aims in the First World War.* London, 1967

Fosten, D. S. V., and Marrion, R. J. *The German Army 1914–18.* London, 1978

Gatzke, H. W. *Germany's Drive to the West: a Study of Germany's Western War Aims during the First World War.* Baltimore, 1950

Gibbons, F. *The Red Knight of Germany.* London, 1927 (Manfred von Richthofen)

Goodspeed, D. J. *Ludendorff.* London, 1966

Herwig, H. *'Luxury' Fleet: the Imperial German Navy 1888–1918.* London, 1980

Hicks, J. E. *German Weapons, Uniform, Insignia 1841–1918.* La Canada, California, 1963 (expanded edn. of *Notes on German Ordnance,* 1937)

Hindenburg, Field Marshal P. L. *Out of My Life.* London, 1920

Hoffman, General M. *War Diaries and other Papers.* London, 1929

Imrie, A. *Pictorial History of the German Air Service 1914–1918.* London, 1971

Kilduff, P. *Germany's First Air Force 1914–1918.* London, 1991

Ludendorff, General E. *My War Memories 1914–1918.* London, 1919

Ludwig, E. *Kaiser Wilhelm II.* London, 1926

Lutz, R. H. (ed.). *Fall of the German Empire 1914–1918.* Stanford, 1932

Nash, D. B. *German Infantry 1914–1918.* London, 1971

— *Imperial German Army Handbook 1914–1918.* London, 1980

Nash, D. B. (ed.). *German Army Handbook April 1918.* London, 1977 (orig. pub. by British General Staff, 1918)

Neame, P. *German Strategy in the Great War.* London, 1923

Neumann, G. P. *The German Air Force in the Great War.* London, 1921

Palmer, A. *The Kaiser: Warlord of the Second Reich.* London, 1977

Rankin, Colonel R. H. *Helmets and Headdress of the Imperial German Army 1870–1918.* New Milford, Connecticut, 1965

Ruhl, M. *Die Deutsche Armee.* Leipzig, n.d.

— *Die Graue Felduniform der Deutschen Armee.* Leipzig, n.d.

Ryder, A. J. *The German Revolution of 1918.* Cambridge, 1967.

Scheer, Admiral R. *Germany's High Seas Fleet in the World War.* London, 1920

Taylor, J. C. *German Warships of World War I.* London, 1969

Waldmann, E. *The Spartacist Rising of 1919.* Milwaukee, 1958

Wheeler–Bennett, J. W. *Hindenburg: the Wooden Titan.* London, 1936

— *The Treaty of Brest–Litovsk and Germany's Eastern Policy.* Oxford, 1929

Wilhelm II, Kaiser. *My Memoirs.* London, 1923

Wilhelm, Crown Prince. *My War Experiences.* London, 1922

Witkop, Dr. P. (ed.). *German Students' War Letters.* London, 1929

GREAT BRITAIN

Although Britain did not mobilize the most men, or suffer the most casualties, of all the Allied nations, it is certain that the Allied war effort could not have been sustained without British participation.

The British system of government was that which still exists: a constitutional monarchy with a parliament of the elected House of Commons and hereditary House of Lords, the latter's power to veto decisions of the Commons having been curtailed in 1911. In contrast to some other sovereigns, King George V (1865–1936), who succeeded to the throne in 1911, did not become unduly involved in internal politics, and as a result of the war against many of his relatives in Germany, on 20 June 1917 decreed that all his family should exchange their German names for British: he adopted the name Windsor, Battenberg became Mountbatten, and Teck became Cambridge.

The most intractable internal problem of the pre-war period was the matter of Irish home rule and the determination of the Ulster Unionists to resist it by force. The 'Irish question' was sidelined for the duration of hostilities, though a major Nationalist rising occurred at Easter 1916,

which was suppressed with considerable loss of life. The problem surfaced again after the war, but not until December 1920 did the Irish Home Rule Act become law; the Irish Free State came into existence a year later, with Ulster remaining part of the United Kingdom.

The Liberal Party had formed the government since the 1906 general election, the prime minister from April 1908 being Herbert H. Asquith (1852–1928). The most important members of his cabinet were the Chancellor of the Exchequer, David Lloyd George (1863–1945), whose 'People's Budget' of 1908–9 was a landmark in the development of social welfare; Foreign Secretary Sir Edward Grey, Bt. (1862–1933); and First Lord of the Admiralty Winston Churchill (1874–1965). Asquith had

King George V (1865–1936).

taken the post of war minister himself in March 1914 when the officers of the Curragh camp had declared that they would resign rather than be used to coerce the Ulster Unionists into accepting Irish Home Rule, but in response to public agitation Asquith appointed as Secretary for War Earl Kitchener of Khartoum (1850–1916), Britain's most famous soldier following the death of 'Bobs', Earl Roberts of Kandahar (1832–1914), at St. Omer in November 1914 while visiting troops at the front. From the outset there was great universality of purpose among the major political parties: the Conservative opposition leader, the Canadian-born Andrew Bonar Law (1858–1923) supported Asquith solidly for the first half-year of the war, as did the leading Irish Nationalist, John Redmond (1851–1918), who declared that Ireland would be protected by the rival Ulster Volunteers and Nationalist Volunteers, so that the British garrison could be deployed elsewhere.

Because of the unwieldy size of the cabinet, on 25 November 1914 a War Council war formed of members of the Committee of Imperial Defence, to control the conduct of the war; the three principals were Asquith, Kitchener and Churchill. Influenced by Churchill and Lloyd George, both of whom favoured an eastern strategic initiative, Asquith sanctioned the Dardanelles expedition, this and other reverses prompting Bonar Law to demand the formation of a coalition government (17 May 1915). This was formed in the Whitsuntide recess, with Asquith, Kitchener and Grey retaining their positions; Bonar Law became colonial secretary, the Labour leader Arthur Henderson became president of the board of education, and the Conservative Arthur Balfour replaced Churchill at the Admiralty. Having been somewhat discredited over the Dardanelles expedition, Churchill became chancellor of the Duchy of Lancaster but, increasingly marginalized, later resigned from the cabinet and left for the Western Front. To solve the great public disquiet over the shortages of ammunition, Lloyd George was appointed minister of munitions, being replaced as chancellor by Reginald McKenna. On 11 November Asquith announced a new War Committee to decide military policy, consisting of himself, Lloyd George, Bonar Law, Balfour and McKenna (Kitchener was absent at Gallipoli). Lloyd George made a conspicuous success of his duties at the ministry of munitions (one of his most significant innovations being the employment of women in the industry), but the government was beset by difficulties including the introduction of conscription, continuing entanglement in the Mediterranean which diverted resources from the Western Front, the 'Easter Rising', and the replacement in December 1915 of Sir John French by Sir Douglas Haig as commander on the Western Front. Upon Kitchener's death in June 1916 (perhaps to the relief of some members of the government as he was not the easiest of colleagues), Lloyd George was appointed Secretary for War.

Amid increasing dissatisfaction with the conduct of the war (the Dardanelles and Mesopotamian expeditions were

David Lloyd George (1863–1945), prime minister from December 1916, having been a most successful minister of munitions.

under investigation by royal commission), in September 1916 Lloyd George declared that the only end to the war was a fight 'to a knock-out', and demanded that Asquith reorganize the War Committee to comprise only four members, with absolute power, but excluding Asquith. When this was refused Lloyd George resigned (5 December), which made Asquith's position untenable; he too resigned, and with Bonar Law's approval, Lloyd George was appointed prime minister on 7 December. Lloyd George constructed his four-man War Cabinet of himself, Henderson and Lords Curzon and Milner, all supporters of his policy, the latter enjoying influence second only to the prime minister. Bonar Law (chancellor) was co-opted onto the War Cabinet and given leadership of the House of Commons to free Lloyd George to conduct the war; Balfour became foreign secretary (Grey favoured a European conference to arrange peace-terms, a view totally opposite to Lloyd George's determination to destroy German militarism, so it was obvious that he could not work with the new prime minister). Although the personnel changed, the War Cabinet remained the principal planning body; the Earl of Derby became war minister and Churchill was recalled to government as minister of munitions in July 1917.

As an ardent supporter of the 'eastern' school (i.e., a concentration of effort in the east, to assail Austria–Hungary instead of continuing the expensive and fruitless assaults on the Western Front), Lloyd George came into conflict with both his Western Front commander, Haig, and the chief of the Imperial General Staff, William 'Wully' Robertson, both convinced 'westerners', and to impose further control agreed that the execution of the new offensive on the Western Front should be under French command, the disastrous 'Nivelle offensive'. In March 1917 Lloyd George convened an Imperial Conference in London to bring the prime ministers of Canada, New Zealand, South Africa and Newfoundland (Hughes of Australia was occupied at home), and the Secretary of State for India, into the policy-making process; it was so successful that it was decided to make it an annual event, and the experienced and capable Jan Smuts of South Africa was appointed a member of the British War Cabinet. At the Allied Rapallo Conference in November 1917 Lloyd George secured his plan for a Supreme War Council to conduct the whole Allied strategy, with Foch as overall commander on the Western Front; to the horror of Robertson, who was dismissed in February 1918 and replaced by Sir Henry Wilson, an intriguer and 'political' soldier more in tune with the prime minister.

The Coalition government was returned to office in the election of December 1918 (the life of the parliament having been extended to avoid a wartime election), with the secession of most of the Labour members, who formed the official opposition with 63 seats (Asquith and his anti-coalition Independent Liberals won only 28 seats, and none of the 73 Sinn Feiners returned in Ireland took their seats at Westminster). Lloyd George remained as prime minister until October 1922, providing a compromising voice in the peace negotiations between Clemenceau's and Woodrow Wilson's conceptions of the way forward.

Army

During the war the British Army was transformed from a voluntary, professional force backed by a voluntary reserve, into a 'national' army recruited by conscription. That it was able to make this transition without a material decline in effectiveness is a considerable tribute to the regimental

The universal khaki service uniform of the British Army is seen worn by a member of the 7th (TF) Battalion, King's (Liverpool) Regiment. The white-metal brooch visible on the right breast is the 'Imperial Service Badge' worn by Territorials who had volunteered for overseas service; the 1/7th King's, based at Bootle, served in the 2nd, 7th and 55th Divisions on the Western Front.

system and the calibre of the personnel. The Hon. Herbert Asquith (son of the prime minister) summarized the qualities evident throughout the war when writing of 1918, his 'inspiring memory' being 'the steadiness and fortitude of the British private soldier combined with his queer ironic humour in days of deep privation and extreme adversity'.[1] Edmund Priestman (killed at Gallipoli) remarked that only in adversity did the real character emerge: 'The greatness comes out when Tommy, after restless days and sleepless nights in Hell, keeps as merry and optimistic as ever, and even when he has bits knocked off him lights his cigarette and cracks jokes with the stretcher-bearers.'[2]

At least in the regular army, there was no overt anti-German feeling in 1914, but instead probably a preparedness to take on any army, as expressed in the Middlesex Regiment's song (written *c.* 1870):

'Be they Russians or Prussians or Spanish or French,
At scaling a rampart or guarding a trench,
Neither bayonet nor bullet our progress retards,
For it's just all the same to the gallant Die-Hards.'[3]

A story quoted by Frank Richards probably represents the general attitude: of a British soldier in Rouen in 1914, threatening a French café owner for not understanding the mixture of Hindustani and Chinese with which he was addressed (presumably in the belief that all foreigners would comprehend bazaar Hindustani). When advised that the French, being allies, should be treated with courtesy, the British soldier remarked that the only way to treat foreigners, from France to Hong Kong, was to knock hell out of them.[4] Traditional attitudes continued despite the conditions, even to the extent of a front-line battery-commander on the Western Front changing into blue patrol uniform for dinner in his dug-out every evening (which, according to one of his subordinates, was no empty gesture but a way of assuring his men that all was in order).

The regular army was recruited entirely by voluntary enlistment, the usual period being seven years with the colours and five with the reserve (six and six for horse and field artillery, eight and four for Household Cavalry and garrison artillery, three and nine for Foot Guards); re-

---

An experience of the military medical establishment in Mesopotamia, when suffering from enteric fever:

'I was awful bad all day ... fainted twice before breakfast ... I eventually came round and was put in front of the Doctor at 1 p.m. but everything seemed to go dark in front of me as soon as I stood up & over I went again, coming round in the Hospital Marquee ... saw the Doctor but he never gave me any idea of what was the matter with me, no strength to stand up even for a wash, had to kneel down to the bucket ... stayed in here till 23rd when I went back to my Unit even worse than when I went in. I shall never forget the Doctor as long as I live, who used to visit us at 7-30 a.m. & then about 12 noon the orderly came & told you who had to draw medicine but you had to walk a good 100 yds for it & there was not a man in our tent strong enough to fetch his Medicine in the broiling sun, so we all had to do without it, I never had a drink of Medicine or a pill the whole time I was in, I asked the Dr. for a bottle of Medicine to take out & he said I must ask at the dispensary before going out but was told by the Sgt. in charge that I could have no medicine as they had no bottle to spare. Reported myself for work on the 24th and as soon as the captain saw me he said I looked more fit for my grave than my duty ...'

(Driver Albert Birch, Army Service Corps)

A Vickers gun team in a rough earthwork, wearing the early gas mask which enveloped the entire head, used before the development of the 'box' respirator.

engagements were permitted, allowing twelve years' service with the colours. The reserve, used to bring units up to full strength on mobilization, was divided into four classes: 'A', liable to be called for any minor emergency, and receiving an extra allowance; 'B', the general reserve; 'C', general reserve men transferred prematurely; and 'D', men whose reserve service had expired but who volunteered to remain on call for a further four years. The special reserve, converted from the previous militia, was to make good deficiencies which existed after the mobilization of the reserve. The Territorial Force, created in 1908 from the previous volunteers and yeomanry, was a separate, self-contained volunteer army of men enrolled for four years, attending a 14–18-day training camp annually and additional drills, intended primarily for home defence but permitted to volunteer for overseas service, as huge numbers did during the World War.

As soon as mobilization was ordered the recruiting-offices were swamped with volunteers (rising to 33,000 per day in September 1914), who could hardly be accommodated in barracks or equipped. After the rush slowed, in July 1915 the National Registration Act provided for the listing of all men aged 18–41, and in October 1915 the 'Derby scheme' (organized by the Earl of Derby) provided for the enlistment of recruits for one day's service, then passing to the reserve for call-up when required; this brought in some two million men by the end of the year. However, as half of these were married men whom the government had pledged would not be called before single men, and as insufficient volunteers were forthcoming, conscription was introduced by the Military Service Act of January 1916, which rendered liable for service all single men aged 18–41, extended to married men in May 1916; exemptions were permitted, from reserved occupation to conscientious objection. The creation of the Ministry of National Service in November 1917 transferred recruiting to civil control, and in April 1918 another Military Service Act extended the age-limit to 51, and the government was compelled to abandon its undertaking not to send abroad troops under the age of nineteen. Conscription was never applied to Ireland due to the resistance from John Redmond and others. Up to February 1916 more than 2,631,000 men volunteered; from then to the armistice more than 2,339,000 were conscripted. A major consequence of such large enrollment was a huge increase in the number of women working in previously male occupations, contributing very materially to the nation's industrial production, a strong support for the principle of women's suffrage.

Higher formations

The Secretary of State for War headed the Army Council composed of the heads of the staff departments. Home forces were divided into seven Commands (Aldershot, Eastern, Irish, Northern, Scottish, Southern and Western) and twelve districts; the principal overseas commands were South Africa and Mediterranean (including Egypt); except

The most common image of the British soldier of the Great War is this, with the steel helmet adopted in 1915–16 and the 'box' respirator: a platoon of the East Lancashire Regiment on the Western Front.

in South Africa, British troops were not stationed in the self-governing colonies. A large proportion of the army was stationed in India, to ensure a ratio of about (or slightly less than) one British soldier to every two Indian; British troops serving in India were borne upon the Indian establishment. At the outbreak of war the strength of the army stood at 247,432 regulars, 154,347 reservists, 63,933 special reservists, 268,777 territorials, and 5,943 others (Channel Islands militia, Isle of Man and Bermuda Volunteers).

The British Expeditionary Force sent to mainland Europe consisted of one cavalry and six infantry divisions, organized in three army corps under Field Marshal Sir John French:

I Army Corps (Sir Douglas Haig): 1st and 2nd Divisions.
II Army Corps (Sir Horace Smith–Dorrien): 3rd and 5th Divisions.
III Army Corps (Sir William Pulteney): 4th and 6th Divisions.
Cavalry Division (Major-General Edmund Allenby).

The 7th Division arrived in October 1914, forming the basis of IV Army Corps, and by the following month the cavalry had been expanded to a corps of three divisions.

Unlike many, Kitchener realized that the war would not be 'over by Christmas' and upon his appointment as secretary for war requested the raising of a huge reinforcement under regular terms of service (rather than using the Territorial Force as a cadre). The first appeal, on 11 August 1914, raised the requested 'first hundred thousand' volunteers within a fortnight, in six divisions, numbered 8–13; when another regular division was formed from units recalled from overseas, it took the number 8 and thus the new formations were numbered 9th–14th. These troops were known as 'Kitchener's Army' or the 'New Army', and after a second appeal (28 August) the first became known as 'K1', with the 'second hundred thousand' 'K2', divisions 15–20. The Third New Army ('K3') followed immediately, divisions 21–26; divisions 27–29 were formed from more regulars withdrawn from overseas, and a Fourth New Army ('K4') comprised the 30th–35th Divisions. In April 1915 it was broken up to reinforce the other New Armies; the Fifth New Army was re-designated Fourth, and its divisions (37–42) were re-numbered 30–35. A new Fifth New Army ('K5'), authorized March 1915, included the 36th–41st Divisions; the 36th (Ulster Division) was recruited *en masse* from the Ulster Volunteer Force, the Protestant organization raised before the war to resist home rule. A feature of the Fourth and Fifth New Armies were battalions formed on a more localized basis than normal, often styled 'Pals', a scheme for attracting recruits by enabling them to serve with their friends from their own town, but with the disadvantage that small communities could be devastated when such a battalion was badly mauled. (The case of the Accrington Pals – 11th Battalion East Lancashire Regiment – almost annihilated on the first day of the Battle of the Somme, has almost passed into folklore.)[5] Succeeding divisions were: 1st line Territorial, 42nd–56th; 2nd line Territorial, 57th–69th; home service 71st–73rd (70th was never formed); 74th and 75th Yeomanry. Some divisions had subsidiary titles, for example the 14th and 20th (Light), 42nd and 66th East Lancashire, 64th Highland, etc.

By late December 1914 the BEF had increased sufficiently for armies to be formed, whereupon army corps were re-titled 'corps'. Two armies were formed initially (First Haig, Second Smith–Dorrien, later Sir Herbert Plumer); Third Army was formed in July 1915 (Sir Charles Monro, later Allenby). In October 1915 they comprised: First Army (I, III, IV and Indian Corps); Second Army (II, V and VI

Royal Fusiliers on the march, c. 1914, showing the use of the 1908 webbing equipment; two of the men in the foreground carry rolled signal-flags, and one has improvised a 'havelock' neck-cloth from a handkerchief. The 1st and 4th Battalions both served in the BEF in 1914.

Corps); Third Army (VII, X, XI and Canadian Corps, and two Indian cavalry divisions). The Cavalry Corps was not allocated to an army.

In September 1916 further reorganization created five armies; Haig having succeeded French in command of the BEF, Monro took over First Army from February 1916. The Cavalry Corps was dispersed from 12 March to 30 September 1916: First Army (I, IV, IX Corps); Second Army (VIII, IX, I and II ANZAC Corps); Third Army (VI, VII, XVII Corps, 2nd Cavalry and 1st Indian Cavalry Divisions); Fourth Army (Sir Henry Rawlinson, III, X, XIV and XV Corps, 1st Cavalry and 2nd Indian Cavalry Divisions); Reserve (later Fifth) Army (Sir Hubert Gough, II, V, XIII and Canadian Corps, 3rd Cavalry Division).

By August 1917 organization was: First Army (Sir Henry Horne, I, XI, XIII, Canadian and Portuguese Corps); Second Army (Plumer, IX, X, I and II ANZAC Corps); Third Army (Sir Julian Byng, III, IV, VI, VII, XVII Corps, 4th Cavalry Division); Fourth Army (XV Corps, 1st Division); Fifth Army (II, V, VIII, XIV, XVIII, XIX Corps); Cavalry Corps (Sir Charles Kavanagh, 1st–3rd, 5th Cavalry Divisions).

At the armistice, organization was as follows (commanders as before, except that Sir William Birdwood led Fifth Army): First Army (VII, VIII, XXII and Canadian Corps); Second Army (II, X, XV, XIX Corps); Third Army (IV, V, VI, XVII Corps); Fourth Army (IX, XIII, Australian Corps); Fifth Army (I, II, XI and Portuguese Corps); Cavalry Corps (1st–3rd Cavalry Divisions).

Divisional organization remained similar, but in the last year of the war shortages of personnel reduced each brigade from four to three battalions (the increase of machine-guns maintained the firepower); and the supporting services were changed by a reduction in artillery, increase of machine-guns (by the introduction of light guns for infantry use and withdrawal of heavy guns into support units), and introduction of trench artillery and pioneers. In 1914 a division comprised three brigades of four battalions each, each with two machine-guns (total 24); three field brigades (54 18pdrs), one field howitzer brigade (eighteen 4.5in howitzers), one heavy battery (four 60pdrs), brigade and divisional ammunition columns; two engineer field companies, one signal company, one cavalry squadron, one cyclist company, three field ambulances, one veterinary section and one divisional train. By mid-1915 each battalion had four Vickers machine-guns, the heavy battery was withdrawn, and the howitzer brigade had eight 4.5in howitzers. By September 1916 each battalion had twelve Lewis guns, and each brigade had a separate machine-gun company, each with sixteen Vickers guns, and a light trench-mortar battery with eight 3in Stokes mortars; artillery comprised four field brigades (total 48 18pdrs, sixteen 4.5in howitzers), three medium trench-mortar batteries (each with four 2in mortars), one heavy trench-mortar battery (four 9.45in mortars) and a divisional column; cavalry and cyclists were withdrawn, and the engineers

were supplemented by a pioneer battalion with eight Lewis guns. In April 1917 each battalion had sixteen Lewis guns; the artillery was reduced to two field brigades (total 36 18pdrs, twelve 4.5in howitzers), and a divisional machine-gun company was formed, with sixteen Vickers guns.

By October 1918 the infantry comprised three brigades of three battalions each (each with 36 Lewis guns, total 324); and each brigade included a light trench-mortar battery with eight 3in Stokes mortars (total 24). Artillery as before, except that there were now just two (medium) trench-mortar batteries (six 2in mortars each); the pioneer battalion had twelve Lewis guns, and the heavy machine-guns were concentrated into a divisional MG battalion, of four companies of sixteen Vickers guns each. The size of the divisional train (four Army Service Corps companies) remained reasonably standard, as did the number of the division's vehicles (877 in 1914, 822 in 1918); 21 motor ambulances were added from 1915, and motor-cycles and motor-cars increased from nine of each (1914) to 44 and eleven respectively (1918). There were, however, many variations on the above; divisions serving at home, for example, had only the machine-guns deployed at battalion level, and neither trench artillery nor pioneers, and initially Territorial divisions had old 15pdr field guns, 5in howitzers and 4.7in heavy guns.

Not including cavalry or Territorial mounted divisions, the following served during the war:

	Existing 1914	Formed during war	Served overseas	Served India	Served home
Regular (inc. Guards Division, formed 1915)	6	6	12	–	–
Territorial	14	14	19	3	6
New Army	–	36	30	–	6
Others (RN, 71st–75th)	–	6	3	–	3

(For the Royal Navy Division, see below; the 75th was formed from June 1917 of six British and three Indian battalions (by September 1918 three and nine respectively) and South African artillery.

Infantry

The amalgamations of 1881 produced infantry regiments of two regular battalions each, the original intention being that one battalion should be abroad and one at home; at the same time the county volunteers were affiliated to the county regiments, which was confirmed by the creation of the Territorial Force in 1908. Battalions were numbered in sequence, generally the 1st and 2nd being the regular battalions, the 3rd the reserve or previous militia battalion, and subsequent battalions Territorials (the Foot Guards had no Territorial battalions, four regiments had four regular battalions each, and some few existed only as Territorials). When the army expanded during the war, no

British corporal on sentry duty on the Western Front; a good illustration of the 1908-pattern webbing equipment, but the scene was probably 'posed' for the photographer, behind the lines: the rifle's mechanism would not be wrapped at the front line, and the observation-hole would probably have had a sacking cover.

new regiments were formed, but additional battalions were added to those existing, New Army battalions being given a number in the regimental sequence and the title 'Service' (e.g., 11th (Service) Battalion, Border Regiment). When a Territorial battalion went on active service, its place was taken by its Territorial reserve battalion, bearing a 'fractional' number (e.g., 1/4th Battalion), which would itself be replaced by a new reserve battalion, designated 2/4th, etc. From March 1915 third reserve battalions were formed, designated 3/4th, etc.

This system permitted the maintenance of regimental traditions, even within New Army and reserve battalions, a factor difficult to over-estimate and fostered to inspire emulation of heroic predecessors. When 86 Brigade landed at Gallipoli, its commander (Brigadier-General S. W. Hare) issued the following exhortation:

'Our task will be no easy one. Let us carry it through in a way worthy of the tradition of the distinguished regiments of which the Fusilier Brigade is composed; in such a way that the men of Albuhera and Minden, of Delhi and Lucknow may hail us as their equals in valour and military achievement, and that future historians may say of us as Napier said of the Fusilier Brigade at Albuhera, "Nothing could stop this astonishing infantry".';[6] and when Lieutenant-Colonel Eric Stephenson of the 3rd Battalion, Middlesex Regiment died on St. George's Day 1915, endeavouring to plug a gap in the line at Ypres, his last words, 'Die hard, boys, die hard' were deliberately those of his predecessor 104 years earlier, William Inglis of the 57th Foot at Albuhera.

The regiments and their field battalions that existed during the war are listed in order of seniority; the first number is the number of regular battalions, the second the number of Territorial battalions, and the third the number of New Army (Service) battalions:

Royal Scots 2, 14, 6; QORW Surrey 2, 6, 5; Buffs (East Kent) 2, 5, 3; KOR Lancaster 2, 5, 5; Northumberland Fusiliers 2, 10, 19; Warwickshire 2, 9, 6; R. Fusiliers 4, 0, 17; King's (Liverpool) 2, 14, 8; Norfolk 2, 8, 3; Lincolnshire 2, 5, 4; Devonshire 2, 10, 3; Suffolk 2, 8, 5; Somerset LI 2, 6, 3; Prince of Wales's (West Yorkshire) 2, 8, 9; East Yorkshire 2, 3, 7; Bedfordshire 2, 3, 3; Leicestershire 2, 4, 5; Royal Irish 2, 0, 2; Green Howards 2, 5, 7; Lancashire Fusiliers 2, 9, 10; Royal Scots Fusiliers 2, 6, 3; Cheshire 2, 9, 8; Royal Welsh Fusiliers 2, 11, 10; South Wales Borderers, 2, 2, 8; King's Own Scottish Borderers 2, 2, 8; Cameronians 2, 9, 4; Royal Inniskilling Fusiliers 2, 0, 7; Gloucestershire 2, 7, 7; Worcestershire 4, 4, 4; East Lancashire 2, 4, 5; East Surrey 2, 4, 5; Duke of Cornwall's LI 2, 3, 4; Duke of Wellington's 2, 8, 3; Border 2, 4, 5; Royal Sussex 2, 8, 6; Hampshire 2, 11, 5; S. Staffordshire 2, 4, 3; Dorset 2, 2, 2; Prince of Wales's (South Lancashire) 2, 5, 6; Welsh 2, 9, 12; Black Watch 2, 10, 3; Oxford & Bucks LI 2, 5, 4; Essex 2, 13, 4; Sherwood Foresters 2, 5, 4; Loyals (North Lancashire) 2, 7, 5; Northants 2, 3, 3; Royal Berkshire 2, 2, 4; QORW Kent 2, 5, 5; KO Yorkshire LI 2, 4, 6; K. Shropshire LI 2, 3, 4; Middlesex 2, 12, 12; King's Royal Rifle Corps 4, 0, 12; Wiltshire 2, 2, 3; Manchester 2, 13, 12; North Staffordshire 2, 4, 3; York & Lancaster 2, 4, 8; Durham LI 2, 12, 10; Highland LI 2, 10, 8; Seaforth Highlanders 2, 6, 3; Gordon Highlanders 2, 8, 3; Q.O. Cameron Highlanders 2, 3, 3; Royal Irish Rifles 2, 0, 11; Royal Irish Fusiliers 2, 0, 5; Connaught Rangers 2, 0, 2; Argyll & Sutherland Highlanders 2, 11, 4; Prince of Wales's Leinster (Royal Canadians) 2, 0, 2; Royal Munster Fusiliers 2, 0, 4; Royal Dublin Fusiliers 2, 0, 5; Rifle Brigade 4, 7, 8; Monmouthshire 0, 7, 0; Cambridgeshire 0, 3, 0; London 0, 62, 0; Hertfordshire 0, 3, 0; Herefordshire 0, 2, 0; Northern Cyclists 0, 2, 0; Highland Cyclists 0, 2, 0; Kent Cyclists 0, 2, 0; Huntingdonshire Cyclists 0, 2, 0.

In addition there existed many reserve battalions (for regulars, Territorials and New Army) and garrison battalions; the Royal Fusiliers, Royal Welsh Fusiliers, Middlesex, Manchester and Durham Light Infantry all had 40 or more battalions in total, and the Northumberland Fusiliers the most of any, 51. The only regiments with ten or less were

the Royal Irish, Wiltshire, Connaught Rangers and Leinster. A typical array of battalions was that of the Prince of Wales's Own (West Yorkshire) Regiment: regulars, 1st and 2nd Battalions; 3rd Reserve; 4th Extra Reserve; Territorials 1/5th, 1/6th, 2/5th, 2/6th, and 1/7th, 1/8th, 2/7th, 2/8th all Leeds Rifles; Territorial reserve 3/5th, 3/6th, 3/7th, 3/8th; New Army 9th–12th, 15th and 17th (1st and 2nd Leeds 'Pals'), 16th and 18th (1st and 2nd Bradford 'Pals'), 21st (Wool Textile Pioneers); New Army reserve 13th, 14th, 19th, 20th; 22nd Labour Battalion; 1st and 2nd (Home Service) Garrison Battalions; 51st and 52nd (Graduated) Battalions; 53rd (Young Soldier) Battalion.

There were four regiments of Foot Guards, with a fifth (Welsh) formed in February 1916. They had the following battalions: Grenadier Guards, four and one reserve; Coldstream three, one reserve, one pioneer; Scots two, one reserve; Irish two, one reserve; Welsh one, one reserve. The machine-gun companies of the Guards Division formed a Guards Machine-Gun Regiment.

A battalion consisted of a headquarters and four rifle companies, between 800 and 1,000 of all ranks (the nominal strength of 30 officers and 977 men was rarely attained in the field: officially six officers and 221 men per company, six officers and 93 men for headquarters (including MG section), and it became usual for a cadre to be withdrawn before an action, the 'Battle Surplus' or 'First Reinforcement', to ensure that some personnel would be left even if the unit were badly mauled). Each company (commanded by a captain) comprised four platoons (commanded by a lieutenant or 2nd lieutenant), each of four sections of one NCO and five to nine other ranks, with a platoon headquarters of a subaltern, platoon sergeant, runner and a combined batman/second runner. By the end of the war the platoon was the most important cog in the battalion machinery, each including a Lewis gun section (2-man gun-

The commonest opinion (in all armies) on staff officers:

'I hear that leave has started again for those Divisions out of the Line. When will G.H.Q. remember that there is a Division with our number? Divs. which have done far less than we, are out at rest. I think we have a record of 3 special mentions in a month for "exceptional gallantry", "immortal valour" &c. We & the 51st – the two most hated Divisions by the Hun – are here together . . .

'I suppose John Copley is a Town Major. I don't envy his job, for they get a rotten time from all officers who despise them. In his case it is totally different being disabled, but in 99.9% of the cases these officers are the windiest & most inefficient of the Division. That's why they get the jobs. All "duds" get excellent jobs, or, like Mitchell, often left out of the line as no good. It pays to be a dud.'

(Officer, 61st Division – alias 'old Sixty-worst' – France, 5 May 1918)

To illustrate the change of organization of an infantry division, the following orders-of-battle show the composition of 29th Division in April 1915 (Gallipoli) and three years later (France); in the latter note the use of the divisional number to identify some of the supporting units:

1915:
86 Brigade: 2/Royal Fusiliers, 1/Lancashire Fusiliers, 1/Royal Munster Fusiliers, 1/Royal Dublin Fusiliers
87 Brigade: 2/South Wales Borderers, I/KOSB, 1/Royal Inniskilling Fusiliers, 1/Border Regiment
88 Brigade: 4/Worcestershire Regiment, 2/Hampshire Regiment, 1/Essex Regiment, 5/Royal Scots
Cavalry: 'C' Squadron Surrey Yeomanry, 29th Division Cyclist Company
Artillery: XV Brigade RHA (three batteries); XVII and CXLVII Brigades RFA (three batteries each); IV (Highland) Mountain Brigade (two batteries); 460 Howitzer, 90 Heavy and 14 Siege Batteries; 29th Divisional Ammunition Column
Engineers: 2/London, 2/Lowland, 1/West Riding Field Companies; 1/London Signal Company
Support: 87th–89th Field Ambulances; 18th Mobile Veterinary Section; 29th Divisional Train.

1918:
86 Brigade: 2/Royal Fusiliers, 1/Lancashire Fusiliers, 1/Guernsey LI (replaced by 1/Royal Dublin Fusiliers 27 April), 86th Trench-Mortar Battery
87 Brigade: 2/South Wales Borderers, 1/ KOSB, 1/Border Regiment, 87th Trench-Mortar Battery
88 Brigade: 4/Worcestershire Regiment, 2/Hampshire Regiment, Royal Newfoundland Regiment (replaced by 2/Leinster Regiment late April), 88th Trench-Mortar Battery
Artillery: XV Brigade RHA (two field, one howitzer battery); XVII Brigade RFA (three field, one howitzer batteries); X29, Y29 medium trench-mortar batteries; 29th Division Ammunition Column
Engineers: 455th, 497th, 510th Field Companies; 1/London Signal Company
Pioneers: 2/Monmouthshire Regiment
Support: 29 Battalion Machine-Gun Corps (86th–88th, 227th MG Companies); 87th–89th Field Hospitals, 18th Mobile Veterinary Section, 29th Divisional Train, 226th Employment Company.

A khaki service uniform was adopted in 1902, including a single-breasted tunic with patch pockets and folding collar, trousers, puttees and ankle-boots. The khaki peaked cap had a crown stiffened with wire, removed on active service to produce a shapeless head-dress colloquially styled a 'Gorblimey'; some had ear- and neck-flaps, and from 1917 a completely soft version was produced (including peak) which could be rolled up or even worn under the steel helmet introduced in 1916. The only regimental identifications were the cap-badge and brass-shoulder titles, the

'One man, a bugler in a county regiment, little more than a child in years, went raving mad as he staggered across a trench and fell, dragging with him a headless Thing which still kept watch with rifle against shoulder. His shrieks, as they pulled the two apart, ring even now in the ears. He died that night, simply from shock after the awful tension of the day.'
(Major A. Corbett-Smith, *The Retreat from Mons, by One who Shared in it*, pp. 105–6, London, 1916)

latter also worn on the single-breasted khaki greatcoat, which had brass buttons like the tunic. The 1908-pattern equipment was made of greenish-khaki or khaki webbing, a waist-belt with five cartridge-pouches on each side of the brass clasp, shoulder-braces, knapsack, at the left a haversack, bayonet and entrenching-tool haft, and at the right the entrenching-tool blade in a webbing cover and a felt-covered canteen. To remedy shortages of the 1908 equipment, an emergency set of leather belts was produced, with one large cartridge-pouch at each side of the brass S-clasp of the waist-belt; this 1914-pattern was intended for home service only, but was soon issued to troops on active service as well. Officers' tunics had open collars, worn with shirt and tie, khaki cloth or cord breeches, puttees or leather gaiters, and Sam Browne belt; their greatcoats were double-breasted, and a wide variety of unregulated, belted trench-coats and mackintoshes were also used. Scottish tunics were originally cut in 'doublet' shape with rounded front corners and gauntlet cuffs for officers, but the ordinary tunic was often worn. The Scottish head-dress was originally a glengarry, which was found unsuitable for active service, and was replaced by a blue Balmoral bonnet (khaki from 1915). Highland regiments retained the kilt of Black Watch tartan (Black Watch, Argyll & Sutherland), Mackenzie (Seaforth), Gordon (Gordon Highlanders), Cameron of Erracht (Queen's Own Cameron Highlanders) or Elcho grey (London Scottish).

NCO rank-badges were khaki on light drab (black on green for rifle corps), worn on the sleeve: one to three chevrons for lance-corporal, corporal and sergeant; crown over three chevrons (company sergeant-major to 1915, and quartermaster-sergeant); crown (regimental sergeant-major to 1915, CSM thereafter); royal arms (RSM after 1915); regimental quartermaster-sergeants before 1915 wore a crown over four chevrons, a crown within a wreath thereafter. Officers' rank-badges were in khaki on large cuff-flaps, with one to four hoops of khaki braid above the cuff: one to three stars for 2nd lieutenant, lieutenant and captain respectively, crown for major, crown and one or two stars for lieutenant-colonel and colonel; Scottish officers wore these on the gauntlet cuff, with no patch. As the badges were unduly conspicuous, from 1915 it became usual for officers' rank insignia to be worn in bronzed metal on the shoulder-straps, as already worn on tropical uniform and the greatcoat, permitted officially from 1917.

A 'brew' in the trenches: British troops receive hot food or tea from a 'dixie', 1917.

team and supporting riflemen) and one section trained as specialist bombers. The platoon system was of comparatively recent introduction: at the start of the war Territorial units were still organized according to the 1909 regulations, under which a battalion comprised eight companies of about 120 in four sections. Until the withdrawal of heavy machine-guns into brigade companies, each battalion had a Maxim (later Vickers) section of two guns, carried by mules and crewed by an officer and twelve other ranks, doubled when the number of guns was increased.

The wartime classification of some battalions as pioneers intended them to act as divisional troops, but although this involved minor variations in equipment (less Lewis guns, the use of crossed pick and rifle collar-badges, etc.) such battalions still retained their infantry capabilities.

Staff appointments were indicated by coloured gorget-patches on the tunic-collar, with a central braid strip: general officers scarlet with gold oakleaves; staff scarlet, red braid; accounts dark-blue, red edge; Army Medical Service black, edged blue, gold braid; Indian Medical Service black, gold or red braid; Veterinary Service scarlet, edged blue, gold braid; administration blue, crimson braid; intelligence green, green braid (from 1916); RFC French-grey, crimson braid (from 1917); Indian Army Supply black, white braid. Staff officers also wore coloured brassards, of which a huge variety existed (at least 62 plus examples bearing divisional insignia), in 'crude stained-glass window colours'[7] including red and blue bands for general HQ ('a chromatic outrage' which 'quite spoiled the appearance of a tunic';[8] corps HQ

red, white and blue bands; divisional HQ red, brigade HQ blue, etc.

A wartime development was the use of 'battle insignia', coloured badges worn on the sleeve, rear collar or helmet, to identify units from battalion to division; some were pictorial (e.g., divisional signs) but for smaller units often simply geometrical shapes, or rough representations of the outline of the regimental cap-badge.

For tropical service the uniform was khaki drill, often with shorts or with tunic removed to produce 'shirt-sleeve orders'; topees were commonly worn, but sometimes Australian-style slouch hats. Both these were also worn in Italy, and in hot weather on the Western Front shorts were quite common, generally worn with puttees rather than stockings.

There existed an organization of part-time home-defence volunteers, styled variously Volunteer Training Corps, National Guard, Volunteer Defence Corps, etc., which only officially became part of HM Forces in April 1916, when the title 'Volunteer Force' was adopted. Initially their uniform was Lovat or grey-green, often cut in the form of a Norfolk jacket; officers were properly commissioned from September 1916, and from December 1916 khaki uniforms began to be issued. Recruiting was no longer entirely voluntary, as those in reserved occupations could be ordered to join; in July 1918, excluding the London corps, units were permitted to style themselves as volunteer battalions of their county regiments.

The principal rifle was the .303in Short, Magazine Lee

Enfield (SMLE), which existed in a number of Marks. A replacement known as 'Pattern 1913' in .276in cal. had been developed before the war but was not produced in time; manufacture, with calibre amended to .303in was transferred to the USA where it became the Pattern 1914 ('P14') which was used alongside the SMLE. Use was also made of the 1907-pattern MLE or 'long Lee Enfield', and for reserve forces even weapons as old as the single-shot Martini-Henry. The principal machine-gun in 1914 was the Maxim, but this was replaced quickly by the .303in Vickers; the standard light machine-gun was the Lewis. Hardly any grenades were available in 1914, and only six men per company of Royal Engineers received any training in their use. Many patterns of hand- and rifle-grenade were produced from 1914, including the Hale rifle-grenade and the so-called 'Mexican' pattern (a Hale hand-grenade originally produced for Mexico), but these were in such short supply that home-made 'jam-tin bombs' were utilized. Spherical and egg-shaped grenades were used before the widespread issue from mid-1915 of the Mills grenade with segmented casing which flew in splinters when the charge exploded. Although the Mills was the most famous grenade of the war, other patterns remained in use to the end; as rodded rifle-grenades like the Hale and its derivatives were not completely reliable, cup-dischargers were used to project Mills grenades from a rifle.

Cavalry

The regular cavalry comprised three Household regiments, seven of Dragoon Guards (numbered 1st–7th), three of dragoons (1st, 2nd, 6th), twelve of hussars (3rd, 4th, 7th, 8th, 10th, 11th, 13th–15th, 18th–20th) and six of lancers (5th, 9th, 12th, 16th, 17th, 21st). Three Household and fourteen line reserve regiments were created in 1914 (reduced to six in 1917) to provide drafts and for home service. There were three Special Reserve regiments (North Irish, South Irish and King Edward's Horse) and 54 of yeomanry (the mounted equivalent of the Territorials), of which one (Welsh Horse) was formed at the outbreak of war.

Excepting the Household regiments (converted to machine-gunners 1918) all the regular cavalry remained horsed, and almost all served on the Western Front (7th, 13th and 14th Hussars served in Mesopotamia, 1st DG moved from France to India in 1917 and 21st Lancers were in India throughout). Apart from the 15th and 19th Hussars, which served briefly as divisional cavalry 1914–15, all were concentrated into the five, later three, cavalry divisions. Some yeomanry were employed as divisional cavalry early in the war, but many were concentrated into Mounted Divisions, and although a few remained in a mounted role most were dismounted from 1915 and served as infantry. Second- and third-line units were formed when the first-line yeomanry were abroad, the majority being converted to cyclists and almost all remaining in Britain.

Regiments were generally organized in three squadrons, each of six officers and 152 other ranks, plus HQ and machine-gun section of eight officers and 67 other ranks. Three regiments formed a brigade, and two to four brigades a division, which also included a horse artillery brigade and the usual supports (field engineer squadron, signal squadron, field ambulances, veterinary section, train, etc.).

Cavalry wore the same service uniform as the infantry, with 1903-pattern leather equipment, including a 90-round bandolier over the left shoulder. The Lee Enfield rifle was the principal weapon, though these were not available initially for all second-line formations (the 2/2nd, later 3rd Mounted Division, for example, was originally issued with Japanese carbines). Lances had been classified as ceremonial weapons in 1903 but were re-issued as a combat weapon in 1909. The 1908-pattern sabre was, ironically, the best-designed weapon ever issued to British cavalry, yet was of hardly any combat use; in mounted action in Palestine, for example, when sabres had been withdrawn or never issued, bayonets had to be pressed into service in this role.

Artillery

The Royal Regiment of Artillery included three branches: Royal Field Artillery, which manned most of the field guns; Royal Horse Artillery, which accompanied the cavalry; and Royal Garrison Artillery, which crewed the heaviest pieces. The 6-gun battery was standard (4-gun batteries for the heaviest ordnance), but Territorial and New Army artillery was initially organized in 4-gun batteries, until the 6-gun battery was made universal in 1916. Battery-strength was originally five officers and 200 other ranks (horse), five and 193 (field), five and 192 (howitzers), five and 163 (heavy) and five and 177 (siege howitzers); batteries were generally grouped in brigades of three, to which were attached ammunition-columns.

Divisional artillery consisted originally of three field brigades (nine batteries, 54 guns), one howitzer brigade (three batteries, eighteen guns) and one heavy battery (four guns). Each battery had two ammunition-wagons per gun, and each brigade a light ammunition column (one extra wagon per gun plus thirteen vehicles for infantry ammunition, in field brigades only). In February 1915 the heavy batteries were withdrawn, and it was found that divisional artillery was too numerous for close-support action, so the number of batteries was reduced and the surplus concentrated in a general reserve, which like the medium and heavy artillery deployed at corps or army level, was available for specific tasks when required. Light trench-mortars were deployed at brigade level, and heavy trench-mortars at divisional. To illustrate the changing formation, the artillery of 1st Division (on the Western Front throughout) was:

1914:
XXV Brigade: 113–115 Batteries, XXV Brigade Ammunition Column (BAC)
XXVI Brigade: 116–118 Batteries, XXVI BAC

The principal British field gun of the war, the 18pdr, here covering a canal-crossing in 1918.

XXXIX Brigade: 46, 51, 54 Batteries, XXXIX BAC
XLIII Howitzer Brigade: 30, 40, 57 Howitzer Batteries, XLIII Howitzer BAC
26 Heavy Battery; 26 Heavy BAC.
1918:
XXV Brigade: 113–115 and 40 Howitzer Batteries
XXXIX Brigade: 46, 51, 54 and 30 Howitzer Batteries
X1 and Y1 heavy trench-mortar batteries.

The principal field gun was the 18pdr quick-firer, which remained in use (with minor improvements) throughout the war; the 13pdr horse artillery gun was a lighter version. Some of the Territorial formations were equipped with older 15pdrs. The principal field howitzer was the 4.5in weapon, the mountain howitzer 3.7in calibre; mountain guns were originally 10pdrs, with a 12½pdr issued in 1914. The original divisional heavy artillery was the 60pdr, supplemented by a 6in howitzer (designed early 1915), which remained in use. At the beginning of the war there were no very heavy guns available for mobile use, so 6in coastal defence guns were mounted on heavy carriages until a purpose-built 6in gun on 8in howitzer carriage was used from 1916. The first 8in howitzer was a re-bored 6in gun with shortened barrel, until a new pattern was produced.

Immensely heavy and less mobile 9.2in howitzers were deployed from November 1914; 12in howitzers were used on road and rail mountings. The bulk of the field artillery remained horse-drawn, but a variety of tractors were also used for transportation, such as the Holt.

Trench-mortars were completely lacking at the beginning of the war, so that the only ones available for use at Gallipoli were a few Japanese weapons. Early mortars included the 2in tubes firing 'toffee-apple' bombs, but the principal weapon became the Stokes mortar, designed in 1915 by Sir Wilfred Stokes, of 3in and 4in calibre, and the heavier Stokes–Newton which operated on the same principal of automatic ignition.

The Royal Artillery wore ordinary service uniform, distinguished only by corps badges and insignia.

Armoured corps

The first armoured vehicles were basically civilian cars with armour-plating added; later armoured cars were purpose-built, many with traversible turrets containing fixed machine-guns. Although Rolls-Royce cars are the most famous, a number of other manufactures were used including Lanchesters, Austins, Wolseleys and a variety of foreign vehicles. Due to the nature of trench warfare, the use of such mobile, armoured machine-gun posts was very restricted on the Western Front, but cars were used to much greater effect in other theatres, including Palestine, Mesopotamia, and with the Russian Army on the Eastern Front.

The earliest armoured vehicles were conversions from civilian vehicles, such as this armoured lorry converted from a B-type omnibus, crewed by Royal Marines and operated by the Royal Naval Air Service in Flanders in 1914.

The earliest units were crewed by the Royal Naval Air Service, and later RN Armoured Car Division; the first army units were the batteries of the Motor Machine-Gun Service, each of eighteen motor-cycle combinations of 2-gun sections. Upon the formation of the Machine-Gun Corps in 1915 the naval and MMGS vehicles were absorbed ito the MGC (Motors), initially of 4-car Armoured Motor Batteries (AMBs, equipped with Rolls-Royces), Light Armoured Batteries (LABs) or Light Armoured Car Batteries (LACBs). Nos. 1–3 AMBs formed the Light Armoured Car Brigade in the Middle East. Eight-car Light Armoured Motor Batteries (LAMBs) were formed later; and the Russian Armoured Car Division, crewed largely by Royal Marines, served with the Russians but remained under naval control.

Although the tank was a British invention, it took some time for the advantages of its large-scale deployment to be appreciated. There existed ten principal patterns of heavy tank, all of the same basic pattern (with tracks passing around the entire vehicle), most with a crew of eight; these were numbered from Mk I to Mk IX, with three Mk Vs (V, V*, V**) and no Mk VI. All were produced in 'male' and 'female' versions, the former with two 6pdr guns and four machine-guns, and the latter with five (Mks I–III) or six machine-guns (Mk IX was designed to carry infantry, had a crew of four and only two machine-guns; like Mk V** and

All British heavy tanks had the same rhomboid configuration, with external tracks and armament mounted on the sides. The rear wheels, however, were soon found to be unnecessary and were discarded.

British Medium Tank, known as a Whippet because of its enhanced speed, although this term was used more loosely at the time and may be found referring to a Renault light tank.

VIII it was never actually used). From late 1917 a new design was introduced, the Medium Tank Mk A (Mk B was produced but not used), known universally as the 'Whippet', with three crew, four machine-guns, and almost double the speed attainable by the heavy tank.

Tanks were crewed by the Machine-Gun Corps heavy branch, re-titled Tank Corps in June 1917. There were originally six companies, each of four sections of three male and three female tanks each, each section with a spare seventh vehicle in reserve. In October 1916 the four companies on the Western Front were ordered to be augmented to twelve and formed into four battalions, with the two companies in England forming the cadre for five further battalions; each battalion was to have three companies, each of four 5-tank combat sections and a 4-tank HQ section. In early 1917 the organization was changed, each company to comprise three 4-tank combat sections and a spare section. From January 1917 brigades of two battalions each were formed. A later development was the creation of supply tanks, Mk IVs with armament removed, for use as supply-vehicles for both tank and infantry units.

Supporting services

Engineering duties were undertaken by the Corps of Royal Engineers, which included the signal service (an independent Signal Corps was not formed until 1920). Each division nominally possessed two (later usually three) field companies (each of six officers, 211 men, eighteen vehicles, a pontoon and 33 bicycles), a divisional staff (four officers, ten men) and a signal company (five officers, 157 men, 32 bicycles, nine motor-cycles). In cavalry divisions there was an engineer squadron (seven officers, 184 men, 20 vehicles, 44 bicycles) and a signal squadron (eight officers, 198 men, 21 vehicles including two motor-cars, 34 bicycles, six motor-

cycles). Field companies and squadrons were numbered, although Territorial units retained local titles until early 1917 (for example, in 42nd Division the 1st–3rd East Lancashire Field Companies received the numbers 427–429 on 3 February). Specialist units were deployed at corps level, for example the bridging train (seven officers, 278 men, 57 vehicles, one bicycle) and tunnelling companies. Engineers wore ordinary service uniform, signallers with a horizontally divided blue and white brassard, engineers in signal companies with a white band on the left arm, and postal service personnel in signal companies with green gorget-patch for officers.

The Army Service Corps provided army transport. Initially a divisional train comprised three companies of five officers and 80 men each, a headquarters company (six officers, 155 men), headquarters (five officers, seven men), 142 vehicles, four motor-cars and 30 bicycles. For units deployed at other than divisional level (for 'army troops') the company comprised seven officers, 93 men, 28 vehicles, one motor-car and nine bicycles. Companies were numbered individually, but the entire train bore the number of the division. Although the bulk of transport was initially horse-drawn, it was acknowledged that motor vehicles would be useful, so from 1911 owners of suitable vehicles were paid a subsidy to keep them in good order and ready for transfer from civilian to military service: these were divided into Class A vehicles to carry 3 tons and Class B 30 cwt. As troop-transports, civilian omnibuses were requisitioned (initially from the London General Omnibus Co. for use with the naval brigade in 1914); some 1,300 AEC 'B'-type buses were uses during the war, in Auxiliary Omnibus Companies of 75 vehicles each. The wartime expansion was enormous: in 1914 there were 500 officers and 6,000 other ranks in the ASC, rising to more than 330,000 personnel by

officer and a small number of orderlies who performed battle first-aid, serious casualties being evacuated to the field ambulances. A divisional field ambulance comprised ten officers, 224 men and 23 vehicles, in three sections; a cavalry field ambulance six officers, 118 men and eighteen vehicles in two sections. The usual sequence of treatment for a casualty was: initial dressing at the Regimental Aid Post (RAP); then to the Advanced Dressing Station (ADS), to the Main Dressing Station, and thence to the Casualty Clearing Station (CCS), the first place for the performance of major surgery. After that a casualty might be sent to a Base Hospital, and then to a convalescent hospital.

'Now that the sword, as a fighting implement, anyhow for an infantry man, seems to have gone the way of the bow and arrow, I think that officers should be armed with some sort of club that could act as a walking-stick as well. A very favourite stick at the Front is the so-called *Canne de St. Omer*. It is a stout ash plant with a good-sized knob at the end, while the grip is bound with leather something after the fashion of a golf club, with the addition of a leather strap to go round the wrist. I believe that they were locally used by pig drovers, but anyhow they make a very useful weapon and could be improved on as to weight, strength and balance without impairing their utility as a walking-stick . . .

'One that particularly took my fancy was a short hunting crop . . . made of strong cane. The handle, which is usually made of horn, was of cast steel, the angle-piece tapering to a point, a truly formidable weapon in the hands of a skilful man . . . a brother officer, who was a very powerful man and sceptical as to the value of the crop as a fighting weapon, offered to bet that he could easily break it with a blow, with the result that he cracked the mess table but not the crop.'

('The Oracle', in *Navy & Army Illustrated*, pp. 61 and 154, 1 & 22 May 1915)

Women's services developed during the war to an unprecedented degree: this handsome young auxiliary appears to wear the cap-badge of the Somerset National Reserve.

the armistice. In 1915 there were 185 horse and 67 motor companies, and six supply units; by 1918 these had increased to 552, 605 and 346 respectively. From 950 motor-trucks and 250 motor-cars in 1914, the service expanded to 33,500 trucks, 13,800 motor-cars and 1,400 tractors by 1918. Railway transport was also vital, and as the French rail service was unable to cope, large numbers of engines and rolling stock were shipped from Britain and run by British administration; by early 1917 there were more than 520 engines and 20,000 wagons serving under War Department control on almost 1,000 miles of British track.

The Royal Army Medical Corps was deployed at all levels from battalion upwards. Each battalion had a medical

Navy

The Royal Navy was Britain's guarantee of communication with the empire and protection of commerce. It was the largest fleet in existence and one of the nation's proudest possessions, and it was thus entirely appropriate that the great innovation of the period, the dreadnought battleship, should have been designed and built by Britain, the most profound of the most beneficial reforms undertaken by Admiral Sir John Fisher, First Sea Lord 1904–10 and who was recalled by Churchill early in the war.

The navy was controlled by the Admiralty's dual heads, the First Lord of the Admiralty (a political appointment) and the First Sea Lord (the senior naval officer). First Lords during the war were: Winston Churchill to May 1915, Arthur Balfour to December 1916, Sir Edward Carson to July 1917 and Sir Eric Geddes thereafter; First Sea Lords were Prince Louis of Battenberg (resigned October 1914 amid allegations of his German ancestry), Sir John Fisher to May 1915, Sir Henry Jackson to December 1916, Sir John Jellicoe to January 1918, and Admiral Rosslyn Wemyss thereafter. They were assisted by a War Staff (titled Naval Staff from May 1917), but not until that year was a truly proficient organizational system insituted. In October 1917 two committees were established, both chaired by the First Lord. The Operations Committee consisted of the First Sea Lord and Chief of Naval Staff (the posts had been merged earlier in the year), the Deputy First Sea Lord (responsible for operations abroad), Deputy and Assistant Chiefs of Naval Staff, and Fifth Sea Lord; the Maintenance Committee comprised the Deputy First Sea Lord, the Second (personnel), Third (material), Fourth (stores and transport) Sea Lords, the Civil Lord, Admiralty Controller and Financial Secretary. The restructuring permitted the First Sea Lord to give his undivided attention to naval policy, free from the burden of administration, and from October 1917 the Chief of Naval Staff was given responsibility of direction of operations, and permission to issue orders in his own name rather than in the name of the Board of Admiralty as before.

The navy had been constructed on the basis of the 'two-power standard', i.e., that Britain's fleet should be the equal of those of any two other nations combined. A comparison prepared in 1910 showed this to be almost the case (in battleships, Britain had 65, the next strongest forces being Germany 41, USA 34, France 23; in armoured cruisers, Britain 41, France 22, USA 15; in protected cruisers, Britain 78, Germany 40, France and Japan 22 each). In order to maintain the 'two-power standard' from 1909 there was an increase in naval expenditure and the beginnings of an imperial naval organization in which the dominions co-operated in a common defence policy.

It was an undoubted disappointment that the one major naval confrontation of the war, Jutland, should end relatively inconclusively, albeit as a British strategic victory; and it might be seen as revealing deficiencies in ship-design, communications, utilization of intelligence (despite a proficient intelligence department, the Admiralty's Room 40) and leadership. Thereafter, the chance of decisive action was thwarted by the unwillingness of the German fleet to engage and the need to protect commerce from the U-boat campaign.

Virtually the entire British fleet was built at home, and repairs were carried out in home or empire bases (the destroyer *Arno* was built by Ansaldo of Genoa, originally for Portuguese service; HMS *Taku*, captured from China in 1900, was built at Elbing, and some submarines were built in Canada and the USA). A singular vessel was the destroyer *Zubian*, patched together from the fore section of HMS *Zulu* and the aft section of HMS *Nubian*, wrecked by mine and torpedo respectively in 1916.

The navy was organized in squadrons of capital ships to form the battle-fleet, of which the battlecruisers formed the reconnaissance element yet capable of engaging the enemy's main body, with lighter cruisers used as a support for the main fleet and to patrol the sea-lanes around the world. The principal capital ships were:

(Ships listed in classes, generally known by the class-name of the first ship listed)

Date	Name displacement (tons)	Main armament only (general for class)
Predreadnought Battleships		
1892	*Revenge* (renamed *Redoubtable* 1915; used as monitor) (14,150)	4 × 12in, 6 × 6in
1895–8	*Majestic* (sunk Dardanelles 1915), *Caesar, Jupiter, Prince George*; the following all disarmed 1915: *Hannibal, Illustrious, Magnificent, Mars* (14,900)	4 × 12in, 12 × 6in
1900–1	*Canopus, Albion, Goliath, Glory, Ocean* (sunk Dardanelles 1915), *Vengeance* (12,950)	4 × 12in, 12 × 6in
1901–2	*Formidable* (sunk Channel 1915), *Implacable, Irresistible* (sunk Dardanelles 1915) (15,000)	4 × 12in, 12 × 6in
1902	*London, Bulwark* (blown up Medway 1914), *Venerable* (15,000)	4 × 12in, 12 × 6in
1903–4	*Duncan, Albemarle, Cornwallis* (sunk Mediterranean 1917), *Exmouth, Russell* (mined Malta 1916) (14,000)	4 × 12in, 12 × 6in
1904	*Queen, Prince of Wales* (15,000)	4 × 12in, 12 × 6in
1904	*Swiftsure* (11,800), *Triumph* (sunk Dardanelles 1915) (11,985) (originally Chilean *Constitucion* and *Libertad* respectively)	4 × 10in, 14 × 7.5in
1905–6	*King Edward* (mined Cape Wrath 1916), *Africa, Britannia* (sunk Trafalgar 1918), *Commonwealth, Dominion, Hibernia, Hindustan, Zealandia* (16,350; *Dominion* 16,500)	4 × 12in, 4 × 9.2in, 10 × 6in
1907–8	*Agamemnon, Lord Nelson*	4 × 12in, 10 × 9.2in
Dreadnought Battleships		
1906	*Dreadnought* (17,900)	10 × 12in
1909	*Bellerophon, Superb, Temeraire* (18,600)	10 × 12in, 16, later 10–11 × 4in
1910	*St. Vincent, Collingwood, Vanguard* (blown up Scapa 1917) (19,250)	10 × 12in, 20, later 12 × 4in

Date	Name displacement (tons)	Main armament only (general for class)
1911	*Neptune* (originally *Foudroyant*) (19,900)	10 × 12in, 20, later 12 × 4in
1911	*Colossus, Hercules* (20,000)	10 × 12in, 12 × 4in
1912	*Orion, Conqueror, Monarch, Thunderer* (22,500)	10 × 13.5in, 16 × 4in
1912–13	*King George V, Ajax, Audacious* (mined Lough Swilly 1914), *Centurion* (23,000)	10 × 13.5in, 12–16 × 4in
1914	*Agincourt* (originally Brazilian *Rio de Janeiro*, then Turkish *Sultan Osman I*) (27,500).	14 × 12in, 20 × 6in
1914	*Iron Duke, Benbow, Emperor of India* (ex-*Delhi*), *Marlborough* (25,000)	10 × 13.5in, 12–14 × 6in
1914	*Erin* (ex-Turkish *Reshadieh*) (23,000)	10 × 13.5in, 16 × 6in
1915	*Canada* (ex-Chilean *Almirante Latorre*) (28,000)	10 × 14in, 14 × 6in
1915–16	*Queen Elizabeth, Barham, Malaya, Valiant, Warspite* (27,500)	8 × 15in, 16, later 12–14 × 6in
1916–17	*Revenge* (ex-*Renown*), *Ramillies, Resolution, Royal Oak, Royal Sovereign* (27,500)	8 × 15in, 14 × 6in

Battlecruisers

1908	*Invincible* (sunk Jutland), *Indomitable, Inflexible* (17,250)	8 × 12in, 16, later 12 × 4in
1911–13	*Indefatigable* (sunk Jutland), *Australia, New Zealand* (18,800–19,200)	8 × 12in, 20 or 16, later 14 or 10 × 4in
1912–13	*Lion, Princess Royal, Queen Mary* (sunk Jutland) (26,350–26,500)	8 × 13.5in, 16 × 4in
1914	*Tiger* (28,500)	8 × 13.5in, 12 × 6in
1916	*Renown, Repulse* (26,500)	6 × 15in, 17 × 4in

Light Battlecruisers (designed with shallower draught for Baltic, but actually employed as aircraft carriers)

1916	*Glorious, Courageous* (18,600)	4 × 15in, 18 × 4in
1917	*Furious* (19,100) (only one 18in gun mounted; converted to aircraft carrier 1918)	2 × 18in, 10 × 5.5in

Cruisers (9,000 tons or more only listed)

1898–1900	*Diadem, Amphitrite* (converted to minelayer 1917, 4 × 6in), *Argonaut, Ariadne* (converted to minelayer 1917, 4 × 6in, 1 × 4in, torpedoed Beachy Head 1917), *Europa, Niobe* (transferred to Canada 1910) (11,000)	16 × 6in
1901–3	*Cressy, Aboukir, Hogue* (all sunk by *U 9* 1914, *Bacchante, Euryalus, Sutlej* (12,000)	2 × 9.2in, 12 × 6in
1902–3	*Drake* (sunk Rathlin Sound 1917), *Good Hope* (ex-*Africa*, sunk Coronel), *King Alfred, Leviathan* (14,100)	2 × 9.2in, 16 × 6in
1903–4	*Monmouth* (sunk Coronel), *Berwick, Cornwall, Cumberland, Donegal, Essex, Kent, Lancaster, Suffolk* (9,800)	14 × 6in
1904–5	*Devonshire, Antrim, Argyll* (wrecked Bell Rock 1915), *Carnarvon, Hampshire* (mined Orkneys 1916 with Kitchener aboard), *Roxburgh* (10,850)	4 × 7.5in, 6 × 6in
1906	*Duke of Edinburgh, Black Prince* (sunk Jutland) (13,550)	6 × 9.2in, 10 × 6in
1907	*Warrior* (sunk Jutland), *Achilles, Cochrane* (wrecked Mersey 1918), *Natal* (blown up Cromarty 1915) (13,550)	6 × 9.2in, 4 × 7.5in
1908	*Minotaur, Defence* (sunk Jutland), *Shannon* (14,600)	4 × 9.2in, 10 × 7.5in

The deployment of cruisers in 1914 and 1918 exemplifies the move away from heavy cruisers and the increasing significance of light cruisers. There were eleven numbered cruiser squadrons plus those on overseas duty: 1st Squadron (Mediterranean, four ships plus four light cruisers); 2nd, 3rd, 6th (Grand Fleet, four each); 4th (North America/Caribbean, five plus two French); 5th (Atlantic, four); 7th (North Sea, five); no 8th Squadron; 9th (Atlantic, Gibraltar, six); 10th (Northern Patrol, seven); 11th (West Ireland Coast Patrol, five); 12th (Western Channel Patrol, four); Cape of Good Hope three; China four; East Indies three; Australia four; New Zealand three; Canada, Pacific, SE coast of S. America one each; 29 others attached to other formations. The first three light cruiser squadrons were formed by early 1915, and by 1918 only the 2nd Cruiser Squadron (Grand Fleet) was still in being, the other eight squadrons being light cruisers, between four and six ships each, the 5th Light Cruiser Squadron (twelve ships) at Harwich, the 8th in the Adriatic and the rest with the Grand Fleet.

Destroyers evolved from the early 'torpedo-boat destroyers' to much larger, swifter and more powerfully-armed 'ocean-going' vessels. Those existing during the war included some 112 under 600 tons (Classes A–E, 1893–1909, the most powerfully armed E Class with 4 × 12pdrs); 71 750–900 tons (classes F–I, 1907–12, the most powerfully armed I Class with 2 × 4in, 2 × 12pdrs); and 249 935–1,100 tons (classes K–M, R and S, all with 3 × 4in guns, 1912–18). Destroyers were organized in flotillas of varying numbers of ships (up to 20 or more), of which there were

HMS Bulwark, *a representative of the pre-dreadnought battleships; 15,000 tons, 4 × 12in, 12 × 6in, 18 × 12pdr guns, 4 × 18in torpedo tubes.* Bulwark *was accidentally blown up in the Medway on 26 November 1914, with only fourteen survivors.*

HMS Cornwallis *fires a final broadside after the evacuation from the Dardanelles; abandoned stores are burning in the background. A pre-dreadnought battleship (14,000 tons, 4 × 12in, 12 × 6in, 12 × 12pdr guns), she was sunk by* U 32 *in the Mediterranean, 9 January 1917.*

The British perception of the submarine may be deduced from the title of an article in Navy & Army Illustrated *in 1915: 'Assassins of the Seas'. This is*

D2, built by Vickers in 1910 and sunk by a German patrol-boat off Wester Eems on 25 November 1914.

nine numbered flotillas in 1914, rising to sixteen in 1916, based in home waters, with a smaller number on foreign stations. As flotilla-leaders light cruisers could be used, or purpose-built 'leaders', up to 2,000 tons; there were some 84 of these, including four each of the Botha and Talisman Classes (built originally for Chile and Turkey respectively), thirteen Marksman Class and 51 V and W classes; most were armed with 4in guns, but HMS *Swift* (1907, 1,825 tons) ultimately had a 6in gun as well as 2 × 4in.

Submarines were a comparatively recent development, under the aegis of Fisher and in the face of some hostility from those who regarded the submarine as representing an underhand and un-English method of waging war. The size of boat increased from A Class, 1903–4, 165 tons displacement, to K Class, 1917–18, 1,880 tons; G and J Classes were the first ocean-going boats, K Class were 'fleet submarines' designed to accompany the battle-fleet, M Class mounted a 12in gun which permitted them to be used for bombardment, and R Class, completed only in 1918, were designed as U-boat hunters.

Other vessels included seaplane-carriers (generally converted from merchant vessels), monitors (heavily armed vessels used for coastal bombardment), merchant cruisers (converted merchant ships) and Q-ships, decoys designed to destroy U-boats on the surface.

Royal Naval Division

Upon the mobilization of naval reservists in 1914, it was discovered that 20,000–30,000 more men could be assembled than there were places aboard ship, so a Naval

Perhaps the most famous military communication of the war:

'To All Ranks of the British Forces in France.

'Three weeks ago to-day the enemy began his terrific attacks upon as on a fifty-mile front. His objects are to separate us from the French, to take the Channel Ports, and destroy the British Army.

'In spite of throwing already 106 divisions into battle, and enduring the most reckless sacrifice of human life, he has as yet made little progress towards his goals.

'We owe this to the determined fighting and self-sacrifice of our troops. Words fail me to express the admiration which I feel for the splendid resistance offered by all ranks of our army under most trying circumstances.

'Many among us now are tired. To those I would say that victory will belong to the side which holds out the longest. The French Army is moving rapidly and in great force to our support.

'There is no other course open to us but to fight it out! Every position must be held to the last man: there must be no retirement. With our backs to the wall, and believing in the justice of our cause, each one of us must fight on to the end. The safety of our homes and the freedom of mankind alike depend on the conduct of each one of us at this critical moment.

D. Haig
Field Marshal.'
(Order of the Day, 11 April 1918).
(Brigadier General John Charteris, in *At GHQ,* London 1931, remarked that he thought this order unwise: if as in 1914, the French never came, it would raise false hopes; it would hearten the enemy; and in any event, he believed that the British Army needed no such exhortation.)

Division was created for service on land, as had occurred in previous wars. Initially it comprised twelve numbered battalions, 1st–8th of Royal Navy personnel and named after admirals (Drake, Hawke, Benbow, Collingwood, Nelson, Howe, Hood and Anson respectively), and 9th–12th of Royal Marines, named after marine bases (Chatham, Portsmouth, Plymouth, Deal). Numbers were soon discarded and brigading varied; in April 1916 the division was transferred from Admiralty to War Office control, and on 19 July was numbered as 63rd Division (the earlier 63rd, 2nd Northumberland Territorial Division, was dispersed in the same month); brigades (hitherto 1st–3rd Naval) were numbered 188th–190th, although 190th was an army formation. Composition in July 1916 was:

188 Brigade: Howe, Anson, 1st and 2nd RM Battalions
189 Brigade: Drake, Hawke, Nelson, Hood Battalions
190 Brigade: 7/Royal Fusiliers, 4/Bedfordshire Regiment, 10/Royal Dublin Fusiliers, 1/1 Honourable Artillery Company.

When first deployed (at Antwerp in 1914) the Naval Division wore naval uniform, but received khaki shortly after, which was worn at Gallipoli and on the Western Front. They retained naval caps with woven name-ribbons for some time, but when taken under army command adopted the army cap, with distinctive battalion-badges (less Battalions Benbow and Collingwood, which had been disbanded before that date).

Aviation service

The Royal Flying Corps was created in May 1912 from the Air Battalion, Royal Engineers, which had been formed as a kite-balloon unit. Until July 1914, naval aviators formed part of the corps, until they were separated by the formation of the Royal Naval Air Service. From January 1914 the service was organized in squadrons of three flights of four aircraft each, plus three reserve aircraft. Upon the outbreak

Allied 'dazzle' camouflage was designed as a method of breaking-up the silhouette of a ship: by interfering with the laws of perspective it became difficult to determine even the course of a ship. Primarily intended to deceive submarines, it was applied to some 4,000 merchant vessels and 400 convoy escorts, and was included in the British Defence of the Realm Act to ensure that the entire merchant fleet was thus painted. That illustrated is one of a number of variations, in three colours, light-grey, black (solid colour above) and medium blue-grey (shaded). The stern (left) and bow (right) are shown below.

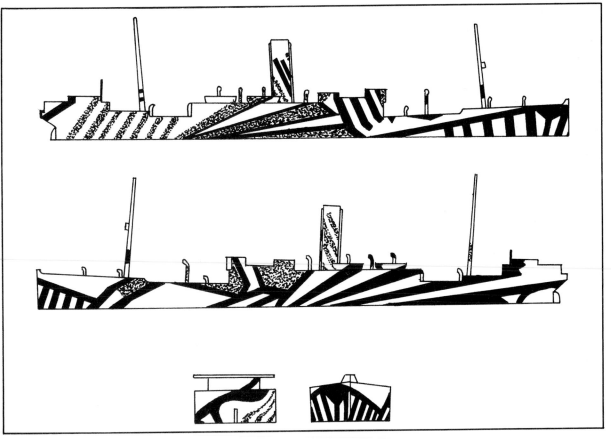

of war, all available RFC machines (four squadrons) were sent to France, under control of army headquarters; in November 1914 'Wings' of two squadrons were formed, 1st Wing to operate with First Army, 2nd with Second Army; 3rd Wing was created in March 1915 and each wing was enlarged to three squadrons. Twelve squadrons were deployed by October 1915, 27 by the following July; in August 1915 it was decided to organize brigades of two wings each, one for artillery-spotting and divisional reconnaissance, and one for bombing, patrols and reconnaissance at corps or army level. Squadrons originally included a number of scout or fighter aircraft in addition to the usual two-seaters, but from early 1916 squadrons were equipped for specific tasks; strength was increased to eighteen machines per squadron, and some fighter squadrons were later increased to 24.

The number of squadrons increased as the war progressed; 200 training squadrons were projected in June 1917, and in February 1918 it was estimated that 240 active squadrons would be required. In November 1917 179 were projected for the Western Front and Italy, composed as follows: 40 squadrons of single-seater fighters; 21 for 'corps' duties (artillery-spotting, etc.); 20 for bombing; fifteen each of single-seater ground-attack and two-seater fighter-reconnaissance, and one each of two-seaters for long-distance reconnaissance and long-distance attack (carrying cannon or quick-firing gun); in addition, a strategic bombing force of 25 squadrons of daylight and 20 of night bombers, 20 of long-distance two- or three-seater fighters, and one long-distance attack squadron with quick-firing guns.

The Royal Naval Air Service did much more than its initial North Sea patrolling; until February 1916 it was responsible for the air defence of Britain (which was then transferred to the RFC), and was the pioneer of strategic bombing (the first raid on German territory, six weeks into the war, was mounted by the RNAS against the Zeppelin hangers at Düsseldorf). In addition, the RNAS continued its naval patrols from coastal air stations (some 126 by 1918) and from ships, reconnaissance aircraft flying from ordinary warships and ultimately vessels converted to aircraft carriers.

The RFC and RNAS were merged on 1 April 1918 to form the Royal Air Force, 188 squadrons strong at the armistice. The expansion of the service owed a great debt to Hugh Trenchard, commander of the RFC in France from August 1915, and selected as first RAF chief of staff (January 1918); but he came into conflict with his political masters and resigned shortly before the RAF actually came into existence. He returned to France to command the Independent Air Force, nine squadrons of strategic bombers

A new development in naval warfare was the aircraft carrier: HMS Furious *was a light battle cruiser converted to a carrier in which role she was completed in March 1918, and launched a successful anti-Zeppelin raid on Tondern in July. Note the dazzle camouflage.*

which carried out more than 500 raids on long-range targets before the end of the war. While fulfilling a crucial role in the war, the British aviation services suffered immense losses; at times the casualty-rate was truly appalling, as in 'black week' of 'bloody April' 1917, when the life-expectancy of a pilot was measured in a very few weeks.

The RFC wore a singular uniform in khaki, including a plastroned lancer-jacket (known as a 'maternity jacket') and side-cap, although officers attached to the RFC mostly continued to wear the uniform of their original unit, sometimes with RFC insignia added; RNAS personnel wore naval uniform. A grey-blue uniform was introduced for the RAF, but the khaki was ordered to be worn on active service, albeit with new rank-markings for officers, one to four rings of khaki lace with sky-blue stripe around the cuff, below a gilt eagle; or, for 2nd lieutenants, a crown above an eagle on the cuff.

Britain's aircraft industry expanded greatly during the war; among the British-produced aircraft in service were:

Airco (De Havilland): DH1/1A was a two-seater pusher reconnaissance biplane employed in small numbers from 1916, as trainers and in combat in the Middle East. DH2 was single-seater pusher fighter, 1916–17; equipped the first fighter squadron (No. 24) and was considerably successful until the new generation of Albatroses and Halberstadts caused it to be relegated to a training role. DH4 was a very effective and prolific two-seater biplane bomber and reconnaissance aircraft, in service from 1917 with RFC and RNAS. DH5 was a single-seater tractor biplane designed to replace the DH2, in service from spring 1917; performed poorly at altitude and most successful as light bomber/ground attack; withdrawn January 1918. DH6 was a prolific two-seater biplane trainer used 1917; flown as a single-seater with a bomb-load from early 1918 by RNAS and US Navy for coastal protection duties around Britain. The DH9 was a two-seater long-range biplane bomber introduced 1918 to replace the DH4, but was a poor substitute, with restricted ceiling and erratic engine (its failings became apparent in July 1918 when 99 Squadron was decimated in a raid on Mainz, seven out of twelve machines being shot down and three falling from engine faults). The DH9A was a much improved version, but saw only limited service before the armistice, with only four squadrons (18, 99, 110 and 205).

Armstrong–Whitworth: the FK3 (from the Dutch designer, Frederick Koolhoven) was a two-seater light bomber and reconnaissance biplane, introduced in autumn 1916 as a trainer, and for combat use in Macedonia only. The FK8 was an improved version, entering combat service in January 1918, flown by five Western Front squadrons (2, 8, 10, 35, 82), 17 and 47 in Macedonia and 142 in Palestine. The FK3 and FK8 were nicknamed 'Little Ack' and 'Big Ack' respectively.

Avro 504: two-seater trainer and reconnaissance biplane in service at the beginning of the war, but by mid-1915 relegated to training; RNAS used it as a light bomber.

A typical routine from a trench diary:
'23 Sept. 1915. Very wet day. I bombarded Huns' wire. Other platoons of 'B' Company went into trenches. Very wet!
24 Sept. Bombarded Huns. Brought my platoon & No. 7 into trenches. Very muddy & wet!
25 Sept. Very wet night. Bombarded wire "8/62".
26 Sept. Patrol from 5th Glos. went out 1 a.m. One officer & 1 Cpl. killed. Very wet night! Very tired.
27 Sept. 7 p.m. "Wind up" opposite "Buck". Huns shout: "Come on, Gloucesters, the Royal Berks led the attack!" Spy reported caught in village, dressed as English officer. Cold night but fine.
28 Sept. Awful night & very dank. German in front of our wire! Huns "wind up" at 4.20 a.m.
29 Sept. Relieved & came to Souastre. Nice billet.
30 Sept. Delightful sleep in bed – the 1st I've seen since I left England. Had bath!
11 Oct. Back to trenches. I rode "bike" up to Hebuterne – awful thing! Slept at "Poste Cambron" [*sic*].
12 Oct. Day's rest on Keep. Saw 18 aeroplanes bomb Achiet-le-Grand station!
13 Oct. Relieved in trenches. Wet – in support trench "Biron".
14 Oct. Up in fire trench. Collins (10th R. Irish Rifles) with me. Rats & mice in dug-out; crawled over me!
16 Oct. Working party in afternoon. London Territorial RFA to tea & lunch, I had lunch early tho'. Lilian sent me a lavender bag.
19 Oct. Awful bombardment. 450 shells but 59 duds on us, on left corner of trench.
20 Oct. Left trenches. Saw German – missed him but Hesketh Pritchard & snipers had him. New billet – dirty!'
(Lieutenant Charles Sharpe, 1/4th Royal Berkshire Regiment)

Beardmore WBIII: a Sopwith Pup (q.v.) amended for aircraft-carrier use, with folding wings and undercarriage, hence nickname 'Folding Pup'.

Blackburn Kangaroo: twin-engined biplane heavy bomber developed from the 1916 GP and SP seaplanes; very limited use as maritime patrol aircraft from spring 1918.

Bristol: F2A and B: splendid, two-seater fighter/reconnaissance biplane, one of the best aircraft of its type of any nationality, ordered for all fighter/reconnaissance squadrons in July 1917. M1C was a single-seater monoplane fighter produced in small numbers, used in Macedonia and Mesopotamia from late 1917, and as a trainer in Egypt. Bristol Scout was a single-seater biplane reconnaissance/fighter, existing in B, C and D marks, initially unarmed; used 1914–16, and by RNAS on coastal and anti-Zeppelin duty. TB8 was a two-seater reconnaissance and light bomber operated by RNAS 1914–15.

Felixstowe: F2A was a twin-engined heavy flying-boat, four crew, used 1917–18 in anti-submarine and anti-Zeppelin duty from coastal stations; a superb aircraft with long-range capability. The F3 had double the bomb-carrying capacity.

Handley-Page: the 0/100 was a twin-engined, heavy biplane night bomber, four crew, flown by RFC and RNAS from late 1916. The 0/400 was a more widely produced and more powerful version, the leading strategic bomber, carrying the 1,650lb bomb, the largest in general use.

Martinsyde: the SI was a single-seater civilian biplane produced by Martin and Handasyde, transformed into a military reconnaissance role in 1914, and withdrawn from all but training in autumn 1915. The G100 was a single-seater biplane fighter used early 1916–late 1917, generally as long-range escort and mostly distributed among the two-seater squadrons; heaviness led to the nickname 'the Elephant' and restricted manoeuvrability so that it was largely transferred to reconnaissance/light bomber role; the later G102 had an increased bomb-capacity. The F4

The Royal Flying Corps uniform included two singular items: a double-breasted tunic (nicknamed 'Maternity Jacket') *with concealed buttons, and a side-cap, both khaki, worn here by flight-sergeant W. H. Duckworth.*

'Buzzard' fighter was one of the fastest British aircraft, but was developed too late in 1918 for use in action.

Norman Thompson: maritime aircraft used in small numbers: the NT2B was a two-seater biplane flying-boat trainer used by RNAS 1917–18; the NT4 was a four-seater light bomber/trainer twin-engined pusher biplane, used by RNAS on coastal patrol duty from 1915, the NT4A with uprated engine.

Royal Aircraft Factory: the BE2 series were two-seater biplanes designed by De Havilland; BE2, 2a and 2b were unarmed reconnaissance aircraft used 1914–15; 2c and 2d (1915–17) and 2e (introduced mid-1916) were long-range, armed, and used for reconnaissance and light bombing, considerably inferior to the Fokker monoplane, Albatros and Halberstadt, and suffered accordingly. The BE8 (1914–15 as reconnaissance and light bomber, then a trainer) was unarmed and saw much less service, its fish-like configuration leading to the nickname 'the Bloater'. The BE12 was a single-seater fighter version of the 2c, used from mid-1915, but its slowness made it unsuitable as a fighter and it was used as a light bomber instead. The FE series ('Fighting Experimental') were two-seater pusher reconnaissance/fighter biplanes, the FE2b a development from the earlier 2a, used from 1916; the FE2d had an improved engine, but both were inferior to the German machines and were converted to a night-bombing role for the rest of the war, though a single-seater version was used for home defence. The BE8 was the last pusher fighter, autumn 1916–mid-1917, but was slow and withdrawn when proven inferior to German machines. The RE series were two-seater reconnaissance and light bomber biplanes; only two RE1s went into service (1914) and only 24 RE5s were built (1915), both unarmed. The RE7 was a light bomber (armed), 1915–16; the RE8 (from 1916) was the most widely-used British two-seater, designed to replace the BE2 series. Unstable and initially unpopular, it was nicknamed 'Harry Tate' (a popular comedian), from the similarity with the number 'RE8' (RE indicated 'Reconnaissance Experimental'). The SE5 and 5a was one of the most famous and successful fighters of the war, a fast, stable and sturdy single-seater biplane with light bomber capacity, in service 1917–18 when it helped restored Allied air superiority.

Short: two-seater biplane seaplanes. The 184, used from 1914, was the first aircraft designed to carry a torpedo, and at the Dardanelles became the first aircraft to sink a ship with an air-launched torpedo. The 827 and 830 were reconnaissance/light bomber seaplanes, the former far more prolific, used by RNAS 1915–18; the 320 was the last wartime seaplane, designed to carry a 1,000lb torpedo but also used to carry anti-submarine bombs. The Short Bomber was a heavy bomber version of the 184, used by RNAS (and on loan to RFC) 1915–17, a large machine with four-wheel undercarriage and a bomb-load increased from 400 to 900 pounds.

Sopwith: the Tabloid was the first of the single-seater Sopwith reconnaissance/light bomber biplanes, used in

A powerful British recruiting-poster designed by Bernard Partridge.

A card dedicated to Lloyd George as Minister of Munitions in the wake of the 'shell scandal': 'We shall shell!' says the Shell Mascot, and crossing his fingers for luck, settles down to it and SHELLS.

small numbers by RFC and RNAS until mid-1915; initially unarmed. The Sopwith 1½-Strutter was the first British two-seater biplane fighter used by RNAS from 1916 and RFC in smaller numbers 1916–17, also used as light bomber (single-seater version permitted an increased bomb-load). It was the first British aircraft to use a synchronized Vickers in action, and the first two-seater to operate from an aircraft-carrier; outmatched in combat, it was withdrawn from the Western Front in 1917, and although 1,520 were used by Britain, no less than 4,200 were used by France. The Sopwith B1 bomber was a development, but although one machine saw action it was not put into production. The Sopwith Baby was a single-seater biplane light bomber seaplane, developed from the Sopwith Schneider, used by RNAS from 1916; based at coastal stations and on seaplane carriers. The Sopwith Camel (F1) was probably the most celebrated British aircraft of the war, a single-seater biplane fighter used from spring 1917, ultimately representing about

40 per cent of the British fighter strength on the Western Front. A superb fighting machine, it was sufficiently versatile to be used as a light ground-attack bomber, night-fighter and in a maritime version for use from ships. The Cuckoo was a two-seater torpedo biplane similar to the abortive B1, intended to operate from carriers, but was developed too late for combat service. The Dolphin was a single-seat biplane fighter/ground-attack light bomber used in limited service from late 1917. The Sopwith Pup was a splendid single-seat biplane fighter also used by RNAS from carriers and on home-defence duties, styled 'Pup' because it looked like a smaller version of the 1½-Strutter. The Snipe (TF1) was a single-seater biplane fighter designed to replace the Camel, but saw only limited service in late 1918; the Salamander (TF2) was a version developed for ground-attack ('TF' indicated 'Trench Fighter'), with armoured fuselage as protection against AA fire, but it entered service too late in 1918 to be used. The Sopwith Triplane was a

single-seater fighter used by the RNAS in 1917 in comparatively small numbers, despite excellent features, especially in rate of climb.

Vickers: the FB5 'Gunbus' was a two-seater pusher reconnaissance/fighter/light bomber biplane used until early 1916, a useful aircraft until outmatched by improved German machines. The FB9 was an improved version which became obsolete at the same time. The FB19 was a mediocre single-seater biplane fighter used in small numbers from late 1916, principally in the Middle East where opposition was limited.

Wight: two-seater biplane seaplane used in small numbers on anti-submarine duty by RNAS.

In addition to home-produced aircraft, Britain used a variety of foreign machines, including the Bleriot XI, Breguet 2/4/5, Caudron G3/4, Curtis H4/12/16/JN, Farman F40, HF20, MF7/11, Morane–Saulnier BB/N/L/P, Nieuport 10–12/16/17/23/24, and Spad VII. (The Morane–Saulnier BB was French-manufactured but not used by France: two-seater reconnaissance biplane used in small numbers 1915–17.)

The traditional humour of the British serviceman is evident in this Christmas card of the Royal Naval Division from the Western Front: a duck-board raft in a flooded trench.

Footnotes

1. *Moments of Memory: Recollections and Impressions*, H. Asquith, London, 1937, p. 347.
2. *With a B–P Scout in Gallipoli.* E. Y. Priestman, London 1916, p. 174.
3. *See: Songs and Music of the Redcoats.* L. Winstock, London, 1970, p. 230.
4. *Old Soldiers Never Die*, F. Richards, London 1933, p. 12.
5. Although of 235 killed on 1–5 July 1916, apparently only 64, plus five died of wounds, came from Accrington itself: see *Pals: The 11th (Service) Battalion (Accrington) East Lancashire Regiment*, W. Turner, Barnsley, n.d.
6. Quoted in *With the 29th Division in Gallipoli*, Revd. O. Creighton, London 1916, p. 46.
7. *G.H.Q.*, 'GSO', London 1920, p. 45.
8. Ibid., pp. 42–3.

References

Anon. *Statistics of the Military Effort of the British Empire*. London, 1922
Ascoli, D. *Mons Star: the British Expeditionary Force 1914*. London, 1981
Babington, A. *For the Sake of Example: Capital Courts-Martial 1914–18*. London, 1983
Barnes, R. M. *The British Army of 1914*. London, 1968
Baynes, J. C. M. *Morale: A Study of Men and Courage* (*2nd Scottish Rifles at the Battle of Neuve Chapelle, 1915*), London, 1967
Becke, Major A. F. *Order of Battle of Divisions*. London, 1934–45 (rep. Nottingham 1987 Newport 1988–90)
Beckett, I. F. W., and Simpson, K. (eds.). *A Nation in Arms: A Social Study of the British Army in the First World War*. Manchester, 1985
Beaverbrook, Lord. *Politicians and the War 1914–1916*. London, 1928–32
— *Men and Power 1917–1918*. London, 1956
Brown, M. *Tommy Goes to War*. London, 1978
Bruce, J. M. *Aeroplanes of the Royal Flying Corps*. London, 1982
Burt, R. A. *British Battleships of World War I*. London, 1986
Carew, T. *The Vanished Army*. London, 1964 (BEF 1914)
Carr, W. G. *By Guess and by God: the Story of British Submarines in the War*. London, 1930
Caulfield, M. *The Easter Rebellion*. London, 1964
Chappell, M. *British Battle Insignia (I): 1914–18*. London, 1986
— *British Soldier in the 20th Century*: series, Hatherleigh, from 1987.
Corbett–Smith, Major A. *The Retreat from Mons*. London, 1916
Craster, J. M. *Fifteen Rounds a Minute: the Grenadiers at War*. London, 1976 (August– December 1914 from diaries of Grenadier Guards officers)
Crutwell, C. R. M. F. *The Role of British Strategy in the Great War*. Cambridge, 1936
Duff, C. *Six Days to Shake an Empire*. London, 1966 (the 'Easter Rising', 1916)
Dunn, Captain J. C. (ed.). *The War the Infantry Knew*. privately published, 1938; rep. with intro. by K. Simpson, London 1987
Fletcher, D. *Landships: British Tanks in the First World War*. London, 1984
Fletcher, D. *War Cars: British Armoured Cars in the First World War*. London, 1987
Fosten, D. S. V., and Marrion, R. J. *The British Army 1914–18*. London, 1978
Foster, A. E. Manning. *The National Guard in the Great War 1914–18*. London, 1920
Gibson, Major E., and Ward, G. K. *Courage Remembered*. London, 1989 (Commonwealth military cemeteries)
'GSO' (Sir Frank Fox). *GHQ*. London, 1920
Guinn, P. *British Strategy and Politics 1914–1918*. Oxford, 1965
Hamilton, E. W. *The First Seven Divisions*. London, 1916
Hankey, Lord. *The Supreme Command 1914–1918*. London, 1961
Hogg, I. *British Artillery Weapons and Ammunition 1914–18*. London, 1972
James, Brig. E. A. *British Regiments 1914–1918*. London, 1978 (combined edn: orig. pub. 1969, 1974)
James, Captain E. A. (later Brigadier). *A Record of the Battles and Engagements of the British Armies in France and Flanders 1914–18*. Aldershot, 1924 (rep. with intro. by T. Cave, London, 1990: names battles according to schedule of Battles Nomenclature Committee, 1921)

Jellicoe, Earl. *The Grand Fleet 1914–1916: Its Creation, Development, and Work*. London, 1919

Jones, T. *Lloyd George*. Oxford, 1951

Jenkins, R. *Asquith*. London, 1964

Keyes, Admiral Sir Roger. *Naval Memoirs of Admiral of the Fleet Sir Roger Keyes*. London, 1934–5 (chief of staff, Dardanelles, and commander of the Dover Patrol)

Liddle, P. H. (ed.). *Home Fires and Foreign Fields: British Social and Military Experience in the First World War*. London, 1985

Lloyd George, D. *War Memoirs*. London, 1933–6

Macdonald, L. *The Roses of No Man's Land*. London, 1980 (nurses, Western Front)

Macmillan, Captain N. *The Royal Air Force in the Great War*. London, 1950

Marder, A. J. *From the Dreadnought to Scapa Flow: the Royal Navy in the Fisher Era 1904–1919*. Oxford, 1964–70

Marwick, A. *The Deluge: British Society and the First World War*. London, 1965

— *Women at War 1914–1918*. London 1977

Norris, G. *The Royal Flying Corps: A History*. London, 1965

Occleshaw, M. *Armour against Fate: British Military Intelligence in the First World War*. London, 1989

Rimell, R. L. *The Royal Flying Corps in World War One*. London, 1985

Roberts, Lieutenant-Colonel F. J. (ed.) *The Wipers Times* (reprint of the immortal trench newspaper: first rep, London, 1918, included only issues up to 10 April 1917; complete edn. with same title, London, 1930)

Robertson, F. M. Sir William. *Soldiers and Statesmen*. London, 1926 (Robertson's period as chief of Imperial General Staff)

Simkins, P. *Kitchener's Army: the Raising of the New Armies 1914–16*. London, 1988

Simpson, K. *The Old Contemptibles*. London, 1981

Spears, Major-General Sir Edward. *Liaison 1914: A Narrative of the Great Retreat*. London, 1930 (further reminiscences of this period appear in *The Picnic Basket*, London, 1967)

Travers, T. H. E. *The Killing Ground: the British Army and the Western Front, and the Emergence of Modern Warfare 1900–1918*. London, 1987

Treves, Sir Frederick, Bt., and Goodchild, G. (eds.). *Made in the Trenches*. London, 1916 (anthology of contributions from those on active service)

Westlake, R. *Kitchener's Army*. Tunbridge Wells, 1989

— *The Territorial Force, 1914*. Newport, 1988

Williams, B. *Raising and Training the New Armies*. London, 1918

Winter, J. M. *The Great War and the British People*. London, 1986

Woodward, D. *Lloyd George and the Generals*. London, 1983

Woodward, Sir Llewellyn. *Great Britain and the War of 1914–1918*. London, 1967

(See also references listed under individual biographies).

Much of the anecdotal material emanating from the war is of dubious provenance, with the same stories being attributed to different events. The following was recounted in 1931 (*Humour in the Army*, J. Aye, p. 158) where it was attributed to the great retreat during Ludendorff's offensive of spring 1918, although this author heard it attributed to the civil disturbances during the British miners' strike of 1984:

Unnerved by the battle, a soldier makes off towards the rear as fast as possible. After some time he is stopped by an officer who asks why he's running away; the soldier tells the officer to mind his own business. The officer replies, 'Do you know who you're talking to? I'm your general!'

'Good Lord,' says the soldier, 'I didn't know I'd run that far!'

GREECE

Greece was a constitutional monarchy (whose sovereign was styled 'King of the Hellenes'), legislative power being shared by the king and a chamber of deputies, elected by male suffrage every four years. Executive power resided with the king, who governed through ministers of his choice but responsible to the chamber of deputies. Political parties were largely based upon the followings of individuals, patronage being a cause of the instability of successive governments, although a law of 1906 which disqualified junior officers from standing for election had eroded the influence of the military in politics.

After the expulsion of King Otto in 1862 the national assembly requested Britain to nominate a successor, who was Prince Christian of Schleswig–Holstein–Sonderburg–Glücksburg (1845–1913), who assumed the title of King George I and married grand duchess Olga Constantinova of Russia; their eldest son, Constantine, Duke of Sparta (1868–1923) succeeded as King Constantine I when George

King Constantine I of Greece (1868–1923).

I was shot to death on 18 March 1913 at Salonika by Alexander Schinas (whose motives were obscure: Bulgarian, Austrian and German intrigues were suspected but unproven). Constantine had graduated from the Berlin military academy, and his admiration for Germany was reinforced by being the Kaiser's brother-in-law, having married Princess Sophia of Prussia. His military career was inauspicious: he led the Greek army to humiliation in the Greco–Turkish War of 1897. In August 1909 a military revolt removed him from his nominal post of commander-in-chief and forced him into a brief exile, from which he returned only after the assumption of political power by Eleutherios Venizelos (1864–1936).

Eleutherios Venizelos (1864–1936).

Venizelos was Cretan-born, and after legal training in Greece espoused the cause of Greek irredentism, the belief that all ethnic Greeks should be united. Following the independence of Crete from Turkish rule (1898, in which he played a considerable part), he became prime minister of Crete and in 1909 gave political advice to the Military League at Athens which executed the bloodless *coup* against Constantine. Enjoying both Greek and Cretan citizenship, Venizelos convinced both the League and the king of the necessity of a revision of the Greek government and constitution, and became prime minister in October 1910 after victory in the election. He revised the constitution, overhauled the Greek armed forces with the aid of British naval and French military missions, and was instrumental in the formation of the Balkan League, which defeated Turkey in the First Balkan War; from this and the Second, against Bulgaria, Greece doubled her territory. The uneasy relationship between king and prime minister, however, had a considerable effect upon Greece's attitude to the World War, and compounded internal divisions, resulting in conflict between the liberal Venezelist faction and the reactionary royalist faction, backed by the military high command.

At the outbreak of the World War King Constantine was probably inclined towards neutrality despite his German sympathies; Venizelos was convinced from the outset that Greece should join the Entente. On 4 August 1914 Germany invited Greece to join the Central Powers; Constantine declined, and on 23 August Venizelos announced that although Greece's place was with the Allies, military considerations made it impossible for her to participate unless Turkey became involved. Against Venizelos' protests, Constantine declared that Greece's neutrality would end only in the event of Turkish attack.

In early 1915, Venizelos acceded to an Allied request for Greek help in bolstering Serbia and in the planned attack on the Dardanelles; Constantine refused to comply, and demanded Venizelos' resignation (6 March). A pro-royalist administration was formed by Dimitrios Gounaris; but in June Venizelos won an electoral victory on an interventionist platform. Not until August was he asked to form a government, by which time a new crisis had arisen in the preparations for a Bulgarian attack upon Serbia. According to the 1913 Greco–Serbian treaty, in such an event Greece was bound to assist Serbia, which Venizelos confirmed; Constantine remonstrated so forcibly that Venizelos resigned. The king assumed political leadership behind a succession of virtual nonentities as prime minister (notably Skouloudis and Zaimes), but was unable to prevent the Anglo–French landing at Salonika to which Venizelos had acceded as a support for Serbia. In protest at the king's behaviour Venizelos requested his party not to participate in the election called for December, and a pro-German assembly resulted. The government was in almost open support of the Central Powers (Bulgarian forces were unopposed when they seized the strategic positions at Fort

Rupel and Kavalla in May and August respectively, in which the Greek IV Corps – 5th and 7th Divisions – surrendered without resistance), and with paramilitary associations of army reservists being formed to support either the royalists or Venizelists, virtual civil war resulted. On 1 September a revolutionary 'Committee of National Defence' was established at Salonika, which was absorbed by a provisional government established by Venizelos. Aided by two influential military figures, General Dankles and Admiral Kountouriotes, Venizelos' government announced the formation of an Army of National Defence to assist the Allies, to which Venizelist volunteers flocked. This included some Greek regulars (although most officers remained loyal to the king) and some conscripts: one of Venizelos' supporters, Captain Kondylis, collected recruits by burning the houses of those who resisted impressment, which caused some resentment against the Venizelists in the post-war period!

On 19 November 1916 the Allied commander in Macedonia, General Sarrail, had the representatives of the Central Powers expelled from Athens by the Allied fleet which stood off the city. On 24 November the Allies demanded the surrender of some Greek artillery, and believing Constantine to have consented to this, landed French, British and Italian marines on 1 December; they were attacked by Greek troops, and royalists and members of the 'Reservist Leagues' took the opportunity to harass known Venizelists under the pretext of a plot to dethrone the king. The Allies demanded reparations, and although the Greek government accepted their terms on 16 January 1917, an Allied blockade was maintained. The Allies regarded Constantine as implicated in the 'battle of Athens', and the fall from power of the French premier Briand left the king friendless. By this time he was in no sense neutral, in regular communication with the Central Powers and in a message to the Kaiser prayed that Germany have a glorious victory. Accordingly, on 11 June the Greek government was presented with an Allied demand for Constantine's abdication. On the following day Constantine left for Switzerland; as the Crown Prince Paul was equally unacceptable to the Allies for his pro-German sympathies, Constantine named his second son, Alexander (1893–1920) as his successor. The pro-Entente camp seems not to have resented such interference in Greek affairs: Venizelos had compared the actions of the 'Protecting Powers' of Greece – France, Britain and Russia – to parents reclaiming a son's birthright; and despite fighting that had been occurring between royalists and Venizelists, which had necessitated the establishment by the Allies of a 'neutral zone', there was little resistance to the virtual Allied *coup d'état*, save a skirmish on 12 June at Larissa between French and Greek royalist forces.

Venizelos returned to Athens on 26 June 1917, formed a national government, and on 29 June Greece declared war on the Central Powers. The Salonika government already had some 60,000 men in three divisions (with a fourth, that

---

The rudimentary nature of battlefield communications is exemplified by the following orders concerning twenty-two tanks of 7th Tank Battalion ordered to collaborate with 37th Division in an attack towards Achiet-le-Petit:

'Signals to Infantry
  (i) Green and White Flag   "Come On"
  (ii) Red and Yellow Flag   "I am Broken Down – Go On"
  (iii) Red White and Blue Flag "I am Withdrawing"

'Infantry to Tank
  Helmet on top of Bayonet held above head – "Tank Wanted"

'Brigade Forward Stations will be provided with the following means of communication –
(1) Telephone (2) Power Buzzer (3) Visual (4) Pigeons (5) Runners (6) Message Carrying Rockets.

'All infantry will carry a 6in circular tin disc for purposes of signalling their position to the aeroplane. These discs will be flashed and WHITE flares lit by the most advanced Infantry when called for by the contact aeroplane sounding a Klaxon horn.'

(37th Divisional Orders nos. 231/3, /6 and /7, 20 August 1918)

---

of the Cyclades and Ionian islands, almost ready), with which Venizelos had wanted to attack the forces of the Athens government, only to be restrained by the Allies. Full mobilization of the Greek forces was put into effect, but not without unrest: Constantine continued pro-German agitation from exile, a large number of officers who refused to take an oath of loyalty to King Alexander were cashiered, and some mutinies had to be suppressed by the execution of ringleaders. Mobilization was completed by April 1918; by July some ten divisions of about a quarter of a million troops were in the field, and in the Allied drive in Macedonia they distinguished themselves in the storming of the Doiran heights (22 September).

After the war, Venizelos' dream for Greek expansionism foundered; though a leading figure at the Versailles conference, his absence from Greece and the continuing conflict in Asia Minor (in the Greco–Turkish War which began in 1919) caused the electorate to sweep him from office in 1920, and though he served as prime minister on two further occasions (1924, 1928–33) he was never again the dominant personality of old, and died in exile in Paris. Constantine returned to the throne after the unexpected death of King Alexander (27 October 1920, of blood-poisoning following a bite from a monkey); Constantine assumed personal direction of the war against Turkey, and its disastrous outcome resulted in his second abdication, 26 September 1922; he died in Palermo some fifteen weeks later.

Army

The Greek Army suffered from years of ineffective admini-stration and political interference. A law of 1904 made military service obligatory from age 21, including two years with the colours followed by ten years in the reserve and eight in the territorials (eight and ten years respectively for cavalry), but conscription was not universal: the intention to raise 13,000 recruits annually was reduced to 10,000 in 1906, and the period of service reduced to fourteen months, recruits in excess of the annual quota being exempted by ballot and passing directly into the reserve after six months' training.

At the outbreak of the Balkan War four active divisions and a cavalry division were organized, plus a similar number of reserve divisions, totalling about 210,000 men by the end of the war. By 1914 a reorganization had formed five army corps, plus an independent cavalry brigade (two regiments), and a regiment of fortress artillery and fortress engineers. Each army corps comprised three infantry divisions and one regiment each of cavalry, field artillery and engineers; each infantry division comprised three regiments and a mountain artillery group of three batteries. Field artillery was thus deployed at corps level, and there was little heavier ordnance. In September 1915 about 150,000 combatants were mobilized as a precaution against Bulgarian aggression, and in addition to the three Venizelist divisions at Salonika, at the Greek entry into the war it was hoped to field ten divisions on the Macedonian Front. In the event, three corps (nine divisions) were formed with arms and equipment from the Allies at Salonika. In addition, internal security was the responsibility of the gendarmerie, initially part of the army but from 1907 recruited separately by voluntary enlistment of drafts of some 700 recruits per year.

From the accession of King George (son of the heir to the throne of Denmark) the army uniform had been in Danish style, including a dark-blue tunic and kepi with 'arm-of-service' piping (staff, infantry and artillery red, engineers crimson) and light-blue trousers, and a green hussar uniform with crimson facings and piping for cavalry. The rifle corps (*evzones*) retained Greek national dress, including a fez and 'skirt' (*fustanella*). From 1912 a greenish-khaki service uniform was introduced, initially with a kepi and later a peaked cap, both with crowned light-blue and white cockade; leatherwork and cap peak and chinstrap were of natural colour. The tunic had patch breast-pockets and a turndown collar, cuffs and shoulder-straps piped in the arm-of-service colour, which was also present as officers' collar-patches, and piping to rank-insignia, kepi, cap and breeches (staff and infantry red, artillery blue, engineers light-blue, train green, medical services crimson). Other items in-cluded gaiters or khaki puttees (knee-boots or leather gaiters for officers), alternative white or off-white trousers, a single-breasted greenish-khaki greatcoat (officers' double-breasted) and a French-style side-cap of white, light-blue or greenish-khaki with arm-of-service piping. Evzones wore a khaki fez, knee-length single-breasted greenish-khaki tunic with folding collar, lower, vertical flapped pockets and red shoulder-straps, and red piping to the collar, pocket-flaps and turned-up cuffs; white or greenish-khaki tight trousers with blue or white garters, and shoes with black pompoms. NCOs wore yellow rank-bars on the cuff (white for cavalry and train), a narrow bar for senior privates, a wide bar for corporals, and two or three silver or gold bars for sergeants. Company officers had one to three khaki lace bands on the kepi and one to three silver stars on the shoulder-straps; field officers had the same cap-lace with an extra wider band, and arm-of-service-colour stripes on the shoulder-straps and one to three gilt stars. Shoulder-straps also bore the regimental number in black (gilt for officers, silver for cavalry and train). General officers had gold shoulder-straps with one or two silver stars and silver crossed baton and sword, and one or two gold kepi-bands above a wider band.

The principal firearm had been the French 11mm Gras rifle, but from 1907 the 1903 Mannlicher–Schoenauer 6.5mm rifle was issued; a 1903 carbine also existed, with a minor modification (Model 1903/14) being issued just before the outbreak of war. The Gras was also in use during the Balkan Wars. The cavalry carried lances. After trials in 1907 some 168 Schneider–Creusot 75mm guns were ordered (36 field and six mountain batteries), though some of the mountain batteries had the 75mm Schneider–Danglis 'screw-guns'). These replaced the 1860–70s 75mm Krupp guns. Heavy artillery, which was in extremely short supply, was all old. The Venizelist forces' equipment was based on that of the regular army, but supplies were more haphazard, and much French uniform, helmet, equipment and weaponry was utilized, including Lebel and Mannlicher–Berthier rifles. The aviation service was small and used Allied *matériel*, for example the Sopwith Camel.

Navy

The navy was manned largely by conscription, on a two-year enlistment followed by four years in the reserve, but despite the seafaring tradition (especially among those from the Aegean), numbers were small. Reorganizations were instituted in 1904 (a plan presented to the government in 1908 by the French Admiral Fournier, which envisaged the Greek forces being composed of submarines and light vessels was rejected), and the naval commission determined to acquire new capital ships, using a fund instituted in 1900, financed in part by a state lottery. Gunnery and navigation training was neglected, and despite the presence of the naval headquarters, dockyard, arsenal and torpedo school at the appropriate and historic location of Salamis, the total number of artificers employed by the navy was less than 400.

At the outbreak of the World War the navy's capital ships were still largely outdated. They included three old 5,000-ton battleships (*Psara* 1897, *Spetsai* 1899, *Hydra* 1900, 3 × 10.8in, 5 × 6in, 1 × 4in guns); two 13,000-ton battleships.

Kilkis and *Lemnos* (acquired 1914, previously the 1905 US battleships *Idaho* and *Mississippi*, 4 × 12in, 8 × 8in, 8 × 7in guns); one armoured cruiser (*G. Averoff*, 1911, 4 × 9.2in, 8 × 7.5in guns) and one light cruiser (*Helle*, 1913, 2 × 6in, 4 × 4in guns). Smaller vessels included six destroyers with 4 × 4in guns, eight destroyers with 2 × 12pdr guns, eight torpedo-boats, two submarines and a torpedo depot-ship (*Kanaris*, 1877, 2 × 4in guns). A dreadnought battleship, a battlecruiser and two light cruisers were ordered.

On 10 October 1916 the Allies demanded that the Greek fleet be handed over, together with the naval yard at Piraeus (the batteries at which port were to be neutralized by the surrender of the breech-blocks). Under protest the Greek government acceded, and the fleet was transferred to Allied control on the following day, the larger units being disarmed and their crews reduced to one-third, and the smaller vessels being transferred entire. In July 1917 the fleet was returned to Venizelos' government.

References

Abbott, G. F. *Greece and the Allies 1914–22*. London, 1922

Alastos, D. *Venizelos: Patriot, Statesman, Revolutionary*. London, 1922

Melas, Major G. M. *Ex-King Constantine and the War*. London, 1920

Ruhl, M. *Die Armee der Balkan-Staaten*. Leipzig, n.d. (includes Greece)

Ure, P. N. *Venizelos and his Fellow-Countrymen*. London, 1917

An anonymous artilleryman gives a most graphic description of the sensations of a bombardment:

'The air was suddenly torn into a thousand pieces; screeched and screamed; and then groaned and shivered as it was lashed again and again and again. Along our section, say, five miles, there must have been 3,000 shells fired in five minutes . . . I wish I could give you some idea of the awful majesty of those few moments . . . The morning, it seemed, was dull . . . but the flashes of the guns were so continuous as to give a light which was almost unbroken. It flickered, but it never failed. The earth itself quivered and shook . . . The air was a tattered, hunted thing, torn whisps of it blown hither and thither by the monstrous explosions . . . On every yard of trench at least four shells must have fallen within five minutes, and each shell would have a radius of destruction of at least 20 yards . . .'

(Quoted in *The Times History of the War*, VI, p. 378, London, 1916)

GUATEMALA

Guatemala was one of the most internally unstable of the Allied nations, yet possessed one of the largest armies in the region and, with a population approaching two million, more than one-third of the inhabitants of Central America. Governed under the 1879 constitution (reformed 1903), the term of presidential office was officially limited to six years; but Manuel Estrada Cabrera, elected in 1898, ruled for 22

years by the suppression of dissent. He survived an invasion in 1906 by the ex-president Manuel Barillas, but after opposition smouldered for years his dictatorship ended in a revolt in 1920, Cabrera having intended to bombard his own capital (Guatemala City) until the army defected to his opponents.

Guatamela included a considerable number of European settlements, among the most productive parts of the economy, including a number of German establishments (more than half the coffee crop, the most important export, was German-owned), and consequently during the war numbers of Germans arrived from Mexico in an attempt to persuade the state from taking the Allied part. They were unsuccessful: Cabrera broke off relations with Germany on 27 April 1917 and later considered this as a declaration of war: he offered the harbours, territorial waters and railways of Guatemala to the USA for use in common defence.

As some 60 per cent of the population were Indians, only the remainder were eligible for military service (Europeans and *Ladinos*, those of Spanish descent, of whom a large proportion were *mestizos* or of mixed blood). For these, military service was compulsory between the ages of 18 and 30, producing an army about 57,000 strong, but only about 7,000 were mobilized at any one time. From the age of 30 to 50 men passed into the reserve, which when mobilized numbered about 29,500.

HAITI

None of the Allied nations had enjoyed such a bloodstained internal history as Haiti. Civil turmoil had been endemic, but reached new heights following the revolution which deposed president Nord Alexis in 1908. His successor, Antoine Simon, was overthrown in 1911; in the following year the new president, Cincinnatus Leconte, was killed when his palace was blown up, and the next three years saw the reign of five presidents. The last of these, Vilbrun Sam, fled to the French legation amid massacre and civil war; two hours before a US warship landed marines to restore order Sam was dragged from the legation and murdered by a mob. US forces occupied the country, disarmed the warring factions and imposed martial law. Sudre Dartiguenave was chosen as president by the Haitian congress in April 1916, and in the following month an American protectorate was proclaimed, to remain for 20 years, including American supervision of finance, customs, armed forces and public works. This somewhat drastic measure was regarded as necessary to bring some order to the country, the condition of which was totally ruinous, with European nations having lodged financial claims against the wrecked Haitian economy. Haiti declared war on Germany on 12 July 1918, but could play no part in the war; indeed, there were revolts against the US occupation in 1918–19, and US forces left only in 1934.

Military and civil administration was synonymous prior

to the American intervention, each of the country's five *départements* and 23 *arrondissements* being governed by a general (these divisions were a result of the historic French influence: French was the official language, but most spoke a derivative styled Creole). The army was originally about 7,000 strong, and the navy had a few small craft; but upon American intervention the armed forces were replaced by a gendarmerie, commanded originally by American officers who were to be succeeded by Haitians once sufficient officers had been trained by the Americans.

HONDURAS

One of the Central American nations to declare war on Germany in the wake of the USA, Honduras was never in a position to play an active part in the war, save for the seizure of German property within its own borders. Nominally governed under the reformed constitution of 1894, the state had recently experienced severe internal turmoil: in the face of an invasion encouraged by Nicaragua, President Manuel Bonilla had had to flee to the security of the US Navy in April 1907; he himself invaded in 1910 and unseated his rival, President Miguel Dávila, was re-elected, and was succeeded upon his death in 1913 by Dr Fransisco Bertrand, who was re-elected as president in 1915. Such instability remained, however, that in January 1912 US Marines landed in Honduras to protect American property. In the wake of American involvement in the war, Honduras severed relations with Germany (17 May 1917) and declared war on 19 July 1918. Bertrand fled the country in September 1919 in the face of a liberal revolt, with the excuse that the forthcoming presidential election would not be held honestly.

Like all the Central American states, Honduras had an insufficient population to support any effective military force for anything other than territorial defence (population in 1905 was assessed at something over half a million, but statistics were unreliable as a large proportion were Indians among whom census-taking was difficult). The regular army comprised about 500 men; the militia, about 20,000 strong, was formed by a selective conscription among males aged between 20 and 30, with an additional reserve service of ten years.

INDIA

The vast territory of India, over which King George V ruled as emperor, was a vital component in the British Empire. Some 1,087,000 square miles were directly under British administration, the remaining 680,000 square miles being semi-autonomous native states. The British territory was divided into thirteen provinces, each with its own administration: Ajmer–Merwara, Andaman and Nicobar Islands, Baluchistan, Bengal, Bombay, Burma, Central Provinces/ Berar, Coorg, Eastern Bengal/Assam, Madras, North-West Frontier, Punjab, and the United Provinces (Agra/Oudh). The native states numbered almost 700, mostly governed by hereditary rulers with varying degrees of autonomy, all assisted by British political officers whose duty was to prevent misgovernment and ensure internal peace. Some of these states were organized into administrative groupings, such as the 148 states of the Central India Agency, and others were subordinate to British provinces, such as the 354 states controlled by Bombay.

The Emperor's rule was exercised through the Secretary of State (a member of the British cabinet), responsible to parliament. Administration was carried out by the Government of India, headed by the Viceroy, appointed by the crown for a five-year period: Charles, Baron Hardinge of Penshurst (grandson of Henry Hardinge, victor of the Sikh War) was succeeded in April 1916 by Frederic, Baron Chelmsford (son of the victor of the Zulu War), Hardinge having exceeded his five-year term by some six months. The Viceroy's executive council of six members (plus the military commander-in-chief) served like a cabinet, with ministerial portfolios distributed among them; it was enlarged for legislative purposes by a further 61 members, including 25 elected. Provincial administrations were headed by governors (for Bombay and Madras), lieutenant-governors (Bengal, Burma, Eastern Bengal/Assam, Punjab, United Provinces) or chief commissioners. In the lower echelons of administration, Eurasians and Indians had considerable influence, so that the whole continent was controlled by only some 6,500 British officials.

British preoccupation with the World War might have been an opportunity for exploitation by the Indian home-rule movement, encouraged by the English theosophist and socialist, Annie Besant, who founded the Indian Home Rule League, of which she became president in 1916, and of the Indian National Congress (formed 1885) in 1917, but there was comparatively little unrest. Some Muslim discontent had been fanned by the Italo–Turkish and Balkan Wars, where the conflict appeared to be between Christianity and Islam, but despite pressure for independence there was no widespread use of force by the nationalists. Attempts were made by Germany to exploit internal discontent, such as support for the *Ghadr* revolutionary movement of Har Dayal, but their efforts were frustrated. Revolutionary societies were especially active in Bengal (they were reputedly responsible for a bomb attack on Hardinge in Delhi in 1912, which injured him and supposedly hastened the death of his wife from shock), and German agents proposed to ship weapons to the Bengal revolutionaries in 1915, but the plan miscarried and the movement was suppressed. The effect that unrest could have had, however, is demonstrated by the events in Singapore, q.v.

Similarly, the years of the World War were largely untroubled by unrest on the frontiers, due partly to the neutrality of the Amir of Afghanistan in the face of Turko–German agitation. There was a minor rising in 1915

One of the most famous Indian personalities of the war: Major-General Sir Pratab (or Pertab) Singh, Regent-Maharaja of Jodhpur.

the armistice, some 1.3 million men having served during the war. Internal security had always been enforced by a nucleus of British regiments, but at one point in the war British forces were reduced to 15,000 (later reinforced by Territorials and garrison troops from Britain), but throughout the war the strength was considerably less than that which had been thought necessary. The Government of India enacted a number of laws to suppress enemy influence (such as the Commercial Intercourse with Enemies Ordinance), and the 1915 Defence of India Act provided the government with wider powers in the interest of national security.

The Indian Army provided troops for service on the Western Front, the Dardanelles, the Middle East and East Africa, such troops passing into British control upon reaching the theatre of operations. Execution of the Mesopotamian expedition was left to the Government of India (although the British government directed policy), a division of responsibility which had unfortunate effects; but by the time the Mesopotamian Commission produced its critical report the worst deficiencies had been rectified. Conflict with the Turks could have influenced their co-religionists in India, but a declaration by the Government of India on its attitude to Islam, and vehement support for Britain from the leading Muslim princes (notably the Nizam of Hyderabad) prevented any serious discontent.

Indian economics were not so strong as to enable the subcontinent to send great quantities of material to the Allies. The Government encouraged the development of Indian industry and controlled grain prices, appropriating stocks and prohibiting private export of wheat; the same restrictions were extended to Burmese rice. Supplies to

by the Mohmands (quelled by a blockade), followed by the Mahsuds (inspired by the deathbed exhortations of the mullah Powindah, described by Kitchener as the 'Pestilential Priest'), who were finally quietened by 1917; but there was no serious trouble until the Third Afghan War of 1919.

During the World War much of the indigenous population gave ungrudging support to Britain, and so satisfactory was the internal situation (revolutionary dacoity in Punjab notwithstanding) that the Government of India was able to divert more than expected of the resources previously regarded as necessary for the maintenance of internal stability. Before the war the British government had requested an assessment of the military forces which would be available in the event of a European war: the reply was that India could supply two divisions and a cavalry brigade, but that the dispatch of a third division would threaten internal security. In the event, from a pre-war strength of 155,000, the Indian Army had risen to 573,000 at

'It has been very hot here the past two days. Just wear a trousers [*sic*] & shirt.

'Jerry has been hot too with bombing & artillery, but we send over 10 shells to his one. Yesterday I had a marvellous escape for a shell burst in one of these rooms. Poor old Lodge, who used to be in the 1/4th R. Berks. & was A/CSM of D. Coy. was killed, Robinson (my OC Coy.) was wounded, 4 of our Servants wounded & two killed. Those wounded were badly so, except Robbie, & how I escaped without a scratch is marvellous. It seems an act of Providence. I was badly shaken that's all. I am quite all right again now, though. I am the only one left of those who were in the Room.

'I am fed up with this War. It ought to be finished with bladders on sticks & then the Bosche would hit you on the head with his stick . . .

'I hope your Battn. was better than its 2nd Line. They are awful & do little but sit on the backs in the Line. Never work, never fight & always let you down. They would give you the pip . . .'

(Officer, 2/4th Battalion, Oxfordshire & Buckinghamshire Light Infantry, 22 May 1918)

Officers of 1st Battalion, 39th Garwhal Rifles, part of the Meerut Division which landed in France in late 1914, inadequately equipped for European conditions, still wearing khaki drill (note the contrast with the serge-uniformed 2nd lieutenant standing at extreme right), shorts and with a tropical helmet visible in the tent. Seated extreme right is a French interpreter, wearing a brassard bearing 'INT'.

Indian Army Maxim gun section, Mesopotamia.

Indian forces serving abroad, and to the Mesopotamian expedition, all came from India, and Chelmsford established a Munitions Board to produce as much as possible within India.

Army

The Indian Army had been reorganized considerably, most notably during Kitchener's tenure as commander-in-chief, India (1902–9). He completed the 'unifications' of the Indian Army begun in 1895, by merging the forces of the old presidencies (Madras, Bombay and Bengal) and others into a unified force (so that henceforth units no longer carried a 'presidential' title: thus the 39th Bengal Infantry took their place in the universal line as the 39th Garwhal Rifles, for example). In the cavalry, the old Bengal regiments retained their numbers 1–19; 21 to 25 were occupied by the Punjab Frontier Force, 26–28 by Madras, 31–37 by Bombay, 38 and 39 by the Central India Horse, and the gaps (20, 29, 30) were filled by the old Hyderabad Contingent. In the infantry the Bengal regiments took the numbers 1–48, 51–59 Punjab Frontier Force, 61–93 Madras, 94–99 Hyderabad Contingent, and 101–130 Bombay.

Recruiting was entirely voluntary (before the war about 15,000 men per annum), concentrated upon the 'martial races', so that Punjab provided fully half the total; the policy of replacing the Madras regiments with more effective Punjabis continued, so that fifteen of the Madras units became Punjabis, and others were disbanded. It was not possible to recruit entire regiments from one tribe or district, some units incorporating companies of several different races, which might bear little similarity to the official title: the 129th Baluchis, for example, which provided the first Indian-born winner of the Victoria Cross (Khudadad Khan, at Hollebeke, 31 October 1914), contained no

Baluchis but Pathans, Mahsuds and Punjabi Mussulmans, while Wilde's Rifles, part of the first contingent to serve on the Western Front, had one company each of Dogras, Pathans, Punjabis and Sikhs. (British supervision and discipline held together such elements traditionally hostile to one another: as *The Times* remarked, if by chance a Brahmin and a Pathan regiment were left together without control, there would not have been a man of the weaker regiment left alive after a day!) As in British service, wartime expansion (which pushed the recruiting service to the limit) was normally accomplished by the addition of new battalions to existing regiments rather than by creating new regiments.

Kitchener identified the Indian Army's main tasks as the defence of the north-west frontier (where the Russian threat declined markedly following the Russo–Japanese War and the 1907 Anglo–Russian convention), and the maintenance of internal tranquillity. Little preparation had been made for taking the field in anything other than *ad hoc* formations. Kitchener instituted a divisional system, but financial restrictions prevented a change of peacetime stations so that these might remain together. Two armies were formed: the Northern Army comprised the 1st (Peshawar), 2nd (Rawalpindi), 3rd (Lahore), 7th (Meerut) and 8th (Lucknow) Divisions and the Bannu, Derajat and Kohat Brigades; the Southern Army the 4th (Quetta), 5th (Mhow), 6th (Poona), 9th (Secundarabad) and Burma Divisions, and the Aden Brigade. The nine numbered divisional areas also included the troops required for internal security (some 80,000, against 152,000 in the field army). A division normally contained three infantry brigades (each of one British and three Indian battalions), an Indian cavalry regiment, a brigade of field artillery (18pdrs), two mountain batteries (10pdrs), a pioneer battalion, two sapper and miner

companies and supports. The eight independent cavalry brigades normally contained one British and two Indian regiments and a horse battery; the British units were included to 'stiffen' the Indian, and excepting twelve Indian mountain batteries, all artillery was British. In addition there were local forces, stationed principally on the frontier, often almost as wild as the tribesmen they were intended to contain; and 'Imperial Service' troops raised by the autonomous states.

Although there existed a lower tier of native officers, each unit's small number of British officers formed its most irreplaceable asset. As the huge expansion caused by the World War had never been envisaged, the reserve of officers numbered only about 40, more than offset by Britain's appropriation of Indian Army officers on leave in Britain at the outbreak of war. Officers could not be supplied to Indian units as easily as to British, due to the singular relationship between officers and men: not only did the British officers need to be able to converse with their men in their own language, but had to understand the nature of Indian regiments, in which the British officer was regarded not only as leader but adviser and father-figure. Casualties among officers could not easily be replaced, and the loss of their mentors in the alien environment of the Western Front was one reason for the decline of morale among the Indian Expeditionary Force.

The first use of Indian troops in the war was the Indian Corps which landed at Marseilles on 26 September 1914. It formed a valuable resource at a time of some difficulty, yet *The Times* found it necessary to justify the use of native troops against a European enemy, which forms a comment upon contemporary attitudes: 'We British are constitutionally the last people in the world to take unfair advantage . . . The instinct which made us such sticklers for propriety

. . . made us more reluctant than other nations . . . to employ coloured troops against a white enemy'; but, as Britain was already allied to 'the yellow people of Japan' and as France was employing Turcos, it would not be fair to refuse the Indian Army 'the privilege of taking its place beside British troops'.[1] The Indian Corps comprised the following.

3rd (Lahore) Division:

Ferozepore Brigade: 1/Connaught Rangers, 9th Bhopal Infantry, 57th Wilde's Rifles, 129th Baluchis

Jullundur Brigade: 1/Manchester Regiment, 15th Ludhiana and 47th Sikhs, 59th Scinde Rifles

Sirhind Brigade: 1/HLI, 125th Napier's Rifles, 1/1st and 1/4th Gurkhas

Cavalry: 15th Lancers (Cureton's Multanis)

Support: 34th Sikh Pioneers; 5, 11 and 18 Brigades RFA, 109 Battery RGA

7th (Meerut) Division:

Dehra Dun Brigade: 1/Seaforth Highlanders, 6th Jat Light Infantry, 2/2nd and 1/9th Gurkhas

Garwhal Brigade: 2/Leicestershire Regiment, 1/ and 2/39th Garwhal Rifles, 2/3rd Gurkhas

Bareilly Brigade: 2/Black Watch, 41st Dogras, 58th Vaughan's Rifles, 2/8th Gurkhas

Cavalry: 4th Cavalry

Support: 4, 9 and 13 Brigades, RFA, 110 Battery RGA.

4th (Secunderabad) Cavalry Brigade:

7th Dragoon Guards, 20th Deccan Horse, 30th Lancers, Jodhpur Lancers, N Battery RHA.

The Indians on the Western Front suffered immense casualties (in a year's service Vaughan's Rifles lost 33 British and 31 Indian officers and more than 1,500 other ranks, in effect wiping it out twice over). Under such conditions it is little wonder that some Indians took on a fatalistic or depressed attitude, yet the few desertions which occurred could be accounted for by the fact that most were Afridis and Pathans who could hardly have been expected to remain loyal, as had they not joined the Indian Army they might well have been fighting the British on the Frontier. The Indians' comparison of the Kaiser with Rawan the ten-headed demon were sentiments which would have found much sympathy with British public opinion, but despite objections from their commander, Sir James Willcocks, it was decided to withdraw the Indian Corps from the Western Front, their losses having been so severe, their trusted leaders gone, and their morale dented by the trauma of an environment totally alien. The presumed prevalence of suspected self-inflicted wounds (a remarkably higher proportion of hand injuries than those of British units) is a pointer towards the decline in morale. The Secunderabad and Sialkot cavalry brigades (expanded into the 4th and 5th Cavalry Divisions in October 1916) remained on the Western Front, but the remainder were withdrawn in late 1915. Thereafter, the Indian Army bore the major share of the Mesopotamian expedition; 29 Brigade (14th Sikhs, 1/5th, 1/6th and 2/10th Gurkhas) served at Gallipoli; Indian troops served in Egypt, East Africa, Aden and Bahrein; and Allenby's army in Palestine included the Lahore and Meerut Divisions and 20 and 49 independent brigades. Although as expected the 'martial races' acquitted themselves well, less was expected of the Marathas; yet such as the 103rd, 110th and 117th Marathas achieved a record in Mesopotamia exceeded by none.

Cavalry

At the outbreak of war there were 38 cavalry regiments, numbered 1–39 (no 24th), plus the cavalry of the Queen's Own Corps of Guides. Only three were 'class corps' (i.e., of one race): the 1st Skinner's Horse was composed of Mohammedans of Hindustan and the southern Punjab, the 14th Lancers of Jats, and the 15th of Multani Pathans. The remainder had 'class squadrons', i.e., squadrons composed exclusively of one tribe. The principal races were Sikhs, Dekhani Mohammedans, Dogras, Jats, Pathans, Punjabis and Rajputs, who could be identified by the method of tying the *lungi* (that part of the turban wrapped around the *kullah* or skull-cap), which was different for each race. All but the 26th–28th (who rode government horses) were organized on the 'silladar system', by which each trooper provided and maintained his own mount in return for a higher rate of pay, popular with the government for its economy and with the men who received a lump sum in return for the horse when discharged; but it was hopelessly impracticable for service abroad and its maintenance demonstrates the unpreparedness of the Indian Army for serving outside the subcontinent.

The regiments were: 1st Duke of York's Own Lancers (Skinner's Horse), 2nd Lancers (Gardner's Horse), 3rd Skinner's Horse, 4th, 5th, 8th, 12th, 16th and 17th Cavalry, 6th King Edward's Own Cavalry, 7th Hariana Lancers, 9th

Hodson's Horse, 10th Duke of Cambridge's Own Lancers (Hodson's Horse), 11th King Edward's Own Lancers (Probyn's Horse), 13th Duke of Connaught's Lancers (Watson's Horse), 14th Murray's Jat Lancers, 15th Lancers (Cureton's Multanis), 18th King George's Own Tiwana Lancers, 19th Lancers (Fane's Horse), 20th Deccan Horse, 21st Prince Albert Victor's Own Cavalry (Frontier Force), 22nd Sam Browne's Cavalry (Frontier Force), 23rd, 25th Cavalry (Frontier Force), 26th King George's Own Light Cavalry, 27th, 28th Light Cavalry, 29th Lancers (Deccan Horse), 30th Lancers (Gordon's Horse), 31st Duke of Connaught's Lancers, 32nd Lancers, 33rd Queen Victoria's Own Light Cavalry, 34th Prince Albert Victor's Own Poona Horse, 35th Scinde Horse, 36th Jacob's Horse, 37th Lancers (Baluch Horse), 38th, 39th King George's Own Central India Horse, Queen's Own Corps of Guides (Frontier Force) (Lumsden's). The 40th–46th Cavalry were formed 1918, the 46th previously the Alwar Lancers.

Organization, uniform and equipment were based upon British models, though in general older patterns were used

Indian cavalry sentry on the Western Front, wearing the characteristic, long-skirted kurta.

by the Indian Army. The service uniform was khaki drill; only latterly did regiments serving on the Western Front receive serge uniforms, despite the unsuitability of drill for the European climate. The cavalry wore a khaki turban (occasionally with coloured ornamentation), a khaki drill tunic or *kurta* with long skirts and steel shoulder-chains, khaki breeches and puttees; ankle boots, Sam Browne belt and British 1903-pattern ammunition bandolier, all brown leather; sabres, rifles and lances were carried. British officers wore a khaki turban, topee (normally restricted to hot climates though some were in evidence on first landing in Europe) or peaked cap (in Europe), a khaki drill tunic with patch pockets and open collar revealing khaki shirt and tie (or white shirt and black tie), khaki drill breeches, brown leather riding-boots and Sam Browne belt. For the cavalry which remained on the Western Front, khaki serge uniforms of British pattern were issued ultimately, and steel helmets.

Infantry

Indian infantry regiments were numbered 1–130 (nos. 49, 50, 60, 68, 70, 77, 78, 85, 100, 111, 115 and 118 vacant), each one battalion strong (the 39th had two), plus the infantry of the Queen's Own Corps of Guides. The same 'class' system operated as in the cavalry (and hence the same variations in turban within a regiment); included were nine Sikh battalions (three of which enlisted Mazbi Sikhs), three of Dogras, two of Brahmins, two of Jats, one of Afghan Hazaras, two of Garwhalis, 41 of Punjabis (of class companies, including Punjabi Mohammedans, Sikhs, Dogras and Pathans), three of Punjabi and frontier Mohammedans, three of Mohammedans from outside the Punjab, and six ostensibly of Mahrattas, but each including two class companies of Dekhani Mohammedans. Although some had not seen active service for years, in general the calibre was high, especially those which had served on the frontier (as part of the Frontier Force and others), and those drawn from the 'martial races' such as those of the Punjab. A number of battalions were classified as pioneers, but although they were trained in engineering they were also fully trained infantry. The regiments were as follows:

1st, 3rd Brahmins; 2nd Queen Victoria's Own Rajput Light Infantry; 4th Prince Albert Victor's Rajputs; 5th Light Infantry; 6th Jat Light Infantry; 7th Duke of Connaught's Own Rajputs; 8th, 11th Rajputs; 9th Bhopal Infantry; 10th Jats; 12th Pioneers (Kelat-i-Ghilzai Regiment); 13th Rajputs (Shekhawati Regiment); 14th King George's Own Ferozepore Sikhs; 15th Ludhiana Sikhs; 16th Rajputs (Lucknow Regiment); 17th Loyal Regiment; 18th, 98th, 108th, 109th, 112th, 113th Infantry; 19th, 21st, 22nd, 24th–31st, 33rd, 46th, 62nd, 64th, 66th, 67th, 69th, 72nd, 74th, 76th, 82nd, 84th, 87th, 89th, 90th, 92nd Punjabis; 20th Duke of Cambridge's Own (Brownlow's Punjabis); 23rd, 32nd, 34th Sikh Pioneers; 35th, 36th, 47th Sikhs; 37th, 38th, 41st Dogras; 39th Garhwal Rifles; 40th Pathans; 42nd Deoli Regiment; 43rd Erinpura Regiment; 44th Mharwara Regiment; 45th Rattray's Sikhs; 48th, 64th, 81st, 107th,

121st, 128th Pioneers; 49th Bengalis; 50th Kumaon Rifles (formed 1918); Queen Victoria's Own Corps of Guides (Frontier Force) (Lumsden's); 51st–54th Sikhs (Frontier Force); 55th Coke's Rifles (Frontier Force); 56th Infantry (Frontier Force); 57th Wilde's Rifles (Frontier Force); 58th Vaughan's Rifles (Frontier Force); 59th Scinde Rifles (Frontier Force); 61st King George's Own Pioneers; 63rd Palamcottah Light Infantry; 65th, 73rd, 75th, 79th, 80th, 86th, 88th Carnatic Infantry; 70th Burma Rifles formed 1917); 71st Coorg Rifles (1917, 71st Punjabis); 83rd Wallajahabad Light Infantry; 85th Burma Rifles (formed 1918); 91st Punjabis (Light Infantry); 93rd Burma Infantry; 94th, 95th Russell's Infantry; 96th Berar Infantry; 97th, 99th Deccan Infantry; 101st Grenadiers; 102nd King Edward's Own Grenadiers; 103rd, 105th Mahratta Light Infantry; 104th Wellesley's Rifles; 106th Hazara Pioneers; 110th Mahratta Light Infantry; 111th (formed 1917), 114th, 116th, 117th Mahrattas; 119th Infantry (Mooltan Regiment); 120th, 122nd Rajputana Infantry; 123rd Outram's Rifles; 124th Duchess of Connaught's Own Baluchistan Infantry; 125th Napier's Rifles; 126th Baluchistan Infantry; 127th Queen Mary's Own Baluchistan Light Infantry; 129th Duke of Connaught's Own Baluchis; 130th King George's Own Baluchis; 131st United Provinces Regiment (formed 1916); 133rd Regiment, 140th Patiala Regiment, 141st Bikanir Infantry, 142nd Jodhpur Infantry, 143rd Narsingh (Dholpur) Infantry, all formed 1918.

In addition were the ten Gurkha regiments (two battalions each), recruited from Nepal and justifiably regarded as the élite of the army: 1st King George's Own Gurkha Rifles (Malaun Regiment); 2nd King Edward's Own Gurkha Rifles (Sirmoor Rifles); 3rd Queen Alexandra's Own Gurkha Rifles; 4th, 6th–10th Gurkha Rifles, 5th Gurkha Rifles (Frontier Force).

Infantry wore a khaki turban, khaki drill blouse buttoned to the waist but with the same 'skirt' as the cavalry, and two patch pockets; khaki drill trousers and khaki puttees. Those units serving on the Western Front eventually received British-pattern khaki serge; equipment was the brown leather, 1903 'bandolier' pattern, the 1908 webbing equipment not being issued during the war. Officers wore a turban or khaki service cap (topee in hot climates), khaki tunic, breeches and puttees with brown ankle boots and Sam Browne belt (with double shoulder-braces for some regiments); Indian officers wore the turban and either an officer's tunic, or an officer's version of the skirted blouse, with four patch pockets. Gurkhas and the two Garhwali battalions wore short khaki jackets, khaki shorts (with puttees) or ordinary trousers, and a khaki felt slouch hat with upturned brim; British officers of these units sometimes wore shorts, which garment spread to other units in hot weather later in the war.

Artillery and Engineers

The twelve Indian mountain batteries were numbered 21–32; British mountain batteries bore the numbers 1–8 and the remainder were vacant. Batteries 21–24 were originally from the Frontier Force, 25 and 26 from the Bombay army and 27 and 28 from Bengal; personnel were half Punjabi Mohammedans and half Sikhs. They were equipped with mule-carried 'screw-guns'. One other unit was the Frontier Garrison Artillery (previously the Punjab Garrison Battery, alias 'the Blokes'), a corps of men no longer fit for field service. British field batteries serving in India had Indian drivers, mainly Punjabis and a few from Hindustan.

As the Royal Engineers supplied only a few NCOs for service in India, the Indian Army's engineer force was entirely 'native', with officers from the Royal Engineers, generally operating as separate companies grouped into three regiments: six companies of the 1st Prince of Wales' Own Sappers and Miners (largely Sikhs, Pathans and Punjabi Mohammedans); six companies of the 2nd Queen's Own Sappers and Miners (five of Madrassis and one of Burmese); and six service and one fortress company of the 3rd Sappers and Miners (Sikhs, Mahrattas, Rajputs and others).

Indian Army insignia was generally restricted to British-styled brass shoulder-titles; head-dress badges were used principally by British officers. Rank-badges were in British style, though Indian terms were used for native ranks:

British	Indian infantry	Indian cavalry
private	sepoy	sowar
lance-corporal	lance-naik	acting lance-daffadar
corporal	naik	lance-daffadar
sergeant	havildar	daffadar
sergeant-major	havildar-major	kot daffadar
2nd lieutenant	jemadar	jemadar
lieutenant	subedar	rissaldar
	subedar-major*	rissaldar-major*

(*These two ranks were the senior Indian officers, not directly comparable with a British rank. All Indian officers, no matter how experienced, were subordinate to the most junior British officer.)

Imperial Service Troops
Although the semi-autonomous Indian states were often overlooked, as the Marquis of Lansdowne remarked, it should not be forgotten that the Nizam of Hyderabad controlled a population three times as great as that of Ireland, or that the Maharaja of Mysore led a people more numerous than that of Sweden. Most maintained an army (about 100,000 men in all at the outbreak of war), although in many cases they were only ceremonial bodyguard units. (Nevertheless, some of these corps were of greater antiquity than any European regiment, even if the lineage was sometimes tenuous: for example, the earliest battle-honour on the colour of the Jaipur guard regiment was Kheench-wada 1621–2.)

A number of Indian state forces had assisted Britain over the previous century (in the Indian mutiny, for example, and the defence of Chitral, 1895, was largely undertaken by Kashmiris), and in 1885 the 'Penjdeh Incident' (in which a war with Russia threatened) numbers of Indian rulers (notably the Nizam) offered large sums in support of the expected war effort. It was suggested that instead of contributing cash, an element of the princes' forces should be trained to the standard of the Indian Army, which proposal was accepted eagerly, the result being the 'Imperial Service Troops'. The expense involved in raising the number of trained 'Imperial Service Troops' to more than 21,000 at the outbreak of war was obtained by reducing the numbers of the ceremonial forces. This collaboration between the British and the princes was described as '. . . a happy one. In addition to providing a satisfactory career for the feudal gentry of the States, it has brought the best class of sirdar into touch with the best class of British officer.'[2] The forces included infantry, cavalry and supporting services, and in Kashmir two mountain batteries were established largely for the defence of the Gilgit frontier.

Upon the outbreak of the World War, a number of Indian rulers offered huge sums towards the expenses of the war: the Nizam of Hyderabad 60 lakhs of rupees, the Maharaja of Mysore 50 lakhs, for example (about £400,000 and £333,000 respectively). Imperial Service contingents were mobilized, and some princes took an active role, none more notably than Major-General Sir Pratab Singh Bahadur, Regent-Maharaja of Jodhpur, who had served in China in 1900 and who again took the field despite his age (70), declaring that as the British were shedding their blood like water, it was time the Rajputs demonstrated their gratitude and similarly shed their blood for the King-Emperor. Support was manifested in other ways than the deployment of troops and gifts of cash; Sir Pratab Singh's nephew, for example, the Jam Saheb of Nawanagar, mobilized every horse and motor-car in his state, equipped a hospital and ambulance-column, and himself served a year on the Western Front. (The Jam, who had declared that the Rajputs 'would consider it a high honour and privilege to

'. . . what a scene of devastation! No crops had been planted here. Certainly the ground had been tilled, but not with the ploughshare. Rank weeds grew where shells had not recently fallen. Wire, tangled and torn, tripped the unwary step. Beyond us lay two curious-looking mounds, a few stray battered leafless and branchless trees stood as sentinels in and about these mounds. Once these mounds were villages, so said the plan; it was difficult to believe it. Truly it was the valley of desolation; the shadow and the substance of death were there too – freshly dug graves with the little wooden crosses above them placed there by some loving comrade with a name pencilled on . . .'
(Anonymous description of the Western Front, in *Made in the Trenches*, ed. Sir Frederick Treves Bt., p. 218, London, 1916)

A veteran mule of the Indian Army, wearing medals for the six campaigns in which it had participated.

fight shoulder to shoulder with the British army in maintaining intact this great Empire and its glorious and untarnished name',[3] was probably the best-known in Britain of the Indian princes: he was K. S. Ranjitsinjhi, the immortal Sussex and England batsman.)

Not all the Imperial Service Troops saw active service, but some important contributions were made, for example by the Bikaner Camel Corps in the Middle East, and in the charge at Haifa by the Hyderabad, Jodhpur and Mysore Lancers. Among the states whose Imperial Service contingents went on active service were:

Alwar: Alwar Infantry (Fateh Paltan) (Egypt and Palestine)

Baria: Baria Ranjit Infantry

Bharatpur: Bharatpur Infantry (East Africa)

Bhavnagar: Bhavnagar Imperial Service Lancers (Egypt, Palestine)

Bhawalpur: Bhawal Imperial Service Mounted Rifles (Egypt, Mesopotamia).

Bikaner: Bikaner Camel Corps (Ganga Risala) (Egypt, Persia, Iraq); Bikaner Sadul Light Infantry (Egypt)

Faridkot: Faridkot Sappers & Miners (East Africa)

Gwalior: Maharaja Scindia's Battalion (3rd Gwalior) (East Africa); Maharaja Bahadur Battalion (4th Gwalior) (Egypt, Palestine); Gwalior Transport Company (Mesopotamia)

Hyderabad: 1st and 2nd (Nizam's Own) Hyderabad Imperial Service Lancers (Egypt, Palestine, Syria)

Indore: Holkar's Imperial Service Mounted Escort (Mesopotamia); Holkar's Imperial Service Transport Corps (France, Suvla, Macedonia, Egypt)

Jaipur: Jaipur Imperial Service Transport Corps (Mesopotamia, Palestine)

Jammu and Kashmir: 1st Jammu and Kashmir Infantry (Palestine); 2nd (East Africa); 3rd Jammu and Kashmir Rifles (East Africa, Palestine)

Jind: Jind Imperial Service Regiment

Jodhpur: Jodhpur Lancers (France, Palestine, Syria)

Kapurthala: Kapurthala Jagjit Infantry (East Africa)

Maler Kotla: Maler Kotla Sappers & Miners (France, Mesopotamia)

Mysore: Mysore Lancers (Egypt, Palestine, Syria)

Patiala: Patiala Lancers (Egypt, Mesopotamia); 1st Patiala Infantry (Rajindra Sikh's) (Egypt, Palestine); 2nd (Egypt, Palestine)

Rampur: 1st Battalion Rampur Imperial Service Infantry (East Africa)

Sirmur: Sirmur Sappers & Miners (Mesopotamia)

Tehri Garhwal: Tehri Garhwal Sappers & Miners (France, Mesopotamia).

In addition, other units were mobilized for service in India.

Footnotes

1. *Times History of the War*, London 1914, I, p. 155.
2. *The Armies of India*, G. F. MacMunn, London, 1911, p. 197.
3. Quoted in *Ranji: Prince of Cricketers*, A. Ross, London, 1983, p. 161.

References

Anon. *India's Contribution to the Great War*. Govt. of India, Calcutta, 1923

Farwell, B. *Armies of the Raj: From the Mutiny to Independence, 1858–1947*. London, 1990

Jaipur, Maharaja of. *History of the Indian State Forces*. New Delhi & London, 1967

MacMunn, G. F., and Lovett, A. C. *The Armies of India*. London, 1911

Mason, P. *A Matter of Honour: An Account of the Indian Army, Its Officers and Men*. London, 1974

Merewether, Lieutenant-Colonel J. W. B., and Smith, Sir Frederick. *The Indian Corps in France*. London, 1919

Mollo, B. *The Indian Army*. Poole, 1981

Willcocks, General Sir James. *With the Indians in France*. London, 1920

ITALY

The Kingdom of Italy, proclaimed on 18 February 1861, was a constitutional monarchy with executive power vested in the king, who shared the legislative power with the parliament of an elected chamber of deputies and a senate of members appointed by the king (plus all royal princes). The prime minister headed a council of eleven ministers. Of the many independent states of which Italy had been composed, only the tiny Vatican state and republic of San Marino retained independence.

King Victor Emmanuel III (Vittorio Emanuele, 1869–1947) succeeded to the throne on 29 July 1900 upon the assassination of his father, Umberto I by the anarchist Angelo Bresci. Victor Emmanuel was content to act as a figurehead during an era of comparative tranquillity and economic prosperity, presided over by the Liberal prime minister Giovanni Giolitti (1842–1928). The Italo–Turkish War (September 1911–October 1912) had ended successfully for Italy with the acquisition of Libya, Rhodes and the Dodecanese islands, but the nation's military reputation had not been enhanced, the faltering Ottoman Empire agreeing to peace only because of the imminence of the Balkan War. It probably influenced the election of October–November 1913, which resulted in a crumbling of Giolitti's support and the election of 79 Socialist and 70 Radical deputies; on 10 March 1914 Giolitti resigned and was replaced by Antonio Salandra (1853–1931). In June there was an upsurge of internal violence, the 'Red Week' instigated by various anarchist and revolutionary groups; barely had this been quietened by troops when the World War began.

From 1882 Italy had been part of the 'Triple Alliance' with Austria–Hungary and Germany, which had been renewed as late as 7 December 1912. It was most unpopular in Italy, largely as a result of the Irredentist movement which sought the unification with Italy of all areas populated by Italian-speakers, principally the Trentino and the Trieste area under Austro–Hungarian control, which heightened the Italo–Austrian rivalry for influence in the Balkans and Adriatic. Italy had also cultivated good relations with the Entente powers, so that upon the outbreak of war there was little question that Italy would be anything other than neutral. (Among the factions demonstrating public opinion were the Garibaldists, led by descendants of the hero, vehemently Irredentist and who raised a corps of anti-Central Powers volunteers who served with the French Foreign Legion until Italy's entry into the war, when they transferred to Italian service. Such organizations encouraged the interventionist movement which led to unrest and rioting in the period before Italy's declaration of war.)

Salandra's inexperience meant that at the beginning of the war, foreign policy was largely in the hands of Antonio Castello, Marquis di San Giuliano (1852–1914); together they endeavoured to maintain neutrality without alienating

King Victor Emmanuel III of Italy (1869–1947).

either of the opposing camps. San Giuliano died on 16 October, and foreign affairs devolved upon Giorgio, Baron Sonnino (1847–1922), a half-Scottish Conservative who had served briefly as prime minister (1906, 1909–10). On 26 April 1915 Italy concluded a secret Pact of London which gave Italy considerable gains in the Adriatic and Brenner frontier in return for Italian participation in the war on the side of the Entente, a policy beset with difficulties as Giolitti's faction was vehemently neutralist. (German business interests controlled a portion of Italian commercial life: its importance can be over-stated, but it is interesting to note that Professor Maffeo Pantaleoni's foreword to G. Preziosi's *La Germania alla Conquista dell'Italia* stated that Irredentism was as much about the re-possession of Italian finance from foreign hands as about the 'liberation' of the Trentino.) On 3 May Italy declared an end to the Triple Alliance, but Allied reverses and Germany's pressure upon Austria–Hungary to make concessions to Italy resulted in only lukewarm support in the Chamber of Deputies for Italian intervention; and on 13 May Salandra resigned.

General Armando Diaz (1861–1928), Cadorna's successor as chief of staff and de facto *commander-in-chief of the Italian Army.*

who formed a widely based national government; Sonnino remained in charge of foreign affairs. The anti-war movement increased in 1917, encouraged by factions which favoured the Central Powers; Giolitti's publication *La Stampa* in Turin, and the encyclical of Pope Benedict XV (1854–1922) aided the movement. There was economic hardship, following poor harvests, and fuel became short: the price of imported British coal rose to almost 30 times its pre-war figure. A strike in Turin in August developed into a revolutionary outbreak, and many of those involved were, after its repression by the military, sent to the army by having their exemptions revoked, and proceeded to foment unrest within their regiments. Boselli, regarded as too old to manage the war with the necessary zeal, was voted out of office on 25 October 1917, and on 30 October was replaced as premier by his interior minister, Vittorio Orlando (1860–1952), a determined proponent of the prosecution of the war. He rallied support and pledged that Italy would continue to fight even if the front were driven in as far as Sicily; this declaration, at the Rapallo Conference on 5 November, contrasted with Cadorna's gloomy message to the government two days earlier, which hinted at the need for a separate peace. Allied demands resulted in Cadorna's relinquishing command on 7 November; in his stead, Orlando appointed Armando Diaz (1861–1928), an officer with a proven combat record who favoured a defensive posture in place of the previous policy of attack, and whose relations with the politicians were good.

Orlando overcame the neutralist movement in the Chamber of Deputies by a call for national resistance, and instituted a War Council of military and political leaders which finally stabilized relations between army and government. Despite British and French reinforcement, Diaz was unwilling to commit his forces, but as the Central Powers collapsed Sonnino indicated that Italian territorial claims would receive little support if they continued to hold back; so under this urging, Diaz attacked at Vittorio Veneto which gave Italy the triumph it desired. At the peace conference, however, Orlando and Sonnino found it impossible to claim everything promised by the Pact of London, even less the additional demands for more Adriatic territory at the expense of a Yugoslavian state, and Orlando's government fell in June 1919 amid accusations that it had accepted only part of Italy's due. Victor Emmanuel was the longest-lasting member of those who had directed the war, but with his influence submerged by that of Mussolini, he became the last king to sit upon the throne of Italy, the monarchy being voted out of existence in June 1946.

Army

The collapse of the Italian Army at Caporetto, and the discontent within the ranks which was a contributory cause, was probably the original reason for the bad reputation accorded to the Italian forces, which became quite widespread. The poor opinion of the Italian military was not

After interventionist demonstrations, the preference of the king for the Entente, and Giolitti's refusal to form a neutralist government, Salandra returned to power on 16 May; Italy declared war on Austria–Hungary on 24 May 1915 (on Bulgaria on 20 October, and on Germany on 28 August 1916).

The king, whose influence had grown considerably during the turmoil, was an enthusiastic supporter of the Entente and spent most of the war near the front, as nominal commander-in-chief (his cousin, the Duke of Genoa, remained in Rome as regent). Actual command was vested in the chief-of-staff, General Luigi Cadorna (1850–1928), who was both uninspired and unpopular as a commander and frequently at odds with the government, with whom the king had to mediate in some cases.

The Austrian drive through the Trentino passes precipitated the fall of Salandra on 10 June 1916; he was replaced as premier by Paolo Boselli (1838–1932), an aged but experienced politician of Liberal and Irredentist persuasion,

restricted only to those British and Allied soldiers who came into contact with them: Rommel remarked that one Württemberg alpine soldier was worth 20 Italians, and Repington records 'Wully' Robertson laughing over Lloyd George's expressions of enthusiasm about the Italians 'just before they had been licked'.[1] Such opinions, however, conceal the fact that Italian troops conducted themselves with considerable fortitude, despite the disintegration after Caporetto.

The Italian Army grew out of that of Piedmont, which had been in the forefront of the unification of Italy. In order to draw together people of different regions, 'territorial' identity of regiments was deliberately eschewed, so that Milanese, Romans and Neapolitans might serve in the same unit. Upon discharge, soldiers returned to their homes throughout the country, so that upon mobilization regiments had to draw upon the nearest reservists, irrespective of the unit to which they belonged. This, and financial restrictions, left the army in a poor state at the outbreak of war; the neglect came from the belief that it was sufficient if Italy maintained only enough troops to ensure public order, and the commission appointed in 1907 to review national defence presented modest recommendations in 1910 which were thought too expensive.

According to the recruiting scheme of 1907, all citizens were liable to serve from their 20th to 39th years, in three classes. In the first, two years were spent with the colours, six in the reserve, four in the mobile militia and seven in the territorial militia; in the second, six months maximum with the colours, 7½ years in the reserve, and the rest as for class 1; and in the third, all nineteen years with the territorial militia, with no training. Only a fraction of those eligible served their period in the 'active' army; in 1911, for example, of more than 487,000 liable for service, less than 123,000 were actually sent for training. The active army consisted of regular officers (never available in sufficient numbers: there was a shortage of 13,000 in 1914, in the active and reserve forces, including 44 per cent of artillery officers), and men from class 1 of conscripts. These were supposed to join every November, but as actual service was deferred until March there was virtually no army during the winter, a gap partially filled from 1907 by scheduling this as the training period for the second-class men. Strengths were so much under establishment that some companies (mobilized strength 250) had only fifteen men, there were hardly any professional NCOs, and most reserve officers had no experience of regular service.

Many units were entirely dispersed as police detachments, and denuded of drafts sent to Libya; upon mobilization, the ranks had to be filled with inexperienced reservists. The mobile militia was intended to act as a support for the active army, and the territorial militia to be used at home and to protect lines of communication; from 1910 it was ordered that every infantry and field artillery unit should have a mobile militia cadre attached, to facilitate mobilization; but this had not been implemented

The body-armour of the early Italian 'death companies' gave a very medieval appearance; the 'pike' is a wire-cutter.

fully even by 1914. Mobilization expanded the army hugely, from its 1914–15 force of an authorized 289,000 men to 5.2 million at the armistice, with about 460,000 having died and 570,000 being invalided out. In effect the three-class system did not operate, so that in general those serving at the front were aged 19–39, those in the second line 40–42, with those out of combat entirely being aged 43–44, and 18-year-olds undergoing training. Until 1917 reinforcement was from central depots, and thereafter each brigade was allocated its own depot battalion. It was a considerable achievement that the army was virtually re-created after the Caporetto disaster, which cost some 300,000 men and 3,000 pieces of artillery.

Initially there were twelve army corps, each of two divisions, with headquarters: 1 Turin, 2 Alessandria, 3 Milan, 4 Genoa, 5 Verona, 6 Bologna, 7 Ancona, 8 Florence, 9 Rome, 10 Naples, 11 Bari, 12 Palermo/Caligari (three divisions). At the outbreak of war there were fourteen army corps in four armies (25 infantry and four cavalry divisions); by October 1917 there were 26 army corps, of 65 infantry and four cavalry divisions (in effect 66 infantry: the division in Macedonia had four brigades and was thus as strong as a corps). There were ultimately nine armies. Each army corps comprised two infantry divisions (two brigades, each of two regiments), a *Bersaglieri* regiment, a cavalry regiment, an artillery regiment (eight batteries), two or three heavy howitzer batteries, and a *carabinieri* section.

Infantry

The infantry comprised two grenadier, 94 line, twelve *Bersaglieri* (rifles) and eight *Alpini* (alpine) regiments. Initially each regiment comprised three battalions of four

The Italian Army's field uniform is seen in this contemporary illustration of a youthful member of the 21st

Regiment being introduced to prime minister Orlando. (Print after J. M. Brock)

companies each, battalions 1,043 strong; two (occasionally four) machine-guns were deployed at regimental level. *Bersaglieri* regiments consisted of four battalions of three companies each (one of cyclists); some *Alpini* regiments had three and some four battalions, with three or four companies per battalion. In 1912, to provide troops for Libya without weakening the home forces, 24 line and three *Bersaglieri* regiments were each given an extra battalion. The militarized customs service had been employed in Libya, and at the start of the war four 3-battalion regiments were formed. Re-organization during the war gave each battalion three companies (each with two light machine-guns), a machine-gun company (eight guns), a mortar section (four tubes) and a pioneer section, and battalion strength 780. Independent machine-gun companies were deployed at brigade (two companies) and divisional level (four companies), the number of guns at the declaration of war (700) rising to 12,000 at the armistice. The mobile militia comprised 51 3-battalion regiments, three allocated to Sardinia and the rest attached to the 48 infantry brigades of the active army; the 20 *Bersaglieri* battalions and 38 *Alpini* companies of the mobile militia were attached to the *Bersaglieri* and *Alpini* depots. The territorial militia comprised 324 line and 26 *Alpini* battalions.

Although a grey-green service uniform had been introduced from 1909, some units still wore the blue 1903 uniform at the beginning of the war. This tunic was single-breasted (double-breasted for officers) with falling collar bearing a patch in the brigade colouring (regiments were linked in pairs), the patches with a pointed rear (grenadiers had red collar and cuffs and parallelogram-shaped patches):

Grenadier Brigade (1st and 2nd Grenadiers, patch white on red); Brigade Re (1st and 2nd Line, patch black, red edges); Piemonte (3rd and 4th, red); Aosta (5th and 6th, red, black stripe); Cuneo (7th and 8th, crimson); Regina (9th and 10th, white); Casale (11th and 12th, yellow); Pinerolo (13th and 14th, red, black edges); Savona (15th and 16th, white, black stripe); Acqui (17th and 18th, yellow, black stripe); Brescia (19th and 20th, crimson, black stripe); Cremona (21st and 22nd, green, red edges); Como (23rd and 24th, blue); Bergamo (25th and 26th, blue, red stripe); Pavia (27th and 28th, green, red stripe); Pisa (29th and 30th, green, black edges); Siena (31st and 32nd, black, yellow edges); Livorno (33rd and 34th, orange); Pistoia (35th and 36th, orange, black stripe); Ravenna (37th and 38th, white, red edges); Bologna (39th and 40th, white, red stripe); Modena (41st and 42nd, white, crimson edges); Forli (43rd and 44th, white, blue edges); Reggio (45th and 46th, white, green edges); Ferrara (47th and 48th, blue, red edges); Parma (49th and 50th, blue, white edges); Alpi (51st and 52nd, green); Umbria (53rd and 54th, green, white stripe); Marche (55th and 56th, blue, white stripe); Abbruzzi (57th and 58th, green, black stripe); Calabria (59th and 60th, red, green stripe); Sicilia (61st and 62nd, red, green edges); Cagliari (63rd and 64th, red, white edges); Valtellina (65th and 66th, white, black edges); Palermo

(67th and 68th, blue, black edges); Ancona (69th and 70th, yellow, black edges); Puglie (71st and 72nd, white, green stripe); Lombardia (73rd and 74th, white, blue stripe); Napoli (75th and 76th, white, crimson stripe); Toscana (77th and 78th, red, white stripe); Roma (79th and 80th, red, yellow edges); Torino (81st and 82nd, blue, yellow stripe); Venezia (83rd and 84th, crimson, light-blue stripe); Verona (85th and 86th, blue, yellow edges); Friuli (87th and 88th, blue, black stripe); Salerno (89th and 90th, crimson, white edges); Basilicata (91st and 92nd, crimson, white stripe); Messina (93rd and 94th, yellow, red edges).

A five-pointed star of the button-colour was carried on the collar of all arms. Trousers were blue-grey with red piping (red stripe for officers), and for service a dark-blue kepi bore crowned crossed rifles (flaming grenade for grenadiers); white buttons, black leather equipment, dark blue-grey greatcoat with turndown collar, single-breasted for all except officers; white cap-covers and ticken trousers were worn on service. *Bersaglieri* had crimson swallow-tailed collar-patches, brass buttons, dark-blue trousers, blue short cloak, and a black leather round hat with flat brim, cock-feather plume, and a brass grenade and horn badge with the regimental number voided in the grenade, upon a national cockade; in undress they wore a soft red fez with blue tassel. *Alpini* had green swallow-tailed patches and a black leather Tyrolean hat with eagle on horn badge, and an eagle feather at the left.

A stretcher-bearer of the Royal Naval Division describes the result of a shrapnel-burst at Gaba Tepe, Gallipoli, 3 May 1915:

'It went in at the side of my left arm . . . in between the ribs, through the lung – pierced it – clean through, and passed between the spine and an artery in going through. The doctor said he had never seen such a case before . . . if I had not been in good condition I should never have come through it. I was dressed on my own stretcher inside sixty seconds . . . I knew what they would have to do; and as I fell I pulled my tunic off. The blood was spurting out of the wound; and they had to plug it . . . I had a lucky horse-shoe attached to my disc . . . When I was brought into hospital the nurse saw the horse-shoe and she said, "That hasn't brought you any luck." "Hasn't it?" I replied. "I lost two mates, one on each side of me in the morning . . ."'

(Thomas Adamson in *The 'Leader' Local War Record*, p. 87, Nelson, 1915)

Italian troops in a trench dug-out at Monfalcone; note the Adrian helmet worn on top of the soft cap by the man second from right.

The 1909 grey-green service uniform which became universal included a loose, single-breasted tunic with low collar bearing the coloured patch as before, and padded rolls at the shoulder, trousers, puttees, ankle-boots, grey-green leather equipment with two cartridge-holders at each side of the waist-belt buckle, and a grey-green stiff kepi with matching or black peak, and badges as before (later black embroidery). It was later replaced by a soft version, and from 1916 by a felt field-cap with grey-green peak; the other ranks' badge was just a crowned number. *Bersaglieri* wore grey-green short capes and grey hat-covers, and cyclists had leather gaiters instead of puttees; the *Alpini* hat was grey felt with a pompom at the base of the feather, coloured red, white, green, blue and yellow for 1st–5th battalions respectively.

The principal rifle was the 1891 6.5mm Mannlicher–Carcano, though the earlier Vetterli, converted to 6.5mm calibre, remained in use with the territorial militia. The Perino machine-gun was clip-fed, and a curious innovation was the Villar Perosa 9mm submachine-gun, designed for aircraft use but employed by the army, double-barrelled and so light (14½ pounds) that it was useful for alpine service.

Wartime expansion involved the creation of new brigades, distinguished by collar-patches which had horizontal or new vertical stripes (e.g., Brigade Avellino, Regiments 231 and 232, had red with yellow vertical stripe). Early in the war regiments formed 'death companies' to cut wire and lead attacks, equipped with metal cuirasses, leg- and arm-guards, pikes and metal skull-caps with neck-protection (known as 'Farina' helmets from the Milan company which produced them); in 1916 it was decided that these men should be styled *militare ardiot* ('bold soldier'), and when assault detachments were formed in 1917 they were termed *Arditi*. These were formed into 'groups' or battalions, armed with carbines, grenades and daggers, and with more light and heavy machine-guns and flame-throwers than the infantry; each army corps had its *Arditi*, and in 1918 a whole army corps of *Arditi* was organized, each infantry regiment also forming a platoon. They wore infantry uniform with the collar cut open, a black swallow-tailed collar-patch, a black *Bersaglieri* fez in undress, and a badge of a grenade bearing the battalion number upon crossed swords. The French Adrian helmet was adopted by the Italian Army, and by 1916 an improved version had been produced, painted in the uniform-colour with regimental insignia stencilled in black. *Bersaglieri* wore their plumes on the steel helmet, as they did upon the tropical helmet in North Africa.

Commissioned rank-insignia were one to three button-coloured stars on the shoulder-straps, with lace edging for field ranks, and one to three metallic (later yellow or grey) lace bands on the cap, plus a wider band for field ranks. General officers had gold crown and stars on silver shoulder-straps, and vandycked lace with foliate edging (*greca*) on the cap. From 1916 rank-badges were transferred to the cuff, one to three stars and the same on a lace-edged patch for field ranks. NCO rank-insignia were one or two red cuff-chevrons for senior private and corporal, one wide and one or two narrow metallic lace chevrons for sergeants; warrant officers had one to three mixed black and metallic laces on the shoulder-straps. From 1916 the chevrons were black, and warrant officers' badges transferred to the cuff, one to three undulating black chevrons.

Cavalry

The 30 cavalry regiments comprised line (*Cavalleria di Linea*, regiments 1–4), lancers (*Lancieri*, 5–10, 25, 26) and light (*Cavalleggieri*, the remainder). Regiments comprised five squadrons (in 1912 five regiments received a 6th squadron to provide for the garrison of Libya), each 142 strong. The mobile militia included 31 cavalry squadrons, used as cadres. During the war the regimental machine-gun sections were transferred to the infantry, and dismounted MG units were formed from cavalry reservists; and two divisions were dismounted for service on the Isonzo and Carso Fronts in 1916.

The original uniform included a dark-blue single-breasted tunic (officers' double-breasted) with coloured collar and often a triple-ended swallow-tailed patch, white buttons, grey-blue trousers with double black stripe (collar-patch colour for officers, or collar-colour for those without patches), white-metal dress helmet with brass comb and black turban for line regiments, and for undress a blue kepi bearing black grenade; others had squat fur busbies with crowned crossed lances or crowned horn badge for lancers and light regiments respectively. The grey-green service uniform was like that of the infantry, but with shoulder-straps instead of padded rolls, a half-belt at the rear, riding breeches, black leather gaiters and ankle boots; the dress head-gear had a grey-green cover bearing the regimental number and a cockade showing the squadron-number; an alternative was a grey-green helmet shaped like the tropical topee, with badge on the front. Collar-distinctions were:

Regiments 1 (Nizza), 7 (Milano) crimson; 2 (Piemonte Reale), 6 (Aosta) red; 3 (Savoia), 25 (Mantova) black; 4 (Genova), 10 (Vittorio Emanuele II) yellow; 5 (Novara) white; 8 (Montebello) green; 9 (Firenze) orange; 11 (Foggia), 15 (Lodi) red, black patch; 12 (Saluzzo) yellow, black patch; 13 (Monferrato) black, crimson patch; 14 (Alessandria) black, orange patch; 16 (Lucca) white, black patch; 17 (Caserta) black, red patch; 18 (Piacenza) green, black patch; 19 (Guide) light blue, white patch; 20 (Roma) black, white patch; 21 (Padova) crimson, black patch; 22 (Catania) orange, black patch; 23 (Umberto I) white, light-blue patch; 24 (Vicenza) white, red patch; 26 (Vercelli) light-blue piped red; 27 (Aquila) crimson, white patch; 28 (Treviso) light blue, red patch; 29 (Udine) white, green patch; 30 (Palermo) yellow, red patch.

Cavalry were armed with the 1891 Mannlicher–Carcano carbine (there was also the 1891 musketoon, 'MoTS': *Moschetto per Truppe Speciali*), and sabres; only the lancers

Italian gunners with 'happy Easter' chalked upon their shells (and 'long live the king' upon the gun), 1916.

carried lances, with blue pennon for 'dress'. Also included in the cavalry were the *Carabinieri* (gendarmerie), part of the regular army and recruited from selected volunteers from other corps; they had ordinary uniform (with puttees for dismounted service), black collar-patch bearing grey-green lace loops, and a black bicorn hat with grey-green service cover bearing a black grenade on the front.

Artillery

There were initially 36 field artillery regiments (289 batteries), and 63 mobile militia batteries; each active regiment had a depot and train company, the militia being attached to regimental depots. The horse artillery regiment had eight batteries. Each battery comprised four guns; and despite the losses in the Caporetto retreat, by the armistice the number of batteries had risen to 490. The guns were 75mm 1906 Krupp or 1911 Deport quick-firers, the latter with opening trail; most batteries were horse-drawn, but two motorized regiments were formed latterly. Initially there were some 60 4-gun mountain batteries (ten regiments plus fifteen mobile militia batteries) equipped with mule-carried 65mm guns, and 20 mule-batteries with older 70mm guns, intended as infantry support; these were progressively equipped with the 65mm gun, so that mountain and mule batteries became indistinguishable, 170 existing at the armistice. Trench artillery was crewed by bombardier companies, organized in some 200 6- to 12-tube batteries, and about the same number of independent sections; these abandoned most of their equipment at Caporetto and served as infantry until the bombardier service was re-formed and re-equipped.

The heavy artillery was very weak at the outset, expanding from 30 to 280 4-gun batteries by the armistice. They were equipped originally with 149mm guns and 210mm howitzers, to which were added 105mm guns, and 102mm and 105mm motor-drawn guns. Not until late 1917 was it possible to make permanent assignments of mixed groups of 105mm and 149mm guns to each army corps, the motorized batteries remaining as an independent reserve; latterly sufficient ordnance was available for three 149mm batteries to be assigned to each infantry division. Garrison (three fortress and three coastal regiments) and siege artillery were also very weak, the old fortress guns being dismounted and taken to the field army; motorized tractors were introduced for them. Most of the outdated ordnance was lost at Caporetto, necessitating a re-equipping with Italian and Allied guns; the siege batteries increased from 40 initially to 750 at the armistice, those with lighter ordnance in 8-gun batteries and the others in 2- to 6-gun batteries. The increase in number of guns permitted the assembly of single-type artillery groups, whereas only mixed batteries were possible initially. The principal calibres were 120, 149, 152, 155 and 381mm guns, 152mm and 305mm howitzers, and 210mm and 260mm mortars.

Artillery wore infantry-style uniform. The old blue uniform had yellow piping and buttons, dark-blue trousers, black leather equipment and shoulder-belts and pouches for horse batteries; the grey-green service uniform had pointed black collar-patches piped yellow, and cap-insignia a bursting grenade over crossed cannon-barrels.

Supporting services

The original four engineer regiments (eleven battalions) were deployed as individual companies initially, one per infantry division (including a telephone and a bridging section); later three-company battalions were formed, one per division, strength increasing from 42 companies to 78 battalions during the war. Engineer uniform was like that of the artillery, with crimson piping on the blue uniform, and with black pointed collar-patches piped crimson on the grey-green service uniform. The cap-insignia was a bursting grenade over crossed axes (over crossed anchors for pontoon sections). Similar expansions occurred in the train and medical branches, the former with a great increase in motor-transport (for efficiency and because of shortages of horses); on the service uniform the train had pointed blue collar-patches, medical units the same in crimson, and veterinary officers light-blue.

Navy

The navy comprised two commands, with headquarters at Taranto and on the island of Maddalena; the coastal installations were divided into three departments, with headquarters at Spezia, Venice and Naples. Although the navy laboured under the same financial constraints as the army, the effects were much less severe, the equipment being considerably more modern than that of much of the army. The separate naval engineering branch was very proficient and was employed in the construction and repair of warships; their re-floating of *Leonardo da Vinci* in 1919 (accidentally blown up in 1916) was regarded as a triumph for the corps. The navy's main duty during the war was the containment of the smaller Austrian fleet in the Adriatic, and operations against German submarines in the Mediterranean. Both sides conducted raids, in which the fast Italian torpedo-boats were conspicuously successful: the Italian naval hero Commander Luigi Rizzo, for example, sank *Wien* with his motor-boat at Trieste in December 1917, and in June 1918 mounted another hit-and-run raid against a whole flotilla, the speed and manoeuvrability of his little craft allowing him to escape unscathed, leaving the dreadnought *Szent Istvan* sinking.

The capital ships existing in 1915 were:

Date	Name and displacement (tons)	Main armament only
1895	*Marco Polo* (4,583)	6 × 6in, 4 × 4.7in
1901–4	*Giuseppe Garibaldi, Varese, Francesco Ferruccio* (7,400)	1 × 10in, 2 × 8in, 14 × 6in
1901	*Ammiraglio Di St. Bon, Emanuele Filiberto* (9,800)	4 × 10in, 8 × 6in; St. Bon also 8 × 4.7in
1904 (refitted)	*Carlo Alberto, Vettor Pisani* (6,500)	12 × 6in, 6 × 4.7in
1904	*Benedetto Brin, Regina Margherita* (13,427)	4 × 12in, 4 × 8in, 12 × 6in
1907–8	*Vittorio Emanuele, Regina Elena, Napoli, Roma* (12,625)	2 × 12in, 12 × 8in
1909	*Pisa, Amalfi* (10,118)	4 × 10in, 8 × 7.5in
1910	*San Giorgio, San Marco* (9,830)	4 × 10in, 8 × 7.5in
Dreadnoughts:		
1912	*Dante Alighieri* (18,400)	12 × 12in, 18 × 4.7in, 14 × 3in
1914	*Conte di Cavour, Giulio Cesare, Leonardo da Vinci* (22,000)	13 × 12in, 18 × 4.7in, 14 × 3in
1915	*Caio Duilio, Andrea Doria* (22,000)	13 × 12in, 16 × 6in, 18 × 3in

In addition, there were two old battleships (*Sicilia, Sardegna*, 4 × 13.5in, 8 × 6in, 16 × 4.7in), sixteen cruisers

The first Italian dreadnought, Dante Alighieri (18,400 tons, 12 × 12in, 20 × 4.7in, 12 × 3in guns, 3 torpedo tubes). She might almost be described as 'double-ended' from the disposition of funnels and turrets, the main armament in four 3-gun turrets, of which two were situated amidships.

(including *Elba*, a balloon-ship), six torpedo-gunboats/minelayers, 49 small gunboat-destroyers, 85 torpedo-boats, 25 submarines, and four super-dreadnoughts under construction.

Initially there were no marines, naval landing-parties being used instead, members of ships' crews trained as soldiers and equipped with the 12pdr field guns carried by some ships (in 1911, for example, landing-parties from the four ships of the *Vittorio Emanuele* Class occupied Tobruk until relieved by the army). In the World War, naval units served on land (beginning with the crew of the sunken *Amalfi*) and manned floating batteries; in autumn 1917 the first naval infantry regiment was formed (San Marco, of three, later four, battalions) initially for the defence of Venice; it also served at Vittorio Veneto. Naval personnel also manned the armoured trains carrying artillery, which patrolled the Adriatic coast as a defence against Austrian naval bombardment.

Aviation service

The *Corpo Aeronautico Militare* at the commencement of the war included only some fifteen squadrons with about 115 aircraft in total, all suitable only for observation. By the end of the war there were 51 'groups' with about 1,750 aircraft, divided into bombardment, fighter and observation units; from 1917 attempts were made to integrate the aviation service with the army, to maximize air-support for ground operations.

Italy had its own aircraft industry; some of the most significant home-produced aircraft were:

Ansaldo: the A-1 *Balilla* ('Hunter') was a single-seater biplane fighter from later 1917; used for home-defence and bombardment-protection, being less manoeuvrable for ordinary fighter work than others in service.

Caproni: the Ca2 was a biplane heavy bomber used 1915–17, with three engines including one pusher, superseded by the improved Ca3, 1917–18, four crew, also used as naval torpedo-bomber. The Ca4 was a similar aircraft but of triplane configuration, more powerfully-engined, much larger but slower, used principally for night-bombing (and as a floatplane torpedo-bomber). The Ca5 combined the best features of the Ca3 and Ca4, a biplane heavy bomber used 1918 for both day and night bombing.

Maachi: the L1, L2, M3 and M8 were successive designs of flying-boat used 1916–18 for coastal patrol work. The Macchi Parasol was a monoplane observation aircraft used early in the war, slow in climb, liable to stall, and replaced as soon as possible by the Caudron G3.

Pomilio: O. Pomilio & Co. of Turin (taken over by Ansaldo 1918) produced a series of two-seater reconnaissance machines, the PC being notably unstable, and succeeded by the PD, PE and PY; the later models, especially the PE, were very successful (at Vittorio Veneto 112 of 199 aircraft available were PEs).

SAML: the SAML Aviatik was a copy of the Aviatik B1 built by the Società Anonima Meccanica Lombardo of Monza, 1915–16, a two-seater reconnaissance biplane, used only for training from 1917. It was succeeded by the SAML 1 and 2, two-seater reconnaissance biplane and occasional bomber.

SIA: the Società Italiana Aviazione, a subsidiary of Fiat, produced two-seater reconnaissance biplanes 1917–18, the 7B1 and 7B2; despite the former breaking the world record for a climb, both were structurally weak and were withdrawn from combat service in mid-1918. The 9B suffered similar weaknesses and was accepted only by the navy as a bomber. SIA became Fiat–Aviazione in 1918, which produced the Fiat R2 from the 7B2, solving the problems; it was primarily a reconnaissance aircraft but could be used as a light bomber, and saw limited service in autumn 1918.

SP: the SP2 and SP3 were two-seater pusher biplane reconnaissance/bombers, bearing the name Savoia–Pomilio but sponsored by Fiat, 1916–18. Low speed and lack of manoeuvrability made them easy prey, their crews claiming that 'SP' indicated *siamo perduti* ('we are doomed') and 'SP2' *sepoltura per due* ('two-seater coffin'). The SP4 was a twin-engined, three-man bomber used late 1917–mid-1918.

SVA: the Savoia–Verduzio–Ansaldo, designed by the former and constructed by Ansaldo was a single-seater biplane designed as a fighter, but its lack of manoeuvrability led to use as a light bomber and for reconnaissance. The SVA 5, in service from February 1918, was a splendid long-range aircraft (it raided Friedrichshaven and Zagreb); a two-seater version (SVA 5B) was not constructed until 1919, but both the SVA 9 (primarily a trainer) and 10 were two-seaters. This excellent series were among the best aircraft flown by Italy, and featured in Gabriele d'Annunzio's famous leaflet-raid on Vienna on 2 August 1918.

In addition, the aviation service used a number of French aircraft including the Bleriot XI, Caudron GIII, Farman MF7 and 5B, Franco–British H, Hanriot (the standard

---

An anonymous poem epitomises the emotions felt by soldiers of all nations, in all theatres:

Mesopotamia

'One place so vast and wondrous desolate,
I'd give the world if it could be my fate
To leave it now and once more go
To England o'er the seas so far away,
How much I'd love this so.
A wilderness – so flat and void of life,
Why is it that there should be so much strife,
About a land so primitive,
Peopled by tribes whose object seems to be
To live and not let live.
It breaks my heart
To think of all the lives
Lost there.'

(The 'tribes' are presumably the warring armies, not the indigenous inhabitants).

('J. Y.', in *The Mesopoluvian*, 15 June 1917)

Italian fighter), Nieuport 10, 11 and 24, and Spad VII and XIII; and the German Etrich Taube, which was the first aircraft to drop a bomb in action, in the Italian campaign in Libya.

Footnote

1. *The First World War.* Lieutenant-Colonel C. à C Repington, London 1920, I, pp. 207–8.

References

Anon. *The War in Italy.* Milan, 1916 (General HQ photographic dept)

Bainville, J. *Italy and the War.* London, 1916

Davanzati, R. F. *The War of Italy.* Varese, 1918 (issued to promote to the Allies greater appreciation of Italy's contribution)

Hurd, A. *Italian Sea-Power and the Great War.* London, 1918

Page, T. N. *Italy and the World War.* London, 1921 (author was US ambassador during the war)

Salandra, A. *Italy and the Great War.* London, 1932

Thayer, A. J. *Italy and the Great War.* Madison, Wisconsin, 1964

Trevelyan, G. M. *Scenes from Italy's War.* London, 1919

JAPAN

In less than 50 years before the outbreak of the World War, Japan had been transformed from virtually a medieval into a modern society. The emperor remained head of state: in July 1912 Crown Prince Yoshihito succeeded his father, Emperor Mutsuhito, and was formally enthroned in November 1914. He remained as emperor until his death in December 1926, but from November 1921 his eldest son Hirohito acted as regent because of Yoshihito's failing mental condition. The first parliament or Diet was convened in November 1890, consisting of an elected house of representatives (*shugi-in*) and an upper house of peers (*kizoku-in*), some elected, some hereditary and some appointed by the emperor. The 'president of state' or prime minister led a ten-member cabinet, and the emperor was also advised by an intermediate body between himself and the cabinet, the *genrō* or 'elder statesmen'.

Japan's recent foreign policy had been dominated by territorial aspirations towards China, Korea and the Pacific, in pursuit of which the Russo–Japanese War had been fought, from which Japan had emerged with a greatly enhanced military reputation. It was also the main reason why Japan entered the war in 1914, rather than in support of the pact made with Britain in 1902 and 1905, and renewed in 1911, which only applied in the event of an attack on Britain's oriental possessions, Hong Kong and Weihaiwei, which Germany had pledged not to menace if Japan would remain neutral. However, some elements in the Japanese government regarded the opportunity as too good to miss, and the pro-British foreign minister, Takaaki Katō, persuaded prime minister Count Okuma and the *genrō* that the war would enable Japan to appropriate German colonies in China and the Pacific. Britain was wary of Japanese expansionism but was unable to impose many restrictions on Japanese action, and after an ultimatum to Germany went unanswered (requiring the removal of German ships from Chinese waters and the surrender to Japan of the leased territory of Kiaochow), Japan declared war on Germany on 23 August 1914.

Virtually all Japanese operations were undertaken in pursuit of their aims towards China and the Pacific. In October 1914 the German territories of the Marshall, Caroline and Mariana Islands fell, which caused some disquiet in Australasia and the USA, but as Britain required Japanese assistance in the elimination of German commerce-raiders, Japan was confident that Britain would not object. The most important Japanese operations of the war began almost immediately, when General Mitsuomi Kamio (1856–1925) landed to besiege the German fortress of Tsingtao, the port of the Kiaochow colony. The German

Japanese heavy artillery at Tsingtao, 1914.

garrison of about 4,000 was outnumbered greatly by Kamio's 23,000 (primarily 18th Division and 29th Infantry Brigade, supported by a fleet which included the British battleship *Triumph*), and in September Kamio was reinforced by a British brigade under General Nathaniel Barnardiston (2/South Wales Borderers and 36th Sikhs). A bombardment of Tsingtao commenced on 31 October (the emperor's birthday), and the garrison surrendered on 7 November 1914.

In 1915 Katō presented to China the '21 Demands' which would give Japan control over Chinese economic and political matters; the Chinese were compelled to concede most of these, but Anglo–American protests resulted in Katō falling from office (July). Okuma resigned in 1916, and on the advice of the *genrō* the emperor appointed Field Marshal Terauchi Masatake as prime minister. Katō formed a new political party (Kensei-kai) in October and with the support of the Nationalist Party (Kokuminto) achieved a majority in the Diet, but in the following general election the government secured a majority. Japan's only other military action was the intervention in the Russian Civil War, other Allied nations urging Japan to land an expedition at Vladivostok to support the Czech Legion. The Japanese contingent which landed in eastern Siberia was not withdrawn until October 1922. Considerable influence on foreign policy was exerted by Shimpei Gotō, who became home secretary in October 1916 and foreign minister in April 1918.

The navy played a more significant role in the World War, co-operating with Allied ships in the Pacific and in operations against German surface-raiders (Japanese ships participated in the hunt for *Emden*, for example). From 1917, to release British resources, Japan took over patrolling the Indian Ocean as far as the Cape of Good Hope, and a cruiser (*Akashi*) and three destroyer groups were sent, at British request, to perform convoy duty in the Mediterranean.

Army

The Japanese forces were organized on European lines. All able-bodied men aged 17–40 (in practice 20–40) were liable for two, later three years' service with the colours; men who were the sole support of their family were exempt, overseas residents were exempt to age 37, and service could be deferred until education was completed. There was also a system of one-year volunteers which, as in the German system, was designed to form a cadre of those capable of acting as reserve officers. There were two reserves, first or *yobi*, second or *kōbi*, of seven-year enlistment (mobilized only twice during this period for training), and a territorial reserve (*ko kumin-hei*) up to age 40, which received no further training. Less than a quarter of those eligible were actually conscripted; the remainder went into the *hoju* or special reserve, of whom one class received brief training and after seven years passed into the territorial reserve, and the second which passed into the territorials untrained. Officers

were inducted via cadet schools and were commissioned after a period of up to a year being trained in the ranks (artillery and engineers received a further year's training).

The emperor was the commander-in-chief, assisted by a war department, general staff and advisory board of field marshals. The empire comprised three military districts; the army was divided into the Guard Division (HQ Tokyo) and eighteen numbered divisions (two more were formed in 1915); divisions on foreign service maintained their allocated recruiting-grounds in Japan. After wartime augmentations, the regular infantry comprised 84 4-battalion regiments, each battalion 600 strong; 26 field artillery regiments, each of six 4-gun batteries; 28 cavalry regiments each of four squadrons about 100 strong; six heavy and three mountain artillery regiments; 20 engineer battalions each of three companies of about 300 men; and four aviation squadrons, each of three flights of twelve aircraft each.

The army uniform consisted of a dark-blue single-breasted tunic, trousers and peaked cap, with collar, tunic- and trouser-piping and cap-band in the arm-of-service colour (staff and infantry red, cavalry green, artillery yellow, engineers crimson, train light-blue; from 1916 dark-brown for engineers and aviation service); officers wore a blue-black *Attila* with five black cord loops on the breast, and no arm-of-service colour, but broad trouser-stripes of this colour. Cavalry wore a dark-blue *Attila* with white looping (Guard red), green collar and cuffs, and red trousers with green stripe; buttons and lace were white (Guard yellow). Equipment was black leather; white calf-length gaiters were worn by dismounted troops. Rank-insignia was one to three cords of the arm-of-service colour for lower NCO ranks, with a wide lower stripe for senior NCOs; ranks were *nitō-sotsu* (2nd class private), *ittō-sotsu* (1st class private), *jotō-hei* (senior private), *gochō* (corporal), *gunsō* (sergeant), and *sōchō* (sergeant-major); for *tokumu-sōchō* (senior sergeant-major) the insignia was a metallic lace stripe below the coloured stripes. Officers had one to six black trefoil cuff-knots, and black stripes around the cap-band, two for company and three for field grades (*shōi*, 2nd lieutenant; *chūi*, lieutenant; *tai*, captain; *shōsa*, major; *chūsa*, lieutenant-colonel; and *taisa*, colonel). General officers had three stripes on the trousers, three black cuff-cords with broad lace edging, and four cap-band stripes (*shōshō*, major-general; *chujō*, lieutenant-general; *taishō*, general; *gensui*, field marshal). In summer and service dress the uniform was of the same cut, in khaki, without arm-of-service colouring or with a coloured collar-patch bearing the arm-of-service device or regimental number, with cap-band and piping in the arm-of-service colour. A brass five-pointed star was borne on the front of both blue and khaki caps; khaki puttees and often brown leather equipment were worn in service dress, with rank-insignia in the form of brass stars and (for officers) gold piping and lace on the shoulder-straps.

The principal rifle was the Arisaka (officially 'Year 38th pattern'), adopted 1905, a Mauser derivative; there were also 'Year 38th' and 'Year 30th' (1897) carbines, and a 'Year 44th' (1911) cavalry carbine with folding bayonet. During the war Japan supplied huge quantities of rifles and artillery to Russia, and also to Britain for the use of reserve or training formations.

Navy

Although a comparatively modern creation, victory in the Russo–Japanese War (especially in the crushing success of Tsushima) raised the prestige of the Japanese Navy to unprecedented heights. From 1891 all naval ordnance was manufactured in Japan, and although some steel had to be imported, the construction of warships could be undertaken in Japan, although much of the fleet was initially of European manufacture. It was crewed partly by conscripts, but more than half were volunteers; officers were trained at the naval cadet academy, staff college, engineering, gunnery and torpedo schools; and there was an engineering school for NCOs and seamen.

As a result of the Russo–Japanese War, it was decided that the most effective organization would be in '8–8' units (squadrons consisting of eight battleships and eight battlecruisers), but financial strictures resulted in the initial organization being planned as '8–4', rising to '8–6' over seven years.

The following were ships of 9,000 tons displacement or more existing in the first year of the war:

Date	Name and displacement (tons)	Main armament only
Battleships:		
1901	Shikishima, Asahi (15,200)	4 × 12in, 14 × 6in
1902	Hizen (12,700; reconstructed 1907)	4 × 12in, 12 × 6in
1902	Mikasa (15,200)	4 × 12in, 14 × 6in
1906	Kashima, Katori (15,950–16,400)	4 × 12in, 4 × 10in, 12 × 6in
1910	Satsuma (19,370)	4 × 12in, 12 × 10in 12 × 4.7in
1911	Aki (19,800)	4 × 12in, 12 × 10in, 8 × 6in
1912–13	Kawachi, Settsu (21,420)	12 × 12in, 10 × 6in, 8 × 4.7in
Battlecruisers:		
1907	Ikoma, Tsukuba (13,750)	4 × 12in, 12 × 6in 12 × 4.7in
1909–10	Ibuki, Kurama (14,600)	4 × 12in, 8 × 8in, 14 × 4.7in
1913–15	Haruna, Hi-yei, Kirishima, Kongo (27,500).	8 × 14in, 16 × 6in
Cruisers:		
1897	Asama, Tokiwa (9,750)	4 × 8in, 14 × 6in
1901	Azuma (9,456)	4 × 8in, 12 × 6in
1901	Yakumo (9,850)	4 × 8in, 12 × 6in
1901	Iwate, Idzumo (9,800)	4 × 8in, 14 × 6in

In addition, there were several old coastal defence battleships, Iki and Tango (1887–93), Fuji (1897), Sagami and Suwo (1901), reconstructed 1908) and Iwami (1904, reconstructed 1906–7); Iwami, Suwo and Tango all participated in the

Japanese battlecruiser Kongo (27,500 tons, 8 × 14in, 16 × 6in, 16 × 14pdr guns, 8 × 21in torpedo tubes), built by Vickers, Barrow; the other three in the class were built in Japan.

bombardment of Tsingtao. (*Sagami*, *Tango* and the cruiser *Soya* were originally the Russian *Peresviet*, *Poltava* and *Variag*, sunk during the Russo–Japanese War but raised and refitted by Japan; they were returned to Russia in March 1916.) There were some six other cruisers and fourteen light cruisers, three lighter, old battleships for coastal defence, four gunboats, 55 torpedo-boat destroyers, 56 torpedo-boats and seventeen submarines.

References

Jansen, M. B. *The Japanese and Sun Yat-Sen*. Cambridge, Massachusetts, 1954

Lowe, P. C. *Great Britain and Japan 1911–1915*: A Study in British Far Eastern Policy. London, 1969

Typical of the self-deprecating humour of the British soldier during the war was the Fred Karno song, of which this is one of several variations (Fred Karno being one of the most popular comedians of the pre-war period); it was sung to the tune of the hymn *The Church's One Foundation* (S. J. Stone, music (*Aurelia*) S. S. Wesley):

'We are Fred Karno's army
Fred Karno's infantree,
We cannot fight
We cannot sh*te,
What bloody good are we?
But when we get to Berlin,
The Kaiser he will say,
'Hoch, hoch, Mein Gott,
What a blody fine lot,
Fred Karno's infantree.'

LATVIA

Latvia occupied the territory of the Russian Baltic provinces of Livonia and Courland, people by the Letts. It suffered severely during the war, from German occupation (Libau was captured in May 1915) and later Bolshevik terrorism: less than three-quarters of the arable land was in use in 1920, the population of Riga had fallen from 517,000 in 1913 to less than 211,000 in 1917, and instead of 550 railway engines in 1914, only eleven were working by August 1919.

During the war Russia formed a Lettish division 50,000 strong (authorized July 1915), partially from Lettish refugees from German occupation (by 1916 there were 735,000 in Russia), among whom Bolshevik sympathies spread. Kerensky granted limited autonomy to Latvia in July 1917, but a Latvian National Council declared independence on 18 November 1918, with K. Ulmanis as president. Latvia was invaded by the Bolsheviks almost immediately, and despite the formation of a Baltic *Landeswehr* to oppose the Reds (December 1918), Riga fell on 3 January, the government escaping in British warships, and a Latvian Soviet Republic was established. With Allied approval, the German-trained Baltic *Landeswehr*, reinforced by German volunteers and Russian and Lett units, drove

back the Reds, recapturing Riga on 23 May. The Germans commanded by Rüdiger von der Goltz who had arrived from Finland in February, attempted to extend German influence, overthrew the White Latvian government and installed a pro-German administration. Recognizing the danger of German influence, the Allies turned from their non-interventionist policy towards support for the Ulmanis government, and the Baltic *Landeswehr* was defeated by Estonian and Lettish forces. The German members of the *Landeswehr* were forced to return home by the armistice of 3 July 1919, the remainder (now commanded by Colonel A. R. Alexander, a British officer) merging with the Lettish army. Further hostilities occurred in October 1919 when the Latvian government (assisted by the Anglo–French Baltic fleet) resisted an attempt by a White Russo–German force to cross Latvian territory to attack the Bolsheviks, which was regarded as compromising Latvian independence. The last Russian Bolsheviks were expelled from Latvian territory in January 1920, and Latvian independence was recognized formally by Russia by the Treaty of Riga, 11 August 1920.

LIBERIA

Liberia was established as a homeland for freed Negro slaves from the USA; it was declared an independent republic in 1847. US influence remained strong, and although Liberia had its own legislature and president, from 1910 much administration (including finance and defence) was in US hands. The World War seriously affected the Liberian economy, as two-thirds of its commerce was controlled by Germans, and Germany used it as their last West African outpost. Neither the Liberian government nor the Allies felt able to interfere with the German presence (which operated the wireless station in the capital, Monrovia) until US entry into the war. In May 1917 Liberia broke relations with Germany, and President Daniel Howard announced Liberian co-operation with the USA, Britain and France. War was declared on Germany on 4 August 1917, and the Germans in the country were deported. Liberia was unable to take any part in the war, as her military forces (a frontier constabulary organized by US officers) were so weak as to be unable to control tribal violence in the outlying regions; and the customs gunboat *President Howard* constituted the navy. In April 1918 a U-boat bombarded Monrovia to destroy the wireless station, and sank the gunboat. As an Allied nation, Liberia attended the peace conference.

LITHUANIA

The Russian province of Lithuania was occupied by Germany from mid-1915. In an attempt to consolidate their hold, Germany attempted to give Lithuania a vestige of independence under the terms of a perpetual alliance; the

German-dominated Lithuanian Council of State (Taryba) proclaimed the state a kingdom and offered the crown to a member of the Württemberg royal family, Prince Wilhelm of Urach. He accepted on 11 July 1918 and took the title King Mindove II (Mindove or Mendowg I was a Lithuanian heathen who had resisted the Teutonic Order and been killed in 1263); but in the event the Taryba cancelled the appointment on 2 November 1918 and proclaimed an independent republic. Upon the withdrawal of the Germans a Red force moved in and established the Soviet Republic of Lithuania at Vilna (5 January 1919); the legitimate government of President A. Smetona was based at Kovno. Poland intervened and dragged Lithuania into the Russo–Polish War, and the newly organized Lithuanian forces engaged the Bolsheviks. Poland also claimed Vilna, and refused to give it up after the expulsion of the Russians. Hostilities ended between Lithuania and Russia by the Peace of Tartu (Dorpat), 12 July 1920; but Vilna was re-occupied by Poland on 9 October 1920, two days after they had recognized it as the Lithuanian capital, and the dispute was not resolved for seven years. The other territorial question, over the originally German area of Memel, was settled when Lithuanian volunteers helped the inhabitants overthrow the German administration governing under French supervision (January 1923), and Memel was transferred to Lithuania, providing the Baltic harbour she desired.

LUXEMBURG

Situated between Germany and the Western Allies, the tiny Grand Duchy of Luxemburg could not hope to be uninvolved in the event of war, despite guarantees of neutrality to which Germany had acceded. Its population was largely francophile, but its economic ties had been close to Germany since entering the German Customs Union in 1842, and following the Franco–Prussian War Germany ran the railways.

German troops entered Luxemburg on 1 August 1914 and took control of the capital on the following day, despite the protests of the reigning Grand Duchess Marie Adelaide and her government. Luxemburg's military force was so meagre that no resistance could be attempted (it consisted of 150 royal guardsmen, who doubled as postmen, and about the same number of gendarmes), and about the only attempt to check the invasion was made by a cabinet minister, M. Myschen, who blocked a road with his car and presented a copy of the guarantee of independence to the leading German officer. Luxemburg remained under German control during the war, its own government being permitted to retain control of internal affairs, but communications were censored and some citizens were conscripted unwillingly into the German forces. Others escaped to volunteer for the Allies.

The US Third Army entered Luxemburg eleven days after the armistice, and Luxemburg's ties with Germany

Grand Duchess Marie Adelaide of Luxemburg.

were severed by the Allies. There was some internal unrest (necessitating the use of French troops to prevent disorder), as some citizens advocated a republic, others favouring union with France or Belgium; Grand Duchess Marie, who had shown some sympathy with Germany, abdicated in favour of her sister Charlotte Adelgonde. In 1919 a referendum decided against the creation of a republic, to keep the Grand Duchess and the existing constitution, and for economic ties with France.

MEXICO

Although Mexico remained neutral during the World War, it exerted considerable influence on US foreign policy. Mexico suffered much disturbance from 1911, when President Diaz was overthrown; the new president, Francisco Madero, was assassinated in February 1913 on the orders of General Victoriano Huerta. Although some nations recognized Huerta as the new president, the USA and others (Argentina, Brazil, Chile) declined to accept a murderer as head of state and thus encouraged the anti-Huerta factions, led by Venustiano Carranza. The USA occupied Vera Cruz (21 April 1914) after the arrest of US Marines at Tampico, and Huerta was pressured into resigning on 14 July. His successor, Francisco Carbajal, ruled for less than a month, and from the chaos which followed Carranza emerged victorious and was recognized as president by the USA on 19 October 1915. His hold on power was somewhat tenuous, as the head of a government in northern Mexico, Francisco (Pancho) Villa, remained

'Nowadays, the loss of one or more limbs may be regarded almost with equanimity. The day of the wooden stump leg and crutch has passed. There is no necessity to limp through life as a cripple; reparation for a limb or limbs lost in the country's cause can be made and to such effect that one need not be deprived of the joys and pleasures of life, but may move about as easily and comfortably as one's fellow-men who have not had the misfortune to encounter mishap . . .'

('The Oracle' (providing advice to officers about to leave for the Front!) in *Navy & Army Illustrated*, p. 60, 1 May 1915)

hostile despite being defeated several times by Carranza's general Alvaro Obregón.

Allied propaganda made much of German interference; Huerta left Mexico in a German ship, and it was believed that Germany was supporting him in an attempt to overthrow Carranza and to initiate hostilities to keep the USA too preoccupied to intervene in Europe.

Villa raided over the US border in March 1916, killing a number of Americans at Columbus, New Mexico (Allied propaganda claimed that Germay had bribed Villa); on 15 March the US 'hot pursuit' of Villa became a punitive expedition of some 10,000 men, led by Brigadier General John J. Pershing. Carranza gave grudging assent to this foreign incursion, but this turned to hostility and in addition to running fights with the *Villistas*, on a number of occasions the US forces were engaged by regular units of Carranza's army, notably at Carrizal (21 June) when two troops of the US 10th Cavalry suffered and inflicted considerable casualties. The USA mobilized the National Guard on the border in the face of imminent war (eventually more than 150,000 men were involved), but with the international situation worsening it became important that the USA be free of the Mexican entanglement, and the expedition evacuated Mexican territory by 5 February 1917. (Villa remained a threat until he was severely mauled by the US cavalry in a brief cross-border operation on 17 June 1919.)

Allied disbelief of Carranza's expressions of neutrality was reinforced when in February 1917 he urged the American nations to place an embargo on food and munitions upon all belligerent nations, which would have benefited only Germany. Most important, however, was the 'Zimmermann Note'. On 19 January 1917 Arthur Zimmermann, German Secretary of State at the Foreign Office, sent a coded cable to the German Ambassador in Mexico, von Eckhardt, which contained an extraordinary proposal: that in the event of US–German hostilities, Germany should assist Mexico to recapture the 'lost' territories of Texas, Arizona, and New Mexico; and that Japan should be invited to join the German–Mexican alliance. British naval intelligence intercepted and decoded the message and passed a copy to Walter Page, US Ambassador to Britain, who transmitted it immediately to the State Department.

President Wilson published the note on 1 March 1917, causing widespread indignation in the USA; and although both Mexico and Japan denied knowledge of it, together with evidence of other German intrigue it had a considerable effect upon both political and public opinion, and helped pave the way for the US declaration of war on Germany on 6 April.

Civil war erupted again in Mexico in April 1920 when Obregón helped lead a revolt; Carranza fled after his defeat and was killed on the night of 21 May while sheltering in a mountain cabin in Puebla. Obregón and his allies triumphed, and he was recognized by the USA as president in August 1923.

References

Clendenen, C. C. *Blood on the Border: the United States Army and the Mexican Irregulars*. New York, 1969

Tuchman, B. W. *The Zimmermann Telegram*. New York, 1958

MONTENEGRO

Montenegrin independence can be said to have begun with the battle of Kossovo (1389) when the wild and mountainous territory of Montenegro became the haven for fugitive Serbs, and from 1479 the Montenegrins fought on alone against the Ottoman Empire. Under leaders like the fabled Ivan the Black (who established the capital at Cettigne) Montenegro remained an independent state controlled by a ruling prince, a hereditary appointment from 1696 (often passing from uncle to nephew, as the early rulers were also bishops of Cettigne and thus celibate). Centuries of bitter warfare for the very existence of the state and its Christian religion produced a society virtually a relic of an earlier age, of little sophistication, in which blood-feud and revenge-murder were admired, and in which the modern world's most obvious intrusion were the firearms with which every Montenegrin male was festooned. (A measure of the country's backward nature is the fact that it possessed no mint, using Turkish and Austrian coinage, with some low-denomination Montenegrin coins struck in Austria.)

The Montenegrins secured official recognition of their existence from the Ottoman Empire in 1799 after centuries of warfare, but conflict continued (Mirko 'the Sword of Montenegro' won a great victory at Grahovo in 1858). Close ties with Russia existed from 1715 (even in the immediate pre-war period, Montenegro received a Russian subsidy, mainly for military purposes), and the country became increasingly associated with Serbia: Montenegro won considerable territory by the Peace of San Stefano which ended the Russo–Turkish War (1877–8), which was instigated by Serbian and Montenegrin opposition to Turkish suppression of Christians in Bosnia–Herzegovina.

The theocratic succession to the throne ended in 1851 with the death of Peter II, the last prince-bishop of Cettigne; his successor, Danilo II, refused holy orders and took the title *Gospodar* (prince) instead. His successor was Nicholas Petrović-Njegoš (1841–1921), who made considerable steps towards modernization and established dynastic attachments with Russia, Italy and Serbia. Although he established the first Montenegrin parliament in October 1906 (the elective senate created in 1831 was largely powerless), the state was very much under his control, and in August 1910 he proclaimed himself king. His ambition was to create a 'greater Serbia' under Montenegrin leadership, but he was eclipsed by the rising influence of Serbia.

From the beginning of the World War Montenegrin forces co-operated with those of Serbia, although Nicholas retained command. He refused to let the Montengrin army withdraw with the Serbs, and as a result it was captured by Austria (25 January 1916). The cabinet had resigned already (4 January), possibly in protest against rumours that the king was attempting to arrange a separate peace with Austria; the king fled to Italy, and thence to France, where the Allies paid him a subsidy. (His second son, Prince Mirko, subsequently went to Vienna – where he died – presumably in an attempt to ensure that one member of the royal family would be on the winning side, no matter what the outcome.)

With Montenegro out of the war as a combatant power, a threat emerged from Serbia, whose Crown Prince Alexander (Nicholas' grandson: the king's daughter Zorka had married King Peter of Serbia) prepared a plan for the merger of Serbia and Montenegro after the war. Suspicions of Nicholas' attempts at negotiation with the Central

King Nicholas of Montenegro (1841–1921).

Powers undermined his position, and opposition to the king was encouraged by Serbia. A Montenegrin committee was established in Switzerland, and its delegates acceded to the Declaration of Corfu (20 July 1917) which decreed a unified kingdom under Serbian monarchy. Serbian troops liberated Montenegro, and after an election the Montenegrin assembly announced the deposition of the king and a union with Serbia (26 November 1918). Minor incursions by pro-royalist factions (financed and organized from Italy) were repelled largely by the Montenegrins themselves (confirming the king's unpopularity), and Nicholas died at Antibes on 1 March 1921. Although his successors were proclaimed (Crown Prince Danilo abdicated after less than a week as king-in-exile over his German connections, his wife being Duchess Jutta of Mecklenburg), both Britain and France withdrew their recognition of the independency of Montenegro, and its union with the 'Southern Slav' state became irreversible.

Army

The entire population regarded themselves as warriors, and habitually bore arms; in 1889 it was reported that a revolver was simply an accepted part of a man's dress. The majority were of the type approved by the militia, an immense, 6-shot weapon of varied barrel-length (the longer barrels were most popular), based on the 1870 Austrian Gasser model, and known by the generic term 'Montenegrin Gasser'. It was reported that the king held a monopoly on the sale of these, no doubt contributing to their being made compulsory possessions (Nicholas had a reputation for avarice, enhanced by his speculation in stocks during the World War). In addition, most Montenegrins kept at least one rifle at home in addition to that issued by the government, which they were instructed to take with them on even short trips from home.

Until 1870 the military system was based upon tribal lines, but from that date modernization included instruction by foreign officers; Russia provided gifts of weapons to supplement the small quantity of munitions that could be produced in Montenegro. There existed a cadre of officers and *pod-ofizieri* (NCOs) but no standing army; permanent forces (including an artillery brigade) had been established in 1896–8, but had been disbanded for reasons of economy in 1905, and the traditional royal bodyguard had been dissolved in 1898. Instead, every able-bodied Montenegrin male was compelled to serve in the militia (Muslims paid a tax instead). All attended a 12-day training course; aspirant officers or NCOs were sent for two years' training, and some to study abroad. These officers supervised the local training of the militia, which when mobilized was intended to form 56 infantry battalions in eleven brigades (4–6 battalions each) and involved every fit man between ages 18 and 62. Battalion-strength varied, each company (*tchete*) having its own clan identity, and each its own standard. The total force on mobilization was expected to be about 32,000 of the first *ban* (class) and about 6,000 of the second *ban* (reserve);

Montenegrin soldiers with improvised protection against the winter weather: blankets and a sheepskin pelt.

The characteristic New Zealand slouch hat in the 'lemon squeezer' shape generally adopted after Gallipoli, worn by a sergeant photographed in France in 1918; the badges may be those of the 10th North Otago Rifles, which contributed personnel to the Otago Regiment.

in total about 50,000 were mobilized during the World War, of whom 3,000 were killed and 10,000 wounded. There was a small artillery park, the heavier guns kept at the Spuzh arsenal and the lighter ones with the militia brigades; no cavalry, due to the unsuitability of the terrain; and organized transport was entirely deficient: draught-animals were registered and a few carts provided, but the drivers and attendants were often the wives and daughters of the militiamen. At the outbreak of the war, and upon the suggestion of the Tsar, the Montenegrin Army received a Serbian chief of staff, General Yankovich (later Colonel Pesich).

From 1910 some militia units began to receive light olive-khaki Russian-style uniform, including a single-breasted tunic with folding collar (standing for officers), long trousers cut tight below the knee and ankle-boots (riding-breeches and boots for officers), and either a light olive-khaki pillbox cap or Russian-style cap with olive-green leather peak and chinstrap. Arm-of-service colours were borne on the shoulder-straps and piping on NCOs' collars: infantry red, artillery yellow, machine-gunners light-blue, engineers green, general officers crimson, ordnance and staff officers white; rank-insignia was in the form of coloured stripes on the shoulder-straps and design of cap-badge. Officers had grey Russian-style greatcoats but the troops had none, wearing civilian cloaks or coats. Many troops received no uniform whatever, so wore civilian clothes, basically the 'national dress' of a white jacket, red under-jacket and black pillbox cap. The standard weapon was the Russian 1891 7.62mm rifle, but older Russian Berdan rifles were also carried.

References

Anon. *Die Serbische und Montenegrische Armee.* Vienna, 1912
Devine, A. *Montenegro in History,*

Politics and War. London, 1918
Ruhl, M. *Die Armeen der Balkan–Staaten.* Leipzig. n. d. (includes Montenegro)

NEWFOUNDLAND

Until 1949, when it became a province of Canada, Newfoundland was an independent British colony to which representative government had been granted in 1832. It was administered by an elected Assembly and a Legislative Council comprising the governor (appointed by Britain), an upper chamber appointed by the governor, and an executive council or cabinet of ministers chosen by the majority party in the Assembly. In the November 1913 election the government of Sir Edward Morris was returned, and upon the outbreak of war party politics were largely abandoned: Newfoundland offered a military force of 500 men and an increase from 500 to 1,000 in the existing naval service (a branch of the British naval reserve, formed 1899). In 1917 Morris formed a National Government with a cabinet increased from seven to twelve members, six seats of government members and six opposition. At the end of 1917 Morris resigned and emigrated to England (he was created Baron Morris of St. John's and Waterford), and was succeeded as prime minister by William Lloyd, previously leader of the opposition and Attorney-General of the National Government, and who was knighted in the following year. His appointment caused the Colonial Secretary, the Hon. Richard Squires (previously Morris' Attorney-General) to resign and go into opposition to the National Government; and after a split in its own support, the Lloyd ministry was defeated in 1919.

Army

The Newfoundland contingent sailed with the original Canadian force for Britain, and was enlarged into the Newfoundland Regiment. It served at Gallipoli, in Egypt, and on the Western Front; it joined 88 Brigade of the British 29th Division at Suvla in September 1915, and served with them until April 1918, as GHQ Troops until September

1918, and then joined 28 Brigade of 9th Division. On the first day of the Battle of the Somme, the 1st Battalion sustained casualties which can scarcely have been equalled by any unit during the war: sent across open ground without any support or anything to distract enemy fire, it lost 684 out of 752 men in less than three-quarters of an hour, a casualty-rate of 90.95 per cent; every officer became a casualty. In recognition of its conduct in the defence of Masnières (1917) the regiment was granted the title 'Royal', a unique distinction in the war. In all, some 6,500 men served in the regiment, of whom some 1,250 were killed. Some 2,000 Newfoundlanders served in the naval reserve, and 500 in a forestry battalion which served in Scotland. Among the most poignant and distinctive of existing memorials are the national monuments of great, sculpted caribou at Beaumont Hamel and Gueudecourt, the former including the memorial to the 800 Newfoundland missing.

References

Cramm, R. *The First Five Hundred: Being an Historical Sketch of the Military Operations of the Royal Newfoundland Regiment in Gallipoli and on the Western Front.* New York, n.d.

Nicholson, Colonel G. W. *The Fighting Newfoundlanders: A History of The Royal Newfoundland Regiment.* 1964

NEW ZEALAND

New Zealand's contribution to the Allied war effort was extensive: from a total population of 1,090,000, more than 124,000 served in the armed forces, of whom more than 100,000 served abroad, virtually half the eligible male population; almost 58,000 casualties were sustained, including more than 17,000 dead. This was most telling evidence of loyalty to the British crown, even though only some 25 per cent of inhabitants of the country were British-born (more than 72 per cent were born in New Zealand), and it extended to the outlying territories: the natives of Niue in the Cook Islands, population about 4,000, sent £164 to the New Zealand government in 1914 and the offer of 200 men, saying that Niue was 'a small child that stands up to help the King to stand fast'.[1]

New Zealand was governed by a 'general assembly' of a governor (appointed by the crown), a legislative council (appointed by the governor) and a House of Representatives elected by the universal suffrage of all adults, conditional upon one year's residence. The governor (re-titled governor-general in June 1917) and commander-in-chief, New Zealand, throughout the war was Arthur, Earl of Liverpool. After the 1912 election the Liberal Party was forced to step down after 21 years in government, and the Reform Party assumed power under William F. Massey, born in Ireland but who had resided in New Zealand since 1870. The December 1914 election was overshadowed by the war, and there was a degree of unanimity between the parties. The Reform Party achieved a majority of one seat, and despite opposition attacks over defence (especially on alleged mismanagement of Trentham Camp), it was possible to form a coalition National Government on 12 August 1915, in which Massey remained as prime minister, with a cabinet including seven Reform members and six Liberals, led by Sir Joseph Ward Bt., the Australian-born former prime minister (1906–12); the small Labour Party refused to participate. The National Government remained in office until August 1919 (the election due in December 1917 was not contested), and though unpopular was able to concentrate the dominion's efforts on the war.

During the absence of Massey and Ward on Imperial War Cabinet affairs in Britain, in 1916, 1917 and 1918, the Australian-born James Allen (Sir James from 1917), defence minister in both the Reform and National Governments, was acting prime minister; as an enthusiastic volunteer officer he was a fortunate choice, and his contribution to the war effort was very considerable. His youngest son fell at Gallipoli. Allen was responsible for the introduction of the Military Service Act which became law in August 1916, introducing conscription to supplement the previous voluntary enlistment. The most serious internal problem faced by the government during the war was the miners' strike of April 1917, supposedly against conscription, which was resolved by giving automatic exemption. Conscription's effect was limited: 92,000 out of 124,000 men were volun-

New Zealand field battery in action on the Western Front.

teers. New Zealand's export trade was the largest in the world in proportion to population, but the war imposed a heavy financial burden; but New Zealand's produce, bought exclusively by Britain, provided good revenue at little cost, as Britain supplied the vessels to ship the frozen meat, wool, dairy produce and minerals.

When the National Government was dissolved by the resignation of Ward and the Liberals in August 1919, Massey formed an entirely Reform Cabinet, which won a decisive victory in the election of the following December. Allen retired from politics to become New Zealand's High Commissioner in London.

Army

Originating with the New Zealand Militia Act of 1845, virtually all New Zealand's military forces were wholly of militia or volunteer nature. The 1909 Defence Act introduced compulsory military training for all able-bodied males, from ages 12–14 in the Junior Cadets, 15–18 in the Senior Cadets and 18–21 in the 'General Training Section'. The Defence Amendment Act of 1910 took into account the recommendations of Kitchener's survey: a 'citizen army' of 20,000 Territorials aged 18–25, with a further five years in the reserve. In 1911 the previous Volunteer system was replaced by a Territorial scheme, which divided the country into four military districts (Auckland, Canterbury, Otago, Wellington), each with three mounted rifle and four infantry regiments, based on the previous volunteer corps. It was never intended that these units should be used for overseas service, but that in the event of war they would provide volunteers for regiments to be formed in each military district, which occurred in 1914. At the outbreak of war there were more than 25,600 Senior Cadets, almost 26,000 Territorials, plus fewer than 600 'permanent forces' (staff and cadres).

The cavalry were mounted rifles, experienced horsemen trained to fight on foot. Major-General A. J. Godley, commander of the New Zealand forces, described how they were selected from shepherds, farm-workers or those employed in occupations 'for which the ubiquitous motor-car or bicycle has not yet replaced the horse . . . all can ride and find their way about', despite the fact that 'every little "cockatoo" farmer now drives a motor-car instead of breeding a hack or horse for his buggy'.[2] Regiments were composed of four squadrons (two of five), but because of the scattered nature of the 'back-blocks' in which the members lived, regular training was usually carried out only by troops. For the Expeditionary Force formed in 1914, one squadron was taken for each provincial regiment, so that the following units were formed: Auckland Mounted Rifles (from 3rd Auckland, 4th Waikato and 11th North Auckland Regiments); Canterbury Mounted Rifles (from 1st Canterbury Yeomanry, 8th South Canterbury and 10th Nelson); Otago Mounted Rifles (from 5th Otago Hussars, 7th Southland and 12th Otago); Wellington Mounted Rifles (from Queen Alexandra's 2nd Wellington West Coast, 6th Manawatu and 9th Wellington East Coast Regiments). The Auckland, Canterbury and Wellington Regiments formed the Mounted Rifle Brigade; the Otago, reduced to squadron strength, served on the Western Front from 1916.

Similarly, existing Territorial infantry regiments were used to form provincial regiments for overseas service (a 17th Territorial Regiment was formed in 1914). The four provincial regiments were organized from the following Territorial units: Auckland Regiment (from 3rd Auckland, 6th Hauraki, 15th North Auckland and 16th Waikato Regiments); Canterbury Regiment (from 1st Canterbury, 2nd South Canterbury, 12th Nelson and 13th North Canterbury & Westland); Otago Regiment (from 4th Otago, 8th Southland, 10th North Otago and 14th South Otago); Wellington Regiment (from 7th Wellington West Coast Rifles, 9th Wellington East Coast Rifles, 11th Taranaki Rifles and 17th Ruahine Regiment). The 5th

A splendid study of an infantry platoon in Western Front battle order, including fabric-covered helmets and 'box' respirators; apparently New Zealanders from the fern-leaf collar-badges. A Lewis gun is posed in the foreground.

Wellington Regiment, not included in the above, sent personnel to the Samoa Expedition, and to a new 4-battalion regiment formed in early 1915, originally the Trentham Regiment (Earl of Liverpool's Own), from October 1915 the New Zealand Rifle Brigade, which in 1916 became 3 Brigade of the New Zealand Division.

From 1911 the artillery was organized into one field brigade (two or three batteries) for each province. The Native Contingent or Maori Contingent was formed in 1914, and went towards the New Zealand Pioneer Battalion formed in February 1916, which was all-Maori from September 1917, when it was re-styled the New Zealand (Maori) Pioneer Battalion. The New Zealand Machine-Gun Corps was formed from the MG sections of the NZ Infantry Division in January 1916, three companies strong (one from each brigade), plus an extra 'divisional company' formed in England; these were formed into a battalion in June 1918, and ultimately two mounted companies were formed in Palestine from the Mounted Rifles MG sections, the 1st in July 1916 and the 2nd (from the NZ companies of the Imperial Camel Corps) in August 1918, the latter serving with the Australian Mounted Division.

Reinforcements were sent out regularly from New Zealand as numbered 'Reinforcement' units, which were drafted to existing corps at the front. From the 12th–14th Mounted Rifle Reinforcements, and reserve squadrons, the New Zealand Cyclist Corps was formed in April 1916, forming part of an ANZAC Cyclist battalion from July 1916, but reverting to wholly NZ composition when the Australian company was withdrawn in January 1918.

The first New Zealanders to serve abroad were in the Samoan Expeditionary Force, companies of 3rd Auckland and 5th Wellington Regiments, an artillery battery and supports, which occupied the German possessions in Samoa without opposition. Two months after the outbreak of war the New Zealand Expeditionary Force left the country; at the Dardanelles it formed part of the combined New Zealand and Australian Division, and in February 1916 was reorganized as a division. The men from Samoa returned to New Zealand in 1915, being replaced by personnel too old to volunteer for the NZEF.

Organization and equipment were based on British models, but there were differences between the Australian and New Zealand troops. Whereas the Australians used a universal badge, the New Zealand units wore distinctive insignia; a huge variety of designs existed for the Reinforcements, these being replaced by ordinary unit-badges or the 'general' pattern when the drafts reached their destination. The original service uniform was a rather more brownish shade than that of the Australians, but the head-dress was most distinctive. Although the peaked cap was worn by all except mounted troops at Gallipoli, the slouch hat was the usual wear; after Gallipoli, to reinforce individuality, Godley (commander of the NZEF) directed that the brim should be worn level and the crown punched up to produce the 'lemon-squeezer' shape which became the New Zealanders' hallmark.

Navy

Although the naval defence of the Dominion rested in the hands of the British government, under the Liberal administration of Sir Joseph Ward (1906–12) New Zealand gave a battlecruiser to Britain. At a cost of more than £1½ million, the *Indefatigable*-Class *New Zealand* (18,800 tons, 8 × 12in, 10 × 4in guns) was completed in January 1912; it was intended originally for Australasian and far-eastern service, but the New Zealand government authorized its use for European service; it was present at Jutland. Allen insisted that the payment of a subsidy to Britain in return for naval protection was not sufficient, and the 1913 Naval Defence Act laid the foundation for an independent naval force, on condition that upon the outbreak of war any New Zealand forces would pass automatically into British Admiralty control. In 1914 the 'New Zealand Division' of the fleet consisted of the old *Pelorus*-Class cruisers *Psyche* and *Pyramus* (1900, 2,135 tons, 8 × 4in, 8 × 3pdrs) and the older *Philomel* (1890, 2,575 tons, 8 × 4.7in, 8 × 3pdrs).

Footnotes

1. *The Great War*, ed. H. W. Wilson, and J. A. Hammerton, London 1915, III, p. 175.
2. 'The New Zealand Mounted Rifles', by Major-General A. J. Godley, in *Cavalry Journal*, London, 1913, VIII, p. 464.

References

Corbett, D. A. *The Regimental Badges of New Zealand*. Auckland, 1970 (contains much on unit-lineages and services)

Drew, H. T. B. (ed.). *The War Effort of New Zealand: a Popular History*. Auckland, 1924

Powles, Lieutenant-Colonel C. G. *The New Zealanders in Sinai and Palestine*. Auckland, 1922

Pugsley, C. *Gallipoli: the New Zealand Story*. Auckland, 1984

Stewart, Colonel H. *The New Zealand Division in the Great War, 1916–19*. Christchurch, 1921.

Waite, Major F. *The New Zealanders at Gallipoli*. Auckland, 1919

The bestowal of the George Cross upon the island of Malta on 15 April 1942 was not the first occasion in which a military decoration was conferred upon a location. A motto inscribed over the gate of Fort St. Michel, Verdun, proclaimed '*S'ensevelier sous les ruines du fort plutôt que de se rendre*' (Bury yourselves under the ruins of the fort rather than yield it), and such sentiments, when carried into practice, led to the award of numerous decorations to the town of Verdun. These included: Légion d'Honneur (France), Military Cross (Britain), Croix de Guerre (France), Cross of St. George (Russia), Al Valore Militare (Italy), Order of Leopold II (Belgium), Medal for Bravery (Serbia), and the Obilitch Medal (Montenegro).

NICARAGUA

Nicaragua was another of the Central American republics to take the Allied part in the war, and to follow the lead of the United States, which had played a considerable part in Nicaraguan affairs. Civil war and rebellion had left the Nicaraguan economy in a ruinous condition, and it was due largely to US assistance that any order was brought out of chaos: in 1912–13 US Marines had to be landed to end factional violence and prop up the regime of President Adolfo Díaz. He was succeeded from January 1917 by Emiliano Chamorro, who presided over Nicaragua's break in diplomatic relations with Germany (18 April 1917) and subsequent declaration of war (8 May). American influence remained sufficiently strong for Nicaragua to be prevented from invading Honduras in 1919.

The Nicaraguan Army was recruited by the conscription of able-bodied men aged 17-55, who served one year with the regulars and transferred to the reserve; but only some 4,000 served in the army at any one time. Military and political affairs were closely linked, so that the political

leader of each of the country's thirteen departments was also commandant of the area's military.

NORTH AFRICA

Excluding the small territory of Spanish Morocco, the whole of North Africa was in the hands of nations which were, or would become, members of the Allies. Among the most significant colonies were:

Algeria. Ruled by France from 1830, Algeria was administered by a governor-general from the capital of Algiers; it returned three senators and six deputies to the French parliament, and a considerable proportion of its population was European (by the 1911 census, more than 750,000 of a total of 5,492,000, of whom more than 558,000 were French). Algeria extended inland to meet French West Africa, the boundary across the Sahara between the two being established in August 1905. The colony's military force comprised the French XIX Army Corps, and a separate territorial reserve and Algerian force (largely Arab) for the defence of the four Algerian Saharan territories. Coastal defence was undertaken by the French Navy.

Morocco. From 1912 the sultanate of Morocco was a French protectorate, following the 1911 'Agadir crisis' with Germany over the increase of French influence. Much of the previous native administration remained, under French supervision; but there was great hostility to the imposition of French rule, which resulted in a series of risings. French campaigning was affected severely by the withdrawal of regular troops to the World War, and the native tribes took the opportunity to revolt, assisted by German finance, munitions and instruction. Some Moroccan tribes remained loyal to France, however, and French military occupation was pushed forward steadily, although hostilities continued until the surrender of the chief Abd el-Krim in 1926.

Tunisia. Tunisia was a French protectorate from 1883 (although France had administered foreign affairs from 1881). The Bey of Tunis remained head of state, and his government administered the affairs of the Berber and Arab inhabitants, but was actually under the control of a French resident-general, in effect a viceroy, who administered directly the affairs of foreigners and Christians.

All three of the French colonies supplied units for the French forces, many of which fought in Europe.

Tripoli. The areas of Tripolitania (capital Tripoli), Cyrenaica (capital Benghazi) and Fezzan (capital Murzuk) were generally termed 'Tripoli', and passed from Ottoman to Italian rule as a result of the Italian victory in the Italo–Turkish War (1911–12). The war did not enhance Italy's military reputation, however, and throughout the World War the territory was beset by native risings; not until 1934 was there a complete pacification. The colonies were united and named Libya by Fascist Italy.

Most military action in North Africa (excluding Egypt,

which appears separately) arose from the hostility of the Senussi (or Senusi). They were principally neither a tribe nor a sect, but a grouping which recognized the authority of the Senussi family, named after Seyyid Mohammed ben Ali ben Es Senussi el Khettabi el Hassani el Idrissi el Meharjiri, born in Algeria at some date between 1791 and 1803, and who died in Jaghbub (Cyrenaica) in 1859 or 1860. Commonly called the Sheikh es Senussi, he founded an Islamic reformist movement centered on Cyrenaica. During the Italo–Turkish War, Ottoman instructors joined the Senussi and partially reformed their military capability, but the end of the war removed most of such support, and in the succeeding years only in Cyrenaica did the Senussi continue to be dominant.

Upon the outbreak of the World War, Turkish and German agents sought to make Tripolitania and Cyrenaica bases for operations again Britain and France. The Turks persuaded the Senussi Sheikh Sidi Ahmad esh Sherif to remain loyal, and with munitions and instruction from the Central Powers, in late 1915 the Senussi invaded British Egypt. They were no longer just undisciplined tribesmen: under Ottoman instruction seven 'regular' battalions (*Muhafizia*) were formed to provide a trained nucleus, equipped with light artillery and machine-guns, and commanded by Ja'afar al Askari (or Ga'far Pasha), an Iraqi general of considerable skill; in overall command of the Senussi war effort was another Turkish officer, Nuri Pasha, Enver's half-brother. Some inroads were made into Egypt, some very ineffectual Egyptian tribesmen (armed largely with flintlock muskets) went over to the Senussi, and the British forces were extremely stretched (the Western Frontier Force was a very scratch formation in November 1915, including British Territorials, Yeomanry, Australian Light Horse, New Zealand Rifle Brigade, the 15th Ludhiana Sikhs, South African infantry and Egyptian supporting troops). As British strength increased they mounted a counter-offensive in which armoured cars gave the British the same level of mobility enjoyed by the Senussi. The decisive action occurred at Aqqaqia on 26 February 1916, when the Senussi forces were routed, culminating in one of the last cavalry charges, launched by the Dorset Yeomanry against Senussis retreating before a determined South African attack; in the course of it Ja'afar was wounded and captured.

Senussi operations continued against France, whose resources were weakened by the transfer of regular troops to Europe, their forces largely the local *saharien* units (including camel corps) and the wild, irregular *goums*. The Senussi were supported by other disaffected tribes, notably the Tuareg, but their military capability was limited. The low point in the French campaign was December 1916, when out-posts were overrun; France recalled the previous commander from Europe, General Laperrine, and undertook a more offensive strategy; lost ground was recovered and the southern Tuaregs were defeated in April 1917. The Senussi, who had been raiding as far as the River Niger,

were dispersed and despite sporadic guerrilla activity the French Sahara was pacified by January 1918.

Following their expulsion from Egypt, the Senussi were pursued by British mechanized columns, although the Allied effort expended was out of all proportion to the number of Senussi under arms, whose guerrilla operations tied down up to 60,000 Italian, 35,000 British and empire, and 15,000 French troops. Military aviation was also important: much of the British patrolling was done by aircraft, and the Italian Caproni heavy bombers proved a potent weapon (an agreement on Anglo–Italian co-operation was concluded in July 1916). Sidi Ahmad retired to the Siwa oasis, a major Senussi centre, where he was attacked on 3 February 1917 by Brigadier-General H. W. Hodgson's motorized column from Matruh. The Senussi held up the attack and Sidi Ahmad escaped. Ottoman and German influence declined, and peace negotiations between Britain, Italy and the Senussi (opened as early as mid-1916) concluded with treaties signed in April 1917. Sidi Ahmad's cousin, Sidi Mohammed el Idris, who had opposed the attack on Egypt, gained sufficient support to lead the Senussi; Sidi Ahmad quit Cyrenaica for Turkey, aboard a German submarine, in August 1918.

Although the peace between Italy and the Senussi was no more than an armed truce, Italy undertook to supply them with munitions in return for support against another anti-Italian resistance movement in Tripolitania, organized by Nuri. The peace lasted until after the end of the World War, when Italy finally defeated the Senussi (1922).

References
Nicolle, D. *Lawrence and the Arab Revolts*. London, 1989 (a good introduction)

> Charles à Court Repington casts an unusual sidelight on Pétain, after they had dined with Nivelle on 27 April 1917:
> 'Pétain discussed women and marriage. He said he was a bachelor but loved children, and after the war he would have to choose between matrimony and suicide. I said that it was often the same thing.'
> (*The First World War*, I, p. 542, London, 1920)

PANAMA

Not surprisingly for a state with no standing army, the Republic of Panama's entry into the war on the Allied side (declaring an intention of supporting the USA on 8 April 1917) had little effect on the conflict. Ties with the USA were very close; indeed, without the USA it is doubtful whether Panama would have existed, for until the Panamanian revolt of November 1903 it was a province of Colombia. The revolt had been encouraged by President Theodore Roosevelt to facilitate the purchase of the territory necessary for the Panama Canal; three days after the revolt (3 November 1903) the USA recognized Panamanian independence, and on 18 November the treaty was signed which granted the Canal Zone to the United States. Panama was governed under the 1904 constitution, with a president elected for a four-year term. Apart from an inherited border dispute with Costa Rica (which resulted in hostilities in 1921) and riots in mid-1912 at the time of the election of President Ramon Valdez (which necessitated some US intervention), Panama remained at peace save for its declaration of war on Germany. Valdez should have served until 1920 but his death in 1918 led to the balance of his term being served by Ciro Urriola. Panama's only forces were four gunboats, of which the most formidable, *Gatan* and *Darian*, were equipped with only three 1pdr guns.

PERSIA

In a state of considerable internal turmoil, the kingdom of Persia was originally the subject of intense Anglo–Russian commercial rivalry. An accord was drawn up in 1907 which divided Persia into a northern zone of Russian influence, a southern zone of British influence, and a central neutral zone in which both might compete; in the event of Persia defaulting on the repayment of foreign debts, Britain and Russia claimed the right to take control of Persian finances within their own spheres of interest. The zones of influence became almost protectorates as a result of the 1909 revolution which deposed the despotic Shah Mahommed Ali in favour of his 13-year-old son, Ahmad Mirza, who ruled under a regent. In 1911 the ex-Shah attempted to return (with Russian encouragement) but was defeated, and in November 1911 Russian forces moved into northern Persia to restore order and protect their interests; Britain moved into south-west Persia to guard her oil interests. Germany, for some two decades before the war, had also attempted to increase her influence in Persia, and to profit from Persian resentment of Anglo–Russian domination.

At the outbreak of the World War, Persia was largely powerless. The 'native' Persian Army – which had always utilized foreign officers, the latest attempts at reorganization being by Austrian and Russian missions in 1879 – was under-strength and generally useless. The only effective forces were the 'Cossack Brigade', some 8,000 strong, formed and commanded by Russians, and 7,000-strong police, known from the nationality of its officers as the Swedish gendarmerie. Neither were wholly committed to the interests of Persia: the Cossack Brigade was Russian-controlled and the gendarmerie was pro-German. Germany intended to use missions and agents to destabilize Anglo–Russian interests, appropriate the Persian banks and raise Persian forces under German control to threaten British India. In the north, their plans were frustrated by the presence of Russian troops; but aided by gangs of assassins the Germans enjoyed success in undermining British interests in the south, so that only the Gulf ports and their British garrisons remained within British influence. In western Persia, Turkish forces drove back the Russians, so that by 1916 the situation was very unpromising for the Allies. However, despite German propaganda (including the absurd story that the Kaiser had been converted to Islam and was henceforth to be styled Hajji Wilhelm!), German instructors were hated almost as much as the Russians, and few recruits were forthcoming. Despite the state of anarchy in parts of Persia, von der Goltz (commanding in Iraq and Persia) was fairly accurate in his assessment: vast expenditure and no return.

With the agreement of the Persian government, Britain proposed to raise a Persian force to restore order. Organized by General Sir Percy Sykes (who had spent many years in Persia), the South Persia Rifles were formed at Bandar Abbas in March 1916, with British and Indian instructors. Aided only by a small Indian contingent (one battalion, a cavalry squadron and a mountain artillery section), and latterly 600 Cossacks who joined at Isfahan, Sykes marched some 1,000 miles through the heart of the country, suppressing brigandage, enlarging his Rifles, and eliminating German influence. The Swedish gendarmerie, on the point of becoming lawless brigands themselves, were partly incorporated into the Rifles, and unruly tribes were brought under control of the Persian government.

The Russian Revolution threw all into confusion, and in north-west Persia a revolt by the brigand Kuchik Khan (who had German, Turkish and Austrian munitions and instructors) could have resulted in his march on Teheran and the forcing of the Persian government to take the part of the Central Powers. He was stopped in early 1918 by the combination of a small British force (that under Major General L. C. Dunsterville which later marched to Baku), and Russians unaffected by Bolshevism. Later in 1918 more British troops moved into north-west Persia to defend it against aggression from the Turks and Russian Bolsheviks; there they remained for some time after the war. In spring 1918 the Persian government declared the South Persia Rifles to be a foreign force, and urged Britain to withdraw from Persian territory. This prompted some mutiny and desertion within the Rifles, and the rebellion of Solat et Dauleh, chief of the Kashgai tribe; after some hostilities he was deposed and the Kashgai revolt suppressed. An Anglo–Persian agreement was achieved in 1919, and following Russian incursions in 1920, the commander of the Cossack Brigade, General Reza Khan Pahlavi, seized power. Ratifying a treaty with the Soviet government, he secured the withdrawal of Russian troops from Persia, and in October 1925 deposed the Shah; in the following April he was himself crowned Shah.

References

Dickson, Brigadier-General
  W. E. R. *East Persia: a Backwater of the Great War*. London, 1924
Moberley, Brigadier-General F. J.
  Military Operations in Persia 1914–19. London, rep. 1987;

(Official history)
Sykes, C. *Wassmuss*. London, 1936 (concerning 'the German Lawrence')
Sykes, Sir Percy. *History of Persia*, London, 1930

PHILIPPINES

The Philippine Islands were ceded to the USA on 10 December 1898, in the wake of the Spanish–American War. During this conflict the Philippine patriot forces had assisted the USA, but dissatisfaction that total independence had not been achieved led to an insurrection against their erstwhile allies, which lasted from February 1899 until 1902 (or 1905 if the campaigns against the Moro tribesmen are included). A US civilian administration was established in 1901, which incorporated an increasing number of Filipinos, until by 1916 the state was in many ways almost autonomous. When the USA entered the World War the Filipinos offered to supply a division of troops and finance the construction of a destroyer and a submarine. Upon the declaration of war, 22 German ships which had been interned in Manila harbour since the beginning of the war were seized. The Philippines possessed no army as such, the Philippines Constabulary being largely responsible for public order and for controlling the tribesmen of the more primitive parts of the archipelago; officers were largely American and rank-and-file partly American and partly Filipino. During the war a Filipino National Guard was raised (disbanded 1919), and many Filipinos enrolled in the US forces. To emphasize the near-independent nature of the Philippines Constabulary, members who served during the war received their own Victory Medal, not that of the USA.

POLAND

From 1795 there was no independent Polish state, save the satellite Duchy of Warsaw established by Napoleon. The old kingdom was partitioned between Austria, Prussia and Russia, and the Congress of Vienna (1815) transformed the previous Duchy of Warsaw into the 'Congress kingdom' under Russian control. Abortive risings in 1830–1 and 1863–4 were crushed, but despite attempts at 'Russification', Polish nationalism survived.

Upon the outbreak of the World War Polish nationalist opinion was divided over whether Austria or Russia provided the best opportunity for gaining independence (hardly any Poles supported Germany). Roman Dmowski, formerly leader of the 'Polish Circle' in the Duma and head of the National Democratic Party, advocated support of Russia in the belief that the Entente would unify those areas of Poland appropriated by Germany and Austria. The alternate view was taken by Joseph Pilsudski (1867–1935), born in Russian Poland but who had fled to Galicia (Austrian Poland) after repeated trouble with the Russian authorities, including five years in Siberia for allegedly conspiring to assassinate Tsar Alexander III. In Galicia from 1908 he began to organize a private Polish army (under the guise of athletic and shooting clubs) with which to liberate his homeland.

As Poland was one of the main theatres of conflict, and as

> The Daily Sketch, 4 February 1928, carried extensive reports of the funeral of the Field Marshal The Earl Haig, Viscount Dawick and Baron Haig of Bemersyde, KT, GCB, OM, GCVO, KCIE, Hon. LLD, DCL, who had received in addition some fourteen foreign awards and a grant of £100,000 at the conclusion of the Great War. The same journal appeals for financial assistance for one of Haig's old soldiers, now 'semi-starved' and who 'lives in one room with his wife and three children, and pays a weekly rent of 6s. 6d. from his pension of 12s. 6d. The pension was awarded because an enemy shell tore away three of his ribs and injured a shoulder. The man now has three silver ribs and has to wear a complete leather case for his body and one arm . . .'

some million Poles were mobilized by one side or the other, the importance of Poland was recognized by both sides. On 14 August 1914, to counter anti-Russian sentiments being encouraged by Germany, the Grand Duke Nicholas issued a proclamation calling on all Poles to support Russia and promising a united, free and democratic Poland under the Russian crown. However, with Russian reverses and the occupation of Poland by the Central Powers, the pro-Russian camp favoured by the National Democrats receded in importance, and Dmowski transferred his base from Petrograd to London and Switzerland, from where he maintained a vigorous propaganda campaign to very limited effect. More attention concentrated upon Pilsudski's Polish Legions being organized under the aegis of the National Council of Galicia. This formation, only some 18,000 strong by mid-1916 but of considerable political significance, was subject to Austrian command but was organized as a separate Polish force, using the Polish language and originally under command of Marshal Durski (a Pole in Austro–Hungarian service), but having taken the Austrian Landsturm oath of allegiance. In mid-1916, observing little progress towards increased autonomy, Pilsudski resigned his command of the Legion's 1st Brigade; Austria–Hungary prepared to make concessions (he had requested the use of Polish colours and the substitution of Polish for Austrian officers), but Germany interfered, Pilsudski was dismissed and in October the Legions were withdrawn from the front.

By now the Central Powers had realized that some diplomatic accord was necessary to maintain Polish support, so on 5 November 1916, amid protests from the Entente at the breach of international law, Germany and Austria–Hungary established a Polish state, semi-independent but under their protection, to be administered by a provisional Council of State, with Pilsudski as head of the state's Military Commission. Realizing that it was an artifice to gain Poland's support in the war, in March 1917 Pilsudski and his army refused to accept a proposed oath of allegiance binding them to support Germany and Austria, and as a result the Polish Auxiliary Corps, as the Polish army was now termed, was disbanded; on 30 July Pilsudski was arrested and a month later the Council of State resigned. It was replaced by a 'regency' council allowed to administer some internal affairs, but with no control over military forces and with the governors-general appointed by Germany and Austria having the right of veto. By this time Austro–Hungarian influence had declined markedly, and with the collapse of Russia Germany had no need of further Polish assistance on the Eastern Front, so no longer made concessions to Polish nationalism: the Polish government was excluded from the negotiations which led to the Treaty of Brest–Litovsk.

The concept of an independent Poland had been recognized by the Russian Provisional Government on 30 March 1917, and a 'Polish Liquidation Committee' was established (its chairman, Lednicki, was given a cabinet seat), and soon after a Polish army (three corps) was created from Poles serving in the Russian forces. Pilsudski was released from his confinement in Magdeburg during the 'German Revolution' of November 1918, and returned to Poland to find the nucleus of an army already in existence. Poland was in a parlous state, with little means of defence, the Council of Regency being dependent upon German support, with threats of anarchy spreading from Russia and with 30,000 rebel German troops still in the country. On 14 November the Council of Regency resigned, leaving Pilsudski in authority; he formed an army on the existing foundations and then a government. A compromise was reached between Dmowski's conservative National Committee and Pilsudski's largely Socialist government: in January 1919 Pilsudski remained as head of state with a coalition cabinet headed by the pianist Ignacy Jan Paderewski (1860–1941) as prime minister and foreign minister; Poland was represented at the peace conference largely by the National Committee, Dmowski and Paderewski. Pilsudski led Poland in the Russo–Polish War of 1920, begun by Poland to pre-empt a Russian attack to expel the Poles from disputed frontier territory. Pilsudski stopped the Russian advance in the Battle of Warsaw (August 1920) and defeated them again at the Battles of the Niemen and the Shchara (September 1920); hostilities ended with an armistice on 12 October, and by the Treaty of Riga (18 March 1921) Russia acceded to all of Poland's territorial claims.

Army
Several independent Polish forces existed during the World War; despite the different national armies in which they served, elements of traditional Polish costume were maintained where possible.

Russian service
In October 1914 the Russians formed the Polish Pulawy Legion in the 'Congress kingdom'. The two lancer squadrons had a dark-blue dress uniform of traditional Polish pattern, with crimson plastron, pointed cuffs, collar, trouser-stripes and shoulder-straps, Russian-style peaked cap with crimson top and white band, and crimson lancer girdle with blue stripe; the service uniform was a light khaki Russian-style shirt and cap and blue breeches, although officers appear to have worn a single-breasted khaki tunic and breeches with crimson collar, pointed cuffs and trouser-stripe. As the Russians were traditionally fearful of Polish nationalism, the Legion was dispersed in February 1915 and its personnel became two cavalry squadrons and an infantry battalion of the Russian Army. As the war progressed, Russia was compelled to re-institute Polish units to obtain recruits, initially a brigade and later a division, with a lancer regiment. The Polish Army formed by the Provisional Government was short-lived: I Polish Corps was constituted in September 1917 but surrendered to the German occupation of Belorussia in the following February, and was returned to Poland (still under Central Powers administration). Under Russian command the Polish units wore Russian uniform with no national symbols, but these appeared after the Revolution to reinforce national identity, including the traditional eagle cap-badge and even the use of a huge embroidered eagle upon the upper arm. The traditional square-topped *czapka* was used, with soft top in light khaki with matching peak, and trimmed in arm-of-service colours: for artillery, for example, it had a black band and crimson piping, and bore a brass crossed cannon badge.

Austrian service
The Polish Legion wore basically Austrian uniform with Polish features. The 1st Brigade (initially six infantry battalions and a cavalry squadron) wore a light-grey peaked cap instead of the Austrian field cap, and the 2nd Brigade a square-topped cloth cap. The 1st Lancers wore a very large grey *czapka* with crimson piping, white-metal chinscales, large brass eagle-on-shield plate, a very light-brown lower band and peak, and white cockade with crimson rosette as worn by the Duchy of Warsaw; a light-grey lancer tunic with crimson facings, and a brownish-grey double-breasted cavalry jacket piped crimson. The 2nd Lancers (and apparently the 1st at a later date) wore a shorter grey *czapka* with light-brown peak and a single line of crimson piping, a braided white cord at the front, suspended from the side corners, and a grey rosette with crimson centre bearing a small white-metal eagle. The headquarters troop of 1st Brigade, described as *Chasseurs à Cheval* or Mounted Rifles (and later absorbed by the 1st Lancers) wore perhaps the most archaic head-dress of the war, a broad-topped black shako with black leather peak and trim and white-metal chinscales and large eagle-plate, virtually identical with the pattern worn a century before. Later all adopted a soft khaki cap with square top in imitation of a *czapka*, bearing on the front either a white cockade with crimson centre bearing a small eagle, or a white-metal eagle upon a crescent-shaped

*1st Lancers of the Polish Legion
in Austrian service.*

shield inscribed '1' or '2' for lancers, 'S' for infantry (*Strzelec*: rifles) or later 'L' (*Legiony*). The 1st Brigade wore rank-insignia on the collar: one to three red lace bars for NCOs (or red collar-edging for sergeants), red zigzag collar-edge and one to three silver stars for company officers, and the same with silver edge and gold stars for field ranks; these were worn on the shoulder-straps by the 1st Lancers, with the stars alone on the collar by officers. The 2nd Brigade wore Austrian rank-badges, but officers removed theirs when ordered to replace the military star with the rosette of non-combatant officers. Facing-colours were worn on the collar-patches (infantry green, 1st Lancers crimson, 2nd Lancers amaranth, artillery black) until the pike-grey uniform was replaced by field-grey in 1916. New rank-distinctions included zigzag collar-lace for all, with one to three stars for NCOs and the same all in silver for officers (gold and silver lace and gold stars for field ranks); towards the end of the year these were replaced by shoulder-strap insignia, one to three transverse silver stripes for NCOs, a silver zigzag for sergeants, and silver longitudinal stripes for officers (gold for field ranks).

French service

On 4 June 1917 President Poincaré authorized the creation of a separate Polish army in French service; Poles serving in the French Army were transferred, and other recruits came from the Russian Expeditionary Force in France and Macedonia, large numbers of Poles resident in the USA joined, and many prisoners of war were recruited (Polish troops previously in German or Austrian service). As early as January 1917 a training establishment had been opened at Camp Borden, north of Toronto, for those Poles from North America, and these men also joined the autonomous Polish army in French service. Often styled 'General Haller's Army' after its commander, Josef Haller (1873–1960), when transferred to Polish service (arriving in Poland from April 1919) it was more than 80,000 strong.

Uniform and equipment was generally of French style, though when Camp Borden was moved to Camp Niagara (known to the Poles as Camp Kosciusko) many were equipped with old Canadian militia uniform until they could be re-supplied; some even wore straw slouch-hats with the red and white Polish colours as a hat-band. The French uniform was horizon-blue with arm-of-service collar-patches bearing a double chevron and unit-number (and horn for infantry), coloured: infantry dark-green on horizon-blue, cavalry white on amaranth, artillery light-blue on red, engineers red on black, train white on green with red number, and medical service white on crimson with blue number. Polish features included a white eagle on the shoulder-straps (silver on circular crimson patch for officers) and a square-topped horizon-blue cloth cap, piped in the branch colour, generally with a peak only for cavalry, artillery and most officers, and badge at the left front (a horn for infantry, and an eagle on the centre front for some officers). Rank-insignia was worn on the cuff by all, and on the front of the cap by officers and some NCOs: diagonal bar for senior private and two for corporals, the same in metallic lace for sergeants and sergeant-majors respectively, a bar with crimson centre for warrant officers, and horizontal metallic bars for officers, one to three for company officers, major four, lieutenant-colonel five and colonel six, for field ranks with bars of opposing metals. On the cap these could be worn in chevron form. Lace was silver for all except artillery, engineers and medical service, gold. Generals had crimson pointed cuffs and cap-band both with zigzag silver lace, with two silver stars below an eagle on the cap-band (two lines of lace and three stars for generals of division). The Adrian helmet bore a pressed-metal eagle badge (within a hunting horn for infantry). A mixture of this French uniform, German, Austrian and Russian styles remained in use with the Polish forces until the implementation of the 1919 uniform regulations.

References

Dziewanowski, M. K. *Joseph Pilsudski*. Stanford, 1962

Gillie, D. R. *Joseph Pilsudski: Memoirs of a Polish Revolutionary and Soldier*. London, 1931

Zygulski, Z., and Wielecki, H. *Polski Mundur Wojskowy*. Cracow, 1988 (contains many relevant illustrations of extant items of uniform and equipment)

PORTUGAL

Until the revolution of 5 October 1910 Portugal was a constitutional monarchy; after that date the royal family was deposed and the king, Manoel II, fled to Britain (he had reigned only since the assassination of his father, King Carlos I, and his elder brother the Duke of Braganza in

February 1908). A republic was proclaimed and the monarchy abolished (1911), with an elected president as head of state and a prime minister to lead the government. Royalist risings occurred in 1911–12, followed by draconian repression, and terrorism by the powerful republican movement of the *Carbonarios* or 'Young Portugal', which had been instrumental in precipitating the revolution. The first president, Dr. Manuel de Arriaga, remained in office with a succession of prime ministers until his resignation in 1915, when after a short interim presidency of Theophilo Braga, Dr. Bernardino Machada became president (6 August 1915), having been premier at the outbreak of the World War. The governmental situation in 1914–15 was chaotic, with regular resignations of premiers, of whom one (General Pimenta de Castro) was transported to the Azores, and another (his successor, Chagas) was shot and wounded by a rival senator.

On 5 December 1917 a revolution broke out against the prime minister, the Democrat Dr Afonso Costa; rebel artillery bombarded the fleet at Lisbon and after some fighting both Costa and President Machado were arrested, the latter being exiled on 15 December. The new president and leader of the revolt was Major Sidonio Paes, who submitted himself for election and was confirmed in office in May 1918, having in January overcome a Radical mutiny in the navy which involved a naval bombardment of Lisbon. Under Paes' government, the offices of president and prime minister were combined. He remained in power until his assassination on 14 December 1918, which opened another chapter of revolt and bloodshed, including another royalist attempt to restore the monarchy in a brief civil war in 1919.

Throughout this chaos, Portugal's external policy remained stable; indeed, in November 1916 King Manoel (from exile) instructed his adherents to suspend their attempts to restore the monarchy and to put the interests of the country before those of party. As early as 7 August 1914 the Portuguese government proclaimed its support of the country's oldest ally, Britain, and on 23 November parlia-

ment authorized military participation; but such were the internal and financial problems that this was no more than a gesture. Conflict with Germany occurred as early as 24 August 1914 on the Mozambique frontier, but engagements in the Portuguese colonies of Angola and Mozambique did not cause a declaration of war. Reinforcements were dispatched to these colonies as early as 11 September 1914, and ultimately some 40,000 Portuguese troops collaborated with Allied forces in Africa, against both German forces and native insurrections encouraged by Germany, such as that in Angola in 1917.

Despite sympathy with the Allies, Portugal did not join the war officially until 1916. In that February Britain encouraged Portugal to seize German ships lying in Portuguese harbours (mainly in the Tagus estuary); 36 were taken (most damaged by their crews to prevent their immediate use) and as a result Germany declared war on Portugal on 9 March. On 16 March war was declared between Portugal and Austria, and German residents of Portugal were banished or interned from 21 April, which countered the German agitation that had existed since the beginning of the war. French and British military missions arrived in Portugal in March–April 1916, and the training of a Portuguese division began. In January 1917 General Fernando Tamagnini de Alorn was appointed to command the Portuguese Expeditionary Force, and by the middle of the year some 40,000 were serving on the Western Front, with 20,000 in support in Portugal; before joining the Allied forces, the Expeditionary Force received further training in southern England. As Portuguese finances were in a parlous state, a loan was agreed from Britain in August 1916, finally amounting to £23 million; nevertheless, Portugal emerged from the war with an immense national debt.

Army

Under the monarchy the Portuguese Army was regulated by acts of 1887, 1899 and 1901, with amendments. Recruitment was by a mixture of voluntary enlistment and conscription;

Portuguese infantry in France, June 1917, wearing their distinctive fluted helmet, and re-equipped with Lee-Enfield rifles to facilitate ammunition supply when serving with British forces.

although exemption could be purchased, theoretically all able-bodied men over the age of 21 were liable for a term of three years in the regular army, followed by five in the 'first reserve' and seven in the 'second reserve'. The effective strength of the army was about 33,000 men and 100 guns, rising upon wartime expansion to some 175,000 with 336 guns, plus some 7,500 extra men from the mobilization of municipal guards. During the World War Portugal mobilized about 100,000 men, and suffered some 21,000 casualties, including more than 7,000 fatalities.

The Portuguese Expeditionary Force on the Western Front was in general not regarded highly by the British, as perhaps indicated by their nicknames 'Geese', 'Gooses' or 'Pork-and-Beans' (all from the name 'Portuguese'). Although comparatively inexperienced, the two Portuguese divisions (four brigades) were assigned part of the British line around Neuve Chapelle, and fled before the great German offensive on 9 April 1918, in the Battle of the Lys. Their almost total disintegration, leaving great numbers of prisoners, tended in British eyes to confirm the opinion they held on the value of the Portuguese.

The service uniform was a shade similar to French horizon-blue, including a single-breasted tunic with pleated breast-pockets and standing collar, breeches and puttees, and a cloth cap with matching peak and brown leather chinstrap (silver lace for officers) with blackened badge (infantry, crossed rifles and regimental number; cavalry crossed sabres; field artillery a grenade; garrison artillery crossed cannon barrels). Some officers wore British-style tunics with open lapels and sometimes external side-pockets, grey shirt and black tie, and brown knee-boots or ankle-boots with brown or black leather gaiters. Before they went to the Western Front, the Expeditionary Force was equipped with steel helmets manufactured in Birmingham (under Portuguese government contract), similar in shape to the British pattern but with a fluted skull for additional strength, and painted in the uniform-colour. Some arm-of-service badges or a regimental number were borne on the sleeve, near the shoulder, in blue embroidery. Rank-insignia was borne upon the shoulder-straps for NCOs (silver diagonal stripe for 1st class privates, one to four silver stripes on dark-blue for NCOs) and one to three gold bars on the cuff for officers, with an additional wider bar for field ranks; three silver stars in the cuff for general officers and seven for the commander-in-chief.

Greatcoats were double-breasted for the rank and file and single-breasted for officers, with folding collar, in the uniform-colour; officers also had grey cloaks with dark-blue collar bearing rank-insignia upon a grey patch. The 1911-pattern equipment was of khaki webbing, very similar to the British 1908-pattern, but with only four cartridge-holders at each side of the waist-belt buckle, and with a flask-shaped canteen similar to the German pattern. The regulation rifle was the Model 1904 .256in Mauser–Virguiero, and a short carbine was also produced; but for service on the Western Front, to facilitate ammunition-supply, the Expeditionary force carried British weapons. The respirator was the British 'box' pattern.

Navy

The navy was recruited under the same system as the army, but had few ships of consequence. A commission was established to reform the navy, which in January 1911 recommended the purchase from Britain of three dreadnoughts, and an increase in the number of smaller vessels, including six submarines; but in the event the naval establishment was actually reduced in 1912, by almost 1,200 men, to 4,500. At the outbreak of the World War, Portugal had one battleship, *Vasco da Gama* (reconstructed 1902, 3,030 tons, 2 × 8in, 1 × 6in, 1 × 12pdr, 8 × 3pdr guns); four cruisers (*Republica*, 1901, 1,683 tons, 4 × 6in, 2 × 4in, 4 × 3pdrs; *Almirante Reis*, 1899, 4,253 tons, 4 × 6in, 8 × 4.7in, 14 × 3pdrs; *Sao Gabriel*, 1899, 1,800 tons, 2 × 6in, 4 × 4.7in, 8 × 3pdrs; and *Adamastor*, 1897, 1,757 tons, 2 × 6in, 4 × 4.7in, 4 × 6pdrs); nine destroyers, four torpedo-boats, and one submarine. The crews of *Vasco da Gama* and *Sao Gabriel* were among those implicated in an attempted Radical *coup d'état* in April 1913, after which part of these crews were transported to the Azores.

Aviation service

The Aviation Service originated in 1912, when three aircraft were bought by public subscription; aviators were trained by Britain and France prior to the opening of Portuguese air school in 1916. The service was expanded during the war but remained very small.

'When attacked by an opponent who tries to kick. Turn sideways and hop towards him on your rear foot, the front leg being raised and bent at an angle to act as a parry and to protect your vulnerable parts. If he kicks with his right leg, turn your left side towards him, and *vice versa*.

'When you have closed with him . . . Force your buttock into the small of your opponent's back, and overbalance him with a strong swing of your arm around his throat . . .'

(*Physical Training: Unarmed Fighting*, p. 74, issued by British General Staff, June 1918)

ROUMANIA[1]

Roumania was different from the other Balkan nations, not least in the use of a Romance language instead of the Slavonic or Magyar of the remainder; it was based upon the Latin spoken in the Roman provinces of Dacia and Moesia, and despite the intrusion of many Slavonic words, the surviving Latin words were often preserved in a purer form than in Italian or Spanish. The language and retention of the Roman alphabet tended to accentuate the differences between the Roumanians and their neighbours.

*King Ferdinand of Roumania
(1865–1927), photographed in
June 1916.*

The Ottoman provinces of Moldavia and Wallachia were unified as the state of Roumania in 1861; independence was declared in 1877 and acknowledged after the Congress of Berlin (1878). In 1866 Prince Charles of Hohenzollern–Sigmaringen (1839–1914) was elected as prince of Roumania by the nation's constituent assembly, and in 1881 was proclaimed king; he is usually known by the Roumanian version of his name, Carol I. The Roumanian parliament comprised an upper house (senate) and a chamber of deputies, elected by wide suffrage; executive power was controlled by a council of which the prime minister was president. Although the king had the right of temporary veto on measures passed by parliament, the influence of the monarchy was limited, and the constitution (1866, modified 1879 and 1884) guaranteed complete freedom of speech and assembly.

Roumania had fought on the Russian side in the Russo–Turkish War, and their decisive intervention against Bulgaria in the Second Balkan War (1913) had resulted by the Treaty of Bucharest in the gain of almost 3,000 square miles in the Dobrudja. At the outbreak of the World War King Carol, as a relative of the Kaiser, was a strong supporter of the Central Powers, and a secret alliance had been concluded with Germany and Austria–Hungary in 1883. Most of Roumania's commerce was in German or Austro–Hungarian hands, her debt to Germany amounted to almost £80 million, and half that amount had been invested in Roumania by Germany. The Central Powers obtained considerable amounts of petroleum from Rou-

mania (in 1915, about a quarter of a million tons by Austria–Hungary and 150,000 tons by Germany), increasing the motivation for the Central Powers to prevent Roumania joining the Allies. Conversely, the population of Roumania was largely antagonistic towards the Central Powers, angered over the alleged ill-treatment of three million ethnic Roumanians who lived under Austro–Hungarian rule in Transylvania; as King Ferdinand stated to the *Times* correspondent Stanley Washburn in October 1916, 'the tie of race and blood underlies all other considerations',[2] and thus popular sentiment favoured the Allies. On 28 July 1914 Carol informed Austria–Hungary that the Translyvanian issue would make it impossible for Roumania to honour its obligations and join the Central Powers, confirmed by a 'crown council' on 3 August.

In the ensuing weeks Carol attempted to support the Central Powers, but his influence waned and he even considered abdication. As his standing in Roumania declined, so that of his prime minister grew. Ion Brătianu (1864–1927), Liberal prime minister from early 1914, was the son of a namesake father who had been a leading associate of Carol's in the early days of Roumanian independence, was very pro-French (educated in Paris) and was the most commanding figure in Roumanian politics. Although a supporter of the Entente, his main concern was for Roumania to profit to the maximum, and in the interests of the acquisition of those lands inhabited by Roumanians he negotiated with both sides, though his dealings with the Central Powers were never serious. Carol I died on 10 October 1914 and was succeeded by his nephew, King Ferdinand I (1865–1927), a modest man whose inherent loyalty was towards the Central Powers: the Kaiser was his cousin, Emperor Franz Josef was a friend, and two of his brothers served in the German Army. Nevertheless, he supported Brătianu's initial policy of neutrality. His wife the British Princess Marie, daughter of the Duke of Edinburgh and grand-daughter of Queen Victoria, who was naturally very pro-Entente, exerted a considerable influence on Ferdinand, and allowed Brătianu to dicate policy. So much had Ferdinand's view changed that he supported Brătianu's decision to enter the war when the opportunity was favourable. Tacit approval to Roumania's territorial claim was given when Britain advanced a £5 million loan on 27 January 1915.

The Allied success in the Brusilov offensive was the spur which brought Roumania into the war. Brătianu eventually achieved Allied acceptance of his terms: Allied munitions, support from both the Russians and from Salonika, and the territorial concessions; on 27 August 1916 Roumania declared war. The unpreparedness of the Roumanian forces led to disaster: thrown back from Translyvania, they tried without success to defend their Carpathian frontier. Bucharest, with its outdated Brialmont fortifications (1880) could not be held, and having lost an estimated 3–400,000 men the shattered army retreated into Moldavia, with king and government establishing themselves in Jassy, the ancient Moldavian capital. The greater part of the oil- and grain-producing areas fell to the Central Powers, although the British M.P., John Norton-Griffiths, sent to Roumania on an intelligence mission, destroyed much of the oil-producing capacity and vast quantities of grain immediately prior to the German occupation. Ferdinand, nominally commander-in-chief, helped Brătianu keep the army together in the north-eastern corner of the country, and endeavoured to maintain popular support by agreeing to land reform and widened suffrage for the lower classes, so a counter-offensive could be launched in mid-1917. The collapse of Russia, however, sealed Roumania's doom, Mackensen being able to concentrate his forces against the Roumanians. With the Russian supporting troops either deserting or becoming bands of brigands, it was clear that Roumania could sustain the fight no longer (Roumanian response to the bad behaviour of the Russians was such that in retaliation, the Roumanian minister at Petrograd was flung into gaol, and in January 1918 the Russian government broke off relations, impounded Roumanian funds and expelled their diplomats). Ferdinand resigned as commander-in-chief in December 1917, and was replaced by General Constantine Prezan (1861–1943), commander of the Fourth Army at the declaration of war and chief-of-staff from late 1916; Brătianu agreed an armistice with Germany on 9 December, and then resigned.

The new prime minister, appointed at Brătianu's instigation on 8 February 1918, was General Alexander Averescu (1859–1938), chief-of-staff in the Second Balkan War and leader of the defence of the Carpathians in 1916 and the 1917 counter-offensive, minister of war in Brătianu's Liberal government in 1907, and suppressor of the peasant revolt of that year. He found the terms of the Central Powers too strict to accept, so Brătianu had him dismissed and on 18 March Alexandru Marghiloman (1854–1925) took office; he was more pro-German, the leader of the Conservative Party, and had remained in Bucharest liaising with the Germans as president of the Roumanian Red Cross. He presided over the conclusion of the Peace of Bucharest (May 1918) by which Roumania left the war; but as Ferdinand astutely avoided having to sign the document, it enabled Brătianu to claim that Roumania had never abandoned the Allies and thus should receive full recompense for her efforts in the post-war settlement. Marghiloman was unable to obtain very advantageous peace terms, but persuaded the Central Powers to allow Roumania to annex Bessarabia, Russian territory long coveted.

As the Central Powers collapsed in autumn 1918, Brătianu persuaded the king to dismiss Marghiloman, and in his place a ministry led by Generals Coandă and Grigorescu was installed (6 November). Brătianu persuaded the king to declare war again (10 November 1918) and in December resumed office himself. Although Brătianu resigned again in September 1919 he remained the dominant figure in Roumanian politics, and as a result of his

Roumanian uniform seen in this portrait of General Iliescu, ultimately chief of staff.

efforts almost all Roumania's claims were accepted at Versailles, and her territory doubled in size. This was an unexpectedly fortunate conclusion to what had been a disastrous intervention in the war, as much the result of Allied unawareness of the true situation of Roumania as of Roumanian miscalculation. The war correspondent Hamilton Fyfe, writing of the Roumanian débâcle, quoted with some justice the proverb: against folly, even the gods fight in vain.

Army

Compulsory service was introduced under Carol I, renewed by the 1908 Army Law and amended in 1910 and 1913. The armed forces comprised four parts: the regular army and its reserve, the teritorial militia, and the *Gloata* or *Landsturm*. From age 21 those conscripts selected by ballot for service joined the regular army for seven years, then passed into the reserve for twelve years, mustering for drill in spring and autumn, and finally spent six years in the militia, which also included those members of the annual conscription who had not been selected for regular service. The *Gloata* consisted of all other citizens aged 36–46, to be mobilized for wartime home service only. The annual conscription was about 50,000 men, from a population of 7½ million.

There were four army corps with headquarters at Bucharest, Jassy, Craiova and Galatz, plus an independent cavalry division (HQ Bucharest) and an independent brigade in the Dobrujda. The peace establishment in 1913 was about 97,000; upon mobilization that year the field army expanded to 382,000, including reserves. Generally an army corps comprised two infantry divisions and a reserve division; each division of two brigades of two 3-battalion regiments each, a *Jäger* battalion, three cavalry squadrons, an artillery brigade (two regiments, six batteries each) and an engineer company. Upon the declaration of war in 1916 about 860,000 trained men were available, 700,000 for service with the field army, a total of 23 infantry and two cavalry divisions, the latter each of two brigades of two regiments and two horse batteries. Equipment was old and not available in sufficient quantities to meet the demands of mobilization: when a Roumanian officer was sent to Britain shortly before the war to purchase artillery ammunition, he found that the munitions required were no longer in production, so outdated was the ordnance; and typical of the shortage of equipment, at the outbreak of war the 10th Cavalry (a regular unit) had only 600 firearms for 1,100 men. The German military attaché at Bucharest, Colonel von Hammerstein, reported succinctly that the expansion for war fatally weakened a good, small army. Excluding Averescu, Prezan and General Dragalina (who was killed at Targu Jiu), most of the command was incapable; General Sosescu was not only cashiered but sentenced to five years' imprisonment for his conduct at the Battle of the Argesul (there was even a suspicion of treachery: he was of Saxon descent and his real name was Sosek). Had the Allies made sufficient inquiries to reveal the true state of Roumanian military capability, they would have been less enthusiastic about Roumania's joining of the Entente.

From early 1917 the army was reorganized, to good effect, by a French military mission under General Berthelot; a British mission also assisted.

Infantry

The peace establishment included 40 infantry regiments, each of three regular and one reserve battalion (eight regiments had only two regular battalions), each regiment with a 3-gun machine-gun company. Upon mobilization the regular battalions expanded to 120 (three per regiment), and each reserve battalions expanded into a 2-battalion regiment (80 battalions in total), and a further 40 battalions were formed from mobilized militia; additional mobilization in 1916 increased the total to about 330 infantry and 80 militia battalions. There were nine *Jäger* battalions, doubling on mobilization, each with a 2-gun machine-gun section.

In February 1912 a new field uniform was ordered, but such were the shortages that older coloured uniforms remained in use in the war: a double-breasted dark-blue tunic with dark-blue collar and pointed cuffs, red piping and pointed collar-patch, dark-grey trousers and dark-blue kepi piped red, and black leather equipment; much of the style was French, even the national cockade being based upon that of France, with yellow substituted for white. The militia wore a similar uniform with light-blue facings; Muslim units

had a red fez with blue tassel and brass crowned cipher (of Carol I) on the front; *Jägers* had double-breasted brown tunics with green facings, dark-grey trousers piped green, and a brimmed leather round hat with a green tuft at the right and bearing the national cockade.

The 1912 field uniform included a grey-green single-breasted tunic with breast- and side-pockets and standing collar bearing a pointed-ended patch in arm-of-service colour, grey-green trousers and puttees, or brown leather gaiters, with ankle-boots, and a grey-green cloth cap with similar or black leather peak, with the crown pointed at front and back, a folding flap to be lowered in bad weather, and on the front a national cockade, braid loop and button. The double-breasted, light- to medium-grey greatcoat had a falling collar with pointed patch, and a black sheepskin cap could be worn in winter. The arm-of-service colour was present on the collar-patches and as piping to the cap (with extra piping on the centre seam for officers), tunic-collar and other ranks' shoulder-straps, dark-red for staff, red for infantry and general officers, and green for *Jägers*; regimental numbers (battalion-numbers for *Jägers*) were carried on the front of the cap and shoulder-straps, preceded by an 'R' for reserve units. Equipment was black or dark-brown leather, with a cartridge-box at each side of the front of the waist-belt, and brown leather shoulder-braces supporting a khaki knapsack with metal mess-tin affixed, plus an off-white or grey haversack over the shoulder. The standard rifle was the 6.5mm 1893 Mannlicher. Among French items adopted latterly were the Adrian helmet and the Chauchat gun.

Rank-insignia on the old uniform were one or two fabric chevrons on the lower sleeve for 1st class private and corporal, the same in metallic lace for sergeants and warrant officers; officers wore stars on the shoulder-straps. On the 1912 uniform all rank-insignia was on the shoulder-strap, one or two yellow stripes for 1st class private and corporal, one to three gold for NCOs, and one to three silver stripes for company officers, with an additional gold stripe for field ranks. In May 1916 another service uniform was decreed, made in France and like the previous one but in horizon-blue; its use was very limited, and probably restricted to

---

'. . . I saw a Scot lying on the ground, plastered from head to foot with mud as with a trowel. I thought I recognized the yellow stripe in the tartan, and stepping gently over an unconscious form between, I touched him and said, "Are you a 1st Gordon, my lad?" His arm was crushed, his leg was twisted, but the white of his eye gleamed through the mud that caked his face as he answered with an unmistakable grin, "A wis this mornin', and A think A'm a half yin yet . . ."'

(Account of Loos by an anonymous padre, quoted in *The Great War*, ed. H. W. Wilson & J. A. Hammerton, VII, p. 234, London 1916).

some officers, the remainder continuing to use the older patterns. The main change was in officers' rank-distinctions: one to three grey braids around the kepi and vertical braid over the crown for company officers, with an additional wider band and a second crown-braid for field ranks; one to three braids and three on the crown, in gold, for general officers. The collars were edged with one to three lines of lace, plus a wider band for field ranks, in gold for general officers, and the same number of laces on the shoulder-straps, which were yellow, white, green, blue or scarlet for I–V Army Corps respectively; general officers' straps were red, covered with gold lace, with one to three silver stripes.

Cavalry

The cavalry was divided into regular regiments (*Rosiori*) and reserve or territorial (*Calarasi*); 112 squadrons were mobilized in 1916. The old uniform was of hussar style, red dolman with black braid for *Rosiori* and blue with red braid for *Calarasi*, white breeches, natural-coloured leather equipment, and a small black busby with cockade and cipher on the front, white tuft, bag of regimental colour at the left, and yellow cords for dress. Officers wore a black kepi with band of regimental colour; the grey greatcoat was double-breasted and had a red collar bearing a regimentally coloured pointed patch. Regimental colours for the ten *Rosiori* regiments were: 1 yellow, 2 white, 3 green, 4 light-blue, 5 light-green, 6 dark-blue, 7 light-brown, 8 lilac, 9 pink, 10 light-grey; and red for all *Calarasi* units. The 1912 grey-green uniform included black trousers and riding-boots, black piping and collar-patches for *Rosiori* and red for *Calarasi* (with black piping on the collar-patch). Regimental numbers were borne on the cap and shoulder-straps. Weapons were a sabre, a lance (adopted 1884 and carried only by the *Rosiori*) with pennon of regimental colour over red, and 1893 Mannlicher carbine.

Artillery and supports

The artillery included twenty field regiments, each of six regular and one reserve battery (four guns each); five howitzer regiments, each of three regular and one reserve battery; a mountain artillery regiment (four batteries); and two regiments (four battalions) of fortress artillery, totalling 41 companies. Upon mobilization a further four regiments of three batteries each were to be formed for support of the reserve infantry divisions. In 1916 there were some 1,300 pieces of ordnance, only about 760 of which were modern; the principal field gun was the 75mm Krupp quick-firer, 1904 pattern (1908 pattern for horse artillery); howitzers were the 120mm light Krupp, replaced by 105mm; mountain batteries used 63mm Armstrong guns, carried on mule-back and equipped with wooden trails. The fortress artillery included a range of 105mm, 160mm and 210mm guns of French and German manufacture.

The old coloured uniform included a double-breasted brown tunic for artillery, with black collar and pointed cuffs,

red piping, dark-grey trousers piped red (black with red double stripe for officers), dark-blue kepi with black band and red piping, grey greatcoat with red pointed collar-patch, and yellow buttons. The train wore a similar dress with white buttons; engineers had a single-breasted dark-blue tunic with black collar and pointed cuffs, red piping and collar-grenade, dark-blue kepi, dark-blue trousers piped red (red stripes for officers), and black leather equipment. With the 1912 uniform the artillery wore black breeches, collar-patch and piping, and regimental number on the cap (with crossed cannon for other ranks), the engineers and technical troops black collar-patches piped red, medical officers black patches piped blue and medical other ranks red. The aviation service was small and used French equipment, e.g., the Farman FH20 series.

Navy

The navy was very small and of little significance. It was divided into two squadrons, one for the Black Sea (based at Constantza) and one for the Danube (at Galatz, where the naval arsenal was situated). At the outbreak of war it consisted of one cruiser (*Elizabetha*, 4 × 6in, 4 × 6 pdrs), four monitors (3 × 4.7in, 3 × 3pdrs, 2 × 4.7in howitzers), four destroyers (3 × 4in, 7 × 12pdrs) and three small torpedo-boats.

Footnotes

1. The most common contemporary English spellings were 'Roumania' or 'Rumania'.
2. Quoted in *The Great War*, ed. H. W. Wilson and J. A. Hammerton, London, 1916, VII, p. 509.

References

Anon. *Die Rumänische Armee.* Vienna, 1913
Carossa, H. *A Roumanian Diary.* London, 1929 (acount by a medical officer of 12th Bavarian Reserve Regiment of the Roumanian campaign)
Fyfe, H. 'The Rumanian Blunder', in *The Great War*, ed. H. W. Wilson and J. A. Hammerton, London, 1919, XIII, pp. 195–204 (interesting account by war correspondent with Roumanian Army, with observations on the causes of Roumanian collapse)
Marie, Queen of Roumania. *Ordeal: The Story of My Life.* New York, 1935
Mitrany, D. *Greater Rumania: A Study in National Ideals.* London, 1917
Ruhl, M. *Die Armeen der Balkan-Staaten.* Leipzig, n.d. (includes Roumania)
Seton-Watson, R. W. *History of the Roumanians.* Cambridge, 1934
— *Roumania and the Great War.* London, 1915

RUSSIA

Arguably the most influential effect of the World War was the revolution in Russia, which not only removed from power one of the oldest dynasties, but introduced to power a political philosophy which had the most profound effect upon the remainder of the century.

The vast territory of the Russian empire was nominally a constitutional monarchy, but the title of the Tsar, 'Emperor and Autocrat of all the Russias' indicated the actual residence of power. The total authority of the Tsar had been challenged periodically by outbursts of violence (Alexander

II had been killed by a bomb in 1881), and pressure for reform had been such that in October 1905 the Tsar acceded to a liberal constitution, but the system which resulted was insufficient to silence the growing unrest. From 1905 the Tsar agreed that no law should be enacted without the consent of parliament, which comprised an upper chamber (Imperial Council), half nominated by the Tsar and half elected by bodies such as the nobility, provincial authorities, etc.; and a lower house (Duma) elected by an extremely limited franchise, constructed to give most power to the landed classes. Military and naval affairs were outside the jurisdiction of the Duma, and members of the Council of Ministers (established 1905) were accountable only to the Tsar; the president of the council was the prime minister, although this post was not necessarily the most important of the Tsar's advisers.

Tsar Nicholas II (1868–1918) succeeded to the throne in 1894; a somewhat indecisive and reactionary character, he was influenced to some degree by the Tsarina, Alexandra of Hesse-Darmstadt, who in turn was said to be under the influence of Grigory Rasputin, a self-proclaimed holy man who claimed an ability to assist the health of the haemophiliac Tsarevitch Alexis. The actual power wielded by Rasputin is uncertain, but his malign influence helped undermine the loyalty of the Duma, as he constantly advised against the extension of its power. The Tsar's resistance to suggestions of liberalization, social and political evolution, helped to ensure that when the change came, it would not be peaceful. President of the Council of

Tsarina Alexandra (1872–1918), wearing Russian lancer uniform.

Nicholas II, last Tsar of Russia (1868–1918).

Ministers at the outbreak of war was Ivan Goremykin (1839–1917), who was installed in this post in 1914 as an aged, somewhat ineffective and very reactionary premier; he had little influence in the decisions regarding the war, in which foreign minister Sergei Sazonov (1860–1927) was more significant. At the beginning of the war, the Tsar was expected to take personal command of the forces; but instead he appointed his uncle, Grand Duke Nicholas (1856–1927); with the chief-of-staff Nikolai Yanushkevich (1868–1918) being inexperienced, actual direction of the war devolved upon deputy chief-of-staff Yuri Danilov (1866–1937).

The Tsar bowed slightly to pressure from the Duma in early 1915, to give them slightly more influence, and in August 1915 dismissed the Grand Duke and assumed supreme command himself, with General Mikhail Alekseev (1857–1918) as chief-of-staff. The Council of Ministers mostly opposed the change, but the Tsar was adamant; opposition within the Duma began to organize into a 'progressive faction'. With the Tsar occupied at military headquarters, routine affairs passed into the hands of the Tsarina and (in public perception at least) her abhorrent adviser Rasputin. The infrastructure of the nation, severely damaged by the war, began to crumble in early 1916, but the Tsar made little effort to implement real changes. The ineffectual Goremykin was dismissed in February 1916, but was succeeded by another premier in the same mould, Boris Sturmer (1848–1917); the Tsarina's reactionary faction caused the dismissal of able ministers, war minister Aleksei Polianov (1855–1920) in March, and Sazonov in July. Sturmer (who took over the foreign ministry himself) was distrusted for his Austrian origin; it was believed, both at home and among the Allies, that not only was he attempting to negotiate a separate peace but that he was actually an agent of the Central Powers. His position was untenable, and he was dismissed on 22 November 1916. His replacements were Alexander Trepov and, in January 1917, Prince Nikolai Golitsyn; but neither exerted much influence and actual power was accorded to interior minister Alexander Protopopov (1866–1918), a favourite of the Tsarina and Rasputin, but ultra-reactionary, incompetent and seriously ill with advanced syphilis. The assassination of Rasputin by a conspiracy of conservative aristocrats on 29–30 December 1916, while removing a malevolent influence, also served to direct criticism for mismanagement of the war towards the Tsar and Tsarina, who now lacked a scapegoat.

Unrest over the war had been suppressed in autumn 1916, but food riots in Petrograd in February 1917 served as the catalyst for the fall of the imperial family. Late in 1916 Grand Duke Nicholas had urged the Tsar to implement radical political reforms to forestall revolution; such suggestions were dismissed. With the explosion of violence, the Tsar was informed in March 1917 that the army commanders could no longer condone his retention of the throne; he abdicated in favour of his brother, Grand Duke Michael, but his refusal brought the monarchy to an end. Its initial replacement was a 'Provisional Government' with Prince George Lvov as premier, but its most influential member was the justice minister, Alexander Kerensky (1881–1970), who represented the left of the Duma. While liberalizing the entire political and social establishment, the Provisional Government continued to prosecute the war; Kerensky became war minister in May, and premier in July, but with further military reverses and increasing demoralization of the army, his position was parlous. The Provisional Government had to share authority with the Petrograd Soviet (a term meaning 'council', the representatives of workers, soldiers and peasants), and came under attack from right and left, especially from the extreme Bolshevik party. This, under Vladimir Lenin (born Ulyanov, 1870–1924), who returned from exile with German assistance, urged a widening of the March revolution, more extreme policies, and an end to the war. General Lavr Kornilov (1870–1918), appointed by Kerensky as supreme commander in August, and hoping to reconstruct the government, marched on Petrograd in early September. Kerensky turned to the Bolsheviks for assistance, which fatally undermined the authority of his government, and Kornilov's forces disintegrated. With Russia effectively in a state of revolution, with the army collapsing and civil unrest increasing, Lenin called for an armed uprising in the name of the Soviets, and on 6–7 November overthrew the Provisional Government. Although it took three years of civil war before Lenin's control was established over the whole of Russia, this act effectively removed Russia from the World War.

Lenin and his chief associate, Leon Trotsky (1879–1940), made overtures of peace to the Central Powers, but with Russian resistance collapsing a German drive eastwards compelled them to accept Germany's terms, by the Treaty of Brest–Litovsk (3 March 1918), which was hugely advantageous to Germany. Counter-revolutions against the Bolsheviks occurred as early as the Don Cossack revolt in December 1917, and provinces declared independence. By the beginning of 1919 a civil war was in full swing, and despite the death in action of Kornilov (leading a 'White' counter-revolution), by late spring the 'Red' armies organized by Trotsky (commissar for war from March 1918) were faced by attacks on several fronts. In November 1918 Admiral Alexander Kolchak (1874–1920) seized power in Siberia, declared himself 'supreme ruler of Russia' and advanced into eastern Russia; but he enjoyed only limited popular support and was dependent upon the assistance of the Allies and the Czech Legion, and throughout 1919 was driven back by Trotsky's Red forces. Kolchak was captured by the Irkutsk local government, tried by a tribunal dominated by Bolsheviks, and shot on 7 February 1920.

The civil war included the landing of small Anglo–French–US expeditionary forces under British command in north Russia, ostensibly to recover munitions supplied to the Tsarist government, but also to co-operate with the Whites in overthrowing the new regime. In summer 1919 a major White offensive, led by General Anton Denikin (1872–1947) made some progress, but was finally repulsed and the survivors evacuated (largely by British ships) from the Black Sea region. In the latter half of 1920 the last White leader, General Peter Wrangel, took advantage of the Russo–Polish War to sally out from the Crimea; the Reds drove him back and again the survivors were evacuated by the British. In a war marked by poor leadership and organization (for despite the military experience of many of the combatants, the Tsarist military system had not survived), critical factors were the lack of unified command among the Whites, and the administrative capability of Trotsky, who assembled his Reds into a proficient fighting force.

As the Provisional Government was unable to secure an overseas sanctuary for the Tsar and his family, just before the November revolution they were sent to Siberia (ultimately to Ekaterinburg) for safety. As they would serve as a rallying-symbol for all anti-Bolshevik factions, and fearing their release by White forces, the local Bolsheviks murdered the imperial family and their remaining entourage on the night of 16/17 July 1918.

Army

The immense territory of the empire provided a resource of manpower superior to that of all other combatants. In 1911–12 it was estimated that the fit male population of military age numbered in excess of 26 million, although the number of different nationalities within the empire, the difficulty of supply, and the vast distances which had to be travelled to reach the scene of operations to some degree negated the numerical superiority. During the war the total mobilization was probably about 12 million, with probably more than 6.5 million casualties (1.7 million dead, and probably about 2 million civilian dead); of combatant troops, the maximum at the front was probably about 2,240,000 in late May 1916. The Russian soldier exhibited those characteristics which were evident in the wars of the previous century: resolution, endurance and loyalty; but the ineptitude of higher leadership, resulting in immense losses, led inevitably towards the eventual collapse of morale, disintegration of the army, and revolt. So enormous were the early losses that Brusilov noted that after a year's combat the trained, regular army had almost ceased to exist, and had been replaced by dunces.

Recruiting was by conscription, a system of obligatory military service having been introduced in 1874 and refined thereafter, with the period of active service being reduced to enable a larger number of men to be trained without increasing the size or expense of the army. Regular army service had been reduced from the original six years to 3½ years with the colours, from age 21, followed by 14½ in the reserve, including two six-weeks' trainings per year, but it was only possible to enforce this in the western areas, as the distances were too great and the population too spread in many other regions. From the reserve until age 43 men transferred to the militia (*opolchenie*), which was divided into two classes (bans), the first of those who had come from the reserve and those who would have served in the regulars had there been places for them, and the second ban of those exempted from regular service and rejected narrowly on physical grounds. Except in dire emergency it was intended to use only the first ban, as reinforcement for the regulars or service in their own units. In Transcaucasia and the Kuban and Terek provinces, conscripts served three years in the regulars and fifteen in the reserve, only Christians being eligible: most Muslims paid a tax instead. The Cossacks held their land in return for military service, and were liable for eighteen years' service (reduced from 20 in 1909), beginning at the end of their 18th year: one year's training, four with the colours, eight at home on furlough but ready for immediate service (with three weeks' annual training in the first four-year period and three weeks in total in the second four years), and the final five years in the reserve. In time of emergency all able-bodied Cossacks were liable for service by a form of *levée en masse*.

NCOs were selected mainly from men who re-enlisted after their service with the colours, to form a professional cadre, but conditions and pension were too poor to attract the most able conscripts. Aspirant officers were trained at military schools, and in their reorganizations following the disasters of the Russo–Japanese War, promotions to field rank were made on merit rather than by seniority, ensuring a greater degree of competence. Many reserve officers were drawn from conscripts whose abilities had gained them a shorter period of service to facilitate further education, the equivalent of the German 'one-year volunteer' system.

Units taking the field upon mobilization were removed from control of the War Ministry, all authority residing with the commander-in-chief, subordinate only to the Tsar (when the Tsar did not command in person), who also had jurisdiction over supports and rear areas. The highest permanent formation in peacetime was the corps, of which 37 existed, distributed over the empire's twelve military districts. The unequal distribution (most concentrated on the western frontier) complicated mobilization, as drafts often had to travel immense distances, which would have been quite impossible without the rail network. Distribution of corps was: 1st Military District (Petrograd): Guard, I, XVIII, XXII Corps; 2nd (Vilna) II–IV, XX; 3rd (Warsaw) VI, XIV, XV, XIX, XXIII; 4th (Kiev) IX–XII, XXI; 5th (Odessa) VII, VIII; 6th (Moscow) Grenadier, V, XIII, XVII, XXV; 7th (Kazan) XVI, XXIV; 8th (Caucasus) I–III Caucasus Corps; 9th (Turkestan) I–II Turkestan Corps; 10th (Omsk) 10th Siberian Rifle Division; 11th (Irkutsk) II–III Siberian Corps; 12th (Pri-Amur) I, IV and

Russian infantry in field uniform in a trench with wood-reinforced sides, Eastern Front.

VI Siberian Corps. In Cossack areas there were eleven Cossack armies, of the Don, Amur, Astrakhan, Kuban, Orenburg, Semerechensk, Siberia, Terek, Trans-Baikal, Ural and Ussuri.

Upon mobilization the various corps were assigned to numbered armies, military districts being administrative areas only; the armies were grouped into 'Fronts', each under a commander subordinate to general headquarters (*Stavka*) of the commander-in-chief. Three 'Fronts' were established: Western (First–Fourth and Tenth Armies), Northern (Fifth, Sixth and Twelfth Armies), and South-Western (Eighth, Ninth and Eleventh Armies); 'Front' commanders had jurisdiction over the entire territory and rear areas of his 'Front', in order to facilitate the local acquisition of supplies.

An ordinary corps comprised two infantry and none to two cavalry divisions, but upon mobilization the cavalry was generally detached to operate as separate divisions, corps cavalry being provided by Cossack units, generally reservists. In addition to divisional artillery, each corps maintained a howitzer division (two 4-gun batteries) and an engineer unit; heavier artillery was not allocated permanently at corps level but deployed where required.

During 1918 the old Russian Army disintegrated completely. The original forces of the revolutionary government was a militia styled the Red Guard, which was replaced by a regular army; but neither the Red Army, nor the various White armies, were based upon the old imperial regiments. However, the presence in the various forces of many thousands of ex-imperial troops resulted in some continuity of practice, uniform and equipment.

> 'The world wasn't made in a day,
> And Eve didn't ride on a 'bus,
> But most of the world's in a sandbag,
> And the rest of it's plastered on us.'
> (*The Wipers Times*, 12 February 1916)

Infantry

Before the war there were 70 field divisions (1st–3rd Guard, 1st–3rd and Circassian Grenadiers, 1st–52nd Infantry, 1st–11th Siberian); each comprised two brigades of two regiments each, each regiment of four battalions. Guard units bore a title, grenadier and infantry regiments had a number and the title of the area to which they were affiliated; reserve regiments were numbered consecutively after the regular regiments. There were also eighteen light or 'rifle' brigades (Guard, 1st–5th, 1st–4th Finnish, 1st–2nd Circassian and 1st–6th Turkestan, the latter including the Kuban–Plastun Brigade), which could be assigned at divisional level; each had four 2-battalion regiments (one had only three regiments, and the Kuban-Plastun Brigade six separate battalions). Infantry battalion-strength was 15–16 officers and 440 combatants, increased on mobilization to eighteen officers and 958 combatants, when from

each first-line unit a cadre was detached to act as a nucleus for the assembly of second-line units; preparation was made for the assembly of 36 such divisions (53rd–85th Infantry, 12th–14th Siberian), and independent brigades could also be expanded into divisions. Each division possessed 36 machine-guns and an artillery brigade of 6–8 batteries.

In 1907 a light olive-khaki field uniform was issued, of tunic, breeches and peaked cap. The other ranks' tunic was withdrawn from 1912; instead, they wore a single-breasted shirt (*Gimnastirka*) with standing collar and detachable shoulder-straps, worn outside the trousers, with the waist-belt on top. Most officers adopted shirts, or looser khaki tunics styled on a British shooting-jacket, with breast- and side-pockets, standing collar and metal or brown leather buttons. The cap had a khaki leather peak and bore an oval white/orange/black cockade on the front; all ranks had blackened knee-boots or ankle-boots and khaki puttees. In winter it was usual to wear the greatcoat (*Shinel*) at all times, a double-breasted, grey-brown garment fastened by hooks and eyes, a half-belt, deep falling collar and deep cuffs; a grey-brown fake-Astrakhan cap (*Papakha*) with the cockade as on the cap; a loose hood which could cover the whole head-dress (*Bashlyk*); and brown cloth mittens with a thumb and two 'fingers' (one for the forefinger, one finger for the other three). The greatcoat could be carried rolled, bandolier-fashion.

Regimental distinctions were evident on the shoulder-straps and greatcoat collar-patches. The shoulder-straps were reversible, khaki for service and coloured for dress, bearing regimental numerals, cipher or arm-of-service badge; red for Guards, grenadiers yellow and rifles crimson. For infantry they were red for the 1st and 2nd regiments in a division, blue for the 3rd and 4th; collar-patches were generally red, blue, white and green for the 1st–4th regiments in a division respectively. Rifles had green patches piped crimson (1st Guard Rifles crimson); yellow, blue, white and green respectively, all piped yellow, for the regiments of the 3rd Guards Division (Regiments Litovski, Kexholm, St. Petersburg, Volynski). Red piping was carried on the patches of the 1st Guards Division (Regiments Preobrajenski, Semenovski, Ismailovski and *Jägers*), and green piping for the 1st Regiment of the 2nd Guards Division (Regiments Moscow, Guard Grenadiers, Pavlov, and Finland). Piping on the opening of the shirt-front of Guard regiments was of the same colour as the collar-patch (save rifles, crimson), and cuff-piping was white, red and yellow respectively for the 1st–3rd Divisions. Red, blue and white piping was borne on the shoulder-straps of the 1st–3rd Grenadier Divisions. Rank-insignia was borne on the shoulder-straps, initially in yellow lace (4th Grenadier Division white, Guards orange), but replaced by red at the start of the war: 1 to 3 transverse stripes for junior NCOs, a metallic lace stripe for sergeants, one longitudinal metallic stripe for warrant officers; officers had shoulder-boards covered with metallic lace with one (company) or two (field ranks) longitudinal coloured stripes, with none to four stars;

Russian 1910 7.62mm Maxim gun, known as the 'Sokolov', showing its elevated mount, *photographed on the Eastern Front.*

metallic zigzag lace with none to three stars for general officers (plus scarlet greatcoat-lapels and piping, and scarlet trouser-stripe); crossed batons on the shoulder-board for field marshals. To be less conspicuous, during the war officers often used soft cloth straps instead of rigid shoulder-boards, with khaki lace, or with the rank-insignia stencilled or drawn on.

Equipment was brown leather (sometimes blackened, and white for the first three regiments of each Guards division), including a 30-round ammunition-pouch at each side of the waist-belt buckle, the Linnemann entrenching tool suspended from the waist-belt, a canvas haversack and canteen (either aluminium or older copper version) over the right shoulder, an ammunition-bandolier over the left (30 rounds: 30 more were carried in a reserve pouch over the right shoulder and fastened to the waist-belt), and over the bandolier the rolled greatcoat containing a spare pair of boots and one-sixth of a tent, with the aluminium mess-tin pulled over the ends of the roll. The principal rifle was the 7.62mm 1891 Mosin-Nagant, but the great expansion of the army on mobilization outstripped resources, so that many older weapons were utilized, and quantities of Japanese Arisakas were supplied to Russia in 1914. The bayonet was habitually fixed on active service, so no scabbard was carried. Machine-guns, also in short supply, were principally the 1910 Russian Maxim (or 'Sokolov'), 7.62mm calibre, generally with a two-wheel carriage; others were also used, for example Colt guns by cavalry. To facilitate ammunition-supply, units serving on the Western Front or in Macedonia were issued with French 8mm Lebel rifles, and appropriate ammunition-pouches and belts; the Adrian

helmet and French side-caps were also issued to these troops.

Cavalry

In wartime the cavalry was generally removed from the corps organization and deployed in divisional strength: there were 24 divisions (1st–15th, 1st–2nd Guard, Circassian, 1st–2nd Cossack, 1st–3rd Circassian Cossack, 1st Turkestan Cossack), each of two brigades of two regiments each, each regiment of six squadrons (*sotnias*) and including a scout and pioneer section. The 1st Guard Division had seven regiments (Chevalier-Guard, Life Guard of Horse, Emperor's and Empress' Cuirassier regiments, and the Lifeguard, Tsarevich's and Combined Cossack regiments); the 2nd Guard Division included the Guard Horse Grenadiers, Empress' Lancers, Guard Dragoons and Hussars; and there existed eight independent brigades of two or three regiments each (one a Guard brigade: Emperor's Lancers and Grodno Hussars). Each division had a horse artillery brigade of two 6-gun batteries, two machine-guns per regiment, and a strength of about 4,500. Line cavalry included twenty numbered dragoon regiments, seventeen numbered and two un-numbered lancer regiments, and eighteen numbered hussar regiments. Their tactical role was generally as mounted infantry, due to some extent to the quality of the mount: small horses of great endurance but, excluding the fine mounts of the Guard, unsuited for more conventional cavalry service.

Service uniform was like that of the infantry, but with pointed shirt-cuffs and dark-blue trousers with regimentally coloured piping (in practice most wore khaki trousers); shoulder-straps were in regimental colours with number and arm-of-service initial in light-blue ('D' dragoons, 'Y' lancers, 'T' hussars). The principal weapons were the carbine of 1910 pattern or 1891 dragoon, and Cossack rifles (a version of the infantry rifle some three inches shorter), with the bayonet carried on the outside of the sabre-scabbard.

Cossacks

The Cossacks were traditionally some of the best (though often most savage) units of the Russian Army. The hardy nature of their small ponies made them ideal reconnaissance forces of great endurance, and reserve units formed much of the corps cavalry. In 1914 some 939 squadrons were mobilized, nominally 100 men strong, of which of which the majority came from the Don (360 squadrons), Kuban (202), Orenburg (107), Terek (66), Siberian and Transbaikal (54 each). They were divided into Steppe and Caucasian groups, each subdivided into *voiskos* or territorial divisions, of which there were nine in the Steppe Cossacks; they wore ordinary service uniform with shoulder-straps and collar-patches blue (Don, shoulder-strap piped red, red collar-patch), green piped yellow (Amur), yellow (Astrakhan, Transbaikal, Ussuri, the latter shoulder-straps piped green), light-blue (Orenburg), crimson (Semerechinsk,

Ural) and red (Siberian), all with silver lace; other ranks had khaki straps with light-blue badge or number. The blue baggy trousers had stripes coloured like the collar-patch (save Amur, yellow). The Caucasian *voikos* (divided into Kuban and Terek units) wore 'tribal' dress of astrakhan busby, grey or black kaftan or single-breasted frock-coat with cartridge-tubes on each side of the breast, ordinary greatcoat or rough-haired woollen cloak, and red shoulder-straps and collar-patches for Kuban units and blue for Terek, and silver lace. Cossacks wore no spurs but carried a knout or whip; arms included the Cossack sabre (*shashqa*), carbine, lances for the front-rank men and, for Caucasians, a tribal dagger (*kindjal*). From 1909 Cossacks were permitted to carry ancient family weapons in place of regulation sabres. Each Cossack had to provide his own uniform, equipment and horse; only his rifle was supplied by the government, and half the cost of it was charged to his tribe.

Also in the Cossack forces were artillery (ordinary uniform, red shoulder-straps, gold lace, black collar-patch piped red) and Kuban infantry (Plastun) who wore a shorter version of the kaftan, with crimson shoulder-straps, gold lace, and black collar-patch piped crimson.

Artillery and supports

Despite advances in industrial capacity and the purchase of ordnance from abroad, guns and ammunition remained in very short supply: the disasters of 1915 were considerably attributable to lack of ammunition, and when compared with western armies, the Russians were desperately short of ordnance. Comparing the French Sixth Army at the opening of the 1916 Somme offensive with the Russian II Corps at Strypa in the same period (both offensives against prepared positions), the French fielded 44.4 field and 64.5 heavy guns per mile; the Russians, 11.4 and 1.6 per mile respectively. This lack of artillery support helped cause the immense casualties suffered by Russia.

At the beginning of the war field batteries had eight guns each, including the 90mm 1880 Krupp and 76.2mm 1902 guns; the 1909 122mm light field howitzer of French design began to be introduced from 1910. Each infantry division included a field artillery brigade (6–8 batteries); cavalry and Cossack divisions had a horse artillery group of two 6-gun batteries. Medium and heavy artillery, deployed at corps level (a howitzer division of two 4- or 6-gun batteries per corps, using for example the light or 1884 150mm howitzer) remained in desperately short supply. Batteries stationed in Asia were normally kept at full strength; those in the west were raised to wartime strength on mobilization. The system of extracting cadres to act as the nucleus of reserve formations was used only in the field artillery; organization of horse batteries was largely unchanged by mobilization.

The artillery service uniform had red shoulder-straps and gold lace, and black collar-patches piped red; shirt-cuffs were piped white, blue and yellow respectively for the 1st–3rd Guard field brigades, and black (with cavalry-style pointed cuffs) for the Guard horse artillery. The khaki shoulder-straps bore a crossed cannon device and brigade-number in red.

An engineer battalion of three companies was attached to each corps; they had red shoulder-straps and silver lace, black collar-patches piped red, and brown devices on the khaki straps (crossed pick and shovel, saw and axe for miners, crossed anchor and oars for pontooneers). Train units were deployed at divisional level, and each corps included a corps train, two telegraph companies and field hospitals (some ambulance units were also deployed at divisional level); transport units had light-blue collar-patches and white shoulder-strap devices. Motor transport was very limited, and restricted largely to motor-cars and a small number of armoured cars (British armoured cars for a period operated with the Russian Army); motor-transport personnel were part of the engineers.

Navy

Prior to the Russo–Japanese War, the navy comprised four fleets, Baltic, Black Sea, Caspian and Pacific. The catas-

Russian 1909 Light field howitzer of 12.2cm calibre, showing the disposition of the crew in action.

trophe of Tsushima destroyed much of the naval capability, but the bulk of the Black Sea Fleet's capital ships served as the basis for the construction of a new naval force. Despite a major building-programme rearmament was not due for completion until 1917, so on outbreak of war the navy's role was largely defensive. Principal naval bases were Kronstadt (Baltic), Sevastopol (Black Sea) and Vladivostok (Pacific). The Baltic Fleet, used to protect Petrograd, was largely contained by U-boat activity, though Russian minelaying was effective; and due to its superiority over the Turkish Navy, the Black Sea Fleet suffered no serious losses in its limited operations (*Imperatriza Maria*, sunk at Sevastopol, was blown up accidentally; she was re-floated upside-down in 1919). The fleet suffered a number of mutinous outbreaks from 1915, and the support of the Baltic Fleet in 1917 helped ensure the success of the Bolshevik revolution; most famous was the participation of the cruiser *Aurora*, which when anchored in the River Neva on 7 November raised the red flag and fired a blank shell towards the Winter Palace in Petrograd. Next most famous was probably the cruiser *Askold*, known to the British as 'the packet of Woodbines' (from the shape of her funnels), which co-operated with the Allies in the Dardanelles operations.

Ships existing in the first year of the war, over 6,000 tons displacement, were:

Date	Name and displacement Main armament only (tons)	
BALTIC FLEET:		
Battleships		
1903	*Tsarevitch* (13,380)	4 × 12in, 12 × 6in
1905	*Slava* (13,500)	4 × 12in, 12 × 6in
1911	*Imperator Pavel, Andrei Pervoswanni* (17,400)	4 × 12in, 14 × 8in, 12 × 4.7in
Dreadnought battlecruisers		
1914–15	*Gangoot, Petropavlovsk, Poltava, Sebastopol* (23,300)	12 × 12in, 16 × 4.7in
Cruisers		
1893	*Rossiya* (12,500)	4 × 8in, 22 × 6in
1899	*Bogatyr, Oleg* (6,650)	12 × 6in
1899	*Aurora, Diana* (7,600)	10 × 6in

Date	Name and displacement Main armament only (tons)	
1901	*Gromoboi* (13,200)	4 × 8in, 22 × 6in
1903	*Askold* (6,500)	12 × 6in
1907–10	*Bayan, Admiral Makaroff* (7,775)	2 × 8in, 8 × 6in
1908	*Rurik* (15,000)	4 × 10in, 8 × 8in, 20 × 4.7in
BLACK SEA FLEET		
Battleships		
1894	*Georgi Pobiedonosets* (10,250)	6 × 12in, 7 × 6in
1897	*Tri Sviatitelia* (12,540)	4 × 12in, 10 × 6in, 4 × 4.7in
1898	*Rostislav* (9,000)	4 × 10in, 8 × 6in
1903	*Pantelimon* (12,800)	4 × 12in, 16 × 6in
1910	*Ievstafi, Ioann Zlatoust* (12,800)	4 × 12in, 4 × 8in, 12 × 6in
Dreadnought battlecruisers		
1914	*Alexander III, Ekaterina II, Imperatriza Maria* (22,500)	10 × 12in, 20 × 5in
Cruisers	*Kagoul, Pamiat Merkooria* (6,750)	12 × 6in

Other vessels included:

Baltic Fleet: 81 torpedo-boat destroyers, plus 36 building or projected; eighteen torpedo-boats; 25 submarines, nineteen building; seventeen river gunboats; two gunnery-school ships (*Imperator Alexander II*, 9,900 tons; *Petr Veliky*, 9,665 tons), eight minelayers; two mine-school ships; and various subsidiary craft.

Black Sea Fleet: 26 torpedo-boat destroyers; ten torpedo-boats; eleven submarines; two minelayers; four gunboats; and various subsidiary craft.

Aviation service

Part of the engineers, the aviation service was of limited significance during the war, despite the considerable interest which had been shown in military aviation. The service was established in 1912, with two permanent training bases (Petrograd and Tashkent) and subsidiary

Russian dreadnought battleship Imperator Alexander III, *of the Black Sea Fleet: 22,500 tons, 12 × 12in, 20 × 5in, 4 × 2½in, 4 × 3pdr guns, 4 torpedo tubes.*

Revolution in Russia: artillery in place behind a barricade in a Petrograd street, with a red flag flying over the defences.

schools at Sevastopol, Odessa and Moscow; there were three aviation battalions, stationed at Petrograd, Warsaw and Vladivostok, with additional companies at Sevastopol and Kiev. At the outbreak of war its aircraft were more numerous than those of other nations, but of some 360 machines many were not fit for service. Expansion was slow, replacements not easy to produce, and only in 1916 were units reorganized into specialist reconnaissance, fighter and bomber squadrons. Technical assistance and aircraft were provided by France, although considerable numbers of aircraft were built in Russia; there were more than 1,000 in service by early 1917, but their impact on the Eastern Front was limited. The operations of the Sikorskii Ilya Mourometz heavy bomber represented the only real Russian aviation success of the war. Russia had some sixteen airships at the outbreak of war, twelve training craft, two French, one Parseval, and one Russian-built Albatros, with an immense craft (the Gigant) under construction at Petrograd.

The aviation service wore a dark-blue *Gimnastirka*, black breeches piped red, black sidecap with silver lace and red piping along the crown, laced leather gaiters and ankleboots. Shoulder-straps (also worn on the black leather jackets favoured by flying personnel) were of engineer pattern, bearing a brown or yellow winged propeller, gilt or bronze for officers (a propeller, sword and eagle by flying officers).

Among the principal Russian aircraft were:

Anatra: produced by the Anatra factory at Odessa, founded by an Italian banker of that name. The 'D' or 'Anade' (contraction of 'Anatra D') was a two-seater reconnaissance biplane similar to the German Aviatik, produced 1916–17 but structurally unsound; the DS or 'Anasal' (Anatra-Salmson, from the Salmson Canton-Unné engine), introduced mid-1917, was more successful. The Anatra VI, a modified Voisin reconnaissance biplane named after its designer ('Voisin-Ivanov') was in service 1915–16 but was very unstable, dangerous and condemned as unfit for active service.

Lebed: two-seater reconnaissance biplane based on the Albatros, built by the Lebedev brothers (hence the contracted name 'Lebed'); Marks 11, 12 and 13 in service from 1916, principally the Lebed 12.

Sikorskii Ilya Mourometz: giant biplane, four-engined bomber, based on pre-war civilian design of Professor Igor Sikorskii; crew of 4–7 in enclosed, glazed cockpit, virtually indestructible (only one lost in combat) and so well-armed as to be capable of destroying almost anything sent against it; bomb-load 1,120 pounds. Five Wings in operation by 1917.

In addition to Russian-manufactured machines, the aviation service operated a variety of Allied machines including the Caudron GIII, Farman HF20, Franco–British H, Morane Parasol and N, Nieuport 6M, 11, 17 and 23, Sopwith 1½-Strutter, Spad VII and A2, and Vickers FB19.

References

Carr, E. H. *The Bolshevik Revolution*. London, 1950

Chamberlin, W. H. *The Russian Revolution 1917–1921*. London, 1935

Deniken, General A. *The Russian Turmoil*. London, 1922

Frankland, N. *Imperial Tragedy: Nicholas II, Last of the Tsars*. New York, 1961

Golovin, Lieutenant-General N. N. *The Russian Army in the World War*. London, 1931

Gourko, General B. *Memories and Impressions of War and Revolution in Russia*. London, 1918 (Russian chief-of-staff from November 1916)

Katkov, G. *Russia 1917*. London, 1967

Kerensky, A. *The Kerensky Memoirs: Russia and History's Turning Point*. London, 1966

Kerensky, A., and Bulygin, P. *The Murder of the Romanovs*. London, 1935

Knox, General Sir Alfred. *With the Russian Army 1914–1917*. London, 1921

Kochan, L. *Russia in Revolution 1890–1918*. London, 1967

Mollo, B. *Uniforms of the Imperial Russian Army*. Poole, 1979

Mollo, E. *Russian Military Swords 1801–1917*. London, 1969

Morse, J. *An Englishman in the Russian Ranks: Ten Months' Fighting in Poland*. London, 1915

Pares, B. (later Sir Bernard). *Day by Day with the Russian Army*. London, 1915

Pares, Sir Bernard. *The Fall of the Russian Monarchy*. London 1939

Perrett, B., and Lord, A. *The Czar's British Squadron*. London, 1981 (Locker Lampson's RNAS Armoured Car unit)

Rutherford, W. *The Russian Army in World War I*. London, 1975

Seaton, A. *The Cossacks*. London, 1972

Stewart, D. *The White Armies of Russia: a Chronicle of Counter-Revolution and Allied Intervention*. New York, 1933

SERBIA[1]

Distinct among the Balkan peoples, the Serbs (*Srbi*) were recorded as long ago as Pliny (1st century AD) and traditionally settled in the Balkans at the invitation of the Emperor Heraclitus; unlike the Croats who were Roman Catholics and used the Roman alphabet, the Serbian religion was Orthodox and their alphabet a variation of Cyrillic. Annexed by the Ottoman Empire in 1459, Serbia's struggle for independence gained a degree of autonomy from 1804, but full independence was attained only after the Russo–Turkish War, by the Treaty of Berlin (1878).

Nineteenth-century Serbian politics were principally a rivalry between the dynasties of Obrenovich (Obrenović) and Karageorgevich (Karadjordjević); with the deposition of the latter family in 1859, Obrenovich rule was assured until 11 June 1903, when King Alexander and his Queen Draga were assassinated in a *coup d'état*, resulting in a call to Peter Karageorgevich (1844–1921) to assume the throne, after 45 years in exile. His popularity was enhanced by being the grandson of George Petrovich, alias 'Karageorge' ('Black George'), who had led the fight for independence in the early 19th century. With his accession the 1889 constitution was revived, establishing a constitutional monarchy with the king as head of state, assisted by a cabinet, with a National Assembly elected by all adult males paying 15 dinars tax annually (excluding members of the army, who had no vote). Civil administration was based on seventeen departments (*okruzhi*), each *okrug* governed by a prefect (*nachalnik*) who also controlled the departmental gendarmerie (*pandurs*).

*King Peter of Serbia
(1844–1921).*

King Peter was educated in liberal Western political tradition (he had translated John Stuart Mill into Serbian!), and in his reign the previous close links with Austria–Hungary declined. The Austrian annexation of Bosnia and Herzegovina in 1908 inflamed Serbian nationalism, the goal of which was a 'Great Serbia' to embrace all ethnic Serbs in Bosnia, Herzegovina, Montenegro and north-western Macedonia. Although Serbia emerged successfully from the Balkan Wars, the Macedonian question caused considerable internal ferment. Prime minister from 1904 was Nikola Pašić (1845–1926), the dominant figure in Serbian politics, but the military regicides of 1903 continued to exercise considerable influence, and the problem came to a head in 1914 over whether Macedonia should be administered by civil or military authority. King Peter, aged and ailing, was compelled to relinquish his throne on 24 June 1914 and his son, Crown Prince Alexander (1888–1934) was appointed prince-regent; perhaps influenced by his education in Russia, he favoured autocracy rather than liberalism. (Peter's eldest son, George, should have been the heir but had been compelled to renounce his position as crown prince in 1909 amid allegations over the death of one of his servants and suggestions of insanity.) The crisis forced Pašić to call an election, the campaign of which was actually in progress when the assassinations at Sarajevo precipitated the war.

For a year Serbia held back its enemies, inspired by the symbol of national resistance of old King Peter, who was present in the front line in times of crisis. Alexander was nominal commander-in-chief, but actual command resided in the capable hands of Field Marshal Radomir Putnik (1847–1917), the dominant military personality in the Balkans. Not in good health, he was convalescing at the Austrian resort of Bad Gleichenberg when the crisis of 1914 occurred, and the Emperor Franz Josef's personal intervention which allowed him to return home was a gesture of chivalry which cost Austria–Hungary dearly.

In autumn 1915 the combined assault by the Central Powers overran all but a small enclave south of Monastir; in response to an offer of peace involving the Serbian surrender of Macedonia and some eastern territory to Bulgaria, Pašić was reported to have remarked that Serbia's path was mapped out: it would remain loyal to the Entente and die an honourable death. The country was divided between Austria–Hungary and Bulgaria; their brutal treatment of the Serbs provoked a major rising around Kuršumlje, which was savagely suppressed, with more than 2,000 evacuations in reprisal and wholesale deportation. The Serbian Army retired into Albania and Montenegro, and was evacuated on Allied ships (principally Italian) to be refitted at Corfu, from where they were sent to the Salonika front; rather than live under occupation, a large number of civilians accompanied them, in conditions and weather so arduous that one estimate suggested that as many as 200,000 perished on the trek. Old Putnik, having supervised a skilled retreat in atrocious weather and over hard terrain, ended the march borne in a sedan chair; his health broke down completely and he relinquished command (he died in Nice in May 1917). His successor was Zivojin Mišić (1855–1921), recently field marshal and commander of the First Army; appointed chief-of-staff under Alexander's nominal authority, his aggressive attitude proved a great asset in the final drive against the Central Powers in the Balkans.

The government accompanied the army to Corfu, where some political turmoil ensured. A threat to Pašić's authority emerged from Ante Trumbić (1864–1938), a Croatian nationalist who had fled Austria–Hungary in 1914; as spokesman for the London-based Yugoslav Committee, his ideas for the unification of the Austrian Empire's southern Slav provinces with Serbia conflicted with Pašić's ideas for smaller territorial acquisitions. Against this divisive background there occurred the 'Conspiracy Trial' of 1917, a number of senior military officers being arrested for treason, most notably Colonel Dragutin Dimitrijević (1876–1917), alias 'Apis', former head of military intelligence, a fervent nationalist and leader of the 'Union or Death' society, better-known as 'the Black Hand'. Convicted of plotting against the royal family, he was executed at Salonika in June 1917, although his guilt is doubtful; though implicated to some degree in the Sarajevo assassinations, it has been suggested that he was removed for his knowledge of Serbian royal complicity, or that it was a preliminary towards a negotiated settlement with Austria–Hungary, but perhaps more likely it was an opportunity to end the interference of the military in Serbian politics.

Although their relationship was difficult, in July 1917

Alexander, Crown Prince Regent of Serbia, later King of Yugoslavia (1888–1934).

Pašić and Trumbić co-operated in the Declaration of Corfu, which announced the intention of establishing a united South Slav state. Serbian forces under Mišić recovered Serbia and pushed into the southern states of Austria–Hungary, and in late November 1918 a meeting was convened in Belgrade of representatives of Serbia, Montenegro and the former Austro–Hungarian provinces of Croatia and Slovenia. Having supported Pašić throughout, Alexander allowed his more extreme views to prevail, and in effect pushed Pašić aside so that Trumbić's united kingdom of Serbs, Croats and Slovenes (ultimately Yugoslavia) was created on 1 December 1918. Old King Peter was given the crown, but he handed power immediately to Alexander, who succeeded as king on Peter's death in August 1921. Pašić headed the delegation to the peace conference, and was recalled to office in 1921 and again in 1924–6. The administration of the new state was dominated by Serbians, which caused resentment among the Croats and Slovenes, and in January 1929 Alexander's beliefs had reached such a stage that he ended democratic government and began to assume the powers of dictator. On a visit to Marseilles in October 1934 he was assassinated by Petrus Keleman, a Croatian nationalist.

Army

The army was reorganized in 1901, comprising a 'national army' (*narodna voyska*) and a *Landsturm*. Recruiting was by conscription, with few exceptions all able-bodied Serbians being liable for military service from the age of 21. The first two years were spent with the colours (in practice only in the artillery: eighteen months was the usual term in other branches), followed by nine years in the 1st-line reserve, six in the 2nd, and the remainder (to age 46) in the 3rd line (forces were organized into 1st–3rd *Ban* or class). Membership of the *Landsturm* was compulsory for those aged 17–21 and 46–50; the first-line reserve existed only as a cadre, and the others were not organized in peacetime.

Original organization was in five divisions, with headquarters at Belgrade, Kraguyevats, Nish, Valyevo and Zayechar; each division comprised four infantry regiments of three battalions each, with field artillery deployed at divisional level. There was an independent cavalry division (four regiments of four squadrons each) and separate mountain and siege artillery; the artillery comprised seven field regiments and two siege battalions, including 45 field, two horse, nine mountain and six howitzer batteries. Supports included 2½ engineer battalions and a mounted telegraph section, but the train service was very inadequate, and almost medieval vehicles had to be pressed into service at the outbreak of war, including solid-wheeled bullock-carts. Total peacetime strength was slightly less than 29,000 men; with wartime mobilization it increased to five regular divisions, five second-line, five third-line and one reserve division (in addition to the first-line men who had gone to reinforce the regular divisions), one cavalry division, and under the commander-in-chief's orders a guard unit (two

Serbian field howitzer, the crew wearing the characteristic cloth field cap (foreground) and officer's-pattern kepi (rear).

squadrons), a heavy field artillery regiment, a siege regiment and some railway companies, a total strength of about 260,000.

After the Balkan Wars, acquisition of territory permitted the formation of five more divisions (Ibar, Kosovo, Monastir, Shtip and Vardar) and ten additional artillery batteries, but reorganization had not been completed before the outbreak of the World War. Some 350,000 men were mobilized in late July 1914, organized in four armies, each intended to include four divisions. Divisional strength was intended to comprise two infantry brigades, each of 6,000 men; two artillery brigades and one cavalry regiment (600 men each), engineers and supports (about 1,300); with the addition of heavy artillery and 'corps troops' the intended strength of each army was about 65,000. In the event the four armies comprised:

First Army: 1st and 2nd Timok, 2nd Danube and 2nd Morava Divisions (52 battalions, seven squadrons, 26 batteries); Second Army: 1st Danube, 1st Morava, 1st Shumaja and Combined Divisions (64 battalions, ten squadrons, 33 batteries); Third Army: 1st and 2nd Drina Divisions (28 battalions, five squadrons, sixteen batteries); Uzhitse Army or 'Army of the West': 2nd Shumaja Division, Uzhitse Brigade (24 battalions, two squadrons, eleven batteries); Cavalry Division (sixteen squadrons, one battery).

In addition there were independent formations, stationed on the frontiers and as the Belgrade and Obrenovats Groups, together about 45 battalions, two squadrons and 28 batteries. Contemporary assessments remarked upon the valour and hardiness of the men, excellence of artillery and quality of leadership of the lower-ranking officers, but doubts were expressed over the flexibility and initiative of the staff.

There had been considerable improvements in weaponry and training, principally during Putnik's tenure as minister

King Peter of Serbia riding in an ox-drawn ammunition-cart during the great retreat; much of the Serbian army's transport was of this rudimentary nature.

of war, during which he introduced new small arms and heavy artillery, and made careful plans for mobilization. An olive-grey/khaki service uniform was introduced from 1912, but by the outbreak of war it had been received only by the 1st *Ban*; the 2nd wore a mixture of pre-1912 coloured uniform and often a 1912 cap and greatcoat, and the 3rd largely civilian clothes. The 1912 uniform included a kepi with brown leather peak and chinstrap, national cockade on the front (red/blue/white) and piping in the arm-of-service colour, for officers; for other ranks the head-dress was a soft sidecap of similar shape, without peak or cockade. The single-breasted tunic had breast- and side-pockets, standing collar (in arm-of-service colour for officers), deep cuffs with coloured piping and shoulder-straps (coloured for officers); long trousers and civilian- or peasant-style boots and anklets (breeches with coloured piping, black riding-boots, or ankle-boots and leather gaiters for officers); double-breasted greatcoat with falling collar, deep cuffs with coloured piping, and coloured collar-patch. Arm-of-service colours were: infantry crimson, artillery black, cavalry dark-blue, engineers cherry-red, staff scarlet, train dark-red; the shoulder-straps generally bore the regimental number (in Roman numerals for engineers and mountain artillery). The old coloured uniform included a single-breasted dark-blue tunic (double-breasted for officers) with red facings for infantry, black for artillery (red piping for officers); black trousers; originally a dark-blue kepi, and blue-grey peaked cap for service, officers and NCOs with a Russian-style dark-blue peaked cap with green band; later a squat fur cap was adopted for winter and dress. The cavalry wore a light-blue tunic (double-breasted for officers) with dark-blue collar and shoulder-straps, red breeches, white buttons and shoulder-strap number, and light-blue cap piped dark-blue. The engineers wore infantry uniform with white buttons and cherry-red facings and cap.

It is likely that old coloured uniforms were re-issued to some of the 2nd *Ban*, but the 3rd generally only received a forage-cap, blue, red or black respectively for infantry, cavalry and medical troops, although some officers and NCOs did have uniforms. Rank-insignia was the same on the coloured and 1912 uniforms: one to three brass stars on the shoulder-strap for senior private, corporal and sergeant; for company officers, coloured shoulder-straps with two metallic lace stripes and 1–4 stars in contrasting metal for 2nd lieutenant, 1st lieutenant, 2nd- and 1st-class captain respectively; field officers had metallic lace straps with 1–3 stars, metallic cap-piping, and trrouser-stripes in arm-of-service colour. In the 2nd and 3rd *Ban*, rank-insignia consisted of strips of lace on the collar-patch, 1–3 in yellow or white for NCOs, 1–3 metallic strips for company officers and a metallic bar for majors; white/silver for 2nd *Ban* and yellow/gold for 3rd.

The brown leather equipment included a waist-belt with three pouches, knapsack on shoulder-belts with a rolled greatcoat on top, and fabric-covered oval canteen, but shortages of equipment led to the use of blanket-bundles in place of the knapsack, or with equipment carried in a rolled blanket or groundsheet, bandolier-fashion. The principal rifle had been the single-shot 10.15mm 1881 Mauser–Milanovic, but this was replaced by the 1893 7.65mm Mauser. Upon the outbreak of the Balkan Wars the artillery was in process of replacing their French 85mm Système de Bange guns with more modern French 75mm field and 70mm mountain guns; the heavy batteries used 12cm and 15cm howitzers. Upon the beginning of the World War, Krupp guns captured from Turkey or lent or sold by Greece were allocated to the 'army troops'; Schneider guns captured from Bulgaria were deployed on the southern front, the other three armies using the French ordnance. At the outset not all reservists could be equipped, and ammunition was in such short supply that the situation was saved only by supplies from France from November 1914.

After the evacuation to Corfu the army was completely re-equipped from Allied stocks, using both French horizon-blue and British khaki uniforms, French weapons (including the Chauchat light machine-gun), and the Adrian helmet bearing an embossed badge of the Serbian crowned, double-headed eagle with a shield upon its breast.

A member of the re-equipped Serbian army wearing French Adrian helmet, and armed with a CSRG (Chauchat) gun.

Footnote

1. In contemporary English publications the name may be found as 'Servia', a form somewhat resented by the Serbs in case it conveyed a suggestion of servility from the Latin *servus*.

References

Anon. *Die Serbische und Montenegrische Armee.* Vienna, 1912
Burgess, A. *The Lovely Sergeant.* London, 1963 (biography of Flora Sandes, one of the most remarkable combatants of the war, a British volunteer nurse but later commissioned in the Serbian Army)
Matthews, C. *Experiences of a Woman Doctor in Serbia.* London, 1918
Paget, Lady R. *With our Serbian Allies.* London, 1915–16
Petrovich, M. B. *History of Modern Serbia 1804–1918.* London, 1976
Price, W. H. Crawfurd. *Serbia's Part in the War.* London, 1918
Ruhl, M. *Die Armeen der Balkan-Staaten.* Leipzig, n.d. (includes Serbia)
Sandes, Captain F. *The Autobiography of a Woman Soldier.* London, 1927

SIAM

Siam declared war on the Central Powers on 22 July 1917, claiming that the motivation was to uphold the rights of small nations and international law in general.

An absolute monarchy, Siam was controlled by the king, who had absolute veto over the decisions of the legislative council which he appointed. Government and administration was run upon European lines, and Siam had close links with a number of European nations; from 1896 Siamese independence was guaranteed jointly by Britain and France, and the majority of European trade was with Britain. When King Chulalongkorn died in 1910 he was succeeded by the Crown Prince, Somdech Phra Ramadhipati Srisindra Maha Vajiravudh, who took the title King Rama VI in 1917; his ties with Britain were strong, having been educated at Eton, Christ Church, Oxford and Sand-

King Rama VI of Siam.

hurst, followed by an attachment to the Durham Light Infantry.

Siam was divided into eighteen administrative districts or *montons*, which formed the basis of the system of recruitment for the armed forces from 1903, that provided for compulsory service. Previously the army had been formed from the descendants of prisoners of war, so that the concept of 'national service' was alien; Rama VI endeavoured to encourage it with the establishment in 1912 of the Wild Tiger Corps, which fulfilled a similar role among the adult population as did the Scouts in Europe. The conscription laws were revised in 1917, by which all able-bodied men aged 21–22 were liable for 2 years' service, after which they passed into the reserve, which had three classes graded according to age; modern, European-style uniforms and weapons were adopted. There was also a quasi-military gendarmerie in seventeen of the *montons* (the eighteenth, Bangkok, was constituted differently from the provinces); it was well-disciplined, numbered about 7,000, and included a number of Danish officers.

The navy was recruited under the same laws, but drew its members from the maritime provinces; about 5,000 men were kept ready for service afloat, with 20,000 in reserve. At the outbreak of the World War Siam had only one capital ship, the cruiser *Maha Chakrkri* (4 × 4.7in, 10 × 6pdr guns), which also doubled as the royal yacht; other vessels included four gunboats (one or two 4.7in, 4 or 5 × 6pdrs), three torpedo-boats (1 × 6pdr, 1 × 2½pdr), a customs ship (1 × 6pdr) and an unarmed transport; and two torpedo-boat destroyers building.

Siam's participation in the war was limited by the small size of her armed forces, but the internment of enemy aliens (ultimately sent to India) ended Germany's intelligence operations and damaged German trade in the area. A Siamese military mission was sent to the Western Front in early 1918, headed by Major-General Phya Bijai Janriddhi, followed by a military contingent consisting of a motorized ambulance unit and a number of aviation personnel, who were to be trained by France; but the war ended before they saw active service. In return for support of the Allies, Siam gained the confiscation of all German property in the country, excluding diplomatic missions.

SINGAPORE

Singapore was an important outpost on the British trade-route to the far east; from 1889 it was an independent command, its first head being Sir Charles Warren, whose recent constabulary duties in London had included a failure to apprehend Jack the Ripper. Singapore merits an entry here as the site of the only serious outbreak of mutiny, caused partly by foreign agitation, to affect the Indian Army during the war. On 15 February 1915 the 5th Light Infantry, in garrison, revolted and began to murder those of its officers and other British men that it could find (women were generally left unmolested). The causes included elements characteristic of every mutiny in the Indian Army throughout history: a regimental grievance, poor officers, and external agitation. The grievance was partly over the recent promotion of an Indian NCO and partly a rumour that the regiment was to be sent to fight the Turks (actually it was bound for Hong Kong), which was the spark that ignited the rising.

The 5th was unusual in that it was composed exclusively of Muslims (principally Ranghars from Delhi and the eastern Punjab, some Baluchis and Pathans). The imam of a local mosque had been preaching of the heresy of helping the British fight fellow-Muslims, and spread propaganda to the effect that the Germans were also Muslim. Compounding this was the agitation of the anti-British *Ghadr* (revolution) movement, founded by Indian nationalists but supported by Germany: the instigator, Har Dayal, had recently been established in Berin by the German government, from where he and the Germans ran a network of agitators throughout the east. In another regiment the British officers would probably have identified and forestalled the unrest, but the 5th's commanding officer had been reported as unfit for command, yet had been confirmed in his place, and was both ineffective and unpopular.

The opposition to the rising was limited to a few artillerymen, the Malay States Volunteer Rifles, and an unarmed detachment of the 36th Sikhs in transit; the Sikhs of the Malay Guides mule battery joined the mutineers, but there was no cohesion and no attempt to use the artillery. The mutineers marched to the local internment camp and killed or overpowered the guards and, in the naïve belief that German or Turkish ships would arrive to support them, invited the internees to join them. This was refused: the civilians wanted no part in the violence, and the German prisoners of war regarded it as totally dishonourable to associate with mutineers. Although a few escaped (including the navigating officer from the surface-raider *Emden*), the remainder cared for the wounded British guards.

The 5th's commanding officer, Lieutenant-Colonel Edward Martin, barricaded himself in his bungalow with a few supporters; the Malay States Volunteers, Indian police and other volunteers barred the way from the cantonments to Singapore. On the following morning Lieutenant-Colonel Charles Brownlow, a 'frontier' veteran, assembled a relief-force of his own few artillerymen, some volunteers (including a body of Methodist clergymen attending a conference), and a landing-party of 80 bluejackets from the survey ship HMS *Cadmus*, advanced to the relief of Martin's bungalow and with a few casualties evacuated the garrison. In the next few days reinforcements assembled, including 200 Japanese civilians sworn in as special constables at the suggestion of the Japanese consul, 90 men and two machine-guns from the French cruiser *Montcalm*, followed by Japanese and Russian landing-parties, and the Sultan of Johore who personally brought 150 of his troops on the Penang mail train. Members of twelve European nations (including non-

belligerents such as Swiss, Swedes, Norwegians and Danes), Americans, Canadians, Australasians, South Africans and Japanese from the civilian population were armed and organized under the command of Brigadier-General Dudley Ridout; but by the time the nearest British unit had arrived (1/4th Territorial Battalion, King's Shropshire Light Infantry) from Rangoon, the mutineers had either surrendered or fled to the jungle, from where the majority were apprehended in the following month, with the assistance of Dyak trackers sent from Borneo. A total of 202 of the mutineers were court-martialled, 201 convicted, 47 shot by firing-squad and the others sentenced to imprisonment, 64 for life in the Andaman Islands penal colony. An Indian merchant also was executed for writing to the Turkish consul at Rangoon requesting a warship to evacuate the mutineers.

Apart from an outbreak at Bombay involving the 130th King George's Own Baluchis, the Singapore mutiny represents the only successful attempt by Indian nationalists and the Central Powers to suborn Indian troops from their duty; which, considering the number of Muslims in the Indian Army who were committed against their co-religionists of the Ottoman Empire, is a considerable testimony to their superintendence and their loyalty to their officers, regiments and ultimately King-Emperor. Following the outbreak, compulsory military training was introduced for all British-born inhabitants of Singapore aged 18–55.

References

Contemporary accounts of the mutiny do not present a completely accurate view (the results of the court of inquiry were not published for 50 years). *The Singapore Mutiny*, R. W. E. Harper and H. Miller, Singapore, 1984, is a full account, and it is also covered in some depth in *Armies of the Raj*, B. Farwell, London, 1990.

SOMALILAND

Three European colonies were established in Somaliland: a British protectorate from 1884, and until 1898 administered with Bombay; French Somaliland (*Côte française des Somalis*), established from 1856; and Italian Somaliland, established from 1892. Some conflict occurred in British Somaliland during the World War, but this was unconnected to the war, being part of a conflict with the Mullah Mahommed bin Abdullah of the Habr Suleiman Ogaden tribe, better known as 'the Mad Mullah', who had been causing uprisings against the British and their many friendly tribes from 1899, which compelled British forces to withdraw to the coast in March 1910, leaving the tribesmen in possession of the interior. With raids becoming more frequent, operations were mounted against them in November 1914 and February 1915, which resulted in the destruction of the rebel fort at Shimber Berris. Raiding on a smaller scale continued until 1919–20 when an expedition was mounted to crush the Mullah's forces once and for all, which was accomplished on 12 February 1920; the Mullah escaped and, destitute and bereft of support, was reported to have died in the Ogaden a year later. The main effect of the World War upon Somaliland was a marked growth of prosperity, the Somalis being major exporters of camels (used by the British forces in Egypt), and sheep and goats (to the Aden Field Force).

SOUTH AFRICA

The Union of South Africa came into existence on 31 May 1910, exactly eight years after the surrender of the forces of Transvaal and Orange Free State, which ended the great Boer War. It comprised the states of Cape Colony, Transvaal, Natal and Orange River Colony (ex-Free State), each with its own administration and a Provincial Council, elected triennially, which returned elected members to the Union's 121-member Assembly and 40-seat Senate. Executive power was held by a ten-man cabinet, with a governor-general appointed by the crown. The 1910 election returned the South African National Party to power, a new creation based upon the Transvaal *Het Volk* Party, whose leader, General Louis Botha, became prime minister. Botha (1862–1919) had been commandant-general of the Transvaal forces during the Boer War and had conducted a brilliant guerrilla campaign against the British until his surrender, after which he became devoted to the reconciliation of Boer and Briton, and remained unswervingly loyal to the British Empire. He was aided by his defence minister, Jan Christiaan Smuts (1870–1950), one of the greatest South Africans, an Afrikaner born in the British province of the Cape, educated in law at Christ's College, Cambridge, and after a career as a superb Boer commando leader during the war like Botha worked for reconciliation and in support of British interests. Among the Afrikaners, however, there was still resentment against the British and sympathy with Germany, which had supported the Boer republics. At the beginning of the World War, Botha and the National Party were supported by the English-speaking community; the disaffected Afrikaners backed James Hertzog, an ex-Boer general who had been justice minister until his anti-British sentiments forced Botha to drop him.

Immediately Britain declared war, Botha undertook to maintain South African defence with local forces, freeing the 6,000-strong British garrison. Britain suggested that South Africa occupy the German colony of South-West Africa, depriving Germany of two naval radio stations and the harbour of Walfisch Bay; having coveted the German colony, the South African government accepted with enthusiasm. On 14 August 1914 Botha and Smuts assembled their military commanders and discussed mobilization, but immediately a rupture occurred: among senior figures who resigned their commissions or declared open opposition were Christian Beyers (1869–1914), commandant-general of the South African Defence Force; Lieutenant-Colonel Solomon Maritz; and Major J. Kemp. On 14 September Beyers and the old Boer general Jacobus de la Rey (1847–1914) set out for the Defence Force camp at Potchefstroom, western

General Louis Botha (1862–1919), prime minister of South Africa and commander of the campaign against South-West Africa.

Transvaal, probably to assist Kemp who was intent on gathering anti-British forces and marching on the capital, Pretoria, to depose the government. Driving to Potchefstroom in a motor-car, Beyers and de la Rey were fired on by a police patrol attempting to catch car-thieves, and de la Rey was killed.

The rising was badly co-ordinated and limited in scale. Maritz, who commanded the Union forces at Upington on the South-West African border, had been in collusion with the Germans since mid-August, and on 10 October announced the independence of South Africa and declared war on Britain. Botha immediately declared martial law and began to organize forces; anti-British elements gathered around Beyers in the Transvaal and around the old Boer general Christiaan de Wet (1854–1922) in the Orange River Colony. As Botha dispersed Beyers' adherents, de Wet announced his intention of collaborating with Maritz, occupying Pretoria and establishing a republic; Kemp also set out to join Maritz. However, most of the South African forces remained loyal to Botha, and the prime minister assumed personal command, holding English-speaking units in reserve so as not to accentuate the hostility between nationalities. On 12 November Botha defeated de Wet's 2,000-strong commando at Mushroom Valley, near Winburg, and de Wet was captured on 1 December, his horses being unable to outrun motorized columns. Beyers was drowned attempting to ford the River Vaal to avoid pursuit (8 December). Kemp and Maritz, having united in German territory, attacked Upington in January 1915; defeated,

Kemp and most of his men surrendered on 3 February. Maritz fled to South-West Africa, and thence to Angola and Portugal.

By mid-December the revolt was suppressed, having cost Botha barely 400 casualties. The rebels' losses are unclear, but some 5,700 were captured or surrendered, emphasizing the small scale of the rising (Botha fielded some 40,000 Afrikaner Defence Force members to oppose them). They were treated leniently; only one was shot (an officer who had deserted on active service to join the rebels); others received fines or prison sentences, few of which were served in full (de Wet, for example, served barely six months of his six-year sentence).

Botha was then able to resume his plans for the occupation of South-West Africa, which involved an advance by four columns. The largest, under Botha, marched from the port of Swakopmund (a station on the South-West African coast, seized shortly after the war began) towards Windhoek; three smaller columns, under Smuts, advanced further south, two from South Africa and one from Lüderitzbucht, another German coastal installation. These operations began in April 1915, Botha having overwhelming superiority (some 50,000 against 2,000 Germans plus 7,000 reservists); Windhoek was entered on 20 May, and after a rapid pursuit the surviving German forces surrendered on 9 July; Botha had lost just over 400 men.

Internal dissent still continued, coalescing around Hertzog's Nationalist Party. Although no difficulty was experienced in raising troops for service in East Africa and on the Western Front, in the 1915 election the Nationalists polled only some 15,000 votes less than Botha's party for the Assembly. Botha remained in office, relying on the support of the largely British Unionist Party; but it was a considerable advance that the division was no longer between British and Boer, but between a sector of the Boer community and all the rest. Hertzog continued to urge neutrality and led the Nationalists towards the concept of a republic.

Smuts served as commander of the Anglo-South African forces in East Africa until January 1917, and then went to London to serve on the British War Cabinet, where he acquitted himself with great credit, and was sent to report on the situation in the Middle East in 1918. Both Botha and Smuts represented South Africa at the peace conference, and upon Botha's death in 1919 Smuts succeeded him as prime minister.

Army

The South African military forces were reorganized by the Defence Act of June 1912, which replaced the previous volunteer units with a small regular force of artillery and five mounted rifle regiments, supported by a part-time 'Active Citizen Force'. For this, all men aged 16–25 were registered, recruits to be chosen by ballot if insufficient volunteers were forthcoming (in the event, no ballot was necessary). Training was for not more than 30 days in the first year, 21 days in the next three years, after which men transferred to the Class A Reserve, where they remained until age 45. The 50 per cent of the eligible men who had not been selected for the ACF were compelled to train in rifle clubs, and formed the Class B Reserve. From age 45–60 reserves from both classes were to pass into the National Reserve. Only men of European descent were permitted to serve in the military forces.

The regular South African Mounted Rifles were converted as follows: 1st from Cape Mounted Rifles; 2nd, Natal and Orange Free State Police; 3rd, Natal Police; 4th, Transvaal Police; 5th, Cape Mounted Police. They were available for police duty in peacetime, and upon mobilization their police duties would be taken over by reservists. Two other 'regular' regiments which were regarded as part of the 'Imperial Army' were the 1st and 2nd South African Rifles, raised in 1915 in Johannesburg, and which served in Nyasaland and German East Africa.

The Active Citizen Force which came into existence on 1 July 1913 comprised most of the existing part-time volun-

South African motorized column, of the type found to be most effective in pursuing the Boer rebels.

teer units of Cape Colony, Natal and Transvaal (Orange Free State had no volunteers). The ACF Mounted Rifles included the following regiments: 1st and 2nd Mounted Rifles (from Natal Carbineers), 3rd (from Natal and Border Mounted Rifles), 4th (Umvoti Mounted Rifles), 5th (Imperial Light Horse), 6th (Cape Light Horse); and infantry: 1st Durban Light Infantry, 2nd Duke of Edinburgh's Own Rifles, 3rd Prince Alfred's Guard (Port Elizabeth), 4th 1st Eastern Rifles (originally 1st City of Grahamstown Volunteers), 5th Kaffrarian Rifles, 6th Cape Town Highlanders, 7th Kimberley Regiment, 8th Transvaal Scottish, 9th Cape Peninsula Rifles, 10th Witwatersrand Rifles, 11th Rand Light Infantry, 12th Princess Alice's Own Pretoria Regiment.

ACF units were mobilized for the 1915 campaign, but thereafter a new expeditionary force was formed for service abroad, similar to the policy adopted by Australia, Canada and New Zealand, to which existing ACF corps contributed personnel. For service in Europe, South Africa contributed

William Tennant, South African Scottish, illustrating the Scottish cutaway-skirted 'doublet'-style tunic. He was posted as missing in July 1916.

heavy artillery, supporting services and an infantry brigade of four regiments, which served in Egypt before transferring to the Western Front: the regiments (formed 1915) were numbered as the 1st South African Infantry (from the Cape), 2nd (Natal, Orange River Colony), 3rd (Transvaal) and 4th (South African Scottish, for which personnel were contributed by the ACF Scottish corps, the Cape Town Highlanders and Transvaal Scottish). Despite the hostility of the Nationalists, there was never much difficulty in finding sufficient personnel for service outside South Africa. Apart from forces used in the suppression of the revolt, some 146,500 whites were raised for active service, of whom 43,000 served in East Africa and 30,000 in Europe; this does not include 8–10,000 South Africans who enrolled in the British forces (in 1918 it was stated that more than 3,000 were serving in the RAF).

Often overlooked is the contribution made by the non-white inhabitants, who were mostly disenfranchised (a few non-Europeans were allowed to vote in Cape Province and Natal), but who provided assistance in a largely non-combatant role, in labour battalions. Including these, the total mobilized forces amounted to almost 231,000. (Offers of service were also made by the protectorates represented by the South African High Commissioner in London, Basutoland, Bechuanaland and Swaziland. Although the offer of combatant units made by the Basuto chief Griffith was turned down, much to their disappointment, they made a generous contribution to war funds, and many Basutos served as non-combatants in South-West and East Africa, and a further 1,400 with the South African Native Labour Contingent on the Western Front, for example.) In all, some 18,600 casualties were sustained by South Africa during the war, including more than 6,600 fatalities.

In organization and equipment, the South African forces followed the British model, with considerable latitude in the dress of the ACF. Many existing volunteer regiments had elaborate dress uniforms, but the service uniform decreed in 1913 consisted of a 'smasher' hat (felt slouch hat, as worn before and during the Boer War), greyish-drab tunic and trousers, brown ankle-boots, and leggings, with dark-green facings, piping and hat-pagri. In effect, most of those who took the field during the rebellion continued to wear the khaki service dress evolved during the units' existence as the earlier volunteers. The service battalions formed for overseas wore British-pattern uniform, with both unit-badges and a 'general service' badge of a springbok-head within a circlet inscribed 'Union is Strength' in English and Dutch; a notable exception was the Scottish-style uniform of the South African Scottish, including Murray of Atholl kilt and tam-o'-shanter bonnet.

References

Buchan, J. *The History of the South African Forces in France*. London, 1920

Hancock, W. K. *Smuts: the Sanguine Years 1870–1919*. Cambridge, 1962

Lawson, J. A. *Memoirs of Delville Wood, South Africa's Great Battle*. Cape Town, 1918

Official History. *The Union of South Africa and the Great War*. Pretoria, 1924

Reitz, D. *Trekking On*. London, 1933 (excellent first-hand account by a distinguished ex-Boer commando who rose to command 7/KSLI and 1/RSF on the Western Front)

Ritchie, M. *With Botha in the Field*. London, 1915

Robinson, J. *With Botha's Army*. London, 1916

Smuts, J. C. *Jan Christian Smuts*. London, 1952

Tylden, G. *Armed Forces of South Africa 1659–1947*. Johannesburg, 1954

> Referring to recent fighting along the Suez Canal:
> '. . . the Pilot Carew has lost one arm & one leg but is expected to recover. He seems a very plucky man, as directly after his injury he requested them to bring him a chair & put him in it & he would pilot the ship to Ismailia, which he succeeded in doing. He deserves the VC.'
> (Unidentified officer's log, 7 February 1915)

SUDAN

The Anglo-Egyptian Sudan was administered by the British and Egyptian governments following a convention of January 1899; a governor-general was appointed by Egypt upon British recommendation, and from 1910 he was assisted by a small council over whose decisions he exercised the right of veto.

Sudan was largely unaffected by the World War, though the demand for Sudanese goods (especially to supply the British forces in Egypt) helped the country recover from economic depression. Most internal security duty was performed by the Egyptian Army (largely under British command), involving periodic minor skirmishing with hostile tribes; most significant in the 1914–18 period were operations against the inhabitants of the Nuba mountains (1917–18) and in 1918 against the Turkana tribe on the Sudan–Uganda border. Most risings were not politically inspired but arose from banditry or religious fanaticism, such as an attack on the Egyptian garrison of the fort at Kassala (on the Eritrean border) in 1918.

Despite the Muslim religion of most inhabitants, Turkish agitation produced little result; Enver's aide, Elmaz Bey, described as a 'witless blackamoor'(!)* landed at Port Sudan intending to call upon the Egyptian troops to revolt, but they promptly arrested him. Sultan Ali Dinar of Darfur rebelled under the influence of Turkey and the Senussites, but was defeated in 1916; Darfur, hitherto a tributary to the Sudan, was annexed and additional irregular forces raised to ensure its internal tranquillity (the Western Arab Corps; the Eastern Arab Corps operated in the east of the country). The military establishment at this period also included one British battalion and an artillery detachment at the capital, Khartoum, and about 14,000 soldiers of the Egyptian Army. During the operations against German East Africa, Sudanese units briefly took over security duties on the northern Ugandan border. One notable loss to the Sudanese service during the war was Sir Rudolph von Slatin ('Slatin Pasha'), who had rendered most valuable service; as an Austrian, he felt it his duty to resign on the outbreak of the World War.

Footnote
* *The Times History of the War*. London, 1915, III, p. 318.

TURKEY

With the exception of a brief period from December 1876 to February 1878, when a constitution was in force, the Ottoman Empire was an absolute monarchy controlled by the Sultan, who as caliph (successor of the prophet) was both a theocratic and temporal ruler. Nominal head of the government, albeit under the Sultan's direction, was the Grand Vizier. Yet the empire was not a complete autocracy; its mix of nationalities, racial groups, languages, and religions was such that some areas of its vast territories were only nominally under the Sultan's control; beset with internal tensions and unrest, and expansionist policies from states upon its boundaries.

The Empire, traditionally 'the sick man of Europe', had suffered the repressive rule of Sultan Abdul Hamid II ('Abdul the Damned') from his accession in 1876; having accepted the 'Midhat Constitution' of that year, he suspended it in 1878 and ruled autocratically until the revolution of 1908. This was instigated by the 'Committee of Union and Progress', better-known as the Young Turks, organized in Paris as a revolutionary, nationalist movement which sought to arrest the decline of Turkey and institute a liberal government. Having gained military support, the Young Turks transferred their base to Salonika, from where in July 1908 they proclaimed a return to the constitution and threatened to march on Constantinople. The Sultan acceded to their demands (24 July) by resurrecting the 1876 constitution and establishing an elected chamber of deputies.

The Young Turk movement had no single leader, but was controlled by a committee of young activists, most significant being Enver Pasha (1881–1922), ultimately War Minister, an army officer whose family was from Macedonia; Mehmed Talaat Pasha (1874–1921), a Thracian who became Interior Minister and who was the political leader of the movement; Achmed Djemal Pasha (1872–1922), born in Constantinople and who became Minister of Marine; and Mehmet Djavid Bey (1875–1926), a Salonikan Jew who was Finance Minister.

Unrest had been endemic in the outer reaches of the empire, and continued with severe revolts by the Albanians and Kurds (1909) and in Arabia (1908), with constant inter-racial and inter-religious conflict, Bedouin raids on the

Sultan Mohammed V of Turkey.

with Britain was almost twice that of Germany and Austria–Hungary combined, German finances assisted Turkey greatly, and the Baghdad–Constantinople railway was dependent upon German construction. The linking of the Ottoman Empire's traditional foe, Russia, with Britain and France in the Triple Entente only confirmed Turkey's need for a German alliance. The Kaiser cultivated friendship with the imperial family, making state visits to Abdul the Damned in 1889 and 1898; a German military mission under General Colmar von der Golz (appointed marshal of the Turkish Army) as early as 1883 had made badly needed reorganizations in the Turkish Army, and many Turkish officers received training with the German Army. By the time of the outbreak of the World War, despite dissenting voices like that of Djemal who favoured a French alliance, the Young Turk government was in accord with that of Germany; Enver, who had been military attaché in Berlin, was an especially enthusiastic supporter of German aims.

Two days before the war began, Germany and Turkey agreed an alliance, but this did not commit Turkey to immediate military action. On the following day, two dreadnought battleships which had been built for Turkey by Britain (*Sultan Osman I* and *Reshadieh*) and which were almost completed, were requisitioned by Britain (as HMSS *Agincourt* and *Erin* respectively), which aroused great Turkish resentment; and as a gesture of friendship, Germany sent the battlecruiser *Goeben* and light cruiser *Breslau* to Turkey, to become part of the Turkish Navy. Enver, putting Turkish before German aims, was considering a Russo–Turkish alliance when he received news that these ships had evaded the British in the Mediterranean and were waiting to enter the Dardanelles; by ordering them to sail through, he confirmed Turkey's desire to be linked with Germany. As the British Naval Mission (which has been training the Turkish Navy) was withdrawn, German control was extended to the navy, and without orders from the government and in contravention of international law the German commander of the Dardanelles fortifications, Weber Pasha, closed the waterway. The impulsion towards war was now virtually unstoppable: on 29–30 October *Goeben*, *Breslau* and supporting vessels, nominally Turkish but commanded and partially crewed by Germans, bombarded Russian establishments on the Black Sea coast; Djemal denied knowledge of the operation, but probably Enver and Talaat had been informed. When a British, French and Russian ultimatum to the Turkish government went unanswered, hostilities began officially on 31 October 1914.

To justify the war, the government emphasized that it was against Russia, the traditional enemy, for the recovery of lost Ottoman territory and for the protection of Islam. The religious dimension was emphasized, but the Sultan's declaration of *Jihad* (holy war) was frustrated by the fact that it was decried and the war opposed by the Sherif of Mecca, which divided the Islamic world and perhaps averted risings in British and French colonies, upon which

Hejaz railway and a Mahdist revolt in the Yemen. Most serious was an attempted counter-revolution in Constantinople, which though suppressed resulted in the National Assembly voting for the deposition of the Sultan (27 April 1909); Abdul the Damned's ineffective younger brother, Mohammed Reshad Effendi, was installed as Sultan Mohammed V. Nationalist movements and foreign expansionism caused a major loss of territory: Crete gained independence in 1910, Libya, Rhodes and the Dodecanese islands were lost in the Italo–Turkish War (1911–12), and the complete defeat of Turkey in the First Balkan War (1912–13) cost virtually all the European possessions.

The Young Turks assumed further power as a result of the Balkan Wars. The government, nominally led by Grand Vizier Kiamil Pasha and Nazim Pasha, War Minister and commander-in-chief, considered sueing for peace at a time when Constantinople was under threat from a Bulgarian army; Enver, who had chosen a military rather than political career after the 1908 revolution, led a party which ousted the government (23 January 1913), Kiamil being deposed and Nazim assassinated. A virtual Young Turk dictatorship resulted, in which Enver, Talaat and Djemal exercised the greatest influence.

Throughout this period, Germany had been increasing its influence deliberately, recognizing the value of an ally whose territory controlled Russia's access to the Mediterranean and threatened the Suez Canal, and whose religion could exert influence from India. Although Turkey's trade

The German light cruiser Breslau (4,550 tons, 12 × 4.1in guns, 2 × 20in torpedo tubes). Re-named Midillu *in Turkish service and seen here flying the Turkish ensign, she was sunk after aerial bombardment and running on to a mine during a raid against Mudros in January 1918.*

Germany had been counting. (Among absurd stories circulated to win Turkish public support were those which claimed that the Kaiser was a Muslim, and that his family was descended from Mohammed's sister!) The war gave an opportunity for a policy of 'Turkification' of Asia Minor from 1915, under Talaat's control; the population of Greek origin which proliferated on the coast was deported to the interior, but most effort was concentrated against the Armenians. Although the scale of the operations has been queried, estimates of the atrocity perpetrated upon the Armenians of Asia Minor put the deaths at between three-quarters to 1½ million, out of some 2 millions, either by organized massacre or starvation and the hardships of forcible deportation to Syria and Mesopotamia. Talaat's instructions to the authorities in Aleppo, for example, while admitting that the measures might be criminal, made it clear that the official policy was one of extermination without regard for age or sex. Only the Armenians of the districts bordering Transcaucasia were able to escape.

As War Minister, Enver played a crucial role in the direction of Turkish strategy, but was a most inept general. He personally led the Third Army to catastrophe in the Caucasus; although the defence of the Dardanelles was successful, it consumed immense Turkish resources, and in Palestine and Mesopotamia the Turks met defeat; and the revolt of Arabia proved a further fatal drain on resources. Only the collapse of Russia allowed Turkish fortunes to be retrieved, Turkey's claims to provinces in 1878 being recognized by the Treaty of Brest-Litovsk; but even this was not fully advantageous, as Enver's ambition to create a new empire diverted Turkish forces needed to combat the British in Palestine, and by autumn 1918 his eastward expansionist plans, threatening the German satellite states in Transcaucasia, had almost destroyed the German alliance.

By late 1918 the Turkish position was untenable, and the situation so critical that Talaat pledged to withdraw from

the German sphere of influence, leaving the Germans in control of such important features as the Baku oilfields. Not even the temporary patching of differences between Germany and Turkey could save the situation, and on 14 October the Young Turk government resigned. A new government was installed under Ahmed Izzet Pasha (1864–1937), who was appointed Grand Vizier, having been the War Minister before Enver (until January 1914), and having led Turkish forces in the Caucasus. His government concluded the armistice of Mudros (30 October 1918) which ended hostilities, gave the Allies control of Constantinople, and ensured the withdrawal of Turkish forces from Transcaucasia. The leading Young Turks fled, the most important in a German ship on 2 November, most to meet a bad end: Talaat and Djemal were assassinated by Armenians in revenge for the atrocities against that nation, Enver died in action in Uzbekistan, fighting against the Soviets, and Djavid was executed for subversion against the new Turkish state. Izzet was believed to have connived at the escape and his government fell on 11 November 1918.

Turkey was reduced to a fraction of its previous size by the Treaty of Sevrès (10 August 1920). Under the leadership of Mustafa Kemal (1881–1938), the only Turkish general to emerge from the World War with a high reputation, a Nationalist government was established which abolished the sultanate (1 November 1922), Kemal becoming first president of the Turkish republic on 29 October 1923. In defending Turkey against Greek expansionism (1920–3) and in instituting a modern, secular and in some respects Westernized state, he probably justified the name he adopted, Kemal Atatürk, father of the Turks.

Army

Whatever the failings of command, the individual Turkish soldier was held in high regard by many of the Allied troops, who rarely questioned the Turks' heroism, determination or martial qualities. A characteristic opinion was expressed in the poem *Anzac* by 'Argent'[1] which mourns the burial of an ANZAC comrade at Gallipoli:

'Better there than in France, though, with the Germans' dirty work;
I reckon the Turk respects us, as we respect the Turk;
Abdul's a good clean fighter – we've fought him, and we know –
And we've left him a letter behind us to tell him we found him so.'

Edmund Priestman expressed the same sentiments: 'I'm jolly sure we'd fight better against the race who did all those gruesome things in Belgium than we do against the Turk, who fights "clean", and is really, when you get to know him, quite lovable.'[2]

Strangled of resources and modernization by Abdul the Damned, the Turkish military system broke down completely in the Balkan Wars. Even reactionary elements recognized the need for radical reform, which was entrusted to a German military mission led by General Otto Liman von Sanders, a capable administrator who showed considerable skills when assigned to command the Turkish forces in the Dardanelles, and later in Palestine. The mission arrived at Constantinople in December 1913, and thus had little time to make major improvements before the outbreak of war, although without the German influence it is uncertain what manner of military effort Turkey could have sustained.

The army was raised by conscription, although universal service had never applied; for example, it was estimated that of some 240,000 men annually liable for service, about half were exempted and only about 70,000 of the remainder actually served. By the Army Act of 12 May 1914 all Turks were liable for service from age 18, actually commencing from the 1 March after the 20th birthday; officially only the Sultan's family was exempt. Terms of service were, for infantry and train, two years in the regular army (*Nizam*) and 23 in the reserve, three and seventeen years respectively for the other arms; students served a shorter term, the physically unfit paid a tax instead, and exemption could be purchased after five months' service, so that the higher social groups avoided having to serve. Christians and Jews were prohibited from combat service, but went instead to labour battalions. In practice, the majority of recruits came from the peasantry of Anatolia and the Arab regions; the former were especially valuable, inured to a life of hardship and able to exist on the miserable rations, yet courageous and stubborn. After *Nizam* service, men passed through the ranks of the regular reserve (*Ikhtiat*) to the 2nd-line reserve (*Redif*), and finally into the territorial militia (*Mustahfiz*). (From 1898 there existed two reserve classes, *Redif* Class I and *Ilaweh*, styled Redif Class II in 1903; both existed as cadres in peacetime, with the intention that in wartime *Redif* Class I would be mobilized rapidly, and Class II absorbed into Class I.) The militia did not even maintain a cadre in

Discipline in 'local forces' was often very different from that pertaining to other services. Perhaps it is characteristic of the times that the following could occur, radically different from the discipline even of the earlier British volunteer corps. The Nelson Volunteer Defence Corps (Lancashire) was marching in formation, led by a mounted officer who was the proprietor of a local steam-laundry. He turned in the saddle and spoke to a private in the front rank:
Officer: "Get in step, there!"
Private: "Ah'm in step wi' back legs of bloody 'oss."
Officer: "How *dare* you? Do you know who I am?"
Private: "Aye, th'art our bloody washer-woman."

peacetime. Upon the mobilization the whole *Ikhtiat* was used to bring up the *Nizam* units to war strength, as they were invariably very weak in peacetime: the peace establishment of 17,000 officers and a quarter of a million other ranks was never remotely approached.

Despite some good 'demonstration' units with German instructors, training was generally poor: the *Ikhtiat* was supposedly trained one month per year, *Redif* one month every two years, but internal unrest and shortage of funds prevented most of it. Officers' training was also poor, excluding the 1,500 who had trained abroad or under German instruction. Some were of extremely dubious background: Muntaz Bey, for example, who commanded the 'Northern Column' of the advance on Egypt, had murdered a fellow-officer at Salonika, escaped from prison at Jaffa and become a bandit, before ingratiating himself with Enver to gain both a pardon and an independent command. Reserve officers were mostly retired from the regular army, existing on pensions so small that many were unfit for service. Despite German efforts, administration and support remained lamentable, beset with peculation and idleness, which compounded grievous shortages of equipment. (Liman von Sanders discovered that uniforms were handed from unit to unit before his inspections, so that he was ignorant of the fact that many were totally unequipped; and when he secured a supply of sandbags to fortify the Gallipoli peninsula he had to issue strict instructions that they were not to be cut up and used as clothing!)

Organization was originally in three armies, increased to four in September 1914 (headquarters Constantinople, Baghdad, Damascus and Erzinjan) and ultimately to nine. The number of corps allocated to each varied with circumstance: in early September 1914, for example, the following applied: First Army: I–IV and VI Corps, one cavalry brigade; Second Army: V Corps, one cavalry brigade; Third Army: X and XI Corps; Fourth Army: VIII and XII Corps. Other forces were unallocated at this time. Two or three divisions formed a corps; in August 1914 36 divisions existed, and ultimately 34 more were mobilized. In peacetime a *Nizam* division comprised thirteen infantry battalions, a cavalry squadron and 24 guns, theoretically 15,500 strong, rising to 19,000 in wartime. It was intended that each *Nizam* division would be accompanied by a *Redif* division, together forming the nucleus of a corps. Such strengths were rarely attained: the 23rd Division in Albania, for example, actually numbered 6,000 men, one-third of whom were conscripts of less than a year's experience. Divisions which were nominally maintained at half the establishment were sometimes only at a quarter-strength, and even after mobilization might only reach one-third of establishment. This great difference between establishment and reality was commented on succinctly in 1915: 'No Government by skilful artifice could be more successful in baffling the curiosity of the outsider than is the Turk by the simpler means of statistical incompetence and a natural disinclination to make practice march with theory'![3]

The increase in number of armies during the war did not imply an increase in overall strength or capacity. Some three million soldiers were estimated to have served during the World War, but records-keeping was so inaccurate that the actual figure may be only two-thirds of this, of whom perhaps three-quarters of a million deserted and half a million were killed or incapacitated, though the actual figure is far from clear and may be much higher. The highest establishment, approaching 1½ million, was attained in early 1916, from which total it declined, quite rapidly from early 1917. It has been estimated that actual strength in action never exceeded 650,000, and the number of divisions operating at any one time never exceeded 43. While many eligible men escape service for a variety of reasons, boys of fifteen and greybeards were impressed into the army and stated to be of military age. Although officially only deputy commander-in-chief (control was ostensibly vested in the Sultan as commander-in-chief), Enver had complete control; his initial policy was for a smaller number of well-organized formations, but as the war progressed he created a large number of new formations. As both manpower and equipment was insufficient, existing formations had to be remodelled so that all became weaker and even less efficient: First Army, for example, declined from about 200,000 men in 1914 to 3,000 in 1917, and none of the three armies in Palestine at the end of the war were stronger than a British division. The huge and unwieldy staff, however, not only maintained its strength but multiplied with the creation of each new formation.

Infantry

Field strength of a division was three regiments of three battalions each, each battalion of four companies, with battalion-strength being 24 officers and about 700 men for *Nizam* units, 24 officers and 900 men for *Redif I* and 24 officers and 800 men for *Redif II*; but in practice some companies were barely 100 strong even before the attrition of warfare. Upon mobilization in August 1914 there were 305 infantry battalions, both regular and reserve, and 64 machine-gun companies.

The Turkish Army had worn a dark-blue uniform (except cavalry), but from 1909 a German-style greenish-khaki uniform was introduced, including a single-breasted tunic with folding collar, breeches and puttees, with arm-of-service colour on the collar (infantry khaki, rifles olive-green, staff crimson, general officers scarlet). Head-dress included the *burnous* for Arab units, but the regulation fez or fur tarboosh (*kalpac*) (grey astrakhan for officers, with facing-coloured cloth crown) was usually replaced on service by a greyish-khaki cloth helmet styled a *kabalac* or *enverieh* ('Enver Pasha helmet'). This most singular item was originally a loose turban stitched into shape, named after Enver who copied it from the Italian sun-helmet and reputedly made a fortune from its patent; later it was constructed by folding the cloth around a light, plaited straw framework. Low brown leather boots were worn (riding-boots by officers), although shortages of equipment

The German-style field uniform of the Turkish army, including the distinctive enverieh *sun-helmet, named after Enver Pasha.*

resulted in many soldiers having only native sandals with rags wrapped around the feet, and either small cloth skull-caps or loose turbans. Rank-markings for senior private and NCOs were one to three chevrons (point up) on the upper arm, in arm-of-service colour, with a fourth gold chevron below for sergeants. Officers had worn rank-markings in the form of lace around the cuffs, but with the 1909 uniform these were replaced by German-style gold cord shoulder-straps, with grade indicated by silver stars. Equipment was German-style, in brown leather, the infantry with multiple ammunition-pouches on the waist-belt. The principle rifle was the 7.65mm Mauser, adopted 1890, in similar calibre to the Belgian pattern but otherwise similar to the 1892 Spanish pattern; older weapons were still in store, including 1887 Mausers and about half a million single-shot Martini-Henry rifles in reserve. Machine-gun companies were armed with Maxim and Hotchkiss guns.

Cavalry

Upon mobilization in August 1914 there were 115 regular and 135 reserve cavalry squadrons. *Nizam* regiments had five squadrons each and *Redif* four squadrons, each squadron supposedly 100 strong. Horses were not of good quality, and the cavalry was probably the least effective of the combatant arms. The reserve squadrons were formed of Kurdish and Arab irregulars, virtually untrained, of little military value but harbouring a deep resentment for Armenians upon whom they could perpetrate atrocities; created originally by Abdul Hamid, the German-inspired

The Turkish War Medal, instituted 1 March 1915 for distinguished service; it is sometimes described (erroneously) as the 'Gallipoli Star'.

reforms had disbanded the original 'Hamidian' cavalry, but the 24 regiments which succeeded them were little better. The cavalry's original uniform had been light-blue, later dark-blue with coloured facings and light-grey trousers (the élite Guard Lancers and Ertugrul Lifeguard blue lancer uniform faced red), with grey astrakhan *kalpac* with facing-coloured crown; the 1909 khaki uniform had light grey arm-of-service colour, and the equipment had single 'box' pouches at each side of the waist-belt clasp. Weapons included Mauser carbines, swords, and revolvers for NCOs and officers.

Artillery and supports

The artillery was traditionally an independent command, and as it was entirely a *Nizam* force, with no *Redif* element, was a cut above the rest. It was divided into Field (including horse, mountain and howitzer batteries), fortress and depot branches; at mobilization in Auguat 1914 there were 211 field and 124 heavy and fortress batteries. Most field artillery was assigned at divisional level, each division supposedly including a field regiment of two or three battalions, each of three 4-gun batteries; each corps of three divisions maintained two mountain battalions of three 4-gun batteries, and a howitzer battalion of three 6-gun batteries; each cavalry brigade included two 4-gun horse batteries. Each division thus possessed from 24 to 36 field guns, but the severe losses sustained in the Balkan War had not been restored completely, and guns were in short supply. The principal equipment was the 75mm Krupp field gun, and 75mm 1905-pattern Krupp and the more modern 75mm Schneider mountain guns, but older 87mm German field guns and even antique smoothbored howitzers were also in service, the latter of very limited value. Only a few modern heavy guns were available (150mm Krupp and Schneider–Creusot howitzers), and the fortress artillery was even more antiquated, dating from the 1880s or earlier.

Although the supporting services have been criticized as ineffective, this was not invariably the case: in the advance on Egypt, for example, camel-transport (about 250 per regiment) was such that they could cover up to 30 miles per day. At mobilization in August 1914 there were 104 pioneer and labour companies of various types, 22 signal companies and 42 searchlight sections. The aviation service was small and controlled, trained and equipped by Germany, using German machines (for example the AEG CIV).

The artillery's coloured uniform had been dark-blue with red facings and grey trousers; with the 1909 uniform arm-of-service colours were artillery dark-blue, engineers light-blue and train red.

The German influence on the Turkish Army was entirely beneficial, yet the number of German officers was comparatively small: some 200 in 1916, rising to 800 in the following year. They were concentrated in the most important posts: in the Palestine/Mesopotamian theatre, for example, some 69 staff appointments were held by Germans and only nine by Turks, which caused some resentment. A large number

The Turkish cruiser Hamidieh; 3,800 tons, 2 × 6in, 8 × 4.7in, 2 × 3pdr, 2 × 1pdr guns, 3 × 18in torpedo tubes.

of German other ranks also served with the Turkish forces, mostiy from 'technical' arms providing skills which the Turks had no time to learn. A few complete units served in the Turkish forces, such as artillery batteries in the Dardanelles, but Enver was unenthusiastic about the employment of larger formations, excluding the so-called 'Yilderim' force (known as 'F Group' by the Germans).

Navy

Having lost much of their skilled seafaring capacity with their Greek territory, the destruction of the Ottoman fleet at Sinope by Russia (1853) was a desperate blow. The Sultan Abdul Aziz (reigned 1861–76) attempted to repair the damage and with the assistance of a British naval mission organized the construction of a number of ironclads at British and French yards; but his deposition was assisted by the fleet he had created. Abdul Hamid neglected the navy entirely, perhaps out of fear that it might turn on him as it had upon his predecessor; the small number of destroyers and torpedo-boats which he did commission abroad were dismantled when they reached Constantinople. Although attempts were made to remedy this neglect in the immediate pre-war years, excluding the two ships impounded by Britain and *Goeben* and *Breslau*, the Turkish naval force was negligible, especially after the 1874 battleship *Messudieh* (rebuilt by Ansaldo of Genoa 1904, 2 × 9.4in, 12 × 6in guns) had been sunk by the British submarine *B 11* on 13 December 1914; although the description of the navy as a 'weird collection of scrap-iron'[4] is probably excessive!

The navy was crewed by conscription (five years' regular service followed by twelve in the reserve). Vessels in commission at the start of the war included two old battleships, built 1891 and sold by Germany to Turkey in 1910 (*Häirredin Barbarosse* and *Torgud Reis*, formerly *Kurfürst Friedrich Wilhelm* and *Weissenburg* respectively, 10,060 tons, 6 × 11in, 8 × 4.1in guns); an old coast defence battleship, *Muin-i-Zaffer* (2,400 tons, rebuilt 1904–7, 4 × 6in, 6 × 3in guns); two cruisers (*Hamidieh*, 1904, 3,800 tons, 2 × 6in, 8 × 4.7in guns, and *Medjideah*, mined near Odessa, April 1915),

and about 30 various torpedo- and gun-boats. *Goeben* and *Breslau* (re-named *Sultan Yawaz Selim* and *Midillu* respectively) were officially elements of the Turkish Navy but maintained largely by German crews.

Footnotes

1. Originally published in *Passing Show*; reprinted in *Trooper Bluegum at the Dardanelles*, O. Hogue, London, 1916, p. 283.
2. *With a B-P Scout in Gallipoli*, E. Y. Priestman, London, 1916, p. 282.
3. *The Times History of the War*, London, 1915, III, p. 55.
4. *The First Phase of Turkey's Share in the War*, A. H. Trapmann, in *The Great War*, ed. H. W. Wilson and J. A. Hammerton, London, 1915, III, p. 39.

References

Anon. *Handbook of the Turkish Army*. War Office, London, 1915
Aaronsohn, A. *With the Turks in Palestine*. London, 1917
Ahmad, F. *The Young Turks: the Committee of Union and Progress in Turkish Politics 1908–1914*. Oxford, 1969
Ahmed-Amin. *Turkey in the World War*. Yale, 1930
Djemal Pasha. *Memories of a Turkish Statesman 1913–1919*. London, 1922
Hagopian, A. P. *Armenia and the War*. London, 1917
Jastrow, M. *The War and the Baghdad Railway*. Philadelphia, 1918
Larcher, Major M. (trans. and ed.). *The Turkish War in the World War*. Washington, 1931
Morgenthau, H. *Secrets of the Bosphorus*. London, 1918 (US Ambassador to Turkey)
Nogales, R. de. *Four Years Beneath the Crescent*. New York, 1926 (Venezuelan mercenary in Turkish service)
Ruhl, M. *Die Armeen der Balkan-Staaten*. Leipzig, n.d. (includes Turkey)
Toynbee, A. J. *Armenian Atrocities: the Murder of a Nation*. London, 1915
Trumpener, U. *Germany and the Ottoman Empire 1914–1918*. Princeton, 1968

TRANSCAUCASIA

The collapse of imperial power in Russia was seen by the inhabitants of the Transcaucasian provinces as an opportunity to assert their independence, and a necessity for organizing their own defence. By August 1917 representatives of the three nations involved, Georgians, Armenians and Azerbaijanis, were elected, and at Tiflis on 17 September the 'Council of the Transcaucasian Peoples' announced the establishment of the Federal Republic of

Transcaucasia (which involved the ejection of the Bolshevik commissar sent to govern from Tiflis). It was a somewhat uneasy alliance, dominated by Georgia, which sought total independence; Armenia or Erivan favoured a continued but looser connection with Russia, and Azerbaijan, predominantly Muslim, favoured a connection with the Islamic peoples farther south: the prospect of foreign invasion or the spread of Bolshevism were all that bound them together. The new government assembled a scratch force of Georgians, Armenians and Russian volunteers to secure the border from Turkish aggression, but the Russian government's commissar for the Caucasus succeeded (with the assistance of Armenian revolutionaries and Bolshevik naval forces) in establishing a Bolshevik government in Baku, whose excesses against the Muslim peoples of the area did much to estrange the Azerbaijanis from the Christians of Georgia and Armenia. After the Treaty of Brest–Litovsk awarded parts of previous Russian territory to Turkey, the Azerbaijanis established their own national government at Elizavetpol, and on 26 May 1918 the republic of Transcaucasia was abolished, to be replaced by the separate states of Georgia, Erivan and Azerbaijan.

Georgia accepted German military and financial assistance (German forces were already in Odessa and Sevastopol), confirming existing ties (a Georgian Legion, officered largely by Germans, had been formed as early as 1915). Germany mediated between Georgia and Turkey, and temporarily quietened Georgian fears over the Black Sea port of Batum, which Brest–Litovsk had awarded to Turkey and which had been occupied by Turkish troops on 15 April 1918; Germany ensured that Georgian rights to use the port would not be compromised, and that Turkey should regard Georgia as a neutral.

With Baku held by Bolsheviks, Elizavetpol became the temporary capital of the Republic of Azerbaijan, which admitted Turkish troops in late May 1918; and with Turkey thus increasing its influence, a small British column ('Dunsterforce', named after its commander, General L. C. Dunsterville, the model of Kipling's 'Stalky') advanced from Mesopotamia and occupied Baku on 16 August 1918. Dunsterville's small command (39 Brigade) received only limited assistance from the Russo–Armenians in Baku, whom it had been sent to support, to curtail German and Turkish influence, and after considerable fighting was compelled by the Turks to evacuate Baku, which fell on 14 September. Erivan was by this time much under the influence of the extreme socialist, revolutionary Dashnakist society, so favoured co-operation with the Bolshevik regime in Russia.

The armistice provided for the evacuation of German and Turkish personnel and their replacement by Allied forces; consequently, Dunsterville's 39 Brigade and a Russo-Armenian force under General Bisherakoff re-occupied Baku on 7 November 1918 (the Turkish armistice having been declared on 30 October), and a British garrison arrived in Batum on 27 December.

In the following months, Transcaucasian independence was crushed under internal conflict and Turkish pressure. Despite British mediation, conflict occurred between Erivan and Georgia in January 1919, partly stemming from old rivalries and partly over disputes concerning the Batum–Erivan railway and Georgian customs-duties; and ethnic violence continued between the Muslims of Azerbaijan and the Armenians of Karabagh, a conflict which was to flare again some 70 years later. British troops withdrew from Azerbaijan in August 1919 and the administration lapsed into confusion. Soviet troops entered Baku on 28 April 1920, coinciding with a rising by the local Bolsheviks; the government was overthrown, opponents of the revolution eliminated, and despite an anti-Bolshevik rising which led to massacre and counter-atrocity, Azerbaijan was firmly back under Russian control.

The Republic of Erivan was the next to fall, assailed in September 1920 by a Turkish army on the western frontier and a Soviet force from Azerbaijan. The Armenians resisted but Bolshevik risings occurred in the cities, the state collapsed and became a Soviet republic allied to Moscow; for their assistance, Turkey was allowed to keep part of the newly occupied territory. Georgia had hesitated to support Erivan actively, being unwilling to send forces outside her boundaries; and perhaps believed that resistance would be futile. Consequently, when a Soviet invasion was launched, Bolshevik risings in Tiflis and elsewhere elicited little serious opposition. With the establishment of the Soviet Republic of Georgia, Transcaucasian independence was finally extinguished, and Russian domination again extended throughout the region.

UNITED STATES OF AMERICA

The USA was governed under the system which still exists, of an elected president, a cabinet of ministers, and a Congress of an upper house (Senate) representing states, and a lower House of Representatives. In November 1912 the Democrat Woodrow Wilson (1856–1924) was elected 28th president of the USA; a lawyer and legal tutor, he was a moderate reformer concerned with the maintenance of neutrality over the war in Europe, although generally in favour of the Allies. He won re-election in 1916 over Charles

---

The easy relations between officers and other ranks of the American forces was remarked upon by European observers, unused to such familiarity:

'It was no uncommon thing to hear a private address his captain by his first name. One day a private said to his captain, "Bill, you got all the wrong dope on this", to which the captain replied severely: "I told you before about this discipline – if you want to quarrel with my orders, you call me mister."'

(*Our Army at the Front*, H. Broun, p. 138, New York, 1918)

Hughes, to some degree because of his having kept the United States out of the war.

Wilson's attitude was not one of pure isolationism, however, for as early as February 1915 he warned Germany that they would be held accountable for any destruction of American shipping. Widespread public indignation followed the sinking of the *Lusitania* and others, and in the face of American threats, Germany temporarily suspended unrestricted U-boat warfare in 1916. In 1915 and 1916 Wilson tried to act as a broker for a negotiated peace, without success; and US involvement in the war became inevitable after Germany renewed unrestricted submarine warfare in January 1917. Early in January Wilson was still declaring that for the USA to become involved would be 'a crime against civilization', but renewed loss of American shipping, and the revelation of the 'Zimmermann telegram' (which suggested German support for a Mexican reconquest of Texas, Arizona and New Mexico) compelled Wilson to ask Congress for permission to declare war. The House of Representatives backed him by a majority of more than 6 to 1, and the Senate by more than 13 to 1, and war was declared on Germany on 6 April (and on Austria on 7 December).

The declaration of war represented a failure for Wilson's previous policy, but once involved he was clear about the nation's aim: '. . . to deliver the free people of the world from the menace and actual power of a vast military establishment . . . which . . . secretly planned to dominate the world . . . which . . . stopped at no barrier, either of law or mercy, swept a whole continent within the tide of blood.'[1] Support was not universal: with the United States having so many inhabitants with a background of one or other of the belligerent nations, some tensions could have been expected, and the anti-war or neutralist movement was considerable; Wilson's protest to Germany over the sinking of *Lusitania* had cost him secretary of state William Jennings Bryan, whose replacement, Robert Lansing, took the opposite view and was advocating US entry into the war by March 1917. The division of opinion is reflected in the disagreement between Admirals Benson and Sims: William Benson, chief of naval operations, informed Sims that it was none of America's business to rescue Britain and that he would as soon fight Britain as Germany; the Canadian-born Sims, naval attaché to Britain and US naval commander in Europe, was so pro-British that he had been reprimanded by President Taft in 1910 for a speech in which he assured Britain of total support from their American kinsmen should the need ever arise, and advocated total integration of US ships into the Allied naval forces.

Wilson encouraged the belief that the war was a national undertaking, instituting the draft system, but to maintain the USA's position as an associated rather than fully Allied power, gave his field commander in Europe (Pershing) freedom to organize the American Expeditionary Force as he wished, to co-operate but not surrender US independence. On 8 January 1918 Wilson made his famous 'Fourteen Points' speech to Congress, his vision of an acceptable plan for peace, which formed the basis on which Germany and Austria–Hungary sought the armistice. It also created the idea of a League of Nations, and acted as the base for the Paris Peace Conference; but Wilson's success at the conference was limited, his idealism not matching the political realities and the Allied determination to exact heavy reparations. Wilson lost support at home (the Senate refused by seven votes to ratify the Treaty of Versailles), and his health broke down during his last period in office.

The effect of US entry into the war was profound, and extended far beyond the purely military assistance which, due to the small size of the peace establishment, took a considerable time to enter the field. The morale effect was enormous, especially considering the exit of Russia from the war, and the provision of resources was crucial. The USA's industrial and agricultural potential was awesome: by July 1918 almost four ships were being delivered per day, warships were being constructed in three to five months, and the record was that of the destroyer *Ward*, which was launched, almost complete, 17½ days after the laying of the keel. By May 1918 the weekly production of Enfield-derived rifles was 45,000, and the annual production target was set at 15,000 field guns. By 1918 agricultural exports were so vast that it was estimated that 43.5 per cent of the inhabitants of Britain, 14.1 per cent of France and 11.1 per cent of Italy were supported by US food. About half the

President Woodrow Wilson (1856–1924).

*Admiral William S. Sims
(1858–1936), the vehemently
pro-British commander of US
naval forces in Europe.*

cluding in France and Serbia. Some were formed under the aegis of the American Red Cross, and among the most celebrated were Richard Norton's American Volunteer Motor-Ambulance Corps, and the Field Service of the American Ambulance, organized by previous US Treasury assistant-secretary Piatt Andrew. The latter body was attached to the French Army (a section served in the Balkans) and was composed principally of US university graduates driving motor-cars.

Replying to a British toast of welcome ('Whether you live or die tomorrow, you can never raise your glasses to a more glorious purpose, the Army of America'), Lieutenant Armitage of the A.E.F. spoke of and for the US Army:

'Before the war they were a mere handful, and were somewhat looked down upon, as a rule, by American people, as being a group of wasters, loafers, who did nothing but drink cock-tails. But subsequent events have proved the injustice of this attitude when the crash came, devolving upon them the great task of whipping into shape the great mass of raw material . . . Political power, wealth, social position has absolutely no influence. The selected draft in America has swept in all men and equally distributed the burdens of our country [upon men] who are itching to get over here and stand side by side with you in the game you have played so well . . . when this terrible struggle is over, there will be bound together by bonds of personal friendship that can never be broken, the two great Anglo-Saxon nations of the world . . . No one realizes better than we do now that only the magnificent resistance of the British and French Armies and the eternal vigilance of the Royal Navy has kept our own dear shores free from invasion, our own women left inviolate, and our own babes safe from being spitted on bayonets . . . We not only thank you, but with that we give the offer of our lives, of our fortunes, and everything we have, everything we are, and everything we hope to be.'

(At the Imperial Hotel, St Anne's, June 1918; *The Return*, pp. 5–7, 7 June 1918).

national income went on the war, and financial credits (in the form of goods advanced for later payment) amounted to $3,345 million to Britain, $2,065 million to France, $760 million to Italy, $325 million to Russia, $154.25 million to Belgium, $15.8 million to Greece, $15 million to Cuba and $12 million to Serbia. (The imminent arrival of US forces was not greeted with universal acclaim: Captain James Dunn's *The War the Infantry Knew* includes a comment of October 1917 to the effect that a victory before the American arrival would be ideal, as the Gallic cock was going to be sufficiently insufferable after the war, without the American eagle claiming its share of the victory as well!)

Many American volunteers enlisted in foreign services before the declaration of war, mostly out of idealism. Most famous were probably the members of the French aviation service's *Escadrille Lafayette* and certain members of the French Foreign Legion, including the Legion's greatest poet, Alan Seeger, who in accord with his own prediction met his 'rendezvous with Death/At some disputed barricade' on the Somme in July 1916. Others served in ordinary regiments of foreign armies, like Dillwyn Starr, who served in both the British Navy and Army, and was a 2nd lieutenant in the 2nd Battalion Coldstream Guards when he was killed leading a charge on German trenches east of Albert in September 1916; or John Poe, a Princeton football star, who was a somewhat unlikely member of the 1st Battalion Black Watch when he was killed with a bombing party in September 1915 (his name was commemorated by Poe Field, Princeton). In addition to combatant volunteers, American ambulance units served on several fronts, in-

Army

Before the United States entered the war, their military forces were insufficient even to execute large-scale manoeuvres, and consequently the staff had had no opportunity of directing large formations. In 1911, for example, deducting coast artillery, the army comprised less than 32,000 regulars, distributed among some 49 establishments throughout the country, supplemented by almost 118,000 state National Guardsmen. A major revision occurred in June 1916 with the passing of the National Defense Act, which permitted the regular forces to be enlarged to about 235,000 by 1921, in stages (although the president was authorized to implement the Act immediately if necessary),

some 517,000 concripts and 233,000 volunteers were assembled, when in December voluntary enlistment of those within the conscription ages was suspended. At the same time all eligible men were divided into five classes according to family commitment and civilian occupation (so as not to deplete industries); in the event only Class I men were called, and an extension of the age–range to 18–45, decreed in July 1918, proved unnecessary as such men were never conscripted. The numbers of men assembled in 1918 amounted to 2,149,000 conscripts and 198,000 volunteers (of men outside the draft ages), which of those conscripted represented about one-quarter of the total eligible. By virtue of intensive training courses, within a year of the declaration of war more than 57,000 officers had been commissioned, from three principal intakes, the first two from civilian candidates (many university graduates and students) and the third largely from ex-enlisted men of the regular army. Commissions from the first two intakes were granted up to the rank of colonel, but the third were largely 2nd lieutenants. The reorganization of the regimental structure for the AEF effected a considerable economy on the number of field officers required.

Plans were prepared for the deployment of an ever-increasing number of American divisions in France; by September 1918 they provided for an eventual 100 combat divisions in France and twelve in the USA, involving the mobilization of more than 5.5 million men. The war ended before even half this programme could be implemented: at the armistice there were seven regular, seventeen National Guard and sixteen national army divisions in France (representing almost one-third of the total Allied forces), of which ten divisions had been used to supply reinforcements for those at the front. By May 1918 there were more than half a million US troops in France, and by July that number had doubled; in all, some 2,084,000 arrived in Europe. Well might an American colonel (Stanton) make his famous remark on the arrival of the AEF in France: 'Lafayette, nous voici!' ('Lafayette, we are here!').

It was intended that the US forces in France by the end of 1918 would comprise five corps, each of four combat, one training and one reserve division (for replacements), and that when at the front, each corps would have two divisions in the line and two in reserve. By the armistice, the 30 combat divisions were organized in three armies of three corps each, comprising some 1,338,000 combat troops; of the more than 264,000 casualties sustained, more than 50,000 had been killed and almost 25,000 had died of disease. Divisional organization established in August 1917 replaced the 'triangular' system used since 1898 (three brigades of three regiments each) with a 'square' system, each division of two infantry brigades of two regiments each, plus a brigade machine-gun battalion, a field artillery brigade (three regiments and trench-mortar battery), a divisional machine-gun battalion, an engineer regiment, a signal battalion, divisional train and ammunition column, four field hospital and four ambulance companies, a total

US troops wearing the British-style steel helmet, entrenching on the Western Front.

which projected 65 infantry, 21 cavalry, 21 field artillery and seven engineer regiments (plus two battalions of mounted engineers). Regular enlistment was henceforth for three years, followed by four in the reserve. The National Guard was to be enlarged to some 457,000 in sixteen divisions, with expenses henceforth borne by the federal, rather than state, government. Some of these were mobilized in support of the expedition that entered Mexico, which provided a valuable opportunity for the practising of field operations.

The strength of the military establishment on 1 April 1917 was 5,791 officers and 121,797 other ranks in the regular service; about 4,000 in the army reserve; and 3,733 officers and 76,713 National Guardsmen, plus a further 97,000 still to take the oath to the federal government. This force was wholly insufficient for the task in hand, but as an immediate gesture one regular division, supplemented by marines, was dispatched to Europe under General John J. Pershing, whose conduct in the Mexican expedition led to his being chosen to command the American Expeditionary Force. The Allies urged that American forces be integrated into the existing command structure, but this was resisted as politically unacceptable for US forces to serve under foreign command, and Pershing was instructed to co-operate as fully as possible while maintaining strict US independence.

The entire National Guard was mobilized on 3 July 1917, but to create a new 'national army' conscription was instituted by the Selective Service Law of 18 May 1917, which empowered the president to call two drafts of half a million men each, from those aged 21–30. The first drafts were called in September 1917, and by the end of the year

US troops fitting gas masks; they are wearing the Adrian helmet, used by units operating with French formations; the man in the left foreground wears the 'overseas cap'.

strength of about 28,000 men, or about twice that of a French or German division.

Despite the insistence on preserving US independence, units did serve with other armies, two divisions with the French IV and VI Corps, the 332nd Infantry in Italy, and forces co-operated with other Allied contingents in Russia. The US government was caused some embarrassment over the question of including Negro troops in the AEF (when America entered the war, a Georgia representative introduced a bill – unsuccessfully – to make illegal the appointment of Negroes as either officers or NCOs, despite the good service rendered by those who had held such positions in the past!). In the event, the 92nd Division was formed of Negro regiments, and four intended for the 93rd Division (369th–372nd) were transferred to the French Army as their 157th Division; the French, being used to the concept of coloured troops, were not so sensitive as the Americans. Segregation and discrimination was widespread: some 380,000 Negro personnel served during the war, but of 200,000 sent to France, only 42,000 were regarded as combat troops. Complete segregation, as practised in the army, was not possible in the navy.

The American troops presented a singular appearance: European observers found many of them not especially smart or well-drilled but of imposing physique: 'Where they were impressive was in their composite build . . . The major part of the soldiers were tall, thin, rangy-looking, with a march that was more lope than anything else'.[2] Training was rapid, especially later in the war, supposedly including an additional two or three months after arrival in France, but late in the war the total training was down to four months, with some being rushed into the line immediately upon disembarkation with no more than ten days' weapons-training; even the regular regiments had a large percentage, perhaps as much as two-thirds, of newly enlisted men. It was reported that so many of the US troops were recent immigrants that fully 10 per cent were unable to speak English when they joined, and language difficulties persisted during their stay in Europe. (When asked to translate

a long speech of Poincaré's to the newly arrived AEF, one American reported that 'he said to give 'em hell'.[3] Allied observers, especially British, remarked upon the lack of distinction between other ranks and officers, who were commonly addressed on first-name terms, which somewhat scandalized the British. As in the Australian forces, discipline was enforced without 'salutin' or 'if-you-pleasin' as one officer remarked.[4]

Infantry

At Pershing's suggestion regiments were reorganized on European lines, which economized on field officers and staff, and the increase in size of regiments helped redress the reduction of regiments within a division caused by the change from 'triangular' to 'square' formation. Instead of comprising three officers and 100 men, companies were now composed of six officers and 250 men, subdivided into four platoons of 58 men each, commanded by a subaltern. Each battalion (commanded by a major) comprised four companies, and each regiment (commanded by a colonel) three battalions plus a regimental machine-gun company, giving a regimental total (including headquarters) of 3,700–3,800 of all ranks. A 3-company machine-gun battalion was deployed at brigade level, and a 4-company battalion at divisional level, each company with sixteen machine-guns. Each rifle platoon included six automatic rifles and six rifle-grenade launchers, increasing firepower considerably. During the war the infantry increased more than elevenfold, from about 85,000 to about 974,000, achieved by the formation of hundreds of new regiments rather than by adding battalions to existing regiments in British fashion.

A khaki service uniform ('olive drab' in US terminology) had first been issued in 1903, including a single-breasted tunic with standing collar (introduced 1903), breast- and side-pockets, bronzed buttons and collar-discs (bearing 'US' on the right and unit-identification on the left), trousers and either puttees or canvas leggings. In warm weather the tunic could be discarded and a drab flannel shirt worn with the same collar-insignia and a light buff tie.

Head-dress was the 1912 khaki felt campaign hat with wide brim and 'lemon-squeezer' or 'Montana peak' crown, and light-blue cords for infantry; but it was impractical and replaced by the 'overseas cap', a peak-less fore-and-aft sidecap; there was also a 'foul weather' cap of light khaki gaberdine with soft cloth peak and ear-flaps. The double-breasted khaki greatcoat had a falling collar and bronzed buttons, and khaki gaberdine trench-coats or raincoats were also worn. NCO rank-insignia were khaki or olive-drab chevrons (point up) on both upper arms, one to three respectively for lance-corporal, corporal and sergeant, three chevrons above a lozenge for 1st sergeants, above a star for colour-sergeants, above two curved laces for battalion- or squadron-sergeant-majors, above three for regimental sergeant-majors, and above horizontal bars for staff and supply NCOs. The 1910-pattern light khaki webbing equipment included five cartridge-holders on each side of the waist-belt clasp, a canteen in webbing cover at the right rear, a haversack on a belt over the right shoulder, and the 'long pack', basically a cylindrical knapsack extending from the back of the neck to below the waist, preventing the wearer from sitting comfortably and catching the rear of the hat, a design generally hated by the troops. The entrenching-tool was strapped vertically to the rear of the pack, the bayonet on the side, and the rolled greatcoat across the top.

The field uniform of the US Army, including the unpopular New Zealand-style campaign hat, which was soon discarded after arrival in Europe.

Officers' uniform included riding boots or leather gaiters and a khaki peaked cap with light khaki band, light-brown peak and chinstrap, and bronzed eagle badge. The cords on their campaign hat were black and gold, and the piping on the overseas cap either the same or in the corps colour. At officers' instruction schools, established in France, hat-bands were adopted to indicate fields of specialization: riflemen green, machine-gunners yellow, rifle-grenadiers red, bombers orange, bayonet-experts white and flame-thrower operators blue. Rank-insignia was carried on the shoulder-straps of the tunic, the shirt-collar and overseas cap: one or two silver bars for 1st lieutenant and captain, gold maple leaf for major, silver for lieutenant colonel, and silver eagle for colonel. 2nd lieutenants initially had no rank-insignia, but latterly adopted one gold bar; generals had gold hat-cords and one to four silver stars on the shoulder-strap. The officers' greatcoat was longer than that of the other ranks, with two rows of horn buttons and a half-belt, with brown (2nd lieutenant) or black braid on the cuffs, 1–5 rows with Austrian knots according to rank, with 1–4 stars for general officers. A leather waist-belt supported the pistol-holster, but in Europe (initially to much official displeasure) the Sam Browne was adopted, and some wore webbing equipment.

The steel helmet was adopted in Europe, mostly of the British pattern, painted khaki; horizon-blue Adrian helmets were worn by units serving with the French. Some evidence exists for the use of a distinctive badge on the latter (Union shield within a wreath) but there is no evidence for its actual issue. Such units adopted French leather equipment to accommodate the French ammunition required by their weapons, and the 27th and 30th Divisions, serving with British formations, used some British uniforms with blackened US buttons. The respirator was of British pattern. Formation insignia (shoulder-patches and devices stencilled on the helmet) were introduced very late in the war, and few were actually in use before the armistice.

The principal weapon was the 1903 .30in Short Magazine Rifle, known as the Springfield, of which some 600,000 were in store before the war. As these were insufficient in number, in May 1917 it was decided to adopt a version of the P14 Lee-Enfield already in production in US factories, modified to take .30in ammunition, and designated the 'Rifle M1917 (Enfield)'. About seven-eighths of rifles manufactured during the war were of this Enfield derivation, but Springfields were used alongside them. Units serving with French formations carried French Lebels and Berthiers. Although the Lewis light machine-gun was originally of American manufacture, the .30in Browning automatic rifle was the principal infantry-support weapon, distributed at a rate of 4–6 per platoon; some 29,000 were sent to France for the AEF, and before these arrived some 34,000 French Chauchat guns were issued, adapted to take the US cartridge (and sometimes styled 'chaut-chaut' guns by the Americans). The US Army had adopted the Maxim machine-gun in 1904, which was superseded in 1909 by the

US howitzer battery, Western Front.

gun known in Europe as the 'Portable Hotchkiss', in the USA as the Benèt-Mercié. Orders were placed for Vickers and Lewis guns, but after a most impressive test in May 1917 the Browning was adopted as the principal machine-gun; some 27,000 Model 1917 .30in Brownings were sent to France.

Cavalry
Cavalry was employed hardly at all in Europe, its only active service at this time being minor actions on the Mexican border. After the declaration of war, eight new regular regiments (18th–25th) and 20 National Army regiments were authorized, but in October 1917 the former, and in August 1918 the latter, were converted to artillery; numbers of cavalry rose from 22,000 to only 29,000 by the armistice. The only detachments to serve with the AEF belonged to the 2nd, 3rd, 6th and 15th Cavalry, largely limited to liaison and remount duty, although Pershing did request eight regiments to be used in the event of breaking through the German line. A provisional squadron drawn from the 2nd Cavalry was the only one to see action. Uniform was like that of the infantry, with yellow arm-of-service colour (hat-cords, etc.), reinforced breeches, canvas leggings or riding-boots, a longer greatcoat, the 1910 infantry equipment and 1913-pattern sabre.

Artillery
Before the war the principal weapon was an early quick-firer designed by Ehrhardt of Düsseldorf, 3in calibre, consider-ably more powerful than the guns of some European armies, and with additional stability provided first by a trail longer than the ordinary Krupp carriage, and then with a split trail designed in 1916. There was no light field howitzer, but the heavier artillery included the 1905 6in howitzer. During the war, however, the principal artillery of the AEF was the French 75mm field gun and 155mm howitzer; a mobile mounting was devised by placing the field gun upon a 5-ton Holt caterpillar tractor. Some British 8in howitzers were used, and some 144 rail-mounted heavy guns were deployed in France, including 14in guns and 16in howitzers.

Batteries were of four guns each. Divisional artillery consisted of a field brigade of three regiments, two equipped with 75mm field guns and one with 155mm medium howitzers, plus a battery of twelve medium trench-mortars. A field-gun regiment consisted of two battalions, each of three batteries; a howitzer regiment comprised three bat-talions, each of two batteries; thus divisional artillery comprised 48 75mm guns and 24 155mm howitzers. The heavier artillery was deployed at corps level, a brigade of two regiments, one of three battalions (two batteries each) of motorized 4.7in guns, a similar regiment of motorized 155mm guns, and four heavy trench-mortar batteries. The reserve deployed at army level was sufficient support for 20 divisions: four motorized brigades, each of three regiments, with 24 6in guns per regiment; and five field regiments organized as for divisional artillery. Rail-mounted artillery was under control of general headquarters.

The artillery establishment expanded more than seven-teenfold during the war, the home-based coastal artillery rising from 21,000 to 137,000 men, and the field artillery from 9,000 to 389,000, an increase of some 43 times over. Artillery wore the ordinary field uniform, with scarlet arm-of-service colour. Ordnance personnel (a branch which expanded from 1,000 to 64,000 strong) had mixed black and red as their arm-of-service colour.

Armoured corps
Unlike most European armies, the Americans were quick to appreciate the potential of armoured units, and by Sep-tember 1917 it was planned to include in the AEF five heavy and 20 light battalions, the latter to be equipped with French Renault tanks and the heavy with a version of the British Mk VIII, powered by a Liberty aero-engine and known as the 'Allied' or 'Liberty' tank. These were to be produced both in the USA and, at Anglo-American expense, in a new factory in France, with a production-target of 300 tanks a month, and a potential expansion to 1,200 per month. The 'Liberty', with British framework and American machinery, was constructed in only very small numbers, and not until November 1918; the war was over

before the factory could be opened in France, and only about 20 Renaults had been sent from the USA before the armistice. The Tank Corps, formed in early 1918, was thus equipped with British and French vehicles, and saw action only in September 1918. Establishment was increased in May 1918 to fifteen brigades, each of one heavy and two light battalions, but only few were mobilized, two light battalions serving at St. Mihiel and a heavy battation with II Corps in the drive on the Hindenburg Line. The Tank Corps arm-of-service colour was grey; it numbered some 14,000 personnel at the armistice.

Engineers and supports

In addition to the divisional deployment described above, there were the usual units deployed at corps and army level. The Engineer Corps had the largest expansion-rate of any of the services existing before the war, rising from some 3,000 men to 394,000, an increase of more than 130-fold. Regiments were numbered, and in addition to field regiments assigned to divisions, others included the following specialist units: 11th, 13th, 15th, 16th (Standard Gauge Railway); 12th, 14th, 21st, 22nd (Light Railway); 23rd (Highway); 24th (Supply); 25th (General Construction); 26th (Water Supply); 27th (Mining); 28th (Quarry); 29th (Surveying/Printing); 37th (Electrical/Mechanical); 40th (Camouflage); 56th (Searchlight). The Signal Corps, of the same strength before the war, rose to 52,000; the engineers' arm-of-service colour was mixed scarlet and white, that of the Signal Corps orange and white. Train duties were shared between the Quartermaster Corps (increasing from 8,000 to 228,000), colour buff, and the Motor Transport Corps, a new creation rising to 103,000 strong, colour purple. Other branches included the Intelligence and Interpreters Corps (colour mixed green and white) and the Chemical Warfare service (also a wartime creation, rising to 18,000 strong), colour mixed blue and yellow, the cords of the campaign hat having a red knot and acorn-ends. The Medical Corps, which expanded from 7,000 to 300,000, had mixed maroon and white as an arm-of-service colour, and was not restricted just to AEF units: to remedy the great shortage of doctors, many were attached to British units in the final year of the war.

Marine Corps

Although not part of the army, the US Marine Corps provided one of the first detachments for service in Europe, forming half the 2nd Division, composed thus:

3 Brigade: 9th and 23rd Infantry, 5th MG Battalion
4 Brigade: 5th and 6th Marines, 6th (Marine) MG Battalion
2 Field Artillery Brigade: 12th, 15th and 17th Field Regiments
Supports: 4th MG Battalion, 2nd Engineers, 1st Field Signal Battalion

These were what John Thomason, one of the Marines' most distinguished authors, termed 'Old Timers': experienced professionals assembled from ships and shore-stations, whose service ranged from the Boxer Rebellion to the Pacific. The Marines were described as being quite distinctive from the army units, in size, *espirit de corps* and resulting comportment, and also because their service uniform was initially 'forester-green', an olive shade. When this wore out, army khaki was issued, but reinforcements arrived in green, giving Marine units a piebald appearance. Weapons and equipment were as for the army, but Thomason describes the use of sawn-off shotguns for trench-fighting. The Marines earned a formidable reputation on the Western Front (their German nickname was 'devil-dogs'), from a spirit epitomized by Colonel Wendell 'Whispering Buck' Neville, who when advised to retire to a less perilous position in Belleau Wood, remarked 'Retreat, hell! We just got here!'[5] The corps expanded from a pre-war total of 13,692 to more than 59,000, from all voluntary enlistment.

Navy

The navy had been somewhat neglected until in 1890 a naval advisory board recommended the assembly of a fleet of 100 vessels, including battleships, and a very considerable impetus was given by the Spanish–American War. The first dreadnoughts were launched in 1908 and a major expansion instituted from August 1915; as Germany was perceived to be the main threat, the fleet was concentrated upon the Atlantic. The speed with which ships were built has been noted above, and a year after the declaration of war the total number of vessels (of all types) in service had increased from 300 to more than 1,000, though many of the capital ships planned in the 1916 programme were not completed until after the war.

The following were the ships of 8,000 tons displacment or over which were available in the first year of the war:

Date	Name and displacement (tons)	Main armament only
Battleships:		
1895–6	*Indiana, Massachusetts, Oregon* (10,288)	4 × 13in, 8 × 8in, 12 × 3in
1897	*Iowa* (11,346)	4 × 12in, 8 × 8in, 10 × 4in
1900	*Kearsage, Kentucky* (11,520)	4 × 13in, 4 × 8in, 18 × 5in
1901–6	*Alabama, Illinois, Wisconsin* (11,552)	4 × 13in, 14 × 6in, 4 × 3in
1902–4	*Maine, Missouri, Ohio* (12,500)	4 × 12in, 16 × 6in, 6 × 3in
1906	*Louisiana, Connecticut* (16,000)	4 × 12in, 8 × 8in, 12 × 7in, 20 × 3in
1906–7	*New Jersey, Georgia, Nebraska, Rhode Island, Virginia* (14,948)	4 × 12in, 8 × 8in, 12 × 6in, 12 × 3in
1906–8	*Kansas, Minnesota, New Hampshire, Vermont* (16,000)	4 × 12in, 8 × 8in, 12 × 7in, 20 × 3in
Dreadnoughts:		
1909	*South Carolina, Michigan* (16,000)	8 × 12in, 22 × 3in

Date	Name and displacement (tons)	Main armament only
1910	*Delaware, North Dakota* (20,000)	10 × 12in, 14 × 5in
1911	*Utah, Florida* (21,825)	10 × 12in, 16 × 5in
1912	*Arkansas, Wyoming* (26,000)	12 × 2in, 21 × 5in
1913–14	*Texas, New York* (27,000)	10 × 14in, 21 × 5in
1915	*Oklahoma, Nevada* (27,500)	10 × 14in, 21 × 5in

Cruisers:

Date	Name and displacement	Main armament only
1893	*Saratoga* (reconstructed 1907, 8,150)	4 × 8in, 10 × 5in, 8 × 3in
1896	*Brooklyn* (reconstructed 1907, 9,215)	8 × 8in, 12 × 5in
1905–6	*St. Louis, Charleston, Milwaukee* (9,700)	14 × 6in, 18 × 3in
1905–8	*California, Colorado, Maryland, Pittsburg, South Dakota, West Virginia* (13,680)	4 × 8in, 14 × 6in, 18 × 3in

Date	Name and displacement (tons)	Main armament only
1907–8	*Montana, North Carolina, Tennesee, Washington* (14,500)	4 × 10in, 16 × 6in, 24 × 3in

Among other vessels were eight coast defence ships, four second-class and thirteen third-class cruisers, 56 torpedo-boat destroyers, ten gunboats, 21 torpedo-boats, 51 submarines and numerous support vessels. The principal capital ships constructed during the war were the battleships *Pennsylvania* and *Arizona* (launched 1915), and *New Mexico, Idaho* and *Mississippi* (launched 1917); the next were *Tennessee* and *California* (launched 1919), and the first launched in accordance with the August 1915 construction programme was *Maryland* (1920). *Lexington*-Class battlecruisers were designed in 1916, but no construction was undertaken before the end of the war. New light or 'scout' cruisers were designed in 1916 and construction authorized

USS Texas *(27,000 tons; 10 × 14in, 21 × 5in, 4 × 3pdr, 2 × 1pdr guns, 4 × 21in torpedo tubes) leaving New York. She served with the British Grand Fleet's American 6th Battle Squadron.*

The Washington-class cruiser USS Montana, *14,500 tons, 4 × 10in, 16 × 6in, 24 × 3in, 4 × 6pdr guns, 4 × 21in torpedo tubes.*

in the following year, but none was built between the 1908 *Salem* Class and the 1920 *Omaha* Class. The majority of ship-construction during the war was of the smaller vessels required for convoy and anti-submarine duty.

Upon entering the war, destroyers and submarines were sent to Europe, but the main battlefleet remained in American waters. In contrast to the independency of the AEF, naval forces were integrated with those of the Allies: in December 1917 the US 4th Squadron of dreadnoughts joined the British Grand Fleet as that force's 6th Battle Squadron: the vessels involved were *New York* (flagship), *Arizona*, *Arkansas*, *Florida*, *Nevada*, *Oklahoma*, *Texas*, *Utah* and *Wyoming*. The US Navy also made a significant contribution in the laying of the anti-submarine North Sea mine barrage. Losses were relatively light and included no capital ships; and among convoy-duties, the US Navy escorted some 62 per cent of the American troops who crossed the Atlantic.

The conscription law did not operate in the navy, so all recruits were volunteers. The number of regular naval personnel was held initially at 87,000, but ultimately Congress sanctioned an increase to 131,485. The greater part of the expansion was accommodated in the various reserve formations: the Fleet Naval Reserve (men with naval training who volunteered for four years' service), the Naval Auxiliary Reserve (men with merchant naval experience), the Naval Coast Defence Reserve (men capable of serving in navy yards and on coastal patrol), the Volunteer Naval Reserve (volunteers who provided their own boats), and the Naval Reserve Flying Corps (which formed the bulk of the expansion of the naval aviation service). The Volunteer Naval Reserve encompassed many hundreds of civilian craft taken into naval service for patrol duty (private yachts and the like), most kept on the Atlantic seaboard and attached to the 1st–5th Naval Districts (Boston, Newport R.I., New York City, Philadelphia and Norfolk Va. respectively).

Aviation service

Although the aircraft was an American invention, military aviation had been neglected, and despite some limited experience gained during the Mexican operations, as a neutral the USA had been unable to profit from developments made by the combatant powers. At the time of the US entry into the war the army air service comprised only 65 officers and 1,120 other ranks, originally part of the Signal Corps, with only about 300 aircraft, not fit for combat service. Expansion was rapid (202,000 strong by the armistice), and an intensive training programme (with British and French instructors) produced more than 11,400 aircrew at the armistice, of whom some 4,300 were overseas but fewer than 1,250 at the front. Instead of the more than 260 squadrons which it was hoped would be operational in France by the end of 1918, there were actually only 45.

Although some American aircraft were used, the majority, including virtually all the combat aircraft, were of foreign design or construction. Allied models were modified

to take American engines, and about half of the almost 7,900 aircraft in service at the armistice were American-built (less than 10 per cent of these in France), and almost three-quarters of the engines. The DH4, and Handley Page and Caproni night-bombers were produced satisfactorily in American versions (the DH4, latterly ordered to be replaced by the DH9, was the principal aircraft of its class in American service), but the Bristol Fighter, which had been constructed in considerable quantities, was abandoned when the Liberty engine was found to be too powerful for it.

Squadron-strength was set at twelve pilots and 250 other personnel, and squadrons were classified as observation, pursuit (i.e., fighters), day bombardment and night bombardment. Squadrons were organized in groups (normally three or four squadrons per group); ultimately the AEF included seven corps and one army observation groups, two day bombardment groups (one of only one squadron) and four pursuit groups. These were deployed slowly, as aircraft and pilots became available; there were, for example, only fifteen squadrons deployed by July 1918, though the first combat deployment was in April 1918 (for pursuit squad-

Raoul Lufbery, probably the most famous of the American volunteers who served with other armies; when the USA entered the war he transferred from the French to the American aviation service, whose uniform he is wearing here; he scored seventeen victories but was killed in 1918 when he jumped from a blazing aircraft rather than be burned during its descent.

rons) and July 1918 (bombing). The most famous squadron was the *Escadrille Lafayette*, the French unit of American volunteers which transferred to US service. Kite-balloon units were organized in corps balloon groups of usually three or four companies each, and an army balloon group of two companies. In January 1918 the AEF had only 20 balloons (all borrowed); by the armistice more than 660 had been deployed.

By Congress approving the expenditure of more than $67 million in 1917, it was possible to increase naval aviation-schools from one to 40. Most naval aviation trainees were from civilian life, only a few from the regular navy, and graduates from these establishments were commissioned into the Naval Reserve; some of the regular navy pilots were not officers, but petty officers. In addition to flying seaplanes from coastal bases and ships, naval aviation stations were established in Europe, for patrolling the French and British coasts.

Among home-produced machines which saw service were:

Curtiss: the H4 ('Small America') and H12 and H16 ('Large America') were successive variants of four-man, twin-engined biplane flying-boats used for maritime patrol, anti-submarine and anti-Zeppelin duty; the H4 was used by the RNAS. The Curtiss JN was a two-seater biplane trainer, also used 1915–16 by Britain, and known as the 'Jenny'; the N9 was a seaplane version used by the US Navy.

Standard: the Standard EI was a single-seater biplane designed as a fighter, but found to be suitable only as an unarmed trainer.

Thomas Morse S4: single-seater fighter found to be suitable only as a trainer.

In addition to those already mentioned, among foreign machines used by the USA were the DH6, Breguet 14, Caudron GIII, Dorand AR1–2, Farman F40, Morane-Saulnier A1, Nieuport 17, 23, 27 and 28, RAF FE2b, Salmson 2, SIA 7B1, Sopwith 1½–Strutter, Sopwith Camel, and Spad VII, XI and XIII.

Footnotes

1. Quoted in *How We Went to War*, N. Lloyd, New York, 1918, pp. 9–10.
2. *Our Army at the Front*, H. Broun, New York, 1918, p. 35.
3. Ibid., p. 128.
4. Ibid., p. 138.
5. Quoted in *The Marine Book*, C. Lawliss, London, 1989 p. 38.

References

Anon. *The Americans in the Great War*. Clermont-Ferrand, 1919 (Michelin Guide)
Anon. *The United States Army in the World War 1917–1919*. Washington, 1948
Broun, H. *Our Army at the Front*. New York, 1918
Bullard, Major General R. L.

Personalities and Reminiscences of the War. New York, 1925 (author ultimately commanded Second Army)
Chambrun, Colonel de, and Marenches, Captain de *The American Army in the European Conflict*. New York, 1920
Clendenen, C. C. *Blood on the Border: the United States Army and the Mexican Irregulars*. New York, 1969
Coffman, E. M. *The War to end all Wars: The American Military Experience in World War I*. New York, 1968
DeWeerd, H. A. *President Wilson Fights his War: World War I and the American Intervention*. New York, 1968
Frothingham, Captain T. G.

The American Reinforcement in the World War. New York, 1927
Gauss, C. *Why We Went to War*. New York, 1918 (justification of US entry into the war)
Gregory, B. *Argonne 1918: the AEF in France*. London, 1972
Harboard, J. G. *The American Army in France 1917–1919*. Boston, 1936
Hudson, J. J. *Hostile Skies: a Combat History of the American Air Service in World War One*. 1968
Katcher, P. *The U.S. Army 1890–1920*. London, 1990
Leighton, J. L. *Simsadus: London*. New York, 1920 (title was the telegraphic address of Admiral Sims: account of his tenure in London)
Liggett, General H. *AEF: Ten Years Ago in France*. New York, 1928 (Hunter Liggett was one of Pershing's chief subordinates)
Link, A. S. *Wilson*. Princeton, 1947–65 (5-volume study of Woodrow Wilson)
Lloyd, N. *How We Went to War*. New York, 1918
May, E. R. *The World War and American Isolation, 1914–1917*. Cambridge, 1959
McMaster, J. B. *The United States in the World War*

1914–1918. London, 1927
Morse, E. W. *The Vanguard of American Volunteers*. New York, 1918 (Americans in foreign and Red Cross service, 1914–17)
Paxson, F. L. *America at War 1917–1918*. Boston, 1939
Perry, L. *Our Navy in the War*. New York, 1918
Sims, Rear-Admiral W. S. *The Victory at Sea*. London, 1920
Smith, D. M. *The Great Departure: the United States and World War I 1914–20*. New York, 1965
Stallings, L. *The Doughboys: the Story of the AEF 1917–1918*. New York, 1963
Thomas, Captain S. *History of the AEF*. New York, 1920
Thomason, J. W. Jnr. *Fix Bayonets: With the U.S. Marine Corps in France 1917–1918*. New York, 1925, rep. London, 1989 (one of the finest accounts, with notable contemporary illustrations)
Tuchman, B. W. *The Zimmermann Telegram*. New York, 1958
Urwin, G. W. *The United States Infantry: an Illustrated History 1775–1918*. London, 1988
(See also under 'Pershing' in Section IV)

WEST INDIES

The British colonies of the West Indies were a mixture of crown colonies and those with governors and representative governments. The World War's main effect upon these territories was to boost their economies (total trade increased by more than 60 per cent); only the Dominican lime industry suffered, while the other principal exports (sugar and sugar-derivatives, cotton, etc.) rose in price. Accordingly, the British West Indies were able to contribute significantly to British funds for the expenses of the war.

Although local-defence units existed, the troops fielded for active service were volunteers for the British West Indies Regiment, which served on the Western Front and in the Middle East. The numbers recruited from the various territories were: Jamaica 10,280; Trinidad and Tobago 1,478; Barbados 831; British Guiana 700; British Honduras 533; Grenada 445; Bahamas 441; St. Lucia 359; St. Vincent 305; Leeward Islands 229. Contingents were also sent to enlist in Britain by the 'Contingent Committees' of Trinidad and Barbados. The extent of West Indian service is demonstrated by the fact that in addition to those in the BWI Regiment, Trinidadian fatalities occurred in the Royal Navy, Royal Flying Corps and 74 British, Indian Army and even French and US units during the war.

IV
BIOGRAPHIES

BIOGRAPHIES

Only the briefest biographical notes of a few of the leading personalities can be accommodated here, and restricted to military and naval, rather than political, figures. A recommended source of extensive biographical information is *Biographical Dictionary of World War I*, H. H. Herwig and N. M. Heyman, Westport, Connecticut, 1982. Useful brief biographies can also be found in *Illustrated Companion to the First World War*, A. Bruce, London, 1989; and in *Who's Who in Military History*, J. Keegan and A. Wheatcroft, London, 1976.

Alekseev (or Alexeyev), Mikhail Vasilevich (1857–1918)

Mikhail Alekseev was the son of an officer who had risen from the ranks (it is thus somewhat misleading to describe him as 'son of a private' which has been done); he graduated from the Russian staff college and survived the Russo–Japanese War (in a staff capacity) with reputation unscathed. In 1914 he was chief of staff to the ineffective Nikolai Ivanov, commander of the South-Western front, and planned the successful operation which resulted in the fall of Przemysl. Transferred to command the North-Western front in March 1915, he maintained his reputation while all were falling around him, and in September was named as the Tsar's chief of staff, thus becoming virtual supreme commander. Despite attempts to co-ordinate the various fronts, and despite the removal of dead wood like Ivanov, his task was probably too great. He failed to support the Brusilov offensive by diverting resources, and had to dissipate forces in unwise operations (such as the support of Roumania) in order to placate Russia's allies. His relations with the Tsar (whom he believed was interfering) were not ideal, and his active command was ended by a heart attack in November 1916. He returned to service in February 1917, and has been criticized for not acting swiftly to extinguish the March revolution. Having helped facilitate the Tsar's abdication, he was appointed commander-in-chief, but, unable to work with the Provisional Government, he was dismissed on 21 May. He was recalled for twelve days in September but again stepped down, and after the November revolution went south to form a White Army. Although nominal leader of the 'Volunteer Army' of Whites, actual command resided with Lavr Kornilov; and at this stage, with his influence thus marginalized, Alekseev died of another heart attack in October 1918. An intelligent man and a good strategist, he was flawed by a degree of indecision, and just as the Tsar was not the right supreme commander, neither was Alekseev the right assistant.

Allenby, Edmund Henry Hyman (1861–1936)

'Bull' Allenby (the nickname came partly from his physical appearance and partly from his violent temper) was Inspector-General of Cavalry from 1909, and commanded the Cavalry Division of the BEF in 1914. Elevated to command Third Army in October 1915, his career was unspectacular, and though his handling of the Battle of Arras (1917) was competent, it perhaps exhibited a dis-

regard for casualties attributed to many British commanders. Allenby and Haig shared a mutual dislike, but Lloyd George had confidence in 'the Bull', and he was appointed commander-in-chief in Egypt in June 1917. Freed of control from headquarters and operating in independent command for the first time, he was a revelation. Raising the morale of his command, he began an offensive in Palestine, capturing Beersheba (31 October), Gaza and Jerusalem (9 December). Deprived of resources by the German offensive on the Western Front, Allenby was unable to resume the attack until September 1918, winning a victory at Megiddo (19 September) and capturing Damascus (1 October), which led to the Turkish exit from the war at the end of the same month.

Allenby's reputation among his troops in Palestine, and with the local inhabitants, could not have been higher; the Arab version of his name, 'al-Nabi' (the prophet) and his entry into Jerusalem was taken as the fulfillment of an ancient prophecy regarding the advent of a messiah to free

Edmund Allenby.

the Arabs from Ottoman control, and is an appropriate comment upon his reputation. Promoted to field marshal and to the peerage as Viscount Allenby of Megiddo, he served as high commissioner in Egypt after the war and presided over its attainment of independence. His military reputation was such that Wavell described him as the best British general of the war which, although perhaps an over-statement (and depends for comparison upon the skill of the other British commanders), is a reflection upon the skill and meticulous planning he displayed when given freedom of action in Palestine.

References

Gardner, B. *Allenby of Arabia: Lawrence's General*. London, 1965
Liddell Hart, Sir Basil. *Reputations*. London, 1928
Savage, R. *Allenby of Armageddon*. London, 1925

Wavell, Field Marshal Viscount. *Allenby: Soldier and Statesman*. London, 1946
Although not biographical, *Allenby's War: The Palestine-Arabian Campaigns 1916–18*. D. L. Bullock, London, 1988, is a good modern study.

Beatty, David (1871–1936)

David Beatty was the youngest officer of the Royal Navy for more than a century to achieve flag rank (aged 39), following a succession of daring exploits in Egypt and China. As Churchill's naval secretary (1911–13) he also acquired influential connections, which together with his undoubted talent led to his appointment as commander of the Grand Fleet's Battlescruiser Squadron in 1913. This was conceived as a force swift enough to reconnoitre and find the enemy, and strong enough to hold it until the main force could arrive. Beatty appeared the ideal commander: he was extremely offensively minded and probably regarded his battlecruisers as the naval equivalent of a cavalry vanguard, most appropriate given his antecedents (his father was a captain in the 4th Hussars); yet he tempered the offensive spirit with prudence, and made a considerable success of his actions at Heligoland Bight and Dogger Bank. He behaved with similar energy at Jutland, though his conduct here appears somewhat impetuous: having found the German High Seas Fleet he engaged it (which cost his force severely) and failed to keep Jellicoe adequately informed, so that the main force arrived too late to achieve complete victory. Nevertheless, it was Beatty who was more generally acclaimed as the hero of Jutland, and upon Jellicoe's translation to First Sea Lord, Beatty succeeded to command of the Grand Fleet. He had no further opportunity for major action, and followed Jellicoe's cautious policy of blockade and protection of Allied convoys. He was rewarded by promotion to Admiral of the Fleet and an earldom, and was himself First Sea Lord from 1921 to 1927. It is the dashing side of his nature which is best remembered, epitomized in public perception by the rakish angle at which he wore his cap, and the laconic comment upon observing the destruction of his squadron at Jutland, popularly rendered as 'there's something wrong with our bloody ships'.

David Beatty.

References

Beatty, Admiral Earl. ed. J. Barnes. *The Beatty Papers I (1908–19)*. London, 1970
Chalmers, Admiral W. S. *The Life*

and Letters of David, Earl Beatty. London, 1951
Roskill, S. *Admiral of the Fleet Earl Beatty: The Last Naval Hero*. London, 1980

Birdwood, Sir William Riddell (1865–1951)

William Birdwood came from a distinguished military family (his grandfather was a general and his wife was a niece of Gonville Bromhead, the Rorke's Drift VC). After much campaign service in India (Hazara, Tirah, Mohmand campaigns) and South Africa he was appointed to command the Australian and New Zealand Army Corps in 1914. The choice could not have been better, for unlike some members of the British command, Birdwood appreciated fully the qualities of the ANZACs; and conversely they

William Birdwood.

the Southern Cross featured prominently on his coat of arms. He remained in command of the AIF throughout the war, but despite his outstanding service and abilities, and the unique rapport established with his troops, he never became governor-general of Australia, a position for which he was uniquely suited and which would have been greeted with rapture in that country.

Footnote

*Special Order, Australian and New Zealand Army Corps, April 1915; quoted in *The Anzac Book*, London 1916, p. 152.

Reference

Birdwood, Field Marshal Lord. *Khaki and Gown: Autobiography of Field-Marshal Lord Birdwood.* London, 1941 (His *In My Time*, London, n.d., is a collection of anecdotes, few concerning the period of the war)

Brusilov, Alexei Alexeevich (1853–1926)

Alexei Brusilov was probably the best Russian commander of the war. From an aristocratic and military family, he spent much of his early career in cavalry staff duties, until appointed to lead Eighth Army at the start of the World War. Energetic, imaginative and capable, he stopped the Austro-Hungarian drive through Galicia by counter-

Alexei Brusilov.

appreciated his soldierly qualities and easy attitude. 'Birdy' (or more familiarly, even to his face, 'Bill'), as he was known to the ANZACs, did not possess a martial bearing (slight, with a stammer and a nervy manner), but was one of the best generals of his day, aptly described by Hamilton as 'the soul of Anzac'. He was one of few commanders to emerge with credit from the Gallipoli débâcle, and the four-point order he issued in April 1915 was the epitome of good sense: 'Concealment wherever possible; covering fire always; control of fire and control of your men; communications never to be neglected',* all of which were often disregarded by other commanders. In August 1915 he was promoted to lieutenant-general and knighted in the same year, created a baronet in 1919, a field marshal in 1925 and a peer in 1938, when his unbounded enthusiasm for his ANZAC troops led to his taking the title Baron Birdwood of Anzac and Totnes;

attacking after a long retreat (autumn 1915), and assumed command of the South-Western Front in March 1916. This permitted him to exercise his first truly independent command, and launch the offensive which bears his name, the only really successful Russian operation of the war. By co-ordinating his forces and compelling his surbordinates to accept his directions, the Brusilov offensive was initially extremely successful, and did much to relieve the severe pressure then being felt by the Allies. Lack of supplies and support (from forces not under his control) and the arrival of German reinforcements caused the offensive to halt, but not until severe casualties had been sustained which were, inevitably, a contributory cause for the unrest which resulted in the March revolution. Brusilov replaced Alekseev as commander-in-chief following the revolution, but his final offensive (July 1917) crumbled due to the declining quality of the Russian army, and in the following month he was replaced by Kornilov. Despite his aristocratic background, Brusilov was one of those who had urged the Tsar to abdicate, and although he was unemployed after the October revolution, in 1920 he accepted the new regime with sufficient enthusiasm to join the Red Army, though not employed in a combat capacity.

References

Brusilov, A. A. *Mémoires du Général Brusilov*. Paris, 1929   — *A Soldier's Note Book 1914–1918*. London, 1930

Bülow, Karl von (1846–1921)

Karl von Bülow was given command of the German Second Army in August 1914, more than 40 years after his last combat service (in the Franco-Prussian War), having spent much of the intervening period in staff appointments. Despite early successes, von Bülow was not optimistic about German prospects, and when a gap of some 30 miles opened between his own and von Kluck's First Army, he determined to retreat unless assured of immediate support. In the event, it was the intelligence chief Colonel Richard Hentsch who ordered the general retreat from the Marne, doubtless influenced by von Bülow's dire predictions of imminent destruction. In January 1915 von Bülow was promoted to field marshal, but a heart attack in March caused him to relinquish his command, and he was never restored to active duty; probably his lack of resolution in 1914 resulted in his illness being taken as an opportunity to dispense with his services. Disappointed in his attempts to resume his career, he resigned from the army in 1916.

References

Bülow, K. von. *Mein Bericht zur Marneschlacht*. Berlin, 1919   Krack, O. *Generalfeldmarschall von Bülow*. Berlin, 1916

Byng, Julian Hedworth George (1862–1935)

Julian Byng came from most distinguished antecedents: his grandfather, Sir John Byng, had led a Guards brigade at Waterloo, in the defence of Hougoumont, and less fortunate

Julian Byng.

ancestors included Admiral John Byng (shot in 1757, *pour encourager les autres* according to Voltaire) and, more distantly, Thomas Wentworth, Earl of Strafford, beheaded by Charles I in 1641. Julian was distinguished in command of the South African Light Horse during the Boer War, and in 1914 was given command of the 3rd Cavalry Division, and the Cavalry Corps in 1915. In August 1915 he was sent to the Dardanelles to command IX Corps (at Suvla), and was an architect of the only successful part of the expedition, its withdrawal. In May 1916 he was given the command which made his name, that of the Canadian Corps, which he led with considerable distinction for more than a year, including the capture of Vimy Ridge. In June 1917 he assumed command of Third Army, planning the Cambrai offensive, and performed well in conceding only limited ground in the great German offensive of spring 1918. In the counter-attack in the autumn, he led Third Army to very considerable success. One of the better generals of the war, Byng was rewarded by a peerage (Baron, ultimately Viscount Byng of Vimy), the post of governor-general of

Canada (1921–6), a most appropriate appointment given his wartime service, and, two years before his death, the rank of field marshal.

Reference
Williams, J. *Byng of Vimy: General and Governor-General*. London, 1983

Cadorna, Count Luigi (1850–1928)

Scion of a Piemontese military family (his father had been a general during the *Risorgimento* and had served in the Crimea), Luigi Cadorna was appointed Italian chief of staff in 1914, after some 46 years' army service. He was instructed to modernize the army, but had made little progress before the war began, whereupon he took command on the northern front. At his best as an administrator, he was a capable field commander but lacked the highest skill. He led the Italian army in eleven battles of the Isonzo, all remarkable for their lack of success and unimaginative frontal assaults which caused immense losses. The débâcle

Luigi Cadorna.

of Caporetto was his downfall: although he did not perform badly in organizing a defence-line after a precipitate retreat, he could not hope to survive, and quit his post on 7 November. His reputation shattered, he retired after a brief spell on the Supreme War Council established by the Rapallo conference. In his defence, it must be stated that his main failings were shared by many generals in the war: lack of awareness of realities, separation from the experiences of the troops at the front, and little understanding of the pressures on morale from unremitting attritional warfare; and latterly he became very pessimistic about the outcome of the war, even considering a negotiated peace. His appointment as field marshal by Mussolini in 1924 did not go far in restoring his reputation, blackened by the official inquiry into Caporetto.

Reference
Cadorna, Count L. *Altre pagine sulla grande guerra*. Milan, 1925

Castelnau, Noël Joseph Edouard de Curières de (1851–1944)

Castelnau was a member of an aristocratic French family with generations of military service. Chosen by Joffre as deputy chief of staff in 1911, he was influential in determining the French Plan XVII, which provided for an offensive posture in the event of war, based upon a flawed assessment of German capabilities. Although he was forced on to the defensive in 1914 (as commander of Second Army), he remained an advocate of offence, and (appointed commander of the Army Group of the Centre in June 1915) directed the Champagne offensive of autumn 1915. Later in the year he was appointed Joffre's chief of staff, and in February 1916 was given authority to oversee the defence of Verdun; it was Castelnau who, it is said, was most responsible for the decision to hold the position and place Pétain in command. When Joffre was removed from command in December 1916, Castelnau was considered as his replacement, but his long association with the ex-commander and his forceful Roman Catholic beliefs (he was nicknamed 'monk-in-boots') made this appointment impossible, and he retired temporarily from active duty. In the last year of the war he took command of the Eastern Army Group and conducted the final offensive into Lorraine. More able than many and a competent tactician, his religious beliefs and their expression probably cost him promotion to the rank of marshal, and his wartime service was beset by the tragedy of the loss of three sons.

Conrad von Hötzendorf, Count Franz (1852–1925)

Austrian chief of staff from 1906, Conrad von Hötzendorf was responsible for much of the modernization and reorganization of the imperial forces, and advocated an aggressive policy against both Italy and Serbia. To this end he not only supported the initiation of war in 1914, but contributed towards determining Austria's attitude towards Serbia. In his conduct of the war, he has been regarded by some as not only a master strategist but even the best general of the war, which would seem to be a difficult case to sustain, for no matter how perceptive his strategic intentions, he failed to realize that his forces were incapable of carrying them through. His record of practical warfare was not impressive, his successes (like the Gorlice–Tarnow offensive of 1915) depending to a considerable extent upon German participation. Although elevated to the rank of field marshal from 1916, his unimpressive record made irresistible the German call for a unified command (under German control), and on 1 March 1917 he was relieved of his post as chief of general staff. He served on, in a considerably downgraded capacity, as commander in the South Tyrol, where success still eluded him, and he was dismissed finally on 15 July 1918. A capable strategist, he was undone by a lack of resolution and ability to turn planning into fact.

References

Conrad von Hötzendorf, Count Franz. *Aus meiner Dienstzeit.* Vienna, 1921–5.

Regele, O. *Feldmarschall Conrad.* Vienna, 1955

Enver Pasha (1881–1922)

Enver was the son of a civil servant from Turkish Macedonia, who entered the Ottoman army and joined the Young Turks movement in Salonika. A leading member of the revolutionary faction which deposed the sultan, he eschewed political advancement and concentrated on a military career, being considerably influenced by Germany during a posting as military attaché in Berlin. He achieved a considerable reputation in the Italo-Turkish and Balkan Wars, and shot the then war minister in the upheaval which pushed the Young Turks into dictatorial power. As war minister from February 1914 he played a crucial role in bringing Turkey into the war on the side of the Central Powers, and was Germany's most powerful supporter in the Young Turks movement, while maintaining the primacy of Turkish interests. His strategy during the war was based upon dreams of expansion into the Caucasus, to the exclusion of other concerns; and his own military leadership was poor. Commanding in the first campaign against Russia, he led the Turks to disaster; his interference in the Dardanelles campaign was lamentable, and his preoccupation with the Caucasus threatened a rupture with Germany, upon whose resources Turkey depended. His reputation was damaged further by outrages against the Armenians, and he fled Turkey at the end of the war. He was killed in 1922 at the head of anti-Soviet rebels in Uzbekistan, having attempted without success to gain support for a return to power in Turkey. Incompetent both as a politican and a diplomat, his own belief in his abilities led to his downfall.

Falkenhayn, Erich von (1861–1922)

From an aristocratic but impoverished background, Erich von Falkenhayn enjoyed a rapid rise to power, due to a considerable extent to the patronage of the Kaiser, who had been impressed by his dispatches from the Boxer Rebellion. Promoted to general in 1912, he became war minister in 1913 and succeeded the crushed von Moltke as chief of general staff on 14 September 1914, initially combining that post with the war ministry, which he headed until February 1915. An over-cautious, even indecisive commander, he hesitated to commit resources fully to any one theatre, although the demands made upon him were insupportable. His decision to release troops to make a major effort on the Eastern Front produced significant results, but after a period of containment on the Western Front he accepted the attritional theory of defeating the French by causing them immense casualties at Verdun. The consequent failures of 1916, and hostility to his command by Hindenburg, Ludendorff and others, resulted in his resignation in late August. In mid-September he accepted a considerable demotion in an active field command, leading Ninth Army against Roumania with complete success, but when sent to Turkey to recapture Mesopotamia, he failed. The Mesopotamian effort proving impossible, he was sent to Pal-

Enver Pasha.

Erich von Falkenhayn.

but were responsible for the condition of proficiency in which the navy was placed at the outbreak of war. His most influential creation was the 'all big-gun ship', a capital ship with main armament of a single calibre and greatly increased striking-power, the *Dreadnought* which revolutionized warship-design. Other innovations were the battle-cruiser (a battleship with the speed of a cruiser) and his recommendation of oil fuel for universal use. He retired from the Admiralty in 1910, but was brought back on 29 October 1914. Fisher's relations with Churchill (First Lord) were initially extremely cordial and productive, but became severely strained over the Dardanelles expedition, which Fisher first supported and then turned against, as more naval resources were demanded. He resigned over this matter on 15 May 1915. Despite the unfortunate end to his career, he was largely responsible for the ability of the navy to fight the war, and, being a deeply religious as well as patriotic man, the motto to his coat of arms as 1st Baron of Kilverstone could not have been more appropriate: 'Fear God and Dread Nought'.

Footnote
*L. Gardiner. *The British Admiralty*. Edinburgh, 1968, p. 302

References
Fisher, Admiral Baron. *Memories*. London, 1919

— *Fear God and Dread Nought: the Correspondence of Admiral of the Fleet Lord Fisher of Kilverstone* (ed. A. J. Marder). London, 1952–9
Mackay, R. F. *Fisher of Kilverstone*. Oxford, 1973

John Fisher.

estine, but was unable to halt the British progress, and was relieved by Liman von Sanders in February 1918. He spent the remainder of the war in relative obscurity, commanding Tenth Army in Lithuania.

References
Falkenhayn, General E. von. *General Headquarters 1914–16 and its Critical Decisions*. London, 1919

Liddell Hart, Sir Basil. *Reputations*. London, 1928

Fisher, John Arbuthnot, 1st Baron (1841–1920)

Admiral John Fisher was one of the most influential and energetic naval personalities of his age. A veteran of the Crimean War, he came from a military family (his great-uncle was Captain William Fisher of the 40th Foot, decapitated by a cannon-ball at Waterloo), but was somewhat unconventional: when first arriving at the Admiralty he hung a notice around his neck inscribed 'I Have No Work To Do!'* Appointed First Sea Lord in 1904, his reforms shook the naval establishment to its foundations,

Foch, Ferdinand (1851–1929)

'My centre is giving way, my right is in retreat; situation excellent: I shall attack.' This famous statement (from the battle of the Marne) is the epitome of Foch's belief that the paramount quality required in war was the will to succeed, and that no general was beaten until he believed he was. It was as a theorist that he made his reputation (he saw no action until 44 years after his first enlistment in 1870). Professor of strategy and tactics at the *Ecole de Guerre* 1895–1900 (where he returned in 1907 as commandant), his influence on French military thought was profound, especially his book *Principes de la Guerre* (1903) which emphasized the need for psychological superiority over the enemy and the importance of acting offensively. Although responsible to a degree for the French reliance on attack at the beginning of the war, he was also flexible and realistic, accepting that offensive spirit alone was not sufficient. From command of XX Corps at the beginning of the war, he was appointed to Ninth Army (28 August) and from 4 October

Ferdinand Foch.

was selected by Joffre as assistant in command of the French forces in the north, becoming commander of the Northern Army Group officially in the following January.

Joffre's decline affected Foch also, and from December 1916 Foch was pushed into a backwater of meaningless consultative jobs. Pétain brought him back as chief of general staff, but the near collapse of Italy thrust Foch to the fore again, co-ordinating Allied support for Italy after Caporetto. His success in this task led to his appointment as co-ordinator of Anglo-French forces on the Western Front (to which Lloyd George acceded with alacrity, as it gave him a lever against Haig), and on 14 April Foch was officially installed as Allied commander-in-chief, over the head of his erstwhile superior, Pétain. In June 1918 his command was extended over the Italian Front as well, and he conducted the final advance which ended the war. While retaining his early optimism and offensive spirit, his conduct was cautious when necessary and always well-planned; he was, unquestionably, one of the greatest commanders of the modern era. He described himself as resembling the conductor of an orchestra who beat time well, which has some truth in it; a decent, brave and resolute man, he was able to co-ordinate the actions of allies through not only his own military skill but his personality. He came into conflict with Clemenceau over post-war policy (Foch advocated even more severe terms be imposed on Germany), but declined to enter the arena of politics to pursue his case. He was loaded with honours after the war, including the almost unique appointment as British field marshal (though he was not, as sometimes stated, the only Frenchman thus honoured: the last before Foch was Jean Louis, Earl Ligonier (1680–1770), but Foch was the only Frenchman given the honour without having served in the British forces). Yet, as he stated himself, he was as conscious of having served Britain as he was of his own country, which is a perfectly fair reflection upon his immense significance on the World War.

References

Aston, Major General. Sir George. *Biography of the late Marshal Foch*. London, 1929

Foch, Marshal F. (ed. Commandant Bugnet.) *Foch Talks*. London 1929, (post-war conversations, covering his military philosophy)

— *Memoirs of Marshal Foch*. London, 1931

— *Principles of War*. London, 1918

Hunter, T. M. *Marshal Foch: a Study in Leadership*. Ottawa, 1961

Liddell Hart, Sir Basil. *Foch: the Man of Orleans*. London, 1931

— *Reputations*. London, 1928

Marshall Cornwall, General Sir James. *Foch as Military Commander*. London, 1972

Recouly, R. *Marshal Foch: His own Words on Many Subjects*. London, 1929

Franchet d'Esperey, Louis Felix Marie François (1856–1942)

One of the most energetic and resolute of French commanders, Franchet d'Esperey was a veteran of colonial wars who had travelled widely in the Balkans. Already in late middle age at the outbreak of war, he acted with an energy which belied his years, commanding I Corps at the start of the war and rising to command Fifth Army before the Battle of the

Marne. Consistently distinguished, he was appointed to command the eastern army group in 1915, then that of the north (1917), and was considered briefly as a possible successor to Joffre; but his religious and political inclinations (an overt Roman Catholic from a royalist family) prevented this possibility. He seemed to have been eclipsed after his army group was severely handled in the German attack along the Chemin des Dames in May 1918, and he was transferred to the Balkans, where he had advocated an Allied offensive as early as 1914. Here he was again conspicuously successful, driving ahead with great vigour, forcing Bulgaria from the war and was propounding a most audacious advance through Austria and into Germany when the war ended. He remained in the Balkans for two years as head of the Allied forces, and was promoted to Marshal of France in 1922; at the age of 77 he was still on active service when he was injured in a motor accident in Tunisia! Unlike some French commanders, he was popular with his British allies from his willing co-operation and

determined behaviour, and was given the affectionate nickname 'Desperate Frankie'.

Reference
Azan, P. *Franchet d'Esperey*. Paris, 1949

French, John Denton Pinkstone, 1st Earl of Ypres (1852–1925)

Sir John French was the first commander of the British Expeditionary Force, to which post he had risen from a career as a cavalry commander, in which he was considerably distinguished in the Gordon Relief Expedition and in the Boer War. Sadly, he was temperamentally unsuited for command of the BEF, and became so depressed about the prospects of success that his only concern was to save his own troops, at the cost of his allies. It required an emergency visit by Kitchener in September 1914 to stiffen his resolve; but after the war of manoeuvre had ended, his mood changed to one of over-optimism, until by autumn 1915 he was again reluctant to collaborate with the French and had to be urged into action. In the campaigning which followed his incapability again became evident, coupled with poor judgement (exemplified by the removal from command of Smith-Dorrien), which compelled his replacement in December 1915 by his deputy, Haig. Thereafter he served as commander-in-chief of home forces and, with a lack of success equalling that of his BEF command, as lord-lieutenant of Ireland (1918–21). A small man, he had the appearance of a caricature, pompous ex-colonel, with a red face and white moustache, and an excitable demeanour which Haig likened to the opening of a soda-water bottle, all froth and bubble, without the ability to think clearly and come to a reasoned decision.

John French.

References
French, Hon. E. G. *Life of Field Marshal Sir John French, Earl of Ypres*. London, 1931

French, Field Marshal Earl. *The Despatches of Lord French 1914–16*, 1917

— *1914*. London, 1919. (French's own study of his BEF command; despite Foch's

preface in which he compares the author with Wellington, it was to some extent a self-justification at the expense of Smith-Dorrien, rather than an accurate account)

Holmes, R. *The Little Field Marshal: Sir John French*. London, 1981

Galliéni, Joseph Simon (1849–1916)

... a distinguished career in France's colonial wars, ...ph Galliéni retired from the army some months before ... outbreak of war, but was recalled as Joffre's deputy and ...inated successor should Joffre be incapacitated. Joffre, regarding him as a rival and a creature of the ministry, refused Galliéni permission to join the French GHQ; but in late August Galliéni was appointed military governor of Paris. In this capacity he played a crucial role in the Battle of the Marne, rushing his command forward with the help of commandeered taxicabs and counter-attacking on the Ourcq. He claimed that had he not been denied reinforcements, a major victory could have been achieved, a belief

Joseph Galliéni.

which has received some support. Galliéni was appointed war minister by Briand in October 1915, but his attempts to sideline Joffre and take overall command himself were frustrated not so much by lack of personal support but by Joffre's popularity with the Allies and Galliéni's own parlous state of health. His criticism of Joffre over Verdun forced the government to back their commander-in-chief, and after a brief interval to preserve the appearance of a united government, Galliéni resigned in March 1916, and, worn-out with over-work, survived barely two months. Bespectacled, white-moustached, thin, frail and looking much older than his 65 years, Galliéni did not appear to be an inspirational leader; but without his poor health, he might have became France's military supremo in place of Joffre. His worth was probably only fully recognized after

the war, with his posthumous appointment of Marshal of France in May 1921.

References

D'Esmard, J. *Galliéni*. Paris, 1965
Galliéni, General J. S. (ed. G. Galliéni). *Les Carnets de Galliéni*. Paris, 1932

— *Memoires du Général Galliéni: Défense de Paris*. Paris, 1920
Liddell Hart, Sir Basil. *Reputations*. London, 1928.
Lyautey, P. *Galliéni*. Paris, 1959

Goltz, Colmar, Freiherr von der (1843–1916)

Although Liman von Sanders is the best-known of Germany's 'Turkish' commanders, Colmar von der Goltz enjoyed a much longer relationship with that country. After active service in the wars of 1866 and 1870–1, and long service in the military history section of the German general staff, he spent the period 1883 to 1896 assisting in the reorganization of the Turkish Army, in which he attained the rank of field marshal, achieving the same rank in German service in 1911. He returned to Turkey in 1909, and again in 1914 as adjutant-general to the Sultan, an ill-defined post which met with some opposition from Liman von Sanders. Although he found little favour with Enver and the 'Young Turks', who regarded him as too old and too connected to the old regime, in October 1915 he was given command of Sixth Army in Iraq, and conducted the operations which ended with the capitulation of Townshend at Kut-al-Amara. His triumph was short-lived, for he died only ten days later, either of some tropical disease or perhaps poisoned by the Young Turks. In addition to his influential role in Turkey, he was also a highly regarded military author, his *Nation in Arms* (*Das Volk in Waffen*) (1883) predicting with great accuracy the concept of the 'national war' waged between nations, not armies, on immense scale and requiring combined land-sea strategy on a scale hitherto unknown. He should not be confused with another German general of the same name, Rüdiger von der Goltz (1865–1946), commander of the German expedition to Finland.

Haig, Sir Douglas, 1st Earl Haig of Bemersyde (1861–1928)

Few commanders have been the subject of such debate as Field Marshal Sir Douglas Haig. The son of an Edinburgh distiller, he owed some degree of his early advancement to patronage, and from command of the 17th Lancers he gained wide experience of staff duties and influence in government, serving as Haldane's military adviser during the Liberal reforms of 1906–8; and via his marriage (to Hon Dorothy Crespigny, maid-of-honour to both Queen Victoria and Queen Alexandra) gained entry to the court circle. From Director of Military Operations he became commander of I Corps of the BEF in 1914, and after performing adequately in 1914–15 (especially in the defence of Ypres) replaced French in overall command on 19 December 1915, having been greatly critical of Sir John in his private reports sent to George V. Haig remained in this office for the remainder of the war, despite having a very uneasy

Douglas Haig.

to initiate an offensive to relieve pressure on the French. Despite his reluctance in having British forces placed under foreign command, he worked well with Foch in 1918, determinedly held on throughout the worst of the German assault, and played an important role in the final, victorious advance. At the time he was never regarded as a great general; one contemporary opinion stated that at best he was a 'safe' man, and that confidence in him came from an apparently imperturbable nature and not being too clever(!); in essence, he was a man 'who would meet set-backs with a stiff upper-lip'.* Despite his achievements, however, he could never overcome the impression formed by the slaughter on the Somme and at Passchendaele. A balanced view of his still much-argued career is that expressed by Churchill: that although he might have been unequal to the task which he was assigned, there was probably no obvious superior candidate, and in truth he was no worse than many World War commanders, and better than some. His unfortunate reputation as 'the butcher' is too simplistic.

Footnote
*Quoted in *The Great War*, ed. H. W. Wilson and J. A. Hammerton, London, 1919, XIII, p. 408.

References
Blake, R. (ed.). *The Private Papers of Douglas Haig 1914–1918*. London, 1952
Boraston, Lieutenant-Colonel J. H. (ed.). *Sir Douglas Haig's Despatches, December 1915 to April 1919*. London, 1919
Charteris, Brigadier-General J. *Field-Marshal Earl Haig*. London, 1929
Davidson, J. *Haig: Master of the Battlefield*. London, 1953 (by Director of Operations, France, 1916–18)
De Groot, G. *Douglas Haig 1861–1928*. London, 1986
Dewar, G. A. B., and Boraston, Lieutenant-Colonel J. H. *Sir Douglas Haig's Command*. London, 1922
Liddell Hart, Sir Basil. *Reputations*. London, 1928
Marshall-Cornwall, General Sir James. *Haig as Military Commander*. London, 1973
Terrain, J. *Douglas Haig: the Educated Soldier*. London, 1963
Winter, D. *Haig's Command: a Reassessment*. London, 1991

relationship with Lloyd George, which tended to push the prime minister into supporting the concept of a French overall Allied commander.

From the Somme until the German breakthrough of March 1918, Haig's tactics were marked by the attrition and 'attack at all costs' mentality with which he has been associated, and for which he has been persistently condemned. There is much justification in the charge, and his standing was not helped by an attitude which at least gave the appearance of coldness and aloofness; and it is true that he was an unimaginative commander not overly receptive to modern ideas. However, it is equally true that he did not receive the support or confidence which a field commander should have had from his government, that his responsibilities were immense, and that he was often under pressure

Hamilton, Sir Ian Standish Monteith (1853–1947)
General Sir Ian Hamilton was universally admired in the British Army as a thoroughly decent, heroic, courteous and kindly man, with a very distinguished record in colonial warfare (including an important command in the Boer War), and a brave and fearless temperament. He was also a genuine intellectual and a gifted writer, but sadly was not equipped for the task which he was given, as commander of the expedition to the Dardanelles. A 'Kitchener man' and standing somewhat in awe of his superior (whose deputy he had been in South Africa), he took on the task with insufficient will to question his chief or insist upon adequate resources, and while personally a capable tactician he was insufficiently ruthless to dismiss incapable subordinates or to give orders rather than suggestions to his deputies. Remote from the realities of the Gallipoli horrors in his island headquarters, he was encumbered by incompetents in some subordinate positions, and was relieved of command after reporting pessimistic opinions about the chances

of a safe evacuation. He was given no further command during the war, a sad end to the career of a brave and not untalented officer, but too nice a man for the task in hand.

References

Hamilton, General Sir Ian.
Gallipoli Diary. London, 1920
— *Sir Ian Hamilton's Despatches
from the* Dardanelles. London,
1917

Hamilton, I. *The Happy Warrior: A
Life of General Sir Ian Hamilton.*
London, 1966

Hindenburg, Paul Ludwig von Beneckendorf und von (1847–1934)

After a somewhat unremarkable career, in which his campaign service all came at the beginning, in the Austro–Prussian and Franco–Prussian Wars, Paul von Hindenburg retired with the rank of general in 1911, envisaging no further chance of promotion. In appearance, he resembled the caricature Prussian army officer: large, squarely-built, with a thick neck, fierce moustache and hair like a brush; and it was the qualities of solidity, duty, and slow, careful thinking suggested by this appearance that he brought to the service of his country in 1914. Recalled in August of that year in the wake of early reverses on the Eastern Front, he was sent to command Eighth Army, with Ludendorff as his chief of staff: the parallels with the previous great German command partnership, Blücher and Gneisenau, are obvious.

Success on the Eastern Front was rapid, and although the essence of the victory had been planned by the staff officer Max Hoffman, Hindenburg was credited with the triumph, promoted to field marshal and given command of the entire Eastern Front. Lack of resources prevented greater triumphs, but when Falkenhayn was deposed as chief of general staff, Hindenburg replaced him (August 1916), with Ludendorff as his quartermaster-general. From this point the focus of power slipped from the government and into the hands of the army, with Ludendorff the *eminence grise* behind the hugely popular Hindenburg, whose resolute appearance formed a rallying symbol to bolster German national morale. By forcing the resignation of Bethmann Hollweg in July 1917, and installing the malleable Michaelis as his successor, the Hindenburg–Ludendorff partnership formed a virtual military dictatorship. It was not a success; but Hindenburg cannot be held fully responsible, for it has been alleged that he was almost a figurehead, lending support to Ludendorff's plans, and there would appear to be some veracity in this belief. The pair decided to hold on the Western Front and knock Russia from the war, which was accomplished; but the following huge attack on the Western Front accelerated the decline of German arms despite its initial successes, and Ludendorff resigned prior to the armistice. Presumably motivated by his belief in duty, Hindenburg stayed on as head of the German Army until July 1919.

Somewhat strangely for an avowed monarchist, Hindenburg successfully ran for the office of president of the Weimar Republic (April 1925), coming out of his second retirement as field marshal to become head of state. He was an honest, even noble character, but probably intellectually unfitted for this office as he probably had been as virtual leader of Germany 1917–18, and his active career ended on an unfortunate note, with the somewhat reluctant appointment of Adolf Hitler as chancellor in 1933. Unlike Ludendorff, however, he never espoused the cause of the Nazi Party, and died in August 1934 before the catastrophe of the Hitler regime became apparent.

Paul von Hindenburg.

References

Dupuy, T. N. *The Military Lives of
Hindenburg and Ludendorff of
Imperial Germany*. New York,
1970
Hindenburg, Field Marshal P. L.

von. *Out of My Life*. London,
1920
Wheeler-Bennett, J. W.
Hindenburg, the Wooden Titan.
London, 1936

Jellicoe, John Rushworth, 1st Earl (1859–1935)

John Jellicoe had led quite an eventful career in the Royal Navy even before the outbreak of the World War, serving in Egypt in 1882, surviving the infamous collision of *Victoria* and *Camperdown* in the Mediterranean in 1893, and being severely wounded in the Boxer Rebellion. His expertise in gunnery led to his appointment as director of naval ordnance (1905), and as early as 1908 he was nominated by Fisher as the best commander of the Grand Fleet in the event of war. He was given this post on 4 August 1914, but the expected major battle did not materialize until May 1916, when Jellicoe commanded the British forces at Jutland. In this action, as in the period which preceded it, he has been criticized for over-caution and an unwillingness to engage to the full, and there is some merit in such opinions. Though a charming man, Jellicoe was unwilling to

John Jellicoe.

delegate and thus became too concerned with less important details rather than the broader scope of his duties; but as Churchill remarked, he was the only man on either side who could have lost the war in an afternoon, and thus his desire to make the preservation of the Grand Fleet the primary objective, rather than the destruction of the German Fleet, has some justification.

Following the apparently disappointing outcome of Jutland (which despite being a British strategic success was criticized for not being a second Trafalgar), Jellicoe was removed from active command and appointed First Sea Lord. His tenure in this position was not great, Lloyd George finding him pessimistic and over-conscientious as well as over-worked, and on 24 December 1917 he was dismissed somewhat summarily, supposedly over his reluctance to introduce the convoy system. He was raised to the peerage in the following month, and promoted to Admiral of the Fleet in 1919, although his remaining period of public service was spent away from the navy, as governor-general of New Zealand. His conduct of Jutland is still a subject of debate, and his reputation has suffered somewhat unfairly by comparison with his subordinate and successor in command of the Grand Fleet, David Beatty, a more flamboyant and offensively minded character, but probably a lesser admiral.

References

Bacon, Admiral Sir Reginald. *The Life of John Rushworth, Earl Jellicoe*. London, 1936
Jellicoe, Admiral Earl. *The Crisis of the Naval War*. London, 1920
— *The Grand Fleet 1914–1916: Its Creation, Development,* and *Work*.
London, 1919
— *The Submarine Peril*. London, 1934
Patterson, A. T. *Jellicoe: A Biography*. London, 1969
Patterson, A. T. (ed.). *The Jellicoe Papers*. London, 1966

Joffre, Joseph Jacques Césaire (1852–1931)

'Papa' Joffre was the dominant figure in the French military in the first part of the war, his large and avuncular figure and stolid determination providing an air of security at a desperate period in the nation's history. Of comparatively humble origin (the son of a cooper), he served in the Franco-Prussian War, made his reputation in colonial campaigns (he led an expedition to Timbuktu in 1894) and as a military engineer; though he was a somewhat surprising choice as chief of general staff in 1911, but was generally acceptable for his lack of political or religious affiliations. With Castelnau's assistance he formulated Plan XVII, though his detractors would claim that when its failings became obvious it was Galliéni who saved the situation on the Marne. Nevertheless, Joffre's imperturbable demeanour and determination did much to stabilize the situation, and his ruthless pruning of the staff was of benefit in raising the quality of the army's leadership. After the Marne, with costly but ineffective attempts to break the German line, his reputation declined, and his political enemies first sought to check his freedom of action by appointing Castelnau to 'assist' him, and finally (December 1916) Briand sacrificed

Joseph Joffre.

Kemal, Mustafa (1881–1938)

Of all the leading commanders of the war, none ultimately had the effect upon his own country as did Mustafa Kemal, although even at the end of the war his position was only that of a subordinate commander. Born in Salonika, the son of a minor civil servant, he received a formal military education (during which one of his instructors dubbed him 'Kemal' or 'perfectionist' which he adopted formally as his name), but fell from favour as a result of revolutionary political leanings, being banished on the day he received his lieutenant's commission in 1904. Suffering from rivalry with Enver, he forsook active politics and devoted himself to a military career, which prospered under the 'Young Turks', in the Italo-Turkish and Balkan Wars. The rise of Enver again swept Kemal into something of a backwater (he was unable to compromise or accommodate opinions divergent from his own), and he was commander of the 19th Division in the Gallipoli peninsula at the time of the Allied landings.

Recognizing his military ability, Liman von Sanders allowed him virtually to command the front line of the Turkish defences, in which he succeeded brilliantly, despite renewed conflicts with Enver. Although his succeeding commands (against the Russians in eastern Anatolia; against the British in Palestine) enjoyed marked lack of success, it was not his fault, and he emerged from the war as the one Turkish commander of real skill, and untouched by the collapse of the Young Turk government. The resulting absence of serious political rivals allowed Kemal to appear as first the nation's saviour (defeating Greek expansionist plans) and, having abolished the Ottoman sultanate, as the first president of the infant Turkish Republic (1924–38), as which he dragged the country into the modern world. He adopted the surname Atatürk, 'father of the Turks', a title for which, as both soldier and statesman, he had considerable justification.

References

Armstrong, H. C. *Grey Wolf.* London, 1932

Kinross, Lord (Patrick Balfour). *Ataturk: The Rebirth of a Nation.* London, 1964

Kitchener, Horatio Herbert, 1st Earl Kitchener of Khartoum (1850–1916)

Field Marshal 'K of K' was, in the popular view, the greatest living British hero, whose experience in colonial campaigns was vast and punctuated with great successes such as the victory of Omdurman, the successful conclusion of the Boer War, and the reorganization of the military forces in India. He was in the course of returning to Egypt to take on the reins of government when he was appointed war minister upon the outbreak of the World War, and for the next year and a half he virtually ran the British war effort. His appointment was somewhat unusual in that it was non-political, and included some good points: he was among the first to realize that the war would not 'be over by Christmas', and thus he planned for at least three years' conflict, and his success in recruiting the 'new armies' was

him to preserve his own government, removing him from operational command by promotion and appointment as Marshal of France; thereafter his role was largely ceremonial despite his presidency of the Supreme War Council. Joffre's apparent disregard for the casualties arising from his offensives, and his unwillingness to accept political control, both served to undermine his position; but he always retained popular support as the saviour of France on the Marne, and the government backed him as long as they did partly to please the British, with whom his relations were cordial.

References

Joffre, Marshal J. J. C. *The Memoirs of Marshal Joffre.* London, 1932
— *The Two Battles of the Marne.* London, 1927

Liddell Hart, Sir Basil. *Reputations.* London, 1928
Recouly, R. *Joffre.* New York, 1931
Varillon, P. *Joffre.* Paris, 1956

astonishing, during the course of which his face and pointing finger featured upon the most famous recruiting-poster in history. He also did much to cement the relationship with France, his concern for support of Britain's ally leading him to intervene in person to put backbone into the timid Sir John French. In other ways, however, he was not a success and infuriating to work alongside: unable to delegate or to establish close relations, contemptuous of politicans and unwilling to act as part of a team. The débâcle of the Dardanelles expedition must be charged in part to his account, in his lack of adequate preparation, consultation with subordinates and practical support (Hamilton, who like so many of his colonial subordinates stood in awe of 'K', said that 'it was as hard to get troops out of him as to get butter out of a dog's mouth'.[1] The final blow to Kitchener's reputation came with the failure at Gallipoli, upon which expedition he had staked much, and his influence declined, his role as the Cabinet's

Horatio Kitchener.

chief military adviser being taken over by Sir William Robertson, as new Chief of Imperial General Staff. Kitchener's manner of conducting war also resulted in the army's becoming semi-independent of political control, and it took some two years to re-establish the primacy of civilian control of strategy. On 5 June 1916 Kitchener was lost at sea when the cruiser *Hampshire* struck a mine en route to Russia, where Kitchener was leading a mission. His death was greeted by the public as a major catastrophe, though some members of the government probably did not much mourn his passing. Repington's comment is probably fair: that his method of working did not fit with modern consensus government, that he was not a good 'cabinet man' and that he made too many mistakes; but that his reputation towered above all others, and that his contribution in the early stage of the war should not be forgotten, when he resembled 'a firm rock which stood out amidst the ranging tempest'.[2]

Footnotes
1. To Repington, 9 December 1915; in *The First World War*, Colonel C. à C Repington, London, 1920, I, p. 83.
2. Ibid., I. p. 213.

References
Arthur, Sir George, *Life of Earl Kitchener*. London, 1920
Cassar, G. H. *Kitchener: Architect of Victory*. London, 1920

Esher, Reginald Viscount. *The Tragedy of Lord Kitchener*. London, 1921
Le Bas, Sir Hedley. *The Lord Kitchener Memorial Book*. London, 1916 (includes an essay on 'Advertising for an Army', on the raising of 'Kitchener's Army')
Magnus, Sir Philip. *Kitchener: Portrait of an Imperialist*. London, 1958

Kluck, Alexander von (1846–1934)

The only senior German commander of the war never to hold a position on the general staff, General Alexander von Kluck was a middle-class officer (ennobled 1909) of considerable experience, who commanded First Army in the 1914 campaign. As the right wing of the hook decreed by the Schlieffen Plan, his was arguably the most responsible command in the army. Aiming to destroy the French Fifth Army, he swung to the east of Paris instead of the west, a change of plan which resulted in a dangerous position which opened the gap between his own army and Bülow's Second. It led to orders to retire, the final blow to the Schlieffen Plan, and left von Kluck convinced that interference by German headquarters (in the person of von Moltke's emissary, Hentsch, who ordered the retirement) had robbed him of a decisive victory. In March 1915 he was badly wounded in the leg by shrapnel, and saw no further active service.

Reference
Kluck, General A. von. *The March on Paris and the Battle of the Marne*. London, 1920

Lanrezac, Charles Louis Marie (1852–1925)

General Charles Lanrezac is one of the most puzzling commanders of the war, apparently gifted with strategical insight but lacking tactical ability, and with an unfortunate

Alexander von Kluck.

pessimism and mistrust of his allies. Born in Guadeloupe, he was something of a protégé of Joffre, and was given command of Fifth Army in 1914. In this role he discerned a major flaw in the dispositions laid down by Plan XVII, and after much badgering of Joffre received permission to reposition his forces along the Sambre. This, in the event, was a vital move, for Fifth Army was barely able to contain the German attack at Charleroi, and was forced to retire. This retreat was regarded as too rapid, as it left the British Expeditionary Force exposed; and one of the main criticisms of Lanrezac was an inability to take regard of, or work with, his British allies. Deeply depressed by the course of events and with his army dwindling in retreat, Lanrezac was not regarded as a suitable candidate to lead the counter-attack on the Marne, and he was relieved of his command on 5 September, to be unemployed for the remainder of the war. His supporters believed him to be an able and clear-sighted commander, undermined by superiors of lesser ability; but despite his valuable contribution in recognizing a potential weakness in dispositions, his tactical handling of his troops was unimpressive, and he was probably not equal to the task he was set.

Reference
Lanrezac, General C. L. M. *Le Plan de Campagne Français et le premier mois de la guerre*. Paris, 1920

Lawrence, Thomas Edward (1888–1935)

No character during the war was as charismatic, or enigmatic, as 'Lawrence of Arabia'. His reputation varies according to the source consulted: from a master of guerrilla tactics and the real victor of the campaigns in Palestine and the Arab Revolt, to a self-publicist of little military significance. The truth probably lies somewhere between, both his literary and military standing having faded from its

Paul von Lettow-Vorbeck.

high point. The illegitimate son of an Anglo-Irish land-owning family, his experience of and concern for the Middle East began before the war; in 1911, for example, he was an archaeologist with the British Museum expedition to Carchemish. This background led to his appointment as an intelligence officer in Egypt, in which capacity he established remarkably good relations with Sherif Husain of Mecca and his son Feisal. Appointed as liaison officer and adviser to the latter, he encouraged the guerrilla operations of the Arab Revolt, and, having convinced Allenby to fund and incorporate Arab forces into the overall British strategy, not only continued harassing operations but persuaded Feisal to advance on Damascus, which the Arab army occupied shortly before Allenby's arrival. Unquestionably, the Arab contribution was important to the success of the campaign, and it is doubtful whether it could have been achieved without Lawrence's cordial relationships with the Arabs, which he reinforced by wearing Arab dress, evidence of his regard for them as a singular nation. Lawrence was disillusioned by the peace settlements (especially the ceding of Syria to France), and after abandoning politics he enlisted in the Tank Corps and Royal Air Force under pseudonyms, though his true identity was known. He was killed in a road accident in 1935. His literary reputation was founded upon his *Revolt in the Desert* (1927) and its expanded version, *Seven Pillars of Wisdom* (commercially published posthumously). This attracted some criticism for matters of detail, but was regarded as being in the top flight of contemporary literature. Like Lawrence's military significance, however, it has been somewhat downgraded in the opinion of some commentators. A fair reflection is probably that Lawrence was not as significant as has been claimed by some, but that his contribution was sufficiently important for him to continue to be regarded as a major character.

References
Brown, M., and Cave, J. *A Touch of Genius: the Life of T. E. Lawrence*. London, 1988
Brown, M. (ed.). *The Letters of T. E. Lawrence*. London, 1988
Knightley, P., and Simpson, C. *The Secret Lives of Lawrence of Arabia*. London, 1969
Lawrence, T. E. *The Seven Pillars of Wisdom*. London, 1935
Liddell Hart, Sir Basil, *T. E. Lawrence*. London, 1934
Mack, J. E. *A Prince of our Disorder: the Life of T. E. Lawrence*. London, 1976
Wilson, J. *Lawrence of Arabia*. London, 1989

Lettow-Vorbeck, Paul Emil von (1870–1946)

Colonel Paul von Lettow-Vorbeck was not one of the major commanders of the war, but in his own field undisputedly one of the best, whose skills exceeded many of those who achieved greater fame. All his active service was spent in colonial campaigns, in the Boxer Rebellion and in the Hottentot and Herero rising in German South-West Africa. In 1913 he was given command of German forces in East Africa, and in January 1914 was appointed the colony's military commander. From the outbreak of war he operated virtually without support, with never more than about 3,000 German and 11,000 native troops, but held at bay an Allied

336 BIOGRAPHIES

force of up to 130,000 men, proving him a master of irregular warfare. The odds against him made his task impossible, and he was finally driven into Portuguese East Africa, where for the final year of the war he led a guerrilla campaign with barely 3,000 men, which won the unstinting admiration even of his enemies. Although he never had any chance of securing the German colony, in occupying so many Allied resources he more than fulfilled his duty, and was never defeated conclusively in the field, surrendering some two weeks after the armistice in Europe. After his return to Germany he led *Frei-korps* against the Spartacist revolt, but his right-wing sympathies led to his forced retirement in 1920.

References

Hoyt, E. P. *Guerilla: Colonel von Lettow-Vorbeck and Germany's East African Empire.* New York

and London, 1981
Lettow-Vorbeck, P. E. von. *My Reminiscences of East Africa.* London, 1920

Liman von Sanders, Otto (1855–1929)

One of the oldest divisional commanders in the German Army, General Liman von Sanders was chosen in December 1913 to lead the German Military Mission tasked with the reconstruction of the Turkish army. On the surface, he was not the ideal choice, coming from Jewish ancestry, being ennobled only in July 1913, and in the opinion of Hans von Seeckt, chief of staff to the Turkish Army from December 1917, only being sent to Turkey because he was considered unfit to command a German corps. (In the German army he was generally known as 'Liman'; the Sanders he adopted upon his ennobling, being the Scottish name of his late wife, Amelia, who had died in 1906.) Von Seeckt's comments seem highly ungenerous, for Liman's task was huge and co-operation with the Turks not easy (he contemplated challenging both their war and navy ministers to a duel!), and following early disagreements with the German ambassador, remained highly distrustful of all attempts to interfere by the appointment of German advisers. Given command of the Turkish First Army in August 1914, he made his reputation in command of Fifth Army in the defence of the Gallipoli peninsula. His actions here were not beyond criticism (he wrongly calculated the Allies' landing points), but he stuck to his task stubbornly, and unlike his British counterpart ruthlessly dismissed incompetent subordinates. He was responsible to a considerable degree for the containment of the Suvla landing, but in his final assignment (from February 1917) he was given a hopeless task, attempting to combat the British drive in Palestine, being denied resources by Enver and von Seeckt. With the conclusion of the armistice of Mudros his active career ended, but despite the difficulties he faced from his enemies and his employers, and despite his limitations, he served his masters well and is justifiably regarded as one of the best Turkish (if not German) commanders of the war.

Reference

Liman von Sanders, General O.

Five Years in Turkey. Annapolis, 1927

Ludendorff, Erich (1865–1937)

Virtual dictator of German policy for the last two years of the war, General Erich Ludendorff resembled the archetypal Prussian officer, with cropped head, heavy appearance, and monocle; but he had not risen by the usual advantages of birth or influence, being the scion of a family of rural merchants in what was originally Polish Prussia. From intelligence and energy he worked his way into a succession of staff appointments, attracting the attention of von Schlieffen and von Moltke junior, and headed the mobilization section 1908–13 before he was demoted to a regimental command for too energetically pressing the case for an increase in the army's establishment. As soon as the war began he resumed his staff career, winning a high reputation by the seizure of Liège. Appointed Hindenburg's chief of staff on 22 August 1914, he began the association which was to form the most important command partner-

Otto Liman von Sanders.

Erich Ludendorff (left), with Max Hoffman.

ship of the war. He rose with Hindenburg (to quarter-master-general, actually deputy chief of staff by August 1916), but although officially in a subordinate position, it was Ludendorff who became *de facto* controller of the war; though Hindenburg was more than just a figurehead, it is not unfair to describe Ludendorff as the brains of the partnership. In this role his success was mixed; Liddell Hart considered him perhaps the greatest of all war-leaders of 1914–18, and his strategic skill – evident especially on the Eastern Front – was great; but in the wider context, he failed to appreciate the realities, and formed somewhat grandiose schemes for eastward expansion (the proverbial *Drang nach Osten* which bedevilled so much German policy), which were insupportable if an outright victory in the west also were to be achieved. Unlike some German leaders, he could hardly claim that his schemes had been frustrated by other members of the administration, for as the power behind Hindenburg he had been effective controller of the army since the fall of von Falkenhayn, and by engineering the removal of Bethmann Hollweg he gained control of the political leadership as well. Upon the failure of his great offensive of March 1918 he proved oddly vaccillating, initially advocating peace at any price and later a continu-ation of the war to the end; he appears not to have appreciated the level of the nation's exhaustion. Compelled to resign on 26 October 1918, his military career ended; but from 1920 he became involved in Nazi politics (as their candidate for the 1924 election for the presidency of the Weimar Republic), an association which has tended to darken his wartime reputation. Although one of the most skilled commanders of the period, the task upon which he embarked was probably too great for any one man, and despite intelligence and drive, his military talent tended to be undone by lack of political vision and appreciation of the realities of the wider situation.

References

Dupuy, T. N. *The Military Lives of Hindenburg and Ludendorff of Imperial Germany*. New York, 1970
Goodspeed, D. J. *Ludendorff*. London, 1966
Liddell Hart, Sir Basil. *Reputations*. London, 1928
Ludendorff, General E. *My War Memories 1914–1918*. London, 1919
Tschuppik, K. *Ludendorff: the Tragedy of a Specialist*. London, 1932

Mackensen, August von (1849–1945)

August von Mackensen was one of the most successful German commanders of the war, one of the most distinctive in appearance (he often wore the uniform of the 1st Leib-Hussars with its death's-head insignia), and most unusually was promoted to field marshal during the war. A cavalry general, his operations were marked where possible by the cavalry attributes of speed and surprise. All his wartime service was on the Eastern Front, originally commanding Eighth Army, then Ninth (under Hindenburg) with which he recaptured Lodz, then Eleventh with which he made the breakthrough at Gorlice-Tarnów, bringing him fame second

only to Hindenburg. His responsibility increased when he was given Army Group Mackensen in July 1915, which continued to drive back the Russians, and with a reinforced Army Group (including Austro-Hungarian and Bulgarian armies) he defeated Serbia; in the following year he invaded Roumania and occupied the greater part of that country. He remained in the area, commanding the army of occupation until the end of the war. Although it is likely that much of his success was due to his skilled chief of staff, General Hans von Seeckt, his military reputation during the war was untarnished, though his later association with Hitler was unfortunate: he frequently appeared with the dictator, still wearing the old 'Death Hussars' uniform, like a relic from a more honourable past. Before the war he apparently boasted of the Scottish ancestry implied by his name, though denied it later; and this, together with his appear-ance (different from the imagined Prussian stereotype, with a trim figure and cavalry moustache) gave rise to a ridiculous rumour that he was actually Hector Macdonald, alias 'Fighting Mac', the great British hero who killed himself in 1903, who had assumed an alias and entered German service, refusing to fight against his own country and thus confining his operations to the East! Despite his association with the Nazis, Mackensen remained a mon-archist: in a gesture redolent of a vanished age, at the funeral of the Kaiser in 1941 the 92-year-old marshal laid his own cavalry cloak over the coffin of his sovereign, a last salute not only to the Kaiser but to the vanished Prussia of old.

Reference

Förster, W. *Mackensen: Briefe und Aufzeichnung*. Leipzig, 1938
Royle, T. *Death before Dishonour: the True Story of Fighting Mac*. Edinburgh, 1982 (biography of Hector Macdonald, which explores the Mackensen/Macdonald myth)

Moltke, Helmuth Johann Ludwig von (1848–1916)

Helmuth von Moltke 'the Younger' was nephew of the great Prussian field marshal of the same name, architect of the victories of 1866 and 1870. After a career as adjutant to his uncle or the Kaiser, Helmuth the younger was appointed chief of general staff in succession to von Schlieffen (1906), presumably in the hope that he had inherited some of his uncle's genius. Manifestly he had not, and while retaining the basis of the 'Schlieffen Plan', he made sufficient alterations to dilute its effect, ignoring von Schlieffen's exhortation to 'keep the right strong'. In addition to conducting a flawed plan, in the early operations von Moltke was proved quite unfit for the task, not maintaining contact with his subordinates, remaining far from the theatre of action, diverting resources not only from the vital 'right hook' on the Western Front to the left, but, almost in panic, sending divisions to the east. At a critical point in the first Battle of the Marne he issued no orders whatever, and proved quite incapable of independent thought, persisting

August von Mackensen.

Helmuth von Moltke.

with the ruined Schlieffen Plan even though it was obviously wrecked beyond redemption. Within six weeks of the beginning of the war he had been replaced by von Falkenhayn (14 September 1914). He made some attempt to regain his position in 1915, but his failings were obvious and it was stillborn; he survived barely a year after, his reputation broken.

References

Moltke, H. von. *Erinnerungen, Briefe, Dokumente 1877–1916.* Stuttgart, 1922

Nicholas, Grand Duke (Nikolai Nikolaevich)

(1856–1929)

The appointment of the Grand Duke Nicholas to supreme command of the Russian forces in 1914 was something of a surprise, despite his connections to the imperial family (grandson of Tsar Nicholas I and uncle of Nicholas II). Apart from service in the Russo-Turkish War as aide to his father, Grand Duke Nicholas 'the elder', his military reputation was limited to that of a reformer, and something of a political liberal; and his appointment in 1914 was unexpected (probably even to him!) and may have been the

Grand Duke Nicholas.

Robert Nivelle.

result of pressure on the Tsar to prevent him from taking personal command, or as a figurehead (with the quartermaster-general, General Yuri Danilov, as the actual guiding hand). In any case, the lack of co-ordination between Russian forces, and the system which allowed army commanders too much latitude, meant that his effect would be limited. Nevertheless, he proved a popular commander and capable within the limitations imposed upon him; but the command system would probably have defeated leaders of genius, and by August 1915 he was removed from command, the Tsar taking over personally (with unfortunate consequences). Nicholas was sent to the Caucasus as governor-general, where his military commander, General Nikolai Yudenich, ensured a succession of victories against the Turks. Nicholas declined to be drawn into liberal plans to replace the Tsar, but urged his nephew to introduce reforms to stave off catastrophe. At the end, the Tsar attempted to restore Nicholas to supreme command of the army, but the idea was unacceptable to the Provisional Government, and in March 1919 the Grand Duke went into exile, living quietly in Italy and France for the final decade

of his life, declining to play any active part in White Russian politics. Although no military genius, he was one of the better Russian commanders, though hampered by impossible conditions.

Nivelle, Robert Georges (1856–1924)

The tenure of high command of General Robert Nivelle was comparatively short, and an almost unmitigated disaster. His promotion was rapid, from commanding an artillery regiment in 1914 to command of III Corps by late 1915, and of Second Army in April 1916. His service until this period had been impressive, and the recapture of Fort Douaumont at Verdun made him a national hero. His innovative artillery tactics utilized the 'creeping barrage' to co-ordinate infantry advance with fire-support, and his grandiose claims to utilize them in a wider sphere, to bring rapid and certain victory, led to his appointment as Joffre's successor in December 1916. An urbane and charming man with a fluent command of English (his mother was British), he so impressed Lloyd George that his appointment was not only received with British approval, but taken as an opportunity o subordinate the unpopular Haig to a general more in Lloyd George's favour, even though it meant placing British forces effectively under foreign command. The planning for the great breakthrough (the 'Nivelle offensive') was imperfect, and its architect's boasts revealed it to the Germans; so that when it came, in April 1917, it was an immensely costly fiasco. Clearly unfitted for his position, Nivelle was removed as soon as politically prudent; his actions and the resulting slaughter having precipitated the mutinies in the French armies, he was replaced by Pétain on 15 May. (It is perhaps a comment upon the French command system that when the British journalist Repington dined with Nivelle and Pétain on 27 April 1917, both Repington and Pétain knew that Pétain was to succeed Nivelle, but Nivelle himself was unaware of the fact!) Nivelle spent the remainder of the war in North Africa, having somehow survived the court of inquiry which found him not guilty of serious misconduct; but his career and reputation were wrecked irretrievably.

Reference

Hellot, F. E. A. *Le Commandement des Généraux Nivelle et Pétain, 1917.* Paris, 1936

Pershing, John Joseph (1860–1948)

General John Pershing was appointed to command the American Expeditionary Force on 26 May 1917, following a distinguished career in the US Army. This included service in the Indian wars, a period as instructor at West Point, in Cuba with the 10th (Negro) Cavalry (hence his nickname

John Pershing.

'Black Jack'), a demonstration of considerable tactical and political ability in the Philippines, an observer in the Russo–Japanese War, and command of the US expedition to Mexico in 1916. The different abilities shown in all these proved that he was the best candidate for supreme command of the US forces in Europe, and during his tenure of office he showed an unbending resolve to command in his own way. From the outset he supported the principle of US command over US forces, refusing to integrate his troops into the overall Allied command structure, but to wait until so huge an American army had been assembled and trained that it could intervene decisively; and no amount of agitation by the Allied commanders could deflect him. The success of the 'Michael offensive' and the parlous plight into which it put the Allies caused him to compromise slightly, in permitting American troops to be deployed in support of the French; but otherwise he maintained his position so strongly that the first major American effort was not until the St. Mihiel offensive of mid-September 1918 (victory being achieved against an enemy already retiring), followed by much harder fighting in the Meuse–Argonne sector from late September. Ultimately these operations ended in success, but initial progress was so slow that Clemenceau (unsuccessfully) petitioned for Pershing's replacement. Throughout, Pershing showed a refreshing tendency to dismiss ineffective subordinates with more alacrity than in most other armies, greatly to the benefit of his troops. After the war (which Pershing advocated should be continued until Germany was forced to surrender unconditionally) he was promoted to the unique rank of 'General of the Armies', although in strategy he was perhaps not in the very front rank. His rather stern demeanour was probably influenced greatly by his personal tragedy: in August 1915 his wife and three daughters died in a fire.

Henri-Philippe Pétain.

References

Liddell Hart, Sir Basil.
    Reputations. London, 1928
Pershing, General J. J. *My
    Experience in the World War.*
    London, 1931

Smythe, P. *Guerilla Warrior: the
    Early Life of John J. Pershing.*
    New York, 1973
Vandiver, F. E. *Black Jack: The
    Life and Times of John J. Pershing.*
    College Station, Texas, 1977

Pétain, Henri-Philippe Benoni Omer Joseph (1856–1951)

Pétain's name is perhaps most associated with his 'collaboration' with the Nazi invaders of France, and the establishment of the Vichy government (for which he was condemned to death, but reprieved) rather than with his distinguished service in the First World War. From a humble background, Pétain was approaching retirement age in 1914, having attained only the rank of colonel after 36 years as a commissioned officer. (In 1914 he commanded the 33rd Regiment, in which, ironically, his future antagonist Charles De Gaulle was then a subaltern.) He had, however, served a period as professor of tactics at the *Ecole de Guerre*, where his views (opposing the popular offensive

spirit and his stress on the importance of firepower) had not found favour. His abilities in action were recognized rapidly, elevating him from brigade command to division (Marne), to XXXIII Corps (October 1914) and to Second Army (July 1915). Sent to direct the defence of Verdun, his resolution and vital organization of supply-lines made him a national hero, and his declaration *'Ils ne passeront pas'* became the watchword for the defence. In May 1916 he was promoted to command the Army Group of the Centre, while still maintaining his interest in Verdun, and after Nivelle's catastrophic period at the helm was appointed to overall command. He rebuilt morale after the Nivelle offensive, quelled the mutinies resulting from it, and (ever in touch with the needs of the individual soldier) improved conditions of service and ensured that no more suicidal attacks would be launched. Caution – perhaps over-caution –

Herbert Plumer.

marked his command, and although he remained in control of the French Army he was made subordinate to his old deputy, Foch. The association was not always easy, and his plans for defence in depth were not pursued by some French formations, to their cost; but Pétain's belief in artillery preparation and prudent advances were a marked improvement upon the slaughter of previous years. In the final advance, he pressed ahead with enthusiasm equal to Foch's own, and received his reward on 18 December 1918 with his appointment as Marshal of France. His contribution to the French Army, and to the success of the war, was immense; yet his reputation was soured irredeemably by his actions in the Second World War.

References

Griffiths, R. *Pétain: a biography of Marshal Philippe Pétain of Vichy.* New York, 1972
Liddell Hart, Sir Basil. *Reputations.* London, 1928
Lottman, H. R. *Pétain: Hero or Traitor, the Untold Story.* New York, 1985
Pétain, Marshal H. P. B. O. J. *Verdun.* London, 1930
Ryan, S. *Pétain the Soldier.* London, 1969

Plumer, Herbert Charles Onslow, 1st Viscount Plumer of Messines (1857–1932)

Of all leaders in the war, probably Herbert Plumer was the general whose appearance belied his talent: his squat figure, ruddy countenance and white moustache provided the inspiration for the cartoonist Low's 'Colonel Blimp'. In reality, he was a meticulous planner, cautious, impossible to fluster and greatly liked by his men; one of (if not *the*) best British generals of the war. He succeeded Smith-Dorrien in command of II Corps and, in May 1915, was given Second Army with which he held the Ypres front for two years. His chance of distinction came at Messines in June 1917 when his attack was planned with such care that all objectives were achieved at a fraction of the expected cost; and after Gough's appalling failures at Passchendaele, he was appointed to salvage the operation, in which he did everything that could have been expected under the circumstances. After being sent to restore order to the disintegrating Italian Front in November 1917, he returned to Second Army in time to conduct the defence against the great German offensive, which he did in his usual imperturbable manner. Plumer was one of those rare commanders who understood the nature of modern 'siege' warfare, had no time for the attritional strategy conducted by most commanders, and was sufficiently independent not to be overawed or cowed by pressure from headquarters; a field marshalcy (1919), peerage and burial in Westminster Abbey were immensely well-deserved.

References

Harington, C. *Plumer of Messines.* London, 1935
Powell, G. *Plumer: the Soldier's General.* London, 1990

Putnik, Radomir (1847–1917)

Radomir Putnik is deservedly regarded as one of Serbia's greatest heroes, the image of his continuing to command his troops though desperately ill forming one of the great epics of the war. Having fought in the wars against Turkey and Bulgaria, he served three periods as Serbian war minister, during which time he made many important reorganizations and modernizations. As chief of staff in the Balkan Wars he combined military skills with the results of his reforms, his victories bringing him promotion to field marshal. At the beginning of the World War he was attempting to recover his health at an Austrian resort when, in an act of exceptionally unwise courtesy, Emperor Franz Josef allowed him to return home to become chief of staff to the nominal commander of the Serbian forces, Crown Prince Alexander (effectively, Putnik was himself in command). In the early campaigns he proved more than a match for the Austrian invaders, but even his talents could not redress the balance tipped irrevocably in favour of the Central Powers by Bulgaria's entry into the war. Avoiding the decisive battle which the Central Powers sought, Putnik conducted a fighting retreat over the mountains to the Adriatic and, with his health in ruins, had to be carried in a litter, but continued to command. Although he survived the ordeal – huge numbers of Serbians did not – the old marshal's health was so broken that he took no further part in the war, but was evacuated and died at Nice in May 1917. Despite the poor health which limited his ability to oversee operations in person, he was incomparably the best general in all the Balkan armies.

Robertson, Sir William Robert (1860–1933)

'Wully' Robertson was that rarest of creatures, the private soldier of humble birth who rose to the highest rank in the army as a result of his own ability and unremitting labour. After ten years in the ranks he passed the commission exam, and later became the first ex-ranker to enter the Staff College, which ultimately he commanded. After a difficult period as French's assistant in 1914–15 (originally quartermaster-general, later as chief of staff against French's inclinations), he

was suggested as a successor to French; but perhaps because of his plebian background, Haig was chosen instead, and Robertson was sent home as chief of Imperial General Staff. In this role his primary objective was to concentrate efforts upon the Western Front, as the leading proponent of the 'western' school in which he was a considerable support to Haig. This policy brought him into conflict with Lloyd George, an advocate of the 'eastern' school. Robertson believed passionately that only a decisive victory on the Western Front could conclude the war, and opposed all eastern 'sideshows' which dissipated resources. Probably in an attempt to circumvent his influence and that of the army staff in general, Lloyd George approved the creation of the Supreme War Council, which brought the conflict between them to a head; Robertson was dismissed in February 1918 and assigned a relatively unimportant home command, and after the war com-

Radomir Putnik.

William Robertson.

manded British forces on the Rhine. His promotion to field marshal and a baronetcy were post-war recognitions of his wartime service, his fall from office resulting from political disagreements rather than any inability on his part. Throughout his career, Robertson remained conscious of his humble origin, spoke in an unpolished manner (never overcoming the dropping of aitches), and remained loyal to Haig perhaps in part because he regarded the latter as a gentleman of higher birth than himself. Repington gave an insight into his philosophy: Robertson once remarked that it was no use worrying, but that one could only do one's best, recalling the story of Wellington's warning to Blücher that the Prussian dispositions would lead to them being 'damnably licked'; but having imparted this information, the Duke rode off to have his dinner and paid no more heed to them!

References

Bonham-Carter, V. *Soldier True: the Life and Times of Field Marshal Sir William Robertson.* London, 1963

Robertson, Field Marshal Sir William. *From Private to Field Marshal.* London, 1921

— *Soldiers and Statesmen.* London, 1926 (concerns his period as chief of Imperial General staff)

Woodward, D. *The Military Correspondence of Field Marshal Sir William Robertson.* London, 1990

Rupprecht, Crown Prince of Bavaria (1869–1955)

As the Bavarian Army retained its independence from the remainder of the Prussian-dominated German military establishment, it was appropriate that Sixth Army (formed of Bavarian troops) in 1914 should be commanded by that country's Crown Prince; but unlike other German princes who also achieved high command, Rupprecht was possessed of genuine military talent, which he exercised to considerable effect on the Western Front. Early successes led to his promotion to field marshal and appointment to command 'Army Group Prince Rupprecht' (July and August 1916 respectively), although he deplored the costly policies of both von Falkenhayn and Ludendorff, relations with the latter being especially strained, and deteriorating further after the virtual *coup* which toppled Bethmann Hollweg. Despite his disquiet with the conduct of the war, Rupprecht led his Army Group with his customary courage in the March 1918 offensive. He realized earlier than most German leaders that the war was irretrievable, but did his duty to the end, and upon the abdication of his father retired to private life; he left Germany during the Second World War and did not return to Bavaria until 1945. By a curious twist of history, though fighting for most of the war against the British on the Western Front, his mother (Marie Thérèse, 1949–1919), and by extension himself, were the Jacobite heirs to the British throne, via a lineage extending back to Charles I's daughter Henrietta.

References

Rupprecht, Crown Prince. *Mein Kriegstagebuch.* Berlin, 1929

Sendtner, K. *Rupprecht von Wittelsbach, Kronprinz von Bayern.* Munich, 1954

Sarrail, Maurice Paul Emmanuel (1856–1929)

The career of Maurice Sarrail exemplifies that of the general who held command by virtue of political connections rather than by military talent. In an army dominated by Catholics, conservatives and crypto-monarchists, Sarrail's vociferous, radical, anti-clerical position made him the darling of the political Left, which as much as his organizational skills pushed him to the fore. Given command of Third Army in 1914, early successes turned to heavy losses, and Joffre took the opportunity to relieve him of his command. This almost precipitated a political crisis, Sarrail being seen as the leading general of the radical wing, and to silence the criticism he was given command of the French 'Army of the Orient' in Macedonia. He continued to meddle in political affairs – he encouraged the pro-Allied revolt against King Constantine of Greece – and the atmosphere of intrigue which surrounded him did little to assist the smooth running of the multi-national forces. In January 1917,

Maurice Sarrail.

however, he was appointed commander-in-chief of all Allied forces in the theatre, but his major offensive was a costly failure, and he retained his position only as a result of his political contacts. The arrival of Clemenceau spelled the end, for although officially a member of the party that had supported Sarrail, 'Tiger' Clemenceau had no opinion of him, and he was relieved of command in December 1917, to the regret of very few of those he had commanded. The 'political general' took no further part in the war, later dabbled in politics and, when his friends resumed power in 1924, was sent as high commissioner to Syria, where his lack of success continued: he was recalled after the Druze revolt of 1925.

References

Coblentz, P. *The Silence of Sarrail.* London, 1930

Sarrail, M. *Mon Commandement en Orient.* Paris, 1920

Tanenbaum, J. K. *General Maurice Sarrail 1856–1929: the French Army and Left-Wing Politics.* Chapel Hill, North Carolina, 1974

Smith-Dorrien, Sir Horace Lockwood (1858–1930)

Potentially one of the best commanders of the war, General Sir Horace Smith-Dorrien suffered the fate which should have been accorded some of his incompetent fellows: immediate dismissal from command. A seasoned soldier with wide colonial experience (he was one of the very few to survive the massacre of Isandhlwana), he was appointed to command II Corps of the BEF upon the unexpected death of Sir James Grierson in August 1914. Taking the majority of the German attack at Mons, Smith-Dorrien was left to his own devices for a week until Sir John French ordered a withdrawal, which Smith-Dorrien upon his own initiative halted to face the attack at Le Cateau. French was exceptionally fulsome in his praise for the saving of the situation (which 'could never have been accomplished unless a commander of rare and unusual coolness, intrepidity, and determination had been present').[1] This was an accurate reflection on Smith-Dorrien's worth, but his conflicts with French grew steadily, especially after his appointment as commander of Second Army. In the actions around Ypres Smith-Dorrien pleaded that to reduce casualties he be allowed to retire to more defensible positions; French refused, and following the first gas attacks Smith-Dorrien was compelled to order more costly attacks. He could stand French's tactics no longer, and protested; French immediately relieved him of command, and even refused the courtesy of a personal interview, sending 'Wully' Robertson to tell Smith-Dorrien, "'Orace, you're for 'ome'.[2]

With this ending of Smith-Dorrien's active career (succeeding appointments were minor, command in East Africa being frustrated by pneumonia), which can be seen as vindictiveness on the part of a less-capable superior, the British Army lost one of its best leaders, and one who would surely not have permitted the slaughter of 1916–17. To deflect criticism, French claimed that Smith-Dorrien's health had broken down, which was manifestly untrue. It has been claimed that Smith-Dorrien was potentially

Horace Smith-Dorrien.

Britain's best general; the tragedy is that he was never able to prove it conclusively, and the manner of his dismissal reflects only discredit upon his superiors. Never adequately rewarded for his invaluable service in the 1914 retreat, he died of injuries sustained in a road accident in 1930, his memory further vilified by inaccuracies in French's book *1914*, which was tantamount to discrediting Smith-Dorrien in an attempt to conceal his own failings.

Footnotes

1. Dispatch dated 7 September.
2. Lord Malise Graham, quoted in Smithers (as below) p. 261.

References

Ballard, Brigadier-General C. *Smith-Dorrien.* London, 1931

Smith-Dorrien, General Sir Horace. *General Sir Horace Smith-Dorrien's statement with regard to the First Edition of Lord French's Book '1914'* (privately published justification, 1919)

— *Memories of Forty-Eight Years Service.* London, 1925

Smithers, A. J. *The Man Who Disobeyed: Sir Horace Smith-Dorrien and his Enemies.* London, 1970

Tirpitz, Alfred von (1849–1930)

Like Fisher, von Tirpitz may be seen as the dominating influence on his country's naval policy prior to the World War, and like Fisher he was deposed before the war had run half its course. After an active naval career which included heading the torpedo service, he was appointed Secretary of State of the Ministry of Marine in 1897, which position he held for almost 19 years, and in 1911 received the unique rank of *Grossadmiral* ('Grand Admiral'). He may justifiably be regarded as the father of the German navy, as it was his

Alfred von Tirpitz.

unrelenting pressure which persuaded the Kaiser and his government to construct a fleet capable of rivalling that of Britain. The development of the dreadnought by Britain meant that the Germans had virtually to begin anew, and the immense expenditure required pushed Germany in the direction of bankruptcy. Faced with opposition to his anti-British policy, and claims for priority of expenditure by the army, Tirpitz's construction programme lagged hopelessly behind schedule. Faced with the collapse of his life's work from the unpreparedness of the fleet, Tirpitz urged peace in 1914; and when war came, his belief that Britain would attack immediately was unfounded. Having ignored submarines in favour of capital ships, Tirpitz became a convert to the theory of unrestricted U-boat warfare; but as his entire naval policy might be seen as a failure, he was increasingly marginalized and excluded from the strategical decision-making process. He threatened resignation in March 1916, whereupon his bluff was called and the Kaiser accepted it; thereafter Tirpitz exerted some minor, but not decisive, political influence. Although his role as the architect of the German navy was important in as far as the creation of a fleet was concerned (albeit a fleet hardly used and founded upon a flawed assessment of the nature of naval operations in the event of war), the consequences of his policy extended further than merely being a drain upon the nation's resources; the obvious anti-British motivation was a principal factor which helped to sour Anglo-German relations, and thus his term of office was doubly damaging.

References

Steinberg, J. *Yesterday's Deterrent: Tirpitz and the Birth of the German Battle Fleet*. London, 1965

Tirpitz, Admiral A. von. *My Memoirs*. London, 1919

Townshend, Sir Charles Vere Ferrers (1861–1924)

An Indian Army officer of modest background and great ambition, Charles Townshend won considerable fame by leading the defence of Chitral in 1895. His reputation initially prospered in the early stages of the World War by his advance up the Tigris, intent on capturing Baghdad; and backed by the government's desire for a Mesopotamian success to redress the failure at the Dardanelles, he pushed on in the face of prudence, without awaiting reinforcements. His advance duly fell into trouble, and his army was besieged at Kut-al-Amara, where it was eventually starved into submission. Immense privations were endured by the troops captured at Kut, not shared by Townshend who was held instead at a comfortable Black Sea resort. In 1918 he was accorded a hero's welcome – having received a knighthood during captivity in October 1917 for services at Kut – but a measure of justice prevailed and he received no further military employment. He attempted to establish a reputation as a Turkish expert (after the war he liaised with Kemal), but presumably his previous conduct was the reason he was unemployed in that sphere also. Despite a reputation for dash and activity, he was a poor general and was largely responsible for one of Britain's most seriou disasters of the war.

References

Barker, A. J. *Townshend of Kut: Major-General Sir Charles Townshend*. London, 1967
Sherson, E. *Townshend of Chitral and Kut*. London, 1928
Townshend, General Sir Charles. *My Campaign in Mesopotamia*. London, 1920

Wilson, Sir Henry Hughes (1864–1922)

Sir Henry Wilson was the most political of soldiers, and is remembered now perhaps as much for his intrigue and his death as for his military duties. After some foreign service he became commandant of the Staff College, during which time he formulated his ideas reagrding the necessity o British support for France in the event of a European war and also established a warm relationship with Foch, his opposite number in France. In 1910 he went to the War Office as director of military operations, and drew up plans for the deployment of the BEF as the French left wing, should war come; and when it did he accompanied the BEF as deputy chief of General Staff. His conduct during the retreat from Mons (filling in after Sir Archibald Murray's breakdown) was mediocre, and he was sidelined by a posting as liaison officer with the French. He spent an unremarkable year as commander of IV Corps (December 1915–November 1916), but returning to his old liaison role was dismissed by Pétain, who apparently hated him. Returning home to minor employment, he cultivated Lloyd George who saw in him an ally in his conflict with Haig; and in an unofficial capacity, Wilson accompanied the prime minister to the Rapallo conference. To the horror of Robertson (then chief of Imperial General Staff), Wilson was appointed as British military representative on the Supreme War Council, and succeeded Robertson when the latter's position became hopeless in his conflict with Lloyd George (18 February 1918). Owing his position to his being a tool in Lloyd George's campaign against Haig and his supporters, Wilson never assumed overall direction of the British war effort, but saw it pass to Foch as Allied generalissimo, which he had himself advocated. Although lacking any outstanding military talent, Wilson was rewarded for his wartime service with a baronetcy and a field marshal's baton, but retired from the army in 1922. An ardent supporter of the Protestant cause in Ireland (he had supported the Curragh 'mutineers' in 1914), he involved himself in Irish politics; and on 22 June 1922 was assassinated outside his London home by two Sinn Fein gunmen, for which murder Joseph O'Sullivan and Reginald Dunn were condemned to death. Ironically for the supreme 'political' soldier, Wilson was thus one of very few field marshals to have died a violent death.

References

Ash, B. *The Lost Dictator: a Biography of Field Marshal Sir Henry Wilson*. London, 1968
Callwell, Major General Sir C. E. *Field Marshal Sir Henry Wilson: His Life and Diaries*. London, 1927
Collier, B. *Brasshat: A Biography of Field Marshal Sir Henry Wilson*. London, 1968

V
SOURCES

SOURCES

The literature of World War I is so immense that even extensive bibliographies cannot be comprehensive. Large numbers of works were published during the war, certainly more than had ever appeared during a previous war, reflecting an increased level of literacy, the emergence of 'national' war which involved the whole of society, and a desire to propagandize, or at least to present a certain viewpoint to the reader. After the end of the war there may be perceived a short hiatus in the production of what were known as 'War Books', followed by an increase in the 1920s and later, presumably in response to an increased interest once the immediacy of the horrors had receded. After a decline during the Second World War, there has been a further upsurge of interest. The more modern works include significant re-assessments or re-interpretations, which range from the most fundamental issues – for example the causes of the war – to the more abstruse, and especially to biography: the discussion of the abilities of Douglas Haig is a clear example.

Much of the material published during the war should be viewed with caution; for obvious reasons material critical of friendly troops or personalities was either suppressed or discouraged, and the most successful emphasis was placed on any event, even acknowledged defeats being given a propagandized gloss. A further failing of contemporary comment was that, irrespective of the propaganda aspect, it was usually impossible to present a balanced verdict because of lack of information from the enemy viewpoint, and thus realistic assessments were often only possible in later years. While some propaganda was subtle, much was quite blatant, and this even extended to official dispatches in which a greater degree of accuracy might have been expected.

An outstanding example of such distortion was Murray's dispatch announcing victory at the First Battle of Gaza (actually a British reverse), which *The Times* (6 April 1917) presented with the equivalent Turkish report:

British version: '. . . We inflicted very heavy losses . . . and have taken 900 prisoners . . . The operation was most successful, and owing to the fog and waterless nature of the country around Gaza fell just short of a complete disaster to the enemy . . .'

Turkish version: '. . . The fight developed in the neighbourhood of Gaza on the afternoon of March 27th, and terminated in a brilliant victory . . . the enemy suffered heavy losses, leaving numbers of dead on the ground . . . the enemy retired in a south-westerly direction, pursued by our troops . . . in spite of the extreme violence with which the fight was contested, our losses were quite small.'

These dispatches were reproduced with the comment that the comparison was 'of interest' by Captain Oskar Teichmann in *The Diary of a Yeomanry M. O.* (London, 1921, p. 123); the comment of this experienced and gallant officer was that the affair was a 'ghastly fiasco' which bore not the slightest resemblance to the 'most successful' operation described by Murray. (In fairness, Murray's dispatch was not intended specifically to deceive the public; it also presented the government with an inaccurate picture of affairs, which led to further difficulty; and the unrestricted publication of the Turkish dispatch presumably suggested to readers that either the enemy was lying, or that all was not as it seemed.)

Propagandized accounts were often recognized for what they were: a skit in *The Mesopoluvian* (15 June 1917) made the unreliability of such reports into a joke and reflected the army's view of such accounts:

'Western Front. During the night 7–8 June the enemy made a violent attack against our new positions. This was easily repulsed. Enemy casualties were very heavy, one of our men alone counting 80,000 killed. Our casualties, we regret to say, consisted of one man slightly wounded. There has been great air activity and many fights; 1,137 German aeroplanes have been brought down. All of ours returned safely.'

An example of old-fashioned 'war illustration' which bore little if any relation to reality: a scene purporting to show the Royal Scots Greys and a Highland regiment at St. Quentin in 1914, imitating an incident at the Battle of Waterloo, 99 years earlier, which almost certainly also never happened, at least in the manner depicted! (Print after R. Caton Woodville)

Censorship was another serious difficulty in the presentation of accurate reports. The problems posed by official censors were described aptly in an American poem, *News from the Front*:

'The Allies at the Germans lunged
  And won a fight at Name-Expunged.
But French's army was defeated
  Upon the field of Place-Deleted.
From Town-Blue-Pencilled, lovely spot,
  The Uhlans galloped, fierce and hot,
But hundreds bit the dust and grass
  In Place-Press-Bureau-Would-Not-Pass.
The hottest work in all the field
  Burst around Locality-Concealed.'[1]

Censorship was not complete, especially in the earlier stages of the war, and certain surprising accounts were published; for example, Private Robert Watson of the 2nd Lancashire Fusiliers described how his unit had bolted during a poison-gas attack:

'. . . a very rapid gun fire started, and some of us looked over the front of the trenches. We saw our front line retiring. We saw what it was, and we were not long before we followed them. We had a mile to run in the open before we dare stop, or we should have been gassed properly, and no doubt. That mile was taken like hell let loose – rifle fire, Maxim fire, Jack Johnsons, and Whistling Willies. I don't know how I escaped being hit. We must have lost a good few men. I saw a good few go over, but we could do nothing for them . . .'[2]

The published statement of sergeant A. Nutter of the same regiment was even more discouraging:

'. . . the Germans gave us a dose of their poisonous gas fumes. My God! It makes me shudder now when I think of it. I thought my number was up that day. It is terrible stuff . . . Oh! it was terrible! I shall never forget it if I live to be a hundred . . . I had to go in hospital suffering from gas poisoning and my nerves. The strain on my nerves was too much for me, for the terrible ordeal we had to go through broke me down. I tell you it is not war, it is scientific murder . . .'[3]

Many personal accounts appeared in the contemporary press, especially earlier in the war, including most lurid tales of daring. Many of these are not of value; as Dr J. C. Dunn remarked in *The War the Infantry Knew* (1938, p. 65) many men invented such stories in the hopes of receiving cash from newspapers which advertised for 'letters from the front'; Dunn stated that as these tales were so fabulous most officers never bothered to censor them in the ordinary way. Some incidents (presumably true as they refer to named individuals) are recounted in a most melodramatic style: 'Lieutenant Steele-Perkins died one of the grandest deaths a British officer could wish for. He was lifted out of the trenches wounded four times, but protested and crawled back again until he was mortally wounded.';[4] 'I don't know how he got knocked over, but one of our fellows told me he died a game 'un. He was one of the best of officers, and there is not a Tommy who would not have gone under for him.'[5]

Some collections of accounts were published for overtly propagandist reasons (the sub-title of *The War Stories of Private Thomas Atkins*, London 1914, 'A Stirring Tale of Great Deeds Done for a Great Cause in a Spirit of Simple Duty and Gallant Gaiety' leaves little to the imagination), and some such stories are quite incredible (including one tale of the formation of a British square to repel a German attack: '. . . steel met steel, and sparks shot out as sword crossed bayonet').[6] Others, however, have the feeling of authenticity, such as a remark when under shell-fire of 'Fall in here for your pay, 'A' Company' by a member of the DCLI,[7] and other 'popular' accounts are confirmed elsewhere, for example the death of Captain Mark Haggard, Welsh Regiment, shouting 'Stick it, Welsh!'[8]

Reports from officially accredited war correspondents similarly presented a censored view of the war, although some had the crusading zeal of Russell of *The Times* who exposed much of the mismanagement of the Crimean War: the reports of the Australian journalist Keith Murdoch and the English newspaper correspondent Ellis Ashmead-Bartlett appear to have had a considerable influence upon the decision to abandon the Dardanelles expedition, for example. Much of the published 'informed comment' upon strategical matters, and indeed the dispatches of war correspondents, were dismissed or treated with scepticism by those with actual experience of war. The following skit appeared in *The Wipers Times*, 26 February 1916, and demonstrates clearly the derision with which such pronouncements were viewed; the supposed author, given the name 'Bellary Helloc', was a skit on Hilaire Belloc.

'. . . under existing conditions, everything points to a speedy disintegration of the enemy . . . let us take as our figures, 12,000,000 as the total fighting population of Germany. Of these 8,000,000 are killed or being killed hence we have 4,000,000 remaining. Of these 1,000,000 are non-combatants, being in the Navy. Of the 3,000,000 remaining, we can write off 2,500,000 as temperamentally unsuitable for fighting, owing to obesity and other ailments engendered by gross mode of living. This leaves us 500,000 as the full strength. Of these 497,250 are known to be suffering from incurable diseases, this leaves us 2,750. Of these 2,150 are on the Eastern Front, and of the remaining 600, 584 are Generals and Staff. Thus we find that there are 16 men on the Western Front. This number I maintain is not enough to give them even a fair chance of resisting four more big pushes, and hence the collapse of the Western Campaign.'

If contemporary accounts were thus limited, more might be expected from 'official histories' written after the war and able to utilize 'enemy' sources; but even these do not always present the whole, or even an unbiased, view. Understandably approaching the subject from one national viewpoint, they do not necessarily include even the truths known to compilers, material which might have proved embarrassing being omitted deliberately: for example,

'Propaganda' art at its most blatant: to portray German 'frightfulness', this unsigned illustration depicts a French Boy Scout being executed by a German firing-squad.

Robert Rhodes James in *Gallipoli* (and repeated by John Laffin in *Damn the Dardanelles!*, p 204) notes the official historian of that campaign, Aspinall-Oglander (whose work is among the best of all official histories) remarking that although he was aware of the truth concerning a certain general, as official historian he was unable to blurt it out.

Of the most important combatant nations, the British official histories are generally written with an attempt to introduce some element of 'human interest', and still provide the starting-point for the study of any campaign. The French official history – *Les Armées Françaises dans la Grande Guerre* – is a more factual, technical record not intended to have any public appeal but is instead a somewhat Gradgrindesque collection of facts, designed for the student. In the post-war period, Germany's *Reichsarchiv* provided two types of their official history: the official history *per se*, *Der Weltkrieg, 1914 bis 1918*, which includes a measure of propaganda or support of one commander's views against those of another; and a separate series of studies of battles or military operations, *Schlachten des Weltkrieges*. National bias is understandable in wartime, but

it should be noted that it also extended to later works (see Cyril Falls' comments on Charles Gautier's *L'Angleterre et Nous*, Paris 1922, in *War Books*, for an example of the level of rancour which could exist between allies!).

Several excellent bibliographies of the war have been published, although the task of listing all relevant titles is quite impossible, and would in any case be outdated before publication because of the number of studies which are still appearing. Among those bibliographies available in English, the most significant include *A Subject Bibliography of the First World War: Books in English*, A. G. S. Enser, London 1979, which attempts to subdivide into categories. *A Subject Index of Books Relating to the European War 1914–1918, Acquired by the British Museum 1914–1920* (anon., though the preface is by A. W. Pollard, and R. F. Sharp is named as supervising the team responsible), London 1922, includes poetry but is restricted largely to those works that appeared during the war. British regimental histories (which generally have been excluded from the bibliography which follows) are listed in *A Bibliography of Regimental Histories of the British Army*, A. S. White, London 1965 (the revised edn., London 1988, includes new entries). One of the most interesting, with entries annotated by an experienced officer and leading historian, is Cyril Falls' *War Books: A Critical Guide*, London 1930, reprinted as *War Books: An Annotated Bibliography of Books about the Great War*, intro. and supplements by R. J. Wyatt, London 1988. *A Biographical Dictionary of World War I*, H. H. Herwig and N. M. Heyman, Westport, Connecticut 1982, contains an extensive and most useful bibliography; specialized bibliographies include *World War I in the Air: a Bibliography and a Chronology*, M. J. Smith Jr., New York 1977, and *World War I Aviation Books in English: an Annotated Bibliography*, J. P. Noffsinger, 1987. A most usefully annotated bibliography concerning the British experience is included in *A Nation in Arms*, I. F. W. Beckett and K. Simpson, Manchester 1985.

A guide to the suppression or falsification of fact may be obtained from such works as *Propaganda Technique in the World War*, H. D. Laswell, London 1927; *Falsehood in Wartime*, A. Ponsonby, London 1928; *The Press and the General Staff*, Hon. N. Lytton, London 1921; *Indiscretions of a Naval Censor*, Rear-Admiral Sir Douglas Brownrigg, Bt., London 1920; *The Press in War-Time*, Sir Edward Cook, London 1920 (on the Press Bureau, etc.); and *British Propaganda during the First World War*, M. Sanders and P. Taylor, London 1982. *Gallipoli to the Somme: The Story of C. E. W. Bean*, D. McCarthy, Sydney 1983, concerns one of the most famous of all war correspondents and later official historian. Among reprinted material, the work of one of the most famous correspondents appears in *The War Dispatches*, Sir Philip Gibbs, Isle of Man, 1964.

The recent production of works concerning the war encompasses the whole genre, from biography to reminiscence (now more likely to be based on extant letters and diaries than on the memory of veterans still living), from illustrated popular histories to academic re-assessments, from social histories to regimental and battalion chronicles. Among the most valuable are those works that comprise, or are built around, the experiences of ordinary soldiers, whose surviving memories would not otherwise have been recorded; the work of Peter Liddle, Lyn Macdonald and Martin Middlebrook is especially valuable in this regard. Another comparatively recent development is the increasing interest in facsimile reprints of First World War 'classics' or works of reference, produced by a considerable number of enterprising publishers, ranging from Greenhill Books' 'Vintage Aviation Library' and others, to the republication of statistical works such as Ray Westlake's re-printing of the British orders of battle. Those readers who benefit from the new availability of such works should bear in mind that for the process to continue, it is important that these ventures be supported.

The lists which follow do not pretend to include all important works, and encompass some early material of anecdotal or almost 'curio' value; and as noted in the introduction, emphasis has been placed almost exclusively upon works available in English.

Notes

1. *The Sphere*, p. 150, 7 November 1914.
2. *The 'Leader' Local War Record 1914–1915*, p. 85, Nelson, 1915.
3. Ibid., pp. 88–9.
4. *Atkins at War*, ed. J. A. Kilpatrick, p. 83, London, 1914; concerns Lieutenant Cyril Steele-Perkins, King's Own, killed in action c.31 August–2 September 1914.
5. Ibid., concerns Captain Hamilton-Hughs Berners, Irish Guards, killed in action 14 September 1914.
6. Ibid., p. 47.
7. Ibid., p. 146.
8. Died of wounds 15 September 1915. He was the nephew of Sir Henry Rider Haggard, who received similar accounts of his death: *see The Private Diaries of Sir Henry Rider Haggard 1914–1925*, p. 13, ed. D. S. Higgins, London, 1980. Private William Fuller was awarded the Victoria Cross for carrying Haggard out of this action.

'General' works

Anon. *'The Times' History of the War*. London, 1914–20

Albertini, L. *The Origins of the War of 1914*. Oxford, 1952–7

Banks, A. *Military Atlas of the First World War*. London, 1975

Barclay, Brigadier C. N. *Armistice 1918*. London, 1968

Barnett, C. *The Swordbearers: Studies in Supreme Command in the First World War*. London, 1963

Beaverbrook, Lord. *Politicians and the War 1914–1918*. New York, 1928

Bruce, A. *Illustrated Companion to the First World War*. London, 1989

Brown, M. *The Imperial War Museum Book·of the First World War*. London, 1991

Churchill, Sir Winston S. *Great Con-temporaries*, London, 1937 (Includes chapters on Asquith, Clemenceau, Foch, French, George V, Haig, Hindenburg, Lawrence, Wilhelm II and, in the expanded edn., Fisher)

— *The World Crisis*. London, 1923–31 (Includes *The Aftermath; The Great War*. London, 1933, is a condensed version)

Cooper, B. *Tank Battles of World War I*. London, 1974

Crutwell, C. R. M. F. *History of the Great War*. Oxford, 1934

Edmonds, Sir James. *Short History of World War I*. Oxford, 1951

Evans, R., and Strandmann, H. von. *The Coming of the First World War*. London, 1989

Falls, C. *The First World War*. London, 1960

Fay, S. B. *The Origins of the World War*. London, 1967

Fleming, D. F. *The Origin and Legacies of World War I*. London, 1969

Garrett, R. *The Final Betrayal: the Armistice 1918 and Afterwards*. London, 1989

Geiss, I. *July 1914: The Outbreak of the First World War*. London, 1967

Gilbert, M. *First World War Atlas*. London, 1970

Gleichen, Major-General Lord Edward (ed.). *Chronology of the War*. London, 1918–20; reprinted as *Chronology of the Great War*, intro. Dr. G. Bayliss. London, 1988

Griffiths, W. R. *The Great War*, Wayne, New Jersey, 1986 (West Point Military History series)

Haythornthwaite, P. J. *Soldiers Fotofax*

series: *World War I: 1914, 1915, 1916, 1917, 1918*, London, 1989–90

Herwig, H. H., and Heyman, N. M. *Biographical Dictionary of World War I.* Westport, Connecticut, 1982 (also includes general history section and bibliography)

Kennedy, P. M. (ed.). *The War Plans of the Great Powers.* London, 1979

Laffin, J. *British Butchers and Bunglers of World War I.* London, 1988

Liddell Hart, Sir Basil. *A History of the World War 1914–1918.* London, 1934 (US edn. titled *The Real War*)

– *Reputations.* London, 1928 (concerning commanders: Allenby, Falkenhayn, Foch, Galliéni, Haig, Joffre, Liggett, Ludendorff, Pershing, Pétain)

Liddle, P. H. *The Soldier's War 1914–1918.* London, 1988

– *Voices of War: Front Line and Home Front.* London, 1988

Livesey, A. *Great Battles of World War I.* London, 1989

Ludwig, E. *July 1914.* London, 1929

Pitt, B., and Young, Brigadier P. (eds.). *History of the First World War.* London, 1969–71

Repington, Lieutenant-Colonel C. à C. *The First World War 1914–1918.* London, 1920 (*The Times*' military correspondent: gossip with leading figures of the war)

Robertson, Field Marshal Sir William. *Soldiers and Statesman 1914–1918.* London, 1926 (concerns his period as Chief of Imperial General Staff)

Seton-Watson, R. W. *Sarajevo: A Study in the Origin of the Great War.* London, 1926

Smyth, Brigadier-General Sir John, VC. *Leadership in Battle 1914–1918.* Newton Abbot, 1975

Taylor, A. J. P. *The First World War: An Illustrated History.* London, 1963

— *The Struggle for Mastery in Europe, 1848–1915.* Oxford, 1954

— *War by Timetable: How the First World War Began.* London, 1969

Temperley, Sir Harold W. V. *A History of the Peace Conference at Paris.* Oxford, 1920

Terraine, J. *The Great War 1914–1918.* London, 1965

— *The Smoke and the Fire: Myths and Anti-Myths of War.* London, 1980

Tuchman, B. *August 1914.* London, 1962 (US ed. title *The Guns of August.* New York, 1962)

Weintraub, S. *A Stillness Heard Around the World: November 1918.* London, 1988

Williams, J. *The Home Fronts: Britain, France and Germany 1914–1918.* London, 1972

Wilson, H. W., and Hammerton, J. A. (eds.). *The Great War: the Standard History of the All-Europe Conflict.* London, 1914–19 (later part subtitled *The Standard History of the World-Wide Conflict*)

The 11th edition of *Encyclopaedia Britannica* (1910–11) contains much information and many statistics on the pre-war conditions of the combatant powers. The three supplementary volumes (XXX–XXXII) were produced in 1922 deliberately to cover the events of the World War, and include material and statistics on technology and weaponry, in addition to outline guides to the events of the war.

The Western Front

Ascoli, D. *The Mons Star: The British Expeditionary Force 1914.* London, 1981 (the campaigning of 1914)

Asprey, R. *The First Battle of the Marne.* London, 1962

Becke, A. F. *The Royal Regiment of Artillery at Le Cateau, Wednesday 26th August 1914.* Woolwich, 1919

Blaxland, G. *Amiens 1918.* London, 1968

Blond, G. *The Marne.* London, 1965

— *Verdun.* London, 1976

Bloem, W. *The Advance from Mons, 1914.* London, 1930 (author served with 12th Brandenburg Grenadiers)

Brice, B. *The Battle Book of Ypres.* London, 1927

Brown, M., and Seaton, S. *Christmas Truce.* London, 1984 (the 1914 truce)

A typical, French patriotic postcard, combining the joint appeals of pretty girl and flag.

GLOIRE AUX POILUS

La France Fête la Victoire

An example of the work of one of the most distinguished of Official War Artists: Muirhead Bone's 'Waiting for the Wounded', a study of British Medical officers at a Divisional Collecting Station on the Somme, published as a print in the series The Western Front *in 1917*.

Carew, T. *Wipers: the First Battle of Ypres.* London, 1974.

Charlton, P. *Pozières 1916.* London, 1986

Cheyne, C. *The Last Great Battle of the Somme: Beaumont Hamel.* London, 1988

Conan Doyle, Sir Arthur. *The British Campaign in France and Flanders 1914–1918.* London, n.d.; the updated version entitled *The British Campaigns in Europe.* London, 1928

Coombs, R. E. B. *Before Endeavours Fade: A Guide to the Battlefields of the First World War.* London, 1976

Dewar, G. A. B., and Boraston, Lieutenant-Colonel J. H. *Sir Douglas Haig's Command 1915–1918.* London, 1922

Edmonds, Brigadier-General Sir James E., and Becke, Major J. F. *Military Operations, France and Belgium, 1914–18,* London, 1925–48 (official history)

Ellis, J. *Eye-Deep in Hell: the Western Front 1914–18.* London, 1976

Farrar-Hockley, A. H. *Death of an Army.* London, 1967 (First Battle of Ypres)

— *The Somme.* London, 1964

Fox, Sir Frank. *The Battles of the Ridges: Arras-Messines, May–June 1917.* London, 1918

French, Field Marshal Earl *1914.* London, 1919

Gardner, B. *The Big Push: A Portrait of the Battle of the Somme.* London, 1961

Gibbs, Sir Philip. *From Bapaume to Passchendaele.* London, 1918 (one of the most distinguished of war correspondents)

— *Open Warfare.* London, 1919

— *Realities of War.* London, 1920

— *The Battles of the Somme.* London, 1917

Giles, J. *The Ypres Salient.* London, 1970

Gliddon, G. *When the Barrage Lifts: a Topographical History and Commentary on the Battle of the Somme 1916.* Norwich, 1987, r/p. London, 1990

Gough, General Sir Hubert. *The March Retreat.* London, 1934 (the German 1918 offensive; a shortened version of the *The Fifth Army.* London, 1931)

Haldane, Lieutenant-General Sir Aylmer. *A Brigade of the Old Army.* London, 1920 (the campaign of August–November 1914)

Harris, J. *The Somme: Death of a Generation.* London, 1966

Horne, A. *The Price of Glory: Verdun 1916.* London, 1962

Isselin, H. *The Battle of the Marne.* London, 1964

Joffre, Marshal J. J. C. *The Two Battles of the Marne.* London, 1927

Kluck, General A. von. *The March on Paris and the Battle of the Marne 1914.* London, 1920

Macdonald, L. *Somme.* London, 1983

— *They Called it Passchendaele,* London 1978

— *1914.* London, 1987

Macksey, K. *The Shadow of Vimy Ridge.* London, 1965 (also covers Marlborough and World War II)

Masefield, J. *The Old Front Line.* London, 1917 (account of the Somme prior to the battle which began on 1 July 1916)

Maurice, Major-General Sir Frederick. *The Last Four Months: the End of the War in the West.* London, 1919

McKee, A. *Vimy Ridge.* London, 1966

Middlebrook, M. *The First Day on the Somme.* London, 1971

— *The Kaiser's Battle: 21 March 1918.* London, 1978

Miller, Lieutenant-Colonel H. W. *The Paris Gun: the Bombardment of Paris by the German Long-range Guns, and the Great German Offensive of 1918.* London, 1930

Moore, W. *A Wood Called Bourlon.* London, 1988

— *See How they Ran: the British Retreat of 1918.* London, 1970

Norman, T. *The Hell they called High Wood: the Somme 1916.* London, 1984

Owen, E. *1914: Glory Departing.* London, 1986 (the BEF in the first campaign)

Palmer, F. *With the New Army on the Somme.* London, 1917 (by an

American war correspondent)

erris, G. *The Battle of the Marne*. London, 1920

étain, Marshal H. P. B. J. O. *Verdun*. London, 1930

itt, B. *1918: The Last Act*. London, 1962

owell, E. *Fighting in Flanders*. London, 1915 (war correspondent on the German invasion of Belgium)

itter, G. G. B. *The Schlieffen Plan: Critique of a Myth*. London, 1958

pears, Major-General Sir Edward. *Liason 1914: a Narrative of the Great Retreat*. London, 1930

pears, Major-General Sir Edward *Prelude to Victory*. London, 1939 (French offensive 1917)

erraine, J. *Mons: the Retreat to Victory*. London, 1960

— *The Road to Passchendaele*. London, 1977

— *The Western Front 1914–1918*. London, 1964

Thomas, Sir William Beach. *With the British on the Somme*. London, 1917 (war correspondent: 'Teech Bomas' of *The Wipers Times* was a skit upon such dispatches)

Tyng, S. *The Campaign of the Marne 1914*. Oxford, 1935

Uys, I. *Delville Wood*. Johannesburg, 1983

Warner, P. *Passchendaele: the Story Behind the Tragic Victory of 1917*. London, 1987

Warner, P. *The Battle of Loos*. London, 1976

Whitton, F. E. *The Marne Campaign*. London, 1925

Wolff, L. *In Flanders Fields*. London, 1958 (the 1917 campaign)

Woollcombe, R. *The First Tank Battle: Cambrai 1917*. London, 1967

The Eastern Front

Churchill, Sir Winston S. *The Eastern Front*. London, 1932

Golovine, Lieutenant-General N. N. *The Russian Campaign of 1914*. London, 1933

Hoffman, General M. *War Diaries and Other Papers*. London, 1929 (German chief of staff, Eastern Front)

Ironside, Field Marshal Lord. *Arch-*

angel 1918–19. London, 1953

— *Tannenberg: the First Thirty Days in East Prussia*. Edinburgh and London, 1925

Jukes, G. *Carpathian Disaster: Death of an Army*. New York, 1971

Magnus, J. P. *Russia and Germany at Brest-Litovsk*. London, 1919

Reed, J. *The War in Eastern Europe* (Vol. V of *The War on All Fronts*). New York, 1919

Stone, N. *The Eastern Front 1914–17*. London, 1975

Washburn, S. *Field Notes from the Russian Front*. London, 1915 (*The Times* correspondent)

Wheeler-Bennett, J. W. (later Sir John). *Brest-Litovsk, the Forgotten Peace, March 1918*. London, 1938, revised edn. 1966

The Italian Front

Anon. *The War in Italy*. Milan, 1916

Allen, W., and Hardie, M. *Our Italian Front*. London, 1920

Bainville, J. *Italy and the War*. London, 1916

Dalton, H. *With British Guns in Italy*. London, 1919

Davanzati, R. F. *The War of Italy*. Varese, 1918

Edmonds, Brigadier-General Sir James, and Davies, H. R. *Military Operations, Italy 1915–19*. London, 1949 (official history).

Falls, C. *Caporetto 1917*. London, 1966

Low, S. *Italy in the War*. London, 1916

Page, T. N. *Italy and the World War*. London, 1921 (author was US ambassador during the war)

Powell, A. *Italy at War*, and the Allies in the West (Vol. IV of *The War on All Fronts*), New York, 1919

Salandra, A. *Italy and the Great War*. London, 1932

Seth, R. *Caporetto: the Scapegoat Battle*. London, 1965

Thayer, J. A. *Italy and the Great War*. Madison, Wisconsin, 1964

Trevelyan, G. M. *Scenes from Italy's War*. London, 1919

Villari, L. *The War on the Italian Front*. London, 1932

The Macedonian Front

Falls, C. *Military Operations, Macedonia*.

London, 1933–5 (official history)

Mann, A. T., and Wood, W. T. *The Salonika Front*. London, 1920

Owen, H. C. *Salonika and After*. London, 1919

Packer, C. *Return to Salonika*. London, 1964

Palmer, A. *The Gardeners of Salonika*. London, 1965

Seligman, V. J. *The Salonika Sideshow*. London, 1919

Villari, L. *The Macedonian Campaign*. London, 1922

Ward Price, G. *The Story of the Salonika Army*. London, 1917

The Dardanelles Campaign

Ashmead-Bartlett, E. *The Uncensored Dardanelles*. London, 1928 (influential war correspondent)

Aspinall-Oglander, Brigadier-General C. *Military Operations, Gallipoli*. London, 1929 (official history)

Callwell, Major-General Sir Charles. *The Dardanelles*. London, 1919

Cassar, G. H. *The French and the Dardanelles: a Study of Failure in the Conduct of War*. London, 1971

Creighton, Revd. O. *With the Twenty-Ninth Division in Gallipoli*. London, 1916 (good personal account)

Denton, K. *Gallipoli: One Long Grave*. Sydney, 1986

Guepratte, Admiral P. E. *L'Expédition des Dardanelles 1914–15*. Paris, 1935 (author was France's most offensively-minded admiral)

Hamilton, General Sir Ian. *Gallipoli Diary*. London, 1920

— *Ian Hamilton's Despatches from the Dardanelles*. London, 1917

Hargrave, J. *The Suvla Bay Landing*. London, 1964

Haythornthwaite, P. J. *Gallipoli 1915: Frontal Assault on Turkey*. London, 1991

James, R. R. *Gallipoli*. London, 1965

Kannengiesser, Colonel H. von. *The Campaign in Gallipoli*. London, 1928

Laffin, J. *Damn the Dardanelles!* London, 1980

Liddle, P. H. *Gallipoli 1915: Pens, Pencils and Cameras at War*. London, 1985

— *Men of Gallipoli*. London, 1976

Masefield, J. *Gallipoli*. London, 1916

Moorehead, A. *Gallipoli*. London, 1956; illustrated edn., with additions by A. Moyal. London, 1989

Nevinson, H. W. *The Dardanelles Campaign*. London, 1918

Pedersen, P. A. *Images of Gallipoli*. Melbourne, 1988

Shakland, P., and Hunter, A. *Dardanelles Patrol: the Story of Submarine E-11*. London, 1964

Wester-Wemyss, Admiral Lord. *The Navy in the Dardanelles Campaign*. London, 1924 (Lord Wester-Wemyss was Sir Rosslyn Wemyss at the time of the campaign)

Wilkinson, N. *The Dardanelles: Colour Sketches from Gallipoli*. London, 1915

The Palestinian Front

Bullock, D. L. *Allenby's War: the Palestine-Arabian Campaigns 1916–1918*. London, 1988

Dane, E. *British Campaigns in the Near and Nearer East 1914–18, from the Outbreak of War with Turkey to the Armistice*. London, 1919 (1918 edn. only covered the period to the fall of Jerusalem)

Falls, C. *Armageddon 1918*. London, 1964 (the final Palestine campaign)

Lawrence, T. E. *Revolt in the Desert*. London, 1927; expanded to *The Seven Pillars of Wisdom*. London, 1935

Liddell Hart, Sir Basil. *T. E. Lawrence in Arabia and After*. London, 1934

Macmunn, Lieutenant-General Sir George, and Falls, C. *Military Operations, Egypt and Palestine*. London, 1928–30 (official history)

Massey, W. T. *The Desert Campaigns*. London, 1918

— *How Jerusalem was Won: A Record of Allenby's Campaign in Palestine*. London, 1919

Maxwell, D. *The Last Crusade*. London, 1920 (official war artist)

Nicolle, D. *Lawrence and the Arab Revolts*. London, 1989

Pirie-Gordon, Lieutenant-Colonel H. (ed.). *Brief Record of the Advance of the Egyptian Expeditionary Force*. London, 1919

Preston, Lieutenant-Colonel R. M. P. *The Desert Mounted Corps: an Account of the Cavalry Operations in Palestine and Syria 1917–1918*. London, 1921

Thomas, L. *With Allenby in the Holy Land*. London, 1938

Wavell, Field Marshal Earl. *Allenby in Egypt*. London, 1943

Wavell, Field-Marshal Earl. *The Palestine Campaigns*. London, 1928

The Mesopotamian Front

Barber. C. *Besieged in Kut and After*. Edinburgh, 1917

Barker, A. J. *The Neglected War: Mesopotamia 1914–1918*. London, 1967

— *Townshend of Kut: Major-General Sir Charles Townshend*. London, 1967

Burne, Lieutenant-Colonel A. H. *Mesopotamia: the Last Phase*. Aldershot, 1936.

Callwell, Major-General Sir Charles. *Life of Lieut. Gen. Sir Stanley Maude*. London, 1920

Dane, E. *British Campaigns in the Near and Nearer East 1914–18, from the Outbreak of War with Turkey to the Armistice*. London, 1919 (1918 edn. covered the period only to the fall of Jerusalem)

Dunsterville, Major-General L. C. *The Adventures of Dunsterforce*. London, 1920

Egan, E. *War in the Cradle of the World: Mesopotamia*. London, 1918 (articles written for New York *Saturday Evening Post*)

Ellis, Colonel C. H. *The Transcaspian Episode*. London, 1963

Kearsey, A. *Study of the Mesopotamian Campaign*. Aldershot, 1934

Maxwell, D. *A Dweller in Mesopotamia*. London, 1920 (official war artist)

Millar, R. *Kut, the Death of an Army*. London, 1969

Moberly, Brigadier-General F. J. *Military Operations: the Campaign in Mesopotamia*. London, 1923–7 (official history)

Sandes, Major E. W. *In Kut and Captivity with the 6th Indian Division*. London, 1919

Townshend, Major-General Sir Charles. *My Campaign in Mesopotamia*. London, 1920

Wilson, Lieutenant-Colonel Sir Arnold T. *Loyalties: Mesopotamia 1914–17*. Oxford, 1934

Naval and Colonial Campaigns

Bacon, Sir Reginald. *Dover Patrol 1915–1917*. London, 1919

Bell, A. C. *The Blockade of Germany*. London, 1937

Bennett, G. *Coronel and the Falklands*. London, 1962

Bennett, G. *Naval Battles of the First World War*. London, 1968

— *The Battle of Jutland*. London, 1964

Burdick, C. B. *The Japanese Siege of Tsingtau: World War I in Asia*. Hamden, Connecticut, 1976

Burt, R. *British Battleships of World War I*. London, 1986

Campbell, Rear-Admiral G., VC. *My Mystery Ships*. London, 1928 (Q Ships)

Chatterton, E. K. *Seas of Adventures: the Story of the Naval Operations in the Mediterranean, Adriatic, and Aegean*. London, 1936

Coles, A. *Three Before Breakfast*. Havant, 1979 (sinking of *Aboukir Cressy* and *Hogue* by Weddigen of U9)

Corbett, Sir Julian, and Newbolt, Sir Henry. *History of the Great War. Naval Operations*. London, 1920–31 (official history)

Costello, J., and Hughes, T. *Jutland 1916*. London, 1976

Dane, E. *British Campaigns in Africa and the Pacific 1914–18*. London, 1919 (includes Tsingtau)

Davis, H. W. C. *A History of the Blockade*. London, 1920

Dixon, T. B. *The Enemy Fought Splendidly*. Poole, 1983 (diary of the Battle of the Falklands)

Evans, A. *The Royal Australian Navy*. Sydney, 1988 (includes First World War)

Fawcett, H. W., and Hooper, G. W. W. (eds.). *The Fighting at Jutland: the Personal Experiences of Sixty Officers and Men of the British Fleet*. London, 1921

Frothingham, Captain T. G. *The Naval History of the World War*. Cambridge, Massachusetts, 1924–6 (American perspective)

Gibson, R. H., and Prendergast, M. *The German Submarine War 1914–18*. London, 1931

Halpern, P. *The Naval War in the*

Mediterranean 1914–1918. London, 1987

Harper, Admiral J. E. T. *The Truth about Jutland.* London, 1927

Hoeling, A. A., and Hoeling, M. *The Last Voyage of the Lusitania.* New York, 1956

Hough, R. *The Great War at Sea 1914–1918.* Oxford, 1983

Hoyt, E. P. *The Last Cruise of the Emden.* London, 1967

Hurd, A. *The British Fleet in the Great War.* London, 1919

Jane, F. T. *Jane's Fighting Ships.* London, 1914, and subsequent; other titles include *The World's Warships,* London, 1915, etc., and *Jane's Fighting Ships of World War I,* ed. J. Moore. London, 1990

Jellicoe, Admiral Earl. *The Crisis of the Naval War.* London, 1920

— *The Grand Fleet 1914–1916: its Creation, Development, and Work.* London, 1919

— *The Submarine Peril.* London, 1934

Le Fleming, H. M. *Warships of World War I.* London, n.d.

Liddle, P. *The Sailor's War 1914–1918.* Poole, 1985

MacIntyre, D. *Jutland.* London, 1957

Marder, A. J. *From the Dreadnought to Scapa Flow: the Royal Navy in the Fisher Era 1904–1919.* Oxford, 1961–70

Milne, Admiral Sir A. Berkeley. *The Flight of the Goeben and Breslau.* London, 1921

Newbolt, Sir Henry. *Naval History of the War.* London, 1920

— *Submarine and Anti-Submarine.* London, 1918

Pitt, B. *Zeebrugge: St. George's Day 1918.* London, 1958

Preston, A. *Battleships of World War I: An Illustrated Encyclopaedia.* London, 1972

Siney, M. C. *The Allied Blockade of Germany 1914–1916.* Ann Arbor,

Michigan, 1957

Taffrail (Captain H. Taprell Dorling). *Swept Channels: Minesweepers in the Great War.* London, 1938

Usborne, Vice-Admiral C. V. *Smoke on the Horizon: Mediterranean Fighting 1914–1918.* London, 1933

Warner, P. *The Zeebrugge Raid.* London, 1978

Aviation

Bishop, W. *Winged Warfare: Hunting the Huns in the Air.* London, 1918

Bowen, E. *Knights of the Air.* Alexandria, Virginia, 1980

Bruce, J. M. *The Aeroplanes of the Royal Flying Corps.* London, 1982

Castle, H. G. *Fire over England: the German Air Raids of World War I.* London, 1982

Clark, A. *Aces High: The War in the Air over the Western Front 1914–18.* London, 1973

Cuneo, J. R. *The Air Weapon 1914–1916.* Harrisburg, Pennsylvania, 1947

Ege, L. *Balloons and Airships 1783–1973.* London, 1973

Fredette, R. H. *The First Battle of Britain 1917–1918 and the Birth of the Royal Air Force.* London, 1966

Gibbons, F. *The Red Knight of Germany: Baron von Richthofen, Germany's Great War Airman.* London, 1932

Gray, R., and Thetford, O. *German Aircraft of the First World War.* London, 1969

Jane, F. T. *Jane's All the World's Aircraft.* C. G. Grey. London 1919; *Jane's Fighting Aircraft of World War I,* ed. M. Taylor. London, 1990

Kiernan, R. H. *The First War in the Air.* London, 1934

Lamberton, W. M. *Reconnaissance and Bomber Aircraft of the 1914–1918 War; Fighter Aircraft of the 1914–1918 War.* Letchworth, 1962

Lehmann, E. A. *Zeppelin: the Story of Lighter-than-Air Craft.* London, 1937

Leigh, H. *Planes of the Great War.* London, 1934

Lewis, C. *Sagittarius Rising.* London, 1936 (perhaps the greatest of all first-hand accounts)

Liddle, P. *The Airman's War 1914–1918.* Poole, 1987

Morris, Captain J. *The German Air*

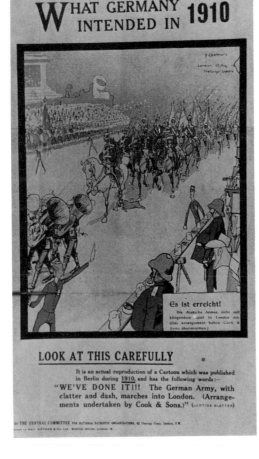

A propaganda poster 'proving' Germany's malevolent intent four years before the war: a German cartoon depicting a triumphal parade through Trafalgar Square, issued for propaganda purposes during the war by the Central Committee for National Patriotic Organizations.

WHAT GERMANY INTENDED IN **1910**

Es ist erreicht!

Die deutsche Armee zieht mit klingendem Spiel in London ein. (Das Arrangement haben Cook & Sons übernommen.)

LOOK AT THIS CAREFULLY

It is an actual reproduction of a Cartoon which was published in Berlin during 1910, and has the following words:—

"WE'VE DONE IT!!! The German Army, with clatter and dash, marches into London. (Arrangements undertaken by Cook & Sons.)" (LUSTIGE BLÄTTER)

Raids on Great Britain. London, 1926

Munson, K. *Aircraft of World War I*. London, 1967

Munson, K. *Pocket Encyclopedia of World Aircraft in Colour* series, Blandford Press. London, various dates, including *Fighters, Attack and Training Aircraft 1914–19; Bombers, Patrol and Reconnaissance Aircraft 1914–19*

Nitske, W. R. *The Zeppelin Story*. New York, 1977

Norman, A. *The Great Air War*. London, 1968

Norris, G. *The Royal Flying Corps: a History*. London, 1965

Raleigh, Sir Walter, and Jones, H. A. *The War in the Air*. Oxford, 1922–37 (official history)

Reynolds, Q. *They Fought for the Sky: the Story of the First War in the Air*. London, 1958

Robinson, D. H. *The Zeppelin in Combat 1912–18*. London, 1962

Simpkins, P. *Air fighting 1914–18: the Struggle for Air Supremacy over the Western Front*. London, 1978

White, C. M. *The Gotha Summer: the German Daytime Air Raids on England*. London, 1988

Whitehouse, A. *The Zeppelin Fighters*. London, 1968

Winter, D. *The First of the Few: Fighter Pilots of the First World War*. London 1982

Woodman, H. *Early Aircraft Armament the Aeroplane and the Gun up to 1918*. London, 1989

Yeates, V. *Winged Victory*. London 1934 (highly regarded fictional account of the nature of air fighting)

Personal accounts

First-hand accounts of the war are invariably of interest, though in some cases the information they contain is not especially relevant and is sometimes considerably biased. As there is only space here for the listing of a limited number, and although evaluation is inevitably subjective, those included are some of the finest, some with comments to emphasize their significance. In some cases the mixture of fact and fiction is unclear: the Sassoon works, for example, might be included in the 'literature' section, while others in that section, for example Renn's much under-rated *War*, might be included here. The titles listed are mostly concerned with an account of the experience of war; a different style of personal account are those by generals, some of which put self-justification above accuracy: French's *1914* is an obvious example; it resulted in a disagreement with Smith-Dorrien that recalled the Napier–Beresford feud of a previous generation of military history writers.

Blunden, E. *Undertones of War*. London, 1928

Carrington, C. *Soldier from the Wars Returning*. London, 1965 (*see also* Edmonds, C., below)

Chapman, G. *A Passionate Prodigality*. London, 1933. (Described by James Agate as one of the few genuine masterpieces of the war.)

Creighton, Revd. O. *With the Twenty-Ninth Division in Gallipoli*. London, 1916 (notable account by a military padre)

Douie, C. *The Weary Road: Recollections of a Subaltern of Infantry*. London, 1929

Dunn, Captain J. C. *The War the Infantry Knew*, privately published 1938; with intro. by K. Simpson, London, 1987 (invaluable compilation by members of the Royal Welch Fusiliers, collated by one of the great (and most heroic) characters of the army, a regimental medical officer; reviewed as one of the finest of all war books, which it still remains)

Edmonds, C. (*actually Carrington, C.*). *A Subaltern's War*. London, 1929

Gibbs, Captain C. C. S. *From the Somme*

LOUVAIN

CROIX ROUGE FRANÇAISE
ASSOCIATION DES DAMES FRANÇAISES
12, rue Gaillon, Paris

The picture postcard was a convenient medium for the dissemination of propaganda; this fund-raiser for the French Red Cross depicts the destruction of Louvain in 1914.

to the Armistice (ed. R. Devonald-Lewis). London, 1986 (includes a notable foreward by Rt. Hon. Enoch Powell)

Graves, R. Good-Bye to All That. London, 1929 (account of major importance by the great author and poet Robert Graves)

Hammerton, Sir John. The Great War: I Was There. Undying Memories of 1914–1918. London, 1938 (anthology of many accounts not published elsewhere)

Herbert, A. Mons, Anzac and Kut. London, 1919

Jünger, E. Copse 125: a Chronicle from the Trench Warfare of 1918. London, 1930

— The Storm of Steel. London, 1929. (These two works, by a fine and extremely gallant German officer, are very much the reverse of the anti-war attitudes sometimes encountered in such first-hand accounts)

Kilpatrick, J. A. Atkins at War. London, 1914. (A typical collection of 'patriotic' first-hand accounts assembled at the time for home consumption)

Laffin, J. On the Western Front: Soldiers' Stories from France and Flanders 1914–1918. Gloucester, 1985

Lewis, C. Sagittarius Rising. London, 1936 (perhaps the greatest of all aviation accounts)

Liveing, E. G. D. Attack on the Somme; orig. pub. in Blackwood's Magazine, December 1917; in book form 1918, rep. Stevenage, 1986. (A notable account)

Macdonald, L. 1914–1918: Voices and Images of the Great War. London, 1988 (notable collection of first-hand accounts)

'Mark VII' (M. Plowman). A Subaltern on the Somme, 1916. London, 1927

Maze, P. A Frenchman in Khaki. London 1934 (noted French artist who served as liaison with the British Army)

Newman, B., and Evans, L. O. Anthology of Armageddon. 1935, rep. London, 1989 (collection of extracts from many sources, including some fictional: e.g., Newman's The Cavalry Went Through appears alongside Foch's Memoirs and Lettow-Vorbeck's Reminiscences, but an excellent compilation giving a good general view of the experience of war)

Purdom, C. B. (ed.). Everyman at War. London, 1930 (collection of first-hand accounts)

Richards, F. Old Soldiers Never Die. London, 1933 (wonderful account of life in the ranks, by a typical British 'squaddy' who by coincidence served in the same regiment as Edmund Blunden, Robert Graves, Dr. Dunn and Siegfried Sassoon; Old Soldier Sahib, London, 1936, covers his pre-war career. Both were reprinted, London, 1983)

Sassoon, S. Memoirs of a Fox-Hunting Man. London, 1928; Memoirs of an Infantry Officer. London, 1930 (perhaps best described as fiction, but based upon the experiences of Siegfried Sassoon, a very gallant officer as well as a major literary personality; his character 'George Sherston' is probably based on Sassoon himself. Associated are Siegfried Sassoon Diaries 1915–1918, ed. R. Hart-Davies, London, 1983; and Sassoon's Long Journey: an Illustrated Selection, ed. P. Fussell. London, 1983)

Talbot Kelly, R. B., ed. R. G. Loosmore. A Subaltern's Odyssey: Memoirs of the Great War 1915–1917. London, 1980 (distinguished by notable contemporary drawings)

Thomason, J. W. Jnr. Fix Bayonets: With the U.S. Marine Corps in France 1917–1918. New York, 1925; rep London, 1989 (one of the finest accounts by any nationality, with notable contemporary drawings)

Vaughan, E. C. Some Desperate Glory: The Diary of a Young Officer, 1917. London, 1979

Witkop, Dr. P. (ed.). German Students' War Letters. London, 1929 (a good contrast to the majority of first-hand accounts available in English and thus written by English-speakers; although, as with many British accounts, they are representative of the higher educational classes)

Young, F. B. Marching on Tanga. London, 1917 (a work of genuine literary as well as historic merit; Francis Brett Young was medical officer of the 2nd Rhodesia Regiment)

LITERATURE

World War I produced a greater outpouring of literary accomplishment, especially poetry, than any previous war. The reason is not difficult to determine: added to a greater degree of literacy than was the case during (say) the Napoleonic Wars, the mass conscription of the Great War swept into the army the type of individual more likely to produce works of poetry or prose than previously had been the case. Few professional soldiers of earlier ages had produced works of the greatest literary merit; a number were military historians with a gift of literary talent, but for every Ewald von Kleist (1715–59, the poet mortally wounded at Kunersdorf) there were thousands like Colonel J. F. Browne who commanded the British 28th Foot in the Peninsular War, who 'never had but one book, and that was the Army List'.[1] The different type of soldier who fought in the Great War, however, resulted in a larger number of memorable works than ever before, and many literary reputations would not have existed without the war, for it was its experiences which produced some of the greatest, though most disturbing, work. It is an interesting speculation whether those major literary figures who emerged from the war would ever have attained such reputation without it: in some cases it was probably only the experience of war which could have provided the necessary material and inspiration, even though so much of that experience was destructive. Owen's *Strange Meeting*, in which the author meets the shade of the literary genius which he wished to be himself, whom he had killed and whose greatest work thus remained unwritten, is an appropriate reflection upon the whole subject, made more poignant by the knowledge that Owen himself, arguably the greatest literary figure produced by the war, was killed before he could finish the poem.

The war produced innumerable works of fiction, of which there is a notable division between those produced during the war and those after. Much of the fiction of the war period was largely didactic in tone and aimed towards reinforcing a certain 'patriotic' viewpoint, some edging so far in this direction that its literary worth is limited. The best of the genre, however, had considerable merit and great influence at the time: notable examples include Ian Hay's *The First Hundred Thousand*, Ernest Raymond's *Tell England* (just post-war), the works of 'Sapper' and lesser-known ones such as Captain R. W. Campbell's *Private Spud Tamson* (Edinburgh and London, 1915). The latter, dedicated to the members of the author's 'gallant Regiment', is perhaps a typical example of this type of novel, in which the hero, a product of the Glasgow slums, saves his colonel, is awarded

the Victoria Cross, survives a desperate bayonet-wound and marries his sweetheart, the narrative ending: 'The whole Empire cried "Well done", and all the world wondered at this hero from the slums.'[2]

A very different type of fiction appeared in the years following the war, altogether more 'realistic' and often harrowing, utilizing or based directly upon the experiences of the authors. In some cases it is difficult to separate fact from fiction: Sassoon's *Memoirs*, for example, are ostensibly fiction, but portray many incidents probably witnessed by, and involving, the author. This is by no means an isolated example: among notable similar works are *Her Privates We* (alias *The Middle Parts of Fortune*), *In Parenthesis* and many others. Even though these do not describe directly eye-witness accounts of identifiable incidents, it is from such works that the most vivid concept of the experience of war can be gained.

Following these novels based on personal experience, the majority of which appeared in the inter-war years, fiction of the Great War declined. Whilst some popular novels have appeared more recently, using the period as a setting or background, the number is much less than those concerning the equivalent treatment of other conflicts, for example the Second World War or even the naval campaigns of the Napoleonic Wars. Perhaps the Great War is not regarded as such a suitable subject, or conceivably the enormity of the catastrophe which was the war is a discouragement both to authors and readers alike. Modern studies of the subject include *Fiction of the First World War: A Study*, G. Parfitt, London 1988; *English Literature of the Great War Revisited*, ed. M. Roucoux, 1986; *English Fiction and Drama of the Great War*, J. Onions, London 1990; and *The First World War in Fiction*, ed. H. Klein, London, 1976.

If the most famous novel of the war – *All Quiet on the Western Front* – were written by a German, the best and most renowned poetry of the war was written by English-speaking poets, mostly British but including other English-speakers such as the American Alan Seeger and Canadian John McCrae. The list of 'war poets' is long, although a small number stand as major literary figures in their own right, not just as the best poets of the war: Wilfred Owen, Robert Graves, Edward Thomas and Siegfried Sassoon are examples. Few of the 'war poets' were established literary figures before the war – Rupert Brooke is an example of those who already had some reputation – and it was the war which provided the spark to ignite some of the greatest work of the era. Other major literary figures had no experience of combat, and although some produced 'war poetry' – the greatest example perhaps Yeats' *An Irish Airman foresees his Death* – it is not difficult to differentiate between those who knew the subject first-hand and those who viewed it from a

'In remembrance of the faithful': a restrained and consequently more effective example of 'patriotic' illustration, depicting *a German cavalryman paying homage at the grave of a comrade. (Print after E. Thönn)*

distance. The difference is generally of tone rather than content, for few of the 'war poets' resorted to the sickening imagery of *Clearing Station* by Wilhelm Klemm, one of the German poets whose war work is less well-known.

Probably the most widely famous poet of the war years was renowned more for his actions than his writing, the Italian Gabriele D'Annunzio, whose robust speeches and addresses to the Italian people contributed markedly towards the movement for intervention in the war. He was not content with acting as a rallying-voice, however, for despite his age (born 1863) he served in all three Italian armed services. His initial duty with the 77th Infantry in the Carso trenches he found insufficiently exciting; transferring first to the navy, he found his niche in the aviation service, where his career became even more fantastic: his wounds included the loss of an eye and his exploits included a famous leaflet-raid over Vienna in August 1918. He retired from active service, profusely medalled, and later led the illegal occupation of Fiume, of which he set himself up as 'commandant' or ruler. His active career, however, over-shadowed the small number of 'war poems' he produced during this period.

It is possible to detect a change of emphasis in the 'war poetry' of the period, with initial idealism being replaced by a sense of futility and despair, a reflection of the general perception of the war, although not all 'war poetry' is necessarily of these natures: Gilbert Frankau, who wrote the moving description of an execution in *The Deserter*, also contributed many humorous and light-hearted pieces to *The Wipers Times*, for example. Unlike the most significant war fiction, the important war poetry was written during the war, by those who were undergoing or had recently undergone the trauma of battle; as if the immediacy of the subject was required for great poetry, and a period of reflection for great novels. It is the more remarkable that so much major poetry was produced considering the relative youth of many of the writers: Isaac Rosenberg was born in 1890, Wilfred Owen in 1893, Robert Graves in 1895 and Edmund Blunden in 1896, for example. Perhaps it proves the veracity of a line by arguably France's greatest literary figure of the war, Guillaume Apollinaire, himself a gallant soldier, terribly wounded in the war and who died from influenza: that the majority of the soldiers were so young that although they had seen death face-to-face a hundred times, they had not yet experienced life.

It is notable that not all the most famous poems of the war were the product of the most famous poets: Lawrence Binyon, for example, is remembered best for *For the Fallen* (published in *The Times* on 21 September 1914, not, as is often thought, as a valediction to the war); a curator of oriental art at the British Museum, Binyon visited the front only in 1916 as a medical orderly at the age of 47. Arguably the single most famous poem of the war, the haunting *In Flanders Fields*, was the only great work of John McCrae, a Canadian doctor who wrote it at his dressing-station during the Second Battle of Ypres.

Despite the huge merit of his work – *The Leveller* is one of the most memorable poems of the war – Robert Graves tended to disregard his war poetry; it recalls Wilfrid Gibson's poem *Back*, in which he suggests that the man with his name who fought and killed in the war was somehow not really him, a theme which doubtless could be appreciated by countless of those who survived and returned to a 'normal' life.

In the following list, in which there is space only to include a few of the most important works, only anthologies of war poetry are listed; any of these provide references to the published collections of the work of individual poets.

Adcock, A. St. J. *For Remembrance: Soldier Poets who have Fallen in the War*. London, 1920

Barbusse, Henri. *Under Fire*. London, 1918 (*Le Feu* was perhaps the most notable work by a French author, but judged as so markedly anti-war as to reduce the reality)

Blaker, Richard. *Medical Without Bar*. London, 1920 (draws heavily upon first-hand experience, concerning life in the field artillery)

Boyd, Donald. *Salute of the Guns*. London, 1930 (a 'novel' built on the experiences of the author, a gunner officer)

Bridgwater, P. *The German Poets of the First World War*. London, 1985

Buchan, J. *Greenmantle*. London, 1916 (an example of the best type of 'romantic-thriller' novels of the war)

Gardner, B. *Up the Line to Death: The War Poets 1914–1918*. London, 1964, rev. 1976 (a splendid introduction, including biographical notices of the poets featured)

Hay, Ian (John Hay Beith). *The First Hundred Thousand*. Edinburgh and London 1915; *Carrying On: After the First Hundred Thousand*. Edinburgh and London, 1917 (popular fiction-cum-fact accounts of 'Kitchener's Army', naturally somewhat 'patriotic' in content but well-written and notable contributions)

Hemingway, Ernest. *A Farewell to Arms*. London, 1929 (based on Hemingway's experience with a volunteer ambulance in Italy: regarded as a major work of literature, but scathingly reviewed by Falls who found it distasteful and impossible to finish!)[3]

Herbert, A. P. *The Secret Battle*. London, 1919 (a moving account of a brave officer worn down by exposure to danger and shot for cowardice. It is often believed to have been based upon the actual case of a Royal Naval Division officer shot for desertion in 1917, a case about which Horatio Bottomley made a notable furore, but while inspired by this, it appears that Herbert did not base his story directly upon it, and it was intended to be entirely fictional)[4]

Jones, David *In Parenthesis*. London, 1937 (fiction based upon personal experience, perhaps in this case written as a form of catharsis by one who suffered severely from his wartime service)

Manning, Frederick. *Her Privates We*. London, 1930 (originally published anonymously under the *nom de*

plume 'Private 19022', and in an unexpurgated version
titled *The Middle Parts of Fortune*; one of the best works,
based upon first-hand experience, of the viewpoint of the
rank-and-file, by an Australian serving in the 7th
Battalion KSLI)

Nichols, R. *Anthology of War Poetry 1914–1918*. London, 1943
(two-thirds of which is a discussion on the nature of war
and its association with literature)

Parsons, I. M. (ed.). *Men Who March Away: Poems of the First
World War*. London, 1965

Raymond, Ernest. *Tell England*. London, 1922 (the best and
most famous of the 'sentimental/patriotic' school of
novel; Falls remarked that it represented not the war as it
was, but as it should have been,[5] but the best
representative of its genre)

Remarque, Erich Maria. *All Quiet on the Western Front*.
London, 1929 (the most famous war – or more accurately
anti-war – novel of the period; probably its original
reputation was over-inflated, and it was not well-
received by some, but it remains a major, powerful work)

Renn, Ludwig. *War*. London, 1929 (overshadowed by *All
Quiet on the Western Front* at the time of publication and
since, this is more like a first-hand account of the life of a
German NCO than fiction, and perhaps should not be
placed in the category of fiction; most significant,
especially in its account of the attritional losses of a
typical unit)

'Sapper' (H. C. McNeile): the more 'popular' end of war
fiction, in such works as *The Lieutenant and Others*. 1915;
Sergeant Michael Cassidy R. E., 1916; *No Man's Land*, 1917;
but a significant author

Sherriff, R. C., and Bartlett, V. *Journey's End*. London, 1930
(novel version of pehaps the most famous war play of all)

Silkin, J. *Penguin Book of First World War Poetry*. rev. edn.
London, 1981

Wharton, James B. *Squad*. New York, 1928 (one of the best
US works of fiction, concerned with a single infantry
section)

Footnotes

1. *Rough Notes of an Old Soldier.*
   Major-General Sir George
   Bell. London, 1867, I, p. 137.
2. *Private Spud Tamson*, p. 291.
3. *War Books*. 1989 edn., p. 279.
4. For an exposition of this case
   and its relation to *The Secret
   Battle*, see *For the Sake of
   Example: Capital Courts Martial
   1914–18*. A. Babington,
   London, 1983.
5. *War Books*. 1989 edn., p. 293.

ART

The art of the World War may be divided loosely into three
sections: the work of the war-illustrator, the war artist, and
the amateur who drew images from life primarily for his
own amusement. Although many nations produced ex-
ponents of all three types, the best and artistically the most
important are generally reckoned to be the British war
artists.

From the mid-19th century a number of illustrated
periodicals had flourished (most famously, perhaps, *The
Illustrated London News* and *The Graphic*), and as 'action'
photographs were hardly possible, these continued to regale
their readers with battle-scenes and similar images, drawn
by very competent illustrators, often with a high degree of
accuracy in regard to military equipment if not in the
realities of combat. Many such illustrations were produced
by home-based artists who worked from sketches contributed by correspondents working at the seat of war
(including serving officers), and some by war illustrators
sent by their publications to cover the campaign: William
Simpson in the Crimea and Melton Prior in a succession of
colonial campaigns are notable examples.

Despite the increasing sophistication of photography and
the ability to reproduce photographs in periodicals, this
process continued during the World War, especially in the

*The influence of the war
extended to every facet of life:
this catalogue of confectionary
was issued by Fryer & Co. of
Nelson, Lancs, one of Britain's
leading sweet-producers, whose
wartime sweets included
'Dreadnought Mixture',
'Belgian Bullets' and even 'John
Bull's Orphans'!*

earlier period. Some artists were war correspondents in their own right, and some of the earlier campaigns were covered by such artists as Frederic Villiers (doyen of the correspondent-artist school), and H. C. Seppings-Wright, who covered the early actions on the Western Front for *The Illustrated London News*, and then transferred to the Eastern Front, from where (accompanying the Russian forces) he sent back many valuable eye-witness depictions of the campaign. (His task was presumably considerably easier than that of Villiers, who was so hounded by press censorship that he once had to hide his drawings in his boots, and after two years threw up his job in despair.) Some of this 'front line' work is not 'finished' artwork in the conventional sense, but is covered with explanatory notes, which give an additional air of realism to the subject. Other notable illustrators at this period included Frédéric de Haenen and Georges Scott.

The home-based illustrator was employed throughout the war to present images of combat for popular consumption. Although some German illustrations in particular tended to show a more realistic view, there was much propaganda implicit in many of these illustrations. Many, as examples of artwork, were superb in execution, and in style followed the Victorian tradition of 'battle painting'; indeed, one of the greatest Victorian battle-illustrators, Richard Caton Woodville, was one of the most prolific artists of the early war period, and it is sometimes forgotten that the most famous of Victorian battle-painters, Lady Elizabeth Butler, produced a number of notable Great War subjects, albeit not primarily for publication. The pervading atmosphere of the Caton Woodville school of battle-painting is one of heroism, of desperate fights conducted at hand-to-hand range, with casualties not exhibiting any disfiguring wounds; in effect, a totally unrealistic view of the realities of battle, but one which had become accepted during the Victorian period and was pursued during the Great War so as not to bring home to the public the true horrors of combat lest it served to affect morale.

Nevertheless, such illustrations form a notable part of the art of the Great War, and include some of the highest artistic merit. Notable is the work of one of the greatest of all illustrators, the Italian Fortunino Matania, whose unmistakable and universally superb artwork graced everything from illustrated books to advertisements for well over half a century, almost all with a historical theme. One of the best draughtsmen of his time, Matania's illustrations have an almost photographic quality, and such was his desire for accuracy that (as an employee of the British Ministry of Propaganda) he not only visited the Western Front but even had a trench built at his home to act as a permanent reference for his subject! Some of his illustrations were based on the advice of wounded veterans whom he interviewed in hospital, when he would take with him a box of toy soldiers to enable the eye-witness to show him the position of the troops he intended to draw.

A different type of artwork was that of the official war artists, who were sent to various fronts to record their impressions of the war, not as journalists or reporters but as artists, a change of British policy which officially had barred artists from the Front prior to 1916. First to be appointed was Muirhead Bone (in August 1916), who was followed by more than 90 others, including Eric Kennington, Christopher Nevinson, Sir William Orpen, Paul and John Nash, William Rothenstein, Stanley Spencer and John Sargent. Although they presented many images very different from those required by the illustrated periodicals, there was still control over what they painted: Paul Nash remarked that as he was not allowed to put dead men into his pictures, he could no longer be considered an artist, but even so hoped that what message he could impart would burn the souls of those who sanitized his work in the cause of propaganda. Censored it may have been, but the effect of the exhibition of war art at Burlington House in 1917 was devastating, and had an immense effect upon the future developments of British art.

Some of the work of the official artists is very traditional in content, if not always in style: one of Eric Kennington's most famous works, for example, *The Kensingtons at Laventie*, is a series of portraits of actual soldiers, identified by their regimental names (e.g., private 'Sweeney' Todd), and incorporating such exact details of uniform and equipment as the number '77' worn in the caps of many members of the 13th London Regiment (Kensingtons) at that time, having exchanged their cap-badges with the French regiment bearing that number. Sir William Orpen's work reflects his pre-war fame as a portraitist; his *The Thinker on the Butte de Walencourt*, based on Rodin's *Le Penseur* but showing a Tommy laden with equipment, is one of the most memorable illustrations, and aptly used on the cover of Douie's *The Weary Road*. Conversely, C. R. W. Nevinson's work includes canvasses of angular lines and planes, akin to the Futurist belief that movement and light destroyed the substance of objects; Nevinson's work has been described as a compromise between Futurism and illustration, though some edge towards complete abstraction. Nevinson himself noted that his work resulted from rapid sketches made on the spot but then worked upon using memory and emotion to produce the finished work, 'as Nature is far too confusing and anarchic to be merely copied on the spot'.[1]

Similarly, the work of Paul Nash is far removed from the orthodoxy of Orpen, involving lunar or nightmarish landscapes, sometimes nocturnal and eerily lit by bursting star-shells, creating an impression of the scene rather than a realistically observed view, yet this impression was described as conveying the most realistic atmosphere by those who had experienced the real thing. Nash himself remarked that no drawing could ever convey the unspeakable, godless and hopeless nature of the landscape, but he came closer to it than most. The human results of the war appear in many works, among the most powerful and poignant being Sargent's immense *Gassed*, one of the most unforgettable images of the war.

Some of the most powerful, 'realistic' drawings to come out of the war were those of the Australian war artist Will Dyson, whose nationalistic background (his father was one of the 'rebels' of the Eureka Stockade) seemed to give additional power to his images of the waste and hopelessness of the Western Front, while still depicting the unquenchable spirit of the Australian soldier. His tendency to show helmets rather smaller than in real life, evident in a number of works, seems to emphasize the vulnerability of the individual amid the horrors of war. Also in the 'realistic' school was the American war artist Hervey Dunn, whose memorable *Out of the Wire* portrays an AEF stretcher-party carrying a casualty amid a wire entanglement and with a somewhat ethereal appearance. No less powerful in its way, though in a different medium (watercolour in very restrained tones, and monochrome drawings) was the work of André Dunoyer de Segonzac, who depicted the *poilu*, a sharp contrast in style to the more traditional French military battle-art exemplified by such artists as François Flameng and Georges Scott.

The work of many official war artists was doubtless influenced by their own military service: Nevinson, for example, although enjoying some artistic fame before the war (albeit in the school of Severini and the Italian Futurists) went to the Western Front in 1914; he was invalided out of active service with rheumatic fever. Kennington served as a Territorial with the 13th Londons until a foot wound ended his active service; Paul Nash was a serving soldier before his appointment as war artist; Norman Wilkinson (designer of the naval 'dazzle camouflage'), whose maritime and Dardanelles scenes are among the finest of the period, served in the Royal Navy; and Wyndham Lewis, better known as the founder of Vorticism and supposedly painter of the first British Cubist picture, served for two years in the artillery before becoming an official war artist for the Canadians.

A more unusual 'war artist' was the German Georg Grosz, one of the foremost satirical artists of the century, who was later one of the founders of Dadaism in Germany. He served in the army during the war, but was court-martialled for insubordination and narrowly escaped being executed; his book of satirical drawings. *Gott Mit Uns* (1920) led to a fine for insulting the army. His drawing *KV* epitomizes his attitude to the military: a medical board passing a decomposing corpse as 'KV' (fit for active service)!

In addition to official war artists, many amateurs painted and drew during their active service, whose work forms an equally valuable record. Some of these had an artistic reputation before the war, for example Captain Robert Gibbings of the Munster Fusiliers, who was severely wounded at Gallipoli. He specialized in wood-block prints in a limited colour-range, of scenes from his own experience as well as images inspired by photographs (most notably a rendition of Putnik's litter carried over a bridge in the Serbian retreat).[2] Other artists of repute produced only limited work during the war, being more occupied with their military duties: the French post-impressionist, Paul Maze, for example, used his artistic skill in the production of military panoramas in his capacity as interpreter and intelligence NCO; although his wartime artistic work was limited, he was much decorated for heroism by both France and Britain. Some very effective 'amateur' work, however, was produced by servicemen with no pre-war artistic background; for example, the sketches by John W. Thomason for his *Fix Bayonets!*, depicting the US Marine Corps and the foreign troops they encountered, are among the finest of all art to emerge from the war, and are a fitting complement to his splendid text.

Apart from the artistic developments it accelerated, the war had a lasting effect upon some artists: most notably, perhaps, Stanley Spencer, whose greatest work is the series of murals in the Sandham Memorial Chapel at Burghclere, near Newbury, nineteen war scenes including perhaps his most distinguished work, *Resurrection of the Soldiers*. Service in Macedonia had left an indelible mark on Spencer, and a map of the Salonika campaigning area actually appears in one of the murals, *Map Reading*.

For obvious reasons, sculpture during the war was limited, though the curious German fund-raising practice of driving nails (the purchase-price of which went into war funds) into wooden statues of war leaders meant that there was a steady demand for enormous carved images of Hindenburg and similar personalities. The most notable sculptural contributions to the art of the war came in the immediate aftermath, when statues were required for memorials and the like; the greatest talent was probably the British sculptor Charles Sargeant Jagger, who had been three times wounded as an officer of the Worcestershire Regiment during the war. He is probably best known for the Royal Artillery Memorial at Hyde Park Corner, though his bas-reliefs have as much power and emotive content as any of the great war paintings.

A very different style of illustration was the cartoon, in which field there were a number of important artists. One of the most significant was the Dutch artist Louis Raemaekers, neutral by nationality but vehemently anti-German by inclination, who produced some of the most bitter cartoons of the period. One of the most widely produced illustrations of the early war was Bert Thomas's *'Arf a Mo, Kaiser!*, showing a Tommy lighting his pipe and addressing this remark in reaction to the German invasion of Belgium; it appeared originally in the *London Evening News*. William Heath Robinson produced a popular series of drawings of fantastic machines, hence the description 'a Heath Robinson' for any patched-up work; but unquestionably the foremost of the war cartoonists, and one of the few artists of the period to achieve massive popularity, was Bruce Bairnsfather. An officer of the Warwickshire Regiment, with which he served from the very first stages of the Western Front campaign, Bairnsfather's sense of humour and unique style was completely in touch with that possessed by the

'The Conscientious Exhilarator', a cartoon by Bruce Bairnsfather which encapsulates the style of his humour, by poking gentle fun at even the most unbearable conditions. The caption reads: '"Every encouragement should be given for singing and whistling" – extract from a Military Manual. That painstaking fellow, Lieutenant Orpheus, does his best, but finds it uphill work at times.'

boost to morale. His cartoons of the enemy were never vicious, caricatured but never over-stated, and Bairnsfather remains one of the genuine artistic giants of the period.

A notable feature of the art of the war was the patriotic poster, whether aimed at recruiting or raising funds. Most famous are undoubtedly the huge Kitchener portrait by Alfred Leete, declaring that he 'wants you' (i.e., to enlist), and Jules Faivre's *On les aura!* ('we'll get them!'), depicting a young and enthusiastic *poilu* encouraging his comrades. A number of German posters are less 'artistic' or carefully-drawn than many of the British, French or American posters, but have greater impact (the whole purpose of a poster), including some of remarkable power; anti-Bolshevik posters are often the most exaggerated, though Germany and the Russian 'Whites' had no monopoly on this: the sculptor Jagger exhibited a striking and most critical picture at the Royal Academy in 1918 depicting a crazed Bolshevik orator, for example. Among the most graphic of war posters were those of the Australian artist Norman Lindsay, which were more akin to the horrors depicted by Raemaekers than the more restrained style of most British posters.

Another notable medium for the expression of patriotic sentiment was the picture postcard. Those most commonly associated with the Great War are probably the French woven silk cards sent as souvenirs from the Western Front, but others depicted battle-scenes, war leaders and patriotic cartoons in addition to the more conventional photographic cards. In some the patriotic appeal was subtle; in others, sickeningly sentimental (often posed by the most unmilitary of models looking totally out of place in their uniforms), while others bore printed authograph exhortations from such leaders as Hindenburg and Ludendorff.

The pin-up postcard saw a huge increase in production during the war, the majority of artwork rather than photography. Unquestionably the leading exponent was the Austrian Raphael Kirchner (1876–1917), who achieved fame through his illustrations in the magazine *La Vie Parisienne*. With all his pictures using his wife Nina as his model, his style was unmistakable and infinitely superior to the general standard of such work, mildly risqué and always idealized. Illustrations in magazine, postcard or print form were collected avidly by troops on the Western Front, and Kirchners and the like were used to decorate virtually every billet and dug-out; the very 'French' ambience of the subjects doubtless added the extra allure of the exotic. Many other artists produced similar artwork – among the best and stylistically most distinctive were 'Ney' and Xavier Sager – but none had quite the style and grace of Kirchner. (He should not be confused with the German expressionist Ernst Kirchner.) Although it might seem unusual to include Kirchner and Bairnsfather with the recognized 'war artists', it should be remembered that they enjoyed immense popularity and had far greater significance to those engaged in the war than did the works of any of the supposedly 'legitimate' artists.

British Army, thousands of members of which collected his works as avidly as the civilians. First published in *The Bystander* magazine, a veritable Bairnsfather industry developed, producing souvenirs and ceramics as well as his immortal series *Fragments from France*. Bairnsfather was recognized as a national asset and sent on drawing missions (much of his later work concerns the American and Italian forces), but his cartoons of the British Army are the most famous, and his character 'Old Bill', the archetypal, morose, sour but indomitable 'old contemptible' became the very symbol of the British Army. His subject-matter, be it flooded trenches, foul dug-outs, the prevalence of plum-and-apple jam or simply war-weariness, was the result of personal experience, and thus appealed directly to the members of the army, and consequently were an immense

Although not 'war art' *per se*, mention should be made of the fine coloured prints published before and after the war by Moritz Ruhl of Leipzig, in the series *Militär-Album aller Lander*, some of the last great series of uniform-plates, of value to the uniform-historian apart from artistic merit. The series included *Die Deutsche Armee, Die Graue Felduniform der Deutschen Armee, Die Armeen der Balkan-Staaten, Die Französischen Armee, Die Französischen Armee in ihrer Uniformerung vor dem Weltkrieg*, and *Die Osterreich–Ungarische Armee*.

A final 'war artist' worthy of mention was the English sculptor F. Derwent Wood, best known for his Machine Gun Corps memorial at Hyde Park Corner, with its appropriate though awful quotation from *I Samuel*, 'Saul hath slain his thousands, and David his ten thousands'; but Wood, an NCO of the RAMC during the war, exercised his talents in another direction, in the production of enamelled copper masks to conceal the most terrible of facial disfigurements. Almost single-handed Wood ran the Masks for Facial Wounds Department, pehaps the most useful practical contribution made by the world of art during the war.

PHOTOGRAPHY

Although military photography came of age in the Crimean War, there were still restrictions on the type of photograph that could be taken, and even more on those that could be published. Although photography had progressed sufficiently for 'action' photographs to be possible, only a small minority of those which came from the war can be so described, partly from technical difficulties and partly because in a war fought at longer range than before, there were fewer opportunities to photograph troops who were obviously locked in combat. Nevertheless, the large numbers of illustrated periodicals which existed before the war, let alone those created to cover the war (such as the British *Illustrated War News, War Illustrated, War Budget*, etc.) required a constant supply of images to fill their pages. These were obtained from journalistic sources and commercial picture-agencies, and from photographs taken on campaign by servicemen: the comparatively recent developments in photographic equipment enabled small, simple cameras to be carried without difficulty, and many of the most effective images of the early years of the war were obtained from such sources, usually captioned as being 'from an officer at the front' or similar. Some remarkable series of photographs resulted from these sources, for example those taken by Lieutenant R. C. Money of the Cameronians during the retreat from Mons.[3]

Censorship was always applied to the publication of war photographs, and stricter control over the taking of photographs was imposed with the appointment of Official Photographers (which occurred in British service, for example, only in 1916). As a result, the quality of photographs improved as full-time photographers could use more sophisticated plate cameras instead of relying on the pocket version employed only when the owner had nothing else to do. Rules of censorship varied: obviously nothing of military value to the enemy could be published, and the need for secrecy was at times taken to unrealistic lengths; for example, photographs of survivors from the British battleship *Audacious* were not de-restricted until four years after the event, as its loss (mined off Tory Island in October 1914) was not admitted publicly until after the war. Photographs of casualties were permitted, but those published showed either long-range views of casualty clearing-stations or of men with survivable injuries; and although photographs of the dead were published, especially in the early stages of the war when agency or private sources were utilized, no horrific pictures were published, but only of corpses lying (as one contemporary magazine described) like so many logs. More graphic pictures were not suppressed for 'patriotic' motives (few could have objected to scenes of enemy casualties), but simply from good taste, it being generally accepted that scenes of dismembered or putrefying bodies were simply unacceptable. Perhaps the most unusual use of photography was that recorded by a French source regarding the death of a popular officer who was killed rushing a German trench. The captain's men stormed the trench and killed the occupants, and despite continuous fire dragged the body of the captain's killer out of the trench and propped it up, and then photographed it with a pocket camera carried by one of the men, to prove to the officer's mother that they had avenged his death!

The numbers of officially appointed photographers seems to have been related to the importance placed upon the propaganda value of photographers: Germany, traditionally leaders in photographic technology, employed an average of about 50, France about 35, but Britain only sixteen, of which Ernest Brooks, John Warwick Brooke and William Rider-Rider each took slightly more than ten per cent of the 'official' photographs of Britain and the Dominions.

Although the Autochrome process had made colour photography possible from 1904, almost all the war photographs were monochrome. Among the very few colour photographs was a notable series taken by Frank Hurley, best known for his work on the Mawson and Shackleton Antarctic expeditions, using the Paget process and depicting the Palestine campaign (examples appear in *The Australian Light Horse*, I. Jones, Sydney 1987).

The most significant question concerning photographs of the World War concerns veracity. Many scenes were posed for the photographer, often quite obviously. Trenches which look too immaculate and inhabitants too smart are typical examples: a noted French 'trench' photograph depicts a cavalry officer in polished boots and a forage-cap, in the cleanest and most symmetrical trench ever seen; and German photographs depicting troops manning barricades and trenches, wearing no field equipment and with officers in best uniform, quite obviously depict behind-the-lines or even home fieldworks, constructed for training purposes. 'Posed' photographs, however, are not 'faked': they still fulfill their original intention of showing fieldworks and

A classic example of the most dubious type of photograph, published in The War Illustrated, *II, p. 202, 17 April 1915. The caption is in typical anti-German propaganda style, although the fallen man is quite clearly also a German, from his* Pickelhaube. *Not only is the caption thus misleading, but the original photograph was very likely posed, as the helmets are without the fabric covers used almost universally on service.*

Definite proof of the Huns' abuse of the rules of war. German ghoul actually caught in the act of robbing a fallen Russian. This snapshot would not have reached England had the culprit seen it being taken.

equipment, and the difference between these and genuine active-service conditions is patently obvious to the viewer. In this way, the claims of illustrated periodicals such as the *Illustrated London News*, 'Guarantees that all its Drawings and Photographs are Authentic', are valid.

Deliberate faking of photographs was rare, as propaganda use could be made of most genuine photographs by skilful captioning. France and Germany, especially the latter, made much greater use of manipulation of photography than did Britain, the British official policy being to broadcast only the 'propaganda of fact', so that British (and associated Australian and Canadian) official photographs were acknowledged to have maximum veracity. Slight tampering, however, was inevitable in the interest of security: thus published photographs may be encountered with cap-badges obscured, for example. Other similar re-touching is evident in pre-'official' days: a notable British example is a remarkable 'action' photograph of the transport wagons of the 1st Battalion, Middlesex Regiment under shrapnel-fire at Signy Signets, 8 September 1914. The actual photograph depicts a staff officer turning away, nursing what appears to be a gash on the head; when published originally, all trace of the wound had been removed so as not to show so dispiriting a scene.

A more confusing practice was the ascribing of photographs as something they were not. This occurred even in the 'official' period, when photographs supposedly depicting troops going 'over the top' appear to have been taken in reserve lines or on occasions other than those stated officially; but for many the true status is unclear, and sometimes only small clues within the photographs can point to mis-attribution. (For example, a well-known Canadian series purports to show an actual attack, whereas it was photographed in training.) A similar case occurred with the British cine film of the Battle of the Somme, in which genuine sequences were mixed with 'staged' operations, albeit ones taken at almost the same time and location

and featuring the same formations. (It is interesting to note that there were only two British film cameramen at work on the Western Front at this time, Geoffrey Malins and J. B. McDowell, and that the Somme film was shown not only at home but to the troops at the front, in some cases accompanied by 'sound effects' from an actual barrage in the distance. Although it depicted nothing especially gruesome, it had an enormous effect at home, and received some criticism for making entertainment out of such a subject.)

A greater amount of mis-representation occurred with the illustrated periodicals and postcard producers. In the early stages of the war in particular, demand for photographs outstripped supply, which resulted in the re-use of old photographs (especially for foreign armies whose subjects were less available to the publishers), suitably but entirely erroneously captioned. Countless photographs published in 1914–15, either captioned or by implication depicting troops on active service, are clearly pre-war manoeuvre pictures, often immediately recognizable by the coloured bands around headdress which was the common way of distinguishing one side from another during field-days; illustrations of German troops published in France and Britain are the commonest. Some photographs were even more blatantly mis-captioned: the Parisian postcard-publisher Levy, fils & cie, for example, issued a photograph in their *Guerre 1914–1915* series showing a British school cadet platoon taking cover on manoeuvres, but purporting to show British infantry; the fractured English caption 'Infantery laring cower' matches the absurdity of the attribution. Other examples include a number of uses in Britain (even in so august a publication as *The Times History of the War*)[4] of French troop-studies depicting the abortive prewar semi-camouflage experiment with the *tenue réséda*. Other photographs are not deliberately but just misleadingly captioned: for example, a picture of fieldworks entitled 'Loos Trench' may well not depict a scene from that battle, but the demonstration trench of that name erected at

Labels within the sketch: *Kettle*, *water bottle*, *This man has his coat P...*, *...fashion*, *Coats very dirty & torn*, *this man's boot is tied together with a*

An example of the work of the last generation of artist-correspondents, whose work was supplanted by photography: sketches of Russian troops on the Eastern Front by the British correspondent H. C. Seppings-Wright.

Blackpool to show the public what a trench looked like.

A more cynical use was made of mis-captioning photographs. For example, in April 1915 the British *War Illustrated* magazine reproduced a photograph of a German soldier bending over a body, with a caption indicating that this was proof of the habit of German ghouls robbing enemy dead. This most inept forgery is easily detected, for the fallen man was obviously not a Russian, as claimed, but clearly a German wearing a *Pickelhaube* like the 'robber'; and the fact that these helmets have no service covers suggests that the original photograph was also faked, showing troops who were not on campaign. Numerous similar examples may be found, such as the French publication in 1915 of a photograph of corpses resulting from a Russian pogrom in 1905, with the caption that it depicted the crimes of the barbarian Boche in Poland, or the photograph reproduced in several Allied periodicals showing German cavalry officers posing with pre-war steeplechase trophies which they had won, captioned to state that they were vandals with their loot from ravaged Allied homes.

For the most spectacular example of faked photographs, however, reference must be made to a post-war publication, *Death in the Air: the War Diary and Photographs of a Flying Corps Pilot*, London 1933, reprinted by Greenhill Books, 1985. This includes some of the most astonishing 'action' photographs of the war, showing aerial combat at close range, with falling and even colliding aircraft. These images gained considerable fame, and even in comparatively recent works have been reproduced with the author's assertion that he took them with an automatic camera fixed to his aircraft.

Sadly, it appears that the author, W. D. Archer, who really had served in the Royal Flying Corps, had taken no photographs at the time but had photographed models to produce his quite remarkable and lucrative work!

Footnotes

1. Preface to the catalogue of his *Exhibition of Pictures* at Leicester Galleries, 1918.
2. See *The Studio*, Vol. 76 No. 311, 14 February 1919.
3. A selection, though uncaptioned, appear in *The Cameronians: 300 Years of Service*, ed. B.A.S. Leishman, 1989.
4. *The Times History of the War*, III, p. 413.

ART AND PHOTOGRAPHY

non. *A Concise Catalogue of Paintings, Drawings and Sculpture of the First World War 1914–1918*. Imperial War Museum, London, 1963

non. *Der Weltkrieg im Bild: Originalausnahmen des Kriegs-Bild-und Filmamtes aus der modernen Materialschlacht*. Munich, 1928

non. *Kriegsfahrten deutscher Maler: Selbsterlebtes im Weltkrieg 1914–1915*. Bielefeld and Leipzig n.d. (selection of German war artists)

Bairnsfather, B. *Bullets and Billets*. London, 1916

— *Fragments from France*. London, 1916

— *From Mud to Mufti: with Old Bill on all Fronts*. London, 1919

Bone, Muirhead. *The Western Front*. London, 1917 (superb drawings from life)

Carmichael, J. *First World War Photographs*. London, 1989 (important study)

Dodd, Francis. *Admirals of the British Navy: Portraits in Colours; and Generals of the British Army: Portraits in Colours*. both London, 1917

Dodgson, C., Montague, C. E., Ross, R., and Salis, J. *British Artists at the Front*. London, 1918 (introductions by those named; a four-part work on C. R. W. Nevinson, Sir John Lavery, Paul Nash and Eric Kennington, Parts I–IV respectively)

Gallating, A. E. *Art and the Great War*. New York, 1919

Hardie, M., and Sabin, A. K. *War Posters*. London, 1920

Heath Robinson, W. *Heath Robinson at War*. London, 1978 (combined edn. of *Some 'Frightful' War Pictures*, 1915;

Hunlikely!, 1916; and *Fly Papers*, 1919)

Holt, T., and Holt, V. *In Search of the Better 'Ole: The Life, the Works and the Collectables of Bruce Bairnsfather*. Portsmouth, 1985

— *Till the Boys Come Home: The Picture Postcards of the First World War*. London, 1977

Johnson, P. *Front Line Artists*. London, 1978 (important study on the correspondent/illustrators, but mostly pre-Great War)

Jonas, Lucien, *Au Grand QG Anglais: carnet de croquis*. Paris, 1915

— *B. E. F.: carnets de croquis de guerre*. Paris, 1917

— *Les Armées Britanniques: carnet de croquis de guerre*. Paris, 1917

Laffin, J. *The Western Front Illustrated 1914–1918*. Stroud, 1991 (covers the work of the war illustrators, but has much useful information on other topics, tactics, weaponry, etc., as exemplified by the war illustrators)

Laffin, J. *World War I in Post-Cards*. Gloucester, 1988

Malins, Lieutenant G. *How I Filmed the War*. London, 1920

Nevinson, C. R. W. *Modern War Paintings* (intro. P. G. Konody). London, 1917

— *The Great War* (intro. J. E. C. Flitch). London, 1918

Orpen, Sir William. *An Onlooker in France 1917–1919*. London, 1921.

— *War: Paintings and Drawings Executed on the Western Front* (intro. Arnold Bennett). London, 1918

Raemaekers, L. *Raemaekers Cartoon History of the War*, ed. J. M. Allison. London, 1919

— *The Great War: a Neutral's Indictment*. London, 1916

— *The War Cartoons of Louis Raemaekers: a catalogue*. London, 1916

Reeves, N. *Official British Film Propaganda during the First World War*. London, 1982

Reid, J. B. *Australian Artists at War*. Melbourne, 1977

Rickards, M. *Posters of the First World War*. London, 1968

Rothenstein, J. *British Artists and the War*. London, 1931

Stanley, P. *What Did You Do in the War, Daddy?: A Visual History of Propaganda Posters; a Selection from the Australian War Memorial*. Melbourne, 1983 (includes Second World War)

Talbot Kelly, R. B. *A Subaltern's Odyssey: A Memoir of the Great War 1915–1917*. London, 1980 (distinguished by notable drawings made at the time)

Thomason, J. W., Jnr. *Fix Bayonets!: With the U.S. Marine Corps in France 1917–18*. New York, 1925, r/p London, 1989 (an outstanding personal account with splendid illustrations drawn at the time)

Wilkinson, Norman. *A Brush with Life*. London, 1969 (autobiography: inventor of dazzle camouflage)

— *The Dardanelles: Colour Sketches from Gallipoli*. London, 1915 (splendid colour illustrations made at the time)

(Some political and other cartoons, including work by Bernard Partridge and H. M. Bateman, in *Mr. Punch's History of the Great War*. London, 1919.)

MYTHS AND LEGENDS

Associated with the evaluation of source-material is the existence of myths and stories which arose during the war. Most were the usual type of transitory rumour which abounds in all wars, but others were of longer duration and attained considerable notoriety. At one time any fanciful story might be described as 'Russians with snow on their boots', referring to a story briefly prevalent in Britain that a Russian army had been sent to Britain and had been seen on troop-trains heading south; a later embellishment to prove their nationality was added to the effect that they still had snow clinging to their boots. The origin of this story may well be the transfer of the Lovat Scouts from Blairgowrie to Huntingdon in 1914, when English civilians, seeing men in unusual bonnets and speaking a foreign dialect, enquired of their origin; and received the reply 'Ross-shire', which in Highland brogue was pronounced 'Roscha'.[1]

Some stories were resurrected later and presented as either 'fact' or as unresolved mysteries. One which surfaced more than forty years after the war was an absurd story that August von Mackensen, one of Germany's most distinguished generals, was actually the British hero Sir Hector Macdonald ('Fighting Mac'), who had committed suicide in 1903 in the face of an alleged homosexual scandal; but who, according to the story, faked his death and entered German service in the place of the real August von Mackensen, who was terminally ill. It is conceivable that the story was started by Germany for propaganda reasons (although no direct evidence of this would appear to exist), or that it was nothing more than the refusal to accept the fact of the death of a revered leader – not an uncommon phenomenon.[2]

To illustrate the nature of the more durable of 'war legends', some are considered here.

The Angel of Mons

A considerably mythology grew up in 1914 concerning the Angel (or Angels) of Mons: the story that the BEF had been saved from destruction by the intervention of one or more denizens of Heaven, whose appearance had caused the Germans to fall back. The legend appears to have originated in a short story published in the London *Evening News* on 29 September 1914, written by Arthur Machen, an author of mildly supernatural stories and sometime member of the mystical society, The Hermetic Order of the Golden Dawn. This story, *The Bowmen*, one of several on the same theme, described (by implication rather than explicit description) how Saint George and the ghosts of medieval archers – doubtless Henry V's 'yew hedge' – came to the aid of the beleaguered British troops at Mons, and helped them repel the German attacks. Machen himself admitted that 'so many queer complications' had entered into the story, with 'such odd and unforeseen consequences', that he ought to apologize for starting it all.[3]

Shortly after, the editors of *The Occult Review* and *Light* inquired about the foundation of the story; Machen assured them that it was fiction. Several parish magazines sough permission to reprint it, one clergyman refuting Machen by insisting that the story *must* have been true. From there Machen wrote, 'the snowball of rumour' was set rolling, 'til it is now swollen to a monstrous size'.[4] From this beginning the story appears to have been transformed into one which described how it was not a spectral army of long-dead Englishmen but one or more Archangels who had come to

Propaganda even spread to official manuals: how to negotiate with the enemy, from the British 1918 Physical Training pamphlet.

Fig. 1.

Fig. 2.

he aid of the BEF, and second- or third-hand reports appeared in which the writers remained anonymous, or had been told by someone who knew a witness of the vision, and so on. A Miss Phyllis Campbell contributed an article to *The Occult Review* (August 1915) entitled *The Angelic Leaders*, in which she stated that not only was the story true, but that 'everyone has seen them who has fought from Mons to Ypres'.[5] As Machen himself commented, if this were so it was unusual that no admitted eye-witnesses had presented themselves (which adherents of the story claimed was for fear of ridicule or damage to their career). Yet some stories which did appear, albeit anonymously, had a convincing level of uncertainty about what *had* been seen; and curiously, a supposed letter from an anonymous lieutenant-colonel, published in the *Evening News* on 14 September, described in a rather sceptical manner how during the night of 27 August his unit had been accompanied by what he 'fancied' were squadron after squadron of cavalry, glimpsed in dim light, which were visible to many members of the column for about twenty minutes. They disappeared when the night became darker, but so convinced were the officers that cavalry had been there, that at the next halt a party was sent out to reconnoitre, and found nothing. The anonymous writer admitted that all were 'dog tired and overtaxed', but remarked how extraordinary it was that so many men should see the same thing, phenomenon, hallucination or whatever.

All manner of strange reports were made in the succeeding months, from Germans suffering from arrow-wounds (reverting to the medieval bowmen) to a story that an account had been given by a brigadier-general, overheard by the Revd. C. M. Chavasse, brother of the double VC winner, Noel Chavasse. Questions might still be posed: was Machen correct in his recollection that the story was entirely his invention, or (though he denied it) had he been influenced by other accounts, perhaps of mass hallucination, or simply the misinterpretation by men who were 'dog tired' of something perfectly explicable? Despite the lack of eye-witness evidence discovered by later inquiries, the story did gain considerable credence (even an *Angel of Mons* waltz was composed!), and there is at least one curious footnote to the story. An employee of the author's grandfather was totally convinced that he *had* seen the angel; and although before the war he was known as a man over-fond of hard drink, after Mons he became not only teetotal but a pillar of the community, apparently for no other reason than what he claimed to have experienced on the retreat.

Atrocities

Probably one of the most contentious issues to arise from the early part of the war were the stories of atrocities perpetrated by the invading German armies upon the civilians of territory they occupied, and to a lesser extent upon wounded or captured enemy soldiers. In the sense used by the Allied press, atrocities were crimes of unbelievable barbarism, not the drunkenness, looting and vandalism from which no army was immune (Frank Richards recorded that upon seeing the glories of Amiens Cathedral, one old soldier remarked that it would be a fine place to loot!) No crime or perversion was too foul to be included in the Allied propaganda, cannibalism being about the only act of which the invading Germans were not accused. The wholesale slaughter of civilians was a common accusation; no less common were the most appalling tales of child-murder, mutilation and every depravity which could be imagined. Official investigations were made and reports published (notably the British Bryce Report) giving catalogues of outrages the like of which, as once contemporary report commented, were believed possible only of the Kurds of Asia Minor,[6] while another stated that even under the Assyrians there could be found 'no such refinement of atrocity'[7] as those which received the official sanction of the German high command and government.

Such stories were exploited to the full: the culprit was not described as Germany but the 'frightfulness' of the Hun, whose ruthless and bestial conduct was described by the Allies as German *Kultur*: 'the aggrandisement by any and every means of Germany and the Germans; the imposition upon the whole world of the German dominion; the ruthless destruction of anything that may stand in the way of that object'.[8] Thus, the reports published by the Allies concerning German outrages were not unbiased (indeed, one section-heading in *German Atrocities: an Official Investigation*, J. H. Morgan, London, 1916, is 'Bestiality of German Officers and Men', which states that 'sodomy and the rape of little children did undoubtedly occur on a very large scale').[9] More careful investigation, however, proved that some of the most lurid cases were either unprovable or untrue: despite financial incentives no photographic evidence for the mutilation of children was forthcoming, and a celebrated case which created a storm in Britain concerning the murder and mutilation of a British nurse was found to have been the invention of an unbalanced girl.

However, it would be naïve to suggest that the atrocity stories were completely without foundation, as any army might be expected to contain a representative selection of society, including the brutal and perverted, and the circumstances of the German invasion of Belgium and France would inevitably give rise to opportunities for such individuals to exercise their passions. There would appear to be authentic examples of revolting acts, but to suggest that the entire German nation was composed of perverted individuals inspired by alcohol or insane blood-lust is so fanciful that it is perhaps surprising that it was believed so widely at the time.

Initially, however, the 'beastliness of the Hun' was not always emphasized even in the most 'patriotic' works; in one such (*Atkins at War*, ed. J. A. Kilpatrick, London, 1914) the opinion of the German army was given predictably ('if it weren't for dread of their officers the Germans would surrender wholesale . . . Their shooting is laughable, they couldn't hit a haystack in an entry'),[10] yet alongside these are stories of German chivalry towards prisoners and wounded, including a statement from a captured British officer who claimed that he 'could not have been better treated had he been the Crown Prince', and that stories of 'brutality are only exceptions, and there are exceptions in every army'.[11]

The prevalence of atrocity stories in the Allied press even affected the attitude of those at the Front; Aubrey Herbert, wounded and briefly captured during the Battle of Mons, felt sure that a red-bearded German with a serrated bayonet who approached him was about to commit an atrocity, having read of such things in English newspapers; he was pleasantly surprised when the German said 'we're all comrades' and gave him water, wine and cigarettes. He could scarcely have been treated with more kindness; the passing German troops looked at him as they passed until shooed on by their officers with, 'Schnell, Kinder!', and their solicitude even extended to stripping German and British corpses for garments with which to cover him. Until liberated by the French a week later, German guards were posted to *protect* the Allied wounded.[12]

Apart from outrages committed by crazed individuals, there was greater foundation for the stories of a different form of atrocity, the mass execution of innocent civilians. These undoubtedly occurred, and were not only tolerated by the German high command but were regarded as an instrument of policy in the subjugation of captured territory.

The invading German army of 1914 was inexperienced in combat, and justifiably afraid of the danger from *francs-tireurs*, a term used somewhat loosely to describe armed civilians acting as snipers in guerrilla activity. German forces had suffered from these in 1870–1, and the spectre of a hostile population in the army's rear required very serious consideration. So concerned were the Germans over the danger from the *franc-tireur* that any shot coming from an unexpected direction might be regarded as originating from this source, even though it might have come from a straggler from the Allied armies. The solution to the problem – which was probably more imagined than real – was collective responsibility: if *franc-tireur* activity were suspected, not only was it acknowledged policy to burn down the area from which the shot came, but to execute civilians by way of reprisal. It was such acts, which might be described as officially-sanctioned atrocity, that were the real horrors of this stage of the war. Neutral observers in Belgium at this time were careful to stress that such acts were not the result of blood-lust or indiscipline, and some American journalists reported the troops as being well-disciplined, disinclined to loot and who treated civilians with respect, and that the only atrocity stories they had encountered were told at second- or third-hand and were quite unprovable.

However, the policy of punishing suspected *franc-tireur* activity, or of overawing the population to prevent such, had the most awful consequences. Individual executions and burning of property were soon followed by mass executions of 'hostages', which were occurring as early as mid-August

1914. Two outrages in particular attracted most attention. The most serious occurred at Dinant, where on 21 and 2[ ] August no less than 639 civilians were shot in cold blood.[ ] The youngest of these hostages was Mariette Fivet, aged [ ] weeks, presumably the child of Fernand Fivet, a joiner, sho[ ] at the same time; more than one-sixth were women an[ ] children. It is interesting to note the reaction of thre[ ] German medical officers who chanced upon the burials c[ ] 135 civilians shot by the 101st Grenadiers in the Quartie[ ] des Rivages. A local barrister was supervising the burial[ ] when the German doctors arrived: he lifted an overcoa[ ] which concealed the bodies of four children (seven aged tw[ ] years or less were numbered among the victims). Th[ ] Germans turned away, one saying 'Malheur! Malheur[ ] Malheur!'[14]

Much importance was placed by Allied propaganda o[ ] vandalism by the German Army, although some of this wa[ ] over-stated and some might even be justified: Reim[ ] Cathedral, for example, shelled by German artillery, ma[ ] have been in use as a French observation-post. Howeve[ ] following a Belgian raid on German positions near th[ ] occupied city of Louvain on 25 August 1914, in the course o[ ] which there was minor suspected *franc-tireur* activity, on th[ ] following day the German military governor of Brussels[ ] General von Luttwitz, ordered German troops to destro[ ] Louvain as a reprisal. Although less of the city was razed[ ] than first reported – only about one-eighth – the damag[ ] was immense, civilians were executed during five days c[ ] pillage, and the world-famous library with its uniqu[ ] collection of medieval maniscripts was destroyed. (Dieri[ ] Bouts' altarpiece in the church of St. Pierre was saved from[ ] the flames only by the intervention of a German officer.[ ] The burning of Louvain and similar incidents, not only[ ] condoned but actually initiated by German commanders in[ ] a deliberate policy of cowing the inhabitants of occupied[ ] areas, provided a factual basis upon which the more[ ] hysterical Allied propaganda stories were built.

Atrocity stories did not originate exclusively on th[ ] Western Front, though these received most publicity. Th[ ] whole of the Central Powers were the target of Allied[ ] attacks, one of which was headed 'The Supreme Develop[ ] ment of Teutonic-Ottoman Methods of Barbarism'[15] and[ ] included such sub-headings as 'Methods by Which Austro-[ ] Hungarians Turned their Men into Devils'; 'League o[ ] Scientific Savagery between Teuton and Turk', etc.[16] Th[ ] same kind of allegations were made about events on th[ ] Eastern Front, though the Turkish massacres of Armenian[ ] were usually not accorded the same coverage as events i[ ] northern Europe. Propaganda was somewhat selective: [ ] photograph of an Austrian trench-club, for example, wa[ ] exhibited as representing 'culture at the stage of canni[ ] balism',[17] though the fact was not mentioned that simila[ ] weapons were not at all unknown in Allied armies. Evidence[ ] of massacres in the Balkans (not unusual for warfare in tha[ ] area) was less easy to obtain, though much was made o[ ] official Austro–Hungarian orders concerning the taking o[ ] hostages (to be executed if any hostile action occurred in the locality), and the fact that no un-uniformed person found under arms was to be taken prisoner (perhaps understandable in an area renowned for its bandits but most unfortunate when it is considered that many genuine Serbian and Montenegrin soldiers had been forced to fight in civilian clothing because of lack of uniforms).

In the later stages of the war the atrocity stories receded, though the Allies made good propaganda use of German deportation of civilians from occupied areas. Among events which caused especial outrage were the execution of the British nurse Edith Cavell (though in the strictest sense she might have been regarded as an enemy agent and thus liable to suffer the death penalty), and the sinking of the liner *Lusitania*. The German contention that this passenger ship was carrying munitions was ignored, and a privately-produced medallion designed by the German sculptor Karl Goetz was reproduced and sold for the benefit of the St. Dunstan's hospital for blinded servicemen. This medal, intended as a criticism of Cunard for allowing the liner to

A typically uncompromising, savage Louis Raemaekers cartoon: 'Neutral America and the Hun', in which Uncle Sam stands by with hands in pockets, observing Germany with hands and apron dripping blood.

Louis Raemaekers.

sail despite the U-boat threat, was portrayed by the Allies as 'proof positive that such crimes are not merely regarded favourably, but are given every encouragement in the land of Kultur'.[18] The fact that Goetz showed artillery on the *Lusitania*'s deck was a boon to the Allies, demonstrating proof of the German untruths.

There were some notable counter-claims over atrocities allegedly committed by the Allies: the Germans issued a 'White Book' of testaments on oath of alleged mutilations and murders perpetrated upon Germans troops by Belgian soldiers and civilians, which were used to justify reprisal killings and burnings; the stories it contained were mostly as unlikely as some of those circulated by the Allies. The German press was equally adept at inventing horrific stories (priests who served poisoned food and drink to German guests was a favourite tale), but the Germans were unable to find many true incidents which could be exaggerated. The shooting of the crew of *U 27* by the British Q-Ship *Baralong* in August 1915 was perhaps a genuine grievance, but probably no worse than the actions of the U-boats themselves. Claims were also made, probably with some justification, about atrocities committed against German troops on the Eastern Front and in the Balkans, though these did not attain the same notoriety as matters on the Western Front.

Few atrocity claims were concerned with actual combat, though some acts of war were condemned as unfair (German shelling of British coastal towns, aerial bombardment of areas away from the seat of war, the use of poison gas, flame-throwers, serrated bayonets, explosive bullets, the firing upon medical parties, and the like). There were, of course, violations in the accepted rules of war: machine-gunners who fired until the last moment and then tried to surrender often did not receive the quarter they sought, and there were probably many instances of prisoners being killed (British accounts, for example, note a trick of dropping a live grenade into a prisoner's pocket), but such deeds were more the result of the stress of battle and the dehumanizing aspect of the war rather than premeditated outrages.

The Lost Battalion

The 'fog of war' was thicker and more impenetrable during much of the Great War than in many previous wars, so that often it is almost impossible to determine the events of an action in minute detail. A case which attained some notoriety was the apparent disappearance of an entire infantry battalion on 12 August 1915, in one of the most curious incidents of the war.

Committed to action with the British 163 Brigade in the area of Kujak Anafarta, part of the attempted breakout from Suvla, the 1/5th Battalion. Norfolk Regiment pushed on ahead of other units, under the bold leadership of Colonel Sir Horace Proctor-Beauchamp, Bt., a veteran of the Sudan, Suakin and the Boer War. Some men fell out with wounds or exhaustion, but then, as described by Sir Ian Hamilton in his official dispatch, 'there happened a very mysterious thing'; the colonel continued to advance with the remains of his battalion, and 'nothing more was ever seen or heard of any of them . . . Not one of them ever came back'.[19]

The mysterious disappearance of the battalion led to inquiries after the war, the Turks denying all knowledge of their fate. Among the wilder theories advanced in later years was one which implied the interference of extra-terrestials, presumably involving the abduction or destruction of the unit by UFOs! A recent study, however,[20] appears to have ended such speculation. Some twelve officers and something over 100 men appear to have been lost (far from an entire battalion but with a high proportion of its officers), most of whom appear to have been discovered in a mass grave by a Graves Registration Unit after the war. A further mystery is raised, however: if 112 of the 1,074 graves at the Azmak Cemetery, Suvla, are of men exhumed at this time, why was the myth of the 'lost battalion' permitted to continue? Despite an officer's watch being discovered in Constantinople (before the discovery of the bodies), why did the Turks deny all knowledge? If the rumour that all 112 bodies were shot in the head were true, is there an implication that an atrocity was not investigated because of concern over political relations with Turkey? There are many such minor mysteries over the events of the war, to which a definitive solution would appear, at this distance in time, to be unobtainable.

Footnotes

1. This story is recounted in full in Lord Lovat's *March Past*, London, 1978, pp. 78–9.
2. See *Death Before Dishonour: the True Story of Fighting Mac*, T. Royle, Edinburgh, 1982, pp. 147–52.
3. *The Angels of Mons: The Bowmen and other Legends of the War*, A. Machen, London 1915, pp. 5, 7.
4. Ibid., p. 15.
5. Quoted in Ibid., p. 83.
6. *German Atrocities: an Official Investigation*, J. H. Morgan, London, 1916, p. 62.
7. *The Great War*, ed. H. W. Wilson and J. A. Hammerton, London, 1917, VIII, p. 470.
8. *The Times History of the War*, London, 1914, I, p. 402.
9. Morgan, op. cit., p. 62.
10. *Atkins at War*, p. 103.
11. Ibid., p. 108.
12. *Mons, Anzac and Kut*. London, 1919, p. 72; the story is also recounted in *Moments of Memory*, p. 206, Hon. H. Asquith, London, 1937.
13. The total of 647 given in *The Atrocities at Dinant*, E. Gerard, Dinant, n.d., includes four townsmen who died in exile and four killed elsewhere.
14. Ibid., p. 23–4.
15. *The Great War*, op. cit., VIII.
16. Ibid., p. 453.
17. Ibid., p. 470.
18. Text which accompanied the re-struck medal.
19. Despatch, 11 December 1915; in *Ian Hamilton's Despatches from the Dardanelles*. London, 1917, p. 231.
20. 'Exploding a Myth: The Vanished Battalion'. H. Giblin, in *Journal of the Orders and Medals Research Society*, spring, 1981.

The poppy is a symbol usually regarded as peculiar to Britain as a token of remembrance; yet it features in this German painting of an isolated Western Front grave of 1914–15. (Print after W. Werner)

VI
MISCELLANEA

MISCELLANEA

PLACE-NAMES

Many place-names mentioned in sources of the 1914–18 War are now changed. Spellings of some have simply been modernized and have altered little (e.g., Cettigne, Nish); others have changed so radically as to be unrecognizable without a guide. The following includes a number of the most significant, but does not include those with a universally accepted anglicized spelling of their proper name (e.g., Brussels/Bruxelles, Vienna/Wien), nor names with more than one accepted non-native spelling, e.g., Pskov/Pskoff.

Old name	New name	Old name	New name	Old name	New name	Old name	New name
Adrianople	Edirne	Danzig	Gdansk	Laibach	Ljubljana	Pressburg	Bratislava
Agram	Zagreb	Dorpat	Tartu	Lemberg	Lvov	Ragusa	Dubrovnik
Altenburg	Magyaróvár	Elisavetpol	Kirovabad	Libau	Liepāja	Revel	Tallinn
Angra Pequena	Luderitz (SW Africa)	Erivan	Yerevan	Marburg	Maribor	Salisbury	Harare
		Esseg	Osijek	Marienburg	Malborg	Salonika	Thessaloniki
Breslau	Wroclaw	Fiume	Rijeka	Memel	Klaipeda	Smyrna	Izmir
Brünn	Brno	Gumbinnen	Gusev	Monastir	Bitola	Tiflis	Tbilisi
Cettigne	Cetinje	Helsingfors	Helsinki	Namaqualand	Southern Namibia	Troppau	Opava
Constantinople	Istanbul	Hermannstadt	Sibiu (Romanian), Nagyszeben (Hungarian)			Uskub	Skopje
Czernowitz	Cernauti (Romanian), Chernovtsy (Russian)			Nish	Nis	Vilna	Vilnyus
		Königsberg	Kaliningrad	Pernau	Pärnu	Weissenburg	Gyula-fehérvár
Damaraland	Northern Namibia	Kovno	Kaunas	Petrograd	St. Petersburg (Leningrad)		
		Kronstadt	Brassó	Philippopolis	Plovdiv		
				Posen	Poznan		

Alternative names used at the time included: Acre/Akko; Aleppo/Haleb; Jaffra/Yafa; Saidon/Saida. Capretto was known as Karfreit to the Austro-Hungarians.

MEASUREMENTS

Although most of the combatant nations used metric or imperial units of measurement, several had distinctive systems, listed here with imperial equivalents:

Length

China: 1 ts'un = 1.41 inches; 10 ts'un = 1 ch'ih; 10 ch'ih = 1 chang; 1 li = approx. ⅓ mile.

Egypt: 1 kirat = 1.125 inches; 1 kadam = 12 inches; 1 pik = 22.83 inches; 1 kassaba = 11.6 feet.

India: 1 ungul = ¾ inches; 48 ungul = 1 guz (1 yard); 1 koss = 2,000 yards.

Japan: 1 sun = 1.1931 inches; 10 sun = 1 shaku; 10 shaku = 1 jo (3.314 yards); 1 ri = 2.44 miles.

Persia: 1 zar = 40.95 inches; 1 farsakh = approx. 3.87 miles.

Russia: 1 arshin = 28 inches; 3 arshin = 1 sajen (7 feet); 500 sajen = 1 verst (1,166.6 yards).

Turkey: used metric system, plus: 1 arshin = 26¾ inches

Weight

China: 1 tael = 1.333 ounces; 16 tael = 1 chin (1.333 pounds); 100 chin = 1 picul (133.3 pounds)

Egypt: 1 rottolo = 0.9804 pounds; 100 rottolo = 1 cantar (98.04 pounds)

India: 1 chittak = approx. 2 ounces; 16 chittak = 1 seer (approx. 2.204 pounds); 1 maund = 82.287 pounds

Japan: 1 fun = 5.797 grams; 10 fun = 1 momme (57.97 grams)

Persia: 1 seer = 1.136 grams; 1 ratal = 1.014 pounds; 1 maun = 6.49 pounds

Russia: 1 zolotnik = 64.84 grams; 1 funt = 0.9028 pounds; 40 funt = 1 pood (36.113 pounds)

Turkey: 1 oke = 22.826 pounds; 44 okes = 1 kantar (124.36 pounds); 78 okes = 100 kilograms.

Capacity

China: 1 ho = 2 pints; 1 shêng = approx. 20 pints.

Egypt: 1 ardeb = 7.4457 bushels.

India: 1 seer = 1.760 pints.

Japan: 1 gö = 0.3176 pints; 10 gö = 1 shö (3.176 pints); 1 to = 3.703 gallons; 1 koku = 4.962 bushels.

Persia: 1 collothun = 1.809 gallons.

Russia: 1 garnets = 2.88 quarts; 1 chetverik = 5.77 gallons; 1 osmina = 2.88 bushels; 1 chetvest = 5.77 bushels.

Turkey: 1 kileh = approx. 1 bushel.

USA: 1 pint (dry measure) = 0.9694 imperial pints; 1 pint (spirit) = 0.8331 imperial pints; 1 pint (beer) = 1.017 imperial pints; 1 gallon = 0.9694 imperial gallons; 1 bushel = 0.9694 imperial bushels.

CURRENCIES

The currencies of the combatant nations are given below, with approximate British value for 1914:

Austria-Hungary: 100 heller or filler = 1 krone (10d. sterling).
Bulgaria: 100 stotinki = 1 lev (9½d.)
Canada: 100 cents = 1 doliar (4s. 1⅓d.)
China: 100 cents = 1 yuan or dollar (2s.)
East Africa: used Indian rupees.
Egypt: 100 piastres = 1 Egyptian pound (£1.0s. 3¾d.)
France: 100 centimes = 1 franc (9½d.)
Germany: 100 pfennige = 1 mark (11¾d.)
Greece: 100 lepta = 1 drachma (9½d.)
India: 192 pies = 64 pice = 16 annas = 1 rupee (1s. 4d.)
Italy: 100 centesimi = 1 lira (9½d.)
Japan: 100 sen = 1 yen (2s. 0½d.)
Newfoundland: 100 cents = 1 dollar (4s. 2d.)
Persia: 1,000 dinaro = 20 shahis = 1 silver kran (4¾d.); 1 gold tomran (7s. 1d.)
Roumania: 100 bani = 1 lei (9½d.)
Russia: 100 kopecks = 1 rouble (2s. 1⅓d.)
Serbia: 100 paras = 1 dinar (9½d.)
Siam: 100 satangs = 1 tical (1s. 6½d.)
Turkey: 100 piastres = 1 Turkish gold pound (lira) (18s.)
Uganda: used Indian rupee.
USA: 100 cents = 1 dollar (4s. 1½d.)

The following is an approximate value of exchange-rate of the currencies of the principal combatants, compared to a British £1 sterling. Figures quoted are for the immediate pre-war period, at the armistice (for currencies of enemy or occupied countries or those not quoted on the London currency market, the highest rate during the war is given), and at the end of 1920 to demonstrate the effects of the war. All figures are approximate as there were many minor fluctuations:

	1914	Armistice	1920
Austria	24.5 kronen (to £1)	wartime, 53	1,550
Belgium	25.2 francs	wartime, 63.5	57
Brazil	15 milreis	17	24
Canada	4.95 dollars	4.86	4.1
China (Shanghai)	8.5 tael	4	5.5
Egypt	97.5 piastres	97.2	97.5
Finland	25.4 marks	wartime, 44.5	115
France	25 francs	25.8	59.5
Germany	20.5 marks	wartime, 32	258

Greece	25.1 drachmas	1918–20, 49.5	48
India	15 rupees	13.3	13.7
Italy	27 lire	30.3	101
Roumania	25.2 lei	1918–20, 325	285
Russia	10.2 roubles	wartime, 43	not quoted
Serbia	25.2 dinar	wartime, 145	130
USA	4.9 dollars	4.77	3.54

The purchasing power of the £1 at the end of 1920 reflects the economic consequences of the war upon various states. Compared with its pre-war value as £1, in late 1920 it was worth 14s. 6d. in New York, 18s. 2d. in India, £2.7s. 4d. in France, £4. 0s. 6d. in Italy, £12.12s. 8d. in Germany, £12.16s. in Czechoslovakia, £63. 9s. 9d. in Austria, and £110 4s. in Poland.

A wartime rule-of-thumb for Allied troops on the Western Front was expressed as the following table of the principal currencies:

German	British	French
20 marks	£1	25 francs
5 marks	5s.	6fr. 25 cent.
1 thaler (3 marks)	3s.	3fr. 75 cent.
1 mark (100 pfennige)	1s.	1fr. 25 cent.
25 pf.	3d.	31¼ cent.

(In *Vade-Mecum for the use of Officers and Interpreters in the Present Campaign*, p. 227, E. Plumon, Paris & London, 1917.)

Prices

The following details the increase in the retail price of food as a result of the war, based on the average food price in July 1914 being represented as 100 units. By January 1919 the comparison in units was as follows:

Belgium	figure not available for 1919; January 1920 396, rising to 493 by January 1921.
Italy (Rome)	259 (in Milan 309)
Germany	253 (328 by July 1919)
France	248 (429 by January 1921)
Great Britain	230
Canada	186
USA	181 (169 by January 1921)
New Zealand	145
Australia	140
South Africa	135

RATIONS

British daily ration, 1914:
1¼lb fresh or frozen meat, or 1lb preserved or salt meat; 1¼lb bread, or 1lb biscuit or flour; 4oz bacon; 3oz cheese; ⅝oz tea; 4oz jam; 3oz sugar; ½oz salt; 1/36oz pepper; 1/20 oz mustard; 8oz fresh or 2oz dried vegetables; ⅒ gill lime juice

if fresh vegetables not issued;* ½ gill rum;* not exceeding 2oz tobacco per week.*
*at discretion of commanding general.
The following substitutions were permitted if necessary: 4oz oatmeal or rice instead of 4oz bread or biscuit; 1/30oz

chocolate instead of 1/6oz tea; 1 pint porter instead of 1 ration spirit; 4oz dried fruit instead of 4oz jam; 4oz butter, lard or margarine, or 1/2gill oil, instead of 4oz bacon.

British daily ration, India:

1lb fresh meat; 1lb bread; 3oz bacon; 1lb potatoes; 1oz tea; 2 1/2oz sugar; 1/2oz salt; 1/36oz pepper.

British daily ration, Indian troops:

1/4lb fresh meat; 1/8lb potatoes; 1/3oz tea; 1/2oz salt; 1 1/2lb atta; 4oz dhall; 2oz ghee; 1/6oz chillies; 1/6oz turmeric; 1/3oz ginger; 1/6oz garlic; 1oz gur.

British iron ration, carried in the field:

1lb preserved meat; 12oz biscuit; 5/8oz tea; 2oz sugar; 1/2oz salt; 3oz cheese; 1oz meat extract (2 cubes).

German daily ration, 1914 measured in grams; ounce equivalent in parentheses):

750g (26 1/2oz) bread, or 500g (17 1/2oz) field biscuit, or 400g (14oz) egg biscuit; 375g (13oz) fresh or frozen meat, or 200g (7oz) preserved meat; 1,500g (53oz) potatoes, or 125–250g (4 1/2–9oz) vegetables, or 60g (2oz) dried vegetables, or 600g (21oz) mixed potatoes and dried vegetables; 25g (9/10oz) coffee, or 3g (1/10oz) tea; 20g (7/10oz) sugar; 25g (9/10oz) salt; two cigars and two cigarettes, or 1oz pipe tobacco, or 9/10oz plug tobacco, or 1/5oz snuff; at discretion of commanding officer: 0.17 pint spirits, 0.44 pint wine, 0.88 pint beer.

The meat ration was reduced progressively during the war, and one meatless day per week was introduced from June 1916; by the end of that year it was 250g (8 3/4oz) fresh meat or 150g (5 1/4oz) preserved, or 200g (7oz) fresh meat for support and train personnel. At the same time the sugar ration was only 17g (6/10oz).

German iron ration:

250g (8.8oz) biscuit; 200g (7oz) preserved meat or 170g (6oz) bacon; 150g (5.3oz) preserved vegetables; 25g (9/10oz) coffee; 25g (9/10oz) salt.

COCKADES

Despite the use of service dress, the armies of a number of states continued the ancient practice of wearing coloured cockades (principally on the head-dress) to indicate national identity; German troops wore two, the *Reich* or imperial cockade, and that of their individual state. The following were worn during the war:

Anhalt: green
Baden: yellow/red/yellow
Bavaria: white/light-blue/white
Belgium: black/yellow/red
Bremen: white/red/white
Brunswick: blue/yellow/blue
Bulgaria: white/green/red
Czechoslovakia: red/white divided diagonally
Estonia: blue/black/white
Finland: white, light-blue ring
Germany (*Reich*): black/white/red
Greece: light-blue/white/light-blue
Hamburg: white with red cross
Hesse: white with two red stripes
Italy: red/white/green
Lippe: yellow/red
Lübeck: white with red Maltese Cross
Mecklenburg: blue/yellow/red
Oldenburg: blue/red/blue
Poland: crimson/white
Prussia: black/white/black
Reuss: yellow/red/black
Roumania: blue/yellow/red
Russia: white/orange/black
Saxe-Weimar: green/
yellow/black
Saxony: white/green/white
Saxon Duchies: green/white/green
Schwarzburg-Rudolstadt: blue/white/blue
Schwarzburg-Sonderhausen: white/blue/white
Serbia: white/blue/red
Waldeck: yellow/red/black
Württemberg: black/red/black

'ACES'

'Ace' status for pilots was first given by France, which considered any aviator with five victories as an 'ace'; other nations followed suit, though Britain never officially adopted the system, and Germany considered a pilot an 'ace' only after he had shot down ten enemy aircraft. The following were pilots with more than 40 victories (including the destruction of balloons):

80   M. von Richthofen (Germany)
75   R. Fonck (France)
73   E. Mannock (Britain)
72   W. Bishop (Britain)
62   E. Udet (Germany)
60   R. Collishaw (Britain)
57   J. McCudden (Britain)

54   A. Beauchamp-Proctor, D. MacLaren (Britain); G. Guynemer (France)
53   W. Barker (Britain); E. Löwenhardt (Germany)
48   W. Voss (Germany)
47   R. Little (Britain)
46   P. Fullard, G. McElroy (Britain)
45   C. Nungesser (France); F. Rumey (Germany)

44   A. Ball, J. Gilmore (Britain); R. Berthold (Germany)
43   P. Bäumer (Germany)
41   T. Hazell (Britain); J. Jacobs, B. Lörzer (Germany); G.

Madon (France)
40   O. Boelcke, F. Büchner, L. von Richthofen (Germany);
      G. Brunowski (Austria-Hungary); J. Jones (Britain)

The most successful pilots of other nations were: Belgium:
W. Coppens, 37; Italy: F. Baracca, 34; USA: E. Ricken-
backer, 26; Russia: A. Kazakov, 17.

NATIONAL STATISTICS

In statistics of area and population, in some cases conflicting information may be encountered in contemporary
sources, partly as a result of the usual fluctuation of
population over a period of time, and partly because in a
number of cases no accurate statistics were available; even
the area of some states could only be estimated, especially in
the case of colonial territories with unresolved boundaries.
Many of the following are approximations; dates are given

for statistics based upon a regular census, but in some
contemporary sources statistics are recorded as uprated
estimates rather than dated ennumerations. In some cases
normal population trends were complicated by such factors
as immigration; the population of the USA, for example,
increased by some 14.9 per cent between 1910 and 1920
(91,972,266 to 105,710,620).

Nations:

Country	Area (sq. miles)	Population
Arabia (not under Turkish control)	about 1 million	12 million
Australia	2,974,581	4,455,005 (1911); 1917 estimate 4.9 million
Austria-Hungary	Austria 115,802	28,568,000
	Hungary 125,609	20,886,000
	Bosnia-Herzegovina 19,768	1,898,000
Belgium	11,373	7,424,784 (1910)
Brazil	3,291,400	24 million[1]
Bulgaria	43,305	5.5 million
Canada	3,729,665	7,206,643 (1911)
China	4 million	320 million[2]
Costa Rica	23,000	421,000
Cuba	44,100	2.4 million
Czechoslovakia	55,000	13,596,000 (1921)
Estonia	18,300	1.5 million[3]
France	207,075 (plus Corsica 3,300)	39,601,509 (1911) (Corsica 289,000)
Germany (main component states):	208,781	64,926,000 (1910)
Prussia	134,619	40,165,000
Bavaria	29,292	6,887,000
Württemberg	7,534	2,438,000
Saxony	5,789	4,807,000
Great Britain	121,432	45,370,530 (1911)
Greece	41,933[4]	4.8 million
Guatemala	47,900	2 million
Haiti	10,000	1.5–2 million
Honduras	44,000	560,000 (1916)
Italy	110,632	35,597,784 (1911)
Japan	147,650	53,596,894 (1914)
Latvia	25,096	1,515,000 (1919)
Liberia	40,000	2 million
Luxemburg	998	259,900

Country	Area (sq. miles)	Population
Montenegro	5,600	515,000
Newfoundland	42,734 (plus about 120,000 Labrador)	242,619 (1911, including Labrador)
New Zealand	104,751	1,099,449 (1916, plus about 50,000 Maoris, not included in census)
Nicaragua	49,000	746,000 (1917)
Panama	32,000	336,700 (1911)[5]
Persia	628,000	9.5 million
Philippines	115,026	10,350,000 (1918)
Portugal	35,490	5.96 million (1911, including Azores & Madeira)
Roumania	53,671[6]	7,510,000
Russia	8,247,624 (of which Russia proper 1,867,737, Siberia 4,831,882; plus Finland 125,689, Poland 43,804, inland lakes 317,468)	158,942,000, of which Russia proper 125,683,800; plus Finland 3,197,000, Poland 11,960,000
Serbia	33,728[7]	2,912,000 (1910); approx. 4.5 million 1914
Siam	195,000	8,150,000 (1910–11)
South Africa	473,954	5,973,394 (1911)
Turkey: component parts:		
Turkey	282,144	14,549,000
Arabia	170,300	1,050,000
Mesopotamia	143,250	2 million
Syria	114,530	3,675,000
USA	3,574,659	91,972,266 (1910)

Colonies:

Country	Area (sq. miles)	Population
Belgium:		
Belgian Congo	900,000 approx.	15 million
France:		
Algeria	222,067	5,492,569 (1911)
American	35,222	451,000
Asian	310,176	14,773,000
Equatorical Africa	668,000	6–9 million
Morocco	220,000 approx.	3–5 million
Oceanian	8,744	81,000
Somaliland	6,000	208,000
Tunisia	50,000	2 million
West Africa	1,500,000	12 million
Germany:		
Cameroon	291,950[8]	3.6 million
East Africa	384,180	7,651,000
SW Africa	322,450	94,000
Togoland	33,700	1,032,000
Others	96,360	889,000
Great Britain:		
Aden	75	12,000
Basutoland	11,716	405,000
Bechuanaland	275,000	125,000
Ceylon	25,481	4,262,000
East Africa	247,600	2,403,000[9]

Country	Area (sq. miles)	Population
Egypt	363,181	12.75 million
Gold Coast	80,235	1,502,000
India	1,802,112	315,086,000 (1911)
N Nigeria	256,200	9,269,000
S Nigeria	79,880	7,858,000
Nyasaland	39,300	1,089,000
Rhodesia	438,575	1,593,676 (1911)
Sierra Leone	31,000 approx.[10]	1,403,000
Somaliland	68,000	310,000
Sudan	985,000 approx.	3 million
Uganda	110,300[11]	2,843,000 (1911)
West Indies	12,227[12]	1,689,000
Italy:		
Eritrea	45,800	450,000
Somaliland	139,000	400,000
Tripoli, Cyrenaica	400,000	528,000
Tientsin	18	17,000
Japan:		
Korea	84,103	16.5 million
Formosa	13,840	3,612,000
Others	13,201	110,000
Portugal:		
East Africa (Mozambique)	293,500	3–3.5 million (1918)

Footnotes

Official estimate 1917 27,475,000, but this is probably too high.
Official estimate (Chinese) for 1916 almost 446,000,000, but this is disputed.
Population of the smaller Russian province of Estonia was estimated 1913 at 492,000.
Before the Balkan Wars, 25,014 sq. miles.

5. Estimate not including the Canal Zone: almost 72,000 extra.
6. After receipt of 2,969 sq. miles in the Dobrudja from Bulgaria 1913.
7. Increased from 18,650 after the Balkan Wars, though the earlier figure appears in some contemporary statistics of the war period.
8. Increased from 191,000 in 1911, which figure still appears in some wartime sources.
9. Alternative figure given in 1917 of 4,235,000.
10. After modification of frontier with Liberia 1911; otherwise given at about 25,000 sq. miles.
11. After exchange of some districts with Sudan 1914.
12. Very different statistics are also quoted in contemporary sources, depending upon definition of what constituted the West Indies: Bahamas 4,400 sq. miles; Barbados 166; Bermuda 19; British Guiana 89,480; British Honduras 8,600; Jamaica 4,600; Leeward Islands 710; Trinidad & Tobago 1,868; Windward Islands 524; and population recorded up to 2,143,000.

Cities

Approximate populations of states' most important cities were:

Australia:
Sydney 828,000 (1921)
Melbourne 743,000
Austria-Hungary:
Vienna 2,031,000
Budapest 880,000
Belgium:
Antwerp 321,000
Brazil:
Rio de Janeiro 976,000 approx.
Bulgaria:
Sofia 103,000 (1910)

Canada:
Montreal 706,600
Toronto 499,278
China:
Shanghai 1 million (estimate 1917, probably too low)
France:
Paris 2,888,000
Marseilles 551,000
Lyons 524,000
Germany:
Prussia: Berlin 2,071,000

Cologne 517,000
Breslau 512,000
Bavaria: Munich 596,000
Saxony: Leipzig 590,000
Dresden 548,000
Others: Hamburg 931,000
Great Britain:
London (county of) 4,521,685 (1911)
Birmingham 840,202
Glasgow 784,455
Liverpool 753,353
Manchester 714,385

Belfast 385,492
Greece:
Athens 300,462 (1920)
Salonika 158,139 (1915)
Italy:
Naples 723,000
Milan 600,000
Rome 580,000
Turin 428,000
Japan:
Tokyo 2,033,000
Osaka 1,425,000
Kyoto 442,000

Newfoundland:
St. John's 32,292 (1911)
New Zealand:
Wellington about 81,300
(1919)
Roumania:
Bucharest 400,000
(1919)

Russia:
Petrograd 2,019,000
Moscow 1,173,000
Warsaw 756,000
Riga 500,000
Odessa 449,700
Serbia:
Belgrade 90,000

South Africa:
Johannesburg 237,104
(1911)
Cape Town 161,759
Turkey:
Constantinople 1,200,000
Smyrna 260,000
Baghdad 150,000

Damascus 150,000
Adrianople 100,000
USA:
New York 4,766,883 (1910)
Chicago 2,185,283
Philadelphia 1,549,008
St. Louis 687,029
Boston 670,585

SHIPPING

Ships' capacity was calculated in tonnage, of which several variations existed, although a universal calculation was that the ton-register was 100 cubic feet. The various tonnages were:

Gross tonnage: all a vessel's enclosed space divided by 100.

Net tonnage: gross tonnage less spaces not used for cargo or passengers (engine-room, crew's quarters, etc.)

Dead-weight tonnage: the number of tons (of 2,240lb) of cargo and fuel coal that a ship could carry when loaded to the load water-line; calculated by multiplying gross tonnage by 1.6.

Displacement tonnage: number of tons of sea-water displaced by the ship when it was loaded to the load water-line

The following records net tonnage of the merchant shipping of some of the belligerents in 1913–14; in some cases there were considerable changes in these statistics during the war, but the most marked was that of the USA, the gross seagoing steam tonnage (i.e., not including shipping restricted to the Great Lakes) rising from 2,027,000 to 9,773,000 between mid-1914 and mid-1919, an increase of some 382 per cent.

Country	Steamers (tons)	Others (tons)	Country	Steamers (tons)	Others (tons)
Austria-Hungary	1,101,347	1,067	Italy	1,274,127	247,815
Belgium	181,637	combined	Japan	1,593,357	619,160
France	1,793,310	417,854	Russia	790,075	184,103
Germany	4,743,046	339,015	Turkey	111,848	45,480
Great Britain and Empire	12,403,231	1,765,043			

The British and Empire figure included the following (both steamers and sailing vessels combined):

Great Britain	12,119,891	New Zealand	159,310	India	107,774	West Indies	71,28
Canada	897,062	Newfoundland	152,715	Straits Settlements	86,416	Hong Kong	62,01
Australia	436,054						

PRIZE MONEY

The ancient practice of 'prize money' awarded to crews of ships which captured or destroyed an enemy vessel still persisted during the Great War, the British practice being to award £5 for every crew member of the vanquished enemy vessel present at the start of the action, 'head money' of which the value had remained unchanged for generations. Traditionally, it was still divided unequally among the crew, and among all ships present, even those that might not have fired a shot. Division was as follows: one-sixtieth of the whole sum to the senior flag officer, and one-sixtieth between the other flag officers present (if only one, he took the whole one-thirtieth). One-tenth of the remainder was divided into equal 'shares' between the commanding officers of ships and commanders second-in-command under a captain, captains taking 6 shares, commanders 2-i-c 3, and other commanding officers 2. The remainder of the sum was

divided in shares between all ships' companies: commanding officers took 80 shares (in addition to their part of the commanding officers' tenth), with lower ranks receiving proportionally lower amounts, for example a commander 40 shares, lieutenant-commander 30, chief petty officer 10, petty officer 8, leading seaman 6, able seaman 5, ordinary seaman 3, boy 1, etc. As a result, prize money varied very considerably: for example, for the sinking of *Blücher* at Dogger Bank, 47 British crews shared the 'head money', amounts ranging from Beatty's £79. 4s. 4d. (as commanding officer) to 1s. 2d. for each ships' boy. Conversely, for sinking *Messudiyeh*, Lieutenant Norman Holbrook of submarine B11 received not only the Victoria Cross but £601. 10s. 2d. 'head money', and the most junior members of his crew more than £120 each.

VII
GLOSSARY

Many contemporary works contain colloquial expressions or technical terms which are incomprehensible by reference only to a modern dictionary. Without knowledge of the argot of the period even simple verses can be obscure:

> 'Sniper, sniper, up a tree,
> Oh how chilly it must be.
> What will happen if you sneeze?
> Just 'Na pooh' and new O.P.s'[1]

The colloquialisms can be perplexing, especially when similar words had different meanings (e.g., the Australian 'possy' and British 'pozzy', although spellings might be interchangeable), 'jippo' and 'gippy', etc. Many British colloquialisms originated in India, reflecting more than a century of service by the British Army in the subcontinent, and others were derived from the phonetic alphabet or 'signalese' designed to facilitate the transmission of messages (e.g., 'Tock Emma' for 'T.M.', etc.). The war saw the first widespread use of abbreviations and acronyms, especially necessary for German terminology (as the British tank officer Frank Mitchell remarked, the German term for 'tank corps' – *Sturmpanzerkraftwagenabteilung* – would have been difficult to fit on a cap-badge!)[2]

This glossary is restricted largely to military terms or those common in the armed services, although some military works of the period include other colloquialisms which might be just as obtuse as the military argot (Major A. Corbett-Smith's *The Retreat from Mons* includes a memorable passage in which he expresses the task of Haig and Smith-Dorrien in the terms of Jessop and Leveson-Gower endeavouring alternately to keep up an end and to hit out against time, perfectly comprehensible to British and Empire readers conversant with cricket, but undoubtedly perplexing for foreign readers!)[3] In the following, those terms without other identification are British; French and German terms are included generally only in those cases where translation from a modern dictionary would be insufficient, i.e., uncomplicated words such as *fusil*, *handgranate*, are not included.

The most important work on contemporary slang is *The Long Trail: What the British Soldier Sang and Said in the Great War of 1914–1918*, J. Brophy & E. Partridge, revised edn. London 1965; similar works in French include *L'Argot de la Guerre*, A. Dauzat, and *L'Argot des Poilus*, F. Dechelette, both 1918. Contemporary glossaries of military terms are also of great value, for example *Vade-Mecum for the use of Officers and Interpreters in the Present Campaign*, E. Plumon, Paris 1914, rev. 1917; and the same author's *Guide Militaire Français-Italien*, and the same for many other nations including even Japanese and Roumanian.

Footnotes

1. *The Return*, 20 April 1917, Blackpool, p. 14.
2. *Tank Warfare: The Story of the Tanks in the Great War*, London, 1933, p. 202 rep. Stevenage, 1987.
3. *The Retreat from Mons*, p. 121.

AA: anti-aircraft.

AA: *Armee-Abteilung*, German Army.

AA & QMG: Assistant Adjutant– and Quartermaster-General.

A Branch: Adjutant-General's Branch of the Staff (responsible for personnel, discipline and training).

Abdul: Anglo-Anzac colloquialism for Turks.

abri: French shelter or dugout.

Abri caverne: French deep dugout.

ABV: Armed Boarding Vessel: civilian ship armed and taken into the navy, smaller than a CES (q.v.).

ACF: Active Citizen Force: South African defence-forces.

Ack Ack: anti-aircraft fire: from phonetic alphabet. (Ack Ack Ack represented a full stop or period on telegraphic messages, thus colloquially an acknowledgement.)

Ack Emma: morning ('A.M.' from phonetic alphabet).

AD: German War Ministry's 'General Department' (*Allgemeines Kriegs-Departement*).

ADMS: Assistant Director of Medical Services.

Adrian helmet: French regulation steel helmet (*casque Adrian*), named after its designer.

Adrian hut: French barrack hut, widening towards ground level to provide extra floor-space.

ADS: Advanced Dressing Station: the most advanced medical post behind the RAP (q.v.).

AEF: American Expeditionary Force.

AEF: French Equatorial Africa (*Afrique Equatoriale Française*)

AEG: German aircraft-manufacturer (*Allgemeine Elektrizitäts Gesellschaft of Berlin*).

aerial torpedo: finned mortar-bomb.

AFO: facetious reference to 'Army Form Nought', a way of expressing disgust at the quantity of paperwork.

A Frame: wooden support shaped like inverted letter 'A', sunk into the bottom of a flooded trench, having a plank-walkway resting upon the cross-bar of the 'A'.

AGO: German aircraft manufacturer (Aerowerke Gustav Otto).

Agru: German corps telegraphic group equipped with Arent sets (q.v.).

AHQ: Army Headquarters

aid post: medical post nearest to firing-line, crewed by battalion medical personnel. *See* 'RAP'.

Ak dum: British Army argot for 'immediately' (from Hindustani). Also used to describe German notice-boards, which were often headed *Achtung*.

AKK: German Army transport-columns (*Armee-Kraftwagen-kollonnen*).

Akofern: German commander of telephone sections (*Armee-Fernsprechkommandeur*).

Akofunk: German commander of wireless sections (*Armee-Funkerkommandeur*).

Akonach: commander of German signal services.

Alleyman: British slang for German (from French *Allemagne*).

ALH: Australian Light Horse.

Ally Sloper's Cavalry: British Army nickname for Army Service Corps, from the initials and a character in the humorous paper *Ally Sloper's Half-Holiday*.

Alpini: Italian mountain troops.

AMB: Armoured Motor Battery: British armoured-car unit.

AMC: Armed Merchant Cruiser: large civilian vessel armed as auxiliary cruiser.

Amiens hut: unpopular temporary structure of canvas on a frame used at British base camps.

ammos: British slang for boots (from 'ammunition boot' = regulation issue).

AMS: Army Medical Staff

ANMEF: Australian Naval and Military Expeditionary Force: the contingent sent to New Britain and New Guinea in 1914.

Ansteckmagazin: enlarged (25-round) magazine for German rifle.

Antennes: main branches of light trench-railways.

Antonio: affectionate nickname for Portuguese troops, more acceptable than 'Pork and Beans'.

ANZAC: Australian and New Zealand Army Corps; used colloquially for any Antipodean soldier.

AOC: Army Ordnance Corps.

AOF: French West Africa (*Afrique Occidentale Française*).

AOK: German Army command (*Armee-Oberkommando*).

AP: Aid Post (q.v.).

APM: Assistant Provost Marshal.

AQ: Adjutant and Quartermaster-General.

Ara: German signal-detachment equipped with Arent set (q.v.).

archie: anti-aircraft fire. To archie: to fire at aircraft.

Arditi: Italian assault troops (lit. 'bold ones').

area shoot: saturation bombardment of a particular area of the enemy positions.

Arent: German telegraphic listening-set, named after designer.

Arko: German artillery command

from 1917 (*Artillerie–Kommandeure*).

armlet: brassard or cloth band worn around the arm to identify a particular duty or function, e.g., staff.

Armstrong hut: small, collapsible British Army hut made of canvas and wood.

Army Troops: unit attached to a division, outside brigade structure, to perform miscellaneous or line-of-communication duties.

ARS: French gas mask (*appareil respiratoire spéciale*).

ASC: Army Service Corps.

askari: African native soldier, orig. German.

Asquith: unreliable French safety-match, named from Asquith's dictum 'wait and see': wait and see if the match lights!.

Asto: German telegraphic listening-stations (*Abhörstationen*).

Attila: braided German hussar tunic.

AV: German medical classification: fit only for labour duties (*Arbeitsverwendungsfähige*).

AVC: Army Veterinary Corps.

Ayrton fan: piece of canvas on a wooden stave, intended to disperse gas when waved; named after lady inventor.

BAB (or 'Bab code'): British telephone code-book from 1916.

BAC: Brigade Ammunition Column.

Bak: German field-guns adapted for anti-aircraft use (*Ballonabwehrkanonen*).

Ban: 'class', as in Serbian army, etc.

bandes molletières: French puttees.

Bangalore torpedo: explosive tube used to clear a path through a wire entanglement.

banjo: Australian slang for a spade (alludes to the shape).

bantam: British and Canadian term for members of battalions composed of men of height between 5ft 1in and 5ft 4in.

barchino saltatore: lit. 'jumping boat'; Italian inshore torpedo-boat with spiked tracks around the hull to enable it to climb net-defences at Pola.

Barjaktar (or *bairaktar*): Montenegrin

ensign (the actual bearer of the company or battalion standard; an hereditary appointment).

barker: a pistol (Irish expression 'barking iron' dates from at least the early 19th century); also a sausage, alluding to the suspected content of dog-meat!

barrage: artillery bombardment (*see also* 'box', 'creeping', 'lifting').

Bashlyk: Russian winter hood worn over the greatcoat and cap.

battle bowler: British slang (principally used by officers) for steel helmet.

battle order: British term for reduced infantry equipment, the pack removed and the haversack put in its place, to reduce weight and facilitate movement in action.

battle police: military police deployed behind an attack to intercept stragglers.

Bayru: Bavarian aircraft manufacturer (Bayerische Rumpler Werke).

BD: German War Ministry 'B. Department'. (Administration).

BEB: German battalion formed from *Ersatz* reserve detachments of a brigade group (*Brigade Ersatz Bataillone*).

BEF: British Expeditionary Force.

belly: a tank was 'bellied' when its underside was caught upon an obstacle so high that its tracks could not grip the earth.

belted: a belted ship was one which carried an armoured 'belt' on the sides.

berm: ledge on a trench parapet on which equipment or ammunition could be stored.

Bersaglieri: Italian rifle corps.

Béton armé: French ferro-concrete, armoured or steel-reinforced concrete.

BF: Austrian mountain guide (*Bergführer*).

BFW: German aircraft manufacturer (*Bayerische Flugzeugwerke*).

BGGS: Brigadier-General, General Staff.

BGRA: Brigadier-General, Royal Artillery (commander of corps artillery).

BGRE: Brigadier-General, Royal Engineers.

BH: Bosnian-Herzegovinian infantry (Austro-Hungarian classification).

BHJ: Bosnian-Herzegovinian *Jägers* (Austro-Hungarian classification).

biff: Bristol Fighter (colloquialism).

Big Bertha: properly the German 42cm Mörser; colloquially, any German heavy artillery.

Bill Harris: colloquial name for bilharzia, a parasitic flatworm named from the helminthologist Theodore Bilharz; a disease commonest in Egypt, believed contracted from the water of the Nile.

Billjim: colloquialism for an Australian, used by themselves.

billy: Australian nickname for a cooking-pot or can.

Biribi: French disciplinary (penal) battalion, serving in Algeria, to which offenders were sent.

bivvy: contraction of 'bivouac'; not just the small tent the term originally implied, but more generally for any temporary shelter or dug-out. To bivvy = to halt for the night.

Black Hand Gang: slang for a raiding-party or a selected group engaged upon some desperate enterprise.

Black Maria: nickname for the explosion of a German shell, from the smoke it emitted. Apparently not connected with *Schwarze Marie* (q.v.).

blanco: whitening agent for full-dress webbing equipment; used more loosely to describe any similar material ('khaki blanco' for service equipment). In slang use, nickname for any man named White.

Blighty: British Army slang for Britain, implying affection and homesickness. Derived from India, either Urdu *belait* or (British version) *belati*, = foreign; or Hindustani *bilaik* = foreign country, adjective *bilati*. A 'Blighty one' was a wound sufficiently disabling to necessitate evacuation home, an injury often not unwelcome.

blimp: airship or balloon (of the smaller variety: a Zeppelin was rarely referred to as a blimp). By extension, any self-important, inefficient wind-bag.

blind pig: Canadian nickname for 9.45in mortar-bomb.

Blue Caps: nickname of Royal Dublin Fusiliers, dating from Indian Mutiny but still in use.

blues: *see* 'hospital blues'.

Boche (alternative English spelling, Bosche): French slang for German. Derivation unclear: perhaps from *tête de boche* (obstinate person), or from *Alleboche* or *Alboche*, an insulting variation of *Allemands*; popularity perhaps enhanced during the war by the similarity between *Alboche* and *sale boche* ('dirty hun').

Bogohl: German (aviation) bomber-squadron (*Bombengeschwader*).

boko: British slang for plenty or many, from French *beaucoup*.

bolo: an officer who refused to move from base duties.

bomb: hand-grenade.

bombardier: Royal Artillery corporal.

bomber: man equipped with hand-grenades.

bomb-proof: splinter-proof.

bomb-stop: traverse or barricade in a trench to hold up the progress of an attacker.

bonhommes: lit. 'good fellows'; description of themselves preferred to *poilus* (q.v.) by French troops.

bonk (verb): to shell.

bonzer (or bonza, boshter or bosker): Australian slang for good.

box barrage: artillery bombardment upon a small 'box' or area.

Boyau: lit. 'gut': French communication-trench (British version, 'boy-oh').

bracket: to bracket a target with artillery-fire was to fire trial shots at either side until the correct range and direction were established.

brand-munition: German incendiary tracer bullets (lit. 'fire-ammunition').

brass: high-ranking staff officers; from 'brass hat', the gold braid on their caps.

brassard: arm-band or 'armlet'.

brigade: smallest tactical formation above battalion: a small number of infantry battalions or cavalry regiments and their supporting services.

British Warm: a heavy greatcoat, generally knee-length.

Brock's benefit: a profusion of flares or rockets at night, from the name of a firework-manufacturer.

B-Stoff: German term for xylyl bromide lachrymatory gas.

buckshee: free, surplus; from Hindustani, bakhsheesh = gratuity.

bull ring: training-ground behind the lines where recruits and convalescents could be prepared for service at the front.

bullocky: Anzac slang for bad language, from that used by bullock-drivers.

bully (or bully beef): canned corned beef, the principal protein ration of the British army.

bundook (correct spelling bandook): British Army slang for a rifle (from Hindustani).

bung: cheese (from its costive effect).

burgoo (or burgew): traditional British Army name for porridge, dating at least from the mid-18th century.

button-stick: a strip of sheet brass with a slot down the centre, slid behind tunic-buttons for cleaning, to keep polish off the cloth.

buzzer: portable telephone with telegraphic facility for tapping messages; from the noise made by incoming calls.

BWI: British West Indies Regiment.

C3: originally the lowest British Army classification of fitness, those only fit for base duty; later used to imply anything useless.

CA: French army corps (*corps d'armee*).

cable: telephone land-line; cable-trench, one dug (deeply) to contain a cable.

cadre: nucleus of officers and men upon which a battalion was built; the reserve held back when a battalion went into action, so that if casualties were severe there would still be enough men to form an effective unit until reinforcements could arrive (also known as 'First Reinforcement' or 'Battle Surplus').

cage: prisoner-of-war camp.

cagnat (or *cagna*): French argot for a trench dugout (orig. Annamite); also used by Canadians.

cagoule: French smoke-helmet.

Calarasi: Roumanian territorial cavalry.

calendrier: French racquet-grenade.

camion: French lorry.

camouflet: counter-mining chamber used for blowing in enemy tunnels.

camp à cheval: French term for a camp pitched astride a river.

canary: British instructor temporarily assigned from the front to base (from the yellow brassard worn).

cap comforter: knitted woollen stocking-cap.

case-shot: short-range artillery projectile, a shell filled with pellets, chain-links, etc., for anti-personnel use.

Casque Adrian: see 'Adrian helmet'.

cat: nickname for a tractor such as the Holt (from 'caterpillar' tracks).

CB: confined to barracks, a minor punishment.

CCS: Casualty Clearing-Station: main medical establishment (tents or huts) immediately behind the lines.

CD: German War Ministry's 'C Dept.' (Law and Pensions).

C de G: Croix de Guerre.

CED: French *Corps Expéditionnaire des Dardanelles*.

CEF: Canadian Expeditionary Force:

CEO: French *Corps Expéditionnaire d'Orient*.

CEP: Portuguese Expeditionary Force, Western Front (*Corpo Expedicionario Português*).

CES: commissioned escort ship: civilian vessel armed and taken into navy, smaller than an AMC (q.v.).

cetnik: Serbian captain.

CGS: Chief of General Staff.

CHA: Commander, Heavy Artillery (of a corps).

Chambre de repos: French dug-out.

char: universal British argot for tea; from Hindustani.

char d'assaut: French armoured car or tank.

charger: metal clip holding several

rounds for use with a magazine rifle.

charpoy: bed (from Hindustani).

chaser: American nickname for French *Chasseurs Alpins*.

Chauchat: French light machine-gun (see CSRG); contrary to one modern glossary this was not derived from 'hot cat'.

chausse-trap: French caltrop.

chéchia: Zouave fez.

cheminement: French approach-trench.

cherb: British slang for beer (from Hindustani).

chevauleger: Bavarian light cavalry (Germanization of French *chevau-léger* = light horse).

chevron: uniform-distinction usually indicative of rank, but in British service rank-chevrons were invariably termed 'stripes'; chevrons instead referred to the service-distinctions worn on the lower right sleeve, red for service in 1914 and a blue one for each succeeding year.

Chinese attack: a fake attack: when a preliminary bombardment ceased, the defending troops would return to their trenches to meet the presumed attack, whereupon the artillery would recommence firing and catch the defenders out of their shelters. (From the use of the word 'Chinese' to describe something false or flawed, eg., a 'Chinese cut' in cricket.)

Chink: British slang for Chinese, e.g., the Chinese Labour Corps employed on the Western Front.

chipperow: British slang for 'shut up' (from Hindustani) (*see* 'chub').

chit: British slang for a note or written message; from Hindustani *chitti*.

chokey (or chowki): gaol or minor punishment (from Hindustani *chauki*).

chub: abbreviated version of *chubarrow*, 'shut up' or 'be quiet', from Hindustani *chuprao*; *see* 'chipperow'.

CIGS: Chief of Imperial General Staff.

circus: British slang for German aviation squadron, especially that of Richthofen; possibly from the bright colouring they favoured.

class corps: Indian Army unit drawn from only one race or tribe; 'class

company regiment' was one in which each company was composed exclusively of one race.

CO: commanding officer, generally in British service referring to a lieutenant-colonel in command of an infantry battalion or cavalry regiment.

coal-box: shell-burst, generally from a heavy gun, causing a cloud of black smoke.

coffin-nails: cigarettes.

colis-postal: lit. French for a packet delivered by parcel-post; French slang for an incoming shell.

colonelle: French tent occupied by commanding officer.

Common Army: Austro–Hungarian regular army.

Communication-trench: narrow trench constructed at an angle to a defensive trench to permit concealed access to the trench.

con camp: convalescent camp.

Concertina wire: coiled wire, sometimes barbed, used for entanglements.

conchie: conscientious objector.

conduroy road: temporary road-surface (mostly over muddy terrain) made by laying cords of wood at right-angles to the direction of the path.

corkscrew: metal post for supporting a wire entanglement, with twisted base enabling it to be screwed into the ground, obviating the use of a hammer which might attract enemy fire.

cossack post: advanced cavalry patrol or vedette (any nationality: 'cossack' in this sense was a generic term).

covering party: detachment protecting a working-party in the front line.

CP: collecting post.

crapaud: lit. 'toad'; French slang for a German disc-shaped hand-grenade; used by the British to describe a French trench-mortar.

crapouillot: French trench-mortar or trench-howitzer.

CRE: Officer Commanding Royal Engineers.

Créneau de canardeur: French loophole or sniping-hole.

eeping barrage: artillery bombardment whose range was extended at timed intervals so as to avoid hitting one's own advancing troops.

ib: wood and metal framework box weighing about 12cwt, used as a bridge to allow tanks to cross wide trenches or streams.

icket ball: Anglo-Australasian nickname for a spherical hand-grenade.

ump: shell or shell-burst.

SM: Company Sergeant-Major.

SRG: French light machine-gun (Chauchat-Sutter-Ribeyrolles-Gladiator), known as 'Chauchat' (q.v.).

-Stoff: German term for mono- or tri-chlormethyl chloroformate gas.

T: communication-trench; also 'com-trench'.

irtain fire: barrage of shellfire designed to form a 'curtain' between a friendly unit and the enemy.

ishy: happy or pleasant (from Hindustani *khush*, happiness).

apka: Polish square-topped cap.

)AC: Divisional Ammunition Column.

)ADMS: Deputy Assistant Director of Medical Services.

)ADOS: Deputy Assistant Director of Ordnance Services (staff officer attached to every divisional HQ).

affadar: Indian cavalry sergeant.

)AG: Deputy Adjutant-General.

laisy cutter: shell with impact fuze to explode immediately on touching ground.

)AMS: Defensively Armed Merchant Ship.

)AN: French *Détachement d'Armée du Nord*.

)AQMG: Deputy Adjutant- and Quartermaster-General

laylight gun: US nickname for the Benèt-Mercié light machine-gun (from the rumour that it could not be loaded in the dark).

)CLI: Duke of Cornwall's Light Infantry.

)CM: Distinguished Conduct Medal.

)DMS: Deputy Director of Medical Services.

DDVS: Deputy Director of Veterinary Services.

dekko: a look (to 'have a dekko', to observe); from Hindustani *dekhna*.

demonstration: a feint attack or bombardment.

Derby Scheme: British system of voluntary recruitment instituted by Lord Derby just before conscription was introduced.

Desecar: Serbian corporal of 2nd and 3rd Ban.

Desetar: Montenegrin corporal.

devil-dogs: *see Teufel-hunden.*

DFPS: *Détachement Français de Palestine et Syrie.*

DFW: German aircraft manufacturer (Deutsche Flugzeugwerke).

DGMS: Director-General of Medical Services.

DI: French *division d'infanterie*, originally of active army; *see* 'DR'.

Difua: German divisional wireless detachment (*Divisions-Funkerabteilung*).

digger: an Australian; orig. from early gold-miners, but made more popular by Hamilton's Gallipoli order to 'dig, dig, dig!'

dinghy: dengue, a tropical epidemic fever.

dinkum: Australian slang for 'good'; 'a dinkum' was a Gallipoli veteran. 'Dinkum oil': authenticated news (and the title of an Anzac trench newspaper at Gallipoli).

dis: 'disconnected', meaning a break in telegraphic communication. To become dis: to lose communication with neighbouring unit.

ditch: a tank became 'ditched' when the ground beneath became so soft or waterlogged as to prevent the tracks from gripping.

division: tactical formation of two or three brigades and supporting services.

divkonach: German divisional signals commander.

dixie: British Army camp-kettle; from Hindustani *degchi*, a cooking-pot.

DKK: German divisional mechanized transport-column (*Divisions-Kraftwagen-Kolonne*).

DLOY: Duke of Lancaster's Own Yeomanry.

DMAP: French central motor-transport depot (*Dépôt Matériel Automobile et Personnel*).

DMC: Desert Mounted Corps.

DMS: Director of Medical Services.

DMT: Director of Motor Transport.

Don R: dispatch rider (from phonetic alphabet for 'DR').

Doolally: mad (from the asylum at Deolali, Bombay; also used to describe a victim of sunstroke).

DORA: Defence of the Realm Act.

doughboy: orig. an American flour dumpling; later a nickname for American troops (their own expression, preferred to other alternatives).

DOW: died of wounds.

DQMG: Deputy Quartermaster-General.

DR: French reserve infantry division (*Division d'infanterie de Réserve*).

draft: reinforcement sent to a unit at the front, to be split up and divided between sub-units upon arrival.

Dreckfresser: lit. 'mud-eater'; German slang for an infantryman.

drift: constant deflection of a shell to the right, caused by the rotation imparted by a rifled barrel.

DRT: Director of Railway Transport.

drum fire: artillery barrage fired not in salvo but by each gun in succession; from the sound made, like a continuous drum-roll.

DSA: French motor transport (*Direction des Services Automobiles*).

DSO: Distinguished Service Order.

DST: Director of Supplies and Transport.

D-Stoff: German term for phosgene gas.

DU: German medical classification: completely unfit for any service (*Dauernd-untaugliche*).

duck-board: slatted wooden planking used for flooring trenches or muddy ground; duck-bord patrol was a nocturnal patrol of unmanned sections of the line, moving between occupied posts. 'Duck-board' was also used to describe the ribbon of the British Military Medal, which resembled slatted woodwork.

dud: a shell which had failed to explode; more loosely, anything of little use (especially a useless staff officer far from the Front); prob. originally from a term descriptive of ragged clothing.

duff: pudding, especially suet; 'to duff', to botch or do a job badly.

dug-out: shelter usually made in the wall of a trench, varying from a scrape just large enough to accommodate one man, to a large subterranean room. Colloquially, a retired officer recalled to active duty and displaying little enthusiasm or ability.

dum-dum: soft-nosed bullet which expanded upon hitting, causing a frightful wound; from the Indian arsenal at Dum Dum.

Dvajesnik: Serbian lance-corporal of 2nd and 3rd Ban.

ED: Excused Duty: medical report on an infirm soldier sufficiently unwell to be relieved of normal duty but not so ill as to justify hospitalization.

EEF: Egyptian Expeditionary Force.

EFC: Expeditionary Forces Canteens: establishments selling food, tobacco, etc. behind the lines (said to represent 'Every Franc Counts' from the mercenary attitude of some of its employees!).

Efreitor: Russian or Bulgarian 1st-class private or lance-corporal.

egg: a bomb.

egg-grenade (or egg-bomb): small egg-shaped hand-grenade.

E-in-C: chief engineer attached to general HQ ('Engineer-in-Chief').

Einjährig-freiwillige: lit. 'one-year volunteer'; German recruit who undertook to equip and clothe himself for a year's training, after which he might become a reserve officer.

elephant: semi-circular-sectioned hut made of curved sheets of corrugated iron; also trench dug-outs reinforced with such sheets.

Emma Gee: phonetic term for 'M–G': machine-gun.

Emma Pip: phonetic term for 'M.P.': millitary policeman.

ENE: French 'corps troops' (*Éléments non endivisionnés*).

Enverieh: Turkish sun-helmet or 'Enver Pasha helmet', named after its designer.

erk: fitter of RFC or RAF (contraction of 'air mechanic').

Ersatz: German reserve forces; used incorrectly by British to denote something substandard.

Esaul: Cossack major.

estaminet: civilian bar-cum-café on the Western Front where Allied troops could relax.

EVK: Russian aviation service bombing wing (*Eskadra Vozdushnykh Korablei*: 'squadron of flying ships').

Evzone: Greek rifle corps or 'highlanders'.

exaspirator: British nickname for 'box' respirator, soon replaced by 'gaspirator'.

eyetie: slang for Italian.

FA: Field Artillery or Field Ambulance; also a euphemistic expression for 'nothing', expanded to 'Fanny Adams' or 'Sweet Fanny Adams' ('sweet F.A.'), from the victim of an infamous murder.

Fahnenjunker: German officer-cadet.

Fahnrich: German ensign.

faire suisse: lit. 'to do Swiss': the most reprehensible act open to a French soldier, to have funds yet not treat one's comrades to a drink or meal.

Fanny (more correctly, FANY): First Aid Nursing Yeomanry or a member of this unit.

fascine: bundle of sticks or brushwood, traditionally used in siegecraft; also carried upon tanks to fill ditches or trenches to allow vehicles to cross.

FB: British aircraft classification: 'fighting biplane'.

FD: field dressing (q.v.); FFD: 'first field dressing'.

Fea: German aviation training-squadrons (*Flieger-Ersatz-Abteilungen*).

Feldfebel: Russian or Bulgarian senior sergeant.

Feldgrau: Field-grey; colloquially, a German soldier (from the colour of the uniform).

Feldwebel: German company sergeant-major of infantry, foot artillery or engineers.

fernleaf: a New Zealander (from the cap-badge of the N.Z. Expeditionary Force).

feu pilote: French Very light.

Fewewa: German Army HQ meteorological station (*Feldwetterwarte*).

FF: Frontier Force, Indian Army.

Fiat: Italian motor and aircraft manufacturer (Fabbrica Italiana di Automobili Torino).

fiche blanche: lit. 'white ticket': French casualty, not movable.

fiche rouge: lit. 'red ticket': French movable casualty.

field dressing: small pouch of bandages and pins carried by each man for application to a wound; smaller than a shell dressing (q.v.).

field postcard: postcard bearing several printed messages to be deleted as appropriate by the sender, used for conveying news that the sender was fit or injured, at maximum speed, no censoring being necessary.

fill: amount of supplies required to make a tank operational; varied with the pattern of tank but in British service comprised about 60 gallons of petrol, 20 gallons water, 10 gallons oil, and 200 6pdr and 6,000 MG rounds (for a 'male' tank; 10,000 rounds MG for a 'female').

fire-bay: part of a trench manned by infantry in preparation for an attack.

fire-step: step upon the forward face of a trench upon which men stood to fire or observe (the floor of the trench being lower so that the inhabitants could walk erect without exposing their heads above the top).

fire-trench: front-line trench.

first reinforcement: *see* 'Cadre'.

five-nine: British term for a German 5.9in shell.

Fixe!: French command for 'eyes front'.

FJ: *Feldjäger* (Austro–Hungarian rifle corps).

FK: German field gun (*Feld-Kanone*).

Flak: anti-aircraft fire (from German *Flugabwehrkanone*).

Flakgruko: corps commander of German anti-aircraft units

(*Flakgruppe-Kommandeur*); *see also* 'Koflak'.

'lamga: German AA MG detachments (*Flugabwehr-Maschinengewehr-Abteilungen*).

'lammenwerfer: flame-thrower.

lank barrage: one directed against, not from, a flank.

leabag: sleeping-bag.

lechette: anti-personnel dart dropped from an aircraft (French, *flèche d'aëro*).

Fliegende Divisionen: German divisions independent of a corps formation.

light: basic RFC unit, five or six aircraft.

lying pig: mortar-bomb.

FMO: full marching order; more correctly, FSMO (q.v.).

OO: artillery spotter ('Forward Observation Officer').

orby: cleaning rag, from 'four-by-two' (q.v.).

Forty Thieves: nickname of 40th Pathans.

ougasse: a mine (small pit with explosive charge, usually packed with stones).

our-by-two: small flannel (4in by 2in) used with the pull-through to clean the bore of a rifle; also 'forby'. The same term was rhyming slang for 'Jew'.

ourragère: shoulder-lanyard used in French service as a mark of distinction (e.g., in the colours of the Croix de Guerre worn by units awarded it).

ourrier: French quartermaster sergeant or corporal.

our-two: British term for a German 4.2in shell.

FP: Field Punishment: draconian punishment involving being tied to a gun-wheel in 'F.P. No. 1', pack-drill and bread-and-water diet.

franc-tireur: irregular rifleman or partisan, a civilian regarded as a terrorist by Germany and shot when apprehended.

Fray Bentos: generic term for corned beef, not just of that brand. Also used on as anglicization of *très bien*.

Fregattenkapitän: German naval officer ranking with army *Oberstleutnant*; literally but *not* actually a 'frigate-captain'.

frightfulness: according to early-war propaganda, German behaviour in general.

Fritz: generic name for Germans (diminutive of Friedrich).

Front: not a 'front-line' *per se*, but forward areas of operation in general.

Fruntas: Roumanian 1st-class private.

FSMO: field service marching order: the full equipment carried by an infantryman.

Fukla: German divisional wireless detachment (*Funker-Kleinabteilung*); later replaced by Difua (q.v.).

funk-hole: dugout, not intended to imply cowardice as in the pre-war noun and verb 'funk' (fear, or exhibition of it), though this was also used in the war.

furfie: (or furphy): Australian slang for a rumour (from the name Furphy, a rubbish-cart contractor in Melbourne).

gambardier: member of Royal Garrison Artillery, or crewman of heavy artillery; prob. from French *guimbardier*, one who drives a *guimbarde* (coach).

GAR: French *Groupes d'armées de réserve*.

Garde à vous!: French command for 'attention'.

gasper: cheap cigarette.

gaspirator: British slang for gas-respirator.

GDR: French corps-like organization of reserve divisions (*Groupe de Divisions de Réserve*).

gearsman: tank crewman responsible for managing the gears.

Gebirgsschützen: Austrian *Landwehr* mountain-troops.

geese: nickname for Portuguese.

Gefreiter: German lance-corporal.

Gekofunk: German commander of corps HQ wireless units.

General der Infanterie/Artillerie/Kavallerie: German general and the service to which he belonged, not necessarily referring to his immediate command.

Generalfeldmarschall: German field marshal.

GHQ: General Headquarters.

gimnastirka: Russian military shirt.

gippy: slang for Egyptian.

girdle: tank caterpillar tracks.

glasshouse: military prison or detention-place; by extension, to be on punishment whether or not confined.

Gloata: Roumanian *Landsturm*.

gnole: French army argot for brandy.

gobbler: slang for Turk (from the noise made by turkeys).

GOC: General Officer Commanding.

gooseberry: reel of barbed wire, or entanglement, from the prickly nature of gooseberry bushes.

gorblimey: cloth Field Service Cap with wire stiffening removed; orig. civilian euphemism for 'God blind me'; presumably applied to the cap by an NCO in dismay at its appearance.

Gorgeous Wrecks: army nickname for home-defence corps, from their 'GR' brassard.

Gotha: generic name for any large German bomber.

GPAR: French base motor-transport park (*Grand Parc Automobile de Réserve*).

GPF: French 155mm Filloux gun (*grande puissance Filloux*).

GQG: French general HQ (*Grand-Quartier-Général*).

GQGA: General HQ of Allied forces in France (*Général Quartier-Général des armées Alliées*).

Granatenwerfer: German grenade-projector.

grand blessé: French term for seriously wounded casualty; equivalent of British 'stretcher-case'.

grand-garde: French party supporting an advanced picquet.

greca: zigzag and foliate lace peculiar to Italian staff.

green cross: German gas-shell containing trichlormethyl (from the mark painted on the shell).

Grenzjäger: Austro–Hungarian frontier rifle corps.

greyback: British Army shirt (from the colour).

GrJ: *Grenzjäger* (q.v.).

GRO: General Routine Order.

Grof: German heavy flame-thrower (*Grossflammenwerfer*).

Grufl: corps commander of German aviation service (*Gruppenführer der Flieger*).

Grufusta: German corps HQ wireless station (*Gruppen-Funkenstation*).

Grukonach: German signal-service commander at Army Group HQ.

GS: General Service: term for any official-issue item, e.g., 'GS Wagon'.

GSO: General Staff Officer (GSO 1 = of 1st Grade, etc.). 'GSO' was the *nom-de-plume* of Sir Frank Fox.

Gulasch-Kanone: lit. 'stew-gun': German wheeled field-kitchen vehicle, so called because the chimney, when lowered for transportation, resembled a gun-barrel.

gunfire: early morning tea; etymology uncertain.

GV: German medical classification, fit for garrison duty only (*Garnisonsverwendungsfähige*).

HAC: Honourable Artillery Company.

HAG: Heavy Artillery Group.

Hans Wurst: lit. 'Hans Sausage'; German slang for a soldier.

hard tack: army biscuit, or by extension 'iron rations'.

Harry: contraction of Harry Tate, a popular music-hall comedian, applied to the aircraft RE8 (from the similarity of pronunciation); also, in rhyming slang, a plate.

hate: bombardment.

Hauptmann: German captain of infantry, artillery or engineers.

Havelock: neck-cover on a cap.

havildar: Indian infantry sergeant.

havildar-major: Indian infantry sergeant-major.

HE: high-explosive.

Heine: American slang for a German.

HF: Home Forces.

HKK: German cavalry corps (*Höheren Kavallerie-Kommandeure*).

homforty: French railway goods-wagon; from the inscription *Hommes 40, Chevaux 8* on the side.

hommes: les hommes (the men) was the preferred description of French troops made by themselves.

hommes de troupes: French 'other ranks', i.e., all excluding officers.

honved: Hungarian *Landwehr* (prior to 1917 also styled KU *Landwehr*).

horse-length: a measurement of 8 feet.

horse-lines: location of draught-animals and transport.

horse-width: a measurement of 3 feet.

hospital blues: blue flannel jacket and trousers, white shirt, red tie and own unit head-dress worn by British convalescent servicemen, to identify them as such.

house (or housey-housey): popular British Army game, now better known as bingo; from this originated a number of colloquialisms for certain numbers, e.g. 'the doctor' (*see* 'number nine'), 'dinky-doo' (22), etc.

housewife: small pouch containing needle, thread, pins, etc.; often pronounced 'hussif'.

hun: slang for German.

Huntley & Palmer: RFC slang for twin Lewis guns mounted on aircraft (from the biscuit-manufacturer of that name).

hush-hush: anything concerned with secrecy or intelligence.

hypo: sodium thiosulphate, anti-gas chemical.

I (or 'I Branch'): staff section concerned with intelligence.

iddy-umpty: a signaller (from dot and dash of Morse Code).

Idflieg: German inspector-general of aviation service (*Inspekteur der Flieger*).

identification disc: name-tag bearing service-number, unit and religion, of metal or (more commonly) 'composition' or compressed fibre. From 1916–17 British servicemen wore two, No. 1 (green) to remain on the body of a slain man to ensure identification for reburial, No. 2 (red) to be removed as proof of death.

IG: Inspector-General.

igaree: Australian slang for 'hurry up'.

Ikhtiat: Turkish reserve for regular army.

Ilaweh: Turkish 2nd-line reserve (Redif Class II).

Iluft: German inspectorate of balloon units (*Inspektion der Luftschiffertruppen*).

Imshi (or *imshee*): Arabic 'go away' used by British and Australian troops in this sense, and also used as a war-cry by Anzacs at Gallipoli.

Infanterie-Ersatz-Truppe: German infantry training establishment.

Infanterie-Geschütz: captured Russian 7.62mm field-gun issued to German assault battalions.

intervalle: French bay in a trench.

iron ration: correctly, 'emergency ration': can of corned beef, tea, sugar and biscuit carried by all soldiers for consumption when circumstances precluded supply of ordinary food.

Irredentism: Italian movement formed 1878 to gain or reclaim territory on language or racial grounds; used more loosely for the same process with other nationalities, e.g., Roumanian claims on Transylvania.

IS: Imperial Service (Indian state troops on loan to government).

Italienisches MG: lit. 'Italian machine-gun'; Austrian designation for Fiat or Villar Perosa submachine-gun, captured and issued for Austrian aviation use.

ITD: Austro–Hungarian infantry divisions (*Infanterie-Truppen-Divisionen*).

IWT: Inland Water Transport: British service responsible for canal-traffic on Western Front.

Jack: slang for a sailor (orig. 'Jack Tar').

Jack Johnson: a shell bursting with black smoke; named after the Negro heavyweight boxing champion who won the world title in 1908 and was defeated by Jess Willard in 1915.

Jacko: slang for a Turk.

Jagdgeschwader: German aviation fighter squadron.

Jagdstaffeln: German aviation fighter flight.

Jäger: lit. 'hunter'; German rifleman; *Jäger zu Pferd*, mounted rifles.

jake: American/Canadian slang for 'good'; not to be confused with the archaic 'jakes' = latrine, still in use.

jankers: minor punishment such as CB

(q.v.) or fatigues.

jannock: straightforward or honest; orig. English dialect expression made more common by army use.

Jasta: abbreviation of *Jagdstaffeln* (q.v.).

Jemadar: Indian 2nd lieutenant.

Jerry: a German, or anything of such origin (adjectival, 'a Jerry tin-hat', etc.).

jippo: gravy or bacon-fat; in Australian usage, stew.

Jock: a Scotsman (or member of a Scottish regiment); also corned beef (more accurately, 'corned jock').

Johnny: a Turk (properly, 'Johnny Turk').

Jonathan: archaic slang for American; still in limited use.

Juldee (or *jildi*): hurry up! (Hindustani).

jump: to jump-off was to begin an attack, from the jumping-off position ('start-line').

K: German War Ministry's War Bureau (responsible for recruiting and labour) (*Kriegs-Amt*).

K (or 'K of K'): Kitchener of Khartoum. K One, K Two, etc.; first, second or successive 100,000 volunteers for the New Armies or 'Kitchener's Army'.

K ammunition: German armour-piercing bullets with steel core (*Kern-Munition*, 'core-ammunition'); alternately 'S.m.K.' (*Spitz mit Kern*, 'pointed with core').

Kabalac: alternative name for *enverieh* (q.v.).

Kagohl: German aviation battle-squadron (*Kampfgeschwader der Obersten Heeresleitung*; 'of the Supreme Command').

Kaiserschützen: Austrian (Tirolean) rifle corps (*Landesschützen* pre-1917).

kalpac: Turkish fur cap.

Kamerad: German lit. 'comrade' or 'pal'; as an English verb ('kamerading'), the act of surrender, from use of the cry of *Kamerad* by Germans wishing to surrender.

Kamerad Schnürschuh: lit. 'pal with laced boots'; German nickname for Austro–Hungarian troops, from their use of such footwear.

kapitan: Russian captain (except cavalry).

kaplar: Serbian 1st class private.

KAR: King's African Rifles.

kazak: lit. 'Cossack'; Cossack private.

KdK: German commander of mechanized transport (*Kommandeur der Kraftfahrtruppen*).

keep: heavily fortified defensive position in a trench system; from the term for a donjon in a medieval castle.

Kest: German aviation fighter flights for defence of strategic sites (*Kampfeinsitzerstaffeln*).

khorunji: Cossack 2nd lieutenant.

KIA: killed in action.

KiH: German field-gun on howitzer carriage (*Kanone in Haubitzlafette*).

kilo: unlike modern usage, 'kilo' was generally used as an abbreviation for kilometre, not kilogram.

Kilometerschwein: lit. 'kilometer pig': German slang for an infantryman (also *Kilometerfresser* = 'kilometer-eater').

Kindjal: Cossack dagger.

kitch: Anzac nickname from British soldier (presumably from Kitchener).

Kitchener's Army: the 'New Armies' raised in response to Kitchener's calls for volunteers.

kite balloon: observation balloon, styled 'kite' from its being controlled by a cable from the ground.

kiwi: a New Zealander. Also (less common) a ground crewman of RFC or RAF (kiwis being flightless birds); or anyone overly concerned with immaculate appearance of uniform (from Kiwi brand shoe-polish).

KJ: *Kaiserjäger*: Austro–Hungarian rifle corps.

KK: *Kaiserlich Königlich*: title of Austrian *Landwehr* formations (see KuK). (Some French jokes were made on the similarity of pronunciation between 'KK' and French *caca*, a childish word for excrement!).

Kleif: German light flame-thrower (*Kleinflammenwerfer*).

knife-rest: portable barbed wire entanglement used for blocking

trenches or gaps in fixed wire; from the X-shaped frame upon which the wire was fastened.

knut: one (often a subaltern) who took undue care over his appearance; from the music-hall song by Arthur Wimperis (1874–1953), *Gilbert the Filbert, the Colonel of the Knuts*.

Kodofea: commander of German aviation training squadron (*Kommandeur der Flieger-Ersatz-Abteilung*).

Kofern: German officer commanding corps HQ telephone section.

Kofl: German commander of an army's aviation service (*Kommandeur der Flieger*).

Koflak: German officer commanding army anti-aircraft units.

Kogenluft: GOC German aviation service (*Kommandierender General der Luftstreitkräfte*).

kokky-olly birds: King's Own Scottish Borderers (archaic nickname from initials of pre-1887 title, King's Own Borderers).

Koluft: German officer commanding army balloon units (*Kommandeur der Luftschiffer*).

kommandir: Montenegrin field officer.

Korvettenkapitän: German naval officer ranking with major; literally but not actually 'corvette-captain'.

Kosbies: King's Own Scottish Borderers (from initial letters of title).

kot daffadar: Indian cavalry sergeant-major.

KOYLI: King's Own Yorkshire Light Infantry.

KR: King's Regulations (official handbook concerning military duties).

Kreuzer: German cruiser.

Kriegsbrot: German sub-standard black bread (lit. 'war-bread').

Kriegsfreiwillige: lit. 'war volunteer'; Germans who volunteered for service in advance of the conscription of their 'class'.

KRRC: King's Royal Rifle Corps.

KS: *Kaiserschützen* (q.v.).

KSLI: King's Shropshire Light Infantry.

KTD: Austro–Hungarian cavalry divisions (*Kavallerie-Truppen-*

Divisionen).

KU: title of Hungarian Landwehr (*Kaiserlich Ungarische*).

KuK: *Kaiserlich und Königlich*: title of Austro–Hungarian 'Common Army'.

kulla (or *khullah*): skull-cap of Indian turban.

Kultur: sarcastic Allied term for German 'frightfulness', German 'culture' being seen as acts of devastation and destruction.

KV: German medical classification: fit for active duty (*Kriegsverwendungsfähige*).

LAB: Light Armoured Battery: British armoured car unit.

LACB: Light Armoured Car Battery.

Lakenpatscher: lit. 'puddle-splasher'; German slang for an infantryman.

LAMB: Light Armoured Motor Battery: British armoured car unit.

lance-daffadar: Indian cavalry corporal.

lance-naik: Indian infantry lance-corporal.

Landsturm: German and Austrian third-line militia.

Landwehr: German reserve units; Austro–Hungarian 'national' forces (i.e., not part of 'Common Army').

larrigan: Canadian waterproof leather knee-boot.

LE: German explosive ammunition, producing a burst of white smoke after travelling about 300 yards, to aid ranging (*Luft-Einschiess* = 'aerial ranging').

Lea: German observation-balloon depot units (*Luftschiffer-Ersatz-Abteilungen*).

leap-frog: system of assault in which the first wave took the first objective, the second wave passing through them to take the second, etc.

Lehr-Kompagnie: German instructional company.

LFG: German aircraft manufacturer (Luftfahrzeug Gesellschaft).

lFH: German light howitzer (*leicht Feldhaubitze*).

LG: Lewis gun.

lifebuoy: British nickname for Wex flame-thrower (from the shape).

lifting barrage: an advancing

bombardment (from the lifting or elevation of gun-barrels as range increased).

light duty: tasks allocated to a convalescent.

Limogé: French colloquialism for being relieved of command; from Limoges, where officers went for reassignment.

line: originally 'front line' or 'firing line'; 'down the line' used to indicate movement away from the front; 'up the line' the reverse, and also used in the same way as 'go west', i.e., die.

Linienschiff: German battleship (lit. 'ship of the line').

listening post: very advanced post, usually in no man's land, crewed at night by sentries listening for enemy movement.

Litzen: double loop of lace on collar and cuffs of German guard regiments.

L of C: line of communication; L of C troops, unit attached to a division for miscellaneous duties, outside brigade structure.

long horn: Farman aircraft with 'horns' or skids at the front.

long tom: long-barrelled artillery-piece; name most popular in the Boer War but continuing in use.

loose: a thief, or thievery; from Hindustani *lus* = thief.

LP (or L-Pip): listening post (q.v.).

LS: German armour-piercing tracer ammunition (*Licht-Spur* = 'luminous trace').

LSB: Austro–Hungarian *Landsturmbataillone*.

lungi: outer wrapping of a turban, generally used for Indian cavalry head-dress.

LVG: German aircraft manufacturer (Luft-Verkehrs Gessellschaft).

LZ: German airship manufacturer (Luftschiffbau Zeppelin); code-letters 'LZ' used to identify individual craft, with a number.

macaroni: slang for an Italian.

Maconochie: canned stew, principally vegetable, from the manufacturer; not overly palatable (it was said that 'MM' indicated 'Maconochie

Medal', reward for eating it).

mafeesh: Arabic for 'nothing', used by British and Anzacs.

maidan: open space or parade-ground, originally used in India.

M and V: canned meat and vegetable ration.

marrons: French slang for bullets (lit. chestnuts).

Marsch: Austrian reinforcement unit.

Massey-Harris: Canadian slang for cheese, from the manufacturer of an agricultural self-binding machine and the 'binding' effect of cheese on the digestive system.

maternity jacket: double-breasted high-necked tunic worn by RFC.

MC: Military Cross.

MCA: French motor-transport repair depot (*Magasin central automobile*).

MD: 'Medicine and Duty', the official designation for treatment of minor illness: dose of medicine and return to duty. Also, the number 9, orig. in game of 'house', from the 'number nine' pill (q.v.).

MED: German military railway directorates (*Militär-Eisenbahn-Direktionen*).

MEF: Mediterranean Expeditionary Force.

mehmedchik: Turkish colloquialism for a soldier.

Mespot: slang for Mesopotamia.

MFW: German aircraft manufacturer (Märkische Flugzeugwerke).

MG: machine-gun.

MGC: Machine-Gun Corps.

MGD: German HQ military railway service (*Militär-General-Direktion*).

MGGS: Major-General, General Staff.

MGK: German machine-gun company (*Maschinengewehr Kompagnie*).

MGO: machine-gun officer.

MGRA: Major-General, Royal Artillery; MGRA (GHQ), the same commanding the artillery of expeditionary force.

mick: an Irishman, or a member of an Irish regiment.

Minenwerfer: German trench-mortar.

minnie: slang for *Minenwerfer*; also 'Moaning Minnie' from the sound made by mortar-bomb in flight.

Mitrailleuse: French term for machine-gun.

mladachi unteroffizier: Russian corporal.

MM: Military Medal.

MMGC: Motor Machine-Gun Corps.

MO: Medical Officer (generally one attached to a unit rather than a hospital doctor).

Moir: prefabricated concrete pillbox erected by British in 1918; from its designer, Sir Ernest Moir.

monkey-meat: American nickname for a particularly odious French ration of Argentinian beef and carrots.

mop: to 'mop up' = to neutralize enemy strongpoints bypassed by an assault; to 'mop down' = to quaff a drink.

Mörser: lit. 'mortar' in German, but in British terms a heavy howitzer, not a trench-mortar.

mot de ralliement: French countersign (answer to a sentry's challenge).

MOTHs: Memorable Order of Tin Hats (ex-service organization founded in South Africa in 1927).

MT: motor transport.

muckim: butter (from Hindustani).

mufti: civilian clothes (from Urdu, = 'free', i.e. not issued and thus not part of uniform).

mulligan: American and Canadian term for stew.

Musketen-Bataillone: German units armed with automatic rifles.

Mutt and Jeff: British war and victory medals, from cartoon characters.

Nachrichtenwesen: German signals service.

naik: Indian infantry corporal.

napoo: gone, finished; from French *il n'y en a plus*, 'there's no more'.

narednik: Serbian sergeant.

nichevo: from Russian, exactly as 'Napoo' (q.v.); used by British forces in Russia and those with experience of German PoW camps.

nijnichin: Russian private.

nizam: Turkish regular army.

no man's land: territory between two front lines; dating from at least the 14th century.

Noper (or Noperforce): North Persian Force (late 1918).

Number Nine: British Army's laxative

pill was 'no. 9'.

numnah: horse's back-cover (orig. Indian Army).

NYD: medical term written on labels attached to casualties: 'Not Yet Diagnosed' (facetiously, 'Not Yet Dead', or for malingerers, 'No You Don't').

NZMR: New Zealand Mounted Rifles.

NZRB: New Zealand Rifle Brigade.

OAW: Austrian aircraft manufacturer (Oesterreichische Albatros Werke), also German (Ostdeutsche Albatros Werke).

OB: order of battle.

Obergefreiter: German artillery bombardier.

Oberjäger: German *Jäger* corporal.

OC: Officer Commanding; 'O i/C' = 'officer in command', generally indicating a temporary appointment or an officer commanding a specialist section within a unit.

odds and sods: unit HQ-personnel or any not serving with a company.

Oeffag: Austrian aircraft manufacturer (Oesterreichische Flugzeugfabrik).

Offizier-Aspiranten: German one-year volunteers during training for a reserve commission.

Offizierstellvertreter: German acting-officer, a senior NCO performing officer's duties in the field.

OHL: German General HQ (*Oberste Heeresleitung*).

oil: Australian slang for truth.

oil-can: German mortar-bomb (from the shape).

old and bold: experienced and by implication incorrigible members of a unit.

old eyes: British Guards (from the eye divisional sign).

old pot and pan: commanding officer (rhyming slang for 'Old Man').

old soldier: a man experienced at avoiding duty; also verb, to come/play the old soldier.

old sweat; an experienced soldier.

OO: Ordnance Officer.

oojah: anything for which the correct name was unknown, same as South

African 'dinges' or 'dingus', or 'thingummybob'; sometimes lengthened to 'oojah-cum-pivvy'.

opanka: Bulgarian sandals.

O Pip: phonetic for 'OP', observation post.

opolchenie: Russian militia.

orderly: soldier detailed for special duty (two per platoon normally detailed each day for routine tasks), or medical attendant.

original: survivor from the initial complement of a unit; in Canadian service, a member of the first contingent.

OS: Ordnance Services.

OTC: Officers' Training Corps.

O-UFA: Austrian aircraft manufacturer (Oesterreichische-Ungarische Flugzeugfabrik Aviatik).

over the top: to leave a trench over the parapet, to make an attack.

padre: military chaplain (from Spanish/Portuguese = father/priest; probably dating from Peninsular War).

pagri: cloth strip wrapped around a helmet, or Indian infantry turban (also 'pugri', 'pugaree', etc.).

Pak: German anti-tank artillery (*Panzerabwehrkanone*).

palanka: Bulgarian sandals, also *opanka* (q.v.).

pals: battalions of 'Kitchener's Army' raised from small locality, to attract volunteers by ensuring they served with their pals).

pantalon rouge: nickname of French soldier, from the original red trousers.

Panzer: German tank (abbreviation of *Sturmpanzerkraftwagen*).

Panzerkreuzer: German battle cruiser (lit. 'armoured cruiser').

papakha: Russian fur winter cap.

parados: side of a trench farthest from the enemy.

parapet: side of trench facing the enemy.

paroli: Austrian collar-patch.

pavé: stone-block roads of northern France and Flanders.

pawnee: slang for water (from Hindustani).

PBI: British slang, 'Poor Bloody Infantry'.

PC: French command-post (*poste de command*).

perisher: trench-periscope.

petite guerre: French field-day or manoeuvres.

petit poste: French advance picket.

PG: French PoW (*prisonnier de guerre*).

P helmet: 'phenol helmet', early gas mask; succeeded by PH helmet, improved PHG helmet, and finally by box-respirator.

phutt: to cease or stop working; from Hindustani. A 'dud' shell might be said to have 'gone phutt'.

phonetic alphabet: to prevent confusion in telephone messages, some letters were given unmistakable pronunciations: A ack, B beer, D don, M emma, P pip, S esses, T toc, V vic; these were taken into everyday speech, hence Don R, Tock Emma, etc.

Pickelhaube: German spiked helmet.

picket: stake for supporting barbed wire; not used much in original meaning, a sentry-party or patrol.

Piffer: ex-Punjab Frontier Force, Indian Army (PFF); archaic.

pigeon: French nickname for German finned grenade, the fins resembling wings.

piggy-stick; entrenching-tool shaft; from the 'bat' in the game of tip-cat or knurr-and-spell.

pillbox: reinforced concrete MG post.

pinard: French army argot for wine.

pineapple: German finned mortar-bomb (from the shape).

piou-piou: alternative to *poilu* (q.v.).

pip: officer's rank-star.

pip emma: phonetic for afternoon ('PM').

pipeline: trench for field telephone wire.

pip-squeak: small or gas-shell.

Pip, Squeak and Wilfrid: British 1914 or 1914–15 Star, War and Victory medals (from cartoon characters thus named).

plastron: French steel body-armour or corselet.

plastun: Kuban Cossack infantry.

platoon: subdivision of infantry company.

plonk: white wine (from *vin blanc*).

plum and apple: the most common jam issued to British troops; 'plum'n'apple' became almost synonymous with jam, irrespective of content.

PM: provost-marshal.

podesaul: Cossack captain.

podnarednik: Serbian corporal of 1st Ban.

podoffizier: Bulgarian NCO.

podofizieri: Montenegrin NCO or aspirant officer.

podpolkovnik: Russian major.

podporuchik: Russian 2nd lieutenant.

poilu: French slang for a soldier, especially an infantryman; orig. meaning 'hairy one'.

point-blank: minimum range requiring no elevation on a gun; slang for white wine (from *vin blanc*).

polkovnik: Russian colonel.

pom fritz: British slang for chipped potatoes, derived from French *pommes de terre frites* and the nickname for Germans, Fritz.

pom-pom: small calibre machine-cannon; from its noise.

poodlefaker: contemptuous term for an officer more concerned with social engagements than military duties.

poruchik: Russian lieutenant.

pork and beans: contemptuous nickname for Portuguese troops, actively discouraged as being insulting to an ally.

portée: artillery carried on lorries.

Portepee: German officer's sword-knot; *Portepeeträger*, German senior NCOs who wore an officer's sword-knot.

possy: Australian slang for a location (from 'position').

postillon: French aviation message-carrier, a bag with streamers attached, dropped from an aircraft.

potato-masher: German stick-grenade (from the shape).

pozzy: jam.

PPCLI: Princess Patricia's Canadian Light Infantry.

praporchik: Russian officer-cadet.

prikazni: Cossack corporal.

provo: provost-sergeant.

PT: physical training (known as 'physical jerks').

PTI: physical training instructor.

puddled (sometimes 'puggled'): crazy, or stupidly drunk; from Low German *purrel* = short and thick.

pukka: genuine, real (from Hindustani *pakkha*).

pull-through: cord for cleaning rifle-bore; colloquially, a very thin man.

push: an attack in strength.

pusher: aircraft with rear-mounted propeller.

puttee: cloth strip wrapped around lower leg as a gaiter.

'Q': quartermaster branch of General Staff.

QF: quick-firing (artillery with hydraulic recoil system obviating re-laying after each shot).

QM: quartermaster.

QMG: quartermaster-general.

QOG: Queen's Own Corps of Guides, Indian Army.

Q-ship: warship disguised as a merchantman to decoy submarines.

quarterbloke: quartermaster (or more loosely any quartermaster personnel).

RAF: Royal Air Force.

rafale: lit, squall; French artillery tactic of laying a carpet of rapid fire within a given area.

R ammunition: German bullets with grooved base intended to prevent stoppages (*Rillen-Munition* = 'grooved ammunition').

ragtime: inefficient or unsoldierly; from ragtime music.

Rainbow Division: US 42nd Division (from their insignia).

RAMC: Royal Army Medical Corps; facetiously, 'Rob All My Comrades' or 'Rats After Mouldy Cheese'.

RAP: Regimental Aid Post.

Raquet-grenade: explosive charge fixed to a wooden handle.

rataplan: onomatopoeic expression for machine-gun fire, orig. French but used in English as well.

RB: Rifle Brigade.

RBVZ: Russian aircraft manufacturer (Russo–Baltic Waggon Factory).

RCN: Royal Canadian Navy.

RDF: Royal Dublin Fusiliers.

RE: Royal Engineers; in French, Foreign Legion regiment (*Régiment Etranger*).

Red cap: military police (from the red cover to the top of their caps).

redif: Turkish 2nd-line reserve.

red hat: staff officer (from the red cap-band).

rednik: Bulgarian private.

redoubt: fortified strongpoint in a trench-system.

red tab: staff officer (from the red gorget-patch on the collar).

red triangle man: YMCA official (US slang, from the YMCA badge).

régiment de marche: French provisional regiment formed from battalions of different units.

register: to fire trial shots when ranging artillery.

respirator: the more sophisticated type of gas mask in which air was inhaled through a metal box of chemicals.

Restanten: German recruits whose service had been deferred.

revally: British phonetic spelling of bugle-calle 'Reveille'.

revers: French parados.

revetment: strengthening of a trench-wall.

revitaillment: French term for supplies, generally food.

RFA: Royal Field Artillery.

RFC: Royal Flying Corps.

RGA: Royal Garrison Artillery.

RI: German War Ministry Remounts Department (*Remonte-Inspektion*).

RICM: *Régiment d'infanterie coloniale de Maroc*.

rissaldar: Indian cavalry lieutenant.

Rittmeister: German cavalry or train captain.

RM: French *régiment de marche* (q.v.).

RMA: Royal Marine Artillery.

RMLE: French Foreign Legion provisional battalion (*régiment de marche de la Légion Etrangère*).

RMLI: Royal Marine Light Infantry.

RMMC: French *régiment mixte de marche de cavalerie*.

RMO: regimental medical officer.

RMT: French *régiment de marche de tirailleurs* (i.e., of North African *tirailleurs*).

RMZT: French *régiment de marche de*

Zouaves et tirailleurs.

RNAS: Royal Navy Air Service.

RNASAAC: Royal Naval Air Service Anti-Aircraft Corps.

RND: Royal Naval Division.

RNVR: Royal Naval Volunteer Reserve.

rocade: light trench-railway running parallel to the Front.

rondins: logs used in construction of 'corduroy road'.

rooti: bread (from Urdu *roti*); rooty gong', a long-service medal, so called from the belief that they were so unimportant that they came with the bread ration!

rosalie: French nickname for a bayonet, and by extension for the doctrine of bayonet-attack.

rosiori: Roumanian regular cavalry.

rotmistre: Russian cavalry captain.

roulement: French rotation of units between front-line and reserve.

route en rondins: French corduroy road.

RSM: regimental sergeant-major.

RTA: French *régiment de tirailleurs Algériens*.

RTO: railway transport officer (staff officer attached to most railway-stations to supervise transit of men and *matériel*).

RTT: French *régiment de tirailleurs Tunisiens*.

RTU: 'return to unit': the fate of those failing a promotion or specialist course.

rum jar: slang for German mortar-bomb (from its shape).

runner: soldier who carried messages by hand when other means of communication failed.

Russian sap: narrow trench dug like a mine-shaft so that the surface of the earth was not disturbed, to allow raiders to approach the enemy undetected.

Russki: slang for a Russian.

RVF: French fresh-meat supply (*Revitaillement en viande fraiche*).

SAA: Small Arms Ammunition.

sac à terre: French sandbag.

salient: trench-system projecting towards the enemy; British position at Ypres was universally known as 'The Salient'.

SAML: Italian aircraft manufacturer (Società Anonima Meccanica Lombarda).

S ammunition: German ordinary bullet (*Spitz-Munition* = 'pointed bullet').

Sammy: French nickname for Americans.

sandbag: sack filled with earth from which defences were built. Verb 'to sandbag': to use a partially-filled bag as a cosh.

san fairy ann: universal British expression of fatalism or resignation, from *ça ne fait rien* ('it doesn't matter').

sangar: wall built as defence against small-arms fire (orig. used in India).

sap: narrow trench, normally for communication, made by digging at an angle from an existing trench.

sapper: enlisted man of Royal Engineers.

Sarg: lit. 'coffin'; nickname for Hansa-Brandenburg D1 aircraft, from the shape rather than from danger of operating it.

sausage: captive barrage balloon.

SB: stretcher-bearer.

Schusta: abbreviation for *Schutzstaffeln* (q.v.).

Schutzstaffeln: German aviation flight detailed for protection of reconnaissance aircraft.

Schützen: German rifle corps.

Schützengrabenvernichtungsautomobil: German term for a tank.

Schwarze Marie: German nickname for heavy naval gun; apparently unconnected with 'Black Maria' (q.v.).

scran: food; orig. described refuse; thus a scranbag might mean either a haversack (where food was carried), or a scruffy person.

SD: German War Ministry medical department (*Sanitäts-Departement*).

sepoy: Indian infantry private.

shashqa: Cossack sabre.

shell dressing: larger version of field dressing (q.v.), including a vial of iodine.

shell-shock: psychological collapse or disorder caused by prolonged exposure to combat; orig. derived from erroneous belief that the cause was physiological concussion from blast.

shinel: Russian greatcoat.

shrapnel: steel balls ejected from a shell upon detonation; more imprecisely, any piece of shell (correctly termed splinters).

SIA: Italian aircraft manufacturer (Società Italiana Aviazione).

Sigarneo: 'OK' (contraction of 'all Sir Garnet', an earlier expression relating to the excellence of Sir Garnet Wolseley).

signalese: phonetic alphabet (q.v.).

silent: 'Silent Percy' was a nickname for a gun firing at such long range that it could not be heard; 'Silent Susan' was a high-velocity shell.

silladar: system by which Indian cavalrymen owned and provided for their own horse.

SIW: self-inflicted wound; a desperate measure of escaping the battle-line, with extreme consequences if detected.

skilly: thin stew or gruel.

skite: Anzac slang for swank; verb 'skiting'.

slack: debris thrown up by explosion of shell (orig. = small coal).

SM: company sergeant-major (officially abbreviated to CSM; regimental sergeant-major always termed 'RSM').

smasher: soft felt slouch-hat.

SmK: German armour-piercing ammunition (*see* 'K ammunition').

snob: soldier employed to repair boots.

Soldier's Friend: proprietary brand of metal-polish.

SOS: coded combination of coloured rockets fired from front-line to call down supporting fire on enemy attack; in US Army. Service of Supply.

sotnia: Russian cavalry squadron.

sotnik: Cossack lieutenant.

souvenir: (verb): to appropriate or steal.

sowar: Indian cavalry trooper.

SP: French mechanical transport (*Section de parc*).

SPAD: French aircraft manufacturer (orig. *Société Provisoire des Aéroplanes Deperdussin*) until the director,

Armand Deperdussin, was imprisoned following a financial scandal in 1913; reconstructed August 1914 under Louis Blériot and titled *Société pour l'Aviation et ses Dérivés*.

splash: pieces of bullet which penetrated a tank's observation-slits; applied less accurately to splinters dislodged from inner faces of tank by impact of bullets striking outside.

spout: 'one up the spout' was a bullet in the breech of a rifle.

spud: most commonly, nickname for potatoes or any man named Murphy; also iron shoes affixed to tank-tracks to provide extra grip.

squaddy: ordinary soldier ('squad-member').

SR: The Cameronians (Scottish Rifles).

SRD: lettering on army rum-jars, 'Service Rum, Dilute' (sometimes rendered as 'Special Rations Dept.'); said to signify 'Seldom Reaches Destination' or 'Soon Runs Dry'!

SS: French field ambulance (*section sanitaire*).

Stabsoffizier: German field officer (not staff officer).

stand-down: order to end a stand-to.

Standschützen: Tirolean reserve mountain troops.

stand-to: the action of manning a trench to repel an attack, or routinely at dawn or dusk in case the enemy attacked out of the half-light.

starshina: Cossack lieutenant-colonel.

starski unteroffizier: Russian sergeant.

Stavka: German General HQ or General Staff.

Stellenbosch (verb): to be relieved of command and sent home (from camp used in the Boer War).

stick-bomb: German hand-grenade on a handle.

stinker: goatskin jerkin for winter use (from the smell when wet).

stinks: soldier employed in use of poison gas.

Stomag: German machine-gun units' staff officer (*Stabsoffizier der Maschinengewehre*).

Stosstruppen: German storm-troops.

Stoverm: German staff officer responsible for military surveying (*Stabsoffizier der Vermessungswesens*).

strafe: bombardment or hail of fire; by extension, to reprimand.

straight: Australian slang for truth.

Stranbaus horn: gas alarm device.

stunt: an attack; a clever trick or action.

Sturmpanzerkraftwagen: German tank (abbreviated to *panzer*); *Sturmpanzerkraftwagenabteilung*: tank corps.

Sturmtruppen: German storm-troops.

subedar: Indian infantry lieutenant.

submarine: British slang for a bloater (fish).

suicide club: bombing-party.

SVA: Italian aircraft manufacturer (Savoia-Verduzio-Ansaldo).

swaddy: private soldier; sometimes rendered as 'squaddy' (q.v.), but derived from an 18th-century term for a bumpkin.

swagger-stick: ornamental short cane carried by soldiers off-duty.

Système D: French colloquialism for a muddle; from verb *se débrouiller*, to manage.

talpack: small fur busby as worn by Belgian artillery.

tank field company: unit responsible for salvaging damaged or bogged-down tanks.

Tankschrecken: lit. 'tank fear'; German deterioration in morale when faced with Allied tanks.

tapes: lines of tape spread on the ground to indicate the 'start-line' of an attack or the direction it would take; to 'have someone taped' was to be aware of their actions or character.

tassie (pronounced 'tazzy'): Australian slang for Tasmanian.

Taube: lit. German 'dove'; early-war description of any monoplane, not just those officially so designated.

TB: torpedo-boat.

TBD: torpedo-boat destroyer.

tchete: Montenegrin company.

teddy-bear: shaggy goatskin jerkin first issued to British Army in winter 1914.

terps: an interpreter.

terrier: member of British Territorial Force.

têtes de veaux: lit. 'calf-heads': French nickname for those serving in a penal battalion, from their shaven heads.

Teufel-hunden: lit. 'devil-dogs': German nickname for US Marines.

three blue lights: cynical remark describing something which would never happen, from the story that peace would be signalled by firing three blue rockets (which would be undetectable by night!)

tickler's: jam, from a common brand-name, which became almost synonymous with jam, irrespective of manufacturer; also used to describe a home-made grenade or 'jam-tin bomb'.

tictac: a signaller.

tin hat: British slang for steel helmet, though the term was used as early as 1914 to describe the *Pickelhaube* (vide *The War Stories of Private Thomas Atkins*, p. 149, London, 1914). Verb 'to tin hat' = to complete.

tin whistle: British nickname for Breguet 1914 aircraft (from metal fuselage).

TJ: Tirolean Jägers.

TM: British, trench-mortar (TMB = trench-mortar battery); French, transport-service for equipment (*section de transport de matériel*).

toc emma: phonetic alphabet from TM, trench-mortar; toc emma beer, trench-mortar battery.

Toc H: the Everyman's Club, Poperinghe, founded 1915 upon the suggestion of Colonel Reginald Talbot, named Talbot House in memory of his brother, Lieutenant Gilbert Talbot. Revd. P. B. 'Tubby' Clayton became first warden; name came from phonetic alphabet, TH. The name continued for the organization founded after the war to perpetuate the ideals.

toffee-apple; mortar-bomb with shaft attached, resembling a toffee-apple.

Tommy: the British soldier, orig. 'Thomas Atkins'; popular with civilians, Empire and foreign troops, but rarely used by the British Army. 'Tommy' was also an ancient nickname for bread, used at least as early as the Napoleonic Wars.

tommy-bar: spanner for unscrewing base of Mills grenades.

tommy cooker: portable stove using solidified alcohol fuel.

Toot sweet: be quick! (from French *tout de suite*).

torpedo-boom: 6-foot wooden beam used for unditching a tank.

tot: rum issue, ½ gill or ⅛th pint.

tour: period of front-line service of a unit, often 4–6 days before a period of rest behind the lines.

town major: staff officer (usually captain or subaltern) responsible for billeting arrangements in a town.

TP: French transport service for personnel (*section de transport de personnel*).

tracer: phosphorescent machine-gun bullet which glowed in flight, indicating course as an aid to aiming; one tracer round would be used to several ordinary rounds.

tractor: aircraft with frontally-mounted propeller; a vehicle which hauled artillery, not exclusively tracked vehicles.

tranchée de départ: French front-line trench.

tranchée doublement: French second-line trench.

tranchée soutien: French support-trench.

traverse: angle in a trench, or a sandbag partition, to limit effect of shell-burst or enfilade fire.

traversor mat: metal mesh mat to allow passage over low wire entanglements.

trench-coat: short, often waterproof, belted overcoat.

trench-foot: fungal infection of the foot which could become gangrenous, caused by continued exposure to wet and cold.

tricoteuse: lit. 'knitter' or 'knitting-machine': French nickname for piece of artillery.

tromblon: French cup-shaped discharger for rifle-grenade.

trooper: cavalry private; colloquialism for a troopship.

trou de loup: lit. 'wolf-pit'; either a shelter, or a pit dug for fortification.

tumpline: Canadian (orig. North American Indian) method of carrying equipment, the pack being supported by a strap around the forehead.

Turco: colloquialism for French North African *tirailleur*.

Turkish Delight: Turkish shrapnel-shell (from a gelatinous sweetmeat).

Uberlandwagen: German transport-vehicle made from a flat top upon a tank base.

UD: German War Ministry's Quartering Department (*Unterkunfts-Departement*).

Uhlan: German lancer.

Ulanka: German lancer tunic

Uncle Charlie: marching order (full equipment).

unditching beam: replacement for the torpedo-boom (q.v.); an iron-reinforced balk of wood used to give additional grip to tracks to allow a tank to drag itself free of obstacle.

Unteroffizier: German NCO, actually a corporal but of equivalent rank to a British sergeant.

uryadnik: Cossack sergeant.

VAD: Voluntary Aid Detachment (volunteer nurses).

Vakhmistre: Russian cavalry sergeant.

valise: the knapsack carried on the back; or an officer's kitbag.

vareuse: French tunic.

VB: French rifle-grenade (Viven-Bessières).

VCO: Viceroy's Commissioned Officer: Indian officer holding a commission signed by the Viceroy, junior to British officers holding the King's commission.

vermorel sprayer: agricultural device used for spraying insecticide; used with chemical filling to disperse low-lying gas.

Very: a Very light was an illumination or signalling flare fired from a Very pistol, both named after the inventor, Samuel W. Very.

VGO: German aircraft manufacturer (Versuchsbau Gotha Ost).

vodnik: Serbian lieutenant.

voisko: Cossack territorial group.

voivode: Serbian commander-in-chief (lit. 'leader').

vrille: corkscrew dive in an aircraft, without losing control.

WAAC: Women's Auxiliary Army Corps.

Wachtmeister: German battery- or squadron-sergeant-major in cavalry, field artillery or train.

wad: a bun.

WAFF: West-African Frontier Force; 'a Waff' was a member of same.

Waffenfarbe: abbreviation of *Waffengattungfarbe*; German term for 'arm-of-service colour', the facing-colour by which infantry, cavalry, artillery, etc. could be distinguished in a number of armies.

waler: robust breed of horse from New South Wales, used especially by Australian Light Horse.

walking wounded: casualties injured sufficiently seriously to be evacuated from the firing-line, but ambulatory.

wallah: man (from Hindustani); generally used with another name to describe a particular duty, e.g. a unit's bombing officer might be called the 'bomb-wallah', etc.

Weary Willie: Gallipoli expression for shrapnel, perhaps named after a Turkish gun.

Westralian: Western Australian.

Whippet: loosely applied to any type of light tank.

Whistling Willie: a shell.

white star: mixture of chlorine and phosgene gas.

whizz-bang: a light shell, from the noise of approach and detonation.

Willie: nickname for any tank, from the prototype 'little Willie'.

WKF: Austrian aircraft manufacturer (Wiener Karosserie und Flugzeugfabrik).

WO: Warrant Officer, or War Office.

wodnik: Montenegrin sergeant.

Woodbine: popular brand of cheap cigarette: from their smoking of such, it became an Australian nickname for British troops.

wooden track (or road): improvised 'corduroy road' made by laying sleepers or wooden planks upon soft ground.

woolly bear: burst of a German shell, named from the black smoke produced.

WRAF: Women's Royal Air Force.

wrist-watch: adjectivally, the best style; a 'wrist-watch uniform' would be one of the best tailoring (from the fact that wrist-watches were regarded as quite fashionable).

WRNS: Women's Royal Naval Service.

Wumba: German War Ministry's Munitions Department (*Waffen-und Munitions-Beschaffungs-Amt*).

'Y': 'the Y' was a term favoured by Americans for YMCA.

Yank: almost universal slang in British Army for an American, in preference to Sammy.

yellow cross: mustard gas (from the symbol painted on the shells).

YMCA: Young Men's Christian Association: organization which established canteens, etc. in the rear areas of the Front; 'the Y' was the favoured American expression, 'Y Emma' more popular with the British.

Ypérite: French name for mustard gas.

'Z': Z-hour was 'Zero-hour', the time an attack commenced.

zastavnik: Serbian 2nd lieutenant.

ZD: German War Ministry Central Department (*Zentral-Departement*).

Zepp: universal abbreviation for a Zeppelin.

INDEX

Personalities are listed by their most familiar names, and those applicable to the period: e.g., H. H. Asquith appears under that name, not under his earldom of Oxford; Mustafa Kemal under that name, not under Atatürk, etc. Ranks are generally applicable to the date at which the entry appears in the text; e.g., Miklós Horthy de Nagybánya appears as captain, rather than as admiral, by which he is best known. In addition to this index, battles are listed in the chronology on pp. 56–60.

A

Abbas Hilmi, khedive of Egypt, 168
Abdul Hamid II, Sultan, 299, 300, 302, 304–5
Abdullah, son of Husein Ibn 'Ali, 130
'aces', list of, 381–2
Acosta, Julio, Costa Rican president, 166
Aden, main text, 123; statistics, 383; 244, 246
aerial warfare, 110–14, 116–20; for aircraft, *see* individual states; 'aces', 381–2
Afghanistan, main text, 123–4; 242–3
Ahmad Fuad (King Fuad I of Egypt), 169
Ahmad Mirza, Shah of Persia, 272
aircraft: 110–14, 116–20; *see also* individual states, principally: Austria–Hungary, 146–7; Belgium, 153; France, 188–90; Germany, 207–10; Great Britain, 231–6; Italy, 258–9; Russia, 288–9; USA, 315–16
airships, 117–18, 208, 289
Aisne, battles of, 17, 92
Aitken, Major-General A. E., 125
Albania, main text, 129–30; 11, 23, 37, 299
Albert, King of the Belgians, 44, 148–9, 174
Alexander, crown prince of Serbia (later king), 265, 290–1, 343
Alexander, King of Greece, 37, 239

Alexander, King of Serbia (*d.* 1903), 290
Alexandra, Tsarina, 282–3
Alexeev, General Mikhail (also Alekseev), biography, 319; 22, 282, 319, 322
Alexis, Nord, Haitian president, 241
Algeria, main text 270; statistics, 383; 174, 177, 186
'Ali, son of Husein Ibn 'Ali, 130
Allen, Sir James (New Zealand politician), 267–9
Allenby, General Edmund, biography, 319–20; 33, 37, 40, 46, 95, 169, 216, 246, 335
Alwar (Imperial Service troops), 249
Andrássy von Czik-Szent, Count Julius (Austrian minister), 139
Angel of Mons, 372–3
Angola, 276
Anthoine, General François, 39
Antwerp, 15, 18, 101, 231
Anzac Cove, 26, 321
ANZACS, *see* Australian Army; New Zealand Army
Aosta, General, duke of, 39
Apollinaire, Guillaume (poet), 363
Aqqaqia, action at, 271
Arabia, 130–1; statistics, 382
'Arab Army, 130–1
Arab revolt, 31, 40, 46, 130–1, 169, 334
Ardennes, battles of, 16
Ardent du Picq, Colonel C. J., 75
Arges, battle of, 36
Armenia, 28, 131, 301, 305–6; casualties, 54
armoured warfare and armoured vehicles, 95–7, 99, 184, 202, 223–5, 287, 312–13
Arnim, General Sixt von, 39, 42
Arras, battle of, 37, 319
Arriaga, Manuel de, Portuguese president, 276
art depicting the war, 364–7 (*see also* names of individual artists)
Artois, battles of, 21
artillery: 74–5, 77–8, 82–4, 86–92, 112, 144–5, 150–1, 156, 162, 182–3, 200,

202, 217, 222–3, 240, 247–8, 256, 281, 287, 293, 304, 312; tactics, 82–4, 86–92; speed of march, 99–101; *see also* under individual states, principally Austria–Hungary, 83–4, 144–5; Belgium, 101, 150–1; Bulgaria, 156; Canada, 162; France, 82–4, 86–8, 181–2, 287, 312; Germany, 83–4, 86–9, 97, 200, 202; Great Britain, 83–4, 86–9, 217, 222–3; Greece, 240; Italy, 256; Russia, 83, 285, 287; Serbia, 293; Turkey, 304; USA, 86, 312
Arz von Straussenberg, General Arthur, 39, 139
Ashmead-Barlett, Ellis (journalist), 352
Asquith, Herbert H., British premier, 37, 53, 148, 211–13
atrocities, 373–5
Australia: main text, 131–7; casualties, 54; prices, 380; shipping, 384; statistics, 382–3; army, 24, 95, 132–6, 271, 302, 320–1; navy, 136; aviation service, 136–7
Austria–Hungary: main text, 137–47; casualties, 54–5; currency, 380; shipping, 384; statistics, 382–3; 11–13, 27, 28, 40, 129–30, 155, 166–7, 191, 213, 250–1, 264–5, 273–4, 276, 278, 290–1, 300, 306–7; army, main text, 140–5; 18–19, 22–3, 28, 36–7, 39, 45, 274–5, 323–4, 338; navy, main text, 145–6; 45, 53, 106, 186, 257; aviation service and aircraft, 146–7; weapons, artillery, 83–4, 144–5; gas, 91; machine-guns, 67–8, 143; rifles, 64, 143–4
Averescu, General Alexandru, 36, 279–80
Aylmer, General Fenton, 31
Aymerich, General, 124
Azerbaijan, 305–6

B

Bairnsfather, Bruce (cartoonist), 366–7